Formations

WARRINGT

MANCHESTER
UNIVERSITY PRESS

Formations is a hybrid print and web-based 'textbook'. The web site was developed with support from the UK's Joint Information Systems Committee through its eLib programme. The ongoing service is sponsored by Lotus. You will find *Formations* on the web at **www.formations.org.uk**

In the Contents, each numbered chapter is accompanied by break-out sections which are further developed on the web. The 'Stop and think' sections are by the editor and do not necessarily reflect the views and opinions of the other authors.

Formations

A 21st-century media studies textbook

edited by

Dan Fleming

Consulting editors:
Henry A. Giroux
Lawrence Grossberg

Manchester University Press

Manchester and New York

distributed exclusively in the USA by Palgrave

Copyright © Manchester University Press 2000

While copyright in the volume as a whole is vested in Manchester University Press, copyright in individual chapters belongs to their respective authors, and no chapter may be reproduced wholly or in part without the express permission in writing of both author and publisher.

Published by Manchester University Press
Oxford Road, Manchester M13 9NR, UK
and Room 400, 175 Fifth Avenue, New York, NY 10010, USA
http://www.manchesteruniversitypress.co.uk

Distributed exclusively in the USA by
Palgrave, 175 Fifth Avenue, New York,
NY 10010, USA

Distributed exclusively in Canada by
UBC Press, University of British Columbia, 2029 West Mall,
Vancouver, BC, Canada V6T 1Z2

British Library Cataloguing-in-Publication Data
A catalogue record for this book is available from the British Library

Library of Congress Cataloging-in-Publication Data applied for

ISBN 0 7190 5845 7 *hardback*
      0 7190 5846 5 *paperback*

First published 2000

07 06 05 04 03 02 01 00   10 9 8 7 6 5 4 3 2 1

Typeset in Photina with Frutiger
by Best-set Typesetter Ltd., Hong Kong

Printed in Great Britain
by Bookcraft (Bath) Ltd, Midsomer Norton

Contents

Contributors

José Arroyo is a lecturer in film studies in the Department of Film and Television Studies at the University of Warwick, England, where his research interests include Spanish and Canadian cinema. Among other publications, José contributed the entry on Almodóvar to *The Oxford Guide to Film Studies* (1998).

Tereza Batista is a community media activist and freelance cultural theorist. Previously a visiting lecturer at the Federal University of Bahia, Salvador, Brazil, Tereza is currently working with a Mayan women's media collective in Guatemala. Her contributions to this volume are her first published output in English.

Cary Bazalgette is Head of Education Projects at the British Film Institute, where she has worked since 1979. From 1989 to 1994 Cary was actively involved with others in lobbying national bodies to ensure a place for media education in the National Curriculum for England and Wales. In 1990 she was joint co-ordinator of the first global conference on media education, in Toulouse, France. She is the author of *Teaching English in the National Curriculum: Media Education* (1991) and co-editor (with D. Buckingham) of *In Front of the Children* (1995).

Conor Beattie is a partner in an independent video shop and, at the time of writing, is a mature student in media studies at the University of Ulster, Coleraine, Northern Ireland.

Marcus Breen teaches in the Department of Communication Studies at the University of North Carolina at Chapel Hill, USA. Before moving to Chapel Hill he taught at the University of Melbourne, Australia. Marcus has worked as a music and film journalist and as a consultant for the State Government of Victoria (Australia) and the Gartner Group on converging industries and regulation policy. His most recent book is *Rock Dogs: Politics and the Australian Music Industry* (1999).

Jim Cook has been involved in film studies since 1967. From 1973 to 1993 he worked in the Education Department of the British Film Institute and since then has been a freelance lecturer and writer, based in London.

Mike Cormack is a senior lecturer in the Department of Film and Media Studies, University of Stirling, Scotland, and a member of the Stirling Media Research Institute. His research interests include minority language broadcasting and issues concerning cultural and national identity, especially in relation to Scotland. His publications include the books *Ideology* (1992) and *Ideology and Cinematography in Hollywood 1930–39* (1994), as well as a number of articles on Gaelic in the Scottish media.

John Corner is Professor in the School of Politics and Communication Studies at the University of Liverpool, England. He has written widely on media topics in books and journals. Recent books include *The Art of Record* (1996), *Studying Media* (1998) and *Critical Ideas in Television Studies* (1999). He is an editor of the journal *Media, Culture and Society*.

Maria Cristina Castilho Costa is Professor in the Arts and Communications School, University of São Paulo, Brazil, and the author, in Portuguese, of *Art's Questions* and *Art: Resistances and Ruptures* (Editora Moderna, São Paulo).

Sarah Edge is lecturer and undergraduate course director in media studies at the University of Ulster, Coleraine, Northern Ireland. Her research and publications are in the areas of post-feminist theory, photography and representations of gender. Sarah is also actively engaged in photographic art practice.

Michael Green is senior lecturer in the Department of Cultural Studies and Sociology at the University of Birmingham, England, where he joined the renowned Centre for Contemporary Cultural Studies in the 1960s. Michael has also taught in Montreal, Montpellier and Munich, and has written widely on cultural policy, educational and media issues. His current media interests include teaching courses on radio and on the politics of representation, and he is also involved with a local multimedia training organisation.

Ramaswami Harindranath is senior lecturer in Cultural and Media Studies at the University of the West of England. He has published on audience research and global media, and was part of the ESRC-funded project team which researched audiences' responses to the controversial film *Crash*. He is currently writing a book on cultural imperialism.

Fred Inglis is Professor of Cultural Studies at the University of Sheffield, England, and director there of the MA in Creative Writing for Film and Television. He has been a member of the Institute for Advanced Study at Princeton, USA, and has had a distinguished career as a radical social and cultural commentator, critic and educator. His many publications include *The Delicious History of the Holiday* (2000), *Raymond Williams: The Life* (1995), *Cultural Studies* (1993), *The Cruel Peace: Everyday Life and the Cold War* (1991) and *Media Theory* (1990).

Julia Knight is senior lecturer in the Department of Media Arts at the University of Luton, England. She is co-editor of *Convergence: The Journal of Research into New Media Technologies* and has written widely on various aspects of the media, in particular video and film.

Lisa Konczal teaches research methods in anthropology and sociology at Florida International University, Miami, and leads a group of researchers in data collection on local migrant neighbourhoods in South Florida under a grant from the US Department of Housing and Urban Development. Her teaching and research specialisms include Hispanic youth in the USA, ethnic identity and minorities in the media. Lisa has done extensive research in Miami and in Central America on the topic of Hispanic youth and how they are represented.

Sonia Livingstone is Professor of Social Psychology at the London School of Economics and Political Science. She has written widely on the television audience and related areas of media research, including children as viewers. Recent publications include *Making Sense of Television: The Psychology of Audience Interpretation* (1998) and (with P. K. Lunt) *Talk on Television: Audience Participation and Public Debate* (1994).

Cameron McCarthy is Research Professor in the Institute of Communication Research at the University of Illinois at Urbana-Champaign, USA, where he teaches mass communications theory and cultural studies. Cameron has published widely on topics related to post-colonialism, problems with neo-Marxist writings on race and education, institutional support for teaching, and school ritual and adolescent identities. Among his authored or co-authored books are: *Race Identity and Representation in Education* (1993), *Racismo y Curriculum* (1994), *The Uses of Culture: Education and the Limits of Ethnic Affiliation* (1998), *Sound Identities: Youth Music and the Cultural Politics of Education* (1999) and (edited with R. Mahalingam) *Multicultural Curriculum: New Directions for Social Theory, Practice and Policy* (2000). Cameron also has a forthcoming book on the work of art in the post-colonial imagination.

Greg McLaughlin lectures in media studies at the University of Ulster, Coleraine, Northern Ireland. His teaching and research specialism is journalism and its role in the reporting and representation of war and conflict. He has a book in press on the subject and has published on news coverage of the peace process in Northern Ireland, the Gulf War and the end of the Cold War. Greg has also worked with the Glasgow Media Group on media representation of mental distress.

Peter Meech is senior lecturer in the Department of Film and Media Studies, University of Stirling, Scotland, and a member of the Stirling Media Research Institute. Having taught in his original specialism – German language, literature and art – at the University of Ulster and the Ruhr-Universität Bochum, Germany, Peter moved into media studies and now teaches courses on journalism and advertising. His published output reflects Peter's particular research interest in marketing communications and public relations.

Shaun Moores is reader in media and cultural studies at the University of Sunderland, England. He has contributed to numerous journals and is the author of the books *Interpreting Audiences: The Ethnography of Media Consumption* (1993), *Satellite Television and Everyday Life: Articulating Technology* (1996) and *Media and Everyday Life in Modern Society* (2000).

Horace Newcomb is the F. J. Heyne Centennial Professor in Communication in the Department of Radio–Television–Film at the University of Texas at Austin. The author and editor of numerous publications, Horace was most recently the editor of *The Museum of Broadcast Communications Encyclopedia of Television* (1997) and of *Television: The Critical View* (6th edition, 2000).

John Orr is Professor of Sociology at the University of Edinburgh, Scotland. His research interests lie in social and cultural theory; film studies; twentieth-century fiction and philosophy; religion, politics and modernity. He has published several monographs on literature, drama and modern society, and co-edited collections on *Terrorism and Modern Drama* (1991) and *Cinema and Fiction* (1992). His most recent books are *Cinema and Modernity* (1993), *Contemporary Cinema* (1998), *The Art and Politics of Contemporary Film* (2000) and the co-edited collection, *Postwar Cinema and Modernism: A Film Reader* (2000).

Tim O'Sullivan is principal lecturer and reader in media education and cultural studies, De Montfort University, Leicester, England. He is also head of the Department of Media and Cultural Production there. His research interests include historical studies of television, radio and advertising; the films of post-war British film directors; and continuing developments in media education. His numerous publications include (with B. Dutton and P. Rayner) *Studying the Media* (1994) and (with Alan Burton and Paul Wells) *Liberal Directions: Basil Dearden and Post-War British Film Culture* (1997). Tim is a co-author of the widely used dictionary of *Key Concepts in Communication and Cultural Studies* (1994) and a co-editor of *The Media Reader: Continuity and Transformation* (1990).

Nikos Papastergiadis is the Simon Research Fellow at the University of Manchester, England. He is the author of *Modernity as Exile* (1993), *Dialogues in the Diasporas* (1998) and *The Turbulence of Migration* (2000). His current research is an exploration of the relationship between the abandoned spaces in post-industrial cities and practices in contemporary art.

Karl Erik Rosengren is Professor Emeritus in the Institute of Sociology at the University of Lund, Sweden. Among his many publications in media sociology and communication studies are the fifth edition (with P. Arvidson) of his popular textbook *Sociological Methodology* (2001); *Communication: An Introduction* (1999); and *Media Effects and Beyond* (ed.) (1994). Karl Erik has written for numerous journals and, in addition to membership of several journal editorial boards, he was a founding co-editor of the *European Journal of Communication* and is a Fellow of the International Communication Association.

Victor Sampedro is Associate Professor of Public Opinion at the University of Salamanca, Spain. His first book, summarised and developed in his contribution to this volume, received an award from the Spanish Constitutional Court as the best research on political science of 1996. He has published in international journals on topics in political communication, audience reception and social movements. Victor is also the author of *Public Opinion and Deliberative Democracy*, a handbook for university students in Spain.

Bill Scott is Professor and head of the division of Media and Journalism at Glasgow Caledonian University, Scotland, Bill is an author, broadcaster, former journalist, media consultant and founder member of the Scottish Communication Association.

Nikhil Sinha is a former associate professor of Radio–Television–Film at the University of Texas at Austin. In 1998 he became President and CEO of iDLX Technology Partners, a software development firm providing support for e-commerce enterprises. In 1999 he was named Executive Vice President for global corporate development at eFunds Corporation, the combined eFunds and iDLX businesses.

Dominic Strinati is a lecturer in sociology at the University of Leicester, England. He is the author of *Capitalism, the State and Industrial Relations* (1982) and *An Introduction to Theories of Popular Culture* (1995). He is also co-editor of *Come on Down? Popular Media Culture in Post-War Britain* (1992).

John Tomlinson is Professor of the Sociology of Culture, and Director of the Centre for Research in International Communication and Culture at Nottingham Trent University, England. He is the author of *Cultural Imperialism* (1991) and *Globalization and Culture* (1999). He is widely involved in the editorial boards of several journals, including the *Asian Journal of International Studies*, is a member of the international advisory board of the Globalisation and Social Exclusion Unit, University of Liverpool, and a managing editor of the Sage book series *Global Power/Cultural Spaces*.

Liza Tsaliki is a senior lecturer in media and cultural studies at the University of Sunderland, England, and is currently also a Marie Curie Fellow at the Department of Communications at the University of Nijmegen, Netherland, working on a project about digital citizenship. Liza has done research on the relationship between national identity and Greek broadcasting, and is writing a book on globlisation, power and identity.

Efrat Tseëlon is lecturer in cultural theory and sociology at University College Dublin, Ireland, having previously taught at Leeds Metropolitan University, England, and the University of California at Davis. Having studied at the Hebrew University, Jerusalem, and the University of Oxford, Efrat's intellectual formation has been distinctly multicultural and her research is no less multidisciplinary, as evidenced by her first book *The Masque of Femininity* (1995). Her current research, writing and editing is in the area of visual culture and the production of identities.

Mike Wayne teaches film, television and video practice at Brunel University, England. He is the editor of an anthology of essays on television, *Dissident Voices: The Politics of Television and Cultural Change* (1998). His forthcoming book on revolutionary cinema is called *Political Film: The Dialectics of Third Cinema*.

Figures

Tables

Introduction

The textbook is something of a rarity in the field of media studies. Most courses at university level rely on reading lists crammed with books and journals that have been written by academics for their peers, leaving learners to become eavesdroppers on academic conversations that must often seem arcane or foreign to them. Doing well in media studies at university often entails working hard to attain sufficient familiarity with these conversations by one's final year to be able to paraphrase their content and offer some acceptable commentary upon them. The idea that today's learners might develop more robust abilities through a more structured programme of reading designed – indeed written – specifically for them seems strangely not to have occurred to those of us who invented the subject during the last twenty years of the twentieth century. But most other fields have their textbooks, so why shouldn't we?

One reason for our reluctance to build university courses around conventional textbooks is that media studies has always placed great emphasis on a loosely formulated sort of 'deconstruction'. This is less the rigorous kind pursued by Derrida and others and more a generalised resistance to authoritative statements, to simplified truth claims, to attempts at comprehensiveness. The conventional textbook would teach students bad habits in these respects. We want the learners in our charge to learn about the constructedness of knowledge, the ideological underpinnings of truth claims, that there is always something left over when one claims to have *the* answer to questions in the human sciences. But these are all problems with one way of writing textbooks, not necessarily problems with the idea of the textbook. The subtitle here – a 21st-century media studies textbook – is meant to signal several things. First, that a new kind of textbook is being attempted. Second, that this newness has an eye on what's happening to the condition of knowledge at this particular moment. Third, it's also a joke: 'Century 21' was the production company behind *Thunderbirds*, the puppet-based science-fiction TV series in Britain that gave a generation of kids (this editor included) their vision of the future from the vantage point of the 1960s. Now that Century 21 is actually here, we might do well to remember what fired our own imaginations as children and how we got from there to here. The 'egghead' character called Brains in *Thunderbirds* was not a bad role model for kids like me who knew they'd never fly a spaceship. There was another way to be part of that future, a way based on ideas.

The true deconstructionists, however, would tell us that we can never evade the will to truth, the fiction of authority – even if we try to disguise it by refusing to write textbooks! Better, perhaps, to recognise this from the outset, to write the textbook anyway and then to let its authority unravel as it inevitably will? In fact we can now do better than that. The web has given us a new medium for writing, teaching, learning and exchanging ideas. What if a textbook could have two parallel existences – the first a conventional print-based one, the second a more open-ended, fluid, unconventional, electronic one? *Formations* does precisely this. Not only is it one of the very few textbooks in media studies to have been constructed from entirely original material (instead of being a reader of previously published stuff) but it has been planned from the outset to exist in print and on the web. The latter does not afford here an additional means to promote the book or a secondary distribution medium; rather, it offers the opportunity to rethink how a book like this works.

Formations opens up the concept of the textbook in new ways. The boxed sections in the print version are where content dimensions of the web version intersect with the more traditional long chapters in the book. The 'Stop and think' sections, an innovation developed on the basis of Manchester University Press's 'Beginnings' series, punctuate the book but flow in a different way on the web. The learner's development has been carefully planned and embedded in this design, not prescriptively but based on the belief that intellectual development needs scaffolding, and the right kind of scaffolding in the right place. The aim has been to support non-introductory work in media studies within higher education: we have had in mind throughout a vital but seldom considered middle zone somewhere between a learner's first encounter with the field and more specialist work such as that pursued in the final year of a degree programme. On the other hand, both beginning and advanced students should find something of interest within these pages. We have not aimed to pack everything in. Academic critics of this book will ask 'what about this . . . ?' 'what about that . . . ?' But aiming for coverage rather than depth would have brought the scaffolding tumbling down. Learning depends first on the building of conceptual structures and only secondarily on coverage of a field. So this is a deliberate refusal of the notion that media studies can be comprehensively captured in a textbook (a briefly held ambition that turned out to be misguided and the cause of a rift with a previous publisher), and the present book offers instead both a series of wayside snapshots of issues, methods and analyses, and a signposted route for the learner to follow. That this route can meander productively between print and web is a benefit of the times.

This hybrid solution to rethinking how a textbook works has depended on several things: Simon Prosser's original encouragement to begin thinking about this, some six years ago now (I'm only sorry that subsequent conceptual differences forced me to break with the venerable publishing house for which Simon then worked); Matthew Frost's conviction that Manchester University Press was becoming the hottest place to publish in media and cultural studies (if unwavering support and encouragement for my odd ideas are any indication then he may well be right); the extremely generous support from the UK university funding councils' Joint Information Systems Committee (through its eLib programme) which gave us access to state-of-the-art web technologies and training and to a community where our ideas seemed not at all odd; Lotus (Ireland) who are sponsoring the *Formations* application server (a term that will surely become as familiar to academic authors as the word 'book' is today); an early set of contributors to this book who showed extraordinary patience with the several false starts and changes of direction that occurred before the project settled down into its present shape; and all the remarkable teachers and writers who have contributed to *Formations* (at a time when conventional research-based publication is more institutionally rewarded).

More personal acknowledgements are due to Lynda Henderson, Simon McLeish and Fiona O'Brien, co-workers on the JISC-funded prototype web-based system on which *Formations* depends; to Nicky Gardner for steering that part of the project so wisely; to Tereza Batista with whom I had long and productive cachaca-fuelled conversations about this project when we were both working at the University of Bahia in Salvador, and to Marcos Palacios and colleagues in the Cyberculture Group there for their hospitality; to my colleagues in media studies at the University of Ulster who have tolerated my preoccupation with this for five years now and to the Faculty of Humanities there for supporting a crucial period of study leave; to my own students over the years (in Falkirk, Aberdeen, Salvador and Coleraine) who have taught me so much; and finally to Joyce Fleming for too many things to list here.

The editor and Manchester University Press would like to thank Polity Press for permission to reproduce extracts and three figures from John B. Thompson's *The Media and Modernity*, and the Johns Hopkins University Press for permission to reproduce a figure from Espen J. Aarseth's *Cybertext: Perspectives on Ergodic Literature*. A version of Sarah Edge's short essay has appeared in the Irish art magazine *Circa* and a few passages from the editorial matter of the present volume appeared in earlier versions in my *Media Teaching* (Blackwell, 1993).

Dan Fleming

Part I
The field

Stop and think

Media studies and you

This book presupposes that you have done some basic work in media or communication studies before – perhaps in the later years at school, in first year at university or at college. It may still be used selectively in first year undergraduate studies but the book as a whole has been designed to take you much further than that. If you have not ventured into media studies before, you can give yourself a good introduction to the field by working through one of the best introductory textbooks – *Studying the Media* (second edition) by Tim O'Sullivan, Brian Dutton and Philip Rayner (1998).

Even if you are not new to the field, you may find it very useful to obtain *Studying the Media* and use it as a revision guide, especially if you encounter topics in the present book that you find difficult. The book that you now have in your hands is for students who are making a substantial commitment to the field of media studies – possibly as their main area of study. Rather than drifting into such further study, it is important for you to stop and think about why media studies is worth doing. In 2000 and beyond it will be impossible for anyone – even in the less developed parts of the world where people may be 'information poor' as well as materially impoverished – to argue that the media of public communication are not now inextricably part of the very fabric of reality. Cheap radios and TVs blare through the alleyways of a Brazilian *favela*, or shanty town, to just as much effect as the media that permeate the leafy suburbs of a northern city.

That much of the content transmitted by the media seems trivial does not mean that media studies is a trivial subject. This is a logical error of the simplest kind but one often made by cynics who argue that media studies is not a 'serious' subject like those longer established in universities. Understanding what values are being negotiated when a *favela* dweller in Brazil wears a Micky Mouse T-shirt, especially where this attempt at understanding is part of a larger project to grasp the media's impact generally, does not make media studies a 'Micky Mouse subject'. Moreover, much of the media's output is not trivial – there are deeply serious questions to be asked about how both news media and entertainment media – often displaying considerable professional and aesthetic qualities – shape our views of the world. We must also ask how people actually use these media, which may not always be what the producers intended.

But where should you start in developing a deeper understanding of twenty-first-century media? You need to get clear in your own mind what some of the basic principles guiding such study are. You need to grasp some of the main reasons for studying particular features of the media (because you won't be able to study them all). You need to know what the main domains of analysis are and what techniques of study are appropriate in these domains. You need to think about how knowledge is produced – how theories and information about relevant social and cultural phenomena are formed into useful knowledge. And finally you need to think about what it means to live responsibly in a media-saturated world and how media education may add something valuable to that, your most fundamental project. You may already have some thoughts on these topics. If you want to pursue them more thoroughly, read on . . .

1

Why media studies is worthwhile

Cary Bazalgette

By deciding to do media studies you have stepped into a controversial, unstable and yet hugely important field. Have you made the right choice? Will it match your hopes and expectations? What difference will it make to your life? Only you can answer these questions, but this introduction may help you to do so.

Media studies is controversial because it is still new and because it deals with things that are not only continuing to change but are also the focus of many anxieties. Newspapers, film, radio, television and, increasingly, computer software and communications networks are generally considered to be immensely powerful in ways that are not fully understood and about which there is little consensus. They are consequently blamed for all kinds of social ills, political problems and cultural degeneracy. Each of these media has also, in its time, been seen as the harbinger of apocalyptic change – for better as well as for worse. But because the oldest of them – the mass circulation press – has only been in existence for little more than a century, the process of change has been too fast for anyone to arrive at definitive conclusions about what its social, political and cultural effects really are.

A century may seem like a long time to you, but in terms of thought and ideas, and the processes by which these become established in 'common sense', it is a remarkably short time. The chances are that your parents, or certainly your grandparents, knew people who were born in the nineteenth century. Anyone born in the first half of the twentieth century is unlikely to have seen television until they were at least five years old and has probably never played a computer game. Many senior politicians and leaders of industry fall into this age bracket. They were taught in school by people for whom films and radio were the novelties of their youth. As much as everyone likes to think they rebel against their parents and teachers, and keep up to date with new ideas and technologies, we are all substantially formed through the frameworks of ideas and thought of earlier generations, and we all find change difficult.

People confront change in different ways. They may try to ignore it, or they may exaggerate its effects. They like to find simple explanations for it, or they may throw up their hands and says 'it's inexplicable'. Change almost always provokes strong feelings: excitement, anxiety, tension, fear, anger. The media, conspicuous and changing objects in a world that is itself changing, are a particularly public focus for these kinds of emotion and argument. There is therefore much disagreement about how the media should be understood, regulated and consumed. You will probably have experienced such disagreement in your own home, from arguments when you were little about what you were and were not allowed to watch on television or video, to debates about whether a particular programme was worth watching. You also know that similar disagreements are rampant in the world at large. Do violent videos cause crime? Should large numbers of television channels and newspapers be owned by one corporation? Should European governments subsidise their film industries to protect their culture and language from American imperialism? You have heard these questions before and you know that they provoke endless arguments.

What may be less apparent to you is that similar disagreements are rife in the academic world as well. The people who teach courses, undertake research and write books in the field of media studies argue among themselves about the subject's content and priorities. Sometimes this sounds like dry academic quibbling. But more often they are passionate arguments with a powerful political edge. They are arguments about things that matter: about people as individuals and as members of groups; about how we communicate – or not; about how – and whether – we are informed about the world; about power and manipulation; about art and entertainment. In this book you will find many of these arguments explored and pondered. What you will not find is simple answers, because there aren't any. Media studies is not, essentially, a subject where you imbibe and regurgitate a lot of information. It is still in the business of generating questions – often challenging and threatening questions – about what we think we know and how we came to know it. It is ultimately for this reason that many people think of it as a problematic and even dangerous subject. It does threaten the established boundaries of academic subjects and the boundaries between the academic world and those of industry and business. Even the people who feel that those boundaries were already well overdue for some breakage find it hard to imagine what new patterns might emerge. Those who believe – sometimes with good reason – that such breakages are going to lose them their jobs and destroy their life's work, are understandably alarmed or despondent. But, fraught though it is, media studies in future stands a good chance of being at the centre of crucial changes in our thinking about what's worth learning and how it should be learned.

A new hybrid

It is essential to recognise that media studies, even as we enter the twenty-first century, is still new. The fact that much of the theory it uses evolved in the 1960s and 1970s – and indeed some of it much earlier – should not distract you from realising that it is a subject still in the process of being formed, full of disagreements and different claims as to what it is 'really about'. It is also a hybrid subject: that is to say, the ideas and approaches that it draws upon come from many different sources. This is inevitable, when you come to think about it. The idea that the modern mass media are worth critical attention has never been the exclusive property of any one academic tradition, and such critical attention began to grow as soon as each medium appeared. The mass circulation press, the cinema, radio, television, digital software and the internet each attracted comment, analysis and speculation from the start. Everyone who spoke or wrote about these media was themselves already educated within existing academic disciplines and motivated by particular interests. But a new object of study can never be approached in exactly the same way as the old. The most alert commentators and analysts start to reach out for new ways of comprehending a new phenomenon.

Imagine what it must have been like in the 1900s to try and figure out the real significance of the new medium, cinema. On the one hand you had the conventional arrangement of an audience seated in rows facing a stage, watching a fictional story or some other form of entertainment being performed, just as millions of people already did in theatres and music halls. But on the other hand it was now possible for each member of the audience to be far closer to the 'performers' than had ever been possible before. From the earliest days of cinema you could see the figures on the screen from an apparent distance of about fifteen feet – closer than the front row of the stalls in most theatres; later, as the technique of 'close-up' developed, you could see a hand clasp, a mouth smiling, a tear falling, as if from merely inches away. What ideas would you have drawn upon to speculate about the impact of such immediacy upon those audiences? Add to this the fact that the very same film could be showing in thousands of cinemas to millions of people: how would you have set about analysing, let alone explaining, such a novelty? The critical traditions of literature and drama would help, but so would psychology and sociology (both of them relatively new disciplines at the time), and indeed political theory (could cinema be used to persuade a whole class or nation to respond in a pre-determined way?); economics (how much demand is there likely to be for this form of entertainment and what is the most profitable way of supplying it?); and even philosophy (can it be said that these audiences are experiencing 'reality' and, if so, on what level?).

Any new medium, therefore, is inevitably 'up for grabs' by critics and theorists of any persuasion, and increasingly so in the modern academic world with its demanding publication schedules and voracious appetite for new research topics. But how do you mix literary theory with economics or linguistics with politics, even when you have recognised that it might be useful to do so? You would not only have to develop a reasonably substantial knowledge of two or more areas; you would also have to contend with the attitudes of present and future colleagues who may be bitterly opposed to the 'dilution' or 'degradation' of the subject to which they have devoted their working lives and public reputations. Nevertheless, hybrid disciplines do appear all the time: semiotics, structuralism, sociolinguistics, and many more. Media studies snaps them all up: there can never be too many different ways of analysing just *what is really going on* in those fleeting images, those rapt audiences, those smoke-filled boardrooms of the owners.

This is how media studies has acquired its reputation for being very theoretical, and a good course should enable you to see why theory is important and exciting, and to use it to develop your own thinking. That said, it has to be admitted that there are still too many courses that offer little more than a dismal trudge through shopping lists of theory, and 'mastering the jargon' appears to be the ultimate aim.

Technology and theory

Academic ivory towers are fewer and further apart with every year that passes, and few students are motivated to choose media studies by a love of pure theory. The media themselves change much faster than any theory. In fact it is often changes in the media – even basic technological changes – that impel changes in the academic construction of the subject. Television study was scarcely possible in any real sense before the advent of the videocassette recorder in the mid 1970s. As I write this in the late 1990s we have moved into a period of what are profound changes brought about by digital technologies. Until the 1980s the term 'media' meant what it said (although it was, and still is, widely misused as a singular noun). It refers to numbers of different ways of physically reproducing and carrying meanings. So, the medium of photography consists of photosensitive papers and chemicals; the medium of video is plastic tape coated with iron oxide; the medium of print is paper and ink, and so on. In the digital world these physical differences are eradicated. Photographs, written words, sounds, drawings and moving images can all be encoded electronically in the same way and stored on disk, transmitted through networks or beamed by satellites. You don't have to move from one expensive machine to another to make images, compose music, write words, combine these and transmit them to other people: you can do all these things with one set of relatively inexpensive equipment with the right software and network links.

The implications of this technology are enormous. Media studies, already well established in the foundation-rocking business, will be rocked to its own foundations as the terms 'producer', 'text' and 'audience' begin to lose the meanings we thought they had. There will be no excuse for media studies courses whose students never engage in production, any more than there is for literature courses whose students never attempt their own creative writing. Luckily such courses are increasingly rare, and most media studies teachers have long recognised the need for students to undertake practical work, even when critical analysis is their main priority. You can see how this has arisen more readily in media studies than in other academic subjects. It is actually harder to study a moving image or a soundtrack sequence than it is to analyse words on a page or cells under a microscope. The whole point of a media text is that it moves and flows: the meaning is never 'there' at a given moment, but in juxtaposition and sequence, in the tension between one moment and another. To analyse a sequence of television or film you have to use a vidoeocassette recorder or editing table and that very process brings you closer to the processes of production than a reader ever gets to a novelist's pen or a printing press. It is thus – or should be – a short step from this kind of analysis to trying out image making, sequencing and soundtrack laying oneself. So although media studies teachers argue – as always – about what the role of practical work on their courses ought to be, and just how it should relate to critical analysis, or to industry standards of competence, they are almost all agreed that it should have some sort of role.

One result of the advent of digital technologies is likely to be that the practice/theory distinction will become increasingly blurred anyway. Once you can integrate moving-image sequences into a written essay (e.g. by submitting it electronically, with hyperlinks to audio-visual material) and demonstrate through 'quotation', for example, the difference between a character appearing to notice X rather than Y when she enters a room, then the way you approach critical analysis in the first place is going to change.

However, these kinds of change will not happen immediately, or all at once, or in the same way. They are obviously dependent upon further technical development and on a wider investment in compatible and reliable systems, especially in accessing and using computer networks, but they are also dependent upon the priorities of different courses. The very name 'media studies' rightly comprises two plurals: different courses prioritise different media, different theories and different learning outcomes. Media studies is thus a catch-all title designating a wide variety of courses, and since these are all embroiled both in developing a coherent theoretical base *and* in keeping up with technological and institutional developments in the media themselves, does it even make sense to lump them all together?

Basic principles

Different versions of media studies do nevertheless have some basic principles in common. Perhaps the most helpful way to characterise these will be to compare media studies with another subject with which you are likely to be familiar. In schools, media studies is often linked to English or taught by people whose academic training was in English literature. It is not difficult to see affinities between the two subjects. English deals with more than just the skills of reading and writing and critical analysis: it engages with students' tastes and personal responses, with moral or ethical issues that are relevant to their lives, and how these are explored through forms of representation such as fictional narrative. But for most students these days, the fictional narratives that are told in films and television programmes provide the basis for such exploration just as much as literature. English teachers usually recognise this and have to find a way of negotiating the gap between the established cultural status of literature and their students' perceptions of what is worthwhile and relevant.

But the difference between English and media studies is not simply the difference between the objects of study that each subject prefers: books for one, film and television for the other. In English you are invited to think of texts as having a single point of origin: the author. You may consider the social or historical context in which that author produced the text, and you may be encouraged to consider aspects of the author's personal life that might have affected his or her writing. You are rarely, if ever, asked to think about a literary text as a commodity: something in which many people have a financial interest and of which copies are sold in order to make a profit. In media studies you *are* asked this. You are asked to look at cinema and television as industries

9

which employ large numbers of people and to understand how they work, how they are financed and why they produce what they do. Book publishing is also an industry that employs large numbers of people but literature students are rarely required to study it.

English also concentrates on individual, personal response. When you study English literature you are asked to think about how novels and poems address you as an individual. In media studies you may be asked to think about films, television programmes or other 'media texts' in the same way. But you will certainly also be asked to think about how they address you – or other people – as a member of a group: as British, say, or as a black person, or as a man, or even – but how often? – as all three. By asking you to think about texts in this way, and by making you investigate who made, say, a film or programme, and why, and in whose interests, media studies is essentially political. Every investigation of even quite short or trivial texts potentially leads into larger questions about power structures in society and how they are organised. This does not necessarily mean national party politics or the daily doings of presidents or armies. It is just as 'political' to be asking questions about who owns this newspaper, who financed this film, and why; or perhaps more interestingly, who *wouldn't* finance that film and why, or how one kind of television programme is more likely to be made than another. The politics of the media affect our lives as much as the politics of Parliament or Congress, and can be more satisfying to investigate since the evidence is all around you every day. What these effects really are, how powerful they may be, and how they may be challenged or changed, is part of the business of media studies and a major reason why this subject is sometimes regarded with suspicion. At the same time it is the inclusion of this political dimension that media students often find the most satisfying and worthwhile aspect of the subject. 'You stop taking things at face value', they say; 'it helps you to take a step back'; 'it makes you always want another perspective'; 'it wakes you up to influences you kind of knew about but weren't fully aware of'.

Some courses, it must be acknowledged, hammer students into the ground with a political 'line'. There are gung-ho versions of media studies whose central objective is to strip away the sugary entertainment coating from any and every media text to reveal the sinister machinery of capitalist manipulation within. You should beware of media courses which render the subject down to a few handy maxims such as 'the basic function of all media is to sell audiences to advertisers'. To object that this can hardly apply to public service broadcasting or a community video workshop is not to deny that these institutions will also have political roles to play and manipulative techniques to use. But it does reassert the principle that there is more than one way to look at any text. A political dimension to critical analysis should add complexity, not simplification.

So far, I have identified two basic principles that media studies courses are likely to have in common: using economic and political perspectives as key ways of understanding the media. These are the most characteristic differences between media studies and most other subjects. But no course will concentrate on these areas alone. I have indicated how diverse a range of other theories may be used and that different courses will prioritise different things.

At a more fundamental level, however, that very diversity is another key principle. One of the strengths – and also the challenges – of media studies is precisely that it asks you to consider texts from different and often sharply contrasting perspectives. It is a long way from thinking about why you wept (and perhaps why your best friend did not) at the ending of Douglas Sirk's film *Imitation of Life* to finding out about the Hollywood studio system of the 1950s, but you could well be doing both in the same week. You could equally well be doing neither. Instead, you might be counting and characterising the number of appearances of women in television news broadcasts over a given week, and shooting and editing your own news item that breaks the 'rules' of gender representation you have uncovered.

What is common to these and any other versions of media studies that you may encounter is the breadth of approaches that will be used and the belief that they do relate to one another in ways that offer you new insights and generate questions you hadn't thought of at first. But does this mean that media studies just doesn't have any boundaries; that it can be about anything and everything? And, if so, how can it have any real status as a subject?

What do you study in media studies?

A familiar criticism of media studies is that it ignores established cultural values, paying undeserved attention to trivial and ephemeral material. The fact that media students may be writing essays about popular television game shows, sports coverage or computer games is assumed to 'prove' that it offers no intellectual challenges and that 'anything' can be chosen to study. It is true that media studies, unlike English, professes not to have a canonical list of high-status texts that everyone ought to have studied; in fact it is as true of media studies as of other arts subjects that certain texts are more accessible than others, have been written about more and are considered to raise more interesting questions. Nevertheless, media studies does assert the principle that texts are not rendered worthy of study simply through some preordained cultural status – unless it is actually the nature of that 'status' which is to be studied. In other words, it can be as important to analyse a Mickey Mouse T-shirt as it is to analyse the classic Japanese film *Seven Samurai*. Indeed, there are some media studies teachers who would assert that it is more important to study the T-shirt since more people have heard of Mickey Mouse than ever have or ever will see *Seven Samurai*. Here we get into one of the most interestingly contentious areas of media studies. Just what – if anything – constitutes a valid argument for studying one text, or one group of texts, rather than another? There are five main ways of answering this question.

Popularity is a powerful argument and the one that most confidently asserts the difference between media studies and other subjects, except perhaps social studies and related fields. Studying television game shows, *Star Wars* movies, chart singles or computer games is justifiable purely and simply because a lot of people like them. The emphasis might be on the phenomenon of mass audience pleasure and on understanding and legitimating the enjoyment people derive from these texts, or, in contrast, the aim of the analysis might be to reveal how audiences are manipulated and deluded by stereotypical or reactionary material. The fact that the object of study may be pretty anodyne is beside the point: what the students are doing – we hope – is developing important critical insights. It is true that, in the hands of inexperienced or poorly trained media teachers, the study of popular cultural forms has sometimes failed to challenge students or move them beyond what they already know, but poor practice does not invalidate the principle that popularity is a significant factor in the media world and we need to try and understand how it works.

Exemplification is an obvious ground for worthiness of study, especially when the aim is to illustrate an aspect of theory, such as genre or representation. This is not a simple matter of 'watch this and then you'll know what film noir (or naturalism, or the dumb blonde stereotype) is'. Single texts rarely function effectively as perfect examples; how would you select an absolutely typical soap opera episode, for example? Would a good example of racist stereotyping be one that was really extreme or one that was rather ambivalent? It is characteristic of media studies that it tests and reviews its own theories, asking students to consider a range of examples and then to figure out not only the usefulness of a theory but also its limitations. So, for example, it would be more interesting to try and select material to help you decide just how helpful the idea of 'genre' is for categorising television drama, than being given established examples of soap opera, crime series, classic serials, and so on, and having to pick out their typical features.

Notoriety is an interesting and useful reason for studying a text that can offer a way in to thinking about social, political and cultural contexts. Texts which are interesting to study in their own right, but whose notoriety reveals much about their conditions of production or consumption, include banned or controversial television documentaries such as Thames TV's *Death on the Rock* (1988), which examined the shooting of IRA terrorists; films such as Hammer Studios' 1955 film *The Quatermass Experiment*, which sparked off a moral panic about horror films as well as a hugely successful cycle of that rare commodity, the exportable British film; and texts which have divided audiences and broken conventional boundaries such as Madonna's *Sex*. Such 'case studies' form the starting point or central exemplar which can illuminate aspects of the media we don't normally think about or see.

Turning points and groundbreaking texts could be included in the previous category, but texts can be significant without being notorious, especially in retrospect. A media course that was concentrating on aspects of stylistic or technological development might well include studies of Orson Welles's 1940 film *Citizen Kane* for its uses of ceilinged sets and deep-focus shot composition, or Alfred Hitchcock's 1929 film *Blackmail* for its use of the then relatively untried technology of synchronised sound. A course that was concentrating on institutional innovation might look at the first night of ITV in Britain in 1954, at the launch of the Madonna Network on the web in 1998, or at the arrival of digital television.

Aesthetic value is a criterion that many media teachers would deny using as a way of selecting or judging texts. In the 1960s and 1970s aesthetics were seen as so closely implicated in elitist attitudes and uncritically accepted value systems that media studies, intent on establishing its political credentials and its difference from established academic tradition, took some pride in a total rejection of judgements about beauty, taste and emotional effects. So, on many courses, out with this particular baby went the bath water of anything not sanctioned by popularity, historical significance or notoriety: many foreign-language films (lumped together as 'art cinema'), experimental films and video, a rich tradition of documentary photography, and so on. This attitude is changing. Most media studies teachers now see it as part of their job to encourage students in experiencing and enjoying a wider range of media than they already know about at the start of the course. But this still does not necessarily grasp the nettle of how media studies should really deal with aesthetic judgements, and we have the strange situation where both teachers and students are making such judgements all the time without really being explicit about them. For example, why is *The Searchers* more frequently studied than many other westerns or films by John Ford? It is because critics have generally found it richer, more ambivalent, more troubling, packed with more meaning, more beautifully shot. It's – well – for many people it's a better film! It is hard enough to come out of the closet on the aesthetic value of a 'classic' from 1956; it is harder still to confront the question of aesthetic judgements in relation to popular texts. What makes you enjoy one sitcom rather than another? For all its assertions that it provides the universal set of critical theories to help you find out all you need to know about any text, media studies has been strangely silent on this question – so far. Recent signs are that the silence is about to be broken and that media aesthetics beyond 2000 will once again become a respectable subject for research, writing and, eventually, teaching.

What is it all for?

Any number of assertions about breadth of approach and student satisfaction will not answer the question of what media studies might be for. What difference should you expect it to make? To what kinds of job or further study might it lead?

Commentators on educational trends often assume that everyone who takes a media studies course wants to work in the media. It is certainly obvious that quite a lot of media students do have such aspirations (and in the USA, university schools of communication are likely to endorse this aspiration) but no one, so far, has actually counted them or tracked the subsequent career or study paths of media studies graduates on a national or international scale. It is also obvious that the media industries themselves are hard to get into and rely increasingly on freelancers, so that most media workers face periods of unemployment and find it hard to predict their pattern of work from month to month, let alone from year to year. However, as other industries are moving into similar employment practices and as short-term contracts, freelance and casual work become more widespread, the prospect of a flexible and varied career path does not seem so terrifying to younger people as it does to those who were brought up to expect jobs for life.

You are bound to be told that employers in the media industries are not necessarily looking for people with media studies qualifications anyway; that a knowledge of history, politics, economics, accountancy, law – you name it – would be equally useful as a basis for working as, say, a journalist or editor. However, 'a job in the media' evokes for most people the idea of the high-profile jobs they already know about from their own media consumption: journalists, editors, cinematographers, presenters, and so on. Taking a media studies course may be the best way for you to get a better idea of the vast range of jobs in the media industries and of how those jobs are changing. There is no doubt that the film and broadcasting industries in particular are experiencing a crisis in training and are likely to face a skills shortage in the future. Some people predict that by the early 2000s as many as 20 per cent of the jobs in Europe will relate in one way or another to the media industries: whether you plan to work in this field or not, you may as well know something about it.

But the 'usefulness' of media studies is, or should be, far wider than simply getting you a job. Employment is (I hope) only one of the roles you will take on. You will also be a citizen, a voter, a consumer, a member of audiences, perhaps a parent. It is increasingly likely that, whatever job you do or whatever your domestic circumstances, there will be more opportunities for you to engage with the media, and not just as a consumer. You may be producing and exchanging multimedia texts (where once written reports were sufficient) or designing web pages; you may be handling press or public relations on your own behalf or for a company; you may be involved in political campaigns whose main tools of communication will be video and narrowcast or 'pirate' programming. Indeed, the field of 'alternative' and subversive media production may be the one that grows fastest over the next few years (who knows? how could you tell?) as access to technology and circulation systems widens. The much-vaunted apocalyptic scenario of 500 television channels available to everyone is unlikely to result in the wall-to-wall soap operas, pornography and video shopping that the big corporations have been predicting for us *ad nauseam*. No society is content for long with a homogenised entertainment diet: sooner or later many, if not most, of those 500 channels will be offering wider access, new voices and kinds of programmes we have not yet imagined. Inside or outside the corporate producers, the new voices will come from the people who are already literate in the new media.

But let us not lose sight of the fact that a media studies course that has been challenging, exciting and satisfying for you will make an important difference to your life even if you never lay hands on a camera, tape recorder or web design software again. 'It makes you more powerful as a reader', students say. 'It gives you the power of choice, the power to question.' Media studies may be engaging with aspects of culture that are central to your life now, and this may well be part of its appeal. It deals with things you already know something about and enjoy, and you know that as you go through the course you won't always have to go to a library or laboratory for your study materials: every time you switch on the television or walk down the street you will be fuelling your critical and creative ideas. But that pre-existing accessibility is just the start. What media studies can really do is to open up your understanding of how things work, how people become informed – or misinformed – and how the myths and ideologies that govern all our lives are created and sustained. These

things are worth learning about in any case. Enjoy them!

2

A student's guide to surviving communication scholarship

Nikhil Sinha and Horace Newcomb

Mapping the field

Planning and presenting a 'survival guide' for students of communication may be likened to approaching the 'Tower of Babel' as described in Biblical history. In that story the peoples of 'the world' gathered to build a tower that would reach to Heaven, but because of their multiple languages they could never agree on plans, and thus the great tower collapsed upon them. In the Western scriptural tradition this is perhaps the principal commentary on the topic of communication. The focus is on distinction, fragmentation and variation, on the folly of trying to construct a common experience or common purpose. And Babel may certainly seem an appropriate analogy for the new student of communication. Communication studies can often seem to be a bewildering arena filled with competing and mutually incomprehensible special languages. At times the speakers and writers of these languages seem to be at odds with one another, hostile to any sense of mutual goals. Indeed, in today's world communication itself seems to be multiplying in form and content, in purpose and method, in technology and price. The Babel of communication styles and strategies may seem to be matched by the Babel of theories, methods, projects and approaches that go to make up communication studies.

If we take this analogy seriously, however, we should remember another story from the same source. We should remember the story of Noah's survival of the Great Flood. Understood symbolically, the animals taken by Noah to the Ark undoubtedly came with different concerns, different backgrounds, different goals, different languages. Once gathered, the Ark was their primary concern, their common experience. It was a meeting place that made possible a common goal. But it allowed for the implications of that goal – life – to be worked out in many ways. Indeed, we should note the shared meanings and etymology of words such as 'common', 'community' and 'communication'. In our view, communication studies is a vessel not unlike the Ark. The field contains different theoretical and methodological species, but all are linked by a common purpose – the study of human communication.

Neither of these analogies is so far-fetched as it might first seem. While we caution against large, universal claims, we do want to suggest that communication, in its many forms, might somehow be central to the survival of all species, humans among them. And despite the apparently contradictory and confused ways of *studying* communication, we want to suggest that it is possible to move through the *field* of communication studies without losing one's way. Let us begin this guide, then, with three propositions that restate some of the previous claims.

First, as emphasised above, communication studies is a 'field'. It is not a discipline in the classical sense. Disciplines have far more precise boundaries than does the study of communication. Disciplines also have clear historical development. While it is possible to trace the history of how communication has been studied, that history would appear more like a swampy river delta than a clear, identifiable channel. Disciplines have bodies of knowledge that are generally agreed upon, common texts with which all who study the discipline should be acquainted. These are 'core' texts, both primary and secondary. Even when these lists of texts are in dispute, as is currently the case with the 'canon' of 'great literature', the terms and objects of the dispute are clear. This is not the case with the study of communication.

Second, communication studies is an intersection, a switchboard of sorts, where various approaches come together in attempts to define and explain some common elements. In order to understand various forms of communication, the field uses many approaches. It draws upon other fields. It even draws heavily upon traditional disciplines such as sociology, economics, literary study, anthropology, philosophy, history, psychology, law, and many more. This is not to suggest that communication scholars have not made important theoretical and methodological contributions to their field. Rather, the real strength of communication studies lies in tying together elements from many different disciplines and forging a new field. These newer approaches are perhaps more suited to the study of a complex phenomenon such as communication in our increasingly interrelated, interdependent and interdisciplinary world.

Third, communication studies as a field is best defined by its *objects of study*. These objects are the various forms and aspects of communication, not all of them human, that nevertheless contribute to our understanding of what it is to be human. Put another way, communication studies, of many sorts, are unified in their attempt to understand communication phenomena and processes.

In this chapter we suggest that scholarship in communication studies can be 'mapped', as it can be in any other field or discipline. The central reference points on such a map will be the major conceptual issues in the field. The student's task becomes much simpler when he or she is aware of existing maps, of the mapping process and of these major conceptual issues. With these features in mind, the student can place scholarship, old and new, the accepted and the challenging, upon the maps. The student can *orient* him- or herself with regard to other features, other approaches, other disputes. This orientation comes when the student sees how one set of sources relates to another, even though the two may use different terms and different methods of study. Or it comes when the student is able to make a claim about a particular issue or problem because he or she has learned how other approaches deal with the topic.

Certainly this orientation allows the student better to understand required readings and to prepare for examinations by having some guidelines and reference points. But it does far more than that. The mapping process, and orienting one's self within it, allows the student to set out his or her own 'destination' in the field, to plan a course of study, a pathway towards personal and professional goals. Indeed, the most interesting work, whether in the form of a required academic essay or in applied work within communication-related professions, is often done in the 'unmapped' terrain of the field. A new problem, a new approach, a new technique or form of communication is discovered by exploring an 'empty' spot on the map.

To establish the utility of this approach as a survival guide to communication scholarship, we suggest that the issues and problems in communication studies can best be first mapped along two dimensions. We refer to these dimensions as (1) the *domains of analysis*, and (2) the *techniques of analysis*. Both these dimensions, in turn, can be broken down along a three-part distinction. The three parts of the communication process we will emphasise go by many names, but we will refer to them as *production, product* and *reception*. In figure 1 we present the approach in outline form. In what follows, we will explore the resulting 'map' in more detail. We will conclude with an example of how the approach might be applied to a specific topic. We will show how it can be used both to study existing communication scholarship and to generate new scholarship.

Helping us to understand and explain communication problems within and among the domains, and guiding our selection of techniques of analysis, are *theories*. Theories are systematic explanations of a set of facts. In the natural and physical sciences scholars and students search for the one theory that best explains a set of facts. In humanistic and social scientific fields such as communication studies, a number of theories may claim to explain the same set of facts. These theories may be drawn from a number of other disciplines.

Domains of analysis provide an outline of the topics and issues confronted by students and scholars of communication. These topics and issues, as presented here, are not meant to be finite. The list can grow and change as new problems emerge and new configurations of industries, products and audiences are formed. These domains represent the three principal levels at which communication problems and issues may be identified. They may be referred to under other terms, such as sender–message–receiver or industry–text–audience, or by yet other terms that indicate the generation/creation of material, the form/content of that material and the users/uses of that material. Distinctions among any of these terms are mainly analytical. They are good for purposes of inquiry. As we shall see, investigating a problem in any one domain will very often blur these distinctions and lead us into another domain. Similarly, the three areas describing techniques of analysis will often be blended, bent or blurred to refine a technique more suitable to understanding a particular problem than to a 'pure' application of method.

Techniques of analysis are the *methods* and *procedures* that scholars employ to gather and analyse facts. They may be *quantitative*, if the analysis requires the use of statistical or mathematical procedures, as in surveys or content analysis. They may be *qualitative*, if they employ non-quantitative but system-

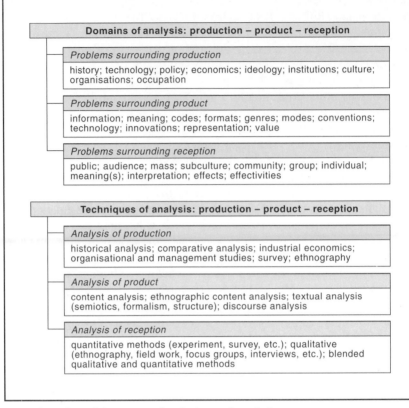

Figure 1 Outline of domains and techniques of analysis

atic techniques of observation and analysis, as in ethnographic or historical work. And they may be *interpretive*, if they depend on subjective but still systematic evaluations, as in various techniques of textual analysis and criticism (see also Part VI of this volume).

These three elements – domains, theories and techniques – can be used to outline the broad conceptual map of the field of communication studies (or any other field). In this chapter we focus on the first and third of these elements. How do we identify problems and how do we identify the techniques to study them? (Theories are dealt with in subsequent sections of the book.)

Stop and think

The student's task

The student confronted with a set of readings for a particular class, confronted with a set of sources in preparing a particular essay, paper or project, should determine what domain is being analysed and what techniques are used in the analysis. The student should recognise that every domain contains many distinct but related problems. The student should realise that each problem can be studied in many different ways. And he or she should realise

that these various analyses can all be valuable. Moreover, the student should recognise that different 'languages' (the languages of economics, aesthetics, sociology, psychology, etc.) can be applied in these varying instances, and that part of studying communication media lies in recognising when different languages are being used to discuss the same problem. Only by being able to 'translate' will the student reap the full benefit of the richness of communication and media studies.

With this overview in mind, consider how various scholars might move across our 'map' in order to study aspects of the same problem, within the same domain, but using different techniques. One might, for example, wish to write about the movie industry. But how does one address such a large topic? A more important question for our purposes is how might a student begin to make her or his way through the vast body of scholarship devoted to the topic? Certainly, a good place to begin is with the history of the movie industry. Historical studies provide good beginnings for any aspect of communication studies, and we strongly recommend that any student learn the history of his or her special interests as a point of departure.

Still, there are many histories within any single history. Looking at our outline, we could choose to focus more precisely on history related to the technology of the cinema. But even this choice does little to narrow the scope of our inquiry. This is a very complex topic, filled with controversy over who invented what apparatus, when and where. Quickly, we would see that our questions would guide us into related questions. Some are questions of economics – who funded these early inventions? Others focus on the organisation of industries – how did Thomas Edison organise his workshop (where some early film technologies were invented or modified)? Our questions might even extend to the institutional arrangements surrounding patents for inventions. Indeed, accounts of the struggle to control patents for the technologies involved in film making are among the most fascinating in communication history. As we move through all these questions we would still be using history as our technique of analysis. And if we are truly involved with the subject we would be studying *historiography*. These are the philosophies of history. They are also varied and can lead to varying explanations of the same phenomena.

But it is equally important to recognise what techniques we *cannot* use in historical analysis. Assuming we continue our work on the same topic, we cannot use *survey techniques* to study the early inventors of cinema technologies – they are, after all, long dead. For the same reason we cannot apply *ethnographic techniques*. Ethnography requires the researcher to be present in order to observe actions and decisions. One of the great frustrations of historical analysis is that we so often wish to be present in the past, to see what was done, how and why. But that remains an impossibility.

If, however, we do not focus on history but choose to study the contemporary development of cinema technologies (our own period is one of the most exciting for the study of new technologies of all sorts), we *can* survey inventors, users and even audiences who view new types of movie. We can arrange to live among inventors and scientists and technicians, constructing our ethnographic explanations of their work. Our techniques of analysis have shifted simply because we have shifted our focus to a different problem, but we have remained within the same domain of analysis.

Shift the example again, and move this time to a different place on our map. Assume that we are now concerned with the product domain. We want to study a specific movie or group of movies. There are many problems here. From our outline we can choose *value*. This will involve us in the study of how to *evaluate* movies, to decide which are 'good' and 'bad,' 'mediocre' or 'great'. Here we may choose *discourse analysis* as our technique. Discourse analysis, as we are using the term, seeks out and describes strong, coherent patterns of ideas. In this case we would be analysing the discourses of 'judgement' or 'evaluation'. How have influential individuals (critics, teachers, film makers) defined 'a good movie', or 'a great movie', in different specific contexts or through periods of time? How have their judgements managed to become accepted by large segments of the population so that 'we' agree on these definitions? These 'agreements' are often unexamined, unquestioned. That is what we mean by 'discourse'. But they do change, and we might wish to study how they change, engaging again in a type of historical analysis.

We may, however, choose to study an entirely different problem related to movies as products, the problem of *representation*, for example. This new focus will involve us in questions of how movies 're-present' the varied worlds of human experience. We can see, for example, that women have often been represented in some ways but not in others. Once again, we have choices to make regarding the techniques of analysis. We can apply *content analysis*. To do so we would construct categories that seem to appear within our sample of movies. We might find these to be Woman as Housewife, Woman as Shrew, Woman as Seductress, Woman as Virgin-Mother. We could then count the instances of each category, compare our tallies with others performing the same count, and decide whether or not we have agreed upon the categorisations. We could then describe our analysis in a paper listing numbers of each category. Usually we would also discuss what these counts mean, perhaps by relating them to our understanding of discourses.

For a different perspective on the same films, we might apply *textual analysis*. Here we would be involved in a more subjective procedure. We might identify the same categories, but our concern would not be for quantifying them. Rather, we would focus our work on how such 'types' function in creating an overall constructed depiction of 'woman'. We would be interested in *interpreting* the significance of that depiction. Very quickly our analysis would blend into other problems: we would link these representations to other forms of *code* found throughout our society, showing how these depictions relate to those found in religion, in educational texts, even in legal structures. We might be interested in seeing how representations of women vary from westerns to film noir, to domestic melodrama, to comedy, to science fiction. If we perform this comparison we are engaged in the study of *genre* as our product-related problem. These approaches could also lead us back to large patterns of social thought, to discourses. And any of these approaches could be conducted as historical studies.

With examples such as these our 'map' quickly becomes more complicated, for it is here that we find we must travel to the 'crossroads' in order to orient ourselves among all these branching options. We might find, for instance, that certain genres have been predominant at certain times rather than others. This is a problem for historical analysis. But we begin to see that the decision to produce those movies, at specific times, came about because of certain *policies* that were driven by *economic* concerns. In other words, our product problem has overlapped, intersected with, and returned us to the domain of production. In communication studies, such intersections are more the rule than the exception. We will have more to say about this below.

First, however, let us look at our final domain of analysis, problems surrounding *reception*. We might want to develop information about reception for a variety of reasons. From a straightforward marketing perspective we might wish to know how many people attended a particular movie. We might be employed by the movie company in a position that collects this information. We would apply various *quantitative measures* to determine this figure. But we might also be asked to find out whether or not those who attended the movie really enjoyed it, whether they would tell others to see it. Here we would be involved in exploring their evaluation of the movie. To find answers to this type of question we would apply techniques of analysis that are more qualitative in nature. We might gather a group of people who have seen the movie, a *focus group*, and interview them about their likes and dislikes. We might, on the other hand, simply interview individuals and compile a profile from their responses.

But we might not be working for the movie company at all. We might, as scholars, be interested in audience interpretations for intellectual reasons, to add to our body of knowledge about how people experience such events. We want to explore what the movie means to a group or to an individual. Here we might apply some of the same techniques as those used for marketing purposes – focus groups, interviews – to gather our information. But we might analyse it quite differently. We might even go further and live with a family for some time, observing the ways in which they choose certain movies rather than others and the ways in which they discuss the movies they see, convincing one another of certain interpretations. This would be an application of *ethnographic analytical techniques*, and would give us still other information. We could use this information to see how people relate to the discourses within the movies, how they relate to the organisation of social power, that is to *ideology*. We could see whether or not certain individuals (fathers, mothers, older siblings) exercise forms of dominance in guiding interpretations, and how others might resist both the ideas in the movie and in their group.

Now, consider another intersection. We are employed by the movie company for marketing purposes, and our task is to find out about audience interpretations. But the goal this time is to decide whether or not to change the ending of a movie before it is released into general circulation. Here we have once again crossed paths with problems surrounding production. And if we are the 'disinterested' scholar, we may study this process as part of our analysis of the movie industry. We may even study the use of this marketing strategy from the earliest days of movie making up to the present – a historical analysis. Or we may study it as part of the way the movie industry decides when to change its representation of women – another form of ideological analysis.

21

The point of this imaginary exercise is very straightforward and is summarised in the accompanying case study. It is about situating oneself, along with the appropriate domains and techniques of analysis, within the complexity of the field. In the case study accompanying this chapter (see box) we examine another specific topic in greater detail in order to demonstrate this complexity yet again.

One of the most highly charged and sensitive aspects of contemporary communication is the issue of pornography, an issue so volatile, in fact, that laws defining pornography, regulating its production, distribution and use, are among the most complex and contested in society. These laws, and the conflicts around them, illustrate struggles over the most fundamental definitions of individual rights and social responsibility, showing how communication is at the heart of our notions of freedom, democracy, restraint and protection. Similarly, the study of issues related to pornography illustrates the enormous complexity of our field. The issues we find here reveal intersections of the domains of analysis and indicate why multiple techniques of analysis must be (cont. p. 27) used to come to a full understanding of the problems we confront.

Pornography: a case study

Over fifty years ago, an early communication scholar, Harold Lasswell (1948), described the process of communication as 'who says what, to whom and with what effect?'. Since then communication research has focused on answering and elaborating one or more of these questions. The question of 'who' has given rise to work that looks at the systems, institutions, organisations and individuals involved in the creation of communication messages. In the outline presented here (figure 1), much of this research would be found in the production category. The analysis of the messages themselves (through content analysis, textual analysis, semiotics or other techniques of textual analysis) has emerged from the question of 'what', our product category. The question of 'to whom' is, of course, linked to the analysis of audiences or, more generally, to questions of the reception of communication messages.

But perhaps none of the questions raised by Lasswell has generated as much research, controversy or debate as the question of 'with what effect?'. Questions related to this topic would also appear in the reception domain of our outline but, as we shall see, the notion of reception may in fact complicate the notion of 'effect'. Still, in a sense it can be argued that the study of communication is always concerned with issues of 'effect', whether implicitly or explicitly. For example, even if the ostensible purpose of the research is to identify the values that guide journalists, the research gains significance from the implicit assumption that identifying journalistic values is important because what journalists produce is important for society – as information, education, entertainment or as cultural products that help construct and reconstruct the world in which we live. Or, even if the stated purpose of the analysis is an aesthetic evaluation of a television programme, the implicit aim is to instruct both programme producers and audiences in how to recognise, and therefore select and support, 'good' television, or perhaps to alter definitions of 'good' television.

Even so, the 'effects' question has given rise to a formidable body of communication research that has attempted to isolate and deal with the problem of the effects of communication messages on individuals, and these studies are often framed to discover effects on particular aspects of human behaviour. The questions, of course, are by no means new. Plato worried over the effects of poetry on the youth of his day, and Aristotle provided analyses and 'handbooks' on how to affect audiences with both dramatic and political communication. But the issue of the impact of communication messages on society has taken on particular salience with the development of modern mass communication technologies such as radio, television, films and, now, computer-based networks. The problems related to this issue have led to further problems that reach far beyond 'communication' in any narrow sense and show us just how central, how fundamental, the study of communication can be.

All societies have struggled with the issue of regulating what should, or should not, be depicted or communicated though modern communication media. Even if countries do not have laws that specify what is permissible mass media content, all countries have laws that identify what is *not* permissible content. These laws and regulations are invariably based on some understanding of the potentially adverse 'effects' such content may have on individuals or on society, and effects research conducted by professional academicians is often cited and used by lawmakers in the debate about what should be excluded from the media. So it is with the question of effects that we begin our case study of pornography.

But, through a series of questions that all students need to put to *any* body of research they are reviewing, we hope to make clear that the effects question cannot be answered without raising issues that fall within all three of our domains of analysis. In pointing to these overlapping issues, we demonstrate that a full understanding of any particular topic within communication studies must utilise many more techniques of analysis than are usually employed within traditional 'effects' research. Indeed, any examination of a topic, issue or problem in communication research should begin, as we do here, with learning what has already been said.

Question 1: What questions are being asked and what answers are provided in the literature?
The first task of the student interested in any topic in communication studies is to gather and examine a body of existing literature. This can be done by using various guides and indexes to the wide range of communication and media studies literature. The next step, the first and crucial analytical step, is to *identify what questions are being asked*. The 'effects' literature on pornography, for example, typically asks what effect exposure to pornographic materials has on men. These anticipated or hypothesised 'effects' usually involve changes in the way men respond to women, their propensity to commit violence against women, their attitudes towards women, and so on. A student reviewing the research on the effects of pornography will, among other issues, commonly come across the following questions: Does exposure to pornography cause men to be more aggressive? Does exposure to pornography cause men to be more aggressive towards women? Does exposure to

pornography cause men to be more callous towards women? Does exposure to pornography trivialise rape? Does exposure to pornography lead to deviant or hyper-sexual practices or attitudes?

Typically, the answers to these questions are in the affirmative. In the past twenty-five years or so a large body of 'evidence' has been accumulated about the potentially deleterious and harmful effects of pornography on both the men exposed to such materials and their potential victims – women. However, the reviewer of such material needs to go beyond the obvious answers provided in the literature and to ask at least three more questions: *what techniques are being used* by researchers to answer the questions they pose; *how appropriate are these techniques for answering these questions*; and *what questions are being ignored* in the literature? (Again, these same questions should be asked when pursuing any research topic in our field.)

Question 2: What 'techniques' are being used to answer the questions?
Since 'effects' are being sought, the researchers usually presume that a *causal* relationship exists between exposure to pornographic material and the observed changes in the behaviour or attitude of men. This cause-and-effect approach inevitably leads researchers towards quantitative techniques of analysis, in particular towards experimental research, and, indeed, experimental research techniques are best suited to the study of causal relationships. Experiments, therefore, become the analytical technique of choice for researchers working in the effects tradition. Typically, experiments involve the manipulation of a 'cause' and the observation of experimental subjects to measure an 'effect' in such a way as to ensure that the changes in the subjects are the result of the 'cause' and not anything else. In the experiments on pornography this procedure has usually taken the form of exposing men to pornographic material, then measuring changes in their behaviour or attitudes towards women as compared with groups that were not exposed to the pornographic material. Since the objective of the experiment is to rule out other possible explanations for the changes in the behaviour or attitude of the experimental subjects, experiments are usually conducted in controlled environments such as university laboratories.

The larger question at stake here, however, is not how exposure to pornographic material affects men in laboratory settings, but what changes it appears to induce in them in social settings. Hence the reliance on experimental research to measure the impact of pornography throws up a number of issues that may challenge the conclusions drawn by that research. At the very least, the student of communication needs to ask: How well does the experimental research lend itself to the analysis and understanding of the social impact of pornography?

Question 3: How well do the 'techniques' of analysis match the requirements of the problem?
The rigorous requirements of experimental research often lead to a number of problems. Since most experiments require controlled environments, they rarely replicate 'real world' conditions. Whatever 'effects' pornographic material may have within the lab setting, there is little certainty that men

exposed to such materials will behave in the same way outside the lab setting. For example, will watching a sexually explicit film have the same effect on a person if the film is viewed in a university lab as it would if the film were viewed in a theatre or at home with or without other people being present? Since experiments are of short duration, there is little evidence to suggest that the changes induced by pornography will outlast the experimental situation.

And what of the pornographic materials themselves? Experiments provide no tools to analyse the materials. Nor do they provide enough differentiation of the subjects. Locked into a specific focus on what we have termed the reception domain of analysis, and relying almost exclusively on the experimental technique of analysis, most researchers of the effects of pornography are forced to leave out of their analysis a number of important questions and issues. These limitations of experimental research, despite the important findings they present, should drive the reviewer to examine what questions are not being asked in the literature, and to consider what would be required to address these unanswered questions.

Question 4: What is ignored in the literature and how can it be addressed?
As important as determining what questions are being posed in the literature is asking what questions are being ignored. In our example, the focus on cause and effect and the reliance on experimental research leave out a number of other important issues. First, as suggested above, the experimental literature either ignores, or deals very poorly with, the question of the materials themselves. Some researchers have tried to differentiate between violent and non-violent pornography and between hard-core and soft-core pornography, but their categorisations are intuitive rather than rigorous. In order to categorise pornographic materials properly, researchers need to engage in what we call the analysis of product and utilise one of the many techniques suitable to that task; for example, content analysis, textual analysis or discourse analysis.

For instance, not all pornographic material depicts heterosexual acts. A significant amount depicts gay or lesbian sexual encounters. Some researchers have argued that, far from instigating violence, such depictions provide avenues of sexual expression for these often marginalised social groups. Or what of pornographic material that depicts women in sexually dominant and men in sexually subservient roles? This sort of material may well have quite the opposite 'effects' to that found in the experimental literature (such as the supposed reinforcement of male aggression). Another approach to the analysis of mass media texts explores their formal or semiotic characteristics and attempts to define patterns of meaning that emerge from these elements. These meanings may be far more subtle and nuanced than the surface material seems to indicate, suggesting that interaction with the material may be equally as complex and relatively undetected in experimental research. Such analysis is largely absent from the study of pornographic material, and certainly experimental research is incapable of such analysis. The important thing to remember is that the study of the material itself may provide further important clues as to the possible 'effects' of pornography (or any other body of visual, aural or printed communication), and researchers need to use techniques appropriate to this analysis. Another way to put this is to recognise that most communication processes and content are very complex. Any research techniques that reduce that complexity in order to meet the requirements of particular methods may reduce the usefulness of the research itself.

Second, the experimental research ignores differences in the audiences for pornographic material. Some experimental researchers have tried to differentiate subjects according to their prior exposure to pornography, but by and large the focus has been on men. Differences related to gender, age, ethnicity or sexual preference have not been examined in detail in this tradition. Researchers outside the mainstream tradition of experimental research have begun to show that pornography performs very different functions in different social groups. For instance, hard-core pornographic films are often the vehicle through which safe-sex messages are conveyed in underground gay clubs. Even among heterosexual men, the main subjects of experimental research, pornographic material may have a number of different effects other than stimulating violent behaviour. A significant determinant of these effects may be the ways in which pornographic material is interpreted by individuals belonging to different social groups. There is growing evidence from studies of other kinds of mass media content that audiences engage in a variety of interpretive practices and that the interpretation or 'reading' process is more complex than experimental research might suggest. Working within the reception domain, researchers need to use very different techniques, such as ethnographic research or interviews, before they can begin to lay bare the complex nature of the audiences for pornography, the uses they make of pornographic materials, and their 'readings' or interpretation of such material. This kind of work, applied to a whole range of problems and situations, is increasingly calling itself 'reception analysis'.

Third, experimental research ignores what we have termed the 'analysis of production'; that is, the process of making pornography. There is no attempt to understand the pornography industry or the wider social and cultural factors that lead to such material being produced. Nor are we given any insights into the actual producers of pornographic materials. Following our earlier example, gay and lesbian producers have been engaged in the production of pornography that challenges many of the assumptions on which the 'effects' tradition is based. While much research on mainstream Hollywood films has been devoted to examining issues such as the industrial structure of production and distribution and the role of individuals in the industry (such as producers or directors), this type of analysis is again largely absent from the examination of pornographic material. As in the case of Hollywood films, these other types of analysis could be essential to determining the nature of the material being produced and, by extension, its 'effects'.

Finally, we must consider the social, cultural and political context of pornography. While researchers in the experimental tradition have focused on the expression of individual behaviours and attitudes in controlled settings, what relationship does this have to the socio-cultural environment of a society? Individual behaviours and attitudes are either constrained to varying degrees or find easy expression, depending upon the dominant normative and cultural climate of the times. It becomes important, therefore, to monitor that climate, and for this we may have to turn to alternative techniques such as large-scale national surveys or careful comparative studies of different historical contexts. Similarly, the judicial climate, particularly laws and court rulings on what is or is not permissible expression or behaviour, may be an important element in determining the extent to which individuals are exposed to pornography and, once exposed, the extent to which they are constrained in their subsequent actions. When these social elements are combined with those found in religious institutions, educational institutions, the military or other professional contexts, we may be able to discern a discourse system at work, a system that guides and directs attitudes and behaviours related to this or other topics.

It is important to recognise the importance of this social context in the evaluation of any body of research; because social research, despite its adherence to objectivity and neutrality, cannot help being implicated in the political and cultural debates of the society at large. One can track, for example, varying intensity of concern with topics such as pornography or violence and link that intensity to specific political and social climates. And perhaps even more significantly, one can trace changes in research *findings* that seem to be grounded in shifting political contexts. In 1970, for example, at the height of the sexual revolution, a US National Commission investigating pornography concluded that there was no reliable evidence that exposure to sexually explicit materials had a role in causing delinquent or criminal behaviour. Sixteen years later, when the ideological pendulum had swung considerably to the right, the Attorney General's Commission (known as the Meese Commission) (1986) found that there was considerable scientific evidence that 'hard porn' could lead to harmful effects on viewers.

While this change in findings may, in part, result from more refined research techniques or from differences in framing the research questions and projects, the student of communication scholarship must keep in mind that research is often implicated, willingly or unwillingly, in the pressing social issues of a society. An analysis of the social, economic and political climate in which research is conducted and digested is often an important element of evaluating that research, since social policy and legislative action are often linked both to the sponsorship of research into specific problems and to research findings.

In a sense, the analysis of such questions, especially when undertaken within a historical perspective, cuts across all three domains of analysis outlined in this chapter. The struggle over communication policy affects the industrial and economic context in which production is carried out. As a result, it affects the products made available for use. And because particular media content is produced, in particular forms, as a result of these social factors, reception is constrained or directed in particular ways.

Nikhil Sinha and Horace Newcomb

What we have tried to show with our case study is not necessarily the 'failure' of one type of communication research and the superiority of others. We certainly have no intention of singling out for attack the methods of experimental research. It is one of the most useful techniques available to us as students and scholars, and findings derived from careful experiments have often guided policy and social attitudes as well as contributed to the ongoing search for answers to communication-related questions. Rather, our aim has been to show that for most problems in the study of communication no single approach will provide complete and definitive answers to the necessary questions. Ours is an inherently interdisciplinary field and, though that term is often used in an imprecise manner, we have tried to demonstrate the ways in which communication studies must constantly re-examine its own fundamental approaches to make sure we have not overlooked other, truly significant, aspects of our problem.

With a carefully laid out map – one that identifies the domains and techniques of analysis – a student of communication can organise and assess a body of scholarly literature by (1) cataloguing the questions that are commonly asked and those that are not; (2) evaluating the techniques of analysis that are employed and discovering additional techniques that need to be used; and (3) placing the literature in the context of the wider social environment. In this way a student can 'survive' what seems at times an overwhelming body of literature by developing a perspective that spans both different domains and different techniques of analysis and, in an important step, shows the relationships between them.

Equally importantly, these same approaches can guide the student who wishes to pursue his or her own scholarship in the field of media and communication studies. That research and scholarship will only be as sound as the questions we ask, the techniques applied to answer them and the care taken to place the work in the larger social environment. The real task for students of the media of public communication is to recognise in their own work that there are powerful advantages in being able to focus and match one's choice of topics with one's choice of analytical techniques.

We note here, of course, that in the study of communication, in the conduct of one's own communication scholarship, and even in preparation for careers in communication, many of these choices are settled by the organisation of the curriculum, the reading lists for a particular class or by professional requirements. Courses in the *history* of specific aspects of communication do not always offer content on *economics*, though they may. A curriculum devoted to examining *technology* may not offer information on *aesthetics*, though it may. Employers concerned with the *effects* of communication may not be concerned with analyses of *industrial organisations*, though they certainly may. And programmes in technical training may deal with none of these 'academic' issues, though they may and many do.

With the domain/technique 'map' in mind, however, a student may discover questions and problems in one course or context that relate to those in another. The student may suggest a project for analysis that does not seem to be part of the organised reading for the course, precisely because he or she has recognised another possible approach to a particular topic or problem. At this juncture, one has begun not only to 'survive' the complex webs of communication scholarship but to weave them anew. And because communication processes and products are among those most central to contemporary society, one has also begun to participate in truly significant work. Even if communication is not the 'ark' upon which we float to social survival, it is surely one compass that aids in leading us towards that goal.

Stop and think

Structure, agency, knowledge and you

The plan of domains and techniques in communication studies (figure 1, p. 18) is the 'big picture' in relation to which you will be pursuing media studies. (Communication studies is a larger field, within which media studies may be joined by studies of interpersonal communication as well as by more applied approaches – courses in advertising, public relations, journalism, and so on. But Nikhil Sinha and Horace Newcomb take very much a 'media studies' perspective in presenting their plan.) The problem you have to think about now is how meaningful knowledge is actually made within those domains and using those techniques.

There are two parts to this: first, there is the question of how knowledge is constructed out of the relationships among theories, models and data; and second there is the question of the position of the constructors – the scholars whose work you are studying but also, importantly, you yourself as you begin to make some of this knowledge your own.

But even before we get to all of that, stop and think about how you already *live* a form of knowledge about the media. What rhythms move you, what celebrities inspire or repel you, what makes you laugh, what opens a sort of emptiness in the pit of your stomach, what makes you feel sexy, what makes you dream of the life you want to live? The media will weave in and out of your answers to these questions – in 2000, in the UK, Fatboy Slim (Norman Cook) and his TV-celebrity spouse Zoe Ball may exercise some power over youthful imaginations, but the names and faces will come and go, while another news report of African famine leaves a lingering unease and *Friends* or some other seductive sitcom urges you to be happy regardless. It's a complex set of influences, but in the end you 'know' something about yourself and your place in the world as a result. The challenge is to take this lived knowledge and construct something more intellectually robust around it.

'Structure' and 'agency' are indispensable terms for beginning to think about that 'lived knowledge' which you have in abundance, thanks to the wealth of information, ideas and values you are exposed to by the media. (The box on 'Lifestyle research' below suggests how we can become a bit more sophisticated in our vocabulary for talking about such exposure.) Structures are the systematic limitations that constrain 'lived' anything – we all live in very particular historical, economic, social and cultural situations, and those situations limit our understanding in specific ways. On the other hand, anything that is 'lived' is also actively engaged in – agency is the activity and growth that distinguish being alive from being a mere cog in a machine. Your lived knowledge about the media and the world they represent for you is precariously balanced between structure and agency. Your particular understanding of yourself and the world is only possible given the specific – and often distorting or limiting – resources available to you. But at the same time you live that understanding as more than a puppet. It's an odd and tanta-lising tension. As you work to make better knowledge for yourself, you will have to grasp how agency can drive the construction of forms of knowledge that challenge the limitations inherent in being rooted within any particular set of circumstances, as we all are.

Two pairs of contrasting terms are helpful in beginning to think about this. The first is 'objectivistic'/'subjectivistic'. Some forms of knowledge lean in one direction or the other – emphasising agency (the subjectivistic) or struc-ture (the objectivistic). The secod pair is 'consensus'/'conflict'. Some forms of knowledge are driven by an assumption that societies, knowledge and just about everything else in the world are inherently contested; while other approaches embody a vision of consensus, of agreement and the reconcilia-tion of differences as somehow the 'natural' process of advancement. Rather than deciding beforehand where one's own understandings and values are going to lie, it is important to see how a range of intellectual work emerges across the terrain defined by these distinctions. So to the domains and tech-niques of figure 1 we have to add a *terrain* of scholarship on which media studies is actually done, and where it involves all sorts of trade-offs and debates among different perspectives, each located somewhere quite spe-cific in relation to the structure/agency and consensus/conflict problems.

The diversity of approaches on this terrain is often a source of great con-fusion to students. This is especially so as the approaches themselves evolve, are replaced or change position over time, so one 'snapshot' of the terrain (see figure 2, p. 32, for instance) will be out of date a few years later. But the important thing is to think about it as a terrain, organised by the sorts of tension outlined here. Particular 'isms' and other approaches will come and go but you need to be able to use the knowledge that they offer in con-structing your own home on that terrain.

3

For lack of models: a field in fragments?

Karl Erik Rosengren

A typology of communication studies

The field of media and communication studies may be understood in terms of a fourfold typology originally devised for sociology by the Anglo-American team Burrell and Morgan (1979), but very well suited also to understand recent developments in communication studies. The typology is based on two very general dimensions, in their turn derived from more specific dimensions, constituting a multidimensional so-called 'property space' for schools of socio-logical thought and research. The two overall dimensions cover assumptions about (1) the nature of social science (objectivistic vs subjectivistic), and (2) the nature of society ('regulatory' consensus vs 'radical change' and conflict).

Crossing the two dimensions we get a fourfold typology: four main para-digms called by Burrell and Morgan 'radical humanism', 'radical structural-ism', 'interpretive sociology' and 'functionalist sociology'. This typology is rendered in figure 2. Each paradigm encompasses a number of different spe-cialist traditions of research which, in spite of their differences, have impor-tant characteristics in common.

For instance, all traditions within both 'radical humanism' and 'radical structuralism' derive their primary inspiration – the perspective on radical change and conflict which is so central to them – from Karl Marx (radical humanism mainly from the young, more subjectivistic Marx; radical struc-turalism mainly from the more mature and objectivistic Marx). Building on classics of sociology from the late nineteenth and early twentieth centuries (say, Durkheim and Weber in Europe, Mead and Cooley in the United States), the two paradigms of 'functionalist sociology' and 'interpretive sociology', on the other hand, regard society in the light of a perspective concerned with regulatory consensus; although the scholars on the right-hand side of the typology have a more objectivistic, 'scientific' view of social science, and those on the left-hand side, a more subjectivistic, individualistic and humanistic view.

Although conceived in the late 1970s, Burrell and Morgan's typology is still a useful instrument when trying to understand the situation not only in social science at large but also, more specifically, in communication studies and related traditions of research. For instance, in terms of this typology, some of the most interesting work in the research tradition of *cultural studies* – a very important source of inspiration to many contemporary students of commu-

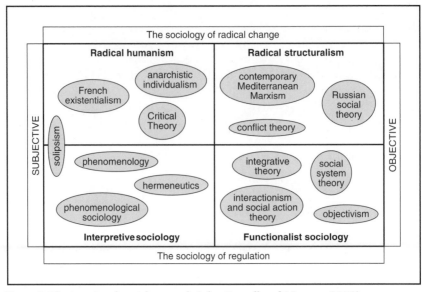

Figure 2 The terrain of social research (after Burrell and Morgan, 1979)

nication and media – is located towards the left-hand side of the typology, the 'subjectivistic' side. Since some research in that tradition is mainly conflict oriented and other research mainly consensus oriented, it occupies both the lower and upper half of that side – in Burrell and Morgan's terms both 'radical humanism' and 'interpretive sociology' (although Gramscian cultural studies is more objectivistic; see 'Afterthoughts' to this Part). Communication research defined in more substantively oriented terms – say, audience research or research on international communications – may be found in all four regions of the typology.

In the late 1970s the conflict/consensus distinction was most topical in both the humanistic and the social science disciplines. Today, it is the subjectivistic/objectivistic dimension which comes to the fore – in the humanities and the social sciences at large, and also within the field of communication. It does not take much thought to understand why this is so.

Because of long-term global political and intellectual change, accelerating since the latter half of the 1980s, the radical schools in the upper part of the typology find themselves in a somewhat awkward situation. From a political point of view, Marxist socialism has proved unviable; intellectually, Marx is on his way back to a niche among other niches in the mausoleum of the classics. In other words, at least since the early 1980s, the horizontal divide of the typology has become less important – or, at least, less visible. Representatives of schools in the upper half of the typology are less anxious to bring up for discussion the very dimension which once defined their existence. Vague terms such as 'critical', 'radical' and 'left', therefore, have recently become more popular, while more precise terms such as 'socialist' or 'Marxist', 'Leninist' or 'Stalinist' are on the wane. Instead, interest has focused on the vertical divide, differentiating between subjectivistically and objectivistically oriented sociology and communication research. Humanistically oriented sociology and communication research, always an important tradition, has grown stronger, vitalising the debate in a way which had only begun in the late 1980s.

This general development manifests itself in two different ways. In the first place, agency – the acting and willing subject, the human individual *qua* human individual – is in focus much more than has previously been the case. Second, the historical perspective has grown ever stronger, a welcome complement to yesterday's sometimes rather one-sided, a-historical perspective of the behavioural and social science approaches located in the right-hand side of the typology. All the same, there remain some very basic problems to take care of.

Above all, productive conflict between different schools and traditions of research seems to have declined. Whatever may be said about the former fights between Marxists and more 'bourgeois' scholars of communication – very bitter and sometimes disruptive as they may have been – they were productive in the sense that they sharpened the wits, forcing everybody to articulate their standpoints as clearly as possible. Unfortunately, the objectivistic/subjectivistic divide does not seem to offer quite the same impetus to productive conflict. Consequently, while in the 1970s and 1980s there was some risk of disruptive conflict, today there is rather a risk of bland indifference.

A case in point is recent developments in audience research, where right now half a dozen research traditions are developing, more or less independently of each other, and – to tell the truth – thus far with only weak signs of either co-operation or confrontation (Jensen and Rosengren, 1990; Rosengren, 1993; Vorderer and Groeben, 1993). I am convinced that a fundamental cause of the bland indifference threatening an imminent fragmentation in media and communication studies is the fact that a basic precondition for cumulative growth is lacking within an increasing number of communication research traditions. Cumulative growth in scholarship presupposes both confrontation and co-operation. In their turn, both these activities presuppose very precise knowledge about what the whole thing is about. This, ultimately, presupposes close relationships between three elements central to all scholarly activity: substantive theories, formal models and empirical data. As we shall see, this basic precondition is not always fulfilled in present-day media and communication research.

Theories, models and data

In modern behavioural and social science, and also in some humanistic disciplines – especially, perhaps, linguistics – there is a growing consensus that it is important, if not downright mandatory, to make a sharp distinction between, on the one hand, the substantive theories of the discipline and, on the other, the formal models in terms of which these substantive theories are explicated and analysed (cf. Rosengren 1995). Substantive theory is usually expressed verbally – using, of course, the special terminology often necessary to express sophisticated thought. The formal models, however, are substantively empty, since they are expressed in terms of logical, mathematical or statistical language (often visualised in terms of graphical models). It is very

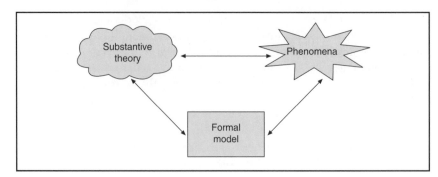

Figure 3 The interplay of theory, models and the world of phenomena

important for scholarly growth and development to let substantive theory, formal models and empirical data interact in a cumulative, spiralling process of knowledge building.

The world of phenomena will always be that buzzing thing 'out there', just as theory is at best only a dim mirror image of that endlessly busy richness. In their clarity and unambiguousness, on the other hand, the formal models call for maximum explicitness in the processes of translation between both theory and model, model and data. It is this demand for explicitness in the process of translation which initiates the spiralling process of knowledge building among substantive theory, formal models and empirical data about phenomena, as visualised in figure 3. It also makes confrontation and co-operation between different traditions of research possible and meaningful.

Actually, it is precisely because of such an interplay between data, theory and models – be the latter graphical, logical, mathematical or statistical – that the modern behavioural, cognitive and social sciences have been able to produce the fantastic development they have demonstrated during the second half of the twentieth century. The insistence on translation between theory and model, model and data, in order to make possible theoretically relevant analysis of empirical data in terms of theoretically derived formal models, has brought about an enormous growth in highly general knowledge. Translation between theory and model has thus made possible strong generalisation. The importance of formal models as such may be seen in the vitalising influence exerted by the use of advanced statistical models found, for instance, in the so-called 'LISREL' approach, which uses computer software of that name (Jöreskog and Sörbom, 1988; for interesting examples of LISREL models in communication studies, see, for instance, Johnsson-Smaragdi, 1994; Johnsson-Smaragdi and Jönsson, 1994). Note, however, that as a rule such processes demand at least a decade or two in order to reach a stage of maturity.

Stop and think

Formalisation

A deeply debilitating problem in media education is the relative scarcity of training for students in the methods of formalisation – especially quantitative formalisation. An absolutely indispensable piece of reading for all media students is, therefore, chapter 5 ('Handling numbers') in David Deacon, Michael Pickering, Peter Golding and Graham Murdock's *Researching Communications* (1999), accompanied perhaps by chapter 14 ('Using computers') of the same book. In their Preface (p. ix) the authors describe a vicious cycle that you must try to avoid: 'Chary of anything smacking of numbers or data analysis, [students] begin to regard all research as suspect and unattractively mundane. Drawn to more qualitative methods, they soon become disenchanted with their imprecision, and what is often a mismatch between aspiration and output.'

They go on to say, in the opening lines of chapter 5:

The use of statistics in the human sciences can evoke strong reactions. For some people numbers inspire an anxiety that verges on phobia. Others object to quantification on principle, perceiving it as a denial of the quality and complexity of our collective and individual worlds. Still others disapprove politically, pointing to the cavalier use of numbers to support all manner of dubious reasoning and partisanship. Conversely, there are some who treat statistics with a deferential respect.' (p. 81)

The authors then present an irresistible case for taking numbers seriously, while remaining careful about what they can tell us. Fred Inglis (1990), in a chapter called 'The books of numbers', also deftly sidesteps the objections just quoted, to issue a reminder that numbers give us permission to proceed to the *strong generalisations* which Karl Erik Rosengren here identifies as the very engine of knowledge production.

So you should stop and think about your own reactions to numbers and to the use of statistics or formal models. If those who teach you are ill disposed to quantitative approaches, find out if their objections are along the lines described above – or perhaps they simply have not been trained in this approach and rationalise this lack of knowledge by evoking one of those objections. In any case, you must make up your own mind, but take into account the argument presented here: that formalisation (whether quantitative or qualitative) is an indispensable component of knowledge production and of the learning process.

Quantitative formalisation is getting easier for students to perform, as relevant computer software becomes cheaper, more powerful and more usable (the LISREL program, for instance, is available in a student version as a free download, and LISREL is also an option within the popular SPSS program that most university computer labs can offer). However, carrying out statistical analysis requires training and you will find yourself either receiving such training or not, depending on what variant of media studies you are pursuing and where you are doing it. If the methods of quantitative formalisation are not accessible to you, though, the importance of formalisation itself need not be lessened. This is especially so as approaches to formalisation are emerging that transcend the old quantitative/qualitative divide.

Software such as NUD*IST (Non-numerical Unstructured Data Indexing, Searching and Theory-building) is becoming more powerful and genuinely useful with each release and currently also interfaces to helpful model-building programs such as Decision Explorer. We can anticipate further developments in formalisation tools of this sort, that take what we might think of as 'qualitative' material (texts, descriptions of images, etc.) and allow reliable formalisation to be carried out on large bodies of such stuff – rather than just intelligent guesswork, which often relies on whatever happens to strike the particular researcher as noteworthy. Moreover, new methods are also emerging – such as Charles Ragin's Qualitative Comparative Analysis (see Ragin, 1987) – that are beginning to explore formalisation techniques for those principles of comparison which tend to be exercised intuitively or subjectively by scholars of social and cultural phenomena. None of this is intended as a substitute for human interpretation but rather to consolidate the relationship between theories and raw material where often insightful ideas are otherwise left unsupported. There is a lot more work to be done in this area, but you can prepare yourself to benefit from it by (1) recognising the role played by formalisation in the process of learning and knowledge production; and (2) familiarising yourself with at least the broad principles involved, whether the formalisation is quantitative, qualitative or some emerging hybrid.

The importance of models has always been recognised in communication studies – witness, for instance, the influence of the book *Models of Communication* by McQuail and Windahl (1993), usefully collating graphical models from half a century of communication studies. But the essential interplay between substantive theory, formal models and empirical data seems to be lacking in some emerging traditions of communication research, both in the humanities and in the social sciences. More specifically, substantive theories in verbal form are directly used to interpret and explain empirical reality and data derived from that reality, without relating either theory or data to explicit, formal models. As time goes by, however, formal models are gradually being introduced to clarify things and this initiates a positive spiral of development, in which theory, formal models and data are combined to produce more precise knowledge. Typical examples of such a development may be found in traditions such as, say, agenda setting (Brosius and Kepplinger, 1993), the spiral of silence (Noelle-Neumann, 1991), uses and gratifications (U&G) research (Blumler and Katz, 1974) and lifestyle research (Rosengren, 1994a, 1995).

Unfortunately, not all emerging traditions follow this course; especially schools of communication research in the two subjectivistic or humanistic regions on the left-hand side of the Burrell and Morgan typology which show a tendency not to draw equally on all three of the elements necessary for cumulative growth. They are often characterised by rich substantive theories, and sometimes also by impressive empirical, qualitative data. But they tend to avoid formal models. The important links between substantive theory and formal model, between formal model and empirical data, are thus weak or even non-existent. One reason for this sad state of affairs is probably a deep mistrust of quantification, where formalisation is often mistaken for quantification. As decades of dramatic developments in linguistics demonstrate, however, the strength of formalised qualitative models is formidable. In other fields of the humanities and social sciences, there have nonetheless been breakthroughs based on qualitative models. A good example with relevance for communication studies is so-called 'social network analysis', which has flourished since the early 1990s as new, formalised, qualitative and quantitative models have been introduced (Wasserman and Faust, 1994). (For a good introduction to the study of formalised qualitative models, see Ragin, 1987.)

There is no reason at all, then, why qualitative studies should not be formalised. Lacking the formal models which alone make the confrontation between substantive theories and empirical data fruitful, strict comparisons between different studies are not possible. Thus key results cannot be carefully compared and, consequently, they cannot be effectively challenged where necessary. The wheat cannot be sifted from the chaff. Instances may be found in the recently emerging traditions of reception analysis and lifestyle-oriented audience research.

The challenge facing any tradition of communication research in the humanities and the social sciences, then, is precisely this: to heed carefully the distinction between substantive theory and formal models, and to start a productive interplay between empirical data and those two vehicles of scholarly analysis. If such an interplay should not come about, even the most promising tradition of communication research will run the risk of being stuck at the basically descriptive, narrative and anecdotal level which marks the beginning of most new lines of communication research. The absence of translation between substantive theory and formal model, between formal model and empirical data, will prevent strong generalisation. Consequently, a line of research can remain a fad among other fads and may ultimately disappear, just like all other fads. Lacking that indispensable interplay among theory, models and data, those productive processes of confrontation and co-operation between various schools of research will also be lacking. Consequently, no general cumulative growth of the field will take place.

Some concrete examples of development in three different traditions of communication research – U&G research, lifestyle-oriented research on media use and reception analysis – may be used to illustrate this proposition.

Models make a difference

Research is a very time-consuming business. The U&G tradition has been around since the 1950s. The roots of lifestyle-oriented mass media research may be traced back at least to the beginning of the twentieth century. The study of developments within old traditions such as these may be used to understand the situation of new lines of research, whose history covers only a decade or so – for instance, the emerging tradition of reception analysis.

The history of U&G research has been traced more than once (cf. Blumler and Katz, 1974). Right from its beginning in the mid 1940s, it has been characterised primarily by a very productive interplay among substantive theory, formal models and empirical data. Empirical data have been collected in a number of ways, ranging from informal interviews through surveys and questionnaires to laboratory experiments. They have been analysed in terms of formal models (for the statistically initiated, ranging in complexity from simple cross-tabulations to advanced multivariate statistical modelling). As a result, the tradition has developed from an initial stage characterised by descriptive studies, through a typological phase to an explanatory phase characterised by a fully fledged interplay among substantive theory, formal models and sophisticated designs for data collection. It has now reached a stage in which detailed and precise comparative studies, spanning time and space, have become possible (see, for example, Liebes and Katz's study of the US TV serial *Dallas* in *The Export of Meaning*, 1993).

Lifestyle-oriented mass communication research has its roots in classical social science, including Veblen, Simmel and Weber (cf. Johansson and Miegel, 1992:7 ff.). Looking back on its long history, it is striking to observe how, after the first insightful, sometimes brilliant observations made by the classic authors, lifestyle research for a very long time never left the stage of verbal description and theories illuminated by notable examples. By and large, when looking at the history of lifestyle research, we find either theoretically informed empirical studies lacking contact with formal models or theoretically uninformed research, the results of which are couched in terms of formal models. Studies based on a fully fledged combination of substantive theories, formal models and empirical data are few and far between.

This paradoxical situation is probably one reason why lifestyle research, in spite of having a history more than twice as long as that of U&G research, needed such a long time to reach its take-off point. Only in the 1990s did any signs of such a development turn up (cf. Rosengren 1994a, 1995). Typically, this new international wave of lifestyle studies has managed to combine typological and other theoretical work with formal models and empirical data, using both quantitative and qualitative methods. Productive criticism and conflicts were thus bound to appear in the field. Consequently, lifestyle research was suddenly able to move relatively quickly from the original descriptive level to the explanatory level. The stage thus seems set for strong, rapid and cumulative development in lifestyle-oriented media research during the next twenty years. What, then, of the relatively new tradition within audience research – reception analysis?

Reception analysis has a number of roots in the humanities and the social sciences (Jensen and Rosengren, 1990). One of the most important roots is located in a discipline which for decades has systematically applied a continuous interplay among theory, models and data – cognitive psychology. (See, for example, the work of Jennings Bryant and Dolf Zillmann at the University of Alabama; for example, *Responding to the Screen: Reception and Reaction Processes*, 1991.) On the other hand, in the type of reception analysis which borrows terms and concepts from modern and not-so-modern linguistics, this type of systematic interplay between substantive theory, formal models and empirical data seems to have been rather sparingly used so far. Prominent contributors to the linguistically oriented branch of reception analysis are by no means unaware of this state of affairs. Indeed, they sometimes even seem to make a point out of it. This specific tradition is dominated by qualitative studies, based on anecdotal data and presented as unformalised, exegetic studies of the meaning of individual experience (cf. Swanson, 1993; Schrøder,

1994). As a rule (in contrast to many qualitative studies in the psychologically oriented branch of reception analysis), these studies neglect otherwise generally accepted tests of reliability, validity and representativeness. The qualitative are said to have an explanatory value in their own right. Precisely what explanatory value they actually have is often not made clear, however. Nonetheless, what has been produced is an impressive number of ingenious and insightful case studies (cf. Jensen and Jankowski, 1991).

Now, there is always that wonderful challenge facing any emerging tradition of research: to confront some interesting qualitative results with formal models, be they qualitative or quantitative, translating them into instruments which may be applied to representative samples from carefully defined populations. Only such processes of translation admit generalisation. Challenges tend to be accepted, sooner or later. So the conclusion of our argument may be formulated as a prediction.

Prediction

Against the background presented above, it does not seem very far fetched to predict that in the near future some enterprising group of communications scholars will concentrate on strategic variables within the substantive theories of so-called 'qualitative reception analysis'. Aiming at empirical and theoretical generalisation, they will start the laborious work of relating the substantive theories to relevant formal models, translating the variables into empirical measurements, applicable in studies of representative samples of carefully defined populations under carefully defined circumstances, analysing the empirical data in terms of both the formal models and the substantive theories.

As a matter of fact, such a development is precisely what happened in U&G research around the middle of the twentieth century (Katz *et al.*, 1973; Elliott, 1974). In that way, a whole body of new knowledge about media use, its causes and consequences, has been produced within the U&G tradition, even if it has taken more than half a century. In that way too, U&G was saved from the fate of being just an interesting fad among so many other fads in communication studies. The same thing happened to lifestyle-oriented media research during the 1980s and 1990s – but only after some fifty years of retardation. It seems to be a fair guess that the same development will soon be taking place around the many interesting results being obtained from qualitative reception analysis. The only question is who will do it. The reception analysts themselves, of course, are first in line. Should most of them prefer not to take their opportunity, instead continuing to grind out more case studies of this or that 'interpretive community', others will do it for them (cf. Schrøder, 1994). Whoever does it, though, it will take time. We can only hope that it will not take half a century.

Summing up

After a period of productive confrontations and rapid growth, media and communication studies seems to run the risk of entering a period of retardation. Those who hoped for more positive confrontation and co-operation have reason to be disappointed. Instead, a bland acceptance of, or indifference towards, traditions of research other than one's own seems to dominate. There is no single cause of this state of affairs. One contributing cause, however, may well be the fact that this basic precondition for cumulative growth is sometimes lacking in present-day communication research – especially in some humanistic traditions: there sometimes seems to be an aversion towards a vital element of all scholarship and research – the formal model, so necessary a complement to substantive theory and empirical data. One reason for this, in turn, may be the mistaken assumption that formalisation means quantification. Qualitative studies, in the strict sense of the word, can be formalised as much as can quantitative studies. What is today traditionally and loosely called 'qualitative studies of reception' (based, for instance, on a few informal conversations with TV viewers, romance readers or Madonna fans) may sometimes produce brilliant ideas. So may a number of other qualitative approaches in communication studies. Brilliant ideas deserve and need hard tests, however. Such tests, I have argued here, call for a combination of theory, models and data. Unfortunately, not all communication scholars seem to be willing or able to draw on this combination. Today's students must learn to.

The solution seems to be twofold. Social science-oriented communication scholars must show themselves willing to draw on the sometimes very productive insights gained by humanistically oriented scholars. Humanistically oriented communication scholars must overcome their aversion to formal models. There is, to state it one more time, an urgent need for the combined use of substantive theory, formal models and empirical data. A promising area in which to undertake a co-ordinated attempt in this direction may well be reception analysis. But there is a host of other options.

Lifestyle research: a case study

Substantive theory should start with reasonably unequivocal definitions, but the concept of lifestyle is often used in a rather loose way – say, something such as *patterns of actions characterising (parts of) populations*. Sometimes such patterns are regarded as being in some way dependent on a more or less consciously made *individual choice*, based on individually held values, attitudes, taste patterns, and so on. In other cases, the notion of lifestyle refers to *structurally determined* patterns of action, characterising, say, most people in industrial and post-industrial societies as opposed to most people in pre-industrial societies. In yet other cases, it refers to *positionally determined* patterns of action, characterising categories of individuals located in a special position within society – say, the positions of being a young man or an old woman.

It is not unusual to find different authors using one or other of these three concepts, and some authors do not care to differentiate between them at all. Obviously, this may cause some confusion in developing any argument. The three different types of phenomenon, as well as the corresponding concepts, should be differentiated by means of different terms. We thus need three different terms for the three concepts by means of which we try to distinguish between three related and yet different phenomena.

Let us call patterns of action which are structurally determined, forms of life. Such patterns of action distinguish, say, populations of industrialised societies from populations of pre-industrial societies; populations of traditional Muslim countries from populations of secularised Protestant societies; populations of large cities from those of small towns or the countryside, and so on.

Let us call patterns of action which are positionally determined, ways of life. In a given society, such patterns distinguish old people from young people; men from women; farm hands from factory workers; factory workers from managers, and so on.

And finally, let us call patterns of action which are individually determined, lifestyles. Such patterns distinguish between individuals who – regardless of the societal structure in which they live, regardless of the position they occupy within that societal structure – more or less consciously choose to shape their actions (and sometimes even their whole lives) in terms of one or the other pattern, a pattern which tends to be formed in accordance with the basic values and the corresponding attitudes embraced by the individual, these values and attitudes in their turn being affected by the very patterns of behaviour which they have called into existence. (In modern societies, music is often used as a means among other means thus to shape and define lifestyles, but obviously there are many other ways and means to build a lifestyle.)

These three definitions, it will be realised, are analytical in the sense that neither forms of life nor ways of life nor lifestyles as such can appear in our everyday world. Actual patterns of individual actions are always *mixta composita* of all three basic types of pattern: forms of life, ways of life and lifestyles. Furthermore, it should also be noted that lifestyles as here defined are phenomena at the aggregate level. They must not be mistaken for the patterns of life of single individuals. Any given individual shows a specific pattern of actions which is unique, an 'individual lifestyle'. Such an individual lifestyle is not at all the same as those aggregated patterns of action which we call lifestyles. To call an individual lifestyle a lifestyle is perfectly correct, of course, as long as the distinction is observed. To mistake a lifestyle for an individual lifestyle, however, is to commit the fallacy of false concretisation; to mistake an individual lifestyle for a lifestyle as here defined is to commit the fallacy of false generalisation.

Having by our definitions created a set of interrelated concepts, we have taken the first steps in creating a substantive theory – a theory of lifestyles. Now, in order to be able more precisely to differentiate between forms of life, ways of life and lifestyles, we must relate our emerging substantive theory to a formal model. As is so often the case, we start by expressing the emerging theory in graphic form, and the basic graphic model is rendered in figure 4. This visualises – much more clearly than can verbal theories – the formal structure of the theory just discussed. We see how, according to the model, all actions are determined by structural, positional and individual characteristics and circumstances. It will also be noted that the three phenomena of form of life, ways of life and lifestyle do not themselves appear in the model. Where are they to be found, then?, one might well ask. They are indirectly represented by the three arrows leading to 'patterns of action' from

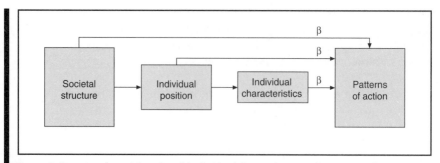

Figure 4 Structural, positional and individual determinants of patterns of action

'societal structure', 'individual position' and 'individual characteristics', respectively. For those three arrows correspond to the verbal definitions of the three types of pattern: structurally, positionally or individually determined patterns of action. Each of the beta coefficients is a formal expression of the strength of a different source of action. The link from 'societal structure' symbolises what makes a form of life, that from 'individual position' a way of life, and from 'individual characteristics' a lifestyle.

So much for the graphic model. In order to refine our theoretical argument further by means of formalisation, we must now translate it not only from verbal theory to graphic model, but from graphic model to formal model, in this case a statistical model. The formal model itself – completely stripped as it is of the substantive content of lifestyle theory – even more clearly and strongly than the graphic model, ruthlessly exposes both strengths and weaknesses of the substantive theory.

There are a couple of statistical models and techniques by means of which one can undertake quantitative analyses of empirical data collected in order to illustrate or test theories of the type visualised in our graphic model. Such statistical models produce so-called 'beta coefficients', denoting the unique causal influence exerted by one variable on another, when the influence of other relevant variables has been controlled for by the statistical model (see the 'Stop and think' section on 'Formalisation' above).

Combining our verbal theories with our graphic and statistical models, we may thus further specify our lifestyle definition: a lifestyle may be formally defined as any pattern of actions which to some considerable extent (as expressed, for instance, in a beta coefficient above a given value) is determined by individual characteristics as differentiated from, and after control for, structural and positional characteristics.

As is so often the case, our definition of lifestyle has been gradually changed in the translation processes from verbal substantive theory to graphic models to statistical models and back again to the verbal definition. What has actually happened is that it has become much more *precise*. We now realise much more clearly that lifestyles are not just any patterns of action which we happen to discern among this or that category of individuals occupying this or that position in this or that society. We realise a

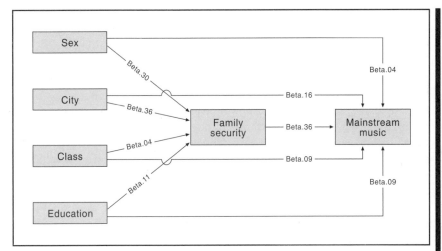

Figure 5 Simplified analysis of the influence of structural, positional and individual variables on a pattern of musical taste (after Johansson and Miegel, 1992)

very simple and very important truth: that all patterns of action are indeed the results of societal, positional and individual influences, so that, at the aggregate level, lifestyles can only be analytically observed – namely, as a given portion of variance, that portion which stems from individual characteristics.

A number of empirical lifestyle studies founded on the processes of translation between theory, model and data summarised above have been carried out within a longitudinal Swedish research programme called the Media Panel Programme (Rosengren, 1994a). For purposes of illustration only, the outcome of one such study will be presented in the form of a highly simplified graphic model. A concrete version of the model in figure 4, figure 5 visualises the influences exerted by one structural characteristic (place of living, which in our terminology represents 'form of life'), three positional characteristics (gender, class and education, which in our terminology represent 'way of life'), and one individual characteristic (the basic value of 'family security', which in our terminology represents 'lifestyle') on patterns of action as represented by a specific variant of musical taste ('mainstream') among some 450 21-year-old inhabitants of the city of Malmö and the town of Växjö in southern Sweden. These influences are expressed in terms of beta coefficients obtained from a number of statistical analyses, one for each arrow. Each beta coefficient expresses the strength of the unique influence of one variable on another, after control for other relevant variables in the model. To simplify the findings we have removed the actual figures for the various characteristics.

We can thus see and measure the strength of lifestyle phenomena. We can also appreciate that strength as compared with the strength exerted by forces related to forms of life and ways of life. We are then in a position to compare the relative importance of patterns of action related to forms of life, ways of life and lifestyles, three quite different types of phenomenon previously often indiscriminately lumped together under one more or less loosely defined notion or another (be it form of life, way of life, lifestyle or whatever).

It will be seen that lifestyle as here defined is by no means an unobtrusive phenomenon. On the contrary. Once we apply the instruments put in our hands by the interplay of substantive theory, formal models and empirical data, lifestyle phenomena become relatively conspicuous. A beta coefficient of .36, denoting the strength of the unique influence exerted by the individually held value of 'family security' on the musical taste of 'mainstream', after control for place of living, gender, social class and education, is relatively high. As it turns out in this case, it is actually much stronger than the beta denoting the structural influences constituting form of life (a beta coefficient of .16 emanating from home city), or the betas denoting the positional influences constituting way of life (beta coefficients emanating from the variables of sex, class and education: .04, .09 and .09).

Similar results have been presented for a number of other lifestyles within the Swedish Media Panel Programme. We thus have quantitative data telling us that lifestyles do indeed exist and can be measured in much the same way in which other social and cultural phenomena may be measured. Combining substantive theory, formal models and empirical data, we make the elusive phenomenon of lifestyle emerge out of that rich, buzzing, bewildering mess called reality.

Karl Erik Rosengren

4

Citizenship and the media

Fred Inglis

In 1988 the BBC broadcast a wistful melodrama about a thorough-goingly socialist prime minister coming to power in Britain after the discovery of corruption on the Tory government benches so appalling as to rouse the stolid and supine portions of the nation's electorate to throw out its rulers in a Labour landslide. During the dazzlingly high-spirited version of election night which opened the drama (all choreographed to Mozart's C Minor Mass), a routinely bullying newspaper editor-owner is interviewed on TV and challenged for his views on the Labour election slogan, 'One man, one newspaper'.

The moment not only lent a delicious frisson to the then baffled and imprisoned left watching television, but pointedly reminded its audience of the utter failure at that time of one elderly democracy to do anything at all about an affront to its principles as gross as the worst that the early nineteenth century could do. It is an agreeable grace-note to recall that when *A Very British Coup* was networked by the public broadcasting service of the United States, the programme was fronted by the honorary Anglo-American Knight Sir Alistair Cooke, who reassured listeners that they would be watching an implausible, amusingly fantastic satire.

For more than two decades the British argument about democracy and the media has turned largely upon the question of ownership, and the American one rather more specifically about the egregious omnipresence of the advertisements as well as the mere awfulness of the programmes themselves. In both versions the case has been put, if not by the protestants of socialism, then certainly by the anti-capitalist intelligentsia.

Even since *A Very British Coup* however, and despite an actual landslide election victory for New Labour, what Edward Luttwak (1995a,b) characterises as 'turbo-capitalism' has careered roaringly into the future, leaving ever-wider depredations behind it and clearing the ground of any obstacles to its progress like a whirlwind. In the epoch of turbo-charged capitalism, legislation to confine one owner to one newspaper in one country has become a lot less relevant to anyone keeping vigil for democracy. It is not without its import, of course, how few people own the newspapers of Britain, nor how a few of the same people own great slices of the television broadcasting spectrum, nor that those men themselves show a striking lack of inhibition about directing the system they own to their own advantage and the eradication of any voices which object.

But what really counts and is observable over hardly more than the last decade of the twentieth century is the advent of this new and savage version of capitalism, a creature which in becoming global has made itself capable of throwing off the never very strong restraints of liberal governments in the name of the profitable casualisation of labour, the reduction of the power of trade unions and therefore of wages, and the application of ruthless productivity criteria in this highly insecure ecology in order to dismiss as many purportedly surplus staff as possible ('downsizing' in the revolting jargon of managerialism).

The march of this fearsome beast has been cheered on by liberal governments of a free market persuasion in the rich nations of the world precisely because of that liberalism. For the principles of liberalism, whether in its tough-egg or its soft-hearted versions, put the freely choosing individual at the centre of life's values and meanings in order to determine the good life (or the bad one) within the space of that freedom, and without too much interrupting the adjacent space of the individual alongside.

New capitalism meets and embraces the free individual and invites him or her to define and fulfil that freedom by buying and consuming the goods it can now so freely produce unhampered by the residual and sentimental weight of welfare, overmanning, inefficiency and state interference. (See Hutton, 1995, to whom much in this synopsis of present politics is due; and Fukuyama, 1993, who welcomes it as an apotheosis.)

In the pure version of this scheme of things, individuals live to the full in their private, leisure and 'free' lives and times, where they can buy and consume what they choose, protected by their civil and political rights from the interference of the state and the political dangers of a totalitarianism still much invoked by populists as the nightmare promise held out by anybody of socialist persuasion.

But the freely consuming, nucleated family is falling victim to a different totalitarianism. The new capitalism in all its sedulously 'deregulated' muscularity has moved smoothly past the merely civil obstacles to its invasion. It has dissolved the strong but unprotected bonds of class and neighbourhood, and where it found itself checked by political barriers, as was the case with trade unions, the unique power of capital itself buckled and broke those barriers until the system was satisfied it could go on its way.

As a result, home, identity, the mutuality of strangers and the meaning of civic pride and, indeed, of patriotism, have been worn pale and thin. They can scarcely hold individuals in a place to which they may belong or in a frame of activity whose narrative is continuous and intelligible. The old story of *work*, key value of the labour culture (see Taylor, 1985) as giving menfolk the confidence and self possession of craft, class and solidarity, and *home* as giving womenfolk authority, neighbourhood, respect and action, has become attenuated. People can see through it. But in the present blank arena of consumer life, they cannot imagine a new story with which to keep capitalism at bay. The only tale to tell at the present replays the limited plot of happy self indulgence, cheerful consumption, 'mobile privatisation'. It is the everyday story of the folk in the advertisements. It is the endlessly iterated fiction of the soaps. One of the two or three unmistakable masterpieces to be broadcast on British television since 1979, *Boys from the Blackstuff*, chronicles its collapse with a wonderful truthfulness which was recognised countrywide.

'Mobile privatisation' is Raymond Williams's slogan by which he sought to catch and hold that large tendency in the well-off two-thirds of the rich nations of the world to shut themselves off from social intercourse either in the home or in the car (itself a rapidly moving extension to the home, as somebody pointed out years ago). The landscapes of culture and politics are then drawn across the television screen or the windscreen, and we watch them, at a safe distance, from our sitting room on the back seat.

There is everything to be said for this sombre account of what Adorno (above all with Horkheimer, 1979) foresaw as consumer totalitarianism but it does not say everything. As Adorno also saw, consumer culture holds out the promise of happiness even as it constantly breaks that promise by staining its fulfilment first with envy, then with disappointment and finally with resentment. What used to be called, in a non-philosophical sense, the materialism of those social classes with neither capital nor savings who bought washing machines and televisions by hire purchase was in truth a deep want for an ideal home which capitalism was happy to answer for a nicely turned price. Washing machines broke the back of the back-breaking labour of women who did the family laundry. Television gave them the delights of absorbingly recognisable fiction to fill and fulfil the time once spent upon that repetitious drudgery.

Nor can these purchases be easily understood by the clumsy metaphor of 'consumption' (as Kumar, 1996, argues). Washing machines are hardly consumer goods; they are inexhaustible and unexploitable substitutes for domestic servants (paid or not). Audiences do not 'consume' television programmes; they use and abuse them according to a plural taxonomy of pleasures both emancipatory and regressive.

These reminders of the queasiness of some of our habitual allocations – 'consumerism', 'privatisation' and the like – can only serve as momentary solace in the face of the malediction to be spoken over turbo-charged capitalism; the retreat of our citizens from public life; the painful reduction of the grand aspirations of Romanticism to the trifling choices of the megamarket, whether shopping in the mall or on the internet.

In the absence of war, that same capitalism has not only made social life abominably insecure, its stooges in government have driven the people from the streets that they may be hemmed in at home as obedient choosers-and-buyers of those delicious goods they cannot quite afford and are encouraged to obtain by means of the magic card which momentarily turns debit into credit.

Beneath a sky filled with these forces, the autonomous individual keeps up some kind of resistance, of course. But without working discipline, the tradition of craft, the settlement of neighbourhood or, indeed, without even the certainty of home, the poor creature can only live for a touch of Saturday night fever or an annual package to the Balearic Islands.

The noble tradition of the citizen has been cut off. Private lives are where we must live; public life will be lived on our behalf by public figures. 'Don't you try to live in public yourself, madam; you'll only get hurt. Far better go home and watch the famous do it for you.'

It has been Quentin Skinner who has solitarily but vigorously pointed out (e.g. in 1984 and 1986) that if liberal societies are to continue to justify their etymological basis in liberty, they had better look to its public defence, for liberty as lived in private is continuously encroached and diminished, and can only be defended and renewed by a display of public spirit. Free choice among trivial goods is not liberty at all.

If this is right, then the rediscovery of an ideal of citizenship is terribly overdue. Liberal individuals seek the liberty to do as they wish, compatible with not infringing the liberty of others similarly in search of their own satisfaction. But where capital seeks always to define and direct wants and purposes to its own advantages, liberty, along with happiness no less than virtue, all become distorted in the name of profit. Society is then run for the benefit of the economy, as happened in Britain for the long duration of Thatcherism.

Beating back this pervasiveness is both a cultural and a political matter, a damned hard distinction to make in practice when the triumphs of new late capitalism have been to transform the political economy into the culture of domestic life. Reinventing citizenship when the space of the citizenry is confined to the audience's seats in front of television's spectacular may simply not be possible. The stirring slogans of the Situationists, long dismissed as a barmy residue of 1968, may now be read as empirical truths:

> The spectacle is not a collection of images, but a social relation among people, mediated by images . . . The oldest social specialisation, the specialisation of power, is at the root of the spectacle . . . The spectacle is *capital* to such a degree of accumulation that it becomes an image . . . This is the principle of commodity fetishism, the domination of society by 'intangible as well as tangible things', which reaches its absolute fulfilment in the spectacle. (Debord, 1977:4,23,34,36)

If this is right, then the best we can do is to diagnose the condition of our own passivity. It is no longer possible to *act* as citizens.

The lie, of course, is given to this serenely French determinism by the events of 1989. In 1989 that traditional agency of history, the *people*, issued into the streets and public squares of Leipzig, Gdansk, Berlin, Prague and Bucharest, in order to object to the forty-year-old vileness, obduracy and incompetence of their dictatorial governments. It took, at first, considerable courage to turn out, watched by television audiences the world over; it fairly took everyone's breath away, the crowds in the street and the crowds on the screen, when this spontaneous gesture of moral revulsion brought down *all* the relevant governments and the Berlin Wall with them, and ended the Cold War in a few weeks.

It was a wonderful dawn to feel blissful at. Of course, in the few years since then things haven't turned out quite so well, and new governments have proved as untrustworthy and as ideological as the old. What is now common *worldwide* is a quite extraordinary degree of contempt and suspicion of politicians as a class and government as an institution. Trust, as Locke was the first to point out in *The Two Treatises on Government*, is the crucial value of any non-despotic polity, and it is trust which is now so seriously corroded in so many places.

This is a tricky matter to interpret. For in the wealthy societies which this chapter addresses, it is plain to see that social structures are rock solid. The spectre of revolution, recently so familiar a familiar in the rhetoric of Europe and the United States, has vanished. The unmistakable dangers of the city street, the violence of the police and the routine miscarriages of justice, threaten no social order. Yet at the same time, politics and politicians are generally believed to be corrupt, self seeking, remote and arbitrary.

They often are. They always have been. At the same time, other corners of politics have been enlightened, generous, open, accessible.

What has changed has been the disappearance of civil society. The rise of the new capitalism and the collapse of old socialism have together wiped out great tracts of that social life where the institutions of power and government mingle with those many configurations of sociable life as they touch upon the questions of state and upon the passages between private and public life, and the easy movement of individuals as they turned into citizens on their way along the corridors of power.

In Britain this change has manifested itself in the shrinking of local government and in the return to a Hanoverian version of patronage where toadies and stooges have been appointed to run local affairs with neither the endorsement of a vote nor a duty to candour or honour. In the United States, the great offices of Senate and Congress are auctioned off to a rich ruling class without a tradition of class responsibility but with an ignorant, sentimental detestation of civic and collective action.

Ruling classes have rarely been any good at ruling, and have always been liable to accurate charges of veniality, cruelty, stupidity and ordinary horribleness. The whole point of the state, ever since its inception in the imaginations of Hobbes, Milton, Carrington and company as they argued over the rights and wrongs of the Commonwealth in seventeenth century England, has been to hold tyrants down and prevent their being quite so tyrannical. Liberal capitalism has so cut down liberty that it has become little more than the freedom to choose the adornments of private lives. Glowing, stupendous as these may certainly be, they can hardly fill a life and they cannot animate a citizen.

As far as the ruling classes are concerned, there is everything to be said for a supine public which lives entirely in private and takes all its pleasures at home. A vigorous civility in the civic places is always difficult to manage in a democracy, and management is always eager to assert the 'right to manage', including manipulating people well away from any space they might invent in order to act in concert.

Television has taught its entranced audiences that meaning is found in the small rooms of private lives; that intimacy is always to be preferred to politeness; that friends matter more than strangers; that home is the only place you can feel at home, and is alone the realm of efficacious action. As for acting anywhere else – at work, for instance, or in the street or the square – well, there's nothing anyone can do, is there?

But this is not all that television has had to teach. For sure it teaches that private life is best; and sure it is. The boredom, the horror and the glory of our domesticities mark the place where we do our living. But television also taught (in 1968 and 1989, for instance) that unless we turn out into the streets from time to time in order to stand up for those private lives, they will not be *worth* living. Citizenship is required of us, if we are to be free in private.

Here we collide with a deep contradiction of modern society. It is that television is now coterminous with politics. Everybody understands this fact intuitively (none more so than politicians). But nobody knows what to do about it. What *can* such a claim signify?

It has four implications, which make the self-reporting self-broadcasting society historically unprecedented, and in need of a quite new self-conception. It may be that this last point leads to the conclusion that in coming to a firm realisation of this self-conception, a polity will conclude that it also needs a new constitution; indeed, if my claim about it is truthful, it has a *new* constitution – it is newly constituted – and this conclusion will also require new kinds of legislative acknowledgement. My point for the time being is, however, about the nature of this self-conception.

It should be said straight away that the self-reporting society is essentially the society as broadcast by radio, print and television, *and the two (self-reported and broadcast) as mutually embedded.*

The political argument, in my judgement, is not affected by the contemporary delirium about the internet and the information superhighway. These are politically important only insofar as they subtend the terrific *authority* of broadcasting, which is a function of its public status and publicity.

This is precisely the first and most prominent of the four features of the self-reporting, self-broadcasting polity. The form, content, genre and detail of public communication combine in its unique authority. This public conversation, and those hired or called to conduct it, embodies a strange mixture of the sacred and the profane, but those holding the conversation wear either set of robes with the spectacular, effortless aura of *celebrity*. What is said in that conversation is rarely casual or efficacious; it is never inconsequential.

The second feature of the self-reporting polity is its *knowledgeability*. This fact takes the measure of the contradiction between the drives of consumer totalitarianism and an unprecedentedly knowledgeable, globally aware (globally anxious also) and politically uncertain audience. It is an audience which lives, as a result of its knowledgeability, in a state of moral and cognitive diffusion. That is to say, it knows more than ever before about the news of the world and the state of the nation, but has no idea what to do about them. Its most obvious feature is its knowledgeability, especially about the present, but its membership lacks the lenses of attention with which to sort and criticise what it knows into a usable hierarchy.

The third feature of the self-reporting polity is its remarkable *narrative grasp*. Raymond Williams (1975:5) wrote:

> we have never as a society acted so much or watched so many others acting . . .
> Drama, in quite new ways, is built into the rhythms of everyday life. On television
> alone it is normal for viewers – the substantial majority of the population – to see
> anything up to three hours of drama, of course drama of several different kinds,

a day. And not just one day; almost every day. This is part of what I mean by the dramatised society.

The human propensity for storytelling has always, I take it, been our best aid in explaining the world to ourselves. Once the available narratives of a culture (and, as Clifford Geertz (1975:445) says, a culture simply *is* its stock of narratives) bound its listeners by the mesmerism of the storyteller into a collective understanding. Those days have been done for by the individualism of the Romantic movement and its transmutation into the thousands of narratives now daily available with which we may probe, interpret, explain, anaesthetise or plan for our everyday experience.

As never before, the tales of film and television make available as the useful and critical instruments of our thought and feeling an endless supply of *theory*. Confidently, clearly, often mistakenly or mendaciously, but nonetheless always, we can offer an opinion on the way things are. Empowerment has no doubt become a cant word, but it cannot be doubted that television empowers, especially the powerless.

But the powerless are still powerless; and that goes for most of us. For the fourth feature of the self-reporting, self-broadcasting polity is its *distanciation* and *disembodiment*. The life pictured on the screen has its lived location somewhere behind the windless spaces from which the particles of light swim up and coalesce along 625 lines irrigated by three primary colours. We know and recognise that life, but we cannot touch it; as a result, it cannot touch us.

Or only rarely. Writing of photographs, Roland Barthes notes that most prompt only 'the *average* effect', what Barthes calls the *studium*, 'a kind of general, enthusiastic commitment . . . but without special acuity' (1982:20). This general ground of our interest is split by what Barthes names the *punctum*, literally a small wound or puncture, which sharpens general attention into human connection. One could say it turns the calm surface of sympathy into a momentum with a clear current (see Inglis, 1990: ch. 8). The movement from calm surface to clear current turns spectator into citizen.

Citizen eh?; under which king? To speak of nation or society, to use the endearing archaism 'polity', is to seem to be blind to the transnational tides of turbo-capitalism, where the demon kings of media – News Corporation, Time Warner, Disney, Viacom-CBS, Bertelsmann, Kirch, Packer – seek whom they may devour in an effort not only to break the power of lesser buccaneers but also of mere public broadcasters in petty nations, by sailing high out of their reach on the satellites, while robbing people of their very own culture in order to sell it back in a dish receptor.

There is no commonly heeded narrative of citizenship which could curb these whirlwinds in space. Citizenship as a political idea was briefly restored to the academic idiom of Britain by T. H. Marshall (1956, 1965, 1981) shortly after the Second World War. In spite of certain privations, the moment of the Attlee government was one of overwhelming optimism. Marshall shared his feelings, and his classic restatement, which J. S. Mill, poised between liberalism and socialism, would have endorsed, identifies three realms of the deserving citizen's roles and of the narratives these roles betoken.

The first of these is the civil realm, in which citizens exercise the classic rights of individual freedom: freedom from arbitrary arrest; from interference with free speech, belief and thought; freedom of property and of legal access. The second is the political realm, in which citizens are free to take part in government without limit as to personal wealth or status. The third is the social or mutual realm, in which a sufficient freedom of personal being and movement is assured by a minimum share in the collective wealth of a society, and the safeties guarded by such benign goods as national insurance, free medical care and social benefits promised in defence against the terrors of time and chance.

These great victories of a hard-won citizenship have found themselves in much reduced circumstances of late. Merely to chronicle them is a reminder of how soundly left and liberal progressives neglected their duties of vigilance over public freedoms during the 1980s, and slept on the watch. But with the most watchful will in the world, it is hard to see what bearing Marshall's tripartite treaty could have upon a world (not a nation) in which the media privateers have swept past such little local defences of honest citizens as rights, representation and a modest wage.

The modern citizen is better educated than ever before, and cognitively more resourceful than any predecessor. This same citizen is also more completely without representation in the face of the viziers and caliphs of knowledge and narrative than anyone answering to the title since the revolutionaries of America and France in 1776 and 1789. He and she have been driven into isolation and helplessness by deliberate government policies and by the omnipresence of consumerism and its irresistible hypnotists, the advertisers. What, then, is to be done?

What it is useless to do is to list expectations of a quite unfeasible sort in present politics. A daydreaming manifesto calling for public ownership of the means of communication and for drastic limitations to be placed upon the acquisitions and distributions of the vast media empires can only command an audience among the dotty sectarians of powerless old Spartacists.

Stop and think

Plan X and you

'Plan X' was a sly coinage by cultural critic Raymond Williams, intended to make graspable something that is otherwise dispersed in social forces and presences that are hard to see, except in their consequences. It is the 'game plan' of high-level political and business alliances, a long way away from any genuine social responsibility and efficiently pursuing high profits and huge power, fully conscious of their own elitism and bolstered by their own success at controlling things – including the future. Williams did not mean any paranoid 'Big Brother' vision of high-level conspiracy here – just the raw, sheerly effective operation of money and power at this level of sophistication. The 'Big Seven' media empires and their second-tier emulators are inevitably, then, part of what Williams intended to draw attention to (see figure 6).

Stop and think about your own place in relation to these empires of power and money. Grasping some connection between their billions of dollars and

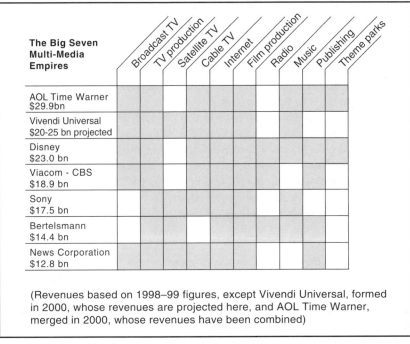

Figure 6 The 'Big Seven' media empires

the media-saturated fabric of your own day-to-day life is a difficult cognitive trick to master. But, ultimately, self projection into those realities is a goal of media education and something that this book as a whole should make easier.

Originally, the public sphere was defined as intrinsically the realm of private citizens. When newspapers and journals of opinion first came into being in post-Restoration England, it was precisely their function to be the organs of critical debate for the operation of the new bourgeoisie in opposition to the calm presumption of power by the Tories of old corruption. Similarly, it was the *point* of the nineteenth-century artisan press, which the state itself attempted to extinguish with the Stamp Tax, that it remain solidly in the hands of this new, self-conscious and insurgent class. Its press would name old corruption for what it was in the accents of William Cobbett and Francis Place, Samuel Bamford and Thomas Frost. It could only do so if that class kept the ownership to itself.

It was across the century and a half from the inception of Addison's *Tatler* to the extraordinary crop of pamphlets about 'the condition of England' in the 1840s that the intelligentsia was born as the voice of bourgeois and artisanal dissent. As public opinion itself came to be the unignorable Polyphemus which power must somehow mollify, the intellectuals formed themselves into what Max Weber termed a *Stand*, or status group, whose business was to serve and sway public opinion and to speak for it against the larger, protean monster which the state was becoming. Habermas (1989:188) writes: 'According to the liberal model of the public sphere, the institutions of the public engaged in rational-critical debate were protected from interference by public authority by virtue of their being in the hands of private people.' Belief in the liberal model held up, and *was* held up as a self-serving piece of mythology by the press barons who kept newspapers privately owned but on a vast scale and of inestimable power to pervade popular passions and keep reason enslaved.

Technology came to their aid. One or two nations, especially Britain and its quondam dominions, kept faith with liberal principles sufficiently to establish semi-independent broadcasting stations. Seventy years after the foundation of the BBC and forty after the Independent Broadcasting Authority, the two British corporations flounder against the sweeping energies of international capital as it strips them of content and beams its theft up to the satellites far beyond the control of individual governments.

The monopolising and global grasp of new capitalism, together with the communicative technology which it commands, now means that instead of informed and educated publics using these media as the arena of public debate and storytelling, the media themselves – supremely television, of course – shape, debate and organise the stories for their own purpose; and that purpose is the marginal rate of profit.

In these circumstances, it is extremely difficult to imagine a picture of citizenship which is not anachronistic and delusive. Naturally, one puts one's faith, with Wordsworth, in 'certain inherent and indestructible properties of the human mind'. Naturally, also, there are active contradictions and oppositions *within* media. Mr Murdoch doesn't get things all his own way. There are still hosts of journals of radical opinion rising and falling. Independent film and television production companies and even the BBC still make their programmes and dramas against the grain of kitsch and commerce. The good citizen needs from time to time to take heart from a specific example of a story capable of calling her and her fellow citizens back to a sense of civic duty. Citizenship must have an imaginative life as well as an institutional one, or it is nothing.

Our example, *Edge of Darkness* (see box) is still shown and still popular. But it is well over fifteen years old and there hasn't been much like it. Moreover, as is obvious, narratives-for-audience may rouse to action; they *are* actions in themselves; but they offer no way of *living* the social and unequal relationship between the sparse institutions of civic life and the massive ubiquity of broadcasting.

For a long time yet, things look bleak for citizens. Our picture of the public interest is shaped by private capital. Television imagines few alternative tales for us with which to criticise the present. Civic society has pretty well shrunk to the clean, well-lighted space of consumer choice.

Some remedies are obvious: assign public events and public moments to public broadcasting. Enlarge the advertising levy to fund production companies. In Britain, turn the BBC into its own licensing authority, and remove the Home Secretary's powers to set the licence. In the United States, fund the Public Broadcasting Service federally. (PBS, headquartered in Alexandria, Virginia, is currently a private, non-profit media enterprise owned and operated by the nation's 348 public television stations.) Control press holdings ('one man, one newspaper') through the Monopolies and Mergers Commission. Encourage (with cash grants) publicly owned local radio. Appoint governors and regulators by vote.

This is the wish-list, however, of the antediluvian left (me, too). There is no chance of it happening. In which case, the only hope for public spirit is to keep up the old labour of the academic intellectual (Raymond Williams); the travelling, bloody-minded journalist (Christopher Hitchens); the dissenting film maker (Ken Loach); the determined independent producer (Phillip White-head); the caustically lucid television interviewer (Eleanor Goodman); the public, political poet (Tony Harrison).

The names are British (non-British readers will have to fill in their own examples, where they exist); the roles are international; the moral meaning irreplaceable. The only thing the intellectual can do today is *warn*. The citizen lives a private life, keeping up his or her education as a citizen, polishing old duties in the quiet of abeyance.

Edge of Darkness: a case study

Edge of Darkness was made by the BBC and shown in 1985. I take it to be one of the most remarkable works of art made for British television.

It is what Vladimir Nabokov once called 'topical trash'. That is to say, its subject matter is the most everyday and urgent of fears. It exudes what at first looks like pious concern for superstitious environmentalism. It is very specific about real events: its action includes the very NATO commanders' conference held at the Gleneagles Hotel in Scotland in 1985, hard by the venerable golf links, at which Reagan's negotiating policy for Reykjavik was prepared.

Television is nothing if not topical. But in addition, *Edge of Darkness* settles viewers into the Cold War frame of feeling and on to the edge of their seats by hanging out all the usual thriller signs – the smell of duplicity, the secret-service paraphernalia. Then it simply walks away from them, and viewers on the edge of their seats are left there, looking for the wrong climax.

The beloved daughter of Ronnie Craven, a widower policeman, is inexplicably murdered as he brings her home in the rain after a student political meeting. She is blasted away with a shotgun as they walk towards their village house in Yorkshire. (Near the end of the five-hour-long serial we learn quite casually that on the spot where she died a spring gushed out where no spring had been before.) Craven discovers that she had been an active member of a secret Green group that has penetrated hidden underground vaults where nuclear waste is stored and uncovered deals being done between US and British corporations in weapons-grade plutonium.

Through the action runs the *leitmotif* of a mysterious freight train carrying a squat ovenful of millions of years of radioactive sludge, trundling and clanking over points, moving as such trains do around us every day.

The police know who the killer is; a hit man from Northern Ireland, where Craven, the mute and anguished hero, was a crack interrogator. Craven baits the killer to his house, again in torrential rain. At the moment when the killer, a shotgun poking into Craven's neck, is about to tell him why he shot the girl, he is shot himself by watcher-police above the house.

The girl, a beautiful, big-eyed, cheerful Yorkshire lass, helps her father as a ghost. Sometimes a little girl, sometimes eerie, more often a reassuring presence as well as a keen blade of loss, she is ghostly in the way the dead are to those who loved them and to whom they were as familiar as breathing or loved music. She disappears only when something in her father's feeling goes wrong.

Craven is joined in his pursuit of the truth by a devil-may-care CIA man, Col. Darius Jedburgh, who is under enigmatic orders to 'break into the ball park and steal the ball'. Jedburgh has already infiltrated the Greens and helped them get into the plutonium store so that he can report to US intelligence the records of their plutonium which the British keep so dark. But now something cheerful and attractive and anarchic breaks out in him, the duplicity in which he thrives subsides, and Jedburgh speaks as simply as Deerslayer of the war between good and evil, the future of the planet. His English ally in this special relationship, rationalist and empirical and domestic to the soles of his caving boots, wants knowledge, not revenge. But in this case, knowledge would be as good as revenge.

They enter the labyrinthine plutonium store together, guided by an old acquaintance of Craven's, a leader of the National Union of Miners who has both secret responsibilities for the underground store and charges of ballot rigging pending against him. The elderly miner helps them out because, as he says, he 'hasn't sold out completely'. The trio silhouette a new political alliance ranged against the reckless new freebooters of an economy run wild who will take any risks with the future of the world for the sake of the profits and a thin line of advantage. They are the most fearsome soldiers guarding the new world order that will replace the Cold War. They are the strategists of what Raymond Williams (1983:248), a couple of years before *Edge of Darkness* was shown, called 'Plan X':

> Plan X is sharp politics and high-risk politics. It is easily presented as a version of masculinity. Plan X is a mode of assessing odds and of determining a game plan . . . To emerge as dominant it has to rid itself, in practice, whatever covering phrases may be retained, of still powerful feelings and habits of mutual concern and responsibility . . . At the levels at which Plan X is already being played, in nuclear arms strategy, in high-capital advanced technologies, in world-market investment policies, and in anti-union strategies, the mere habits of struggling and competing individuals and families, the mere entertainment of ordinary gambling, the simplicities of local and national loyalties . . . are in quite another world. Plan X, that is to say, is by its nature not for everybody. It is the emerging rationality of self-conscious elites . . . [and] it is its emergence as the open common sense of high-level politics which is really serious. As distinct from mere greedy muddle, and from shuffling day-to-day management, it is a way – a limited but powerful way – of grasping and attempting to control the future.

Plan X in *Edge of Darkness* is enacted by an insolent Tory minister, a cold, hard, youthful English businessman who owns the mines and drowns all trespassers, and a neat, boyish, middle-aged American who is an evangelical of the space-travelling future and the vizier of the plutonium bazaar.

The two heroes find the hot cell by way of tunnels and vaulted rooms hollowed out by miners' hands more than a hundred years before – 'Victorian values, Mr Craven'. (They also find a nuclear war retreat and museum store built just after the Cuban crisis, sheltering a whole vintage of chateau-bottled St Julien and the best concert LPs of the day.) After breaking into the cell, they shoot their way out and, fatally irradiated, steal two blocks of plutonium in a green Harrods bag, and escape to break the news.

Driven by their different recklessnesses, each is now doomed to die. Jedburgh goes off to Gleneagles, leaving a trail of CIA corpses behind him. At the hotel, in an effort to push the story out into the public domain and thereby to save it, he clashes his two plutonium pieces together in the face of his evangelical enemy. The generals, admirals and technocrats pile out of the conference hall in undignified terror.

No news escapes. Jedburgh primes his deadly stuff into a crude but serviceable atom bomb. ('Plutonium may not be user-friendly but as a means of restoring one's self-respect it has a lot going for it.') Craven tracks him down and, for Scotland's sake, reports his whereabouts. Craven's ghost-daughter visits him and leaves him a flower of the hardy black alpine perennial that she loved and which lives above the snow line of the unreceded ice age. Jedburgh chooses death in a bloody shoot-out; Craven sits it out with whisky in the kitchen. In the last shots, the plutonium in its improvised bomb is safely winched from the loch while the dying man watches alone from the top of a rock face. The wind whistles thinly through clumps of the black flower as the credits roll.

Maybe some improbabilities are too much. The news of Jedburgh's conjuring with plutonium would certainly have leaked out. The underground gun battle would not have been quite so crass. The Greenpeace environmentalism is a bit kitsch, and Jedburgh is too much altogether. (In one exquisite touch, we learn that his passion besides golf is watching TV ballroom dancing.) But these faults are trifles in a narrative that so masterfully gathers up the themes of Plan X and connects them with the ordinary details of British political life. *Edge of Darkness* ties together the commonplace murderousness of Northern Ireland, the arrogance of a party then too long in power, the always faltering nature of an economy whose leaders will try anything for the sake of profitability, and the lived concerns of a new, intelligent generation convinced that the rich world must revere the authority of the planet before that authority exacts the obedience that is due.

Fred Inglis

Afterthoughts

As we strive to pay attention to each other and to construct more comprehensive theories within our respective approaches, it seems to me that the type of research that has come to be called reception analysis may have a special role to play, in something like the way Jensen (1987) has suggested. This approach encompasses the various styles of research we often describe as qualitative and (loosely) ethnographic, which involve interviewing audience members about the experience of media content, and which, as characterized by Jensen and Rosengren, 'to different degrees, seek to integrate social-scientific and humanistic perspectives on reception' (1990:213).

There are several distinctive features of reception analysis that are potentially important to the effort toward comprehensiveness. In my own experience, I often have found that theoretical ideas which seem obscure and arcane are more easily grasped when I see them used in reception analysis. This is so, I believe, because in the tradition of 'thick description', theory hovers quite close to the ground in reception analysis. The researcher's constant movement back and forth between data and analytical characterizations makes the theoretical accomplishments of reception analysis accessible to the wide community of persons who are interested in audiences, not just to those who share the researcher's own theoretical and ideological preferences, and does so in a way that allows diverse readers to argue about the adequacy of the study's evidence and the appropriateness of its conclusions. That is, reception analysis allows dialogue among readers who themselves hold different theoretical views in a way that most other approaches do not. (Swanson, 1996:59)

Edge of Darkness was released on video in 1986, a year after it was broadcast by the BBC. Fred Inglis celebrates it, not just as a major achievement of twentieth-century television drama, but as an exemplification of how 'topical trash' (in a very special sense) offers good citizens an opportunity to take heart from a story that calls them back to a sense of civic duty. 'Citizenship must have an imaginative life', claims Inglis. This is an important claim. If he is right – and his argument here is persuasively reinforced by his other writings – it is a claim with deep consequences for the business of media and communication studies and for why you are 'doing' media studies at all.

But there is a serious problem here, as our formation of domains, techniques and terrains takes shape into a workable starting point for media studies, one which the learner might act upon and the teacher develop. *Edge of Darkness*, despite what Inglis says about its lasting impact, is a lost text in many ways. The large claim for the importance of it and its like (for other examples might have been taken) is counterbalanced by the fact that such texts come and go so easily these days. We have, in the humanities especially, so successfully dismantled the notion of a canon – of key works in a lineage of fiction preserved for continual celebration – that singling out *Edge of Darkness* fifteen years later seems like an act of nostalgia. At the very least it is a difficult act to follow – today's student is unlikely to have seen it and quite unlikely to find an opportunity to see it, not least because media output has proliferated and the shared experience of any example is less likely than it was in the early days of more limited choice.

Fred Inglis may still be right about the importance of identifying the best resources for the imaginary life of citizenship, but what are we to do with this insight as learners and teachers, where the recovery of distant examples is not only difficult but seems too much like the reinvention of an alternative canon? Moreover, to watch *Edge of Darkness* now, with a view to developing a reception analysis perhaps, is to experience something that has less grip on contemporary circumstances. It had a very precise fit with its moment in the Britain of the mid 1980s and everything that Inglis claims for it was undoubtedly true in that context. Therein resides, however, the answer to our conundrum.

If we have access to, and choose to study, *Edge of Darkness*, we must recover as much as we can of its context – as part of our reception analysis, we must learn about Britain in the mid 1980s. We might then imagine ourselves being spoken to by *Edge of Darkness* in that situation or look for evidence of how people then felt themselves addressed. If we manage to achieve this – and it is hard work – we will, perhaps quite suddenly, realise what is meant by the claim that the imaginative life of the viewer as 'good citizen' is energised by such material. It is this realisation that we can take away from the hard work of understanding such a thing and use in other contexts, including not least our own at this moment. Indeed that realisation, and the work that underpins it, is more important than celebrating *Edge of Darkness per se*, or elevating it and any other texts to some new form of canonical status. At the same time, we have to realise that *Edge of Darkness* and its like are special because of what they achieve in their own specific circumstances. And if anything of those circumstances remains – as is often the case – a piece of drama such as *Edge of Darkness* may retain some, if not all, of its special power, a power to affect that most television of the time would have entirely lacked. There is, in short, little point in just singling something out at random, studying it and feeling that we are doing some meaningful form of media studies, whether reception analysis or anything else. Some things are worth understanding more than others, not least for the sorts of reason Fred Inglis eloquently suggests.

But there is more to this as well. We can go back to Horace Newcomb and Nikhil Sinha's outline of domains and techniques of analysis and locate our chosen example – it may be *Edge of Darkness* – in many different ways. We might use it as a way into the genre of the thriller, across various media. We might use it as our entry point through which to explore the history of British television drama, its institutional organisation, significant personnel, and so

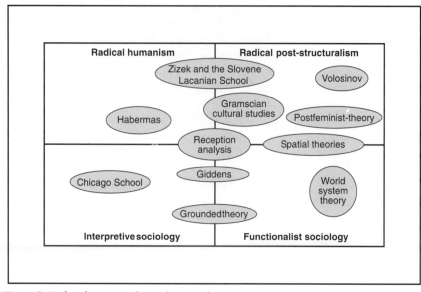

Figure 7 Updated terrain of social research
Note: This figure is based on figure 2, p. 32

on. A good deal of such work was done at that time on another 'landmark' in British television drama, *Boys From the Blackstuff*, and it would be interesting to develop our study of *Edge of Darkness* along those lines. On the other hand, as we begin to unpack such a text into the bigger space of domains and techniques of analysis, it becomes difficult to retain some sense of organisation and perspective in our studies. This is where schools of research often come in: adopting a post-structuralist, feminist, psychoanalytic or some other approach allows one to cut through the sprawling complexity of domains and techniques and to construct a recognisable perspective, because these are in fact genres of academic writing (just as the thriller genre makes *Edge of Darkness* quickly recognisable and lends it a coherent perspective, at least for a while).

Should you then also begin with a specific 'school', and allow it to determine how you select from and deploy the various options in Sinha and Newcomb's outline? To suggest a usable answer to this question, we need to revisit the map of schools of research reproduced in chapter 3. That map dates from 1979. It is a useful historical snapshot (the various terms and approaches are explained in glossary entries here), and today's student should be aware of these academic traditions and their relations with each other. Whatever the oversimplifications, Burrell and Morgan usefully provided a framework that still allows the student to see how such schools are more than randomly distributed groupings of ideas. But it needs to be updated for our moment (see figure 7).

In our version for 2000, a number of things are obvious. The structuralist region has been renamed post-structuralist, because the most exciting work in the various areas within this region has questioned its own earlier assumptions in profound ways and moved on. The boundaries have been ruptured. Important spatial analyses and theories of various kinds have emerged across the boundary that once divided the structuralists from the more mainstream sociological tradition. Anthony Giddens has emerged as perhaps the world's most influential sociologist in this twenty year period, and his work has transcended the older distinction between interpretive and functionalist sociology. Slavoj Žižek has emerged as by far the most influential member of the Slovene Lacanian School, and has revitalised the (previously often rather shaky) ways in which the work of the French psychoanalyst Jacques Lacan is used in cultural analysis. Reception analysis, as Rosengren explains, has developed into a promising claimant to the occupation of some sort of middle ground, if only it can get right that relationship of formal models to empirical data and theory. The various permutations of Russian social theory have faded somewhat, leaving the ideas of Valentin Volosinov more clearly exposed and more influential than ever. The lifelong project of Jürgen Habermas now towers magisterially over the whole previous tradition of critical theory. Italian and French Marxism we now tend to see through the more immediately significant claim to attention of what is here labelled Gramscian cultural studies (a development within what used to be called British cultural studies), thanks to an expanded role for the always important concepts of the Italian Marxist Antonio Gramsci. Post-feminist theory has emerged as simply the most important place to find the legacy of 'grand theory' in the humanities and social sciences being worked through, re-interrogated and new ideas being generated.

There are many other ways of re-mapping some of the relevant fields of intellectual inquiry between Burrell and Morgan's 1979 summary and today. What is offered here is merely a version that allows us to proceed. You do not have to feel that you must soon master these 'schools' or theorists' work – it is enough at this stage to appreciate how the terrain of inquiry is constituted by such shifting, developing, sometimes competing, clusters of ideas; and to note, for instance, how the old subjectivistic/objectivistic barrier (the agency/structure problem) is the location of much of the most interesting work today.

Looking now towards the following Parts of this book, we should note that media studies as a field remains troubled by divided loyalties – between those who are principally interested in how fictional texts, say films and television drama, carry forms of knowledge, and those whose concern is more literally with the knowledge-producing processes of information media, such as journalism, news and the documentary, the avowedly factual form of public communication. Many academics will deny this split (there are approaches that claim to transcend it) but, in fact, few working in the field can genuinely divide their interests between both sides. The allegiances, and the consequent forms of work, go deep into and energise media studies' complex inner workings – the books and papers that are written, the journals read, the conferences organised, the courses delivered, the sense of things worth discovering still out there somewhere. And, described in this way, there is more to it than merely two traditions – whether characterised as the humanities and the social sciences, textual criticism and the sociology of mass communication, the interpretive and the empirical.

What is important here – especially for the student coming to grips with the field – is not to delude ourselves that some ultimate rapprochement awaits, when the intellectual work of the field is sufficiently advanced, but rather to recognise that, if not common ground, then at least a point of contact exists in the very recognition that *forms of knowledge production* are being examined by both traditions. A Tarantino film offers us forms of knowledge, just as much as a news report of inner-city crime. But they are very different in what they ask us to understand as knowledge. In fact, the contrast between the two knowledge claims, as we might call them, has the potential to sharpen our sense that 'knowledge' is not a straightforward thing. The emotional insights of a Tarantino film query the comprehensiveness – the capacity to capture a truth – of a factual news report and vice versa. It is in the concept of the socially symbolic, especially on the fictional side, that we can see the point of contact – the point where fictional texts can be recognised as recoding knowledge in the forms of characters and their interactions, narrative structures, mise-en-scène, music, lighting, spaces, and so on. Not all of these things will be socially symbolic. Rather, they are the material resources out of which something socially symbolic can be constructed, not necessarily in any conscious act by their producers but because human culture (in ways that we are only beginning to understand) distils the socially symbolic out of the dross that it also spontaneously and continually generates.

One early and influential example of 'reading' the fictional media text as socially symbolic was Fredric Jameson's 1979 interpretation of the 1975 film *Dog Day Afternoon*. Jameson's discovery of social symbolism here – of a form of knowledge embedded in the very organisation of the filmic text – should not be taken as representative in any easy sense; he is widely hailed as the foremost Marxist critic still writing in the English language, so he has an interest in reading things a certain way. But it was still an eye-opener. Jameson took three sets of terms and drew out their relationships. The first set consisted of the film's protagonist, Sonny (played by Al Pacino), a confused, angry, would-be bank robber; the concept of 'Hollywood star', of the individually recognisable actor; and the social category of *lumpen* proletariat, the poor and dispossessed. The second set of terms consisted of a character called Maretti, a policeman caught between his local responsibilities and the impersonal federal forces descending on his neighbourhood as Sonny's attempted bank robbery escalated; the concept of the 'character actor', the recognisable type; and the category of national bourgeoisie, of authority located at the level of middle-class self confidence. The third set of terms consisted of the FBI, the anonymous functionaries of the federal policing agency who descend on Maretti's local 'patch'; of the television actor (who plays the FBI agent) as an 'unknown' in cinematic terms, and yet recognisably the representative of a powerful media system beyond the enclave of cinema; and the category of the multinationals, the owners of transnational capital and power (see figure 8).

Fredric Jameson read these three sets of terms as constituting, in their interrelationships, a socially symbolic pattern of meaning which he depicted in simplified form. Each of the three linkages across the sets of terms – the characters, the types of actor, the social categories – Jameson drew as an analogue (or what he termed an 'analogon') of the others. In so doing, he claimed to have revealed how a film such as *Dog Day Afternoon*, because it is a kind of 'symptom' of its own time and circumstances, represents a reality that is impossible to represent literally or directly – a reality encoded in the depicted relationships. The dispossessed here 'star' in a dramatisation that plays out the

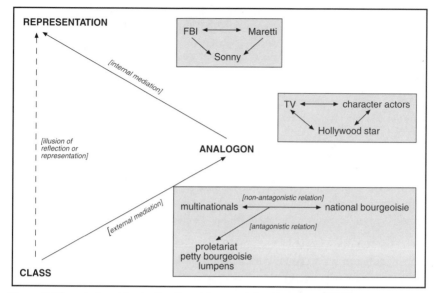

Figure 8 The relationships in *Dog Day Afternoon* (after Jameson, 1979)

great late twentieth-century shift of power away from nation states and their citizens to global forces. Jameson might well now regret some of the crudeness in this early reading – his later work claimed less for these skeletal formalisations of complex texts into bare relationships – but it remains an exercise worth noting, not least because it captured vividly the idea of reading texts for their encoded social symbolism and for their 'knowledge' of larger realities outside the text.

So we find that we can represent *Edge of Darkness* in a similar way (figure 9), not because all texts suddenly become variants of Jameson's model but because this particular text, as Fred Inglis describes it, taps into much the same general circumstances, though subtly nuanced in terms of 1980s Britain. Here the vast forces of Plan X are ranged about the two representatives of the national bourgeoisie, the symbols of old, patriarchal authority, of law rendered irrelevant (and interestingly the CIA character here is made obsolete, post-Cold War, where once he might have been represented on the side of Plan X). It is the ghost citizen, the dead daughter, who returns as a voice of conscience and a call to duty, who tantalisingly represents what Fred Inglis calls 'a new, intelligent generation' (he's talking about you!). In her spectral form, she is little more than a way of imagining such intelligence as a possibility yet to be fully realised, the ghost of citizenship yet to come, a ghost that haunts the project of this book.

With our interest inflected towards reception analysis it is not, in fact, *Edge of Darkness* that will finally engage our attention here – but the 1998 release of Michael Kamen's CD *The Michael Kamen Soundtrack Album* (released as *Opus* in the USA). Alongside soundtrack compositions from movies such as *Highlander, Robin Hood Prince of Thieves, Die Hard* and *Brazil*, this CD includes 'Nuclear Train', the theme Kamen co-wrote with Eric Clapton for *Edge of Dark-*

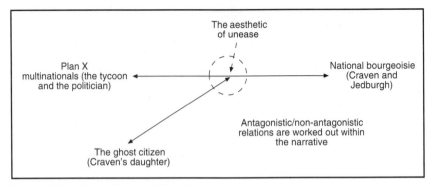

Figure 9 The relationships in *Edge of Darkness*
Note: This figure is based on figure 8, p. 63

ness. This is a mainstream music album, aimed more at the *Die Hard* audience than at anyone who remembers *Edge of Darkness*. Nonetheless, the track is there, in a new arrangement with the unnerving guitar solo played by Japanese cult musician Tomoyasu Hotei, and with the opening sound effects of clanking plutonium-carrying rail wagons preserved. We can borrow one of the findings employed by Karl Erik Rosengren to illustrate his argument about knowledge production, and remind ourselves that 'family security' is a lifestyle value linked to the taste for mainstream music. The aesthetic of unease – the growling menace of the sound – deployed by Kamen's 'Nuclear Train' is a residual deposit left years later amid that security by both the TV drama's call to responsibility *and* Plan X's voracious appetite for recycled media content. In the end, making sense of such connections is what media studies is all about.

Glossary to Part I

Note: Glossaries to subsequent Parts are provided at the *Formations* website.

Aesthetics A term first used in German philosophy in the eighteenth century, aesthetics derives from the ancient Greek distinction between the intellectually known and the sensorily perceived (*aestheta*). Philosophically concerned with understanding the impact of 'beauty' and 'art' on our senses, aesthetics as an intellectual pursuit is divided between those who think such things are universal and those who believe that aesthetic judgements are specific to particular times and places. The former have tended to be the dominant users of the term 'aesthetics', so it has fallen rather out of favour among those deeply suspicious of claims to universality (i.e. most media scholars). But – not least because we all still stubbornly display aesthetic responses – media studies requires some understanding of aesthetics in more localised, specific contexts and is rediscovering the term. *Reading*: Eagleton, T. (1990), *The Ideology of the Aesthetic*. Benjamin, A. and P. Osborne (1991), *Thinking Art: Beyond Traditional Aesthetics*.

Agency If a billiard ball bounces off another ball, its action is determined by external forces. If a person reacts to his or her surroundings, his or her action is both determined by external forces and lived. The living of actions and reactions within the determining structures of a social world is called 'agency'. It is where intelligences, awareness and knowledge are brought to bear on behaviour that would otherwise be purely reactive and mechanical. It does not imply, however, the transcendance of circumstances or an escape from structure, whether the structures of social organisation, cultures, institutions or ideologies (unless one subscribes to liberal humanism's faith in the individual as an unrestricted actor on the social stage, improvising without a script). Marx's adage that men (*sic*) make their own histories but not in circumstances of their own choosing remains a key perspective in understandings of agency. Where those cicumstances are especially dehumanising, people are denied agency (alienated). Non-humanist points of view insist that human society is inevitably 'dehumanising' in this sense and they deny agency from the outset (history makes history, in that impersonal forces structure and fully determine all human action). Theoretical non-humanism can, however, be combined with political humanism. A 'decentred' human subject (not liberal humanism's free-standing actor) can be conceived of as nonetheless capable of acting as more than a mere mechanical puppet, in certain circumstances. Critical pedagogy is devoted to nurturing that capacity. *Reading*: Pickering, M. (1997), *History, Experience and Cultural Studies*. Grossberg, L. (1992), *We Gotta Get Out of This Place: Popular Conservatism and Postmodern Culture*. McLaren, P. (1995), *Critical Pedagogy and Predatory Culture: Oppositional Politics in a Postmodern Era*.

Bourgeoisie Originally the townsmen in feudal Europe (French *bourg*, town), this

65

became a Marxist description of the class of capitalists, the owners of capital, along with those professional groups who directly service their interests (lawyers, teachers, accountants, managers, civil servants, etc.). The lower echelons of this grouping, aspiring to full membership, have been referred to as the petite (little) or 'petty' bourgeoisie. Classes have been defined in terms of economic position, consciousness (or lived experience) and behaviour. Marx's view – that these factors determined highly rigid and inevitable distinctions which crystallised into two opposed groups, the bourgeoisie and the proletariat (possessors and dispossessed) – is counterbalanced by that of Weber, who argued that classes are much more fluid, multidimensional social strata that cannot be so neatly reduced. Neo-Marxist and neo-Weberian variations abound on the theme of social class but the term 'bourgeois' remains useful, if in a looser sense, to describe those who understand their place in the world according to their valuable possessions, mainstream lifestyles and secure social status (of which possessions are usually a sign) – within a so-called 'enchanted' vision of capitalism. The consequent value system may not be irrevocably attached to certain social groupings but is a dominant tendency from which many people have consciously to opt out if they are to evade it. At the start of the 21st century, the old notion of an 'upper class' (e.g. an aristocracy) that wields power has been superseded by that of a consumption-oriented bourgeois world (containing varied social and cultural groupings) cushioning and absorbing the rampant effects of international turbo-capitalism, while the world's dispossessed are more clearly visible in geographical terms, from American inner city to famine-threatened African plain. So the term 'middle class', which has been used interchangeably with bourgeoisie, really has very little literal meaning left, although it is still deeply evocative of a bourgeois form of life in Anglo-American cultures. While an earlier bourgeois world included a 'public sphere' of town squares, coffee houses, and so on, where citizens maintained their engagement with public affairs, it is questionable whether any meaningful public sphere in this sense survives, although the internet has been the focus of some renewed hope about its revival. *Reading*: Marwick, A. (1980), *Class: Image and Reality in Britain, France and the USA Since 1930*. Giddens, A. (1973), *The Class Structure of the Advanced Societies*. Ritzer, G. (1999), *Enchanting a Disenchanted World: Revolutionizing the Means of Consumption*.

Capitalism An economic system based on privately owned enterprises – competing with each other in a free market – rather than on state planning. The latter characterised communist states and since the fall of the Berlin Wall and the collapse of those regimes at the end of the twentieth century, the universality of capitalism has been over-optimistically hailed as the end of history, where history is understood as conflict arising between alternative systems. Against the Marxist argument that capitalism inevitably involves exploitation of a working class – the proletariat – which provides the labour for the owners of capital to use and abuse, capitalism has dovetailed with liberal political institutions to confer a high degree of personal freedom in advanced capitalist societies. Nor has capitalism fallen foul of the deepening economic crises predicted by Marxism, displaying instead a resilience that limits the long-term effects of crisis. Limited state intervention is now frequently deployed to add checks and balances to the capitalist system, where social goals are not otherwise adequately met (an approach formalised as 'social democracy'). Nor has the majority of the middle class in capitalist societies become 'proletarianised', as many Marxist thinkers predicted, by recognising that they are in fact enslaved to the owners of capital. Instead, increasingly efficient, technologically advanced capitalism ('turbo-capitalism') has become 'enchanted' for the bourgeoisie – offering a continuing plenitude of consumption and lifestyle satisfactions. Various theories of a 'new working class' have emerged from this recognition of capitalism's resilience and ability to deliver widespread satisfactions. While many manual workers are now fully part of the bourgeois world, especially with the increased skill level and education required by new technologies, an 'ethnic poor' has emerged at the bottom of the class structure in most European and American cities, paralleling the circumstances of the dispossessed in many underdeveloped countries. Whether or not there is here a new 'class' within capitalism, defined by their remoteness from affluence rather than by their role as labour, for these lumpen millions capitalism will remain resolutely 'disenchanted'. *Reading*: Clarke, J., C. Critcher and R. Johnson (1979), *Working Class Culture: Studies in History and Theory*. Schumpeter, J. (1976), *Capitalism, Socialism and Democracy*. Sakwa, R. (1999), *Postcommunism*.

Chicago School Here intended to refer to the Chicago School of Sociology, although the University of Chicago in the 1920s and 1930s spawned influential 'schools' of thought in architecture, social psychology and social anthropology as well. Chicago had the world's first sociology department, and its second Chairman, Robert Park, was at the centre of an extraordinarily productive group of scholars engaged in urban sociology in the years between the two world wars. They studied Chicago's neighbourhoods, social segregation and 'subcultures', and related their findings in these areas to a spatial analysis of the city's growth, developing new quantitative and qualitative methods along the way and introducing the principle of supervised doctoral research. The deep roots of much of this work were in Park's studies under Berliner George Simmel, often acknowledged to be a co-founder of modern sociology along with Emile Durkheim. Little respected by colleagues at the University of Berlin where he taught, Simmel nonetheless delivered popular lectures and ran an intellectual salon for discussion at his home. In contrast to Durkheim's advocacy of statistical data, Simmel urged a broader interpretive engagement with social topics and an attention to the communication processes that he saw as the main organising features of a society. In this spirit, Park and colleagues such as Charles Horton Cooley became the first theorists of mass communication (Park researched the role of the press among immigrant populations, for example), but after the Chicago School declined in the late 1930s other American communication scholars (notably the 'four founders', Lasswell, Lewin, Lazarsfeld and Hovland) introduced a more limited focus on the 'effects' of mass communication, culminating in Shannon's linear model of communication in 1948. The Chicago School remains a significant touchstone for a more interdisciplinary, interpretive and socially aware approach to communication and media. *Reading*: Rogers, E. M. (1997), *A History of Communication Study: A Biographical Approach*. Faris, R. E. L. (1970), *Chicago Sociology 1920–1932*. Hammersley, M. (1989), *The Dilemma of Qualitative Method*.

Cognitive diffusion Distinct from feelings and immediate sense perceptions, cognition is the process of mentally processing information and organising knowledge, which can include making sense of feelings and perceptions and centrally involves both the functioning of memory and the achievement of reflection (thinking about what one knows). Increasingly the concern is being voiced that, in a world of exponentially growing and accessible information, people may be knowledgeable in a helpless way. We may all know a good deal about the world but be unable to interconnect and structure the proliferating pieces of this knowledge into anything that we can act upon or use. This can be termed 'cognitive diffusion' – what is known diffuses or disperses without meaningful connection – or 'cognitive disintegration' – what is known is already too fragmented to add up to any coherent picture of the world that one can act upon. These are both metaphorical ways of speaking about a cognitive problem in people's thinking which blocks meaningful reflection, despite – or perhaps because of – the availability of so much information 'input'. This is a more general hypothesis than that of 'cognitive dissonance', which proposes that a person will work to minimise cognitively incompatible material, as when the dissonance between moral values and the order to kill is resolved by the concept of 'war'; but cognitive diffusion may increase the tolerance for dissonance. Postmodern architectural spaces have often reflected this cognitive 'problem' by deliberately disorienting the occupant of the space (as with the famous example of the Bonaventure Hotel in Los Angeles), leading critic Fredric Jameson to propose a need for new forms of 'cognitive mapping' to find our way around; a notion that has been generalised to the larger contemporary information spaces of media and culture. *Reading*: Jameson, F. (1991), '*Postmodernism, or, The Cultural Logic of Late Capitalism*. Kellner, D. (ed.) (1989), *Postmodernism/Jameson/Critique*.

Critical Theory Often erroneously used to refer to contemporary theoretically informed criticism in general, Critical Theory, capitalised, was a specific and hugely influential school of thought also known loosely as the 'Frankfurt School', prominently involving Theodor Adorno, Leo Lowenthal, Herbert Marcuse and Max Horkheimer. Beginning as the University of Frankfurt's Institute for Social Research in 1923, the school left Germany for New York in the 1930s because its leading members were Jewish, and only returned to Frankfurt in 1950. Much preoccupied by 'mass' society in the 1930s and early 1940s, when fascism so successfully mobilised mass opinion and action, Critical Theory's most influential work was Adorno and Horkheimer's *Dialectic of Enlightenment* (1979), which argued that the Western intellectual tradition of instrumental rationality – using reason as a tool to manipulate the world – was complicit with capitalism's managerial approach to organising human life in the interests of production and ultimately with the totalitarian impulse to use people as mere disposable raw material. The ferocity of this Marxist-influenced critique was especially directed at the mass media and the 'culture industry' that they sustained (a key chapter in *Dialectic*), the latter viewed as manipulative, deleterious and distracting people from any political consciousness. While this may make Critical Theory sound unrelentingly extreme in its hostility to the media and to contemporary culture, the Frankfurt theorists, in fleshing out their critique, actually generated an astonishing wealth of insights into how modern mass-mediated societies work. To read them today is to be vividly reminded of how much these things matter. Their personal experiences of fascism lent their theorising a realistic edge. Specific studies, such as those documented in Lowenthal's essays, explain much about the emergence of phenomena such as 'celebrity' in popular culture (marking the shift to consumerist media culture). And the associated figure of Walter Benjamin, in essays such as 'The Work of Art in the Age of Mechanical Reproduction', opened up for debate the democratic possibilities of mass reproduced art, such as the Chaplin films that he so ambiguously enjoyed. Later, Habermas's work would be deeply indebted to Critical Theory. *Reading*: Inglis, F. (1990), *Media Theory: An Introduction*, chapter 2. Bottomore, T. (1984), *The Frankfurt School*. Arato, A. and E. Gebhardt (eds) (1978), *The Essential Frankfurt School Reader*. Adorno, T. W. and M. Horkheimer (1979), 'The Culture Industry: Enlightenment as Mass Deception', in *Dialectic of Enlightenment*. Lowenthal, L. (1961), *Literature, Popular Culture and Society*.

Culture One of the most difficult words in the English language, according to Raymond Williams (1988) and rather over-rated in significance, according to Terry Eagleton (2000), culture is perhaps a little less problematic after several decades of effort to make something sensible out of it in fields such as media and cultural studies, but that very effort has certainly contributed to the word's over-valuation. Long burdened by the connotations of 'cultivation', which could so easily imply a social refinement or superiority of taste, culture has in recent years been freed to refer more objectively to the forms of life (including values, social rules, cultural artefacts, etc.) of whole groupings of people, whether defined geographically or historically or both. Where those whose form of life it is use particular resources within their culture to exercise influence, we can refer to their deployment of 'cultural capital'. Where one form of life exercises particular influence over another, especially between nations and where backed by other forces, we may refer to 'cultural imperialism'. *Reading*: Bassnett, S. (1997), *Studying British Cultures: An Introduction*. Willis, P. (1990), *Common Culture*. Du Gay, P. (1997), *Production of Culture/Cultures of Production*. Eagleton, T. (2000), *The Idea of Culture*.

Digital Digital devices – potentially the most powerful machines we have ever devised and rapidly replacing most other machines – work by turning on or off a series of electronic switches. A switch turned on is represented by a 1, a switch turned off by 0. Extreme miniaturisation has placed millions of such switches on the circuits of microprocessors (chips). The 1s and 0s are both binary digits and 'bits' (tiny bursts of electricity). Binary digits can be used as a code to carry immensely complex information. Bits can be used as the transport mechanism to move that information around. This powerful reduction of both information complexity and the process of communication to bits was the great technological achievement of the twentieth century. The mass media were all analogue technologies. In radio and TV a continuous electrical current varies its frequency (develops 'waves') in order to carry information. In photography and cinema, light waves affect sensitive chemicals in film in order to carry information. As these media convert to much more efficient digital devices, vastly more information can be carried and its susceptibility to interference is greatly reduced (because 'on' and 'off' are clear-cut states with no fuzzy variations). Bits are also more flexible, underpinning a move away from mass media to personalised media, where users confronted by greater choice and increased flexibility will fine tune their media consumption to suit themselves. *Reading*: White, R. (1998), *How Computers Work* (fourth edition). Negroponte, N. (1995), *Being Digital*.

Discourse Often loosely taken to mean 'talk', discourse has also developed a more specialist meaning through which it has virtually displaced the term 'language'. It identifies the social process of making meanings through languages (which can include non-verbal languages, such as that of cinematic sounds and images). A central problem in understandings of discourse is whether it answers to any reason, any critical faculty, that is independent of discourse. In other words, is 'reality' ultimately just what we say it is or is what we say ultimately constrained by 'reason', something that is not itself finally reducible to discourse? As multiple discourses are clearly possible, considerable attention is given to the power relations among discourses (e.g. dominant and marginal discourses) and to the question of whether 'reality' can be contested as a result of these differences. *Reading*: MacDonell, D. (1986), *Theories of Discourse: An Introduction*. Foucault, M. (1974), *The Archaeology of Knowledge*. Stubbs, M. (1983), *Discourse Analysis*.

Existentialism Once highly fashionable, now perhaps too readily dismissed, existentialism is a philosophical attitude that raises still unresolved issues about agency and structure. Originating with Kierkegaard, existentialism's period of fashionability in the 1950s and early 1960s was prompted by the work and public reputation of Jean-Paul Sartre (who turned down the Nobel Prize for Literature in 1964). Its general impulse is to insist that the problem of knowing, with which the Western intellectual tradition has been preoccupied, is secondary to the problem of being – which cannot itself be dealt with by objective knowledge but rather involves the individual in reflecting on his or her own existence in concrete moments and situations. Existentialism has been much preoccupied with 'authentic' experience – for some, achieving a reflective awareness that transcends one's determining circumstances, for others (who question the possibility of transcending one's own situation) a matter of maintaining a personal moral identity where one will otherwise be merely acting out a role. In existentialism, the gap between structure and agency often seems so small as to be illusory (Sartre describes a waiter whose 'eyes express an interest' that extends beyond a reaction to the customer's order), especially to those looking for clearer evidence one way or the other on the question of human freedom in relation to constraining circumstances. Sartre saw Marxism as the dominant twentieth-century philosophy and sought to find a place in it for the existentialist attitude, especially through his last work, the magisterial *Critique of Dialectical Reason* (1960), where he elaborated a method of social and cultural analysis (the 'progressive-regressive method') that moves back and forth between the intelligible (the rationally known) and the comprehensible (the reflectively experienced). Engagement with this proposed method, and its underpinning argument, has not yet been widespread, so existentialism may still have something to contribute to the human sciences generally and to media studies specifically. *Reading*: Flynn, T. R. (1984), *Sartre and Marxist Existentialism.*

Gramscian cultural studies Antonio Gramsci was an Italian thinker who worked as a journalist and sometime politician who died in 1937 but whose influence on intellectual activity in the humanities and social sciences at the end of the twentieth century was as substantial as it may be thought unexpected. This influence stems from continuing elaborations of his doctrine of 'civil hegemony', Gramsci's solution to the perceived problem that human history did not always neatly follow Marxism's deterministic predictions. Like Sartre, Gramsci instinctively wished to 'humanise' Marxism's mechanistic model of society (especially as Russian communism became increasingly ruthless in applying that model). In his prison writings he developed a set of ideas that continue to be deeply influential (a founder of the Italian Communist Party, he spent the final decade of his life as a political prisoner of the fascists). Gramsci argued that the struggle for dominance in social, cultural and moral values is every bit as important as economic or political power. Thus the proletariat, far from inevitably emerging as a revolutionary force, might conspire in its own subordination to the owners of capital because people had accepted a value system not just 'injected' as propaganda messages but constructed through diverse cultural means – the exercise of hegemony. In Gramscian cultural studies, cultural consumption is understood as a form of agency (something Sartre grappled with when he discussed 'top ten' musical hits in the *Critique of Dialectical Reason* but never quite came to terms with). The central process here is understood to be the articulation of meaning in and around the consumption of cultural objects (clothes, music, films, TV programmes, etc., etc.). 'Articulation' means a process of exchange and negotiation between the meanings given in the process of production and the meanings made in the process of reception. While dominant meanings may be 'pushed' through this process of articulation, there is always some room for negotiation, which is why the overall process of hegemony in any culture has to be worked at and actively sustained against countervailing tendencies. Agency and structure are always locked in a process of negotiation – without it, agency vanishes. *Reading*: Storey, J. (1999), *Cultural Consumption and Everyday Life.* Gramsci, A. (1971), *Selections from Prison Notebooks.*

Grounded theory A methodology developed by two American sociologists, Barney Glaser and Anselm Strauss (the latter explicitly influenced by the Chicago School, the former by the more quantitative approach of Paul Lazarsfeld). It seeks to support the development of substantive theory with concrete procedures for gathering evidence, structuring research, formalising findings, and so on. The methodological steps are defined in detail but are relatively easy to follow. *Reading*: Strauss, A. and J.

Corbin (1990), *Basics of Qualitative Research: Grounded Theory Procedures and Techniques*.

Hermeneutics Originally a theological term for the interpretation of religious texts such as the Christian Bible, it was borrowed for social philosophy by the nineteenth-century German thinker Wilhelm Dilthey, and by later scholars who used it to describe the interpretation of intentional human meaning, especially as expressed in texts. Although the term is sometimes loosely used to mean the same as 'interpretation', hermeneutics has a more fundamental interest in the nature of human understanding which it sees expressed in interpretation. This German tradition was largely ignored in the 1970s and 1980s when Anglo-American critical and theoretical debate in literary, media and cultural studies was at its most intense but was preoccupied with French theory. It is a tradition consolidated by the work of Hans-Georg Gadamer, whose *Truth and Method* was first published in German in 1960. Dilthey had originally used the term 'hermeneutics' in deliberate contrast to science's forms of explanation based on evidence. For Dilthey, human society and culture could not be explained in the same way as the natural world but required a different interpretive approach. One method within hermeneutics has sought to refine this approach into a state of objective truthfulness on a par with the methods of the natural sciences, based largely on discovering the intended meanings of author, speaker, and so on (see E. D. Hirsch, for example), an approach that sits uneasily with contemporary understandings of how meaning is articulated in more negotiated exchanges. But Gadamer's work has taken hermeneutics in a different and less conservative direction. He opposes 'truth' and 'method', rather than seeing the latter as a route to the former. Gadamer returns to a central theme of the tradition – the paradoxical hermeneutic circle, which suggests that a whole can only be understood by understanding its parts, while the parts can only be understood by understanding the whole. For Gadamer, this paradox consolidates our entrapment in our circumstances – the great problem confronted by so much twentieth-century thought, the entrapment of agency by structure – and constitutes the existential condition of human understanding. There is no 'outside' from where the part can suddenly see the whole objectively, as a scientist looks at something through a microscope. As part of what we are trying to understand – human society and cultures – our viewpoint is always the insider's, or what Gadamer terms the condition of 'prejudice'. Prejudice then becomes the central and unavoidable element of the hermeneutic process. The best we can achieve is a 'fusion of horizons', where part and whole recognise each other in some way – like the ant on the elephant's back suddenly recognising that it is not walking across a plain while the elephant recognises that the ant is not just an itch. *Reading*: Madison, G. B. (1990), *The Hermeneutics of Postmodernity: Figures and Themes*. Gadamer, H.-G. (1979), *Truth and Method* (2nd edn).

Liberal For at least four hundred years, liberalism has been an influential way of thinking about human life and politics. Because other political philosophies habitually define themselves in terms of differences from the liberal tradition, liberalism can be closely identified with 'Western civilisation', a hegemonic construct (see Gramscian cultural studies) that has successfully passed itself off as 'natural' for a considerable part of recorded history. A diverse cluster of ideas, liberalism is founded on the view that politics and government are unnatural but necessary inventions that have to be kept from encroaching too far on something that *is* natural – human freedom. With roots in the tolerant, pragmatic Dutch and Venetian republics, the liberal world view took its most focused form in 1642–49, in the English Revolution, and then in the explicitly liberal philosophy of the American Revolutionaries in the eighteenth century. The French Revolution of 1789 was more of a melting pot for competing political ideas, where liberalism jostled uneasily with rival thinking. Individual human beings remain the fundamental components of the liberal world view, rather than other groupings such as family, community or society, although most liberal thinking does not dispense with such larger components in developing its politics. Where an older Lockean liberal tradition (derived from the English philosopher John Locke, whose ideas informed the English Revolution) attempted to combine utilitarian and rights-based approaches, these have tended to go their separate ways within the range of liberal thinking – some adhering to the view that what promotes individual happiness, without infringing the happiness of others, is right, while others tend to the view that human good is better defended by explicitly defining individual rights. Both assume unencumbered selves, whereas people tend to be embedded in specific communities and larger societies where more complex issues of responsibility somewhat confound the relative simplicity of the liberal world view, something which tends also to encourage 'libertarians', especially in the United States, who hold stubbornly to an even simpler belief in individual freedom. Confronting the complexity of social responsibility, rather than running away from it, the emerging approach of 'communitarian liberalism' re-positions the 'freely choosing individual' within a network of responsibilities to others where that freedom is explicitly constrained, although the individual may still have to make many of the choices. Life is, therefore, full of messy decisions for the communitarian liberal, where individual freedoms and social responsibility often have to be worked through case by case. As with other political philosophies, this has yet to demonstrate that it has the definitive vision of the goal they all share – that of *the good life*. *Reading*: Sandel, M. (ed.) (1984), *Liberalism and Its Critics*. Brown, A. (1986), *Modern Political Philosophy: Theories of the Just Society*.

Phenomenology One of the richest, most profoundly challenging philosophical traditions, though one driven to the margins of the human sciences in Anglo-American academic work in the 1970s by the ascendancy of structuralist thinking. Developed by Edmund Husserl, who also influenced the hermeneutic tradition, phenomenology begins with consciousness of one's own mental processes, when all external influences on thought have to be held at bay ('bracketed'). Though easily dismissed as navel gazing or mere introspection, this starting point gives phenomenology a continuing sensitivity to how things out there are experienced in consciousness, whereas other philosophies tend either to be more readily seduced by the 'reality' of 'out there' as something already given or to consider all human understandings of reality as mere social constructions. The phenomenological slogan, however, is that consciousness is always consciousness of something, so it is not some sort of introspection that loses touch with reality. Husserl posited an ongoing process in consciousness of casting off the detritus to leave more constant, more carefully worked over 'objects' which increasingly approximated to a reality outside consciousness – what he called an 'eidetic' method, from the Greek word *eidos*, form. (In relation to one of academic philosophy's defining arguments, this was supposed to answer Kant's problem of how the mind could ever know things that were forever outside itself.) Some of those interested in art, literature and the other products of the human imagination have been attracted to the possibility that such cultural artefacts, at their best, externalise or project this eidetic process. Of course, this would involve discriminating between cultural objects that contribute to such a process and those that merely reflect the local detritus which the mind should be trying to rid itself of – not an idea that appealed to those media and cultural theorists who wished to mimimise any discrimination among cultural products in the interests of a more even-handed and politically correct treatment. The Geneva School (associated with that university), all but unknown within media studies (in part because its interest has been in literature) has continued to pursue the phenomenological approach.

Georges Poulet, for instance, has argued that 'reading' is a matter of bracketing off one's personal perceptions of an outside world and re-imagining things from inside the text (a recommendation that might help a good deal in realising the achievement of a Tarkovsky film, perhaps). In film studies, a phenomenological tradition has sought to assert itself with only limited success, although the work of Gaston Bachelard remains suggestive. In the late 1930s, Bachelard started to develop a phenomenologically influenced theory of images as a parallel form of discovery to that of scientific thought. Deeply influenced by the new theories of relativity and quantum physics, Bachelard argued that images (by which he meant primarily poetic images but, by extension, photographic and cinematic images) can create in consciousness a 'vertical time', a time of reverie that escapes the linearity of 'out there's' time; a time perhaps that offers a necessary precondition of Husserl's eidetic method and of Poulet's re-imagining? *Reading*: McAllester, M. (1991), *Gaston Bachelard, Subversive Humanist*. Luckmann, T. (ed.) (1978), *Phenomenology and Sociology*. Schutz, A. (1967), *The Phenomenology of the Social World*. Bachelard, G. (1969), *The Poetics of Space*. Andrew, D. (1984), *Concepts in Film Theory*.

Post-feminism Sometimes unhelpfully used, for example by journalists, to suggest that feminism is no longer necessary as its goals have been achieved, 'post-feminism' has also emerged as a more robust term for forms of critical thinking that question the essentialism of the categories 'woman' and 'man', and consequently the goal of achieving 'equality' between them, while retaining the moral victories and many of the theoretical insights of feminist thinking. (Many mainstream feminists allow that 'woman' and 'man' are biological categories while it is 'feminine'and 'masculine' that are the socially constructed terms.) Post-feminism distils many of the most radical ideas from several decades of feminist thinking and frees them from the equality agenda in order to conceptualise new challenges – not least how women can be different rather than merely 'equal'. The MLF (Movement de Libération des Femmes) in France was marked by a split between the mainstream feminists and the 'po et psych' group (a shortened form of *politique et psychanalyse*) who marched through Paris on International Women's Day in 1968 waving 'Down with Feminism!' placards. Thirty years later, it is possible to see that – while mainstream feminism achieved huge concrete changes of attitude and social practice – the po et psych group was anticipating some profound questions about identity that have still to be thoroughly worked through. MLF co-founder and later Member of the European Parliament, Antoinette Fouque spoke for the po et psych group when she pointed out that equality too easily implies a quest for sameness whereas the key task for women would ultimately be that of understanding uniqueness and difference and rethinking identity. Fouque undertook psychoanalysis for several years with the notoriously maverick French analyst Jacques Lacan, underscoring what would become postfeminism's reliance on psychoanalytically derived theory as distinct from mainstream feminism's more pragmatic approaches to consciousness raising and social activism. The work of Luce Irigaray, Julia Kristeva and Hélène Cixous provides central ideas for post-feminism's ongoing encounter with questions of difference, while recent work in 'cyberfeminism' has energetically opened up the debate to new questions about the very nature of human identity when confronted by machine intelligence and human–machine hybrids. Both Irigaray and Kristeva, though with important variations in approach, try to conceptualise a pre-patriarchal space before language created differences by naming and claiming everything in the name of man. They suggest that something of this space can be reactivated as a creative force, evoked in Kristeva's use of the ancient Greek term *chora*, the space that existed before nameable forms in Plato's philosophy. Irigaray and Kristeva both challenge many of Lacan's formulations (Irigaray was expelled from his school of analysis), especially his notion that the 'Imaginary', the realm of being which precedes language and the symbolic order of meaning but remains a constitutive part of identity even after the latter is caught up in language, is regressively comforting and escapist. Post-feminism attempts to rediscover the disruptive potential of this 'space', which may be actualised in certain forms of aesthetic practice (so considerable interest has been directed towards artists such as Cindy Sherman and Louise Bourgeois, for example). It remains to be seen whether this convergence of post-feminist theory and aesthetic practices will produce fundamentally new understandings of identity, rather than revealing itself as either the phenomenological project with a new vocabulary or merely a utopian interest in a non-existent 'place' where women can speak as women in some purer sense. *Reading*: Whitford, M. (ed.) (1991), *The Irigaray Reader*. Irigaray, L. (1996), *I Love To You: Sketch of a Possible Felicity in History*.

Slovene Lacanian School Impossible to summarise because it is not a systematic set of ideas, the work of French psychoanalytic theorist Jacques Lacan has nonetheless proved fertile ground for some of the more adventurous thinking in media and cultural studies since the 1970s. For Lacanians the self is a fluid non-object that is 'objectified' – along with the rest of the world – through language, the basis of a 'Symbolic' order with which we are all complicit in trying to find some solidity for our 'selves' (e.g. when a child stares into a mirror and sees mother and baby as distinct for the first time). Such solidity is illusory because it is based on phantasmic identification with symbolic constructs. The Lacanian 'Imaginary' is the pre-symbolic order that persists in identity as a reminder of the fluid, non-objectified state. While much work in film studies was devoted to developing a Lacanian understanding of the cinematic experience (the screen as mirror, etc.), the long-term success of the approach has been questionable. Much post-feminist thinking is still engaged in debate with the Lacanians. Meanwhile, a startlingly insightful and provocative appropriation of Lacan's ideas for cultural studies took place in an unexpected quarter – the University of Ljubljana in Slovenia (one of the republics of the former Yugoslavia) in the 1980s and 1990s, around the influential figure of Slavoj Žižek, senior researcher at the university's Institute for Social Sciences. Punk rock was at the centre of an influential social movement in Slovenia – a pluralist opposition of diverse groups – that questioned the runaway managerialism of the Yugoslav state bureaucracy in the early 1980s, creating the cultural conditions for ideas concerned with externalising inner experience as a response to the alienating bureaucratisation of life there. Appropriating the term 'liberal' as a defence against rising nationalist populism (Žižek is a prominent Liberal Party member), one intellectual current within this movement has sought to marshal social and cultural theories in defence of openness and inclusiveness against the threat of nationalist closure and exclusiveness (as seen in Serbia). In Žižek's work, Lacan's understanding of identity as the location of phantasmic identifications becomes a deeply resistant impulse to set against exclusionary and essentialising forms of nationalist identification, and it becomes vital – in recognition of the power of hegemony – to explore and expose the phantasmic identifications at work in so much popular culture. 'We are dying in flames because we don't have enough Hitchcock', he has said, evoking perhaps a culture that celebrates phantasmic identifications to the point where the phantasy becomes visible as such and can do less damage in its other forms. *Reading*: Salecl, R. (1994), *The Spoils of Freedom: Psychoanalysis and Feminism After the Fall of Socialism*. Wright, E. and E. Wright (eds) (1999), *The Žižek Reader*.

Volosinov A prominent member of the so-called 'Bakhtin Circle' of Russian intellectuals in the early period of the Soviet Union (the group was active for some six years following the end of the First World War). Although M. M. Bakhtin later claimed to have written some of the work published under his name, Valentin Volosinov's ideas have become increasingly influential in media and cultural studies. He disappeared in Stalin's purges of the 1930s. Volosinov critiques a long-established tradition of thinking about language and human communication as objectively knowable systems made up of structured units of meaning, such as the 'signs' examined by Ferdinand de Saussure and subsequent semioticians and structuralists. For Volosinov the 'sign' or unit of meaning is always already ideological, because caught up in social and historical usage (we will look in more detail at the notion of 'ideology' in Part II) and the world of subjective experience is that of 'inner speech', where the outer signs of the social world are internalised. While Volosinov's writing was often laboured and unclear, realisation dawned late in the twentieth century that it has profound implications for media and cultural studies (even if Bakhtin wrote some of it or, indeed, if Bakhtin and Volosinov were one and the same person). First, he used the term 'speech' more often than 'language', emphasising that human communication is always the *expression* of a language, its articulation, its accenting, its implication in dialogue and the social, rather than some objectively accessible underlying structure or system. This is a shift of emphasis but an important one. The underpinning structures may necessarily exist but, for us, communication is always already 'social-ideological', where 'ideological' means carrying particular values, limited perspectives, particular points of view, intentions to persuade, and so on. In particular, Volosinov focused on indirect speech as the most obvious location of language's inevitably ideological character. When I report someone else's words (as here), I am adding something to them – an evaluative 'accent' or perspective that was not theirs. These inflections organise all our social relations and are deeply characteristic of human communication because all communication, in a Volosinovian sense, is about invitations to orient ourselves towards the communication's particular inflection. If we understand culture and cultural artefacts in this way – including the material circulated by the media – then cultural reception and consumption will involve participation in dialogues about meaning (articulation) rather than mere reception of messages. As this insight is assimilated into media and cultural theory, Volosinov himself may continue to be little read, but his influence will have been considerable. *Reading*: Barker, M. (1989), *Comics: Ideology, Power and the Critics*. Williams, R. (1977), *Marxism and Literature*. Volosinov, V. N. (1976), *Marxism and the Philosophy of Language* (originally 1929).

World-system theory Associated with the work of Immanuel Wallerstein in particular, this approach sees capitalism as a world system that has given rise, especially since the symbolic social unrest of 1968 in the West, to new anti-systemic social movements. While social movements may be diverse in origin, location and objectives, understanding many of them to be anti-systemic in this sense allows overall patterns of social change to be described and new movements to be related to anti-systemic social processes that first began to emerge around 1848, prior to which the capitalist world system had not faced organised social movements. For Wallerstein and colleagues, the demands of gender, ethnicity, race, generation, sexuality, disability, anti-militarism, and so on, are both specific struggles that take different forms in different places and components of a global anti-systemic pressure. So too, however, are nationalist movements (which have shadowed social movements since the mid nineteenth century). *Reading*: Arrighi, G., T. K. Hopkins and I. Wallerstein (1989), *Antisystemic Movements*. Giddens, A. (1989), *Sociology*.

Part II

Public knowledge

5

Broadcast journalism and public knowledge

John Corner

How do the media contribute to the production and the distribution of 'public knowledge', the kind of knowledge upon which any effective exercising of the rights of citizenship must be based and the kind of knowledge which is therefore essential to any adequate notion of modern democracy? In the history both of media research and of political and public debate about the media, this question has been asked frequently and often anxiously. Upon the kind of answers that have been given, a general political evaluation of modern media as a force for good or bad has often been offered. The focus has mostly been placed on journalism because journalism has been seen as the pre-eminent genre, or set of genres, in which information about the world is produced and disseminated to the public (as, variously, readerships and audiences). Journalism of one sort or another is the primary form of most newspaper communication of course, whereas it is only one form among others in radio and television, whose output includes a very large amount of drama and entertainment. It would be wrong to underestimate the informational character of non-journalistic forms, whose 'messages' about the world often have resonance and affective as well as informative power, but it is the *specific referentiality* of journalism, concerned with reporting day-to-day developments through description, analysis and evaluation, which still requires it to be given separate consideration in any analysis of mediated knowledge.

Journalism's relationship to knowledge is direct and explicit; it offers itself as a selective guide to 'what has happened and what is happening', and its function of providing regularly updated reporting about events and conditions in the world has made it far more than an adjunct to modern political life – it has made it one of political modernity's key components. This centrality of journalism to ideas of 'public opinion' and to the processes of modern government is reflected in the way in which the 'classic' tradition of mass communications sociology, developed mostly within North America, has focused extensively on notions such as 'gatekeeping' and 'agenda setting' in an attempt to conceptualise and measure the mediating functions which journalism actually performs. These notions, whatever useful purpose they once had in opening up discussion about the journalism/public knowledge relationship, now serve only to oversimplify a process which is widely recognised as being much more complex than this kind of metaphoric usage suggests.

My aim here is to look at some questions concerning the way in which television journalism is an agency of public knowledge. I want to do this by first of all looking generally at the 'informational aesthetics' of television, clearly very different from those of radio and of print. I then want to consider the broader contexts and processes within whose terms 'public knowledge' is produced, and of which the viewing of television news is clearly only one factor. These general ideas can be given some grounding by selective reference to published studies.

We can regard the relationship between broadcast journalism and public knowledge as involving five linked factors as follows:

1   The sources from which journalism derives its 'stories'.
2   The institutional routines which journalists employ in collecting data from these various sources and in constructing accounts from them.
3   The various forms of depiction, visual and verbal, which are used in the descriptive, analytical and evaluative work of journalistic storytelling, both by journalists themselves and by editors, directors and producers.
4   The interpretive frameworks which audiences and readerships bring to bear on journalistic accounts, turning them both into sense (what they say about the world and show of it) and significance (how this relates to broader knowledge and evaluation).
5   The use which audiences and readerships then make of this significance, as it informs their attitudes, dispositions and actions.

Researching across all five factors of this scheme requires very different research methodologies. Until recently, there was a relative neglect of work on sources and on the often highly proactive ways in which sources are connected with journalistic routines (for instance, through the agency of press relations officers). In this chapter, however, I am going to be primarily concerned with the relationship between factors 3 and 4, that is between journalistic forms and audience interpretation. For the 'gap' here is probably the most widely contentious and perhaps the most central, a 'gap' between those things which happen on the *production* side of the line and those things which belong to *reception*. I am also going to be largely concerned with television, since it is around television journalism that the most intensive research interest has been generated. This is largely to do with the primary role which television now has within most modern public communication systems. The relative neglect of radio, still an important news medium (particularly so at regional and local level) and often the medium in which major news stories are first broken and developed, needs redress. However, my intention here is to follow the main direction of international research and to concentrate on television.

Television's informational aesthetic

Television journalism, whether in news, current affairs or documentary programme format, clearly has a distinctive communicative profile when compared with radio, let alone with print reporting. This is largely due to television's capacity to 'show' things as well as to describe them and comment upon them. Three consequences follow immediately from this capacity, no matter what the specific style of visualisation employed. First of all, television reporting's *evidential* status is greatly enhanced by its ability to image the real, no matter whether this imaging is live or recorded or what directness of relationship obtains between image and topic (as we shall see, this relationship is sometimes highly indirect). Second, the degree of *sensory engagement* which television can elicit from its viewers is richer than print or radio communication. The act of looking at images and responding to them variously as realistic representations or as symbolic expression (often a mixture of the two) draws on the subjectivity (the 'selfhood', the social identity) of viewers very differently from the act of reading a newspaper article or listening to a radio report. This is not to set up implicit hierarchies of representational prowess, nor is it to deny the high levels of imaginative activity which other media can generate from audiences (to some extent, the need to imagine what things look like when attending to print or radio reportage contributes to this). It is simply to note the distinct character of electronic visual representation. Moreover, television's 'showing' places viewers in the position of vicarious onlookers to events, people and places. The onlooking can have various levels of *immediacy* ('this is happening in front of me right now') according to the degree of real or contrived liveness of the visualisation. The sensory appeal of television also has important implications for the strength and the kind of *pleasures* which it can afford the viewer (pleasures which have increasingly become a crucial, competitive element in the economics of television news reporting as various news outlets compete for ratings and for a measure of viewer loyalty). Third, in part as a result of the combination of evidential and sensory factors, taken together with other technical/conventional aspects of its representational character, television can present *people* (faces, voices, bodies, activities) in a way which is strongly affective and empathetic. Unlike cinema images, which are most suited to the projection of intensive, dramatic personhood (the realm of fiction, of fantasy, perhaps of idealistic forms of sexual attractiveness), television images have a more relaxed sociability, they can portray the ordinary, the informal, the everyday and the casual. Television reporting teams can do this when covering the horror of a bomb outrage or when covering a school concert. The placing of people in television journalism, including television professionals themselves as they appear before the camera, has led to charges that the medium unduly 'personalises' issues. These charges have been applied widely to a number of forms of television, particularly the newer styles of 'people show' (talk shows, daytime discussion programmes, 'problem' shows, shows based on do-it-yourself camcorder clips), but they have also featured in discussion of television news output. Not only, it is claimed, has the relationship between news reporters and viewers become too cosy and informal, serving to mask questions of evaluation and the real complexity of the events being reported, but the dominance of personalities in the news, ranging from heads of state (with their almost continuous news profiles) to 'ordinary' people (who usually appear in the news only once, in circumstances variously tragic, celebratory or comical) has skewed the entire pattern of coverage, seriously diverting much television journalism from its proper, public duties as a knowledge agency.

Having noted the evidential, sensorily engaging, personalising character of television 'showing', it is worth remarking too on the way in which a medium so inclined towards the depiction of action (after all, its pictures move) is also, and perhaps necessarily, inclined towards the 'dramatic'. That is to say, it is inclined towards moments of intense, physically observable eventuality or activity (a bridge collapsing, a woman jumping from a burning house, a survivor in closeup telling of his ordeal, the reunion of a hostage with her family). Such moments have evidential power, they frequently personalise, they engage the senses of the viewer strongly, if sometimes only briefly. The way in which the styles of 'showing' of television news emphasise the 'dramatic' happening and, indeed, build whole programme formats around it, has also, like personalisation, been a frequent point of criticism in both academic and public debate.

News 'narrative', the connecting up of the parts of the item into a semi-continuous story, is one way in which dramatic events can receive maximum projection and the news as a whole can generate maximum viewer appeal. However, although newsrooms often work with 'strong storylines' insofar as they can, it would be a mistake not to note the radical differences between the degree of narrativisation open to television journalists and that available to fictional television. Even within the terms of a short filmed report about a high-intensity event, television journalism has little of the scopic mobility of fiction and usually finds it hard to sustain narrative drive for long. More typically, its narrative is a matter of broken sequences, overlaid with *exposition*, often in voiceover (see Corner, 1995).

So far I have talked of television journalism's capacity (much more limited than it often seems) to 'show the news'. But there is still a very important role for speech. Indeed, it is possible to argue that, although pictures are absolutely vital to keep viewers watching, it is words which do the primary job of getting information across and connecting highly discrete sequences. Try watching the news with the sound turned down, if you want to test this point. It will be a much harder business to make sense of it than with the vision turned down. How is this 'telling' organised in relation to the 'showing'? Television journalism has a large number of modes and combinations for mixing speech with image. Among the most prominent of these are:

1   Direct speech to camera by news presenter behind studio desk.
2   Direct speech to camera by reporter 'on location'.
3   Voiceover of news presenter over news images.
4   Voiceover of reporter over news images.
5   Interview speech of people variously 'in' the news or called to comment upon it, whether reporter questioning is heard or not.
6   Speech exchange between news presenter in studio and location reporter seen on studio monitor.

There are many more, of course (Corner (1995) offers a longer and more refined list), but this brings out the main forms currently in use, often in combination with a range of electronically generated graphics and captions. They show considerable variation. In the case of the interview, for example, the speech is absolutely primary; the face of the speaker, though perhaps significant, is communicatively of secondary importance. In a report about a flooded village, however, or a rail disaster, the images are much more consequential. They serve to 'access' us to the reality of the events reported, they engage us as evidence. It will often not be possible to show 'hard news' action directly (although the use of amateur camcorder footage has increasingly filled this 'gap' in news visualisation), but its location and its aftermath can be filmed and 'action impressions' generated from this material. This is not at all the same as actually 'being there' certainly, but it does have some of the feeling of co-presence, including a certain affective power, the power to make us shocked, horrified and distressed in a way which is possibly a good deal stronger than would be produced by a print report or even a radio report. Frequently however, despite the centrality of action values to the world of TV news, journalism's pictures do *not* contain such moments of heightened visual engagement. They serve, instead, to connect us with the ongoing events of the world in less intensive ways. Here, we must note how the extended visual repertoire of current affairs and documentary programming allows for us to be 'accessed' to events in a more sustained and intricate manner than is possible in conventional news items, weaving into and out of various social spaces as unseen observers, propelled by a narrative continuity which may be (but see my provisos above) much more like that of fictional narrative. It would be wrong to suggest *too* sharp a division here however, since most news programmes include 'field reports' of some length, which can in many respects be regarded as 'mini documentaries'. Nowadays, such reports can even include short sections of *dramatisation* too (the reconstruction of events leading to a drugs raid, for instance).

It is frequently the job of journalistic speech to do the main work in 'naming' what has happened and in describing it; perhaps, subsequently, in accessing various judgements upon it through interview. The pictures, despite their engaging general function of allowing us to 'see for ourselves' (if rarely allowing us to see an unplanned news event actually occurring), need speech to pin down the 'what, where, when, how' of the story. We use the words to get information from the images, we use the images as a context, perhaps a strongly affective one, within which to interpret the words. The interconnection between images and speech deserves more study than it has so far received (though see Davis and Walton, 1983; Graddol, 1994; and Meinhof, 1994) but what is clear is that a degree of 'circular confirmation' is possible whereby the words tell us how to read the images and the images 'prove' the truth of the words. A classic case of this, coming not from television but from Second World War propaganda, concerns the use by the Allies of a film purporting to show a German sausage factory producing sausages filled with sawdust, so hard up was the German economy due to the Allied war effort. In fact, the film showed edited sequences from normal sausage production – it was only in the voiceover that the information about 'sawdust' was contained. Yet many people claimed to have 'seen' the astonishing business of sawdust-filled sausages being produced. An element of speech was first of all 'read into' the image, and then this image was used to support the veracity of the spoken commentary! It is not often that broadcast journalism resorts to this level of trickery (although see the examples collected in Ericson *et al.*, 1987), but the basic communicative questions which are raised by this instance – about the slippery relationships which link the activities of seeing, hearing and knowing – are often posed in less blatant form.

I have looked at television journalism's 'showing' and 'telling' functions in the most provisional of ways. There are many more questions to be raised about television journalistic discourse but I want next to ask some questions about what happens when viewers watch television journalism, make sense of

(cont. p. 86) it and variously use it.

Popular newspapers

Popular tabloid titles account for four out of five national newspapers bought in the UK. Sales total approximately 13 million for dailies and 14 million for Sundays (1999 figures), or one paper for every three adults in the country. This criterion alone justifies their description as 'popular' newspapers, by contrast with the 'quality' or 'serious' press, with its relatively small circulation figures. But it is in form and content that the two types of newspaper have distinguished themselves from each other more conspicuously during the twentieth century.

In the UK the larger *broadsheet* format of the national quality papers is associated with the kind of information, news and comment on political, economic and cultural matters which by convention appeal to readers with higher socio-economic status. By contrast, the compact *tabloid* format has come to be linked with material produced for a mass readership: bite-sized items centring mainly on sport, human interest, television, crime, sex and sensationalism. 'Tabloid' also suggests a visual appearance dominated by banner headlines, large photos, and brashly displayed competitions and promotional offers; while 'tabloidese' defines a variety of written English distinguished by its macho snappiness (Waterhouse, 1989).

In reality this binary distinction is less stable and clear-cut. There are middle-market tabloids; some broadsheets now publish supplements in reduced size and give far more space than previously to photos; and a title such as *USA Today* is broadsheet in size but largely populist in character. Yet despite these developments, the association of format with readers' socio-economic status and cultural capital remains one of the distinctive features of the press in the UK and the USA. By contrast, other countries such as France and Spain have a tradition of compact, quality newspapers.

It is customary to date the birth of British popular journalism to the end of the nineteenth century, in particular to the launch of the British *Daily Mail* in 1896 by the press baron Lord Northcliffe (as he later became) and to the contemporary 'yellow press' of the United States. By that time, however, Sunday papers such as the *News of the World* for over fifty years had been successfully producing an early form of the now familiar mix of crime, sport and sensation for working people on their day of rest. Earlier still, the so-called 'pauper press' of the late eighteenth and early nineteenth centuries provided a politically radical education for thousands of working people. Despite state harassment, titles such as *The Poor Man's Guardian* had circulations greater than mainstream titles such as *The Times* (Lee, 1976). But ultimately it is to the seventeenth century that we need to look in tracing origins, for, as Smith (1979) argues, popular journalism had its roots in the street journalism of the English Civil War. (Inglis, in chapter 4, reminds us of the importance of the bourgeois press of this period (Ed.).)

Over the intervening three centuries the term 'popular' has evolved to become a synonym by and large for 'widely favoured' or 'well liked' (Williams, 1988). In relation to the British press at least, it has forfeited any hint of left-wing political radicalism. Today popular newspapers in the UK are often credited with decisively mobilising support for the Conservative Party at elections since 1979 (Miller, 1991). Partisanship has long been a feature of the British press, but tabloids such as *The Sun* have frequently been accused of systematically publishing misinformation and mixing factual reporting and comment from political motives. More generally, critics also attack the dissemination of an ideology which is reactionary, xenophobic, racist and sexist.

For some, the capitalist system itself is to blame. People have become alienated from the centres of political and economic power and amuse themselves instead by reading about sport and television. Sparks (1988), for instance, maintains that as bourgeois democracies become more stable so the mass of the population becomes more apolitical (less interested in how the system works) and the popular press more 'trivial'.

Another widespread indictment of popular newspapers is that they are prepared to stop at nothing in order to boost circulation and thereby also enhance their attractiveness to advertisers. Cut-throat competition has led to violations of journalistic ethics: gross intrusions of privacy, 'chequebook journalism' and invented news stories (Chippindale and Horrie, 1990). Such tabloid excesses have produced a sense of moral outrage, which in turn has prompted calls from some politicians and members of the public alike for tighter, statutory controls, even though this would seriously limit the freedom of the press to act as a public watchdog. But there is an underlying paradox here. While the tabloid press does not lack detractors and critics, these cannot always be neatly distinguished from those who buy, and even benefit from, such papers. An element of hypocrisy consequently bedevils discussion of popular journalism.

In general, readership of the UK national press is not as dichotomous as is often thought. What appeals to readers of all kinds is surprisingly similar, with human interest stories in particular crossing demographic categories (Curran *et al.*, 1980). While the readers of tabloids remain predominantly working class, a sizeable minority is middle class in origin, some of whom will buy a broadsheet paper as well.

The advent of the web poses a potential threat to newspapers in general. The range and instant availability of news and information have a competitive advantage over papers which appear only on a daily basis. Popular titles, which lack the broadsheets' detailed analyses and lengthy background coverage of news stories, are especially vulnerable, a situation merely exacerbated by the growing tabloidisation of television news and current affairs. But despite an overall decline in sales in the 1990s, the tabloid press shows little sign of imminent demise. People of all types who want their news and entertainment in brief, presented in a lively manner and packaged in a format that makes for ease of handling, continue to make them daily bestsellers.

Peter Meech

Interpretive contexts of television viewing

One of the most important features of media research over the 1990s was the recognition, carried into a number of different kinds of study, that the 'meanings' of television do not somehow exist 'inside' the television programme (or sequence, or shot) itself, but are given by viewers to what they see and hear. Viewers therefore quite literally 'make sense' of their viewing, using their own previous cultural understanding, including their familiarity with how television portrays the world and how its various genres involve different kinds of relationship to reality. They 'convert' the images and sounds coming from the television set into 'meanings' and further convert these meanings into significance. Some of these acts of conversion may be relatively unproblematic; the speech of newscasters should not pose too many problems for those reasonably familiar with the language being used. Even here, however, there can be difficulties. One of the areas of journalism I will refer to (see the accompanying case study box) is economic news. This is a realm which has posed considerable challenges for journalistic language. For if journalists reporting an economic story use the conventional language of economists, then there is a very good chance that a lot of people will either 'convert' very little meaning from what they hear or perhaps convert none at all. If, however, journalists choose to render the item in more familiar terms, they may well stand accused of oversimplifying or trivialising the issue.

When it comes to pictures, meanings are, immediately, less stable than they usually are within language. While one person may see in the shot of an inner city residential street a rather rundown, crime-prone district, another may see a quite attractive milieu. While one person may get from the shot of a group of youths playing on the beach a sense of fun and recreation, others may read indications of 'trouble' and the potential for crime. The kinds of meaning which people attach to images can often be decisive in guiding the interpretation they make of a whole news item. Journalists hope that understandings will be broadly in line with their intentions, but, as we shall see below, this is often not the case. One of the problems with the older approach to researching the media and public knowledge was that it tended to assume a highly stable set of meanings in the text (verifiable by a rather simplistic content analysis) and then only ask questions about whether these had been received or not. Seeing media meanings as contingent upon interpretive action complicates this position greatly. Questions have to be asked not about whether people 'got the meaning' but about 'what meaning they got'.

There are also equivalent limitations built into the assumption that, just as people get (or don't get) one specific meaning from a television item, they are likely always to form coherent attitudes or opinions as a result of attending to news items and using them in combination with other sources of knowledge. The notion of 'agenda setting' (still widely used in media research; for a brief account see McQuail, 1987:275–6) tends to assume this relatively straightforward connection, just as the notion of 'gatekeeping' (also widely used; see McQuail, 1987:162–7) tends to give a stable, unproblematic status to that which 'gets through the gate'. In fact, most recent research on the process of public knowledge production shows that many people have a much more inconsistent, partial and often self-contradictory set of ideas, dispositions and understandings out of which they fashion a response to issues (nuclear energy, abortion, genetically modified foods, defence policy, economic change, etc.). Alongside matters of straight cognition (of what is known) there are matters, too, of affective relationships, of how people *feel* about the various, sometimes complex and inconsistent, things which they *know*. The business of research-ing into journalism's meanings and uses thus faces far more instability and flux, is open to far more variables, than was generally assumed to be the case in the old, linear models of public opinion formation. These, as I have sug-gested, often worked with questions about how a determinate 'input' impacted upon the production of a unified mental state.

As with the analysis of journalistic form, I have done no more here than open up some questions. These questions have been widely treated in the media research literature and some useful overviews are available (see, for instance, Morley, 1992; Moores, 1993).

A few commentators have regarded the complexities introduced by the vari-ables of reception, when these are joined by a recognition of textual instabil-ity, as being so extensive as to make the search for journalism's influence upon knowledge a futile one. While it is true that we can no longer work with the same confidence about cause and effect which characterised many earlier studies, I do not believe that this prevents social inquiry from discovering important and accurate things both about the functions of journalism and the way in which public knowledge is constituted. It does mean, of course, that the research methodology has to be one which is aware at every stage of the potential hazards of its methods of data collection and the limitations which have to be placed on the propositions which it can legitimately generate from its data. But, such hazard and limitation allowed for, there is still a lot for media researchers and students to find out, and a lot that is 'findable out' too.

Studies in the journalism/knowledge relationship

So far, I have developed a general account. A look at one or two specific studies would be the best way of developing some detail and substance. A significant and much-cited breakthrough in linking the devices of television journalism to viewer knowledge occurred with the publication of the *Nationwide* studies, undertaken by David Morley and Charlotte Brunsdon in the late 1970s. The first publication from this study (Brunsdon and Morley, 1978) showed a subtle analytical engagement with the modes of address, visualisations, reporter presentations, interviews and links of an early evening BBC news magazine, *Nationwide*. This was a 'soft' news programme, working with a high level of sociability and humour and depending mainly on 'features' rather than on short, hard news items (though these were included). Working from detailed sequence lists and transcripts, Brunsdon and Morley analysed just how various 'positions of knowledge' (often implicitly cued by the audio-visual structure of the material itself) were made available to audiences. They were particularly interested in the way in which the programme 'naturalised' its discourse (i.e. presented it as revealing of 'the obvious' rather than being an exercise in cultural authorship), moving between shots and between different speech sequences with continuity maintained by the voiceover comments of presenter or reporter. By drawing on current film theories about the relation between representation and audience, Brunsdon and Morley gave a new sense of complexity and dynamics to the analysis of news, seeing individual items as crafted artefacts whose narrative formats, though different from those of fiction, exercised an equivalent control over the viewer's knowledge and pleasure.

This was illuminating, but it risked overstating the power of the television discourse (seen within the terms of a 'dominant ideology') and understating the range of interpretive responses that might be made to it. In its own way, and allowing for its sensitivity to textual form, such an approach had a tendency to distort the television/knowledge process in a manner rather like that of some earlier sociological studies by assuming too much fixity at the 'message end'. It was a risk which also distorted a good deal of contemporary film analysis. In the follow-up study, however, Morley (1980) corrected this emphasis and produced a classic of media reception research, attempting to plot how a range of sample viewers had actually understood certain editions of the programme. His work has been the subject of much debate and development (see the discussion in Corner, 1996), but one of the main conclusions to emerge from it was an increased sense of the variety of interpretive positions which viewers used to make sense of television and the ways in which pre-existing knowledge was employed to 'negotiate' the meanings and evaluations at work in journalistic accounts, sometimes leading to part or wholesale rejection of these.

Morley's conclusions remain important, but the fact that his work is conceptualised largely within the terms of ideological analysis (see chapter 6) means that it is concerned primarily with the *socially evaluative frameworks* within which people respond to the programme rather than with specific questions of comprehension. Significant differences were found to occur at this socially evaluative level (for instance, in how people judged the credibility of various interviewees), but questions about basic *comprehension*, about the lower levels of that process by which programme material is converted into knowledge, also need asking. Of course, activity at lower levels may well be informed by evaluative differences and this has to be taken into account when researching them.

Perhaps the most striking piece of research to address questions about 'comprehension' and news knowledge is that by Justin Lewis (1985). Lewis focused on just one edition of the long-running British nightly news programme, *News at Ten* (replaced in 1999 by a later slot) and explored with fifty sample viewers how its items were understood, attempting to take his analysis right down to the level of what viewers thought an item said and showed, as well as noting how they responded to it. At this level, Lewis traced a very wide range of variables. Questions of selective perception in relation to previous knowledge were raised. For instance, Lewis notes how many viewers misunderstood a news item about the standing ovation given to a government minister after he had spoken at a public meeting. They *mis*understood, says Lewis, because they failed to register and use the information on the voiceover commentary. This placed the ovation in the context of the minister's broader public standing in his party – he had recently been through a highly controversial period during which some critics had questioned his fitness for continued office. However, most viewers read the applause in exclusive relationship to the speech he had just given, thus missing the wider implications altogether. Similarly, in looking at foreign and industrial stories, Lewis plots how 'blanks' in viewers' knowledge led to interpretations which often made causal connections very different from those projected in the accounts themselves. In short, Lewis shows the disjunctions possible between journalistic discourses and the kinds of meaning and assessment viewers construct. Viewed from Morley's Marxian position, this might be seen as a good thing (the more disjunction, the less the definitional power exerted by the media). To Lewis, however, such disparities are not positive at all. They are inefficiencies in a public communications process which should aim for optimal understanding. If people are to disagree with the news, he feels, then they should be reasonably clear in their minds (and reasonably accurate too) about what it actually *says* is going on and about what it shows!

Lewis actually connects many of these variant readings back to problems in the journalistic format itself. Far from seeing it as a 'closed' form, exerting its controls on reception willy-nilly, he sees it as vulnerably 'loose', not providing the continuity of narrative line or the emphases to get across its information to viewers. In particular, he sees the convention of including crucial information in the first half-minute or so of a story as one which is detrimental to communicative efficiency. Viewers use this period to refocus their attention and are very likely not to pick up any major 'cues' given them, he suggests. Far better to place, and repeat, such information further into the item.

Lewis's work displays a zeal for getting to grips with the fundamental processes of 'television knowledge' which many other studies can still learn from. Of the few other empirical projects which give such processes an equivalent degree of attention, I would recommend the work of the Danish researcher, Klaus Jensen (Jensen, 1986) and the Swedish researchers Peter Dahlgren (for instance, Dahlgren, 1988) and Birgitta Hoijer (Hoijer (1990) is a thoughtful review of conceptual issues). Scandinavian researchers have generally been more illuminating on these questions, theoretically and practically, than British and American scholars. (*cont. p. 91*)

Economic news in the UK: a case study in forms and understandings

I want to look briefly here at research which, with colleagues, I have recently concluded at Liverpool University in England and which is reported more fully in Gavin (1998). This is research for which Justin Lewis's work has certainly provided a useful point of departure, as have our own earlier studies on the relationship between broadcast form, understanding and response (see Corner *et al.*, 1990).

Given the importance of knowledge of the 'economy' to modern citizenship, we are trying to investigate both the range of devices which television news uses in depicting economic affairs and the range of interpretations which coverage receives. 'The economy' is essentially an abstract, systemic notion – what it indicates is a set of relationships or states between various indicators, such as unemployment, inflation, interest rates, growth rates, trade figures, and so on. Politically, the economy is contentious in terms both of what *should* be included in the system and what *should* be the relationship between the system parts (the economy 'in balance'). Historically, talk of the economy has often made extensive use of either organic metaphors (e.g. the economy as garden, requiring tending; the economy as sick body, requiring healing) or mechanistic metaphors (e.g. the economy as machine, with 'levers'). Journalists often make use of both metaphoric realms in their coverage, but they are drawn inevitably to a highly *statistical* depiction too, relying on figures and, frequently, on graphs and charts. Unlike reporters in many other areas, economic journalists on television have little by way of direct picturing to offer. They can offer 'stock shots' of job centres (unemployment), dealing floors (the City), docks (trade figures), factories (industry), but these often merely provide a visual plane over which speech information is placed. A good deal of economic reporting is organised around the noting of shifts (as indicated, for instance, in the regular release of official statistics). In the early 1990s in Britain, perceived (though often contested) shifts were intensively organised around two key words: 'recession' and 'recovery'. The question was, 'are we pulling *out* of the recession; are we *into* recovery?'. More recently, the threshold of recovery has been seen to be crossed, but the question of whether or not it is 'sustainable' and whether it will generate a 'feel-good factor' among the public strong enough to encourage increased consumer spending and business confidence has been the new focus of speculation.

Part of our analysis of economic news has involved:

1 Looking at how various system parts are related in any one story and at the overall frequency of their occurrence. Questions of causality and of 'cure' (e.g. 'raise X and Y will fall') are of particular interest.
2 Looking at the metaphoric phrases and technical vocabulary used by journalists and others in describing and evaluating the economy.
3 Looking at the kinds of pictorial representation used in economic stories, including the use of graphs.
4 Looking at the type of people routinely interviewed in developing economic stories, including politicians.
5 Looking at the underlying 'story logic' of economic items, and at those features which give them their principal news value. Frequently, it is a *change* in one of the main indicators which forms the core of the story. This change is measured against *expectations* and the resultant fulfilled expectation or surprise gives the main narrative theme for commentary. Studying this aspect leads us to investigate the working assumptions which journalists use, including ideas about the likely rate, scale and direction of economic change.

With information of this kind gathered, we worked with groups of viewers, showing them taped materials and discussing with them the kinds of sense and use they got from the items. There is not space enough here to indicate the findings in any detail but among the most important points to emerge are the following:

1 Television, not surprisingly, is a primary form of information about the economy for most viewers.
2 There is widespread cynicism about the 'truth' status of statistics; items relying heavily on statistical accounts tend to be treated with suspicion. Where the statistics are issued by a government department and are not subject to an explicit scepticism by journalists, this suspicion is increased.
3 The 'economic system' as reported on television is often far more complex than the 'system' people have in their heads. Not only are particular notions (e.g. public sector borrowing) unclear in popular understanding, inhibiting a sense of systemic relations, but the normative relationships which *might* be obtained between parts (what politicians argue about achieving within various policy perspectives) are often only partly grasped.
4 There is a complex play-off between perceptions of 'national good' and of 'personal good' in assessment of news items. Attempts by the news to frame economic shifts in terms of a national-consensual evaluation of the whole system often collapse in favour of interpretations based on the viewers' own specific material interests and the consequent selective focus of their concerns.
5 There is widespread distrust of the role which the 'City' (the finance sector) plays in economic affairs. The use of 'City analysts' within economic news items as objective assessors of economic health, is also often regarded with disquiet. (It would be interesting to compare this with the role Wall Street plays in US television news.)

A generalised and terse list of this kind does no justice to the depth of commentary which our pilot study produced, engaging with the question of how specific items worked, as well as indicating what kind of other knowledge is drawn on in routinely attending to the news and in what ways factors such as age, gender and party political affiliation might work to shape interpretive activity (all developed further in Gavin, 1998). But such a list does indicate some of the main items on our agenda. Our project has cut into the interface between journalistic discourse and public understanding on one of the most important of public issues, and we hope to broaden it in future studies by looking more closely at the *non*-media components of 'common knowledge' (see Neuman *et al.*, 1992).

John Corner

Conclusions

Modern society is a heavily mediated society. Modern democracy, in its various versions, is mediated democracy. Television is in most parts of the world a primary agency by which definitions, relationships and evaluations are produced and circulated. How much this production and circulation registers the differences and the conflict of political and social life will depend on the political and social complexion of the particular society in which a given television system is situated. The full range of television genres, from comedy through food programmes to documentaries, is involved in the production of public knowledge (for further discussion, see Corner, 1999). However, television journalism, in its internationally conventionalised formats, is the key site for providing audiences with specific and direct information about the conditions of their society and of other societies too. Rather than being reducible to a series of discrete 'messages', as some earlier researchers were inclined to think, television journalism is a rich (and varied) cultural form, with strong narrative and symbolic qualities supporting its informational functions, engaging many viewers in a frequent, routine and often entertaining 'look' at the world. We need to keep on asking questions about how it is put together and how it works as public communication.

Many viewers routinely depend on television journalism for their first (and most trusted) source of information about domestic/national events as well as international ones. In interpreting what they see and hear, they draw on a wide variety of sometimes contradictory knowledge obtained from other sources, including newspapers and radio and the increasingly accessible resources of information technology (especially the internet), although their previous experience as television news watchers constitutes a vital part of their viewing 'competence' too. The 'seeing' capacities of television connect it with viewer imagination in quite distinctive ways.

Nevertheless, despite the defining power and imaginative 'reach' of television news within modern culture, there is no evidence to show that viewers are simply placed 'in thrall' to broadcast journalism, dupes to its scopic appeal, its descriptive facility or its institutionalised authority. There is, indeed, a high degree of scepticism about television's capacity (despite the best intentions of many of those who work in it) to 'tell the truth'. However, the interface between (changing) news forms and the processes by which viewers get knowledge from the screen remains a key focus for media research all over the world. And rightly so.

6

The reassessment of ideology

Mike Cormack

The concept of ideology has had an uneasy existence within media studies in recent years. On the one hand, it has been a central concept in much media analysis, particularly in a teaching context. On the other hand, its inherent problems, as revealed under the force of feminist and postmodernist critiques, quite apart from the more internal critiques associated with the term 'post-Marxism', have led some to abandon it completely. Yet the concept still appears, whether in relation to film studies (Turner, 1993), cultural studies (McGuigan, 1992) or feminist media studies (Van Zoonen, 1994). At the very least this suggests that, despite theoretical problems, the concept of ideology can be used to say something important about the media and that, as a mode of analysis, it serves a particular purpose which other concepts are unable to match.

The classic view of ideology, relating ways of thinking about and seeing the world to economic and social structure, does, however, need to be rethought if it is to retain its usefulness. Three areas in particular have appeared as problems for any use of the concept of ideology in relation to the media. The first derives from criticisms of the theory of ideology from writers engaged with issues concerning collective identity. These criticisms have centred around the traditional view's focus on economic structure, which saw social class as the central determining factor. It has now become clear that other forms of collective identity apart from social class (such as gender, race and nationality) can be important determining factors, and so the interrelation of such identities with ideology needs clarification.

The second problematic area concerns ideological analysis. How can ideology be analysed in media texts? Many recent writers have put more emphasis on the concept of discourse – that is, structured relations of concepts which underlie and support the specific statements and judgements which we make. But if this makes certain kinds of analysis clearer, it also raises questions as to the relation between ideology and discourse.

The third problematic area concerns media effects. What ideological effects do media products have and how can these be detected? For anyone concerned with ideology, this is the central question. After all, if ideology has no effects whatsoever, then any concern with it becomes of purely academic interest. This is particularly important given, on the one hand, the ascription of overwhelming power to ideology evident in some writings about the media in the

1970s and early 1980s (particularly writers influenced by the Marxist philosopher Louis Althusser and by the post-Freudian psychoanalyst Jacques Lacan), and, on the other hand, an influential critique which denied any real power to ideology (Abercrombie *et al.*, 1980; Abercrombie *et al.*, 1990). However, before tackling these questions we need to be clear as to precisely what the 'classic' view of ideology is.

The classic account of ideology

Immediately another problem presents itself. How do we identify a 'classic account'? In the early 1990s two books on ideology had to start with a list of different definitions as a way of demonstrating the problems involved in attempting to pin down this concept (Eagleton, 1991; Cormack, 1992). Even an attempt to trace earlier uses of the term will find different definitions (e.g. those of Marx, Lenin and Mannheim, all of which vary in important ways). This at once tells us that what we are dealing with is not a straightforward concept but one which has always been argued over – there has *never* been a single, generally accepted definition of ideology. This in turn should tell us something else – that what ideology as a concept is trying to grasp is something which is not just controversial by, as it were, historical accident, but which is inherently controversial. At its core, ideology is a concept of radical social critique, and its attack on vested interests of one kind or another is bound to give rise to disagreement.

In its most famous early use, however (that of Marx and Engels in *The German Ideology*, written in 1843), an account of ideology is presented which has been particularly influential, at least as a starting point for later debates. This view can be reorganised and represented in the form of the following statements:

1   Ideology is a false (or at least a distorted) way of seeing the world of social relations (i.e. the ways in which people, or groups of people, interrelate with each other).
2   It is based on the economic and social structure of society, to the extent that it is seen as arising naturally from that structure. Thus the economic structure of society gives rise to a particular social structure and out of this ideology emerges.
3   It is linked only to the dominant class in society, which attempts to impose its way of seeing the world on to the subordinate classes.
4   Its essential character is to present as natural, and almost God given, a form of society which systematically works in favour of a few (those who profit from the organisation of society by being in the dominant class), against the interests of the majority (those whose work supports the dominant class but who do not themselves greatly profit by this work).
5   It is thus not a conspiracy invented by the dominant class, but rather a way of seeing the world which even the members of the dominant class see as only natural.

Marx and Engels did not refer to the mass media in *The German Ideology* but a view of the media's role can be extrapolated from their account as follows:

6   The mass media are implicated through their being owned by members of the dominant class or controlled (at some level) by them. The media accept this dominant view since without it their own institutional structures (such as the private ownership of newspapers or public broadcasters' dependence on government finance) are undermined – but once again this acceptance is not (usually) a conscious decision, but rather simply part of the attitudes into which media workers are educated as they are trained. Media professionalism is thus (at least partly) an ideological construction.

7   Media output simply replicates and supports the dominant ideology, as media professionals exercise their judgement in the production of such media products as newspapers, television programmes, popular films, broadcast news and advertisements.

8   Media output results in the quiescence of the subordinate classes, as they come to agree with and accept the status quo (the Italian writer Antonio Gramsci described this as the dominant class's 'hegemony', by which he meant in part its leadership in society, accepted by subordinate classes).

The problems in this account are many and have given rise to later versions of the theory, both within and outwith the Marxist tradition. Each of the points numbered above has given rise to debate. The fullest discussion of these points can be found in the books of Jorge Larrain (1979, 1983), but see also Eagleton (1991). The problem with point 1 is that it implies that it is possible to have a non-ideological (sometimes characterised as 'scientific') view of the world. How else would we know that ideology is false, if not by comparison with a standard of truth? But this raises further questions. If, by its very nature, ideology is unconscious and the person talking from within ideology is not aware of his or her ideological position, then how can anyone be sure that he or she is not talking from within ideology? How can the critic of ideology avoid being him- or herself a 'victim' of ideology as well?

The problem with point 2 – the economic basis of ideology – has already been alluded to. Feminist writings during the 1970s and 1980s have made very clear that gender ideology (particularly that form described as 'patriarchy'; that is, male domination over females), cuts across class boundaries (which is not to deny that there are class differences concerning gender). To put it another way, socio-economic structures are not *in themselves* sufficient to explain gender ideology. Similarly, racial and ethnic ideologies cannot be explained completely on the economic class model. And, although this is more controversial, it is arguable that nationality similarly escapes the traditional model, in that its appeal crosses class differences but not simply in order to defend a dominant class. All of these, then, are forms of behaviour and belief which cut across class boundaries.

Point 3 – that ideology is linked to the dominant class only – has been debated even within the Marxist tradition for a long time, with Lenin, for example, arguing that there existed working-class ideologies, as much as there were dominant ideologies (see, for example, the account in Larrain, 1979, pp. 73–8). Points 4 and 5 have been, perhaps, the least controversial   **95** of these arguments, but even these are clearly bound up with the idea of a dominant ideology.

Points 6, 7 and 8 take us to the study of the media, and here controversy redoubles. The most general criticism affecting all three points is simply that media texts do not, in fact, function as straightforward channels for a unified dominant ideology, and therefore they cannot have the wide effects which some writers have suggested. Writers who have criticised these points have ranged widely in their views. Some have accepted that media texts, especially popular ones, by their very nature include widely differing points of view and even show the signs of ideological conflict within them. This view has often been described as 'Gramscian', being linked to Gramsci's view of hegemony, that different ideologies are in a constant process of struggle, as the dominant attempts to retain its leadership.

Other writers have gone further and argued that the consequences of abandoning the traditional view of the dominant ideology mean that such analysis becomes redundant. In his essay 'Popular Culture and Ideological Effects', Nicholas Abercrombie has argued this position:

> The conclusion of these arguments is that the notion of textual ideology has its limitations. It is often possible to detect a dominant discourse within any one text which gives a certain coherence. However the connection between this and discourses that have a social dominance is not always made and textually subordinate discourses are always present to provide a potentially discordant note. (Abercrombie *et al.*, 1990:211)

Thus, for Abercrombie, textual analysis of ideology becomes a rather pointless activity.

Still others have argued that, regardless of what goes into the making of media products, the audience is still in a position to resist such ideological output, and can even interpret and use media products in ways which are opposed to the intentions of the producers. John Fiske is the best-known exponent of this view, using the term 'excorporation' to describe the way in which 'the subordinate make their own culture out of the resources and commodities provided by the dominant system' (Fiske, 1989a:15). Indeed Fiske (in a very arbitrary move) simply defines popular culture as that which is made 'by various formations of subordinated or disempowered people out of the resources, both discursive and material, that are provided by the social system that disempowers them' (Fiske, 1989b:1–2). He is thus using the term 'popular culture' in a rather idiosyncratic way, which does not reflect either prevailing popular or academic usage.

Stop and think

The working class and culture

The term 'working class' is extremely important in any discussions of ideology and culture but is also increasingly problematic. A social class long understood to consist of those involved in manual or 'blue collar' (as distinct from 'white collar') occupations, the term is still widely used and is seldom questioned despite a considerable blurring of the distinctions on which it traditionally depended – a blurring caused, for example, by the phenomenal growth of the service sector in which many 'working class' employees are no longer 'blue collar' in the old sense. Moreover, other social divisions – such as those of race, gender and nationality – have been recognised to be just as deeply implicated in the social construction of identities as any notion of class. Deep differences in material prosperity, cultural capital and power remain, but they are not so easily mapped on to a socio-economic class structure as was once thought possible. Inherited wealth no longer so clearly secures political power, for instance, as in Britain where the upper chamber of Parliament was reformed in the late 1990s to sever aristocratic inheritance from automatic political influence; so the notion of a clearly defined, self-reproducing 'upper class' holding both wealth and power is increasingly an oversimplification.

In industrialised societies an 'upper working class' has clearly emerged, with high skill levels and job security, and incomes that can be considerably higher than those of the 'lower' middle class (office workers, nurses, etc.). While this also signals a merging of working conditions, clear differences in values, motivations for work and longer-term aspirations often remain. The 'lower' working class (largely unskilled labour) sits unstably atop an increasingly larger group (unstable in the sense that they either drop into it or rise to 'upper working class' status as a result of training) – that of the 'underclass', *lumpen* or dispossessed (in Europe and North America often including disproportionate numbers of non-white groups, including migrant workers).

As the old notion of a monolithic social block – the 'working class' – breaks down, we have to be very careful about any attempts to define a working-class culture as such. In *Uses of Literacy*, Richard Hoggart (1957) was able to celebrate a current of English popular culture fed by the streams of working-class values and experience, but it was a historical scene that could not remain static and the tributaries of the main current would find new sources soon enough. Today, the impulse to claim any special authenticity for working-class experience and 'culture' is a form of existentialist thinking gone astray. Instead the enchantment has moved from activities of working-class community building (such as the now near mythical miners' choirs of the Welsh valleys) to the consumption of media-celebrated goods, including the symbolic goods of the media themselves, and the bourgeois world has expanded exponentially.

However, in his 1974 book *Meet Your Friendly Social System*, Peter Laurie redescribed the working class as the product of a process of 'de-education', as a socio-cultural construction as much as an emergent reality of socio-economic circumstances: posters to teach reading in a London school 'illustrate the word "Mummy" by a neatly permed blonde figure in a light summer frock sitting on greensward next to rosebushes and a lily pond' (p. 16). From this perspective, the working class is created by a convergence of actual socio-economic circumstances, with consequent experiences of self and world, *and* a de-education that mismatches proffered 'knowledge' with that experience. One important consequence of this alienating mismatch is that 'knowledge' is severed from agency, control and empowerment and tied instead to 'learning one's place' in what is really someone else's picture of the world. Laurie quotes educationalist Basil Bernstein's version of this explanation: 'Only a tiny proportion of the population has been socialised into knowledge at the levels of the meta-languages of control and innovation, whereas the mass of the population has been socialised into knowledge at the level of context tied operations'. With a grand sense of irony, Laurie then memorably places that explanation into the working-class heads to which it refers as 'the mass': 'Only a tiny buzz of the population has been buzzed into buzz of the buzz-buzzes of buzz and buzz, whereas the mass of the population has been buzzed into buzz at the buzz of buzz tied buzz' (1974:19).

Revealingly, Mandelson and Liddle's influential manifesto for New Labour in Britain – *The Blair Revolution: Can New Labour Deliver?* (1996), written on the brink of the party's landslide victory – uses the term 'working class' only once or twice and always in inverted commas, as here. If we are to remove the inverted commas, it will perhaps be by shifting from the old Marxist notion of that class as economically produced, which the Blairites reject, towards the idea that a working class is still socially constructed in the kind of mismatch between experience and knowledge evoked here, a site of perpetual friction where sexism, racism, and so on, may then also operate. But who actually experiences this mismatch is something that is less clearly determined on rigid economically defined class grounds than before. That does not stop it from being experienced by huge numbers of young people. Working-class students are implicated in ideology through that experience of mismatch, rather than merely through exposure to ideological 'messages', as carried by the media for instance. This realisation depends on a Gramscian notion of ideology – of contested ground where identities are multiply constructed but also open to reconstruction:

> Students cannot learn about ideology simply by being taught how meanings get socially constructed in the media, and other aspects of daily life. Working-class students also have to understand how they participate in ideology through their own experiences and needs. It is their own experiences and needs that have to be made problematic to provide the basis for exploring the interface between their own lives and the constraints and possibilities of the wider society. Thus a radical pedagogy must take seriously the task of providing the conditions for changing subjectivity as it is constituted in the individual's needs, drives, passions and intelligence. (Giroux, 1997:81)

So you should stop and think about whether – for you – education has been largely a match or a mismatch, whether the 'buzz' that may have been generated by your mismatched experiences and needs blanks out whole areas of knowledge (a phenomenon itself hilariously spoofed in a school-room scene in the 1999 movie *South Park: Bigger, Larger and Uncut*). Whatever answer you come up with will have consequences for how you think of yourself in class terms, in relation to other learners, to culture, to the public knowledge that is available to you, and to the very idea of ideology. If there has been a fairly comfortable match, you should pause and wonder about what that comfort tells you regarding the sort of world that has been constructed for you to know. If there has been largely a mismatch, and you have still got this far, you should stop and think about that problematic experience as itself deeply revealing of the socially determined processes of knowledge production.

Whatever particular positions one takes on the questions raised above, it is evident that any use of the concept of ideology needs to make very clear precisely how the concept is being used. It may be, of course, that the most obvious way out of these arguments is simply to abandon the concept altogether. However, as suggested earlier, something useful is lost if this is done – something which cannot be retained simply by using other analytical concepts. To defend this view I will go back to the three general problems mentioned in the opening paragraphs – the problems of (1) collective identities, (2) ideological analysis and (3) media effects.

Ideology and collective identity

Central to any reworking of ideology must be a satisfactory answer to the question of collective identity. In recent years the concept of collective identity has come to be seen as of central importance in the social sciences (see, for example, Schlesinger, 1991:152–75). It has become the central concept which brings together a number of specific identities, such as those of class, gender, sexual orientation, race, ethnicity, nationality and even occupation. These identities are distinguished by being instances of what Benedict Anderson has described as an 'imagined community', since the members of these large communities cannot know all the other members personally (unlike in a small community such as a village, for example) and therefore can only *imagine* an identity with the group as a whole. As Anderson (whose principal concern was nationalism) puts it: 'in the minds of each lives the image of their communion' (Anderson, 1991:6). The individual imagines him- or herself as part of a community even though he or she can never meet all the other members of that community. Such communities are typically defined in two ways – by insiders, that is, by members of the group (the consciousness of being, for example, female, working class, gay or of belonging to a particular nation) and by outsiders, that is, members of other and possibly opposing groups (the 'us and them' syndrome). Richard Jenkins (1994) has described these two facets of identity as the 'virtual' (the experience of being a member of a particular cultural group) and the 'nominal' (the naming or identifying of the group, and of individuals as members of that group, by outsiders). The potential of the media both to express the virtual experience of belonging to a community (through, for example, fictional drama) and to exercise the nominal power of naming groups, particularly minorities (through, for example, news broadcasts) should be clear. Such identities do not, of course, arise in a vacuum, and are related in complex ways to economic conditions. However, the argument here is that ideology emerges from such identities as part of the process by which the collective aspect of identity is developed and strengthened. It is a way of understanding the social world which gives the power of primary definition (i.e. the supplying of the discourse through which the world is experienced) to the community concerned. Even in groups which have little or no power, it is a way of attempting to empower the group by at least defining the world in the group's own terms. This is not to say that the group's definitions are either necessarily right or wrong, but rather simply a way of seeing the world.

It will be obvious that we are all members of several such collectivities or communities (class, nationality, occupation, etc.), even if we do not normally think of them in these terms, and some of these collectivities contain widely varying views. Take, for example, gender. We all belong to one of two genders. Even those who wish to change or be regarded as of both or neither gender will be categorised by others as one or the other, and this categorisation will have social implications for that individual. Also, in particular circumstances (such as times of social change or conflict) any one of the various collectivities to which we belong can seem to be the most important. This has implications for what has been described as the question of 'subjectivity', that is, the question of how we are constituted as individuals within ideology (a particular issue in writings on ideology derived from Althusser and Lacan). If we are always members of various collectivities, it follows that our own individual identity is not an easily defined product of one ideological formation, but is rather a product of a number of identities, which may well influence us in different ways at different times. It should not be surprising, therefore, that the personal identity of any one individual cannot be predicted simply by noting their class position. Ideology is not as simple or predictable as that – particularly as different identities may well be in conflict.

Discourse and the problem of textual analysis

Seeing ideology as linked to collective identity, however, increases the complexity of the ideological analysis of media texts. As a way into this, it will be useful to consider further a term already referred to and which has been much used in recent years – the notion of 'discourse'. This concept has various meanings (see, for example, O'Sullivan *et al.*, 1994) but the meaning appropriate for our use is that which has developed from the work of the philosopher Michel Foucault. In discussing the use of this term in media studies and cultural studies, Graeme Turner has defined 'discourse' as 'socially produced groups of ideas or ways of thinking that can be tracked in individual texts or groups of texts, but that also demand to be located within wider historical and social structures of relations' (Turner, 1990:32–3). Leaving aside for a moment the rather odd use of the term 'demand', this definition reflects the concept's use in ideological analysis. The idea is that discourses enact systems of power relations by structuring relationships between concepts.

Thus, in relation to gender for example, patriarchal discourse organises series of terms into patterns so that man/male/masculine immediately all link up with other words (active, strong, non-emotional, dominant, etc.) which are opposed to another series linked to the terms woman/female/feminine. To use one of these terms within this discourse ('He's a real man') immediately implies a series of other judgements ('But she's only a woman, and that other person is not masculine at all'). In some postmodernist writing these discourses become not only the defining features of society but the only features (Laclau and Mouffe, 1985; Collins, 1989). This, however, does little more than mystify the processes involved since the discourses seem to be free floating and undetermined by any material reality. Indeed, since by this account discourse defines reality, there is a sense in which they are the only reality. Such a use of the concept becomes mystificatory since it denies any human agency in the construction of discourses and denies the reality of material life (and the problem with Turner's use of the word 'demand' is that, despite the rest of his definition, it seems to indicate a conceptual slippage towards this view). To avoid this we need to link discourses to social structures. This can be done by seeing discourses as arising from collective identities. These discourses have the function of perpetuating the status quo and this in turn enforces the structures, particularly by making them seem natural or desirable. Such discourses can be contradictory. The gender discourse of patriarchy is closely linked to the economic and social discourses of capitalism, but is not *necessarily* linked. The very variety and number of such discourses gives rise to hegemony, that is, to the linking of discourses in order to broaden their appeal and force.

Thus ideology can be seen as a set of discourses (a way of thinking, talking, seeing, understanding, etc.) which is in fact based on collective identities and on their need to perpetuate and defend themselves, but *it presents itself as independent of these identities*. Part of how a discourse works is by presenting a position for the individual to fill (the process which Althusser called 'interpellation'). All of this should make clear the central importance of the mass media as purveyors of discourse and as sites of struggle, since in the typical media product several different discourses may be involved. Occupational ideologies also fit easily into this model, since they typically take the form of a discourse which emphasises the importance of the occupation concerned and its autonomy from other occupations, that is, it builds up the importance of the occupation. An example from the media industries would be the position of cinematographers in traditional Hollywood. By being in charge of the definitions of what constituted professional cinematography (so that, for example, using a handheld camera in films was defined as non-professional during the 1930s), and by emphasising their own contribution and technical expertise (it is not difficult to find evidence of cinematographers making very dismissive statements about the skills of directors, for example), cinematographers protected their own position. (Typesetters long did the same in the newspaper industry; programmers are doing much the same in relation to our use of computers today; and so it goes on.) This approach also, of course, problematises the idea of the dominant ideology since it can no longer be regarded as monolithic. More appropriate would be what I have elsewhere called 'the minimal conception of the dominant ideology' (Cormack, 1994:10–12) This would see the dominant ideology as a set of dominant discourses (on class, on gender, on race, on professionalism, etc.) which are frequently contested, particularly in times of social change, but which *only require minimal assent (rather than total agreement) in order to retain their dominance*.

It has to be asked, then, whether it is worth keeping the idea of ideology since the concept of discourse seems to work well enough on its own. Foucault, for example, abandoned the notion of ideology altogether. The answer argued here, however, is 'yes', since the concept of ideology emphasises social and material links which discourse alone does not do (as is evident from the work of some of the postmodernist writers mentioned earlier). It also emphasises the impossibility of speaking outside of ideology, although we can at least become aware of the discourses within which we ourselves function.

How, then, can we analyse media texts such as films, music videos, newspapers, and radio or television programmes? Such analysis has been central to media studies (indeed one of the sources out of which media studies developed in Britain was the textual analysis of films), with many kinds of analysis being offered. Textual analysis, however, raises all sorts of problems. How can we interpret texts so as to 'read' the ideology which has formed them? As argued, we cannot simply assume an expression of a unified and coherent dominant ideology, despite Roland Barthes's famously misleading assertion that ideology 'cannot but be single for a given society and history' (Barthes, 1977:49). This does not mean, however, that no analysis is possible. Analysis must be sensitive to discursive variety and contradiction, and the analyst must recognise that textual analysis cannot deliver the only meaning but can describe a range of relevant meanings (even if other meanings can always be found). It can also relate such ranges of meaning to a range of viewing positions. Indeed, in one sense an analysis of a text, such as a film or a newspaper, is simply the description of one or more viewing positions – that from which it is being analysed. It is the invitation to 'look at it this way'. Ideological analysis takes the form of describing the structures of the discourses which lie behind a media text, discourses that are linked to collective identities in the society which has produced those texts. It cannot ultimately 'prove' that such links exist, but it can lay open the text for examination. Whether such analysis is accepted or not will depend not just on the quality of the analysis but also on the ideological position of the reader of the analysis (and, after all, a textual analysis simply produces another text – for example, a chapter in a book or a lecture in a college – which will itself be subject to ideological influences).

Approaching ideological analysis

Both Terry Eagleton and John B. Thompson have published lists of typical ideological strategies (Thompson, 1990:61–6; Eagleton, 1991:45–58). Although their lists vary, with Thompson listing five strategies and Eagleton listing six, and with only partial overlap, they can be usefully combined (with a certain amount of revision) into a list of eight strategies. These should be seen as ways in which discourses are structured; that is, they describe how concepts are positioned in relation to other concepts.

The first strategy is *legitimation*, that is, making something seem to be worthy of legitimate support. Most obviously this applies to a form of government but also, for example, to social differences based on gender – ideological discourses will try to present such elements as legitimate, often by simply assuming their legitimacy, as if there could be no questioning of this. The second strategy is *universalisation*, that is, the making of a specific group interest into a universal principle – 'capitalism is the universal law of humankind', 'men and women always have different roles to play in society'. Thompson puts this category as a sub-category under 'legitimation', since it serves to legitimate a particular practice. The third strategy is *rationalisation*, that is, giving 'plausible explanations and justifications' to a belief or practice (Eagleton, 1991:52) or, as Eagleton puts it on the previous page, 'defending the indefensible'. He gives the example of the racist who rationalises a belief in stopping immigration by saying that more people in Britain will use up all the available air (an extreme instance of a strategy that is often more subtle!). The fourth strategy is *naturalisation* by which beliefs or practices are seen as natural, common sense or obvious – 'It's only natural that women should stay at home to do the housework.' In his book *Mythologies*, Roland Barthes describes a basic ideological move at work in making the historical (i.e. something rooted in a particular time and place) seem natural (and thus applicable in all times and in all places) (Barthes, 1993:129).

Fifth comes *reification*, the making of a process or a practice into a thing. This is perhaps the most difficult strategy to grasp, but some examples should make it clear. A country's traditions become 'Tradition' which must be obeyed, economic practices become 'The Economy' which makes its own demands on individuals. Note how capital letters are frequently used here. Generally this process of reification removes causes from humans to something superhuman (some Marxists have been prone to this, with statements about the Law of History and the Law of Capital). The sixth strategy is *unification*, that is, the creation of a symbolic unity. This is most obvious in discourse about nations – 'We are a People', 'Britain speaks', 'God Bless America'. It is also much in evidence in talk of social classes – 'the middle class says no to higher taxes'. Symbols are very important here, such as flags, songs, images of leaders, and so on. A seventh strategy is *differentiation*. This is closely linked to the preceding category in that unity is created by differentiating ourselves from others, creating 'us and them', with the latter being 'the common enemy'. This was most obvious during the Cold War, but now Islam can be seen as taking this role in Western political discourse. As an example of differentiation, Thompson cites an editorial in the British newspaper *The Sun* about an industrial workers' strike in the early 1980s – 'we' won't be defeated by the strikers, 'we' will fight them as 'we' fought the Falklands War – thus the strikers and the Argentinians are bracketed together as the 'others' who oppose 'us'. The final strategy is *dissimulation*, that is, hiding, concealing or creating absences, for example in the statement 'There is no poverty in Britain today'. It works even more obviously by simply not mentioning something – consider how child abuse was formerly simply ignored and 'therefore' it did not exist.

These strategies, then, show the ways in which discourses work and are particularly linked to verbal language. There are still other ways in which media texts can be structured by discursive formations. Narrative structure, for example, can be seen as a discursive strategy since the question of how a narrative begins, develops and ends is a question of how a series of events is shaped by discourse. Even questions of cinematic style can be analysed in this way, when the discursive power of cinematic conventions is considered (for an ideological analysis of cinematic style, see Cormack (1994), although the term 'discourse' is not used there).

Ideological effects

Questions about textual analysis naturally lead us on to the problem of ideological effects. Arguments about media effects have been engaged in since the first studies of the media took place (indeed one could argue that the entire discipline of media studies is based on the assumed impact of media products; that is, on their having important effects on society and on individuals). The concept of ideology was originally applied within media studies as a way of predicting these effects when empirical audience studies seemed to have reached an impasse (see Stuart Hall's (1982) essay 'The Rediscovery of "Ideology"'). The problem with ideological studies, however, has been precisely this tendency to assume audience reactions (and usually ignoring the analyst's own position; that is, treating him or her as somehow outside the audience). This has led some writers to go in the opposite direction and argue that audiences have the power to resist whatever ideological structures can be found in texts. As noted earlier, John Fiske in particular has been associated with this position. The view of ideology as various discourses, interrelated as described here, should make clear the problems involved. It is not difficult to criticise Fiske – the fact that some members of an audience *can* resist domination does not remove the problem. And that very resistance may have its roots in other ideological discourses. In addition, of course, a few resisting viewers on their own are not of great interest to anyone (apart from themselves) – as media analysts and students we need to know what the majority is doing, or how such pockets of resistance might be linked to other things.

How, then, can we actually trace media 'effects' of an ideological kind? It cannot be done simply by interviewing audiences, or at least not by taking their comments at face value. These comments are themselves texts to be analysed. Audience studies have been an important and useful part of media studies, but just as textual analyses have tended to overplay the power of the text, so many audience studies have tended until recently to ignore texts or play down their importance, and to treat statements of individual audience members as if they were some kind of highly privileged knowledge. The answer is rather to note that discourses are not causal agents (in fact they are not 'agents' of any kind) and they do not *make* someone act or react in a particular way. However, if one is already placed within a discourse – that is, if one already participates in it by accepting its presuppositions – then repetition of that discourse is likely to reinforce it. Non-participation in such a discourse will likely result in what used to be called an 'aberrant' or 'deviant' reading of the media product; that is, an understanding of it which runs against the grain of the producer's intentions (making the big assumption that it is possible to know what those intentions were). Tracing ideological discourses in media texts can, however, tell us something about the producers of those texts and can also tell us something about the likely range of audience reactions, even if it cannot predict the effect on any specific audience or audience member (see also chapter 5).

Conclusion

I have argued that, despite the problems associated with the traditional theory of ideology, it is still a useful concept, but more difficult to work with than some had previously thought. It is less predictive, more complex and also more involving for the analyst. However, it remains a useful way of emphasising the vested interests expressed in media products, and of linking those products to social identities. It cannot be seen as the only, or even necessarily as the primary, method of media analysis and study, but it can add something useful to other approaches. Its quality of radical social critique is its central importance, something which postmodernist approaches to the media, for example, cannot match. Without it media studies is conceptually much the poorer.

Taking popular culture seriously

Popular culture has been taken seriously for a long time now. The history of the theories it has attracted (Storey, 1993; Strinati, 1995), and its prominence in the life of modern societies, show this. Indeed, nowadays it may sometimes be taken too seriously. Here we can say what is required if we are to take popular culture seriously as an object for academic study. We can leave the question of whether it is taken too seriously for the time being. What we can do is outline some of the things involved in studying popular culture.

The first point concerns how the popular culture we come across is usually made available to us because it is a commodity. Popular culture has to be produced and consumed. In the societies in which it is prevalent and with which we are familiar, popular culture is something which has to be profitable or which has the potential to be profitable. To do this, it has succeeded, or will succeed, for its producers, in finding profitable outlets or markets. Popular culture is therefore a marketable commodity. It is usually produced by very large and global, multimedia conglomerates such as AOL Time Warner, Disney and the Rupert Murdoch empire (News Corporation), because it makes a profit. And this entails a constant search for markets.

Popular culture, then, has to be understood, first, by this process, which is called *commodification*. It is possibly the best way of beginning to understand what happens in contemporary capitalist societies. There are many good examples of this. One is the spread of multi-channel, digital and cable television with some channels devoted to direct selling and others to facilitating the consumption of products. Another is the televising of football and the associated expansion of marketing and merchandising. Both involve the extensive spread of advertising and sponsorship. This does not mean that everything has to become a commodity. There may be forces such as audiences or governments which oppose specific instances of it, or areas where it may not work, that is, which are not profitable. But the idea of popular culture as a commodity, as something which is sold and bought, is the best way to start to take it seriously.

The importance of the commodity is not confined to the context it provides for popular culture. It can directly shape the popular culture we consume. To illustrate this, we can refer to the way in which an increasing number of television programmes have become consumer guides in all but name. They are about organising an appropriate consumer lifestyle for viewers, be it in the area of clothes, cooking, travel, motoring, entertainment, and so on, or are, more generally, about how to be a good consumer. Even in the making of films which acquire prestige and cult status, such as *Blade Runner* (1982), market considerations can override those of clarity and aesthetics (Instrell, 1992). The turn to science fiction in recent Hollywood blockbusters, such as *Jurassic Park* (1993), *Independence Day* (1996), *The Lost World* (1997), *Men in Black* (1997) and *The Matrix* (1999), rests upon the merchandising opportunities provided (spin-off goods) and the use of the most up-to-date special effects technology. The successful commodity form of the special effects film is not confined to science fiction, but can be found across a range of film genres.

Second, one consequence of this is that audiences have to be regarded, at least initially, as consumers. This is the way in which popular culture produced as a commodity treats them. They are evaluated by producers as potential buyers – not only, say, of a film, but of the products associated with it, including CDs, books, posters, T-shirts, toys, computer games, fast food specials, and so on. This may be the first word on audiences but it is obviously not the last. The reservations we had about the extent to which popular culture need be turned into a commodity also apply here about the extent to which audiences need become consumers. Many studies show how audiences can react in a variety of ways to popular culture (Morley, 1992; Moores, 1993; cf. Ang, 1991). They can be passive, active or indifferent towards what they consume, and interpret it from a range of perspectives. They can, for example, accept the ideas or meanings presented, reject them or turn them into something new. However, it is rare for them not to be addressed, in the first instance, by popular culture as consumers or potential consumers. This is again the context in which popular culture becomes available to us, although it does not mean that audiences can be thought of only as consumers.

It does mean, however, as was the case with production, that popular culture is directly shaped by the need to treat audiences as consumers. As Graham Murdock (1990, 1994) has shown, treating audiences as consumers, as people who are there to be sold things, increasingly clashes with, and threatens, their citizenship rights. In particular, it threatens to undermine their right to free access to the information, knowledge and culture they need to enable them to participate as citizens in a democratic society. Murdock's case is that, in the end, consumerism and citizenship are incompatible but that the forces behind the former are much more powerful and therefore more likely to succeed. Popular culture will therefore be shaped by this process in that it will focus more and more on audiences as consumers. This is a compelling and relevant reason, in its own right, for taking popular culture seriously.

We can return to the example of the film *Blade Runner* to introduce our third point. This is that it is not very useful to study popular culture seriously by confining our attention to the so-called 'texts' of popular culture, which include such things as films, television programmes, books and magazines.

This point should already be evident from the stress we have placed upon the production and consumption of popular culture. What these factors do is not only determine the context in which popular culture is presented to us but also directly shape its content. Therefore popular culture does not exist in isolation but can be directly shaped by outside influences. Instrell notes in his study of *Blade Runner* how a key set of images, which suggest the hero is not a human but a 'replicant' (an artificially manufactured 'human'), was cut from the first version of the film. A more optimistic ending was also added. These changes were insisted upon by the production company after preview audiences reacted angrily to the first version and the film looked as if it might be a financial failure (1992:164, 166). This provides a good way of illustrating the point at hand. However, this kind of research and argument concerned with the manufacture of texts has not yet become very prominent in the study of popular culture.

There are, in any event, a number of problems with a purely textual analysis of popular culture which assumes that popular culture gives collective expression to the general culture of a society (cf. Neale, 1990:54). First, there is no reason why the decisions of audiences as consumers should by themselves add up to a type of collective cultural expression. The former cannot be reduced to the latter. Second, there is no reason why producers should have the knowledge of the wider culture that would enable them to express it in the various strands of popular culture. This is anyway likely to be incidental to the drive for profitability. Third, it is difficult to assume that there is a *direct* relationship between the 'texts' of popular culture and the wider society. (See the 'Afterthoughts' section in Part I on the possibility of indirect relationships (Ed.).) This is because the industries which produce popular culture for markets of consumers always come between the two. As we have seen, the demands of this can directly organise the form and content of popular cultural texts. Fourth, the texts of popular culture need not reflect the wider culture or society at all, but may be inaccurate, misleading, deceptive or illusory.

The fifth and last point is that not all groups in society have equal access (most do not have any access) to the production and circulation of culture and ideas, except as consumers. Even here they are not all equal. This means that the prevalent character of popular culture may not reflect the ideas and concerns of the society as a whole. Rather, it may be more directly related to the interests and ideas of those groups with access to the production and circulation of culture, ideas and knowledge.

These criticisms suggest that an awareness of *ideology* may be needed if we are to take the texts of popular culture seriously. This is the fourth general point that we need to make. This means that the ideas and values to be found in popular culture have to be related to the interests and ideas of the groups involved in its production and distribution, as well as its consumption. They have also to be related to the inequalities between these groups and those excluded from production and distribution. However, they equally have to be related to these excluded groups since popular culture regards them as consumers too, and their interests have therefore to be accommodated.

This is quite a fertile area for the study of popular culture, though observers clearly differ over how powerful and effective a force ideology is in society (Abercrombie *et al.*, 1980; Barker, 1989; McLellan, 1995; Strinati, 1995: chapters 4 and 7). For example, a question can be raised about how successful the ideology of consumerism used by companies and advertisers is in getting people to buy the goods they produce and promote. The idea of ideology has a long history and has been subject to differing interpretations, as well as being rejected by some as a way of analysing society. But in view of how the study of popular culture has developed, there may be a case for its reassessment (see chapter 6).

What this suggests is the fifth and last point we need to make. This is that taking popular culture seriously requires the use of ideas relevant to its study and interpretation. *Commodity* is one possible idea, and *ideology* is another. These are fairly familiar ideas in the social science literature, though they may have gone out of fashion a little. But they still need to be adapted in order to study popular culture.

Another idea that we can look at briefly to illustrate this point is *genre*, an idea which, though also familiar, comes from textual criticism rather than sociology. Genre is a way of distinguishing particular types of culture and showing how they differ from each other. We can refer, for example, to different film genres such as horror, science fiction, crime, comedy, action-adventure and drama. The categories of genre can be strictly defined by critics.

What is more important, however, is that genres are also defined, used and promoted by the producers and consumers of popular culture. This means that they are more loosely defined and more historically various. Producers use them to sell their products as commodities, and audiences use them to organise their consumption. Genre as an idea can therefore be used to interpret the production and consumption of popular culture, remembering that this is an unequal and changing relationship (Neale, 1990). It describes one aspect of the production of popular culture as a commodity, and one way in which its consumption occurs. Genres also embody ideas and values, which means they can be assessed for their ideological content and power. Genre is an idea which can capture a general pattern of popular culture, as we have noted. However, it can equally focus on the tastes and preferences of individuals and groups, since choices are made about which genres to produce and consume. It can, therefore, provide a way of understanding some aspects of the collective and individual features of popular culture.

There may be something to the view that popular culture can be taken too seriously. This can sometimes be found in the textual analysis of popular culture, where almost any aspect of popular culture, no matter how superfluous or obscure, can be scrutinised in minute detail for some significance. The influence of semiotics illustrates this point (Strinati, 1995: ch. 3). It provides an often arbitrary method to identify the codes an item may be supposed to carry but has no way of judging its significance. However, taking popular culture seriously need not mean being this arbitrary or relative. Specific items of popular culture may be insignificant, irrelevant or unimportant, and some deserve their obscurity. It should be the argument about theories, ideas and evidence, some of which have been noted above, that identifies the significance of popular culture. It is the general nature of popular culture which makes it interesting and important. This is one reason why ideas such as genre, commodity and ideology may be useful. They refer us to the general nature of popular culture in modern capitalistic societies without investing every item of popular culture with significance. The points we have raised in this brief sidebar may help us in taking popular culture seriously.

Dominic Strinati

Stop and think

The relationship between public knowledge and popular culture

There are two levels of reception to which we need to pay attention if we are to understand what is going on in the complex process of knowledge production involving the media. The first is the level of basic comprehension. The second is the socially evaluative level, where basic comprehension gets caught up in larger patterns of meaning and we evaluate what we comprehend through social norms. On the first level, the long-held assumption that 'messages' are fairly unproblematically transmitted through medium to audience is no longer tenable. People comprehend things differently and unpredictably. On the second level, the equally long-held view (at least in some quarters) that 'ideological' messages are also fairly unproblematically transmitted has given way as well to the realities of a more complex situation.

The socially evaluative level is certainly where 'ideology' can be found at work – for example, in the sense of sustaining dominant discourses that require only minimal assent from people in order to be effective – but it is no longer assumed that this is just a matter of the wholesale transmission and reception of a distorted view of the world. As long as you assent *to some degree* to the dominant ideas, values and practices that structure schooling, consumer culture, gender relations, career, and so on – and it is all but inevitable that you will – then your knowledge on this socially evaluative level will be ideologically coloured; but you will not necessarily have received and accepted a single, distorted 'world view' that it serves somebody else's interests to have communicated to you.

Setting aside for the moment how the media are deeply implicated in the construction of dominant discourses, you should stop and think about how the popular culture sustained by the media may be hugely influential at the level of basic comprehension as well, even where it appears to be 'news' that is carrying the information being comprehended. This is where how people feel about what they know comes into play too.

The 1998 US-funded feature film *Savior*, directed by Serb-born Peter Antonijevic, co-produced by Oliver Stone and starring Hollywood actor Dennis Quaid, harrowingly depicts the war in Bosnia (shot in neighbouring Montenegro) from the point of view of an embittered mercenary (Quaid). In revenge for a Muslim fundamentalist bomb attack that killed his wife and son, Quaid's character massacres a group of Muslims, then fights for the Serbs and is thoroughly dehumanised until circumstances make him responsible for rescuing a baby, the offspring of a Serb woman raped by a Muslim. Reluctantly at first, but with eventual tenderness, the character rediscovers a timeless compassion that transcends the horrific circumstances. This is a fundamentally liberal way of understanding the war in Bosnia. Director Antonijevic, revealingly, appeared on the programme at a national 'teach-in' about the war in the former Yugoslavia, organised in May 1999 by ADA (Americans for Democratic Action), one of the USA's most influential liberal organisations working 'for the promotion of the general welfare in a world at peace'. His film was honoured at the 1998 'Friends of the United Nations' awards, marking International Tolerance Day.

It is also a way of understanding the war that is deeply implicated in the 'war genre' of popular film. War films work most effectively (i.e. exercise broadest appeal) by stripping back the too easily confusing contextual details of a conflict and focusing instead on the 'existential' problem of the protagonists' experience – the problem of being human in dehumanising circumstances. Whether in fact widely seen or not, a film such as *Savior* represents a way of thinking and feeling about war that (1) works within the commodity form of popular cinema (it's the sort of story that 'sells'), and (2) has become firmly established as a common-sense way of comprehending war from a distance, from a relatively unproblematic liberal stance. News reporting – in this case from the Balkans – then has to compete even at the level of basic comprehension with this already established way of understanding things (which *Savior* both taps into and sustains). It may not be surprising, therefore, that one of the most memorable news 'stories' to come out of Bosnia was that of Irma, a rescued child – not so far from the plot of *Savior*.

Indeed, public comprehension of the post-communist world may be as deeply influenced by the bestselling novels, for instance, of Gerald Seymour, as by the reports of his ex-colleagues at Independent Television News. A growing trend sees journalists and ex-journalists turning to writing topical thrillers (Fredrick Forsyth, Tim Sebastian . . .) and Seymour's have taken in Iran, Afghanistan, Northern Ireland and the former East Germany, among other 'hot' locations. For instance, *The Waiting Time* made the paperback bestseller lists in 1999 after its TV adaptation aired on British screens. In it, a young female British army intelligence corps clerk goes on a personal revenge vendetta against the East German secret police who killed her former lover. Helped by an ageing legal assistant with a military intelligence background (played with archetypal dependability by John Thaw, famed as British TV detective Inspector Morse), she embarks on a pursuit of the truth, the odds stacked against them by the whole post-communist fudging of old distinctions between 'us' and 'them'. This could have been an *Edge of Darkness* for the millennium – the 'daughter' teaching the 'father' about responsibility – but is thoroughly trapped within the thriller genre instead, rendering the 'background' of post-communist Eastern Europe an incomprehensibility that the protagonists have to rise above, as in *Savior's* Bosnia.

How is this sort of thing likely to affect the basic comprehension of news material dealing with the same situations? Unfortunately, this has been seriously under-researched in media studies (still a young field remember). Scholars interested in textual interpretation are reluctant to leave the nuances of textual detail for the more mundane world of audience comprehension, and yet the sorts of understanding of places and issues encouraged by popular culture's handling of them must impact on the comprehension of news reports on the same matters, especially now that we are recognising the unpredictability of such comprehension. Public knowledge becomes in some measure a question of the articulation of one with the other, especially around the matter of *genre*, so closely related – as Dominic Strinati points out above – to the commodification of popular culture.

The genres of the thriller bestseller or the action-adventure movie provide their own 'explanatory' templates for events where explanation may in reality be a much harder business. The 'star system' that turns some journalists into celebrities dovetails with the genres available for them to exercise a fictional form of explanation (and make more money doing so), where journalism proper has been running out of explanatory templates or finding those it is hanging on to increasingly inadequate.

An extraordinary exception to all of this is *The Journey is the Destination: The Journals of Dan Eldon*, a published version of the scrapbook journals kept by a young photojournalist who was stoned to death on assignment in 1993 by a Somali mob reacting against a United Nations bombing. Also developed into a TV documentary produced by his sister Amy (*Dying to Tell the Story*) and optioned for a Hollywood movie, Eldon's journals have their own unique impact. As one reviewer expressed it, 'For young people who doubt that a life grander than MTV and the mall can be achieved in this age, Eldon's journals prove otherwise' (*Washington Post*). Densely collaged cuttings, notes and photographs interweave to document this young man's uncertain but deeply responsible transition into an adulthood that was being achieved amid the dilemmas of how to report contemporary conflicts, such as the one that took his life, while at the same time experiencing sex and fun. If the citizen-ghost in *Edge of Darkness* is your first role model then here is a second, if only in your own imagining of how to live a life today and how to make some knowledge in that living.

7

War reporting at the end of the twentieth century

Greg McLaughlin

Delve into any history of war reporting, indeed look at any history of journalism, and the name William Russell stands out as a reporter who broke the mould, going to the Crimean front (1854–55) and sending back first-hand observations to a hitherto information-starved public (Knightley, 1982; Lambert, 1994). His despatches were remarkable testaments of war, distinguished by breadth and depth of detail and an appreciation of military strategy and tactics. He often clashed with field officers at the front to such a degree that they clamoured for his own summary despatch back to Britain. Yet by the time he moved on to report on the American Civil War, barely six years later, Russell was already a journalistic dinosaur. His abrasive individualism and prosaic style had become, it seemed, ill suited to the new realities of reporting from the front. The new technology of the telegraph had become commercially viable as a means of high-speed communication and it demanded spare, concise copy from the reporter. Russell returned home before the war's end embittered by his clashes with the editors and his difficulties in gaining access to the front; but, as Neumann (1996:34–5) remarks, 'journalism was almost too enamoured of the new speed of information to notice his departure'.

Russell's fate reminds us that there have always been external and internal forces corroding the potential of mainstream journalism to make sense of military conflict. It helps put into essential historical context the rapid changes that contributed to a crisis in the role and function of the war reporter in the 1990s: developments in military and media technologies, in sophisticated propaganda and military public relations, and in media politics and economics, have transformed the practice and content of mainstream commercial journalism. It puts into question the ability or willingness of journalists to resist, or even to negotiate, these changes and probe the causes, conditions and consequences of modern warfare.

One of the features of conflicts in the post-Cold War era has been their 'liveness', their status as instant news. We turn on our televisions, flick through the channels, and suddenly we see events unfold half way round the world, in East Timor, the Balkans or the Persian Gulf. It is this liveness that concentrates the minds of policy makers, analysts, the military and media professionals alike. They have identified something called the 'CNN curve', a strange effect by which live instant news appears to encourage instant decision making, diplomacy on the hoof. Television journalists will argue that this plays a vital Fourth Estate role, checking government control over information. Yet live saturation cable and satellite coverage of Tiananmen Square (1989) did not stop the Chinese government from eventually pulling the plug on the live satellite feed. Technology in that regard is only as powerful and free as human agency allows.

As the West built up for war in the Gulf in late 1990, there were hopes and fears (depending on one's point of view) that news organisations would simply circumvent censorship by transmitting instantaneously via satellite. But the US military had long been constructing a media strategy around the perceived lessons of the Vietnam War, using tactics that would meet this very challenge. They modified and fine tuned it for a working balance of control and public relations: controlling the movement and output of the news media in pools but giving journalists what they wanted most – pictures and stories, interviews with 'the boys' and those cockpit videos of missiles hitting their targets. The aftermath of that war may well have been marked by an outpouring of articles, essays and even books by journalists questioning the nature and extent of military control over media coverage, but the general media response to military PR at the time was, by and large, submissive and co-operative. It certainly set the tone for coverage of further Western attacks on Iraq although, by December 1998, as the USA launched its most sustained bombardment of Iraq since 1991, sections of the British media – television news in particular – were at least more alert to the realities of military propaganda on 'the home front'. (The gung-ho headlines of the popular press in Britain struck a familiar chord, though: 'Ding Dong Hell', *Daily Star*; 'Blasted', *The Sun*; 'Execute!', *Daily Record*. Even the liberal *Guardian* proposed that the US bombing would 'help' the people of Iraq. All references, 17 December 1998.) The BBC reported on the Ministry of Defence's role in the 'propaganda war'; while Channel Four News spent time looking out for the things we were not being told by cockpit videos and smooth MoD presentations. They scrutinised those impressive satellite photographs and questioned their verifiability, their status as evidence.

However, it is not just a matter of military public relations. War reporters operate in a professional culture increasingly defined by a 'star system': a hierarchy determined by pay, status and profile. A conflict may be defined as much by the presence of a top correspondent as by the 'facts' he or she reports: thus the 'It must be bad, it's Kate Adie!' response to coverage from the latest front line. Adie is the BBC's best-known woman reporter and her knack of turning up to report from the latest trouble spot with steely public service cool has earned her admiration, cynicism and loathing in equal measure. 'Take Kate Adie on patrol?', joked a British army officer in Bosnia. 'I'd rather take Lucrezia Borgia' (*Daily Mail*, magazine, 14 February 1998). The focus of this star system is reporter centred: concerned with how he or she is coping with the rigours and dangers of the job, the daring escapes from kidnap, the brushes with injury or even death, and even at times the joys and thrills of war reporting. For many journalists, the Gulf War was the ultimate spectacle, a hugely exciting media event that fulfilled their *Boy's Own* fantasies. In a special BBC programme on coverage of the war, several journalists admitted to their personal fascination. Richard Dowden of the *Independent* confessed that 'Half of me never wants to do anything like that ever again, and another part of me says, "Where's the next one? That was great!"'. For *Newsweek* editor, Tony Clifton, the 'media war' was something akin to sex: 'a hell of a lot of foreplay and one final orgasm that lasted eight and a half seconds'. Robert Fox of the *Daily Telegraph*, 'a kid of the sixties . . . brought up on Camus and the existentialists', felt 'a mad, depersonalised' sense of excitement; for him, it was 'the lunatic on the edge . . . the moment when things come together' (speaking on the BBC2 *Late Show* special, 'Tales From the Gulf', 19 July 1991).

Yet the reporter is meant to report the story, not become part of it. Do we really have to or want to know about the personal experience of a reporter on the front line? Mick Hume (1997:5) notes the 'difference between reporting from the midst of a conflict and writing as if you were the one at war, so that journalists and their feelings become the news'. In some ways the theatre of war becomes a surreal space for 'infotainment' and this can extend beyond the limits of the front line. The best war reporters obtain, whether they actively seek it out or not, a measure of cultural capital exchangeable at the front line between media and other public spaces. Frederick Forsyth, who reported on the Nigerian Civil War, is of course better known now as a bestselling fiction writer of thrillers such as *Day of the Jackal*. More recently, Martin Bell resigned his post as a BBC war correspondent to stand as an independent candidate in the British general election of 1997. His move into the electoral battleground was covered by none other than his former colleague Kate Adie (on special assignment!) and supported by his army friend from Bosnia days, Colonel Bob Stewart, who appeared in a British personnel carrier coloured in United Nations blue and white.

All this seemed a clumsy, if not cynical, exploitation of the Bosnian war which Bell and his colleagues covered with some credit and at considerable personal risk. For none of this is to deny that, like the soldiers they report, death for the war correspondent is an occupational hazard. The statistics are striking: in a 10 year period from 1988 to 1997, no less than 474 journalists were killed doing their job, the majority reporting a war somewhere in the world; 26 died in Bosnia and 60 have fallen in Algeria since civil war broke out in 1992, most of them local correspondents (*The Guardian*, 20 July 1998, p. 8). By the time NATO forces moved into Kosovo in June 1999, more journalists had lost their lives reporting the crisis than NATO personnel dealing with it. Part of this may be explained by the distinctly military apparel that some journalists chose to wear, marking themselves out to combatants as legitimate military targets, and part of it has much to do with simple recklessness. There is no doubt, however, that some journalists take extraordinary risks just to report *that* battle, or to capture *that* image, in a way that might transform public opinion at home about a conflict of which many people know or care little.

In the 1990s, especially, journalists seem to have been more willing to question and rethink their role beyond professional neutrality and self promotion. Arguments about news judgements, 'worthy' and 'unworthy' wars, 'good guys' and 'bad guys', objective and subjective journalism, coalesced into a heated and prolonged debate during and after the war in Bosnia. Some, such as Martin Bell, have gone so far as to ask themselves, can and do they want to make a difference in a turbulent world seemingly bereft of political and moral certainties? And if they do, then what difference should that be? If the reporter cannot go to the front and try to make a difference, or care about what happens to people, then what, he or she wonders, is the point? Perhaps the presence of reporters ensures that wars are not as brutal and terrible as they might otherwise be, making war crimes harder to commit, the guilt harder to deny, the sentence harder to escape (Bell, 1998)? Indeed, Bell came out of the war in Bosnia proposing an alternative journalism, a *journalism of attachment*, a journalism 'that cares as well as knows'. It does not take sides any more than do international aid agencies or charities but it 'is aware of the moral ground on which it operates'. He wonders about the meaning of objectivity, whether it really exists and, in almost heretical terms, he states: 'I was trained in a tradition of objective and dispassionate journalism. I believed in it once. I don't believe in it anymore' (1998:102). He insists that he still believes in impartiality, and that he still believes in facts. Impartial, dispassionate journalism has its place, he says – in the reporting of domestic politics, for example – but it is inadequate in the midst of some brutal war or human calamity. Then it becomes 'bystanders' journalism' and it ill equips the reporter for 'the challenges of the times'. For Bell, reporting a conflict such as Bosnia according to the traditional norms of objective journalism removes any sort of moral content from the story and leaves only an empty spectacle (1998:103).

Martin Bell's advocacy for a more subjective, partisan approach to reporting attracted considerable criticism from within and without the journalistic profession. The most sustained critique so far has come from Mick Hume of *Living Marxism* magazine. In his pamphlet, 'Whose War Is It Anyway?'(1997), Hume sees this brand of crusading journalism as a 'menace to good journalism – and to those whose lives it invades'. It neglects the historical and political context of the conflict it reports and portrays it instead as merely a metaphysical struggle between good and evil, the guilty and the innocent, the oppressor and the victim. Journalists who adhere to this kind of reporting set themselves up – intentionally or by default – as judge and jury. Their mission is not to explain and contextualise but to promulgate the morally correct line and this, says Hume, obscures and undermines their role as impartial and objective reporters. 'The journalism of attachment', he says, 'is self-righteous. Worse, it is repressive.' He goes on: 'Those who fall the wrong side of the line the press corps draws between Good and Evil . . . can expect to be on the receiving end of more than a bad press'(p. 4). Hume argues that there is nothing wrong with taking sides in a conflict. But when the facts are suppressed because they do not fit the moral framework reporters have constructed for themselves, then the audience is the loser. 'There is a difference', he says, 'between taking sides and taking liberties with the facts in order to promote your favoured cause. There is a difference between expressing an opinion and presenting your personal passions and prejudices as objective reporting' (p. 5). Beyond the basic requirement that they are well informed, check the facts and carefully source the evidence, in this view reporters must also adopt a balanced view of a conflict. Hume concludes that, 'Those who pursue the Journalism of Attachment . . . are playing a dangerous game for high stakes' (p. 27).

In spite of its protracted time span, the Bosnian war attracted more intensive coverage than anything given to wars in Algeria or Afghanistan, even though those conflicts have been as terrible and as tragic as those in the Balkans. These discrepancies are partly explained by eurocentrism and by the interrelationships among media coverage, news values and the foreign policy agendas of major regional or global powers. Furthermore, the media-led interventions in the Kurdish refugee crisis, post-Gulf War 1991 – or Operation Irma in which the British government airlifted a Bosnian child, Irma, to London for emergency surgery – are cited as proof of how the media can often drive foreign policy making (Schorr, 1995; Shaw, 1996). (Irma's name was subsequently turned into an acronym: Instant Response to Media Attention.) But as Nik Gowing (1994) argues, 'real time television coverage of [such] regional conflicts will create emotions but ultimately make no difference to the fundamental calculations in foreign policy making'. Gowing suggests that these had more to do with pragmatic short termism and crisis management than those long-term calculations that insure policy making against any number of risks, including changes of government. Coverage of some of the worst incidents of the Bosnian war – the market-place massacre in Sarajevo, the siege of Srebenica, the 'concentration camps' – provoked tough talking from NATO about what would happen to the Serbs if they continued their actions. But it did not affect the Western policy of non-intervention.

Having said that, however, pictures of dead US rangers being dragged through the streets of Mogadishu in Somalia revulsed public opinion in America and led to the most definitive policy decision possible: complete withdrawal. Significantly, it appears that this experience of policy humiliation shaped and influenced the UN's attitude to what happened a year later in Rwanda, in Central Africa. According to a BBC report, the UN ignored on-the-ground warnings that orchestrated massacres were being carried out by the majority Hutus against the minority Tutu population. One of the key factors influencing this policy was the experience of Somalia and the negative global television coverage it generated. It must certainly have been a factor explaining NATO's reluctance to commit ground forces to its operation in Kosovo (1999). It is the dread fear of the body-bag on camera: Vietnam (cont. p. 119) revisited.

The Kosovo conflict on the web: a case study

The war in Kosovo from March to June 1999 was the first major modern conflict during and after which all the involved parties made extensive use of the internet to disseminate information and communicate their views. In the United Kingdom, the Ministry of Defence and the Foreign and Commonwealth Office jointly operated a highly detailed and rapidly updated site on the web combining latest news with background material, including transcripts of government statements and speeches and a cleverly judged FAQs (Frequently Asked Questions) section ('Can Milosevic, now an indicted war criminal, remain in power? How can we get him out?' etc. where the bias was in the form of posed questions from an imagined interlocutor). The main component of the war waged by NATO was 'Operation Allied Force', a bombing campaign directed at Serbian targets and intended to force Serb President Milosevic to order a withdrawal of Serbian forces from the province of Kosovo, where they were pursuing a policy of 'ethnic cleansing' to remove Kosovo Albanians. Kosovo Serbs, in turn, were threatened by reprisals from their Albanian neighbours, especially in the form of the Kosovo Liberation Army (UÇK).

The information office of the existing NATO-led Balkan 'Stabilisation Force' in Bosnia and Herzegovina (SFOR) had its own web site called 'SFOR Informer Online', containing the texts of the various international agreements that legitimised SFOR's operations, and had been developing an online information source that combined 'objectively' usable resources (copies of documents, a photo gallery, regional maps, etc.) with a persuasive and 'softer' overall slant that clearly communicated NATO's interests. They achieved this with a design and content that used many of the techniques developed by both e-commerce sites and online newspapers (including public relations devices such as a downloadable NATO 'screensaver' which users could run on their own computers). The NATO web site during the Kosovo conflict rapidly deployed many of these techniques in a sophisticated way, centred around scheduled daily updates – two based on the morning and afternoon press briefings at NATO headquarters. Frequent updating and depth of background material were combined to create a compelling picture of NATO's operation, one that even included numerous video game-style shots of air attacks, a favourite of the TV news coverage, in 'streaming' versions that played over the web.

The Serbian Ministry of Information countered by running its own web site, 'SerbiaInfo', which became especially active after the NATO military operation in offering its interpretation of events, as summarised by one of their army commanders:

> The terrorist character of the aggression is detected in the preparation of the ethnic Albanian secession, their armed rebellion, the forming of their paramilitary formations, in the delivery and trafficking of arms, the holding of allegedly political negotiations, in Rambouillet and in Paris, in fomenting an armed ethnic Albanian rebellion, in lending logistic support to that rebellion and finally air support (story carried on SerbiaInfo, 20 October 1999).

This perspective was filled out in the form of online newspaper-style pages with 'News of the Day' headlines (linking to detailed stories) and background sidebars on 'Facts', 'Media Watch' (links to other media coverage), and so on. The SerbiaInfo site embedded this newspaper-style coverage and editorial material within the Ministry of Information's pages on Serbian culture, religion, sport, etc., rather effectively countering the NATO sites' reduction of Serbia to tactical maps and fuzzy video footage of military targets. Human interest photographs (e.g. 'Serbian old lady beaten') were effectively used to personalise many of the stories.

So both NATO and the Serbian government made sophisticated use of the web to present their positions and influence public opinion. Both employed by then familiar techniques of professional web design and presentation, some derived from the practices of electronic newspapers, others from electronic commerce, adapted in these instances to communicate reliability and currency and to 'sell' a point of view. Where NATO developed an emphasis on detailed 'briefings' and extensive official background documentation, SerbiaInfo adopted a more newspaper-style approach, with a clear editorial voice coming through in tone and style. By providing web links to the texts of international agreements, NATO constructed a legitimising framework that would not otherwise have been so publicly accessible, except in reported form. Its approach appeared to work well during the months of the bombing campaign in 1999, when the sheer volume of material accumulated by its daily briefings was unmatched, but thereafter SerbiaInfo became an increasingly effective means of 'fleshing out' the Serbian perspective and recontextualising the military events, as when its soccer results pages carried an eye-catching logo, in the form of a bull's eye target, for the 'Athletes Against NATO Bombing' campaign.

It remains to be seen how international public opinion might be swayed one way or the other by these sophisticated efforts to combine information provision with propaganda slants – we have to remind ourselves that neither of these official web-based operations was journalism as widely understood, although both worked hard to evoke such connotations; NATO coming across as a sort of news service like Reuters, while SerbiaInfo projected itself as a serious and responsible daily newspaper. The smartly judged approach of SerbiaInfo suggests that how such events are reworked subsequently may be just as important in the long term as how they are presented at the time. On this evidence, the web is emerging as a highly significant medium for such reworkings and for contested representations to maintain their struggle for public 'mindshare'. Perhaps by its nature it is a medium more suited to this than the older mass media, the importance of the latter nonetheless emphasised when NATO bombed the Serbian TV station in Belgrade.

The Provisional Government of Kosovo, formed in April 1999 to represent the various factions seeking independence, maintained its own web site which attempted a conservative, 'official' look and tone. But the most significant use of the web during the Kosovo conflict undoubtedly came from the Kosovo Albanians generally, from the UÇK and from their international supporters. The UÇK (the paramilitary liberation army), the principal resistance to the Serbian army on the ground, maintained a striking – if much more unashamedly propagandist – presence on the web. Its red, yellow and black badge was evocatively used, often collaged with photographs of bearded guerrilla fighters, to trigger associations with other romanticised peoples' armies – from Che Guevara's or the Viet Cong to the Mexican Zapatistas (the latter also sophisticated users of the internet). By the end of 1999, the UÇK had published over twenty-five 'Political Declarations' on the web. Alongside this almost traditional 'resistance movement' style, the UÇK web sites carried list after list of massacres by Serb 'ethnic cleansing' operations, accompanied by albums of carefully dated photographs of corpses – snapshots on the web of everyday life turned to terror in European villages, the do-it-yourself dissemination of which will remain one of the enduring features that the new medium brought to the 'reporting' of conflict at the end of the twentieth century. On one UÇK-sympathetic web site, these massacre images were poignantly displayed alongside a link (to a database of survivors) labelled 'Find Your Relatives'.

An independent Kosovo Web Ring, including chat forums, was set up to link various sites produced by, or sympathetic to, the Kosovo Albanians. Established by a group of radio journalists in Prishtina in Kosovo, Radio 21, the first internet radio station in Albanian (transmitting streaming sound via the web instead of broadcasting on radio frequencies), developed an English-language version with regularly posted and archived news reports. This relied on the 'Real Player' web software also used by CNN, among others – a nice example of the relatively level playing field available on the web for small-scale news operations to compete for attention with the major news media.

On a more detached level, the web has been excellently employed by the Association for Democratic Initiatives, based in Macedonia where many refugees fled, to set up a user-searchable database of refugees (which contained over 70,000 records of individuals by the end of 1999). Names and towns of origin could be entered to search the records for family members and friends. If the online search failed, the user read this message: 'We are still in the first days of what has been Europe's worst human catastrophe for fifty years – hundreds of thousands of people are scattered all over the continent cut off from their friends and family. But gradually, they *will* come back into contact. This too will pass.' There is perhaps no better sign than this, at the start of the 21st century, that the media of public communication, in some of their forms, are re-wiring the connections between technology and ethics.

Dan Fleming

No amount of optimistic hype about the new millennium, or the 'new world order', is going to change the hard economic and political realities that generate and sustain conflict around the world. There will always be 'wars and rumours of wars' and there will always be media to report them. The questions for the future must centre around the professional and economic trends in war reporting, and in journalism in general, that will continue to develop apace and have serious implications for public understanding of war and its causes, conduct and consequences. The war in Serbia/Kosovo demonstrated more than any recent major conflict the potential of the internet for offering both a conformity and diversity of sources of latest news about the conflict to a new public of web users. That major global players such as NATO and the Pentagon have official web pages offering their version of events shows just how seriously they take the internet as a medium of communication. But is it a medium of *mass* communication in the same sense as the commercial newspaper or public service television? Is it, in other words, an inevitable medium for effective propaganda, rather than simply for the construction and juxtaposition of contested representations? The same question applies to television in the 'digital age'. The assumption that digital technology will offer us a greater choice of television channels, in terms of quantity if not quality, implies further fragmentation of audiences whose value to advertisers will be determined by differentiated lifestyles and incomes. If we really are heading into a century when we can no longer refer to 'mass communication' or to a 'mass audience' (should we ever have in any case?), then this must present new challenges to those whose task is propaganda and persuasion. For the war reporter, however, the challenge remains the same: to report a conflict as accurately as possible without undue risk to self and without compromise to professional integrity. However, the precise nature of that integrity has been opened up to debate as the twentieth century closes. Despite what some of the reporters quoted here have said, war is not sex. It is not even existentialism. It is a failure of the human condition that we need to comprehend amid the warspeak, the video games and the *Boy's Own* adventures.

Afterthoughts

In any consideration of public knowledge, the question of narrative is unavoidable. To what extent and how do narratives – stories and their embodiment in storytelling forms – carry knowledge? This question is overshadowed by what we can call the 'narrative of modernity' – that narrative of security, trust, explanatory confidence – perhaps even promising 'truth' – that Anthony Giddens, for example, so succinctly evokes in *The Consequences of Modernity* (1990): the security of knowing that science leads to progress, that villains can be nailed for any misfortunes along the way; trust in forms of public communication that seem responsive to our needs and values. But there is also another side, undermining confidence – the possibility that misfortunes, even on a global scale, are often built into the system, are part of the narrative of modernity, are even consequent upon it; the growing sense that forms of public communication are caught in a vicious circle of endlessly seeking favour by amplifying what most of us in our weakest moments most want to be told, rather than producing public knowledge in any really meaningful sense. The criteria of competence – what we might actually do with what's on offer – as defined by this master narrative, when it insinuates itself through the stuff of the modern media, are insubstantial indeed – know how to consume, when to applaud, what environmental villainy to agonise over, what heroes to admire, which celebrities to trust.

As the social and cultural apparatus of modernity grew in complexity, especially on entering its late globalised phase, the dimensions of danger and risk inherent in it came more insistently to the fore (the millennium computer 'bug' was deeply symbolic of larger fears). But at the same time, the rich and complex culture of modernity seemed to offer its inhabitants – or at least those of them who 'mattered' – ample resources for making meaning, for telling meaningful stories about their criteria of competence, their ideas of a good life. When it all becomes too complex, however, there is an overload, a fragmentation, a loss of confidence and the narratives will not hold. Attempts have been made to capture all of this in one term – postmodernism – but it is perhaps too large and diffuse a set a circumstances, and insufficiently a matter of a break or an after-state to be adequately summed up as a 'post' anything. Instead of a clean master-narrative of progress based on steadily advancing – and somehow shared or public – knowledge, we seem instead to be up to our necks in the litter of many small stories, the claim to knowledge of each coming across as attenuated and uncertain.

The following stories all appeared in one month in the pages of two popular British newspapers: the civil servant accused of 'pinching a woman's bottom' in Victoria Underground station in London takes up a new career as an impressionist; the Texas businessman who is selling powdered urine to people worried about passing drug tests; 'We don't want girls sailing off with our men, say Navy wives' as the British Admiralty defends its policy of recruiting women for sea-going duty; the man who turned his council house in England into a 'giant dustbin', hoarding 20 lorry-loads of rubbish, including 900 overdue books from the public library, which it took the local council 6 days to cart away; the Valentine's Day story of a pending court showdown between ex-lovers over custody of a dog, following one party's unsuccessful attempt to kidnap it; the Scunthorpe woodcutter whose severed hand was found in a forest clearing after an accident with a circular saw and was stitched back on in a twelve hour operation, having been rushed to the hospital by a traffic policeman; the woman who was dragged for ten minutes round the floor of her flat by a twelve foot pet python which had sunk its teeth into her hand; Tenterden is declared 'the most honest town in Britain' after a local man loses £700 in high winds and £695 of it are handed in throughout the day to astonished police; a clandestinely circulated videotape in a recession-hit capital purportedly shows the wife of an Eastern European president in a sequence of expensive dresses, smiling and waving her way through Europe's swankiest shopping districts with her American Express card at the ready.

Those stories are typical and randomly selected from only two popular newspapers. This kind of material – the human interest story – makes up the largest single category of content in many popular newspapers, and reappears in more polished and detailed form in many magazines. Moreover, stories such as those quoted far outnumber the items on pop stars, TV personalities and other celebrities, contrary to an often voiced preconception that the latter are the standard fare of human interest stories. It is important to notice the marked extent to which such stories work *against* the assumptions which John Hartley sees, quite rightly, as the basis of so much other news. According to these assumptions, society is:

1. Fragmented into distinct spheres – sport, politics, family life, etc. 2. Composed of individual persons who are in control of their destiny, so that actions are the result of their personal intentions, motives and choices. 'Newsworthy' people are usually associated with only one sphere of society. 3. Hierarchical by nature: some people, events, spheres are more important than others. And the hierarchy is centralized both socially and regionally. 4. Consensual by nature. The notion of 'the consensus' is a basic organizing principle in news production. (1982:81–2)

The exemplary human interest stories listed above flaunt the first of these assumptions, assumptions which hold good in most other news coverage. Human interest stories are plucked from any and every sphere of life. The participants are most often experiencing the twists of fortune, the weird turns that human relationships can take, the idiosyncrasies of their own deepest passions or fears, the moments when control and intention break down and they do something that is precisely 'out of character' (like the government minister who made the front page for dragging two six-year-old girls into his house when he caught them picking his flowers). The woodcutter is as newsworthy, in this respect, as the president's wife, and the story is as valid whether it comes from London or the Outer Hebrides – human interest has no social or regional centre. Moreover, it is often the complex entanglements with other people that emerge, rather than the focus on individualism which typifies so much other news. Nor does it really matter that the 'bottom pinching' impressionist was a civil servant or the python owner a secretary. What *is* important is how these stories undermine an implicit hierarchy: the civil servant loses his job while the secretary's life becomes anything but mundane. What matters most, though, are clearly the dilemmas to which they fall prey.

The fourth assumption, that society is 'consensual', based on given agreements about where the boundaries lie, is the one with which human interest stories engage. But rather than merely illustrating a consensus, such stories typically ask where its boundaries lie. Hall *et al.* (1978) describe the consensus in terms of three horizons – outside the safe zone of 'civilised society' is the first horizon, the *permissiveness* threshold, then the *legality* threshold and finally the *extreme violence* threshold. Disturbing or provocative events are positioned somewhere in an imaginary space defined by these three concentric boundaries, an act of terrorism beyond the final one, a pornographic video perhaps somewhere between the first two, and so on. While politics establishes the boundaries of the extreme violence threshold where it manifests itself particularly in war and terrorism, and the law establishes the boundaries of the legality threshold, it falls frequently to human interest stories to raise questions about the permissiveness threshold – and *in doing so to resist the tendency for this also to be only 'officially' established*. Is 'bottom pinching' on the tube train an example of properly repugnant sexual assault? Should dangerous pets be allowed, whether pythons or Rottweiler dogs? Is a person's home their own to do what they will in, including hoarding tons of rubbish? Is finding money and keeping it a form of theft? And so on, endlessly raising questions about where the boundaries of permissiveness might lie in every conceivable area of life. Some of these questions are raised obliquely – like stories about genetic research which implicitly wonder about medical technology's increasing power of life and death – but very few human interest stories fail to connect at some point with such issues of boundary definition.

Important to note, of course, is the fact that the human interest story is only the raw material for questions of boundary definition. Rarely are these questions debated in print in the course of the story. Rather, the stories are of the kind that people repeat to each other ('did you hear about . . . ?'), keeping questions about the permissiveness threshold publicly on the simmer. Television soap opera works in a very similar way and so too, increasingly, does a whole loose category of 'people shows' on television, from air-your-problem-in-public shows to the so-called 'docu-soaps' that started to appear around 1997 and elaborate 'group confinement' shows like *Big Brother*.

A more stark category of such material can be found in the 'urban legends' which often appear as fact in popular newspapers: the cat in the microwave;

the 'lovers'lane' incident involving a close encounter with a maniac ('we didn't know until later how close we'd come to . . .'); the horrendous discovery theme (of which the houseful of rubbish is a mild version); the pet that turns on its owner; the elaborate and unlikely turn of events that leaves someone naked in a public place. There are many other themes to the urban legend, some of them detailed in *The Vanishing Hitchhiker* by Jan Harold Brunvand. Brunvand, for instance, traces the cement-filled car story (typically an act of revenge). One example of it appeared in a popular British Sunday newspaper, while at about the same time variations were appearing in the Copenhagen *Politiken* and Stockholm *Aftonbladet*. Earlier it had been circulating on Norwegian news bureau wire services (it reportedly happened in Bergen) and later it appeared under the headline 'Concrete Revenge' in Nairobi's *Daily Nation*. In fact, no Bergen garage had been called to retrieve a cement-filled car, the police had no record of the incident, no insurance company had ever encountered the phenomenon – indeed the story was just one manifestation of an urban legend that has been cropping up from time to time since the 1960s.

From the examples marshalled by Brunvand, an academic folklorist, it looks as though the urban legend category of human interest story provides the extreme cases that do not otherwise appear regularly enough to keep the full range of questions about the permissiveness threshold sufficiently active. For instance, the very many examples involving unexpected nudity in formal and 'respectable' settings (such as the surprise party, often involving a clergyman, which catches the guest of honour in an embarrassing situation) quite clearly, if implicitly, ask where the boundaries of decorum lie. And the point about the cement-filled car stories is that they are always acts of revenge, again raising obliquely the question of what constitutes just deserts.

Although the urban legends, human interest stories and related 'people shows' on TV do finally invite us to submit to a consensus within which the permissiveness threshold is settled, we glimpse here the fact that this consensus is not a given. It it were, the stories would not exist as a way of endlessly settling, unsettling and resettling it. We might identify here a 'conversational appetite', closely related to notions of gossip but more clearly implicated in processes of public knowledge production. We can call it this in order to engage with Fredric Jameson's explanation of appetite, where contemporary cultural and psychoanalytic theory might instead prefer the term 'desire' to explain what people want (a want more fraught, more complicatedly self conscious and less robust than what is intended here):

> Desire – even as a concept – emerges from a reflection on hysteria, on the absence of desire, the desire to desire, and the like. Sheer appetite does not need to pass through that narrow gap [*défilé*]: it is already there, knife in one hand and fork in the other, drumming on the table. (Jameson, 1998:7)

Jameson sees appetite (a sort of filling out of the hollow term 'consumption') deeply at work in popular culture, in the manic activities of figures such as Harpo Marx, and we begin to see the link with the permissiveness threshold and the racket of conversation that goes on around it:

> they are the archetypes of appetite, surging up from popular culture (rather than, as with supreme villains and manifestations of evil, from the lettered).

Early Chaplin, the tramp in the first short films, was like that – revoltingly possessive, repeatedly kicking the gouty man (who, no doubt, represents society's warning against indulgence) down the stairs, lecherous, distracted impolitely by a variety of new objects, disrespectful and violent (not out of a violent nature or essence but, rather, in some immediate reactions to his surroundings). The first appearances of Mickey Mouse – in *Steamboat Willie*, for instance (1928) – were like that as well; both of them surging before the veneer of culture. (1998:8)

What we are heading for here is that latest surge before the veneer of culture – and one very much in the tradition of appetite in popular culture: *South Park*. This odd trajectory of argument will take us back shortly to the question of public knowledge, where we are going to set up alongside the 'lettered' knowledge of the serious journalists' constructions another sort of knowledge making, the conversations of human interest that go on all the time in and around the consumption of popular culture and its commodities. Moreover, the purpose here is to relate these two very different forms of knowledge in a specific way. One turns out to be the other's spectral companion, at the very moments when – for instance – television news or documentary content is consumed.

At a time when *South Park*'s success had still left most media critics dazed and confused, David Thomson, writing in *The Independent* (1999), offered real insight into the phenomenon, spurred by having taken his own nine-year-old son to the movie (*South Park: Bigger, Larger and Uncut* (1999)) based on the TV series, a movie of which he says:

> Insolent, raunchy, breathtakingly offensive, it's not just the movie of the season but the most truly radical American movie in years, the talking point at cocktail parties, and an event at which kids are jumping up and down like freed slaves while elders groan and clutch their heads against the pain that will not go away. Above all, this mongrel, whiplash movie has made a mockery of the whole question, 'What is a kid?'.

What clearer evocation might we have than that, of the whole messy business of the permissiveness threshold, boundary explorations and the appetite for conversation that focuses on such things (and Thomson underscores the point by noting the moral panic in the USA around school shootings, such as that in Littleton, Colorado, eerily close in the imagination to the mountain town of South Park)? But he goes on:

> You may be shocked to hear that I took my nine-year-old to the film. My reasons were as follows: though nine, he is a devotee of the TV series (where the language is bleeped in America), who educated his parents in seeing its satire and its politics; though nine, he will only get older – we have found no way to arrest his development; though nine, he has heard adults – his parents even – use the word 'fuck', and there is no way of asking the jury in him to forget the word; and, though nine, when he asked what the clitoris was [the characters in the movie go on a clitoral quest], or what it was for, he listened carefully to our answers, was tolerant of our shyness and ineptness, but learned. We talked about the film for a solid hour – and we all learned a good deal about what adults and children think, know, pretend to know, and try to ignore. We were a family. (1999)

David Thomson is describing a knowledge-making experience here, and one, moreover, that requires of us an extended grasp of the nature of consumption when its appetite is focused on popular culture of this sort and it becomes conversational in this way – conversation often highly charged by the culture's archetypes of appetite of which *South Park*'s characters are only the latest manifestation. They probe the boundaries of the permissiveness threshold more sharply even than the urban legends and render the stuff of human interest stories mere background noise. But what has any of this to do with, for example, broadcast journalism and the question of public knowledge? If we return to one of the seminal studies of television news reception, what becomes clear is not just a connection but an explanation of sorts.

Justin Lewis's (1985) study of audience responses to the now defunct but long-running British television news programme *News at Ten* came to three telling conclusions:

1   We can assume very little about the meaning of a news item – a story that was intended to be about a politician's relations with his own party was, for example, decoded as a variety of quite different stories. News broadcasters, in fact, know remarkably little about what they are communicating to the outside world.

2   The ambiguity of the news is based on its narrative structure (or rather, lack of it). News 'stories' on TV are, most of the time, not stories at all. They are fragmented collections of information and images. Programmes with tight narrative structures – such as *EastEnders* or, in a different way, *Blind Date* – would be far more successful at communicating an agreed set of meanings.

3   The images and words we select when we decode TV programmes will be based upon the meaning systems available in our heads. This, in turn, forces us to construct different stories.

Lewis recounts often vastly different 'decodings' of the information presented by the news, often dependent on viewers' prior personal experiences. It is with his second point, however, that we see where different stories most often come from. Human interest stories in popular newspapers, soap opera and 'people shows' of various kinds on TV and, from time to time, eruptions in popular culture such as *South Park*, all feed the conversational appetite and support a looser, less deliberate, less controlled, more amorphous sort of public knowledge making. This is a process achieved at the very heart of what Dominic Strinati describes here as popular culture's relentless commodification (it doesn't come more commodified than *South Park*). But it is not a process on which one would wish to hang too many hopes for clearer, better forms of understanding based on the knowledge being communicated. The final point here is that broadcast journalism, where such hope might seem more safely focused, has evidently little real control in the end over what knowledge it is communicating. So public knowledge becomes something much messier and unpredictable, where the solemn announcement of a public figure's assassination has to take its chances alongside the more manic cry of 'Oh my god, they've killed Kenny!'.

Part III

Cultural identity

Cultural imperialism

Cultural imperialism is a generic term used to describe and criticise relations of cultural domination and subordination in the modern world. As 'imperialism' implies, one of its main uses has been to describe these relations in the 'post-colonial' world – the enduring cultural influence of the Western developed industrial nations over those of the 'Third World'. But this is not its exclusive focus and the term is also used to describe one-way flows of cultural influence within the West: most particularly the influence of American culture in Europe, but also, for example, US–Canadian relations.

The term first appeared in the 1960s and was most current during the 1970s and early 1980s, when it was invoked, along with a subsidiary term 'media imperialism', in policy debates in bodies such as UNESCO, particularly in the call for a 'new world information and communications order'(NWICO) which represented perhaps the most concerted attack by the non-aligned countries on the perceived cultural and communications hegemony of the West. It was during this time that the most forceful formulations of the cultural imperialism 'thesis' emerged in the work of, for example, Herbert Schiller (1976) and Armand Mattelart (1979). Since then, however, the concept has gradually fallen from favour in academic writings, partly on account of the sustained criticism it has received on a number of fronts (Boyd-Barrett, 1982; Schlesinger, 1991; Tomlinson, 1991; Sinclair, 1992), partly because of recent rapid changes in global power structures, and partly because of its displacement by more sophisticated theories of cultural 'globalisation' (see box, p. 153). But though McGuigan scarcely exaggerates in describing cultural imperialism as a 'deeply unfashionable problematic' (1992:229) among academics in the 1990s, this does not mean the term has become obsolete. Not only does it continue to find voice in the work of some major cultural critics (e.g. Hall, 1991; Said, 1993) but it is also very much alive in certain cultural–economic policy debates. For instance, fear of US cultural imperialism was invoked in relation to the stalling of the final stages of the Uruguay round of GATT (the General Agreement on Tariffs and Trade) in 1993 over European (particularly French) resistance to including the trade in audio-visual products – film and television imports – in the agreement.

Although the central idea of cultural imperialism – that certain dominant cultures threaten to overwhelm other weaker ones – looks like a fairly straightforward claim, things turn out to be more complicated at the conceptual level, making a clear empirical answer to the cultural imperialism question difficult to arrive at. One way to understand these conceptual difficulties is to consider the two constituent parts of the term.

The word 'imperialism' has itself been used with two quite different emphases: first as a description of a political and, broadly, cultural project of domination – as, for example, in the empires of the ancient world – and second (particularly in Marxist theory) as primarily economic domination – as the global extension of capitalism. Of course, all historical forms of imperialism have contained both cultural–political and economic elements. But the way the cultural imperialism claim is understood depends on which of these senses is foregrounded. Sometimes it can appear that what is at stake is the extension of cultural influence for its own sake, as in the ideas of 'Westernisation' or 'Americanisation': simply the incorporation of ideologies and cultural practices into one dominant version of the way life should be lived. This is sometimes linked to the idea of the threat of cultural homogenisation. At other times, it can appear that culture – for example, consumer culture – is something employed in the service of extending the world capitalist system (Schiller, 1976). And often these two senses become elided, so that the West, America and transnational capitalism can become almost indistinguishable as the generalised enemy of cultural autonomy.

The other constituent term, 'culture', is of course even more complicated, embracing most aspects of human existence. Among the problems thrown up by this complexity is the tendency to focus simply on the distribution of cultural *goods*. Here a strong *prima facie* case can easily be established for cultural imperialism in relation, for instance, to food (McDonalds, Coca-Cola), clothing ('Western' dress codes, jeans, etc.), music (Michael Jackson, The Spice Girls), architecture (the 'International' style), business and media language (American-English) and the various aspects of the mass media – in particular film (Hollywood) and television (CNN, MTV).

What this case generally neglects, however, is another crucial aspect of the concept of culture: that is, the complexity of *meanings* that people attach to cultural goods. So often the case for cultural influence is made simply on the basis of tracking the sheer flow of cultural goods: for example, monitoring the proportion of American shows on Dutch or Zambian television. This certainly demonstrates some sort of domination – but is it really *cultural*? It is perhaps better described as evidence of 'imperialism' in the political economy of cultural exchange. This might have cultural *implications* – for example, 'programme dumping' by the West may inhibit the development of domestic media production in the Third World – but it does not demonstrate direct cultural *influence*. To do this, as Fejes (1981) has pointed out, analysis needs to focus on the way in which people 'read' media texts and construct cultural meanings out of them. Some critics of cultural imperialism have tried to engage with the substance of media texts, for example Dorfman and Mattelart's celebrated study *How to Read Donald Duck* (1975). But here, though the authors claim to reveal a huge edifice of US imperialist ideology in the Disney comic, there is no attempt at all to consider how readers in the Third World actually interpret these texts, and ideological influence is simply attributed. A very different picture emerges from cross-cultural empirical studies of audience reception of television texts. Liebes and Katz's (1993) study of the audience of *Dallas* demonstrates that, far from being passive imbibers of the cultural values of the programme, viewers entered into a complex active negotiation with the text, bringing their own values and beliefs firmly to bear on their readings. (*Dallas* was a glossy American series that achieved near-global popularity in the late 1970s and early 1980s, with the notable exception of Japan.)

It is for these reasons that critical media theorists have now largely rejected the cultural imperialism thesis in its crudest and most polemical formulations. However, with the increasing globalisation of media and cultural processes and practices, it seems likely that related concerns – for the autonomy of local cultures and the local control of media and communications practices – will become increasingly significant issues in media and cultural studies.

John Tomlinson

8

The elastic metaphor: towards a theoretical outline of cultural identity

Nikos Papastergiadis

The questions 'Who am I?' and 'Where do I belong?' have assumed, in modern times, an unparalleled degree of urgency and complexity. Never before has the self been the site of such intense cultivation and place of origin such a determining force in our destiny. Psychoanalysis and passports were introduced at almost the same time. To break out of the past and to venture across to new territories has been a dominant drive in modernity. However, what also haunted this expansionist epoch was the fear of the eternal return (that the 'escape' would prove illusory). The concepts of identity and culture were also bound in this ambivalent relationship between continuity and rupture.

During the period of early modernity the term 'culture' was either reserved for the aesthetic and philosophical discourses which sought to elevate the subject above their banal existence, or projected on to the exotic practices of premodern societies. Culture had a split identity: it was restricted to either the exalted and refined expressions of 'high' society in the metropolitan centres, or the premodern traditions and primitive practices of the peripheries. On both sides of the divide was the view that, in modernity, culture was beyond the sphere of everyday life.

The crisis of identity had also been a recurring theme throughout modernity. The characteristic feature of modernity was a restless dynamic towards change. Social structures which had previously secured the place of old identities were fragmenting and unleashing new identities. The crisis of identity, which is coeval with modernity, has been articulated in different forms, and it would be a mistake to seek an equivalence between the crisis of identity in the early forms of modernist culture and the questioning of cultural identity in recent debates.

In the early period of modernity there was a binary division of identities. To be modern was not to be part of any particular culture because the cultural parameters of modernity were defined in terms of universals. Cultural identity was thus reserved for those who were outside the metropolitan zones of modernity; it represented the identities of people who were locked into traditional and primitive practices. The space of cultural identity was thus constructed as the opposite of modern identity. It was closed and conservative. Cultural identity was seen as the embodiment of traditions which had been developed within a specific place and over a long period of time. Cultural identity was not linked to the way an individual or a community could make sense of the world, in all its messy totality, but rather was restricted to a specific set of coherent and distinctly defined practices for repeating the past. The preservation of the past became the duty and objective of cultural identity.

To be modern, in contrast, was to be part of the flows and ruptures of history. Modern identity was not rooted in a particular place, nor exclusively linked to fixed practices. Fashions changed, tastes were fickle, conformity and blind belief were unacceptable, mobility was the sign of success, and change was adored for its own sake. Marx's phrase from *The Communist Manifesto*, 'all that is solid melts into air', captured the *zeitgeist* of early modernity. After the progressive march of modernity had gained momentum it was assumed that the idea of cultural identity would be superseded. If some remnants of the past hung on, this was relegated to being either a transitional phase or the mere display of sentiment and nostalgia for the lost home. Modernity picked up the idea of home, broke its links to the past and irrevocably situated it in the forever inaccessible horizons of the future. Home was no longer something you returned to, but rather a place you could never quite reach. Settling down was akin to giving up and pulling out of the modern quest. In this restless sensibility and homeless epoch there was no place for cultural identity.

The dominant ideologies of early modernity, both liberalism and Marxism, were premised on the assumption that particularistic cultural attachments would be displaced by universal values and identities. Local identities and exclusive forms of ethnicity would disappear under the force of modernity. According to these perspectives, the irrational and traditional identities would be replaced by an enlightened and universal identity. Modernity never delivered such promises. If anything, the ruptures and migrations of this period have revealed the hollowness that lurked within such triumphalist discourses. The displacements and transformations associated with globalisation have forced us to rethink the status of cultural identity.

The necessity for a cultural identity is not the problem that only migrants carry with them, nor is it the burden that shackles backward people to the past. Cultural identity has been configured in these limited and patronising terms partly because it was originally articulated within sociological and anthropological paradigms, which highlighted the exploited and melancholic conditions of migrants and savages, and tended to suggest that their cultural identity was disfigured by the fatal contact with modernity. Cultural identity was thus defined *for others*, those who either arrived belatedly or had been bypassed by the dynamics of modern history. This in turn allowed those who found themselves in the centres of modernity to turn a blind eye to their own cultural identity. As their own sense of identity was inextricably linked to the modern dynamic of change and progress they could assume that their cultural identity was subsumed by the gestures of being modern. During spasmodic moments, when the modern sensibility was able partially to acknowledge its own crisis, the cultural identity of the other was celebrated, but again only according to the binary logic of a counter-position, one which could appropriate the mythical integrity of the primitive in order to highlight the material decadence and spiritual poverty of modernity. As Hal Foster observed, 'the primitive is a modern problem, a crisis in cultural identity' (1985:204).

Stop and think

Modernity and the critique of the self

The word 'modern' is often loosely used to mean contemporary, up to date, and so on. It is important for any student of media and cultural studies to grasp a more specific usage of the terms 'modern' and 'modernity' (the time and condition of the modern). Taking a long view, of course, all times can think of themselves as 'modern' from their own perspective. If it's a point of view far in the future then what's modern for us will one day be ancient history. But our point of view is inescapably here and now, and the terms we use have an effectiveness now. So, for us, modernity is the condition of a here and now that we experience as distinctly different from the past, which we only have access to in the history books.

More particularly, modernity has come to be thought of as qualitatively new in some profound ways. Since the period of the eighteenth-century Enlightenment, informed by the rapid growth of the sciences, we have been able to periodise European history more clearly (antiquity, Middle Ages, Renaissance, etc.) based on the view that previous periods had distinctive social and cultural qualities and were 'completed' and then supplanted by something different. History is, of course, never quite so neat in actuality, but the distinctions have proved useful. So modernity has been aware of itself since at least the middle of the nineteenth century, as emerging out of industrial and political revolutions and breaking with its own past in distinctive ways. Aesthetic 'modernism' – new forms of painting, music, architecture and writing – consolidated this self awareness; but so too did the feeling in the late twentieth century that modernity was 'completing' itself in some way and being supplanted by something else – the 'postmodern'. Many social critics, however, broadly share the view of German philosopher Jürgen Habermas that modernity is an 'incomplete project' and that postmodernism is more of a self-parodying, ironic, hyper-intensified turn in relation to aesthetic modernism and a self-critically 'late' phase of modernity than a new 'period' in any fundamentally different sense.

'Modernisation' refers to economic and technological development and identifies the underlying engine of modernity – the pace of change in the advanced industrialised societies where the cultural impact of wave after wave of new technologies throughout the late nineteenth and twentieth centuries was profound (from steam engines to jet aircraft, from telegraph to internet). So you should stop and think about your own position in relation to these changes. Perhaps the most profound has been in our very sense of 'self'.

You can think of modernity as having a temporal dimension, a conceptual dimension and various levels. The temporal dimension separates the modern from its past and always raises the question of what might come next and how we will recognise it. The conceptual dimension distinguishes among various forms of modernity, such as the economic and technical (modernisation) or the aesthetic (modernism). The various levels of modernity would include the overarching social conditions, the intervening cultural manifestations and the subjective level – which is where you actually experience being 'in' modernity. On this level, the most striking feature of later modernity has been an increasingly unavoidable challenge to the idea that the 'self' is a given essence (which usually meant that the European male was the essential prototype of selfhood). This 'critique of the subject' (where 'subject' means self) comes out of the general realisation that, given the right tools, everything in our world is 'makeable', even ourselves.

The idea of the *makeable self* can be both unsettling and empowering. You can experience it as a threatening dissolving away of your certainties about who you are. But you can also begin to see the challenge posed by Anthony Giddens: 'The reflexive project of the self, which consists in the sustaining of coherent, yet continuously revised, biographical narratives, takes place in the context of multiple choice as filtered through abstract systems' (1991:5). Among the most powerful abstract systems offering you these multiple choices and tools for the makeable self – for 'performative construction' of agency – are those of the modern media. The problem of structure and agency remains, of course: to what extent is the makeable self 'made' by its socio-cultural circumstances and how free are you to remake yourself? For the moment, you may feel that the best way to think of this is in terms of multiple choices determined by structure but specific choice open to some degree of determination by agency. In fact, the question of *cultural* identity is where this tension is most clearly confronted and negotiated.

The recognition that the primitive did not belong in a space outside of the modern, and that this opposition was itself symptomatic of a deeper crisis in cultural identity, was enabled by a rethinking of the relationship between culture and identity. There was a direct challenge against the prevailing view in the early modernist literature, and in the social sciences more generally, which had externalised the relationship between identity formation and cultural development. It presupposed that, at first, individuals have little choice in determining what sort of culture surrounds and constructs their everyday life. Culture was defined as a given which is imposed upon the self; that is, as an entity which always precedes and extends beyond the identity of an individual. However, in recent years the debates on cultural identity have both reversed and exploded this relationship. The critique of the self in both philosophical and psychoanalytic discourses has challenged the fundamental categories of Western metaphysics. The recent feminist and post-colonial perspectives have also assumed an influential role in redefining the relationship between subjectivity and what Stuart Hall calls the 'politics of representation'. The notions of a unified identity and a discrete culture have now undergone strenuous critiques and new perspectives have emerged which argue in favour of anti-essentialist views of cultural formation and of performative constructions of agency. Identity, it is now argued, begins as it constructs a shape out of its cultural surroundings, and a culture only takes form through the process of identification and articulation. Concepts such as the 'location of culture' and the 'possession of identity' became problematical. They were both scrutinised from the perspective of a more radical form of historicisation and recon-figured within frameworks which sought to break out of the binary codes of Western metaphysics. The decisive break with the eurocentric and binary views of culture did not occur until the crisis of modernism was compounded by the emergent cultural politics of decolonisation and globalisation. As Stuart Hall argues, the issues of cultural identity have assumed a significance of global dimensions:

> The re-emergence of questions of ethnicity, of nationalism – the obduracy, the dangers and the pleasures of the rediscovery of identity in the modern world, inside and outside of Europe – places the question of cultural identity at the very centre of the contemporary political agenda. (1995:4)

Through this turbulent epoch the distinctions between the insider and the outsider, the citizen and the stranger, have been violently unsettled. Popula-tions and cultures have been on the move and the idea of the homeland bit-terly contested. In this context, debates about cultural identity have taken a prominent role. Once seen from the perspective of rupture and displacement, the concepts of culture and identity could no longer be represented as being exclusively rooted in one location, or that authenticity was abandoned at the point of departure. Though migrants and displaced peoples around the world often invoked their cultural identity in terms of the name of their place of origin and sought to emphasise a continuity with the past, they were also compelled to negotiate the differences between these locations and forms of subjectivity.

This process of cross-cultural negotiation was at first considered to be a 'problem' that only migrants would have to resolve. It was assumed that, with time and the inevitable gravity of acculturation, these 'problems' would fade. However, what was once a marginal concern within the debates in the sociol-ogy of migration and the institutional politics of migrant welfare, has now become one of the central concerns of modern culture. Cultural identity showed unexpected forms of resilience, it resisted acculturation and sharpened the crisis in the dominant discourses of the self within the West. Under this pressure the concepts of culture and identity required a radical overhaul. It became necessary to see how cultures are constituted across differences, rather than being consolidated within closed traditions, and that identity was always constructed through an unending play and oscillation within the polarities of past and present, the self and the other. There was, consequently, a revision of the linear view of cultural progress which had predicted that premodern forms of cultural identity would be successively superseded.

Once the idea of culture was extended to incorporate the dynamic exchange between the social context and the forms of knowledge in everyday life, and the conception of identity was liberated from the essentialist categories of authentic inner being, then the internal and external relationships which con-struct a cultural identity could begin to be understood in ways that did not fix the categories of belonging and identification within exclusivist paradigms. As the debates on modern subjectivity began to move out of *a priori* notions of origin and destiny, culture was also no longer either confined to a closed space or restricted to the repetition of a distinct set of practices that distinguished one locale from another. Culture was not just the organisation of objects and rituals which defined a sense of place, but also an optic, a way of seeing and making sense of the world.

The aim of this chapter is, therefore, twofold: to examine the ways we have come to understand the connections between culture and identity, and to outline a framework for representing cultural identity.

The constitution of cultural identity

The properties of cultural identity are paradoxical and elusive. The question of identity takes its most delicate and barbed form when a sense of belonging is in doubt. When there is uncertainty of where to locate the self in relation to the place, taste and traditions of others, then the question of identity appears in its most precarious form. The determination of a cultural identity is always coterminous with the practice of defining a position in the world and is inter-connected with the way we recognise our relation to others. Displacement is always double: stability is lost in relation to both one's place in the world and one's sense of self as an integrated subject (see Hall, 1992:275). Cultural identity exists through a process of differentiation. Its form is shaped as much by what it excludes as by that which it includes. While politicians summon the term 'cultural identity' to connote a stable and clear sense of self, the consti-tution of cultural identity is inexorably dependent upon the fluid and unstable practices of *incorporation*. There is a fundamental contradiction between the dominant political discourses, which represent cultural identity in terms of overarching national categories and place emphasis on the qualities of exclusivity and uniqueness, and the recent theoretical understanding that stresses the dynamic practice of incorporation which defies the principle that identity can be based on fixed and pure categories. Cultural identity in the polit-ical discourse is a bounded concept, reflecting back the territorial integrity and mythical self image of the unified nation state. This effectively reduces cultural identity from a dynamic process to an object that can only be defended or preserved.

Cultural identity cannot exist as a petrified emblem or as an icon suspended in a time frame of its own. It is a living process, it exists in the basic practice of internalisation and exchange, which is so fundamental to social relation-ships that it is safe to say that cultural identity is a universal. What are always in dispute are the particular forms of cultural identity and its given status. Zygmunt Bauman is surely right to remind us that, while the question of iden-tity cuts across the debates on modernity, its articulation has changed: 'Indeed, if the *modern* "problem of identity" was how to construct an identity and keep it solid and stable, the *postmodern* "problem of identity" is primarily how to avoid fixation and keep the options open' (1996:18).

There are no standards against which a cultural identity can be measured, nor is there an assured position of authenticity from which other forms can be judged. Yet the debates on cultural identity are replete with judgements that condemn others as being in a state of either denial or exaggeration. These responses are part of the manoeuvres for positioning in the 'politics of repre-sentation', whereby it appears that some forms of cultural identity are so secure that they have the luxury of taking their own name for granted, while others consider their own integrity to be at risk whenever an external force seeks to cross its border. The retreat into a form of ethnic absolutism is not a strategy that is confined to minority communities. While minorities may articulate their own identity by means of a rigid identification with their culture of origin, the dominant communities have also adopted displays of aggressivity towards difference in order to bolster the project of nation building. Both the oblivious and vigilant forms of cultural identity tend to presume that security is based on the durability and consistency of their symbols and practices.

Cultural identity is not a coherent and consistent body of symbols, ideas and practices. It is more like what Gramsci called the 'strangely composite' formation of common sense (see Hall, 1996a:433), comprising symbols which are both ancient and modern, ideas which are both traditional and novel, and practices which are securely embedded in a known past as well as those novel ones whose paths are barely mapped. This combination cannot be represented purely in terms of a juxtaposition. It is not simply the positioning of the past hard up against the present, the old with the new, but also the reconfiguring
(cont. p. 141) of both.

Bordertowns: a case study

In 1993 Noam Chomsky wrote a short piece that would become the Preface to an extraordinary book of photographs and essays, *Juárez: The Laboratory of Our Future* (1998). There he detailed what he called the 'international class war' that – among other consequences worldwide – has left border towns such as Juárez, on the Mexico–US frontier, exposed to crippling social, economic and cultural contradictions. The photographs gathered for this book presented a shockingly different view of the world as the twentieth century ended, not least because they could not be neatly allocated either to a 'here' (the West, the developed nations) or to a 'there' (the remote places where human catastrophes normally happen). The carefully documented Juárez book can be taken alongside Gifford and Perry's collaged photo-essay volume *Bordertown* (1998) as key contemporary documents for the debate about cultural identity, since they both challenge the here/there distinction in such profoundly unsettling ways.

As itself a significant media artefact, Barry Gifford and David Perry's book of images explores the conventions of framing and contextualisation by blurring the boundaries between image and text, while undermining the normal authority of text using smudgy typewritten material, handwriting, white space and provocative juxtapositions. More than that, though, Perry's photographs are jarringly unexpected – often decentred, swallowing up the border people in unstable spaces, in blur, in the visual detritus of their own environments. The monotone bleakness of his work – not cool, detached, aesthetically and self-consciously 'bleak' so much as darkly unstable, as if about to slide into a grey emptiness devoid of meaning – contrasts with the crisp colours and careful framing of the more conventional photojournalism in the Juárez book. But the two styles and their accompanying texts triangulate the

Mexican border towns and their inhabitants (Gifford and Perry are documenting Agua Prieta) in order to represent the virtually unrepresentable.

Douglas, Arizona (over the border from Agua Prieta) and El Paso, Texas (over the border from Juárez) exist as absent presences in these photographs, lights in the distance through the dirty windscreen of a car as loose signifiers of somewhere else. The border towns themselves are not captured in post-card-style overviews; rather, they are the accumulated particularities – motion blur of figures across a seedy barroom, pouting lips of a prostitute, endless grubby signs pointing aimlessly, the street musician with an expression of implacability, fingering his accordion on auto-pilot, the leathery face of a woman hunched under blankets as a low sun casts chilly shadows, people hurrying past, streets emptily gaping. But none of this – these are Perry's images – is stereotypically seeking the easy sympathy reaction. The images have their own disconcerting strangeness and don't reach out in any pleading way to the viewer, who remains unsettled but removed from the habitual response to the media's more usual humanitarian appeals with their easy heart-tugging representations of needy otherness. Here the other is determinedly other, with nothing at all to say to 'us'. The photographs don't speak for them, in the usual act of contrived ventriloquism, but momentarily rupture the separating film between viewer and a somewhere that's suddenly 'here', not 'there', at the moment of viewing. The identity of these border people, insofar as it is communicated here, is in these particularities, these localities, and the photographs – for once – don't generalise.

The photographs in *Juárez: The Laboratory of Our Future* present a different challenge as well. From the opening image of a buried woman's heels sticking out of the sand – a victim of *narcotraficantes*, drug traffickers – the book juxtaposes snapshots of everyday life with everyday horror. Female shift workers in the foreign-owned factories, on lunch break drinking Coke with their enchiladas, or crowded together on a bus back to the *colonias*, are shadowed by images of corpses, by blood turned black and hard on the sidewalks. Chomsky's voice intones, dirge-like, in the background: 'These . . . are natural consequences of the great successes of the past years in reducing democracy to empty forms', a claim which his Preface supports drily with detailed discussion of industrial policy, World Trade Organisation and International Monetary Fund practices, the only commentary that can hope to touch the reality which places high-repression, low-wage production behind the images of lives rendered disposable in Juárez. But the viewer has to judge too between conflicting claims in the represented spaces – between the ugly evidence of these border people's brutality to each other and the sense that many of the faces captured here are those of people doing the best they can to live a borderline identity.

The question of the nation state permeates both of these remarkable books and colours their depictions of cultural identity. The United States is there in signs, advertisements, in the distant horizon that defines these places as borderline. Mexico is there as the subject, ironically enough, of the Eastman Kodak Chairman's comment about the need to 'lock in the opening of Mexico's economy' so that US economic interests would not be challenged there. Here is a direct link between the Kodak-processed photographs of cardboard shanty towns, the identities forged there, and the nation states locked in their sado-masochistic mutual embrace. Questions of class and gender permeate these two books as well. David Gifford's camera captures unsettling images of gender stretched taut in shadowy places, the peeling poster of a bullfighter, lacework against newspaper cuttings of kidnapping and rape. The Mexican city police and *federales* figure prominently in *Juárez*; frozen male postures around bodies – often female – dragged from the sand. Rows of women's tights flutter like pennants on clothes lines in the shanty town. One of the photographers for *Juárez* was beaten when he tried to photograph a rabbit hopping across a mansion's lawn.

Finally, both of these books about the border towns reveal the cultural identities of the inhabitants as caught up in symbolic processes that reveal some underlying, barely conscious reality, and as deeply heterological in character. There is not 'one people' here but a cultural identity made up of all the accumulated particularities of people and places: ghostly shelves of white stetson hats in one of Perry's photographs; white-stetsoned Mexican farmers with shiny pick-up trucks protesting about their own government outside the US consulate in Juárez and demanding 'economic asylum' in the USA; a do-it-yourself 'wanted' poster with a boy's photograph and the scrawled plea of 'Come Home Travis (We're Staying Motel Edlades Till Monday)'.

The Enlightenment vision of inevitable progress, modernity's self confidence, crumbles visibly in these bordertown photographs. Here are some of the leftovers from that way of thinking about and visualising the world, and the knowledge produced, especially around Perry's photographs, is deeply 'postmodern' in a way far removed from the clever pastiches and ironically playful self referentiality that sometimes passes for the aesthetically postmodern. Even – or perhaps especially – *work* as represented in these pictures is treacherously self denying instead of being the solid linchpin of self identity. But we still have to be very careful about generalising to any broader notion of 'border' identities, as somehow exemplary of general processes of cultural identity in the contemporary world. Nikos Papastergiadis, here, outlines seven ways of tracing the contours of cultural identity. All seven are clearly apt for the work of knowledge production being done through these two books of bordertown photographs. But all seven turn on acknowledging the specificity of what is being observed. Nonetheless, a careful encounter with these two books of photographs is capable of deeply affecting one's understanding of cultural identity, an effect that in its turn becomes more understandable in light of Arjun Appadurai's (1996) identification of five dimensions of global cultural 'flows': ethnoscapes (flows of people, for example as here around borders); mediascapes (flows of images, for example as here through the published books of photographs); technoscapes (flows of production, for example as here in the foreign-owned factories of the bordertowns); finanscapes (flows of money, for example as described by Chomsky in his Preface to the Juárez book); and ideoscapes (flows of ideology, for example as here in the 'hollow forms' of modernity that are so viciously mismatched with the depicted lives). Our understanding of cultural identity, as informed say by these specific photographs, has to recognise the particularity of the ethnoscape being represented, but it can also recognise – as the brief account offered here is meant to suggest – how the other flows intersect with this particular ethnoscape. It is then possible to see how these flows will also intersect similarly with other ethnoscapes, where the cultural identities being formed will be no less particular and non-generalisable. The borders – with their various crossovers and intersections – may be different but the underlying dynamic of 'flows' will be similar, and the capacity of any border (whether based on nationality, class, gender or some other division) to interrupt the easy movement of these 'flows' and render them visible remains deeply instructive.

See Bowden, C. (1998), *Juárez: The Laboratory of Our Future*. Gifford, B. and D. Perry (1998), *Bordertown*.

Dan Fleming

Imagining cultural identity in the form of a mosaic can be very misleading, for it exaggerates the distinctiveness of its components and overlooks the more dynamic play at the internal and external borders of identity. The energy of cultural identity, its potential for renewal, its subtle rhythms of extension, are most potent and focused when there is a dual coding of past and present, foreign and familiar, known and unknown. Cultural identity is a fragmentary, disjointed and contradictory phenomenon which is experienced as if it were a unified and stable formation, precisely because the boundaries between the constituent symbols, ideas and practices become excited through the process of interaction. The power of cultural identity is thus in a state of exquisite vibrancy, when the juxtaposition between different elements is not only taken for granted but also experienced as if it were part of a continuous historical process. It is when the old is experienced within the contours of the new, and vice versa, that cultural identity can claim a pernicious as well as an enlightening purchase on contemporaneity. Cultural identity is not just the preservation of the past, but is the future-oriented process of claiming a space within the present and ultimately a projection of how a life should be lived. Stuart Hall has captured this double dynamic when he notes that:

> No cultural identity is produced out of thin air. It is produced out of those historical experiences, those cultural traditions, those lost and marginal languages, those marginalized experiences, those peoples and histories which remain unwritten. Those are the specific roots of identity. On the other hand, identity itself is not the rediscovery of them, but what they as cultural resources allow a people to produce. Identity is not in the past to be found, but in the future to be constructed. (1995:14)

Following from Hall, it could be stated that cultural identity is the process by which the conceptions and categories are articulated in everyday consciousness. It is not just a static and closed system of knowledge but the active means by which meanings are shaped and transformed. The vitality of cultural identity is thus experienced in the simultaneity of being both vividly spontaneous and deeply historical. The recent debates on cultural identity have the potential to renew the difficult and unresolved questions of agency in social theory. Aided by the feminist scholarship of Judith Butler and Lois McNay, Hall (1996b) has already re-examined the Althusserian and Foucauldian legacy on agency and crossed this with a re-reading of the Freudian and Lacanian work on identification. The agency of cultural identity is, according to Hall, not an essence but a positioning across 'the unstable points of identification or suture, which are made within the discourses of history and culture' (1990:226). The subject that is constituted by these complex networks of relationships will invariably have a plurality of identities. Contradictory elements cannot be simply dismissed as an expression of false consciousness, or judged as a man-ifestation of an underdeveloped cultural formation. For it is from *within* these contradictions and fragmentary compositions that cultural identity draws its catalytic dynamism. Recognition and affirmation are not dependent on a unified and integrated image, even when the public discourse that promotes a specific cultural identity is loudly projecting the existence of such ideological projections of purity and exclusivity.

Stop and think

Identity and oppositions

One of the important ways in which you can 'tune in' to what may often seem obscure and difficult current debates about identity is to appreciate how the question of oppositions is frequently at the centre of these debates. Think about how your own notions of identity may be often little more than ver-sions of 'us' and 'them'. You know who you are and who you're not. That is the beginning of an opposition, no matter how innocent it seems in the begin-ning. History tells us rather convincingly how quickly such simple – indeed, seemingly inevitable – oppositions can grow into elaborate political and ide-ological distinctions and conflicts (Arab and Israeli, Aryan and Jew, Catholic and Protestant, Serb and Albanian, working class and middle class, etc.).

One liberal response to this historical tendency is to try and strip back the content of the opposition, as it were, so that differences can be recognised but without building elborate confrontations upon them. The problem with this is that people do not easily abandon long-standing antagonisms in the interest of some liberally imagined happy ending; usually because they simply do not believe that both sides of the opposition are equally right and wrong – why should they, as they are inevitably seeing things from one side of the divide, no matter how 'enlightened' they might be attempting to be?

So is it possible to think about identity without falling into the trap of thinking in oppositional terms in the first place? The critic Homi Bhabha (1994) has suggested that it is, but that this involves considerable disorien-tation of our normal ways of thinking (hence the difficulty of much of the writing associated with the attempt to do so). The key concept for Bhabha is that of the 'hyrid moment', when and where neither side of the opposi-tion – self and other – is capable of resisting the experience of 'something else besides'. Hybridity, the name of this 'something else', is not like the liberal vision of an outside position that somehow transcends an opposition; rather, it is an alternative condition *inside* the given circumstances. For Bhabha, any attempts to theorise such a position have always been antici-pated in historical actuality by the identities of those people caught in the border zones between cultures, as in colonial British India, for instance. In such circumstances, colonial power, deployed (e.g. through governmental discourses, schooling, etc.) in the interests of a particular 'us' against a particular 'them', in actuality generated complex and contradictory spaces of identity where the defining power could never entirely succeed in maintaining pure separations, but instead frequently generated hybrid results. We tend to think of the coloniser taking over and pushing the native into the margins, the coloniser speaking while the native is forced into silence, and so on. But these are retrospective oversimplifications. Even where power is most nakedly deployed to define an 'us' and a 'them', realities are usually more complex; the repressed returns in unanticipated ways, the superficial confidence of the 'us' is fractured by paranoid uncertainties or by secret attractions to the identity of the other.

Even post-colonial academic work can fall into the trap of believing that its task is to rediscover the silenced, invisible 'other' – in so doing it may be imposing the opposition yet again. So Bhabha asks us to think about whether there is a *third space*, not somehow 'beyond' or 'outside' the separate spaces of the opposed identities but in the same times and places.

These sorts of difficult issue are bringing into the heart of media studies a whole range of profoundly important work from cultural studies, much of which has yet to be carefully worked through in any real detail: for example, South Asian Cultural Studies (see Lal, 1996); the work of the Centre for the Study of Developing Societies in Delhi and the Subaltern Studies Collective; and work influenced by (though not always uncritical of) Edward Said's studies of Orientalism (the West's imagining of the East). (See also Ahmad, 1992; Nandy, 1997.)

So you should devote some effort to considering what is involved in trying to think of a 'something else besides' those oppositions in terms of which we habitually think about identity.

Cultures on the move and the changing self

It is crucial to note that cultural identity is in a constant state of regeneration. Its dynamic for change is a complex process of internalisation and supplementation. The models for explaining this process have undergone a subtle shift. Renewal was often understood as a form of differentiation, whereby the relationship between the old and the new was experienced in such a way that the new enhances a quality that was latent in the old. This process of internalising difference, by relating it to what has already existed within the boundaries of the cultural identity, has the effect of dissolving the contradiction between the inside and the outside, the old and the new. The subordination of one element to another thus ensured a sense of continuity where there was otherwise a rupture or clash between opposing planes. The modernist strategies of incorporation, or what has been more critically referred to as the 'cannibalising of the other', has been understood as operating according to an 'economy of the same': difference is introduced into a body but only to confirm and bolster its own priorities.

More recently there have been attempts to explain the extensions to, and transformations of, cultural identity in terms of the way incommensurable elements are fastened together. Where a cultural identity is compelled to fulfil a need which has no historical reference point, this does not imply that (since there was no such prior calling or similar resonance within that identity) it will simply bypass or exclude that need; rather, it seeks to incorporate the new forms of subjectivity through supplementation. Discordant pieces are added on and these disjointed supplements can have the effect of disrupting the conventional order and realigning the priorities of the dominant self image. However, the supplement may be granted a form of existence without a direct acknowledgement that it marks a rupture to the structure of the whole. While this appendage may have a precarious status it is nevertheless a vital feature in the self preservation of all cultural identities. In a multicultural context, when cultural identities are not easily translatable according to their own terms, the dynamic role of difference takes on crucial responsibility in expanding the framework of identification and understanding. As Peter Caws argues, cultural identity is never defined from a singular and internally consistent source:

> The enlargement of individual horizons is one of the characteristics of multicultural identity. What is found beyond the old limited horizon may appear to be in conflict with what lies within it; cultures may be, as is sometimes said (borrowing an image, none too helpfully, from Greek mathematics) 'incommensurable'. But this need not be an occasion for despair since incommensurables can be comfortably accommodated in lifeworlds not dedicated to monocultural ideas of completeness and consistency. It is hard to resist quoting Whitman here, clichéd as the passage may have become: 'I contradict myself: very well, I contradict myself. I am large, I contain multitudes'. (1994: 382)

A more subtle reading of cultural identity would not seek to convert the stigma of difference into a badge of pride, or compensate for the historical projections of lack with a counter-claim of cultural surplus, but would aim to subvert the very code which can only create identification through binary oppositions. Drawing from Fanon's statement that the 'colonial subject is always overdetermined from without', Homi Bhabha argues that alienation is positioned in all the configurations of identity. Identity is no more, but no less, than a constant process of negotiation between image and fantasy, in which there is no pre-alienated self which can be redeemed, but rather the 'Otherness of the Self' is what is 'inscribed in the perverse palimpsest of colonial identity' (Bhabha *et al.*, 1987:119). The condition of the colonial subject in Bhabha's writing explicitly opens up the splitting within the processual forms of imaging an identity. In an early essay he attacked the conception of identity which presupposed the prior essence of the ego:

> The postmodern perspective insists that the question of identity can never be seen 'beyond representation', as a psychological problem of personality or even an ethical problem of personhood . . . We are no longer confronted with an ontological problem of being but with a discursive strategy of the 'moment' of interrogation; a moment in which the demand for identification becomes, primarily, a response to other questions of signification and desire, culture and politics . . . it is the priority (and Play) of the signifier that reveals the Third Space of absence or lack or doubling (not depth) which is the very principle of discourse. (1987:6–7)

In Bhabha's later essay on the formation of national identity, he goes even further in deconstructing the logic which confined the sign of otherness to the position of the margin. By pushing the question of identification to the point where all subject conditions are revealed to be split and partial, he reveals a process which constitutes the knowledge of the self as always dependent on the other. There is never a singular form of cultural identity which acquires the benchmark status of stability and unity against which others can be judged. The significance of this deconstructive reading of the narrative of subject formation is not only evident in the ways it heralds the existence of those forms of cultural identity which were previously ignored and margin-alised by the dominant discourse, but also in the aim to expose the logic which both authorises a hierarchic construction of cultural identities and blurs the constitution of the self through a process of interdependency with, and split-ting from, the other:

> Once the liminality of the nation state is established, and its signifying difference is turned from the boundary 'outside' to its finitude 'within', the threat of cultural difference is no longer a problem of 'other' people. It becomes a question of otherness of the people-as-one. (Bhabha, 1994:150)

By situating cultural identity in the modern nation as the sign of the irre-ducibility of difference, Bhabha is thus not just pointing to the range in the pluralist national self image but also highlighting the process through which all forms of identification occur. Phrases such as 'the moment of liminality', 'the disjunctive breaks of difference', 'the ruptures of the in-between space', are all expressive of his attempt to reconceptualise temporal and spatial frame-works of identification. These phrases seek to heighten attention to both those symbols whose meaning is not bound to either the transferral of fixed values along correspondent tracks, and those formations which are never more than the summation of their constitutive references. These forms of identity, which Bhabha is referring to, are always incomplete and mixed. The condition of their emergence exceeds the boundaries of their anticipation, and their naming appears belated and in a partial form. Defining such identities accord-ing to the logic of the supplement is not, for Bhabha, a despairing moment but the precise point upon which a new politics of negotiation and inclusion can be initiated. It marks a way of acknowledging the sign of difference without repeating the modernist economy of the same. The cultural effect of this inter-ruptive presence or disjunctive voice is to acknowledge that the presence of the other always occurs within the terms of reference of the dominant discourse, but that it does not seek to be confined to mirroring back an alternate space. The identity that emerges from this position is one which resists the demands of solidarity and extension according to the logic of the same, and rather inscribes a presence out of the conjunctural modality which oscillates between the monumental position of authority and the equivocal moment of emer-gence. This perplexing state is best described by Bhabha in the form of questions:

> How does one encounter the past as an anteriority that continually introduces an otherness or alterity into the present? How does one then narrate the present as a form of contemporaneity that is neither punctual nor synchronous? In what

historical time do such configurations of cultural difference assume forms of cultural and political authority? (Bhabha, 1994:157)

The form of identification that Bhabha is referring to is not dependent on the principles of common origin, shared history or a solidarity that is confined to those of the 'one blood'. Similarly, the semantic field of identification extends beyond the boundaries of shared characteristics. What Bhabha is referring to, and it is a theme which is developed in a later essay by Stuart Hall, is the conditional and contingent process of articulation. Identification is a process which is always incomplete and excessive (see Hall, 1996b). Both Bhabha and Hall note that identification always operates *across* differences. Identity is never fully constituted or utterly lost. By drawing on both the linguistic turn in critical theory and the recent psychoanalytic constructions of identification, they emphasise the role of the constitutive outside in the formation of identity. Just as the relationship between the image and the identity of signs is one in which they never quite fit each other, and it is this looseness of symbolic marking which entails further signification and allows the play of differences, similarly the process of identification is in a constant state of oscillation across the boundaries of the self and other.

Tracing the contours of cultural identity

From this perspective, which is clearly indebted to Stuart Hall and Homi Bhabha, there are a number of conceptual advances and modifications which need to be highlighted in order to construct a broader theoretical framework within which the formations of cultural identity can be understood. Both Hall and Bhabha have alerted us to the need for a transformation of the existing theories and paradigms if we are to present an adequate account of the nature of cultural identity in the modern world. The points I would like to emphasise are by no means an exhaustive list, nor the blueprint to a universal model for defining cultural identity. Rather, this preliminary set of points merely provides an outline for a theory of cultural identity. It should be emphasised that the theoretical effect of this outline is to abandon a schematic and deterministic conception of cultural identity. It seeks to acknowledge that cultural identity has its own 'relatively autonomous' formations, whose structural orientations and discursive representations need to be understood according to their own distinctive categories and not as the mere effects of other forces.

First, while the general features of cultural identity are universal, it needs to be understood in terms of its historical specificity. To discuss cultural identity at the level of universality can only produce the banal conclusion that it is simply part of the human condition and an inevitable part of all social relations. What is more significant about cultural identity is the production of distinctive ways of being human and the construction of particular forms of social relations. It is in the understanding of the particularity and the specificity of cultural identity that there lies a challenge to our broader conceptualisations of subjectivity and sociality in the modern world. Politically, it was, in the first instance, useful to speak of cultural identity in an abstract and general way, in order to counter the racist ideologies that either promoted the inherent superiority of certain identities or dismissed cultural identity as a sign of inferiority. It also served as a useful category for the promotion of cultural rights which had been hitherto marginalised and ignored by the state. The political strategy of making visible an awareness of cultural identity which was previously invisible must now be redefined at two levels. Cultural identity must be simultaneously defined in terms of its own specificity and particularity while also developing a new mode of solidarity and affinity between counter-hegemonic subject positions. What Stuart Hall termed the end of innocence for the 'essential black subject' applies more generally for the conception of cultural identity in the modern world (Hall, 1989). Once cultural identity is de-essentialised and it is no longer represented within the binary logic of either good or bad, advanced or backward, then this entails a recognition of the ways its subjectivity is formed across a number of other categories and social divisions.

Second, the appreciation of the uniqueness of cultural identity demands a framework for both understanding and relating to the different formations of cultural identity. If not all cultural identities are the same, then how do we address the complex levels of interaction that emerge when different cultural identities meet? The eurocentric and absolutist methods of ranking cultural identities in terms of the vertical hierarchies of developed or undeveloped, modern or traditional, Western or non-Western, are no longer tenable. Similarly, while the relativist position grants a form of recognition to all cultural identities on the putatively flat horizontal grounds that they have intrinsic values and equal rights to survival, this does not, however, provide a framework for judging between conflicting claims when different cultural identities compete for space. One of the most demanding legal and cultural challenges that lies before us is to conceive of a framework which will be able to negotiate across the boundaries of cultural identities. This would require an understanding of both the orientation and status given to a cultural identity by its own members and the socio-political context within which these cultural identities are operating.

Third, while only a minority of cultural identities is defined in relation to national characteristics and in the absence of global structures for the evaluation and protection of the rights to cultural identity, it is necessary to understand the definition of cultural identity in relation to the social and juridical structures of the nation state. In some contexts the development of cultural identities within certain parameters is encouraged as expressive of the diversity of a multicultural polity, whereas in others the articulation of a non-hegemonic cultural identity is perceived as a threat to the coherence and stability of the nation state. The tensions and contradictions of cultural identity cannot be understood unless they are also situated in relation to the projects of nation building. Both the civic and communal institutions that operate within the state, ranging from education, welfare and health to religion, social movements and cultural organisations, play an active role in either sustaining or inhibiting the formations of cultural identity. These institutions, and their interrelationship with cultural identity, need to be examined, not simply as neutral instruments or as exclusively coercive regimes, but in terms of the agonistic construction of hegemonic and counter-hegemonic identities.

Fourth, cultural identity has to be situated in a non-reductive relationship with the other social divisions of class and gender. The articulation of a given cultural identity may impact on the way class and gender relations are conducted within a specific community, but also affects the way relations are expressed across various social boundaries. Class relations and gender rules that are considered as part of the code of cultural identity can be perceived as oppressive and restrictive by some members. There needs to be a greater appreciation of the way cultural identities are contested within certain communities in order to highlight the complex nexus among class, gender and cultural identity. To privilege class or gender over cultural identity is to presume that there are some aspects of social relations which are either determined by, or subordinate to, others. This approach would obscure the way these categories, of either class or gender, are also formed in a culturally specific way.

Fifth, the process of identification in cultural identity needs to be understood in a context of ambivalence. The conditions of belonging to – and the upholding of – a cultural identity are uneven and contestatory. The aspects of cultural identity which are desirable to one member may be repulsive to another. The strength of cultural identity is often tested by the way these tensions, which may occur inter-generationally or across class and gender boundaries, are negotiated. Furthermore, in the racist contexts of post-colonialism and the emergence of diasporic communities in pluralist societies, the formations of cultural identity are pincered between stigma and stereotypes. These forms of identification, which precede and invariably constrain subjectivity, create negative pressures on the articulation of a cultural identity. However, it must also be noted that loathing and loving have a tendency to switch in what Hall calls a doubling act, whereby 'fear and desire double for one another and play across the structures of otherness, complicating its politics' (1989:28). What is violently rejected in one phase may be celebrated in another. The names given in scorn may be subsequently adopted as badges of pride. The burden of the past, which may appear unbearable in one time, can be transformed into a vaulting board in another. Hence the role of the past and the significance of symbols may present us with unexpected forms of resilience and yield unanticipated consequences. Cultural identities which are dismissed outright by a subject in one political setting have a tendency to return and haunt the beholder in another. It is therefore important to consider the resources with which a cultural identity is formed and their associative values. Stereotypes, both positive and negative, are a crucial index of the contestation that occurs both at the borders and within the notion of cultural identity.

Sixth, cultural identity is formed through unconscious processes, it is not an innate and predetermined category. The desires and drives of cultural identity have a distinctive logic which is often contrary to the rational and instrumental structures that are paraded in hegemonic discourse. By definition, the unconscious side of cultural identity is not representable in a straightforward manner, it can only be glimpsed by excavating and 'working through' the symbolic processes of language and dreams. Four of the key concepts in Bhabha's writing – fetish, stereotype, mimicry and splitting – can serve as useful tropes for investigating the complex processes of the unconscious in cultural identity.

Seventh, this approach would encourage us to identify the heterological character of cultural identity. The name of a given cultural identity can contain within it a variety of subjectivities. The process of identification within a cultural identity is always generative and incomplete. There is no absolute standard which defines the fullness or emptiness, the maturity or backwardness, of a cultural identity. One never arrives at the point where a cultural identity is settled and fixed into place, and one cannot achieve a sense of cultural identity which can block out further changes. Given that the dynamic of cultural identity is driven towards renewal and transformation, it must therefore be accepted that there will be an ongoing antagonism and conflict in the structural orientation and discursive representation of its self image. There can be no assumed correspondence between all the forms of subjectivity within the concept of cultural identity.

Conclusion

In the period of early modernism the sign of cultural identity was confined to what was left behind, a trace of what had been lost or superseded by the advances of modernity. Within the vaulted chambers of high culture and the penile skyscrapers of Manhattan, cultural identity was relegated to the dustbin of history. The modernist myths of progress and individualism were premised on the transcendence of cultural identity. This promise was as illusory as the presumption that the European male was the universal subject of history. With the decolonisation of the Third World, the shift of global power from the Atlantic to the Pacific and the internal critique of modernity, there emerged a re-evaluation of cultural identity. The sign of cultural identity became fused with the call for roots in a rootless world, and it began to shift from a sign of weakness and embarrassment to a sign of strength and celebration. From neo-primitivism to multiculturalism, we have witnessed a redrawing of the boundaries of difference. The selective incorporation of the other and the (restricted) permission to celebrate diversity have emerged as the dominant modes for articulating new forms of cultural identity. This inversion of the status of cultural identity has generated a new range of personal choices in private lives and stimulated the gastronomic options in the leisure industry of metropolitan cities, but it has also left within its wake the ghoulish strategies of 'ethnic cleansing' and the lazy tolerance of cultural relativism which, as Warren Christopher noted, is the last refuge of repression. The 'resurgence of ethnicity has also produced the most abject forms of cultural racism and the most extreme reactions against the homogenizing force of globalization' (see Bauman, 1996:26).

More than ever the conceptual terms of cultural identity need to be revisited. It can no longer be used as the concept which legitimates an inward-looking vision and demarcates the exclusivity of social practices. Cultural identity is best understood as a metaphor for the way we understand and make sense of our position in the world. It is an elastic metaphor, one which stretches and embraces the ways in which we live. This broadening and positive re-evaluation of the concept is related to three fundamental changes. First, the distinction between tradition and modern is no longer conceived in terms of a binary opposition. Second, the concept of culture has been given a broader scope. Third, the certitudes of modernity have been revealed as impossible, illusive, distorted, counterproductive and exhausted. In the context of postmodernity, the sign of cultural identity has been embraced as a sign of renewal and depth. Within the context of postmodernism, and its deep fascination with difference, the sign of cultural identity has shifted from a signifier of loss to one of surplus. It stands apart from the idealised subject of early modernity, the square-jawed, forward-looking and techno-driven individual that adorned the posters of both socialist and nationalist regimes.

Mixture and experimentation, displacement and reconfiguration, collage and juxtaposition, have become the cultural practices which are now seen as most expressive of our times. While the project of identity was once seen as leading towards stability and durability, and the settled citizen was the subject of history, the project of identity is now preoccupied with, as Zygmunt Bauman (1996:26) reminds us, how to maximise mobility and minimise attachment, and the exemplary subject is now seen as a migrant, an exile, a stranger. Identities are made on the move. Cultural survival is increasingly defined according to the ability to keep moving. Forms of identity, Bauman argues, such as the stroller, the vagabond, the tourist and the player, which were once only found on the margins of society or experienced during the liminal moments of personal development, are now constituted as the lifestyles which are most suited to the contingencies of the postmodern condition. In this context the reconceptualisation of cultural identity in the guise of the hybrid, creolised, diasporic subject has presented a number of very positive gains. It has enabled the debates on identity to go beyond the binary logic of us and them, it has presented a new mode of internalising the fragments of modernity while also excavating marginalised traditions, and it has encouraged a 'passionate research' into the intellectual challenges of the time without disengaging the body from its emotional range. Cultural identity is thereby defined by the way ideas and practices which have crossed frontiers find new homes; it is a way of coming to terms with the past without ignoring the pressures of the present, an expression of belonging which does not lock the individual into a single place. *The dream of a single home is gone, but in has come the promise of multiple affiliation. The image of integrated and unified being has been replaced by a process of translation which is marked by a consciousness that is more open to the contradictory passages of becoming. The integrity of traditions which were previously premised on spurious notions of purity is now being traced out in terms of the complex crossovers and intersections of cultural exchange.* These new conjunctions and innovations in cultural identity have heightened what Edward Said (1993:336) calls 'contrapuntal, sympathetic and concrete' perspectives, which may ultimately enable us slowly to dismantle the hierarchies of a colonising mentality.

9

'Out there' and 'in here': towards resolving the global–indigenous debate

Ramaswami Harindranath

One of Anthony Giddens's conceptualisations of the nature of globalisation highlights some of the fiercest debates surrounding the global–local dialectic. In suggesting that globalisation is 'not just an "out there" phenomenon. It refers not only to the emergence of large-scale world systems, but to transformations in the very texture of everyday life. It is an "in-here" phenomenon, affecting even intimacies of personal identity' (1996:367), Giddens draws attention to the constitution of global forces and their relationship with local societies and cultures. Though admittedly Giddens's primary concern here is not with the perceived link between global forces and local non-Western cultures, it is, of course, this very relationship which is the object of scrutiny and theoretical concern for those academics and researchers who are interested in issues of global economics, cultural imperialism, modernity and development, media empires, Westernisation and representation of the other in Western texts and museums, to name only a few.

Underlying this variety of concerns is the question of whether globalisation – the buzzword of the 1990s and a term with which no self-respecting cultural studies academic would profess not to be familiar – creates homogenisation: a slow, insidious spread of one 'superior' culture aided by the 'juggernaut of modernity' and international capitalism, drowning other, indigenous, more 'authentic' cultures; or whether, on the contrary, globalisation causes the opposite: the further fragmentation and diversification of cultural differences, aided by a self-conscious assertion of collective identities based on ethnic, national, religious, or linguistic exclusivity and difference. There are those, like Axford (1995), who believe that to conceive of globalisation as resulting in either of these eventualities is simplistic: 'Fragmentation and homogenization are both apparent in the global system, and neither is an imposter; and just as it is possible to underestimate the forces of cultural resistance and systemic transformation, so it is easy to overstate the degree of entropy in the Western cultural account as a global geoculture' (p. 159). Yet another position is adopted by Amin who, using Held's idea of the reciprocal effects of global and local, argues forcefully that globalisation 'should not be misconstrued or demonized as an "out there" phenomenon standing above, and set to destroy, the geography of territorial states, economies and identities' (1997:129). To him, the 'multiple and assymetric interdependencies' which characterise the global–local connectivity imply that it is wrong to consider either the global or the local as separate spheres: 'to think of the global as flows of dominance and transformation and the local as fixities of tradition and continuity is to miss the point' (1997:129).

This slight caricaturing of the different positions with regard to the global–indigenous relationship is deliberate: I want to suggest that beneath them and holding them up are assumptions which need to be interrogated, political stances which require to be clarified. This chapter attempts to do this in a slightly roundabout fashion, since *en route* I would like to avail of the opportunity to voice my own preoccupations with these issues, which are coloured by my concerns as an academic from the developing world teaching and researching in the 'metropolitan' West – the contours of, as Rajan (1997) puts it, my 'geography of intellectual labor' (p. 596). As a Third World academic in another place my own 'post-colonial' (a term whose implications we shall explore later) history is linked to the questions and concerns which form the bases of my intellectual efforts. The growing interest in cultural studies within higher education institutions in the developing world, particularly India, calls for a re-examination of the frameworks which constitute the field. This chapter is therefore more exploratory and meditative than conclusive and unequivocal.

One of the manifestations of cultural imperialism is considered to be in the form of global media: the patterns of its ownership and control, its reach, the global flow of news, images and programme material, and the likely hegemonic potential of global media content. The latter ties media imperialism to concerns regarding the international spread of capitalist values representing largely Western commercial interests. For some time now it has been argued (Dorfman and Mattelart, 1975; Schiller, 1979) that global media networks and empires support and maintain the new form of colonialism which is less about occupation of geographical spaces and more about the exploitation of foreign markets and workers. Global media products are seen to herald and contribute to the creation of global consumerism, benefiting transnational corporations, some of which own and control both media products and the means of dissemination and broadcasting. This is obviously not an uncontested position. While political economists present convincing data concerning the increasing dependency of the developing world on the West for support ranging from technology to news services (Boyd-Barrett, 1982), and the increasing concentration of ownership and control of global media production and representation (Schiller, 1991; Kellner, 1992), whose ideology and hegemonic discourses reflect specifically Western interests, counterarguments are posed by those involved in audience research (Liebes and Katz, 1993). The latter question the former's acceptance that ideological content of the media text necessarily transforms audiences into dupes who unquestioningly assume the position dictated by the text. A few of these researchers assume extreme positions on the continuum from passive receptors to active audience, arguing that the essentially polysemic nature of texts creates a 'semiotic democracy' which undermines the easy assumption that audiences merely absorb the 'dominant' meaning of the text (Fiske, 1986).

In many ways this debate remains unresolved, and the continuing efforts by researchers in both camps to reinforce their arguments imply that the debate may be unresolvable. On the one hand, those who continue to put forward the political economy perspective point to the increasing concentration of owner-ship and control of global media as evidence of a global 'synchronisation' of cultures (Hamelink, 1994), building on Wallerstein's division of nation states into central and peripheral countries which to a large extent reproduces the coloniser–colonised relationship. Intrinsic to this is the belief that the repre-sentation of consumerist aspirations and Western ideas 'out there' influences local cultural values 'in here'. On the opposing side are those who produce evi-dence of 'oppositional' and critical readings of various media texts and genres (Liebes and Katz, 1993; Gillespie, 1995), arguing not only that it is wrong to assume an uncritical acceptance of the dominant ideologies contained in the text, but also that different interpretations by audiences from different social positions and cultures indicate a process of 'indigenisation' – absorption of foreign material into local cultures, thus rendering them relatively harmless. Gillespie goes even further to assert that media products are used creatively by youth in Southall, London (and by extension elsewhere in the world) actively to construct their hybrid identities. I shall return to this later; but it is impor-tant to note here that these debates concerning media imperialism are indica-tive of larger and more fundamental issues and questions.

This quarrel within the family of international communication scholars echoes the theoretical and empirical debates concerning the 'effects' of glob-alisation (see Sreberny-Mohammadi, 1991). From, first, prognostications of doom riding on interpretations of globalisation as the triumphant worldwide spread of capitalism and Western domination (creating one 'global culture' and destroying not only alternative forms of economy, but also local auton-omy) to, second, globalisation as the celebration of differences, as the further augmentation of local identities and values – as Featherstone puts it, a post-modernist recognition of the 'diversity, variety and richness of popular and local discourses, codes and practices which resist and play-back systemicity and order' (1990:2), and, then, a third position which calls for a more naunced exploration of the global–local connectivity (Amin, 1997:123), there are fun-damental disparities in the manner in which the process linking the global and the local, the global and the indigenous, has been interpreted and theorised. Giddens's (1990) definition of globalisation as 'the intensification of world-wide social relations which link distant localities in such a way that local hap-penings are shaped by events occurring many miles away and vice versa' (p. 64) clearly underlines the process of globalisation as 'dialectical . . . because local happenings may move in an obverse direction from the very distanciated relations that shape them' (p. 64). This is the notion which Amin builds on, recognising that it acknowledges the complexity of the local–global links. The rest of this chapter will touch on a few of the implications of this idea in the search for a more adequate theorisation of cultural and media imperialism. (*cont. p. 156*)

Globalisation theory

The term 'globalisation' has become as fashionable in recent years as 'post-modernism' was in the 1980s, so much so that one commentator suggests it 'may be the concept of the 1990s, a key idea by which we understand the transition of human society into the third millennium' (Waters, 1995:1). Like postmodernism, it has been used across a wide range of academic disciplines – sociology, political theory, international relations, geography, media and cultural studies – as well as in the discourses of business corporations, governments, environmentalists and journalists. And, also like postmodernism, it is a term that has been used fairly loosely, with different assumptions and implications depending on the context. Thus what Ted Turner of CNN might understand by 'globalisation' – roughly the global reach of his media business – is very different from what a social theorist such as Anthony Giddens means – apart from the common reference to 'world embracing' processes.

Going beyond this lowest common denominator, however, we can say that globalisation generally refers to the rapidly developing process of complex interconnections between societies, cultures, institutions and individuals worldwide. It is a process which involves a compression of time and space (Harvey, 1989), shrinking distances through a dramatic reduction in the time taken – either physically or representationally – to cross them, so making the world seem smaller and in a sense bringing human beings 'closer' to one another. But it is also a process which 'stretches' social relations – removing the relationships which govern our everyday lives from local contexts to global ones.

There is no shortage of examples of these processes: the complex interdependency of the global money markets shifting millions of dollars around the world in seconds; the 'global assembly line' of the motor industry producing components from factories on every continent; the global environmental risk revealed by the fall-out from disasters such as Chernobyl and the fears of global warming, the pollution of the oceans or genetically modified foods; television pictures of the war in Kosovo beamed live into living rooms around the world; the growth of the web.

Immediate and intuitive responses to all this frequently polarise into the optimistic and the sceptical. On the one hand there is the rather awe-struck techno-enthusiasm of *Wired* magazine which launched its first UK edition in 1995 with a quotation from Thomas Paine: 'We have it in our power to begin the world over again.' (Interestingly, the UK edition was short lived, demonstrating that the US *Wired* was already a global commodity.) This position aligns with a revived interest in the ideas of Marshall McLuhan (*Wired*'s 'patron saint'), in particular his stress on communications media and his notion of the 'global village' (McLuhan, 1987). But on the other hand we find the extreme scepticism of some neo-Marxist theorists who would assimilate the whole process to the relentless extension of the global capitalist system. Globalisation, then, is often intuitively linked to ideas of cultural imperialism.

The intention of globalisation theory is to make coherent sense of all these events without such immediate polarisations. Thus globalisation theorists tend to see the process as ambiguous in its cultural and political implications, and best understood in 'dialectical' terms – as involving tendencies towards *both* cultural massification *and* differentiation, and having the potential for *both* social unification *and* fragmentation. Among the growing body of theorists of globalisation, two sociologists have been particularly influential.

Roland Robertson, one of the first to use the term in a consistent way in the mid 1980s, has developed a considerable body of theory (collected in Robertson, 1992). His work is wide ranging and difficult to summarise, but essentially culturally inflected and concerned with the way the world is both constituted and experienced as 'a single place'. His analysis centres on a model of this global 'unicity' relating four dimensions: individuals, national societies, the world system of societies and 'humankind' as a whole. Though criticised for its lack of reference to the political–economic basis of globalisation, Robertson's work has been influential, particularly in cultural theory.

Anthony Giddens's work contrasts strongly with Robertson's, not least in tying the development of globalisation firmly to that of social *modernity*. For Giddens, the institutional forms of modern societies are 'inherently globalising'. Industrialism involves 'a worldwide diffusion of machine technology', and in particular produces globalising communications technologies. Capitalism inherently tends to become transnational in both the division of labour involved in its production process and the market it creates. And the nation state system is globally encompassing: there is no geographical area of the world – apart from the polar regions – which is not claimed as the political domain of some nation state. Behind all this, according to Giddens, stand certain dynamic properties peculiar to modern societies and marking them off from earlier social formations. Perhaps the most significant of these properties is that of 'disembedding', which Giddens describes as 'the lifting out of social relations from local contexts of interaction and their restructuring across indefinite spans of time-space' (1990:21). The development of money as an abstract medium of exchange is a prime example of a 'disembedding mechanism' allowing economic relations to be 'stretched' across large tracts of time–space. Thus, for Giddens, concrete instances of globalisation such as the global money markets can be traced to fundamental and rather 'abstract' properties of modern societies: the way in which they are able to co-ordinate time and space. In one formulation (1994) he hones down his definition of globalisation simply to 'action at distance'.

Although Giddens stresses that globalisation is a *multidimensional* consequence of modernity, there are times when he hints at the particular significance of communications technology in the 'disembedding' of social relations. (For example, he suggests (1994) that we might fix globalisation's point of origin at the first satellite broadcast transmission.) Though not extensively developed, the significance of globalising media technologies implicitly looms large in his – and arguably any – theory of globalisation. And this invites reflection on, for example, the possibilities for emerging forms of global electronically mediated 'communities' of shared cultural experience (Giddens, 1990; Tomlinson, 1994). Such reflection has to be careful not to reduce globalisation to one dimension and certainly has to avoid the sometimes extravagant claims made for the cultural significance of the particular technology of the moment – for example, for the internet. But, at the very least, globalisation theory needs to be able to engage with that striking, if taken for granted, feature of cultural modernity noted by Joshua Meyrowitz (1985:283) that, 'television . . . now escorts children across the globe even before they have permission to cross the street'.

John Tomlinson

Nationalism and the intellectuals

To return to the example of international communication, satellite broadcasting contributes to the creation of a seemingly borderless world in terms not only of the availability of nationally and culturally diverse audiences but also of instantaneous transmission of globally covered events, while new technologies such as the internet add to this the dimension of transnationalism, facilitating the maintenance of global diasporic cultural identities (Mitra, 1997). Given the various arguments relating to the debate concerning media or cultural imperialism, their apparently selective interpretation, as seen in recent instances of proclamations of local cultural authenticity, is deeply ironic.

The arguments made by the champions of Third World interests are being used by political leaders in the developing world – in countries such as Malaysia and India – to justify the adoption of (or, in the case of India, the arguments for) isolationist and protective measures ostensibly to 'protect' local cultures from Western influence. Buoyed by, and in turn supporting, nationalist ideologies and discourses, such legislations ride on exclusionary politics in the name of aspirations to protect local 'traditions'. Yet, even within these two countries the nationalist picture assumes different colours: while Malaysian control of satellite channels is blatantly disregarded by the peoples of Sarawak in a gesture of defiance which illustrates their own inchoate separatist ideologies, in India the fundamentalist BJP government elected in 1997 saw all representations of non-Hindu values as invidious. An opposing, but equally problematic, position is adopted in arguments which perceive the introduction of satellite broadcasting in regions such as China as the necessary precursor to democratic reform, all in the name of consumer 'choice', with Rupert Murdoch as the unlikely champion of values of democracy.

There is an abundance of academic literature on the topic of nationalism and national identity examining such cases (Schlesinger, 1991 is a good example) in the light of globalisation theories; of how, for instance, both supranational forces from above and separatist discourses from below are threatening, and indeed actually fragmenting, nation states. However, in order to fully comprehend recent developments even in terms of global media empires and local audiences – the influences of 'out there' on events 'in here' – it is necessary to re-examine both normative concepts, such as nationalism, and the politics of global intellectual production.

The ideas of nationalism and national culture are fundamental aspects of indigenous writing during the colonial period. Nationalist figures as diverse as Fanon and Gandhi highlighted, in different ways, the importance of the idea of a 'nation' to the struggle for freedom. This nation was constructed on ideas of local tradition, forms of knowledge and value systems – opposing overtly those of the colonial powers – and which were then called upon to contribute to national self sufficiency (all of which to Gandhi was symbolised by the 'home spun'). Developments on the global scale during the latter part of the twentieth century, however, have made international borders more 'porous', calling into question this notion of a nation as coterminous with a single cultural identity, implicitly demanding a more sophisticated concepualising of culture and imperialism. Moreover, the whole concept of nationalism is now received with a great deal less sympathy, since it is seen as being often based on fundamentalist and politically extreme discourses.

This poses a dilemma for the intellectuals from the developing world – the former colonies – attempting to find an alternative concept to nationalism with which to oppose cultural imperialism. It has not been an easy task – the argument that ideas of development and modernisation, which were foisted on the newly independent states in the 1950s and 1960s, were instances of the continuation of colonial domination, for example, has rarely been accompanied by viable substitutes. DuBois's (1991) convincing Foucauldian critique of the rhetoric of development still uses a Western paradigm (which itself, as we shall see, has been critiqued as being imperialistic); Shiva's (1989) work illustrates attempts to provide a more 'organic' intervention in the form of alternative epistemologies to that of Western science, and she argues her case persuasively, examining the notion of environment from the perspective of Indian (largely Hindu) philosophy. But these are interventions at the intellectual level, not pragmatic solutions.

What we are faced with here is essentially the question of how to engage critically with what is happening 'in here' in terms of 'out there' – the local–global connectivity – and how to take on the task of presenting the case of the local and the indigenous in the face of universalist discourses. Discussions of the indigenous in terms of 'cultural nationalism' often favour 'tradition' (local culture) over modernity, perceived as Western and imperialistic. But these pose problems on different levels. Thematically, the bringing together of 'nationalism' and 'culture' allows for theoretical slippage. As Ahmad (1992) argues, such categories have an 'inherent tendency towards national and civilizational singularization. The ideology of cultural nationalism is based explicitly on this singularizing tendency and lends itself much too easily to parochialism, inverse racism, and indigenist obscurantism' (p. 8).

Such 'singularising' tendencies are much in evidence in the rhetoric of fundamentalist positions from the white supremacists in the United States to the Hindu nationalists in the current Indian government. Cultural essentialism is the common category among such diverse cases. These could be interpreted as further evidence of the 'fragmentation' that has resulted from globalisation, as indicative of the undermining of the nation state by local attempts to reaffirm identities – an example of the seemingly paradoxical nature of the local–global connectivity. But responses from theorists have been far from convincing. As Appadurai (1996) observes, despite the increasing engagement by anthropologists with the issue of nationalism and the nation state, we have yet to see an adequate framework for relating the global, the national and the local.

These developments are further compounded by positions adopted by a few theorists from the South. Ahmad is perhaps a bit harsh in his estimation that:

'cultural nationalism' resonates . . . frequently with 'tradition', simply inverting the tradition/modernity binary of the modernization theorists in an indigenist direction, so that 'tradition' is said to be for the 'Third World' always better than 'modernity', which then opens up a space for defence of the most obscurantist positions in the name of cultural nationalism. (1992:9)

But his criticism is valid insofar as the idea of indigenous 'tradition' is accepted as self-evidently anti-imperialistic, as the source of anti-colonial struggles which are the fountainhead for 'local' values and ideas necessary for constructing an alternative framework to that based on Western values.

This is not to say that attempts by theorists from the South are doomed from the start, that it is impossible for them to identify a viable alternative. While Ahmad's polemic stems from a Marxist perspective, my concern arises from a need for more assurance with regard to the espousal of indigenous alternatives. This is obviously crucial to the debate on cultural imperialism, to theorising the global–local connectivity: on what basis can we legitimately construct a critique of the imposition of value systems from 'out there'? How do we theorise what is 'in here'?

Some scholars, such as Nandy, have attempted to rehabilitate the alternative theoretical frameworks which provided the intellectual grounding for anti-colonial struggles, building on their historical relevance and locating their legitimacy in the argument that a similar set of criteria exist in neo-colonialism. Nandy's (1994) stance is overtly anti-Western in its suspicion of scientism which, for instance, often underpins the rhetoric of development. But his return to Gandhian principles can be seen as an instance of what Ahmad (1992:321, note 8) condemns as inverted logic which simply privileges tradition over modernity as self-evidently superior simply *because* it is its binary opposite. Positions like that of Nandy, while their efforts are to achieve the very opposite, are nevertheless worryingly proximate to the nationalist and communalist politics of the right in its invocation of 'tradition'.

Nationalism as a unitary force is itself a flawed critical concept. While it projects a (mythical?) locally based oppositional stance to the logic of the global, nationalist ideology conceals deep divisions and inequalities within the nation state. This dimension has been highlighted in the historical analysis of the colonial period by the Subaltern Studies Collective, which, identifying in the power structure a local elite who supported the status quo of colonial domination, attempted to unearth writings and other historical evidence of the struggle by local non-elites: an alternative history, in other words, examining the realities of the lives of the 'subaltern', the relatively powerless whose cultural and social identities can be traced to the pre-colonial period.

Post-colonial studies

Subaltern studies, and the whole post-colonial project within the humanities and, to a lesser extent, the social sciences, thus starts from an informed critique of nationalism, which was for some time 'designated . . . as the determinate source of ideological energy in the Third World' (Ahmad, 1992:68). This appears a reasonable premise, since, as we saw earlier, the uncritical celebration of nationalism (or what is argued to be 'cultural nationalism') as *de facto* anti-imperialistic is problematic. The project's enterprise to reveal the voice of the subaltern behind conventional accounts of colonial history, to re-present history by including the accounts of those who had been silenced, tacitly recognises the flaws in theoretical accounts which treat concepts such as 'nation' and 'tradition'. It acknowledges the assumption of the heterogeneity of the colonised. The attempts to exhume subaltern experiences during the colonial era consequently seem, at least on the surface, a commendable enterprise. The reconstitution of the past in terms of the grassroots and the marginal appears a potentially enabling condition for the critical examination of similar aspects of local worlds in relation to contemporary forces of globalisation and imperialism.

In the case of post-colonial studies the problem originates from a different direction – that of the language and epistemology of critical discourse as well as the politics of the institutional and geographic location of the critic. Does the critic *enable* the subaltern to 'speak' or does he or she perform a ventriloquist function, speaking *for* the subaltern? From what position does he or she speak, and to whom?

Some of the issues have been raised by leading figures within post-colonial studies. Spivak's famous essay asking the fundamental question, 'Can the subaltern speak?' (1988), questions the theoretical foundations of subaltern studies. She recognises the political validity of the 'people's history' as opposed to elitist accounts. However, in her view – and to paraphrase her highly naunced argument – the subaltern who speaks ceases to be one: the inability to 'know and speak itself' is a defining characteristic of the 'true subaltern'.

On the other hand, Spivak's position itself has come to be critiqued. Parry (1987; reproduced in Ashcroft *et al.*, 1995) is not convinced by Spivak's conceptualisation of the subaltern woman as doubly oppressed, her advocating of 'a strategy of reading which will speak to' the colonised woman dominated both by the colonial power and by the local patriarchy. But Parry's strongest criticism is that Spivak is deliberately deaf 'to the native voice where it is to be heard', that 'Spivak in her own writings severely restricts (eliminates?) the space in which the colonized can be written back into history' (1987:40; see also Spivak, 1988).

Dirlik (1994) examines the term 'post-colonial' from the perspective of both the intellectual and the practice of literary and cultural criticism and finds both problematic. He presents two basic arguments in his critique of the present state of post-colonial theory: first, that it 'begins' when 'Third World intellectuals have arrived in First World academe', its popularity has to do with the 'increased visibility of academic intellectuals of Third World origin as pacesetters in cultural criticism' (p. 329). The significance of the location of these theorists and practitioners of post-colonial cultural criticism lies for Dirlik in their consequent distancing from the pressing issues of neo-imperialism and their retreat into post-structuralist abstraction. He shares this sentiment with Ahmad, who bemoans what he (following Perry Anderson) calls the 'exhorbitation of language' evident in postmodern (and post-colonial?) theories. Dirlik's other accusation is even more serious: that global capitalism, the enabling condition for the advent of these theorists (as well as their location and transnational status as migrant intellectuals), is also the reason why 'a concept that is intended to achieve a radical revision in our comprehension of the world should appear to be complicitous in the consecration of hegemony. . . . [T]he term [post-colonial] mystifies both politically and methodologically a situation that represents not the abolition but the reconfiguration of earlier forms of domination' (p. 331). This is a grave charge. To put it in the context of our present concerns, Dirlik's criticism is that the intellectuals from the former colonies ('out there') who are now resident in the centres of Western academe ('in here') are unable or, worse, unwilling to engage with the realities of their places of origin and the continuing political, economic and social domination of them by the West. The main reason for this is that their metropolitan privilege – based not only on geographical and institutional location, as in the instance of university academics (and the economic benefits which accrue as a result), but also on their intellectual and theoretical orientations (e.g. following the current fashions of post-structuralism and postmodernism) – has made them willing partners in 'the reconfiguration of earlier forms of domination'. 'Postcolonial criticism', Dirlik suggests, 'has been silent about its own status as a possible ideological effect of a new world situation after colonialism' (1994:331). This ideological effect may be the substitution of abstract theory building for engaged culture building.

In the eyes of some critics, post-colonialism, which originated as a more sensitive substitute for the term 'Third World', has become in its institutional manifestation so reified that it no longer makes any distinction between different post-colonial experiences. McClintock (1994) makes several charges: ' "post-colonial" is haunted by the very figure of linear "development" that it sets out to dismantle'; 'theory is . . . shifted from the binary axis of power to the binary axis of time [which] does not distinguish between the beneficiaries of colonialism (the ex-colonisers) and the casualties of colonialism (the ex-colonised)'; and 'the term [post-colonial] also signals a reluctance to surrender the privilege of seeing the world in terms of a singular and a historical abstraction' (pp. 254–5). The most worrying development for her is that, first, the theory does not account for the diversity of post-independence experiences of different regions – the singularity which has come to characterise 'post-colonial' has difficulty with the heterogeneity of the histories and social contexts which make up the 'Third World' – and, second, few theorists engage with the new, contemporary forms of colonialism evident in regions such as Central and South America.

Radical rethinking and border zones

To summarise, I have outlined, all too briefly, two broad sets of concerns which fall under the rubric of globalisation: the rather inconclusive debates regarding cultural imperialism, and the other academic field which has become a battleground of ideas – post-colonial theory. It seems to me that these two areas of inquiry can usefully benefit from each other's concerns and conceptual strengths. As we saw earlier, the cultural imperialism thesis has fallen between the stools of political economy on the macro level – pointing an accusing finger at the media conglomerates and their global reach – and micro-level audience research which relies, for example, on qualitative analysis of interviews with sample respondents. Both sides have strengthened their own camps, with the flags of capitalist ideology and audience autonomy flying on the respective poles. But their quarrel appears to be based on spurious grounds. While, on the one hand, critics of the idea of media imperialism assert that it is merely grounded in a variant of the old 'effects' hypothesis (in which behaviourist research was conducted on the possible harmful effects of television and film), and on the questionable presumption of the existence of 'authentic' cultures and essentialised identities (Sreberny-Mohammadi, 1991), those who present evidence of cultural imperialism argue that the entire theoretical edifice of the opposition is shaky, whimsical and inadequate. There is a marked absence of a dialogue, suggesting a retrenching of the 'in here' camp against the 'out there' one. In order for a conversation to take place which would enable the exploration of the global–local connectivity, a dismantling and reorientation of the theoretical concerns is a necessary prerequisite. We may do well to visit post-colonial theory again to achieve this.

As we have seen, the entire field of post-colonial studies appears to be in turmoil and it seems to have lost its way, stepping out from its original intentions and aspirations towards critical reflections on the state of the world after colonialism. It is useful, however, to remind ourselves of the original themes of post-colonial discourse: 'one of the distinct effects of the recent emergence of post-colonial criticism has been to force a radical re-thinking and re-formulation of forms of knowledge and social identities authored and authorized by colonialism and western domination. For this reason, it has also created a ferment in the field of knowledge' (Prakash, quoted in Dirlik, 1994:333). From the different charges levelled against the present state of post-colonial criticism it becomes evident that the time is ripe for another theoretical shake-up, to raise questions about explanatory adequacy and political responsibilities in the light of the desire to re-ignite the 'radical re-thinking' mentioned by Prakash.

I believe that this rethinking of theoretical orthodoxy can be helped on its way by audience research in international communication. The subaltern *can* speak. Ethnographically oriented reception analysis, which goes beyond the comparison of audience interpretations of specific content to the examination of the socio-cultural context of media reception, could lead to a proper investigation of the new structures of domination which exist in the developing countries. As Rosaldo (1993) and others have reminded us, the anthropological enterprise itself has to be purged of its colonial legacy within which culture was a monolithic entity and the inhabitants of the colonies were usually considered inherently inferior to the anthropologists. More recently however, there has been a growing avowal of more complex 'cultural borderlands', a notion in which 'the fiction of the uniformly shared culture increasingly seems more tenuous than useful. Although most metropolitan typifications continue to suppress border zones, human cultures are neither necessarily coherent nor always homogeneous' (Rosaldo, 1993:207). Such a conception coincides with the new ethnographic move from 'closed communities' to the idea of 'open borders', reconstituting the task of social analysis from that of discovering law-like intractable variables to exploring heterogeneity and the way culture changes and is changed by both human behaviour and structural forces.

Given this turn in ethnography favouring the investigation of heterogeneity and change, the theoretical dimension of the cultural imperialism debate can and ought to be reconstituted to take on board some of the insights of post-colonial studies. One such is Spivak's re-presentation of the domination of the colonised not as mere subjugation but as a form of hegemonic appropriation of the colonised population into the discursive frameworks of domination:

> For the purpose of administration the native was constructed as a 'nearly selved' other of the European and not as its binary opposite . . . Instead of recounting a struggle between a monolithic, near-deliberative colonial power and an unidenti-fied oppressed mass, this reconstitution displays a process more insidious than naked repression, since here the native is prevailed upon to internalise as self-knowledge, the knowledge concocted by the master. (Parry, 1987:37–8).

It is obvious what such a reconstitution will contribute to the debate on media and cultural imperialism. In the place of the 'effects' of the global media on local cultures, conceived as an imposition, such a formulation enables us to begin rearranging the ways in which the links between 'out there' and 'in here' have thus far been conceptualised, and to start understanding and theorising this relationship as more subtle and insidious. This has obvious implications for the empirical aspects of the ethnographic exercise but, conversely, as I have argued elsewhere (Harindranath, 1998), it also provides us with a more sophisticated framework to explain interpretive differences and distinctions, in the contexts of 'local' media use, as reflecting new forms of domination and internal colonisation.

This reconceptualisation is necessary in order to give the subaltern a voice, to place this voice in the context of indigenous knowledges, traditions and lifeworlds. In the place of an 'imagined' tradition then, the post-colonial ethnographer would have the 'native's' own voice. What Lele demands as the (migrant) Indian intellectuals' task – 'to return to their own past, and be able to appreciate the rationality of the discourses of the underprivileged embed-ded in their own tradition and encrusted in the sedimentations of centuries of hegemonic and ideological distortions' (1993:69) – can be extended to include post-colonial intellectuals and the particular histories of their regions of origin in general. In addition, this investigation into 'the production of locality', as Appadurai (1996: ch. 9) terms it, which would recognise the role of the media in that production, would form part of the ethnographic study of diasporic communities where the spatial dimensions which constitute post-colonial regions give way to more heavily inscribed social and cultural dimensions.

What I am highlighting here is the urgent need for more imaginative theo-retical and empirical interventions into the global–local connectivity. As McClintock suggests, 'a proliferation of historically naunced theories and strategies is called for, which may enable us to engage more effectively in the politics of affiliation, and the currently catastrophic dispensations of power' (1994:266). In this regard, a marriage between post-colonial theory and inter-national communication research is devoutly to be wished, the consummation of which might be able to provide answers to questions concerning, among others, the reciprocal relations between 'out there' and 'in here'.

The Brazilian telenovela: a case study

Introduction

Picture this: a dusty, tree-lined street in Salvador, north-east Brazil, Portugese colonial house facades crumbling with age, cobbled pavements now pitted and holed, spilling white sand. On the corner stands a McDonalds like every other you've ever seen. In front of it stands a street hawker, selling candomblé charms – coloured strips of ribbon, tiny metal figa or talismans, miniature drums – evoking a massive revival of interest in that Afro-Brazilian religious cult. This is the still unsolved mystery about globalisation. Does it lead to 'McDonaldisation' or to the resurgence of different 'cultural identities'? Both McDonalds and the tourist version of candomblé are merely metaphors here but behind them lie forceful realities – of a global culture of sameness and a local resurgence of difference.

Once the great colonial powers repressed local differences 'out there' and the metropolitan European centres of Lisbon, London and the rest levitated above the question of cultural identity, because 'culture' was not yet a word in our sense and if the concept existed at all it was simply as the taken-for-granted tastes that characterised those centres of power (or more accurately those who held power there). When they were considered at all, the ways of life of the colonised – in the Americas, Africa, the Orient – were viewed as fixed residual traditions and practices, hung over from a past that the colonial project had swept through and beyond, and as objects of exotic fascination. As such, they could later be rediscovered as representing an almost mythical integrity to juxtapose against the decadence of the colonial and the modern, for those whose faith in the latter was waning. But that was still to consign the cultural identity of the other to some never-never land outside of history, as 'primitive', premodern and as the preservation of traditions rather than something living, adapting and forward looking.

When new nation states emerged out of the old empires, the question of cultural identity often became one of constructing a new sameness to hold things together and fill the supposed vacuum left by colonial cultural occupation. Instead of an eruption of diversity, countries such as Brazil saw sustained attempts by new regimes to impose the illusion of a common culture – often through the new media of broadcasting which developed at roughly the same time – and to suppress alternatives (in Brazil candomblé temples were frequently raided by the police during the military dictatorship of the 1960s and 1970s). It was not until the phenomenon of globalisation began to take hold in the late twentieth century – the interconnection of the world's economies, the wiring together of a new global media system, an end to the isolation of the nation state (and to its capacity to get away with murder, if it chose, out of sight of the rest of the world) – that cultural identity came into view as a new sort of problem, poised between McDonaldisation and the resurgence of indigenous cultural practices.

An enduring image for Brazilians is that of Eriberto Freire on their TV screens in July 1992. One of President Collor's drivers, Freire, wearing a dark suit, white shirt and thin tie, perspired under the TV lights and leaned nervously towards a microphone, a tall glass of water on the table before him and suited figures walling him in behind. This was TV Globo's coverage of a congresssional hearing into abuses of power by the president, and Freire unexpectedly catalogued a series of illegal presidential pay-offs to cronies. This appearance, and an interview Freire gave to the Brazilian current affairs magazine *Veja*, turned into the country's equivalent of the USA's Watergate scandal and 'Collorgate' permanently tainted most Brazilians' optimism about their post-dictatorship leaders. The national broadcaster, TV Globo, had been massively strengthened during the period of dictatorship, its propaganda potential consolidated by technological development and investment and owner Roberto Marinho moving comfortably through the corridors of power. But now it was broadcasting a testimony and subsequent impeachment proceedings that would topple a president. Far from claiming any crusading zeal for the truth, Marinho simply noted that TV Globo, out of economic self interest, would 'follow' whichever was most powerful – the politicians or the people. Like Televisa in Mexico, TV Globo had become a huge nationally monopolistic broadcaster, exporting large amounts of programming, and representing a new sort of power in a globalised world – the power of economically self-interested media 'empires', now largely unhooked from past political masters and from the propaganda role in the nation state.

It is against this background that the popular telenovelas, Brazilian TV soap operas, have to be seen. Exported to and dubbed in Spain, Russia, China, Poland and elsewhere, the telenovelas remain a central feature of Brazilian popular culture. Indeed, the huge impact of such popular cultural forms has forced a reconsideration, among many Latin American media researchers, of previous claims for various forms of alternative media as the sites of more 'authentic' popular expression – whether this was defined socially (e.g. tin miners' radio in Bolivia, Mayan women's media collectives in Guatemala) or religiously (e.g. various forms of broadcasting loosely associated with 'liberation theology'). Indeed, the Latin American phenomenon of 'syncretic' religious cults, such as candomblé in Brazil, may have provided a sort of cultural model through which to understand a different kind of popular expression. Just as candomblé, in the colonial period, 'disguised' its West African deities as Catholic saints, so the telenovela began to be seen as some sort of 'disguised' syncretic intermingling of many interests, capable of supporting local community health and family planning programmes while also being blended into a gobally marketable form. A guilty conscience is still often detectable among researchers of popular media in Latin America, who fear that they may be legitimising escapism and colluding with the profit motive of the media empires while real social and cultural problems proliferate. But 'reading' the telenovela as an inescapable context for questions of cultural identity remains an important task.

Telenovela as a cultural form

Some cultural manifestations in a society turn out to play a central role in its members' 'imaginary' (the constructed world of communal aspiration) – like knots in the network of culture. They occupy a privileged space in people's daily lives and can have a highly integrating effect in the processes of cultural identity. They can promote interrelation among a society's members, independently of the striking differences set by ethnicity, social class, gender or generation. They turn out to be, in some sense, true 'total social facts', as Marcell Mauss defined those cultural manifestations in which the most diversified social levels are represented. It may be said that these cultural forms bring shared memory and a symbolic rearticulation of differences to a culture.

In contemporary Brazil, one of the cultural forms which is able to integrate, on the imaginary level, the most diversified social classes – constructing a source of shared recognitions that sustains cultural cohabitation – is the *telenovela* (see Rowe and Schelling, 1991:part 2).

What is the Brazilian telenovela like? It is a genre of television narrative fiction that appeared in 1950, simultaneously with the implantation of television itself in the country, and that since the 1970s has achieved the largest audiences among all television programmes. The PROJAC studio complex in Jacarepaguá, Rio de Janeiro, rivals Hollywood in its heyday as a factory for producing entertainment – in this case the telenovela. It has sustained unmatched audience levels, not only in Brazil but wherever it has been exported, and it has become Brazil's third main export product. At the same time as it achieved national and international recognition, the Brazilian telenovela, whose origins lie both in the American soap operas and in the Latin American variant created in Cuba, began defining its own unique features. Like the soaps generally, the telenovelas are romantic stories with a limited number of characters who move in familiar surroundings, acting out personal conflicts. They do not have a series pattern based on unitary episodes containing a relatively self-contained story every time. The Brazilian telenovela's extended narratives may last the best part of a year, with daily episodes which are broken off at their highest point of interest, suspense or tension until the next day (in a model that has become well established in Anglo-American television as well).

That is also the telenovela model deployed in Cuba, Mexico and Argentina, where the genre is essentially melodramatic: the characters face exaggerated conflicts involving personal desires and the threatening or settling of social norms. So the successful plots present illegitimate children, unknown parents, adulteries, incest and disputes over inheritances. In Brazil, the telenovelas of the 1950s and 1960s tried to adapt this format, often by having Mexican and Cuban stories imported, translated or copied.

In the late 1960s, however, several factors allowed a more distinctively national appropriation of this form, revealing what is now recognised as the Brazilian telenovela. Among the facts that help explain this transformation, it is first of all necessary to note that several renowned playwrights, scriptwriters (*roteiristas*) and film makers decided, after initial reluctance, to work for the television medium. These artists and intellectuals, many influenced by leftist ideas, brought to the television 'imaginary' a critical vision of Brazilian realities and an interest in representing that naturalistically. Hoping that they could turn the 'escapist' time enjoyed by the telnovela's audience into moments of reflection, those authors, directors and actors made what used to be a minor genre into a product more visibly intent on the comprehension of contemporary social reality. A new model of TV storytelling was thus created in Brazil – one that, even while keeping some elements of the earlier Latin American telenovelas and the American soaps, went well beyond them in its naturalism, extended narrative cohesion, solidly constructed dramaturgy and even, at times, its critical intent. Thus, in contrast with what happened in other countries, in Brazil many of the best playwrights and theatre actors turned to the genre. Playwrights such as Dias Gomes, Braulio Pedroso and Jorge Andrade have contributed to giving the telenovela a serious language and quality.

These authors, however, were not turning to television in this way as an isolated cultural phenomenon – a strong current within Brazilian literature, especially with the modernists who emerged at the beginning of the twentieth century, had already concerned itself with the discovery of 'Brazilianness'. There was an ongoing attempt to create a cultural identity in language, enriched by regionalism, making it possible to identify 'our' likeness and unlikeness, representing the different shades of our supposed identity. This literature, which has outstanding authors such as Mario de Andrade, Graciliano Ramos, Jorge Amado and Erico Veríssimo, is characterised by novels with local colour, extremely rich and detailed descriptions of places and people, and poetic dialogues often concerned to express 'Brazilianness'. Contrary to the more universalist European literature, these Brazilian novels gave birth to a grounded 'imaginary', or shared representational landscape, with strong visual and oral appeal. It can be argued that, contemporary with the development of the mass communication media, modern Brazilian literature displayed the influences of emerging 'languages', such as that of the cinema. Several novels produced out of this cultural moment, such as Gabriela, cravo e canela, have been successful as both book and telenovela. In this respect, the telenovela authors who reinvented the genre in Brazil found their path already opened by literature. There were novels suited to adaptation to an audio-visual language and there was an approach which valued plots with local colour and indigenous realism. In any case, the liaison between the television authors and the modernist writers resulted in unforgettable products that have elevated the status of the Brazilian telenovela.

The political context has also played an important role in this. In the 1960s and 1970s, Brazil underwent a period of military dictatorship, which saw the media, especially television, heavily censored. The authors referred to here needed to use all their creativity to dodge censorship, so that they could critically communicate themes that were considered vital to the political scene. The effort to devise metaphors in order to duck the censors' surveillance produced plots, characters and dialogue of rich – if often oblique – symbolic significance.

Importantly though, the same political situation actually favoured television's development, given that the medium had the potential to integrate the country culturally – a fact that has always been of central interest to dictators. In the attempt to turn television into a means of social control, spreading sanctioned ideas and information, the military government invested heavily in the creation of a widespread national telecommunications network.

The TV channels that took part in that enterprise amassed great benefits to themselves and became Brazil's communication empires, such as the Globo TV network. As a large-scale enterprise, in Latin American terms, and counting on official support for its development, the network owned by Roberto Marinho (who has been dubbed Citizen Kane) was able to transform the production values of the telenovela, making it into a high-gloss, technically excellent product. It evolved in a Hollywood-style production system, with its own dedicated studios, provided with high levels of investment, requiring actors and authors' 'professionalisation' (including exclusive work contracts), public opinion research, and a strong commercial and marketing infrastructure. Undoubtedly all this entrepreneurial apparatus was the decisive factor in the evolution of the telenovela genre into its privileged space in the TV broadcasting environment of today.

We have mentioned the major contemporary factors that have contributed to the formation of a television narrative genre of recognisably national significance, but at the same time it is necessary to include other features of Brazilian culture and history that have provided a foundation for establishing the telenovela as a meaningful fabricator of our cultural identity.

With any aspect of Brazilian culture, it is always necessary to take into account centuries of cultural formation based on colonialism and the Portuguese settlers' bequest. The Portuguese, with truly colonialist enthusiasm and imbued with Catholic missionary zeal, established in Brazil a culture intent on the verbal expression of catechisation. Among the native Indians, who were divided into countless linguistic groups, the settlers introduced the dramatic colonial rhetoric of 'convincing and converting'. This often emotional *oratória* was eventually assimilated by politicians, poets and scholars, who became adept at preaching and public speaking, even as a mode of writing. The Baroque, the main artistic movement of colonial times, is evidence of the success achieved, in the colony, by theatrical and sentimental forms of expression. It seems clear that the melodrama did not come just with the French culture that reached Brazil in the nineteenth century; it had in fact been there longer, mingled in the Portuguese–Indian culture as a sort of dispersed oratory that often played on the sentimental. It should be taken into account that Indian culture itself abounds with magical and melodramatic elements. The native inhabitants' legends and myths met this rhetorical strand of the Brazilian imaginary, in which intensively symbolic fables have always had an important position. In addition, there is that no less fantastic contribution bequeathed by the black slaves. Having left Africa with nothing but a strong oral tradition, in Brazil they nurtured and enhanced the power of the word as a bewitched manifestation of ethnic identity, making it a weapon against the evil condition of bondage. Their stories and verbal expressions of identity blended with the Indian heritage and eventually mingled with the theatrical culture of the Portugese Baroque. It was these ethnically and culturally mixed people who enthusiastically welcomed, across the boundaries of social class, the first publications of the French *feuilleton* that came to Brazil.

Those *feuilleton* stories, published in 'parts' in the European newspapers, brimmed with vicissitudes, mystery, drama and exaggerated action, and achieved a roaring success in Brazil. In the plantation manor houses, the *sinhá* – as the matriarch of the house was called – traditionally read the *feuilleton* aloud, with rhetorical flourishes, to a gathering of relatives, live-ins and slaves. Where illiteracy pervaded, people looked forward to the arrival of the *feuilleton* with an appetite for the narrative satisfactions of the part-work stories, but also a taste for the melodrama of the reading as performed entertainment.

These factors also partly account for the great success of radio in early twentieth-century Brazil. The radionovela reached huge audiences. Using new technology, with new styles and subject matter, the radionovela updated the manor house *soirée*, when the *sinhá* read stories to a domestic audience. Enhanced by the marvels of sound effects and background music, those stories with their plenitude of ongoing drama trained audiences in a daily routine, starting the long-lasting habit of tuning in regularly to learn of the new narrative developments. When television became the privileged means of mass communication, we observe the migration of the radio *feuilleton* to television. Authors and actors joined the electronic migration, helping to constitute long-running professional casts. Despite the fact that the image acquired greater importance in the new medium, the verbal expression – primarily conversation, gossip and scandal – kept its narrative hegemony. According to Décio Pignatari, a telenovela researcher, the telenovela is action moved by dialogue.

What is conspicuous in the historical trajectory that we have traced here is the remarkable route taken by the *feuilleton*. This summary of the sources of the telenovela makes it clear that the Indian and African cultural legacy mingled, in some respects, with the Portuguese Baroque and was the cradle of an eloquent and strongly oral narrative model. Taken over by the culture industry, it was used by the different media in their own ways. Along these migratory routes, it aggregated features, meshed various trends, but still reaffirmed a kind of storytelling that is characterised by the 'conversational' relationship established between narrator and public – daily, familiar and domestic. Such considerations are of great importance to an understanding of the question of cultural identity in Brazil. The telenovela's scope and penetration of the mass market leads us to conclude that its accomplishment is not only due to the inherent power of the medium and its technical effectiveness, as has sometimes been claimed, but also to the route that this particular cultural form traces through the histories of the peoples that constitute Brazil.

Other conclusions may be drawn from such an analysis: for example, that the erudite and the popular (or 'high' and 'low') cultural manifestations, instead of opposing each other, as suggested by some analyses, can create integrative cultural forms in which the contributions of both may be traced. A complex dialogic process takes place between historic and social factors which interpenetrate and intersect with one another. Being one of the main manifestations of cultural identity, the telenovela readily responds to an uncovering of its historical trajectory and background, as well as the ties established among the other knots of this socio-cultural net.

Maria Cristina Castilho Costa

Afterthoughts

In *Joik and the Theory of knowledge* (Haavelsrud, 1995:17), Ánde Somby describes a Laplandic chanting tradition which – while easy to listen to – is profoundly difficult to explain using established Western European notions of singing, referentiality and knowledge. A highly successful moderniser and performer of yoik (as it is more commonly spelled and pronounced), Wimme Saari performed at the gala ceremony for the 1999 Europrix Multimedia awards, held in Tampere, Finland, as part of 'Mindtrek', a week of new media events organised there in November 1999, during Finland's presidency of the European Union. So Wimme Saari was, in some sense, being called on to represent 'authentic' Finnish culture to an international audience (the awards were televised and also 'streamed' via the web). Wearing traditional costume and chanting amid the paraphernalia of new digital media, he was presumably intended to signify tradition and to connect with deeper notions of cultural identity than those explicitly represented by the awards.

In fact Wimme Saari has released two successful CDs with Rockadillo Records of Tampere and the yoik has been even more successfully updated for contemporary media consumption by the Girls of Angeli, a sibling duo whose music and image combine 'tradition' with a determined sense of contemporaneity – their 1997 CD was called *The New Voice of the North*. Wimme Saari and the Angeli duo (Ursula and Tuuni Länsman) are from the Sami, an ethnic minority distributed across northern Scandinavia (Angeli is a village in Finland). In 1988 an article was added to the Norwegian constitution stating: 'It is the responsibility of the authorities of the State to create conditions enabling the Sami people to preserve and develop its language, culture and way of life.' Their own parliament (Sameting) convened for the first time the following year, representing an estimated 70,000 Sami. In the eighteenth century, Christian missionaries had strongly opposed the Sami's shamanistic practices, with which the yoik has been strongly associated – a suspicion that carried down to the twentieth century (e.g. in the early years of the century a process of deliberate 'Norwegianisation' was attempted against the Sami living there). The defining feature, legally and constitutionally, of the Sami identity has been taken to be their language, of which the yoik is an integrally expressive part.

So what happens when the yoik is modernised, released on CD, and marketed and consumed as popular music by many non-Sami listeners, indeed by many non-Scandinavians? To think about this, I want to put myself (DF) into the question, as I first heard the commercial form of yoik when Wimme performed at that gala in Tampere, which I attended. At a moment in my life when I was deeply bored by much of the popular music I had once enjoyed, the encounter with the live performance and then the recordings of Wimme Saari and, to a lesser degree, the Länsman sisters, was revitalising, emotionally engaging and persistently affecting in the longer term. This is how popular music seems to work – grabbing us unexpectedly and wrenching our feelings around its rhythms. Now there is a 'functional' approach to understanding my response – an approach well established within cultural studies – that would look for some *homology* between my circumstances as Northern Irish listener and Wimme's circumstances as Northern Finnish performer (am I Irish or British, is he Finnish or Sami?, etc.). The music's appeal would then be explained in terms of a fit across these circumstances, where the music 'reflects' the particular configuration of social forces at their point of impact on these circumstances and fits both contexts (performer and listener). The problem with this explanation is that the music itself and my experience of it have to be reduced to being some sort of background soundtrack to cultural identity where the meaning comes from the identities converging momentarily on the music, rather than from the aesthetic value of the music. In reality, the latter just seems to be far too powerful to be reduced in this way.

While I am happy enough to concede that there may be some form of Northern European experience here, this seems to be more of an aesthetic tendency than any specific homology of circumstances lying 'behind' the music. What is important in my unexpectedly positive and affecting response to Wimme's versions of yoik seems to be much more clearly *in* the experiencing of popular music this way than in anything the music supposedly reflects. So perhaps my sense of cultural identity is being created – or re-created – *in* the moments of musical consumption, rather than determining those moments in some *a priori* manner? Am I imagining my cultural identity in these moments, as I deliberately place myself in a relation with the music?

The problem with getting our heads round this distinction is that we are locked rationally into a way of explaining what things are 'about'. We automatically ask of a film, 'What's it about?' Similarly, even a piece of popular music has to be 'about' something in this way of thinking. It is then an easy step to move from saying that this song is 'about' a lost love to saying that it is really about (reflects) modernity's fractured social relationships. Or that cultural identities are somehow 'reflected' in popular music (that's what the music is really 'about'). Usefully, however, the yoik itself is a form of expression that refuses this distinction between expression and 'aboutness'. One does not yoik about friendship, about the sounds of the woods, about a reindeer. One yoiks friendship, yoiks the woods, yoiks the deer. There is no intervening 'about'. Perhaps the yoik then tells us something with regard to popular music generally that is easier to grasp here because yoiking comes already equipped with a more helpful theory of knowledge? In listening to Wimme's songs I am yoiking cultural identity ('out there' and 'in here' merge), just as he is yoiking cultural identity in performing them, as well as yoiking the importance of moss, the full moon or the boiling spring. For this reason, of all the contemporary media, popular music may often be the most revealing about the multiple affiliations of cultural identity and about its nature as a living process.

Part IV
Broadcasting

10

Television and the active audience

Sonia Livingstone

It is something of a cliché in social science research to imagine a Martian arriving on Earth and being bewildered by what it sees. Yet as an exercise, it defamiliarises the familiar, allowing us to understand reality as a social construction and so to recognise the 'work' which goes into making sense of things which otherwise appear obvious to us. Television is a prime example of the obvious, in this sense: for regular viewers, a mere glance at the box in the corner reveals the latest development in the narrative, whether a narrative in the news or in our favourite soap opera. The meanings appear given, unavoidable, they exist 'in' the programmes and leap out at us when we watch. Taking in these meanings seems a routine and effortless process for most people. Kubey and Csikszentmihalyi's (1990) research on the television audience confirms our common-sense view that television viewing is a mindless and relaxing experience, for although television in its early years was startling and new, it has rapidly become 'moving wallpaper' in most homes. This common-sense view of television as moving wallpaper and of viewers as mindless absorbers of images fits with a long-standing trend in mass communication theory. Whether influenced by sociological theories of ideology and hegemony, or by social psychological theories of media effects and attitude or behaviour change, many media researchers have regarded the audience as homogeneous, vulnerable and easily manipulated in the face of a powerful and all-pervasive mass media.

Yet certain traditions of mass communications, both old and new (Curran, 1990), contradict this view and argue instead for active, resourceful and motivated audiences. Children are often in the position of the Martian, and research into children's understanding of television in particular has served to counter the notion of television viewing as an effortless experience. Many of young children's experiences of television show vividly the kinds of work that experienced viewers do in making sense of television. Greenfield (1984) reports her three-year-old son's confusion when his mother, while appearing on television, failed to wave back at her son at home. Dorr (1986) describes how children cannot understand how the Six Million Dollar Man (in an old US action-adventure series) ever catches anybody, for he is always shown in slow motion at the point of capture. She also notes how five-year-olds regard advertisements as helpful displays of available products, with no idea that they are also persuasive, designed to sell to children. As Dorr (1986) and Hodge and Tripp (1986) reveal, even when children begin to understand the conventions of television – the use of televisual codes such as ellipsis, action replay and special effects – they remain confused for some time. Dorr describes a seven-year-old who, knowing that bullets in an action-adventure drama were fake, nonetheless remained anxious about the stray real bullet which may have been included by mistake. Christenson (1986) shows that even when children have figured out the relations between characters, actions, motives and conse-quences, they still find it hard even by the age of twelve to abstract the intended moral message in 'pro-social' children's drama (i.e. programmes intended to educate, directly or indirectly).

None of this is to disparage children: as new members of society, they must learn the codes and conventions of all aspects of their culture, including tele-vision, if they are to become part of the culture, and they are inventive, sophis-ticated and motivated in doing this. However, in so doing, children's efforts to make sense of television point up the kinds of work which adults also do when viewing television. This invites a more general critique of the notion of viewing as mindless and passive, and of the many metaphors used to describe viewers in both common-sense and academic discourses (the passive absorption of messages, the viewer as a *tabula rasa*, the media as a hypodermic needle, etc.). To point to viewers' work specifically (Katz, 1996) is to identify a set of cogni-tive or interpretive processes, but is not necessarily to presume a conscious sense of effort or a straining after meaning. The ease with which viewers rou-tinely make sense of television is evidence of the routine familiarity of these interpretive processes rather than evidence that such processes are unneces-sary. Most important, and often surprising to viewers and researchers, is the fact that even the routine ease with which we generally make sense of televi-sion does not necessarily imply that everyone makes sense of television in the same way. Indeed, it is divergences in interpretation which often make appar-ent the operation of interpretive processes in the first place. And the nature of these divergences raises the question of why different people, or the same people under different circumstances, make sense of television in different ways.

Much contemporary audience research argues against the common-sense assumption that the meanings of television are obvious and require no inter-pretation to receive them. Such research points to the effort and confusions of children (and Martians) in making sense of television as a way of de-familiarising the familiar and pointing up the problematic of viewers' work as a significant area for research. This fits with another widespread discourse of television viewing, one particularly developed by uses and gratifications researchers, namely that of motivated and selective viewers making their own decisions about what to view and what to think about what they see (Blumler and Katz, 1974). Uses and gratifications researchers were concerned about the assumption of audience passivity and media power, an assumption which they felt represented a patronising and elitist approach to audiences. This led these researchers to take a more inductive approach to the audience, asking diverse audiences of diverse programmes about why they watched them and what they got out of them (Rosengren *et al.*, 1985). The answers included media uses characterised as entertainment, relaxation and escapism but, in almost equal measure, they also included media uses reflecting an active and motivated involvement in television. People are emotionally engaged by television; they talk of television meeting personal identity needs such as the legitimation of their values or gaining insight into themselves; they feel television keeps them connected to the rest of the world through a shared imagined community, through knowing what is happening in other places and through having common topics to discuss with others in their everyday lives. They even enjoy being critical of television, working out the production processes behind the programmes, speculating about the real lives of the actors, laughing at the conventions, and decoding complex advertisements designed to tease them (Liebes and Katz, 1993). If we understand the viewing experience in this way, then the very effort after meaning may be seen to be pleasurable. While the media transmit a blur of colours and sounds, the fact that they are seen by viewers to provide a resource for the satisfaction of needs concerning identity, relationships and social connectedness makes clear the interpretive work which viewers must be doing.

Stop and think

Learning the media

Learning to understand the media is not something that any of us is very conscious of having to do. And yet the media are all difficult to understand in various ways for anybody who has not been brought up with constant exposure to them. There is, however, a process of 'remediation' by which new media tend to borrow some of the conventions of existing media, thus speeding up the learning process. So TV borrowed an audio-visual language (the shot, framing, editing, etc.) from cinema and, even though TV developed its own often quite distinctive variations on these conventions, people were quick to pick up how television was representing things. Similarly, the web – at least in the beginning – borrowed many of the conventions of magazine publishing (it had 'pages' with images and columns of text). In other words, the learning process does not have to start anew with each new medium.

It is important to realise, though, that this process of learning is largely one of coming unquestioningly to accept the supposed naturalness of how the media communicate. So TV can seem to offer straightforward pictures of the world, with techniques and conventions that no longer seem invented or artificial to us at all, just as our native language seems to label reality effortlessly. Shifting to a foreign language reminds us that language is a human invention and that the links between words and the things to which they refer are entirely arbitrary. So there is a potential second level to learning the media – the one you are now engaged upon. Now the point is *to make strange in your own mind what you already take for granted* because of prior unreflective learning (i.e. adopting, if you can, the Martian's perspective). This is not easily achieved, but the sometimes dizzying consequences of achieving it – of seeing what you've accepted as 'natural' dissolve away into a multiplicity of artifical techniques and procedures – are a pre-condition of the genuinely reflective learning that underpins media studies as an educational project.

Why place broadcasting so prominently within this project? Whatever specific claims we might proceed to make for the huge influence of radio and TV in the twentieth century, the first reason is precisely because broadcasting is so much taken for granted, even so 'natural' to us now – it constitutes our environment just as much as (for some people more than) the natural world does. In a way it *is* our sense of the world both 'out there' and 'in here'.

We have at least three arguments for the active engagement of audiences with the mass media. First, audiences must interpret what they see even to construct the message as meaningful and orderly, however routine this interpretation may be. Second, audiences diverge in their interpretations, generating different understandings from the same text. Third, the experience of viewing stands at the interface between the media (and their interpretations) and the rest of viewers' lives, with all the concerns, experiences and knowledge which this involves. Over the past twenty years or so, audience research has been a site of debate over these issues, in an attempt to fill out the now commonplace though still contested notion of *the active audience*. Some of this work, from a more 'administrative' tradition (Lazarsfeld, 1941), draws directly on uses and gratifications theory (Levy and Windahl, 1985; Liebes and Katz, 1993), while those from a more 'critical' position define themselves against this work, emphasising the social and material contexts of both production and reception (Morley, 1992). Contentious issues include the following: In principle, is the media text inherently open to multiple interpretations or is it rather an empirical observation that multiple interpretations arise from viewing? Should the experience of viewing be located primarily within a psychological or a socio-demographic context, by identifying either motivations and interests or cultural resources and material conditions as the factors which shape patterns of exposure and interpretation? How far do the media restrict or direct the interpretations that arise on viewing, so that particular meanings, rather than any and every meaning, may result from viewing (Livingstone, 1998)?

This last issue brings us back to the question of the effects of viewing on the audience, which is probably the most central and most contentious question in media research (Livingstone, 1996). We are beginning to work out the ways in which effects do not simply result from the qualities of media texts but rather depend both on selectivity in exposure and on interpretation or the construction of meanings. For both these processes, research shows that viewers draw on the diverse resources in their lives. Katz proposed some time ago 'that individuals seek information that will support their beliefs and practices and avoid information that challenges them' (Katz, 1968:795), thereby arguing for the existence of cognitive defences against the power of the media. More positively, he suggests that viewers 'impress the media into the service of individual needs and values' (Katz, 1979:75). Yet insufficient research exists which effectively investigates the linked processes of exposure, interpretation and effects.

However, we do know, for example, that media effects appear to differ depending on viewers' judgements of the realism of a programme (Himmelweit *et al.*, 1958; Dorr, 1986); on the closeness or similarity of what is viewed to one's own life (Collins and Wellman, 1982; Ettema *et al.*, 1983); on the strength of one's prior assumptions regarding the subject matter of a programme (Pingree, 1978; Drabman *et al.*, 1981); and on whether one has comprehended the relationship between motive, action and consequences in the programme (Dorr, 1986).

The emergence of audience reception analysis

Why did audience reception become such a focus for media research during the 1980s and 1990s? Hall (1980:131) identified the growth of empirical reception research as 'a new and exciting phase in so-called audience research' which emphasised the role of active viewers in a dynamic process of negotiating the meanings of television. For Blumler *et al.* (1985), this new focus offered a route 'to build the bridge we have been hoping might arise between gratifications studies and cultural studies' (Katz, 1979:75). One can identify several strands of thought which led to this particular convergence of diverse researchers on the same project at the same time. One strand was the growing recognition that critical mass communications research, with its focus on the ideological power and institutional production of texts, had tended to ignore, presume or underestimate the interpretive activity of the audience (Fejes, 1984). Meanwhile, traditional audience research – whether uses and gratifications or effects research – suffered from an impoverished conception of both the (almost effaced) television text (Blumler *et al.*, 1985) and the cultural contexts of viewing (Morley, 1986).

Another strand was the development of reception theory or reader-response theory within literary criticism as a more interactionist means of analysing culture, at least by comparison with traditional structural approaches (Suleiman and Crosman, 1980; Holub, 1984). The emphasis shifted from an analysis of the meanings 'in' the text, central to the text-based and content-analytic approaches to television programmes, to an analysis of the process of reading a text, where the meanings which are activated on reading depend on the interaction between text and reader. One reception theorist challenged prior assumptions of both texts and readers, arguing that:

> The work itself cannot be identical with the text or with its actualization but must be situated somewhere between the two . . . As the reader passes through the various perspectives offered by the text, and relates the different views and patterns to one another, he sets the work in motion, and so sets himself in motion too. (Iser, 1980:106)

In Britain, many cultural studies researchers were more strongly influenced by Hall's encoding/decoding model (Hall, 1980) which proposed that 'the degrees of "understanding" and "misunderstanding" in the communicative exchange – depend on the degrees of symmetry/asymmetry . . . between the positions of the "personifications", encoder–producer and decoder–receiver' (p. 131). The differences between encoding and decoding, and the location of these differences in the cultural and material contexts of encoding and decoding, were key theoretical moves. Hall's argument was close to that of the reception theorists when they argued that an implied or model reader is encoded into the text, specifying the 'horizon of expectations' (Jauss, 1982) or the 'textual competencies' (Eco, 1979) required to decode the text. Similarly, both Hall and the reception theorists also stressed that the particular circumstances in which the text is interpreted may or may not actually meet this specification of the ideal reader. The advantage of the more literary approaches over the encoding/decoding model lies in the closer specification of the relation between texts and readers, which details the nature of the codes and the nature of textual and extra-textual resources presumed by texts and available to audiences.

Eco's (1979) concept of the 'role of the reader' focused analysis at the point of interpretation, at the interface between text and reader (or programme and viewer):

> The existence of various codes and subcodes, the variety of sociocultural circumstances in which a message is emitted (where the codes of the addressee can be different from those of the sender) and the rate of initiative displayed by the addressee in making presuppositions and abductions – all result in making a message . . . an empty form to which various possible senses can be attributed. (p. 5)

His detailed outline of the kinds of code, presupposition, forms of knowledge and frames of interpretation in *The Role of the Reader* allows us to emphasise the dialectic between text and reader: 'A well-organised text on the one hand presupposes a model of competence coming, so to speak, from outside the text, but on the other hand works to build up, by merely textual means, such a competence' (p. 8). The notion of the role of the reader has provided a single concept through which we can investigate the textual strategies which construct the 'model reader' as well as the interpretive strategies which actual audiences use in particular, everyday contexts (Livingstone, 1998).

The investigation of audience reception rapidly became an empirical rather than a purely theoretical project. In so doing, it moved from careful consideration of particular reception theories such as those of Iser, Eco and Hall to a rather loose grounding in the blanket notion of 'reception theory' or 'audience reception analysis'. Having argued that texts are dynamic, that meanings are context dependent and that readings may be divergent, it became obvious that researchers must investigate the activities of actual audiences in order to know how they interpret programmes in everyday contexts. Despite the many methodological problems which arose from this shift to empirical reception research (Morley, 1981; Hoijer, 1990), this project quickly justified itself through the joint discoveries that, first, audiences often differed from researchers in their understanding of the media text and, second, that audiences were themselves heterogeneous. Both discoveries undermined the possibility of arguing for a direct link between the meanings supposedly inherent in the text and the consequent effects of those meanings on the audience. As a result, attention was redirected to studying the interpretive contexts which framed and informed viewers' understandings of television.

Examples of resourceful readers

Three widely cited examples of empirical reception research illustrate the use of cultural, class and gender codes as resources in the interpretation of different genres of popular culture.

In the *Export of Meaning* project, Liebes and Katz (1993) examined processes of, and resistance to, so-called 'Americanisation' or cultural imperialism by exploring the reception of *Dallas* (a glossy US drama series) by diverse cultural groups. They analysed focus group discussions held during and after viewing an episode of *Dallas* in people's homes. The researchers' analysis of the text had suggested that *Dallas* concerned primordial cultural themes such as lineage, inheritance, sibling rivalry, property, sex and marriage. Yet the empirical audience study found that viewers of different social and cultural backgrounds generated very different interpretations of the same episode. Thus Russian Jews made ideological readings centred on the moral and political themes underlying the narratives, Americans focused on the personalities and motivations of the characters to make their readings coherent, and Moroccan Arabs emphasised event sequencing and narrative continuity. Each group's reading was clearly constrained by the text and yet the interaction between diverse cultural resources and at least some degree of textual openness resulted in divergent readings.

Morley's study (1980, 1981, 1992) of audience readings or decodings of the TV current affairs magazine, *Nationwide*, showed how audiences diverged as a function of their socio-economic or labour position. Predictably, given that Morley was exploring understandings of the news, audiences' interpretations were politically framed. Bank managers and schoolboys were found to make the most normative readings, consistent with the ideologically dominant assumptions which structured the programme. Trainee teachers and trade union officials made politically inconsistent, ambivalent or negotiated readings. Other groups took a clearly oppositional position, using the resources of the text to construct a critical reading quite unintended by the text. A few viewers were wholly alienated from the text as it did not afford them a reading congruent with their own cultural position (e.g. black college students; while in the *Export of Meaning* project, it was Japanese viewers who occupied this position). This division of audience reception into dominant, negotiated and oppositional positions (Hall, 1980) has influenced much subsequent research.

Radway (1985) revealed the contrast between the readings of popular romance novels made by ordinary women readers and those of literary critics. She argued that 'different readers read differently because they belong to what are known as various interpretive communities, each of which acts upon print differently and for different purposes' (Radway, 1985:341). In the case of 'Harlequin' romances (a publishing brand), women readers were found to emphasise the literal meaning and the factual nature of language in preference to narrative consistency (preferred by the critics), when the two conflicted. For example, the heroine in these books is typically described initially as strong and independent and yet ultimately she appears to submit to her hero's demands. Feminist critics have generally emphasised the significance of the latter capitulation, yet Radway found ordinary women readers emphasising the former, thereby resisting the normative patriarchal message and generating their own meanings. On this account, the heroine is seen subtly to win over her hero, unbeknownst to him, thus revealing her true strength, which had often been stated quite literally at the outset of the novel.

Filling out the text–reader metaphor

Many studies have since supported the notion of ideologically resistant readings. These include studies which focus on gender (Seiter *et al.*, 1989; Brown, 1990; Van Zoonen, 1994), while other studies have investigated the influence on reception of social class or labour market position (Press, 1991; Kitzinger, 1993). Each has been concerned with the ways in which texts attempt to position readers as particular kinds of subject through specific modes of address. Viewers have been found to accept or neglect such textual invitations in the construction of their subject position. Sometimes we can see that they read against the grain by exploiting the inevitable degree of openness in the text, they make aberrant readings and play with textual conventions, thereby jointly constructing different meanings on different occasions (Seiter *et al.*, 1989; Buckingham, 1987; Lewis, 1987; Livingstone and Lunt, 1994).

From the point of view of audience studies, in order to elaborate this text–reader metaphor, we need a theory of the viewer's interpretive resources – a theory of what viewers bring to the moment of reception from their past and present life circumstances. We also need a theory of the text that provides a space for the deployment of these resources. One useful concept is that of the schema – a dynamic, representational structure which operates by balancing processes of assimilation and accommodation in integrating old with new experiences (Bartlett, 1932; Piaget, 1968). For reception theorists, the frameworks which structure a media text are best understood as schematic rather than complete, with the role of the reader being to fill out this schema. To fill out the schema in unexpected ways, without breaking the boundaries of the schema, is to read against the grain; going further and breaking these boundaries is to make an aberrant or wrong reading. Generally, television programmes are designed with sufficient knowledge of the audience's interests so that audiences may fill out rather than conflict with the encoded textual schema. Thus the 'texts of experience' contribute to interpretation in a 'slot filling' capacity, where the location and nature of the gaps to be filled are specified by the 'skeletal' structure of the text (Iser, 1980) rather than by the reader's concerns. For example, when we read a book we fill out our image of the main characters by drawing on our own social knowledge and imagination as readers. Then when we see the film of the book our images are often contradicted and our interpretive activities – what we have added to the text – become visible to us. Yet the overall meaning of the book or film is rarely undermined in this way, although the pleasure – that of actively generating images meaningful to ourselves – may have been reduced.

Such an approach to texts and readers is illuminating, and allows us to keep a handle on the often 'disappearing message' (the textual meanings effaced if we go too far in the direction of the reader). Yet the reader or viewer is an incomplete or partial concept in such analysis, for the invitations to fill out the text are under the control of the text not the reader, and textual coherence is prioritised over the reader's experience. Precisely in order to prevent such a fragmentation, the psychology of textual interpretation reverses this bias (Mandler, 1984; Van Dijk, 1987). Here, the reader's resources are themselves conceived in terms of schemata which provide integrative, knowledge-based frameworks for active interpretation and which leave gaps or slots to be filled according to the particularities of the text. For example, as viewers we share a cultural repertoire that includes the romance as a narrative form. A particular television drama merely fills out the specific details – who is the hero, what does the heroine do, what kinds of problem beset them – which particularise the programme as one instance of our general schema. For this approach, an analysis of the reader's socio-cognitive resources is needed to understand both how viewers fill out textual schemata and how they impose their own schemata on the viewing experience (Livingstone, 1998).

Research on everyday 'lay theories' illuminates the ways in which viewers make sense of television characters and narratives. Such social knowledge is dynamic and integrative, directing and informing interpretations of television, rather than a static and disjointed set of facts which television may simply replace with its own given set of meanings. For example, research on social cognition reveals people's biases towards seeking confirmatory rather than falsifying evidence to fit their preconceptions, as well as their 'scripted' knowledge of standard event sequences (e.g. Reeves *et al.*, 1982). It also shows how they draw on cognitive story grammars to interpret narrative (Van Dijk, 1987), on attributional schemata to understand causality (Kelley, 1972), and how they use a variety of interpretive heuristics to determine the relevance and typicality of the events portrayed (Kahneman *et al.*, 1982). As social knowledge is shared within, indeed is constituted by the activities of, groups or cultures, theorising the role of the viewer in this way avoids the psychological reductionism which implies that audience readings are entirely unpredictable or idiosyncratic. Consequently, we can use social cognition to explain how and why viewers who differ in gender, class or culture actually achieve their divergent readings, for these differences in social context are manifested in the interpretive resources of the viewers. (*cont. p. 188*)

A brief history of television

The French artist and author Albert Robida, who lived from 1848 to 1926, produced a series of startlingly original illustrated novels: *Le vingtième siècle* (*The Twentieth Century*) (1882), *Le vingtième siècle, la vie electrique* (*The Twentieth Century, Life with Electricity*) (1890) and *La guerre au vingtième siècle* (War in the Twentieth Century) (1887). Among his illustrations in the first of these is one showing a family gathered around a large screen in their living room and being astonished by pictures of a desert war – television imagined when the telephone was just emerging from the inventors' workshops and six years before television pioneer John Logie Baird was born. So as an idea television had not been unthinkable before inventors got to work on it.

Two years after Robida's vision (and completely unconnected with it) Paul Nipkow, a German scientist, patented a scanning disk – a metal plate with spiralling holes punched through it that would, in theory, spin between an object to be 'televised' and a photosensitive receptor (e.g. using selenium, discovered in 1873), breaking the image up into small reproducible points of light. Although technically out of reach at the time, this was the key idea that would drive research and in the end give us analogue TV as we came to know it in the twentieth century, until more flexible digital alternatives began to appear in the 1990s. The twentieth-century TV picture was made up of scanned light fired back down a tube at a photosensitive screen where a version of the original image was re-created out of 'dots' that only became visible when one looked at it from a few inches away. Between Nipkow's patent and usable cameras, transmitting equipment, and receivers and screens, numerous scientists and technologists collaborated, competed or worked independently to realise what was fast becoming a widespread vision of a technology that could be made to work, even if the form it would take remained open to considerable speculation. As early as 1879, for instance, a cartoon in British magazine *Punch* had depicted 'Edison's Telephonoscope' with which, 'Every evening, before going to bed, Pater- and Materfamilias set up an electric camera-obscura over their bedroom mantel-piece, and gladden their eyes with the sight of their Children at the Antipodes, and converse gaily with them through the wire.' In the cartoon, the actual form this takes is of daughter Beatrice in Ceylon breaking off from her tennis match (the whole court visible in widescreen) to talk to her parents down a telephone mouthpiece.

The technologists and inventors who would contribute to realising at least a version of that awesome scene included the Russian Boris Rosing and Englishman A. A. Campbell Swinton (who independently realised in 1907–8 that Nipkow's mechanical disk would be replaced by electronic scanning using a cathode-ray tube, itself invented by German Karl Braun in 1897); John Logie Baird, the Scot whose 'Televisor' achieved the best results yet attained with mechanical scanning, when he transmitted the image of a ventriloquist's dummy's head on to a screen, demonstrated at the Royal Institution in London in 1926; Hungarian Von Mihaly who got a mechanical mirrored drum, derived from Nipkow's idea, to scan and transmit tiny pictures, exhibited at the Berlin Radio Exhibition of 1928; Kenjiro Takayanagi in Japan who transmitted an image of a handwritten Japanese character in 1927; Russian Boris Grabovsky who developed an electronic scanning system and transmitted 'the movement of a hand' in a fleeting image in an apartment in Tashkent in 1926; American Charles Francis Jenkins who demonstrated successful mechanical scanning shortly after Baird; Russian Vladimir Zworykin, who had emigrated to the USA in 1919, and who developed electronic scanning for the Westinghouse company; and American Philo T. Farnsworth who pulled it all together to design a complete electronic television system in 1927 (effectively consigning the mechanical scanning systems of Baird, Von Mihaly and Jenkins to the history books). In England, a 1908 letter from Campbell Swinton to the magazine *Nature* had, in fact, described in theory what Farnsworth would realise in practice only nineteen years later – 'distant electric vision'.

Philo Farnsworth is, in many ways, the most unjustly invisible figure in our recollections of twentieth-century media – most people have never heard his name. But Farnsworth has the strongest claim to be plucked out of that short history sketched above and to be recognised as the creator of television. That he hasn't been is perhaps due to a messy legal dispute that clouded the facts. The Radio Corporation of America had, by the early 1930s, adopted Zworykin's camera tube and refused to acknowledge Farnsworth's claim to having developed an earlier working system. In fact we now know that Farnsworth had first sketched his system while at school and in 1934 the US Patent Office recognised the priority of his invention. However, history had by then evidently moved on too far to notice Farnsworth except in passing.

To understand the confidence that inspired the 'invention' of television across this comparatively short timespan, we have to bear in mind a hugely symbolic moment – 12 December 1901, at 12.30 p.m. local time, in St Johns, Newfoundland. Italian Guglielmo Marconi was listening to the first wireless telegraphy message (tapped out in Morse Code) to be sent across the Atlantic (from Cornwall, England). Wireless telegraphy – freeing the great nineteenth-century communication technology, the telegraph, from the wires of bureaucratic control that snaked across the British and other Empires – would rapidly lead to radio and, in its turn, 'distant electric vision' would be the adaptation of radio broadcasting to carry picture as well as sound information encoded on the electromagnetic waves (a continuous spectrum of frequencies in the Earth's atmosphere). While the pioneers of electrically encoding, or scanning, pictorial information are justifiably celebrated (although Baird perhaps a little too much in the Anglophone world, compared with the others), it is important to locate the technical development of television squarely within this underpinning context of development in wireless telegraphy and radio. The deep roots of all of this were in the work of German physicist Heinrich Rudolph Hertz (1857–94) who, in the 1880s, created and measured the electromagnetic waves on which 'broadcasting' would later be carried.

As the technologies of broadcasting rapidly advanced beyond Farnsworth, our attention necessarily shifts to the question of how the new broadcast media would be used and how they might be controlled. Briefly interrupted by the Second World War (Hitler never spoke on live television, Churchill asked for a screen test but decided that radio was his medium), television spread rapidly thereafter, with the number of receiving sets exceeding 130 million worldwide by 1965. In this phase, the question of regulation became even more important than that of further technological development. Roger Silverstone nicely summarises the way that broadcasting regulation and social regulation inevitably dovetail:

> it is possible to suggest that almost all our regulatory impulses, those that engage with the ownership of media industries on the one hand and those that concern the welfare of the family on the other, are between them concerned with the protection of home. What links them, of course, is *content*:

the images, sounds and meanings that are transmitted and communicated daily, and over which governments feel they have increasingly little control. Content is important because it is presumed to be meaningful. Banal though it may seem, the media are seen to be important because of the power they are presumed to exercise over us, *at home*. They can breach the sanctuary as well as secure it. This is the struggle. This is the struggle over the family too; a struggle to protect it in its innocence and in its centrality as an institution where public and private moralities are supposed to coincide. This is a struggle for control, a struggle which propagandists and advertisers understood and still understand. And it is a struggle which parents understand too, as they argue with their children over their viewing habits or the time spent on-line, and which in part defines, across lines of age and gender, the particular politics of individual households. (Silverstone, 1999:94)

So television sits right in the middle of twentieth-century struggles for control of the kinds evoked here. The key debates – about commercial interests in tension with a public service ideal (control over value and its definitions), about power inside and outside families (control over morality), about content and 'effects' (control over ideas, pleasures and behaviour) – are well documented and readily accessible to the student of media, as is the other major area of debate around television, the question of how national broadcasting relates to globalisation.

Historically, the phased arrival of terrestrial broadcasting channels in most of the technologically advanced countries allowed the domestic base of content production talent, supported by appropriate organisational and commercial structures, to grow in tandem. For instance, as summarised by Richard Collins, the limited channels available for broadcast TV in any European nation (because of the need to keep them largely confinable within tightly packed national boundaries), led almost inevitably to a situation in which

> in a number of European countries a fortuitous 'fit' developed between the resources available for national programme (software) *production* and the (limited by spectrum availability) capacity of the *distribution* system. This 'fit' resulted in a stable broadcasting system ecology in which national broadcasting systems distributing substantially indigenous product developed, offering a model instance of the planned evolution of a viable and popular national cultural industry. (Collins, 1990:128)

While the internal arrangements (the broadcasting companies, conditions of competition, state regulation, production capacity, resistance to proliferating US programme content, etc.) differed across different nations, we can still think of this period of a relatively 'stable broadcasting ecology' as having characterised television for the second half of the twentieth century. The scarcity of available space on the electromagnetic spectrum (carefully regulated by governments and their agencies, for example by the Federal Communications Commission in the USA) and, in a sense therefore, of television itself (widely available but growing relatively slowly in terms of channels available and volume of content), contributed to this period of stability which lasted from the late 1940s to the early 1980s, thirty or so years which largely determined how we still thought of television as a cultural form as the twentieth century ended.

This despite a twenty-year transitional period during which the stable regulatory frameworks, forms of content and relationships with audiences had begun to change, not least as a global entertainment and information market-place emerged to upset the delicately balanced 'ecology' described by Collins. Satellite TV, thoroughly disrespectful of most national aspirations to regulate and control, was central to this creeping change. By 2000 it had become clear that television as a whole was changing in some absolutely fundamental ways, hastened by the move from analogue to digital technology which finally released TV (and related technologies) from the scarcity of analogue bandwidth. These broad changes clustered around three developments: (1) high-definition television (HDTV), which began to replace the old standards with bigger, better pictures, including the move towards widescreen (because a digital signal typically transmits at least eight times more information than the analogue equivalent, information that can be used to enlarge and improve the display); (2) more flexible forms of programming, including multi-casting (several programme choices simultaneously carried on one channel), a degree of interactivity (inputting responses via the remote control handset) and 'personal' digital video recorders that can pause and restart 'live' broadcasts and assist in the compilation of programming based on personal preferences; and (3) the addition of CD ROM-style 'added value' to programme content, with browsable background or contextual information, assisted by television content providers' increasing use of the web and the latter's convergence (e.g. as WebTV) with the TV set.

With analogue TV being phased out during the first decade of the twenty-first century, these changes will be consolidated and will take a range of concrete forms – new services and types of programming, new relationships between TV and individual users. In the 1990s the web established a new way of thinking about 'audience' groupings that is becoming central to TV too as it evolves. By addressing an 'audience of one' but automatically gathering data on the individual's preferences, tastes and choices, web content providers and electronic retailers found that they could correlate that data with their databases of hundreds of thousands, sometimes millions, of other users and 'recognise' new groupings based on affinities. Content satisfactions could be predicted with increasing reliability and presented to users as 'recommendations' or customised material. As TV moves gradually into the world of the web's digital flexibility, 'Me-TV' is beginning to emerge, based not on atomisation but on new kinds of affinity groupings that cut across the old notions of audience with their national, geographical and traditional social boundaries. The briefly held fear, that the 'new' technologies would place atomised viewers in front of isolated TVs, anti-socially absorbed in a chosen stream of content shared with nobody else, has turned out to be entirely misplaced. What has happened instead is that TV has started to move from addressing predominantly national audiences to entirely new social groupings, identified and brought together using digital technology's ability to sift large volumes of (sometimes global) data about users and to identify patterns of commonality that had hitherto been impossible to recognise and address. 'Me-TV' is turning out to be the basis of a new sense of discovered affinity with remote others – others like 'me' – in place of the imposed 'us'ness of the twentieth century's view of audience. As students of the media, we have to work hard to understand how these changes are impacting on viewers' comprehension of TV and its content, and how new types of virtually microscopic analysis of users' behaviours may constitute an extraordinary force for manipulation of digital TV contents as commodities (e.g. developing out of the existing 'Viewtime' minute-by-minute audience analysis tools already used by fifteen major TV stations and two leading radio networks spanning five countries in Europe).

Dan Fleming

Comprehension and interpretation of television programmes

Having discussed the resources available to viewers, let us now consider how these resources are used. Two broad approaches to the sense-making process exist in the research literature which, while often presented as opposed to each other, could instead be integrated. In figures 10 and 11, I present two examples of how different approaches can be combined to offer a more coherent and comprehensive approach to audience reception. The horizontal dimension of each figure divides textual codes (put simply, what programmes 'expect' or 'invite' from audiences) from extra-textual codes (in effect, what audiences 'bring' to the text from the context of their daily lives). This is relatively straightforward, and emphasises that viewers draw upon both kinds of code, as indeed programme makers presume they will (Livingstone, 1998). The effect of integrating theory across this dimension is to facilitate connections between theories of media literacy – of how viewers build up an understanding of specifically televisual conventions (Anderson, 1983) – with theories of everyday understanding, in which everyday social knowledge is used to decode 'mass' as well as interpersonal communication. This would allow us to begin to explore the relations, overlaps and contradictions between these two categories of knowledge, as well as the overlapping and different contextual determinants of each.

The vertical dimension of the two figures facilitates the integration of two traditionally opposed approaches to sense making, one focusing on comprehension and the other on interpretation. To put it another way, one is concerned with how viewers understand the denotational level of the text while the other is concerned with the connotational level of the text. Hall (1980:133) defines these two levels of analysis by distinguishing 'those aspects of a sign which appear to be taken, in any language community at any point in time, as its "literal" meaning (denotation) from the more associative meanings for the sign which it is possible to generate (connotation)'. By stressing that both denotation and connotation are coded rather than natural, Hall is inviting the study of audience reception on both levels, for they represent 'the different levels at which ideologies and discourses intersect' (p. 133). Yet most work following the encoding/decoding model investigates audience reception of connotative meanings as part of the broader project of studying the 'ritual'

Interpretive resources: Focus on processes of:	Predominant use of textual codes	Predominant use of extra-textual codes
Denotation in text, comprehension of viewer	Collins et al. (1978) showed that children comprehend narratives better if textual cues to narrative structure were provided	Collins and Wellman (1982) showed that children comprehended the narrative better if the social background of the characters matched their own
Connotation in text, interpretation of viewer	Buckingham (1987) showed that children used their knowledge of the genre and the history of the programme to interpret the significance of soap opera happenings	Palmer (1986) showed how children integrated their response to television drama and play experiences with friends and siblings

Figure 10 Resources used in comprehending and interpreting television: examples from children's understanding of drama

Interpretive resources: Focus on processes of:	Predominant use of textual codes	Predominant use of extra-textual codes
Denotation in text, comprehension of viewer	Findahl and Hoijer (1976) showed that news comprehension is improved by textual provision of explanation or background.	Robinson and Levy (1986) showed that prior information (measured by educational level) aids comprehension of the news.
Connotation in text, interpretation of viewer	Jensen (1986) and Gamson (1992) showed how different interpretative frames or 'super-themes' cued by the text result in divergent understandings of the same news event.	Liebes (1992) showed how the same news event is differently interpreted in families of differing political persuasion.

Figure 11 Resources used in comprehending and interpreting television: examples from adults' understanding of the news

or symbolic functions of cultural communication. Thus it regards studying the decoding of denotation as a reversion to the much-criticised and supposedly oversimplistic transmission model of communication (Carey, 1989). Instead, I would suggest – as indeed Carey does when proposing his very useful distinction between these two models of communication – that both transmission of meanings and the construction of meaning-sharing communities are implicated in the reception of television programmes.

If both are involved in reception, why is it useful to distinguish comprehension from interpretation? 'Comprehension' concerns whether viewers receive specific programme information or whether specific textual biases are mirrored by the viewers. Thus cognitive psychologists ask whether children can decode a narrative to discover 'who done it' or whether they can tell the 'baddies' from the 'goodies' (e.g. Reeves and Garramone, 1982; Collins, 1983). Using similar assumptions, researchers who check the psychological reality of content analyses ask whether particular contents are accurately received by viewers. It should be clear that these questions are rather different from those focused on 'interpretation' which typify audience reception studies (including those referred to earlier in this chapter). For, in these studies, 'interpretation' rather concerns evaluation, contextualisation, connotation and the many divergences in opinion or perspective that also contribute to the process of 'making sense of television'. The underlying assumption behind studies of comprehension draws rather problematically on information-processing theory, conceiving of meaning as unitary and as given by the text, thus only giving viewers the power to agree or disagree with this meaning. However, advances in both semiotic and audience theories require that this match/mismatch conception of the role of the viewer be developed so as to permit both a view of the text as polysemic and open, and a view of audiences as actively constructive in their interpretations.

In short, as proposed schematically in figures 10 and 11, studying processes of comprehension or interpretation involves focusing on two different facets of the same phenomenon, that of audience reception. If we want to know how well people remember the news, what they gain from a public information campaign or whether they learn from election broadcasts, a focus on comprehension is appropriate. But if we want to know what meanings are actually generated through media exposure and what resources direct the construction of those meanings, rather than whether certain *a priori* meanings are successfully transmitted or not, then we should analyse the viewers in context and focus on the connotational level of the text for which it is more likely that 'situational ideologies alter and transform signification' (Hall, 1980:133). Whether one studies comprehension (of denotation) or interpretation (of connotation) should depend less on whether one adheres in principle to a transmission or a ritual model of communication than on which aspects of the text or audience are relevant to one's research questions.

Consider the example in figure 10. Palmer's study of 'the lively audience' shows how the symbolic and identity relations between children and television change as children develop intellectually: 'with the development of an understanding of narratives, of story and character, older children make more complex demands on their favourite TV shows' (Palmer, 1986:121). Thus, after the age of eight or nine, children begin to prefer more realistic and more complex programmes instead of the cartoons or toy animal shows they liked earlier. The link between comprehension and interpretation is twofold. First, comprehension of the basic narrative is a prerequisite for the more differentiated or motivated modes of interpretation which emerge when children begin to make more subtle judgements about genre, about the realism of what is portrayed and about the relation between the drama and their own lives. Second, through the interpretation of these more subtle, connotative aspects of programmes, older children can incorporate television into their relations with friends and family. By this I mean the various activities of fitting television's meanings and images to their symbolic needs, using what they see not merely to copy televised events or display shared media experiences but also to define their particular identities, to negotiate friendships through role play, or to work out the rules for social interaction in the playground (Livingstone and Bovill, 1999). Consequently, it would be inappropriate to explore children's interpretations and the incorporation of television into their daily lives without first knowing how they comprehend the connections, sequencing and conclusions of the narratives, how they determine the modality or realism of different genres, or what they know of the production and purpose of programmes. There are important differences of gender and social class here, and these contribute to the different interpretations or uses of television for children, but the differences among children of different ages, reflecting different phases of intellectual development, are the most striking, affecting children's basic comprehension of the narratives.

A parallel argument can be made for adults' comprehension of the news (figure 11). Robinson and Levy (1986) compared the features of better- and worse-comprehended stories, and found that stories are better comprehended depending on factors such as personalisation, use of a standard narrative structure, degree of human interest, and so forth. Findahl and Hoijer (1976) add that news which includes causal information in the story is also better comprehended (stories often include who, what, where and when, but not why, information which is needed by viewers to integrate the other information). The importance of these textual features makes sense from the point of view of the viewers' resources. Viewers apply story grammars used in interpersonal communication to mediated communication, and they connect everyday patterns in the attribution of causality and responsibility to the comprehension of the news, while human interest stories would encourage them to use everyday social knowledge when 'slot filling' in the news stories. However, as Gamson (1992) shows, there are different ways of providing this kind of information within the text. The news may offer different explanatory frames for the same narrative, casting an event into a frame which, for example, polarises 'us' and 'them' or which characterises participants as 'feuding neighbours'. Different news events tend to be framed according to different but familiar cultural frames which then resonate with other domains of socio-cultural knowledge or experience. The textual characteristics that enhance comprehension, one might argue, do so by directing viewers towards particular kinds of interpretation of the news, and these interpretations resonate with yet further cultural understandings, depending on the knowledge, experience and position of the viewer. Consequently, more than 'comprehending what happened yesterday' is at stake, raising questions of the political consciousness and identity of the citizen-viewer (Corner, 1991; Livingstone and Lunt, 1994; chapters 4 and 5 of this volume).

Conclusions: next steps for audience reception research

Reviewing research since the mid 1970s, it is apparent that the once new idea of audience reception has become so taken for granted that studies of media forms or processes now frequently include a study of the audience. Moreover, audience research now tends to mean research on reception not, as previously, research on effects. However, the rapidity of these developments has meant that accumulating problems have not yet been adequately resolved (Livingstone, 1998). For example, the ways in which audience reception may mediate effects remain to be explored. Indeed, as long as the mediated transmission of meanings is neglected in favour of the ritual significance of the media, the problem of effects will remain (although the argument for resistant readings made of normative texts is often implicitly an argument about media effects). It is also problematic that the recent 'ethnographic turn' (Seiter *et al.*, 1989; Lull, 1990), which has successfully contextualised viewing within the practices of everyday life, seems at times to lose sight of the direct interaction between actual programmes and audiences and, hence, of their more indirect consequences in everyday life.

In conclusion, I have argued that viewing must be understood in terms of the diversity of specific daily practices of media involvement which themselves gain significance through their specific socio-demographic contexts. Yet by emphasising the relation between programme interpretation and local cultural contexts, media theory often begins to lose itself and the specificity of its research agenda in the rapidly expanding domain of interdisciplinary cultural theory. Rather than being distracted by the truth that everything is connected, as part of the 'context', we should recall that it may be useful to maintain analytical distinctions between different approaches. For example, at the level of theory, the many kinds of resource on which viewers may draw (social psychological, familial, material/domestic, gender, class, ethnicity, subculture, etc.) can and indeed should be integrated to illuminate television viewing. However, unless we are to be restricted to case studies, empirical investigation of such a multiplicity of factors must proceed through a range of separate studies whose conclusions then require integration with each other within a comparative framework.

Through meeting this challenge, certain future directions for media studies will become apparent. For example, is the blanket notion of reception theory sufficient or need we retain the specificity of different approaches to reception? Where are the gaps in the empirical research (e.g. what about some studies of the male soap opera viewer or female sports fan, surely necessary if we are to sustain and elaborate the argument for gendered readings of gendered genres)? Have certain rules of evidence (Katz, 1996) emerged to ground empirical research or is there still methodological dissent? And, in relation to the resourceful reader in particular, in what ways do the different resources of the viewer combine or compete in practice? For this last question, we could begin by cataloguing the types of interpretive resource used in viewing, and then specifying the different processes by which these resources are deployed. This would then allow us to understand how the text – here, the television programme – invites, directs or constrains the resourceful reader in both comprehension and interpretation, and how these processes are incorporated into the flow of everyday life.

Public service broadcasting

One of the defining characteristics of the experience of modernity in the twentieth century was the emergence of broadcasting and its consequences. The technologies, social institutions and cultural forms of broadcasting, first in radio and then in television, first terrestrial and then via satellite, first in analogue form and then in digital, have been subject to a range of forces which have shaped and regulated them in a number of ways. Foremost among these forces have been the pressures of commercial markets and the drive towards profitability, whereby broadcast programmes are regarded as commodities to be produced, sold and distributed primarily for profit by private, competing companies and advertisers. This commercial pattern of broadcast provision has characterised the development of radio and television in North America and has come to predominate in a number of other national cultures worldwide. On the other hand, the historical expansion of broadcasting has been decisively influenced by the operations of governments and state agencies which have sought to intervene in, and restrict the power of, commercial, market interests. Public service broadcasting entails the provision and organisation of radio and television channels primarily as public utilities and resources rather than as profitable commodities. This emphasis has entailed their organisation as national, cultural institutions, owned, regulated and run in the public interest and dedicated to the public provision of information and entertainment, part and parcel of the requirements of modern democratic societies. In contrast to the view of broadcast audiences as consumers to be attracted for profit – which is associated with the commercial model – public service broadcasting has been motivated much more by a commitment to the socially responsible provision of information and culture – to which, it is argued, all citizens have rights of access, above and beyond their abilities to pay.

The history of the development of broadcasting systems in many nation states from the 1920s onwards has been profoundly influenced by the values and discourses of public service. This has been either in the form of complete, publicly owned state monopolies or, more recently, as a significant public element within mixed systems which allow for competition between commercial and public variants of radio and TV. In the United Kingdom, the key components of public service broadcasting as embodied by the BBC have been guided by a number of principles.

First, as a public service, broadcasting should be available to all. Provision should be *universal* in both geographical and cultural terms, and should be obliged to recognise and cater for the unity *and* the diversity of citizens within the national culture and its constituent communities. A second, defining feature of public service systems concerns their financing, accountability and autonomy. The services provided should be funded by a simple and egalitarian system of public sponsorship – as, for instance, in the case of the licence fee in Britain. This system should, as far as possible, distance and insulate broadcasters from the vested interests of political parties, governments, and corporate or commercial intervention. Only by guaranteeing this degree of autonomy to broadcasters, it is argued, can the broadcast institution genuinely serve the public interest in the 'balanced' provision of programmes; in its mission to what has historically been understood as informing, educating and entertaining audiences. A third and final component of the public service ethos relates to the nature of the services and programmes provided by broadcasters for public consumption. These, it is claimed, should be of the highest possible *'quality'* – a key term in recent debates about the future of broadcasting – and should be motivated by, and dedicated to, achieving high cultural standards. Public service broadcasters are obliged as a result to demonstrate a commitment to cultural 'excellence' in their provision of radio and television programmes and services. This obligation has generally assumed that there are singular, widespread and agreed criteria whereby high cultural quality or value may be discerned; but public service broadcasters have also been obliged to recognise and respond in a 'balanced' fashion to the needs and views of all groups in modern, plural cultures and communities, regardless of their relative status, power or influence.

In historical terms it is important to consider some central contradictions and shifts in both the ethos and the practices associated with public service broadcasting. In Britain as in many other European systems, long-established criticisms of cultural elitism and paternalism, especially associated with the stance and influence of Lord Reith, the first Director General of the BBC, have claimed that it was 'out of touch', complacent and did not give the public 'what it wanted'. These criticisms have been accompanied in the post-war period by a set of commercial, market-based, deregulatory attacks which have focused on the claimed inefficiencies of large-scale public broadcast provision and its inability to deliver *popular* programming in tune with the many and varied demands of modern audiences. In recent years, these views have also coincided with the expansion of new multi-channel systems: cable, satellite, video and digital technologies which have threatened to overturn the very concept of 'broadcasting' – public or otherwise – as well as providing fuel for the challenge to the older, established rigidities and hegemony of many national broadcasting systems. As a result of this alliance, and in spite of counter-criticisms of commercial broadcast environments – that they provide 'wall to wall *Dallas*' or 'fifty-four channels but nothing on' – many contemporary writers have suggested that public service broadcasting is a monolithic concept which has outlived its time and relevance in the early twenty-first century. Against this, and in the light of experiencing the tendencies often clearly manifest within commercially dominated, deregulated systems – narrowing of choice, exclusion of many voices from the public domain, lowering of 'quality' – some recent reassessments of public service broadcasting have sought to restate the importance and viability, for modern mass democracies, of equality of access to a *shared public broadcast culture*. From this point of view, the erosion of this public resource and its utility has been understood as the political weakening of an important historical right of democratic citizenship as well as an index of modern social and cultural fragmentation. In dealing with the political and technological challenges of modern times, public service broadcasters undoubtedly face a number of intractable financial and cultural contradictions.

Tim O'Sullivan

11

Who Wants To Be A Millionaire? Contextual analysis and the endgame of public service television

Mike Wayne

Introduction

This chapter has two distinct but linked aims. First, it offers a methodology for the contextual analysis of television. Second, it engages with the political debates concerning the nature of that context, essentially what is at stake between public service and market-led television. There is an urgent need to develop and popularise contextual analysis in order to engage with political debates that feed (or potentially feed) directly into government policy making affecting the broadcasting environment. The absence of contextual analysis limits the influence of media studies on the media. It is also required for the simple reason that contextual analysis is little practised by academics and therefore students of television. Textual analysis dominates the study of television (although audience studies have also become popular in recent years). For example, *How To Study Television* (Selby and Cowdrey, 1995) and *Television, Critical Methods and Applications* (Butler, 1994) are comprehensive introductions to the study of the language and grammar of television, how it constructs its meanings and the political implications of those signifying practices. These are important questions but there is an extraordinary silence in both books concerning the contexts in which television is produced. Unless those contexts are factored into the analysis, we cannot understand why television produces the meanings which it does, what the limits to those meanings are and why alternative meanings cannot be accommodated in a given historical moment.

Such questions can only partially be explained by the 'intentions' of those working at the point of production, for we would have also to explain why those intentions and not others are deemed appropriate. How, in other words, has a particular set of intentions become institutionalised? Contextual analysis thus implies a causal effect between X (an aspect of the context) and Y (an aspect of the text). The key issue facing any contextual discussion of television today, the issue on which any student of television must clarify where they stand, is the question of public service television versus the market. Indeed, much depends on whether we retain the very notion of 'versus' or whether, in the language of New Labour and the era of the Private Finance Initiative, it is better to talk of public–private 'partnerships'. This chapter will offer a case study of the quiz show *Who Wants To Be A Millionaire?* in order to explore the gravitational pull of commercialisation which is warping what is left of public service television.

As a way of developing a contextual analysis we can start by making an analytical distinction between three different types of context. It is an analytical distinction because, in practice, the different types of context overlap and interact with each other. Nevertheless, it may be useful to designate: (1) the socio-cultural context, (2) the institutional context and (3) the production context.

Contexts defined

1 Socio-cultural context. This is the widest contextual frame, the most general or abstract in its concepts. It may draw on empirical examples to illustrate the general arguments, but this level of analysis does not deal with the details of history. The 'socio' part of this contextual frame should refer to the fundamental structural relationships of society, in their economic, political and social manifestations. The analysis may draw links, causal connections and parallels between the specific medium in question (here, television) and other political and economic developments. The 'cultural' part of the term does not designate a special, highly valued type of symbolic production/consumption (e.g. 'high' culture), but is used here in a more anthropological sense: culture as a site where meanings and values and identities are constructed, forged, fought over and renegotiated.

2 Institutional context. At this level, analysis would be concerned to start mapping the organisation and bodies involved in, or having an impact on, television production. This would include production companies, broadcasters, regulatory bodies, sponsors, advertising agencies, government and government policy making, and so on. If the socio-cultural context is characterised by a certain historical generality, the institutional level of analysis requires more detail in the histories of these interlocking forces. Since this is a large, shifting field, the task of the researcher or student is to *locate* the salient features of these institutional arrangements and their relevant histories in terms of the specific text under investigation. The researcher or student must identify those institutional factors which made the production of the given text *possible* or *likely*.

3 Production context. Once (1) and (2) have been mapped, we can then move to the third level of analysis, the immediate production context for the text in question, that is to say the process of production directly responsible for the making of the programme. Some questions which arise here are: How has a specific group of social agents come together within the institutional context to actualise its cultural labour? The programme will be made for a particular channel and for a particular place in the schedule. How do these factors impinge on the programme?

Genre

Contextual analysis does not make textual analysis redundant, nor are they absolutely distinct operations, the latter beginning when the former has been completed. Although contexts (1) and (2) pre-exist any given text, the cultural resources which the text mobilises are also already in circulation. The concept which describes this cultural resource, this reservoir of potential meanings, is genre. *Who Wants To be A Millionaire?* belongs to the genre of the quiz show. Defining genres is a tricky business, however. One cannot formulate a definition without some sense of which texts might qualify for being grouped together as sharing the characteristics which make up a genre. Yet a definition which is based on an already existing body of work risks being unable to accommodate new directions and developments in the genre (see Tudor, 1976:121). Generic definition, then, is an exercise in gauging cultural consensus among producers, audiences or critics as to what constitutes the genre, and recognising the possibility for considerable diversity at any given point in time and flexibility over time as the genre changes. It is not about constructing watertight, scholastic definitions and then fiercely guarding what may or may not be admitted.

The quiz show (or the more physically oriented game show) may be broadly defined as a programme in which games of physical skill, knowledge and/or chance are played, usually (although not always) by ordinary members of the public, individually or collectively, usually (although not exclusively) in competition with others, where an accumulation of points allows progress through to different 'levels' and where proceedings are mediated by a figure of authority, often a well-known celebrity or television presenter. This will do as a starting point although it by no means encompasses every example of the genre (in Britain, Channel 5's extra-cheap quiz show, *100 Per Cent*, for example, merely has a voiceover orchestrating the proceedings). Nor does it fix in stone such variables as the types of interaction between competitors and studio audience (if there is one). It does however provide us with a useful sense of the cultural resources being mobilised by the specific contextual determinants in play.

Socio-cultural context

Contextual analysis is often conceived of by students and teachers alike as 'boring' compared with actually analysing something as tangible as a television text (Wollen, 1991:82). One way of addressing this is to foreground the political issues at stake around the questions of ownership, technology, finance, group structures and dynamics, and so on. In Britain, under Conservative Party governments during the 1980s and early 1990s, commercial forces were systematically introduced into television just as they were, to varying degrees of intensity, into other formerly public spheres, such as the natural utilities (water, gas, electricity), transport (buses, railways), health and now, under New Labour, education.

In a seminal article in 1983, Nicholas Garnham anticipated the new waves of commercialisation about to hit British broadcasting. He identified a number of forces driving the free market revolution. Chief among these was the fact that much Western capital had shifted into electronics and communications (hardware and software) and away from older heavy manufacturing industries, much of which had been relocated to the developing and underdeveloped countries. However, capital investment in the electronics and communications sector found its potential growth and profit margins blocked by the regulated television environments of Western Europe. In the UK as elsewhere in Europe, television was founded on the principles and practices of public service broadcasting. In the UK, this meant a television system whose programmes were universally available to all; a programme range that recognised that all viewers sometimes occupied 'minority' taste preferences which should be catered for; that the cost did not include squeezing viewers for shareholder profits; and that, with a broad mission to inform, educate and entertain, it addressed viewers as citizens participating in a democratic body politic rather than private consumers. It was this system which had to be substantially dismantled if the new private media outfits were to profit. Countering the arguments of Conservative politicians, business leaders and pro-market ideologues, Garnham (1983:14) offered a long historical perspective:

> What we are in fact being offered is not a more socially responsive, politically accountable, diverse mode of cultural interchange in the electronic sphere, but on the contrary the expansion of price and profit, of commodity exchange, as the dominating mode of organization in yet another area of cultural production and consumption, as though this were a new phenomenon. Instead we are witnessing merely the latest phase in a process integral to the capitalist mode of production.

Understanding this integral process is actually quite simple and involves a brief digression on the nature of the commodity. In his analysis of the commodity, Marx argued that it is composed of two attributes: use value and exchange value. By use value Marx was referring to all the uses – personal, cultural, political, and so on – to which a commodity can be put by the individuals and groups who consume it – whether it is a coat or a book. By exchange value, he referred to the economic, financial value of the commodity, *how much* it 'exchanges' for. Under capitalism, it is this quantitative measure, this exchange value which dominates the production of commodities. The more exchange value can be increased, the greater the profitability of the commodity for capital. The fundamental dynamic of capitalism is accumulation (of profits) for the sake of accumulation. Exchange value is the concept which describes this dynamic. This may sound very abstract, and unfashionably Marxian, but in fact the terms 'use value' and 'exchange value', and the conflicting dynamics which they describe, are the basic conceptual tools required to understand how the society we all live in actually works on a day-to-day basis.

Here is an example involving an industry adjacent to television, the ratings industry. I found this just scanning the pages of a trade magazine, *Broadcast*. Such trade magazines are interesting precisely because, while we as viewers are interested in the use values of television, the trade papers reveal how television texts circulate as commodities under capitalism. As commercial pressures increase, so too does the need to hold on to audiences and, with that need, so too does the technological capacity to monitor, record, assess and ultimately control (or try and control) audiences. Thus a new software system called Viewtime has been developed (by Anglo-French company Primetime).

Viewtime transforms, for example, the Broadcasters' Audience Research Board's (BARB's) ratings statistics into a minute-by-minute analysis of the ebb **199** and flow of audiences, complete with graphs and images from the programmes. This technology allowed one industry analyst to note that the television game show *Gladiators* loses audiences once the winner is announced, 'but the presenters stay there for the next two minutes. If the last spot on a magazine show isn't good enough, people switch off and you *lose all your promos and advertising . . .* 60 seconds is a long time in TV' (White, 1999:21, my emphasis). It is clear here how technology is developed and used in the interests of exchange value and how this could have a direct effect on the text in question. Of course *Gladiators* is already a cultural commodity, but the beauty of the commodity (from the point of view of capitalism) is that it is always possible to *commodify the commodity further.* Thus what constitutes 'good enough' is simply the economic value of audiences to the programme makers and the successful delivery of them to the advertisers (Masterman, 1985:106–13). Once that becomes a dominating principle of television production, the possibility for other criteria of 'good' to have a presence is severely limited.

The distinction and tension between use value and exchange value can be easily mapped on to the issue of public service broadcasting versus market-led television. Under capitalism, television is both a cultural good and a commodity, and this duality is true even for public service television (see, for example, Wayne, 1998). But within public service television there is a tilt towards allowing more space and autonomy for use values to be part of the production of the text. Conversely, the more television is market led, the more decisions are consciously and unconsciously implemented to secure the exchange value of the programme in question. This has implications for the genre we are concerned with here. Under public service broadcasting, examples of the quiz show/game show genre tend to foreground such values as camaraderie, for example *It's A Knock-Out* (BBC) and *The Generation Game* (BBC); or specialist knowledge, e.g. *Mastermind* (BBC) or *University Challenge* (BBC); or physical/problem-solving skills such as *The Crystal Maze* (C4); but the more exchange value permeates television, the more we can expect consumerism, consumer goods, individualism and hard cash to be at the centre of the game show. *Trading Up*, for example, a game show based around car ownership and status, would have been unthinkable on Britain's Channel Four only a few years ago. There is, then, a fundamental tension between the different television systems of public service broadcasting and the market.

Not everyone, however, would agree with this argument. Richard Collins, for example, asks whether a public sphere could be delivered by the market and privately owned institutions. Recognising that hitherto commercial television in Britain (ITV and Channel Four) has been operating within a strongly regulated public service environment, Collins cannot come up with an actual example of the market delivering a public sphere in television. Undeterred by this, he turns to the print media: 'The UK's elite national press, for example, comprises five daily newspapers each owned by a different corporation and each of which has a distinctive political position' (Collins, 1993:252). This is a most unfortunate example, at least for Collins's argument. Let us leave aside the point that the Murdoch-owned *Times* and *Sunday Times* campaigned vigorously against the BBC and public service broadcasting during the 1980s, simply and crudely because it suited the proprietor's financial interests (O'Malley, 1994:31–46). The key word here is *elite*. For the middle class, there is a public forum of some political debate and diversity, but for the majority who constitute the readership of the tabloid press, information, education, political debate and diversity are squeezed out in favour of celebrities, scandals, gossip, competitions and prizes. Where politics does appear, it is invariably opportunistic and strident – the declaration of an editorial position rather than a forum for any sense of political debate.

What the split between the tabloid and elite press reveals is the way the market reinforces what Pierre Bourdieu (1996) calls unequal cultural competences and dispositions. In a class society, consumers do not have equal access to cultural competences (acquired at home and through formal education), that is, the knowledges required to decode cultural forms, from music to photography. Competences are also reinforced by cultural dispositions, that is, the sense that a person has of a congruence between their preferences and the object consumed. It is such dispositions which encourage working-class readers to think that the elite press is 'not for the likes of us' and is thus a deeply internalised and powerfully effective way of reproducing cultural consumption along class lines.

The quiz show is also an interesting site where the disjuncture between class-determined cultural dispositions manifests itself. The genre, as we shall see, predominantly attracts precisely the audience who cannot take for granted the kinds of material good and financial prize which the show holds out for the winning contestants. Conversely, the genre tends to do less well in attracting materially better off audiences higher up the class ladder, where the blatant consumerism, the celebration of consumer products, the brandishing of prizes, tends to be seen as vulgar and lacking in 'taste'. Such unexamined attitudes have even undermined academic studies of the genre (White, 1994:119). Since the unequal distribution of cultural capital helps constitute ready-made markets, commercial media often have little incentive to overcome these divisions. However, sometimes it does make financial sense to try and bind audiences from different classes together, and, as we shall see, *Who Wants To Be A Millionaire?* attempts to do just that. The catch, however, is that the programme does not call into question or even acknowledge the divisions which exist within society. Indeed, my analysis will show how it perpetuates those divisions while trying to make them invisible.

Public service broadcasting at its best has a duality within its mode of address. On the one hand it constructs a shared forum, a civic space; yet it also, paradoxically, acknowledges that this shared space is characterised by social and cultural divisions. Now of course, as Collins points out, the shared but divided public space of public service broadcasting has often been a hierarchical one, reverential of authority, patrician and paternalistic. This constitutes the Arnoldian and Reithian traditions of cultural provision – giving the masses what elites decide is good for them (see Collins, 1993:245–6). While this tradition has been influential among the personnel, policies and programmes of the BBC in particular, it is an influence that has been gradually declining since the 1960s. Along with its residual Reithian identity, the BBC now openly embraces a discourse sensitive to regional and cultural diversity **201** (see, for example, Hall, 1999:22) and even includes radical grassroots voices which significantly extend and transform our notion of 'the popular' through such initiatives as the Community Programmes Unit. (*cont. p. 205*)

Radio: a twenty-first-century medium

Broadcast radio throughout TV's second era (roughly the 1980s and 1990s) went about anticipating, in its own varied practices and development throughout the world, many of the transformations that television was not to begin seeing until the 2000s. That period for TV was one of widespread availability and still also of relative stability in terms of content genres, relationships with audiences, regulatory frameworks, and so on, even as massive forces of change – digitalisation, globalisation – mustered for TV's transformation towards the twentieth century's end. The world that TV found itself moving into was one of multiple niches for content and services, the loss forever of the gigantic national audiences who could be brought together simultaneously around their TV sets, and an altered balance between use value and exchange value. In a fully market oriented – exchange-value driven – broadcasting environment, the public service ideal itself has to work within niches – no longer can it be *claimed* as an ethos characterising a whole monolithic and dominant broadcasting operation from the ground up, as with the old BBC. But even within the BBC, radio has not operated in precisely that way for some time. Unashamedly populist and relatively shallow radio channels indirectly subsidised with their large numbers the more clearly public service output of other channels. Radio has long tended to operate with more closely defined 'niches' of listeners, especially since radio receivers became small, light and battery powered, in part because radio insinuates itself more easily into a vast range of listening contexts, including the mobile and those where radio is always a background for other activities.

For a long time we seem to have believed that the true vocation of broadcasting was to gather and address large national audiences, something that radio itself had done before TV, of course; most famously with US President Franklin D. Roosevelt's 'fireside chats': 12 March 1933 – 'I want to talk for a few minutes with the people of the United States about banking . . .'. But when TV took over this mission, radio found a largely different role for itself through proliferating channels, programme types, audience relationships, niche objectives – the very sort of 'ecology' to which TV is now having to adapt. Ironically, then, radio got to the twenty-first century better equipped than TV, not least in its rapid and relatively unproblematic assimilation of digital technology. While TV distracted our critical and scholarly attention, radio reached every nook and cranny of the planet with an amazing diversity of aims, organisational arrangements and methods for realising 'use value' within the broadcasting market-place. A few examples here will have to suffice to indicate something of this diversity.

Radio Sagarmatha, a Nepalese community radio station, was the first of its kind in South Asia when it started broadcasting in 1997. In a country with formidable geographical barriers to communication and a level of poverty and illiteracy that limits the accessibility of print media, Radio Sagarmatha took advantage of a newly liberal, if unstable, political climate following the 1990 change from a monarchical to a parliamentary system. In the early 1990s, a new political and regulatory framework for media was pieced together in Nepal, culminating in a 1993 National Broadcasting Act which opened the way for alternatives to the state broadcaster, Radio Nepal. A lobbying group, the Nepal Forum of Environmental Journalists, drove the campaign to secure a licence for Radio Sagarmatha, while Western-style commercial radio stations rapidly proliferated in the more liberal communications environment that was developing there. Broadcasting six hours a day, Radio Sagarmatha (the Nepali name for Mount Everest) offers a diet of public affairs journalism, on-the-street coverage of human interest stories and vox-pop, folk music, community news bulletins and an access slot called 'It's My Turn Now'. Funding is derived from a mix of co-production with local groups, sponsorship, various 'bartering' arrangements with other organisations, paid public service announcements and a controlled degree of commercial advertising.

Based in Belgrade, Serbia, Real Radio B2-92 in late 1999 was still broadcasting on a frequency owned by political opposition leader Vuk Draskovic. Early in the year, station B92 had been closed down by President Milosevic's ruling Socialist Party of Serbia, its studio occupied by police, equipment confiscated and staff ordered out. An appeal for public financial support, including a successful internet-based campaign, allowed the station to return to the air, but by then the supposedly 'original' station B92 was broadcasting again, now with pro-Milosevic personnel installed. Back on air as B2-92, the independent group of broadcasters set about reclaiming their identity with the help of international recognition – they had, for example, won the MTV Europe Music Award in the 'Human Rights' category in 1998 – and campaigning for the return of their original studios and equipment. First started as a youth station primarily broadcasting rock music, B92 had transformed itself into a forum for independent journalism during the ongoing unrest triggered by Milosevic's ethnic cleansing policy (including the March–June 1999 war with NATO over Kosovo). Perhaps its most remarkable achievement – and one which underscores the way radio has been pushed to the fore in the broadcasting environment of a post-Cold War world of multiplying cultural identities – was the establishment of ANEM (the Association of Independent Electronic Media) in June 1997. B92's output was transmitted to London via digital telephone lines. There it was re-transmitted to a satellite and beamed back over the former Yugoslavia, where it could be freely captured and re-broadcast as FM radio. Some thirty-three radio stations accepted this 'feed', constituting a significant alternative source of information to the sate-controlled stations. ANEM partner stations got internet access as part of the arrangement, extending their reach to a potentially global community of interest even as they focused on very local and regional needs. However, along with other independent media in Serbia as 1999 ended, B2-92 was facing the new Serbian Law on Public Information which allowed the state to instigate forty-eight-hour legal proceedings and fines against dissenting media groups, a procedure deliberately designed to prevent adequate defences from being prepared or public sympathy aroused. It remains to be seen whether opposition radio in Serbia can continue to find niches from which to operate successfully. B2-92 continues to rely largely on donations for its financing.

Studio Ijambo in Burundi was set up in 1995 by the US-based non-governmental organisation (NGO) 'Search for Common Ground' which, in partnership with the European Centre for Common Ground, operated throughout the 1990s as an international, non-profit, self-styled 'peace and conflict resolution' organisation with a particular emphasis on using the media to effect changes in attitude. The organisation also has its own spin-off company, 'Common Ground Productions' (based in Washington) which produces radio, TV and internet content. Studio Ijambo operates as a radio production studio, with local staff, to provide independent content for the national radio broadcaster in Burundi. Ijambo's particular focus has been on sending reporting teams into areas where tension was high between the rival ethnic groups, Tutsi and Hutu, often including journalists or programme makers from both groups, where they would develop stories that presented the different perspectives. There is a deliberate 'Common Ground' method-ology here, which the NGO has used in Bosnia and elsewhere; in Burundi the objective was to intervene in the way the ethnic conflict was being defined and reported. Most notably, this resulted in the production of a popular radio soap opera, *Our Neighbours Ourselves*, based on the lives of neighbouring Hutu and Tutsi families, in which the story lines typically 'discover' that sup-posed ethnic difficulties are actually underpinned by shared economic prob-lems or other common social ills that can be addressed together. In 1993 there were an estimated 100,000 ethnic killings in Burundi, with even more in neighbouring Rwanda, and the violence continues. 'Hate radio' remains a common feature of broadcasting in Burundi – radio stations, often using mobile transmitters, that broadcast propaganda directed against the other side, as notoriously with Radio Rutomorangingo ('the radio that tells the truth'), a viciously anti-Tutsi station which broadcast from 1994 to 1996.

These three examples illustrate how deeply radio is embedded in the com-plexities of the twenty-first century and how important it is for us to direct renewed attention towards understanding its roles and impact, especially as television is encountering some of the same issues in its new era of plenty and fragmentation. Disentangling whose interests are represented in these and similar examples is not always easy. What is a US-based NGO really doing funding radio content production in Burundi, however worthy its expressed aims and however unsavoury may be some of the alternatives with which it is trying to compete for listeners' attention? On 28 October 1998, another Washington-based organisation, WorldSpace, launched its powerful AfriStar satellite for digital radio. Five per cent of the content carried by AfriStar (which has three overlapping beams covering the entirety of Africa and much of the Middle East) is related to education and 'social development', while the rest includes CNN International, Radio France International, 'UltraPop' (predominantly Anglo-American pop music) and even 'Up Country', a channel entirely devoted to American country and western music. WorldSpace will be launching AsiaStar and AmeriStar (Latin America) radio services in the wake of AfriStar.

Meanwhile, at the low end of the technological scale, Rwandan refugees in eastern Zaire in 1999 were sent 1,300 clockwork radio receivers, funded by Britain's overseas aid programme and distributed through the UN High Commission for Refugees. Invented by Englishman Trevor Bayliss, the 'BayGen' radio is being promoted by others as a way for refugees to tune in to the BBC's World Service, although once in their hands it can of course be used to tune in to anything, including the 'hate radio' stations from which the refugees might otherwise have been isolated in the camps. The clockwork radios have also been enthusiastically supported by the South African government as a way of taking radio into areas without electricity or access to batteries. So radio enters the twenty-first century as an omnipresent, global medium, and the complexity of its entanglement in such a variety of circumstances (idealistic, regionally sensitive, globally commercial, propagandistic) is something that is still seriously under-researched and, as a consequence, inadequately understood.

Dan Fleming

A third 'face' of the BBC (in addition to the 'Reithian' and the 'regional') testifies to the impact of the Thatcher/Major years (the last two British Conservative Prime Ministers of the twentieth century); this is the entrepreneurial, commercial BBC (Garnham, 1993:26–8). The BBC's decision to buy the rights to broadcast the National Lottery may be taken to symbolise its embrace of an ethic quite antithetical to public service. It is symptomatic first of all of the BBC's determination to compete with ITV. As Marcus Plantin, ITV's chief scheduler put it: 'The Lottery provides an appointment to view, which other channels have to fight their way around' (Culf, 1996a:12). There is a broader politics to this decision. At a time when high-income earners have escaped paying higher taxes, the National Lottery is a deeply regressive 'game'. It is overwhelmingly played by lower-income groups (i.e. the socially desperate) who pay out more as a proportion of their income to play than those middle- and high-income earners who do buy tickets. Where progressive income tax distributes resources from the elites to the majority, the National Lottery reverses such enlightened rationality and distributes resources from the majority to the few – both in the small number of winners it creates and the amount of money channelled to 'good causes' which favour Establishment projects. Such is the absurd fate of a society governed by exchange value.

Institutional context

At this level of analysis we must start to fill in the empirical details of events which make the actual production of our chosen text possible and, indeed, likely. The shift towards a more commercial broadcasting system was confirmed by the Peacock Committee into Broadcasting, set up by the British government in 1985. Its report in 1986 set the tone for developing a market-oriented broadcasting system. This was the result then, not of technological developments in satellite and cable delivery systems, but of a conscious, political strategy. A White Paper on broadcasting followed in 1988: this signalled the government's intention of creating a more commercially driven ITV. The ITV regulatory body, the IBA, was to be replaced by a 'lighter touch' body, the

ITC. The Independent Television Commission which came into operation in 1990 relaxed, for example, the old IBA's rules concerning prizes for quiz shows. The IBA had fixed as an absolute maximum a prize equal in value to the price of a small new car (Tunstall, 1993:146) – the star prize in the old quiz show, *The Sale Of The Century*. *Who Wants To Be A Millionaire?* is clearly operating in a very different environment.

The 1990 Broadcasting Act ushered in 'a relatively deregulated commercial TV, satellite, cable and radio sector' (O'Malley, 1994:134). Where once public service had been the founding ethos of television, now it was merely one component and an increasingly embattled one at that. The Act also obliged the BBC and ITV to commission a minimum 25 per cent of their programmes from 'independent' producers. As we shall see, independence is a rather problematic concept.

The 1990 Act was in effect an advertisers' charter. They had been key lobbyers in wanting to open up television to more commercial forces and competition, since this would simultaneously expand the market for their clients, increase their influence over the medium and drive down the prices they had to pay for air time.

One significant indication of the greater role advertising would play was the increase in programme sponsorship which the Act ushered in. The ITC immediately revised the old IBA's guidelines on programme sponsorship, greatly expanding its possibilities. The new guidelines allow a ten second aural and visual credit at the start of a programme, a seven second credit at the end, a similar credit before and after advertising breaks and a five second mention in any trailers (Murdock, 1992:222). The first sponsorship was Powergen's link with ITV's national weather forecasts ('Whatever the weather') in 1989. The first sponsorships for drama programmes were *Rumpole of the Bailey* (Croft Port) in 1991 and *Inspector Morse* (Beamish Stout) in 1992. What is happening here is that the image and associations already established for a commodity by advertising and marketing are being merged with the characters and their 'lifestyles' in the programmes. Inevitably, with advertising revenue spread more thinly across more channels, broadcasters will be looking for the possibility of sponsorship deals even before a programme idea is commissioned.

There is a public service issue here: that of whether television can articulate a diverse range of voices, whether it can raise difficult questions about social and cultural life, address uncomfortable contradictions and bring the marginalised, neglected social strata and areas of living into the mainstream of representation (Murdock, 1992:224). The problem which sponsorship poses for such ambitions is the same with advertising generally. As Sut Jhally (1990:91) notes, '[p]rogramming . . . has to provide the right *environment* for the advertising that will be inserted within it. Advertisers seek compatible programming vehicles that stress the lifestyles of consumption.' Sponsorship merely extends this logic further by blurring the boundaries between programming and advertising.

One result of the growth of programme sponsorship has been the increased cross-promotion between newspapers and quiz shows. Rupert Murdoch's *Sun* newspaper launched a scratchcard game in conjunction with ITV's *Wheel Of Fortune* in 1994. TV advertising, plus heavy (front page) newspaper promotion of the scratchcard in *The Sun* and the *News of the World* helped boost *Wheel Of Fortune*'s Monday night scrap for audiences with the BBC's *EastEnders*. Simultaneously, *The Sun*'s circulation was reported to have increased by a quarter of a million with the promise of winning £40,000 if people played the scratchcard, which required watching the show (O'Carroll, 1994:49). Such cross-media promotions mean that public service broadcasting faces increasing competition not just from its television rivals but from other commercial media as well.

Who Wants To Be A Millionaire? also used cross-promotion between media to increase its profile. It was originally sponsored by *The Sun*, which used a game card both to sell newspapers and to increase audiences for the programme. The game card shows a series of numbers alongside cash prizes ranging from £100 to £1,000,000. During *The Sun*'s sponsor's credits at the beginning of the show, at the beginning *and* end of commercial breaks and at the end of the programme, numbers are flashed up on the television screen. If the numbers correspond to those associated with one of the cash prizes, then the lucky card holder has won. The more programmes you watch, the more likely you are to win a prize. If we recall the *Gladiators* example, I have suggested that advertisers and commercial broadcasters are worried that they cannot control people and ensure that they sit and watch the adverts during commercial breaks. The game card, however, tries to solve this problem by anchoring people to their seats in the hope that their numbers will come up. Such sponsorship, then, is not just about generating extra revenue for the broadcaster, but is also used to build and control audiences.

A further indication of the commercialisation of ITV and British television generally has been ITV's reorganisation of the prime time schedule. Pressure grew in the mid 1990s from ITV's chief executives to shift *News At Ten* because it made it impossible to show films and feature-length dramas uninterrupted after the 9 p.m. watershed. In 1994, the ITC, backed by the then Prime Minister, John Major, successfully resisted pressure from ITV to move the flagship programme to an early evening spot. ITV's attempt to test the ITC's resolve further came with an attempt to delay an edition of *News At Ten* to accommodate a 'specially' extended edition of the drama series *Cracker*. This again was rebuffed by the ITC (Culf, 1996b:10). However, with New Labour 'not minded', as Will Hutton (1999:30) observed, 'to confront private business interests', the ITC bowed to the inevitable in November 1998 and agreed to shift *News At Ten*, provided that ITV maintained its commitment to public service values. Since the removal of *News At Ten* from prime time was itself symptomatic of the slow death of public service values, this was a pious wish indeed.

Production context

A key resource for performing contextual analysis now comes into play at this contextual level: and that is the people involved in the production of the text to be studied. The interview and any access you can get to their data ought to be a key part of your methodology. This can provide you with details and insights into the production context and process and answers to your own specific questions which cannot be gleaned from newspaper and magazine cuttings. Who you talk to depends upon what kinds of issue and area you want to address. For example, because I want to look at the impact of advertising on *Who Wants To Be A Millionaire?* I approached Sponsorvision, the company responsible for making the adverts promoting the name of a programme's sponsors. I also talked to Celador, the company which originated and produced *Who Wants To Be A Millionaire?*. Any information or data generated by interviewees cannot be accepted at face value: its foundational assumptions must be brought to light and the significance of the information integrated into a theoretical and critical framework.

Within the UK there are a small number of dominant players in the international quiz show/game show market. They are Endemol, Action Time, Pearson Television and Celador (which also produces a range of light entertainment programmes). These companies work in the so-called 'independent' sector – meaning they are not broadcasters. But, in fact, the tendency to monopoly which is a characteristic pressure within capitalism is at work here as well. The 'independents' are becoming tied in with the broadcasters, with each other or with major conglomerates. In 1989, the US studio Paramount acquired 49 per cent of Action Time. In 1992, the Action Time directors made a brief last stand for the small independent business by staging a management buyout; but they quickly conceded to the inexorable logic of competition and convergence, and in 1996 Carlton television acquired 100 per cent of Action Time (Walker, 1998:47). Celador meanwhile is a wholly owned subsidiary of a larger media corporation called Complete Communications. Celador's turnover for 1998–99 was in the region of £14 million. (Incidentally, the prize money for *Who Wants To Be A Millionaire* is generated by the viewers themselves, paying premium rate telephone calls in order to try and get on the programme.)

These monopolistic tendencies, of course, narrow the number of production units and it makes those production units entirely *dependent* on the mainstream commercial logics and forces at work, thus narrowing the possibilities for the quiz show genre. And Celador is operating not only in the national, but also the international market. As is common with successful quiz shows, it has optioned the format of *Who Wants To Be A Millionaire?* to thirty-one countries to date. However, as theorists have often noted, while the formulaic qualities of genre play an important role in standardising output, any genre must also accommodate some level of *differentiation*. For there is also an economic drive for innovation and variation which encourages producers to 'sift through the constantly shifting cultural fund for trends, gimmicks, and novelties' (Meehan, 1993:570). Innovation, however, occurs within firmly policed boundaries. As Trish Kinane of Action Time puts it: 'It became apparent to us very quickly that there was no point having the best idea in the world if it didn't solve a broadcaster's problem' (Walker, 1998:47).

Bearing in mind our widest contextual frame, a socio-cultural context in which the profit motive is dominant, there is no mystery as to what that problem is: how to deliver audiences to the advertisers. However, bearing in mind also our more historically and empirically detailed institutional and production contexts, we have to recognise that Celador's *Who Wants To Be A Millionaire* sets out to solve a *specific* problem for the broadcaster. One of the enduring criticisms which advertisers have had of ITV in Britain is that its programmes attract a predominantly older and poorer audience than is entirely desirable. Ideally, advertisers would like to have access to a wider range of socio-economic spectators. Thus advertisers were increasingly critical of the homogenisation of ITV's schedule during the mid 1990s. The problem was acute because ITV companies were cutting investment having poured money into the Treasury after the 1991 'auctions' of the broadcasting franchise (Corner *et al.*, 1994:10). As one commentator noted, the channel's brand image was rapidly becoming a 'repetitive parade of flashing blue lights, flapping white coats and Beadle-ish bloopers' (Phillips, 1995:16; Jeremy Beadle hosted a show of camcorder pratfalls sent in by viewers). Here we have a major contradiction. The advertisers actually want diversity! But they also want large numbers of viewers and they want the 'masses' even more than they want specialised audience markets. Thus *The South Bank Show*, covering the arts, which has 45 per cent of its audience drawn from the higher-income brackets and 25 per cent aged in the crucial 16–24 bracket, does *not* enjoy prime time scheduling (Culf, 1995:2).

Now, according to Celador, in the mid 1990s the head scheduler of the ITV network, Marcus Plantin, decided that there would be no more quiz shows during prime time television. Here we have an interesting methodological problem. I have not interviewed Plantin to ask why this was the case and, even if I had, there is no guarantee that his explanation would carry any great explanatory power. However, we can construct a plausible motivation for this decision by locating Plantin in his institutional context. The reason for Plantin's resistance to commissioning quiz shows was not, I wager, aesthetic, but economic: quiz shows are one of the prime culprits in drawing in predominantly older and poorer audiences.

Faced with mounting criticism about the 'quality' and range of the schedule, and a slide in ratings (Culf, 1997:11), Plantin invested new ITV money in 'quality' drama. Nevertheless, Plantin's decision is a curious anomaly, since it goes against the grain of the commercial forces which I have been mapping and which are at this time accumulating to such a degree that a programme like *Who Wants To Be A Millionaire?* becomes both possible and likely. During this period, the idea for the programme is in development, but also somewhat stalled because of Plantin's agenda. But given the increasing commercialisation of broadcasting and given the contradictory demands of the advertisers, who want large audiences more than they want diverse audiences, it was inevitable that the quiz show would return to prime time sooner rather than later. The opening was provided when Plantin left ITV in the autumn of 1997. The new head scheduler, David Liddiment, quickly commissioned *Who Wants To Be A Millionaire?*.

It was Liddiment who has been credited with devising the scheduling of the programme which saw it running on consecutive nights over ten or twelve days. This, along with *The Sun's* promotions, helped build increasing audience figures for each of the three series. Some 65.8 per cent of the adult population saw one episode of the first series and 49.8 per cent saw it at least four times. By the third series those figures had climbed respectively to 78 per cent and 64 per cent (statistics supplied by Sponsorvision). By the third series, audience figures touched 19 million, just behind long-running soap opera *Coronation Street* (*Broadcast*, 26 March 1999:31). The industry calls this kind of scheduling 'stripping' a programme across the schedules. Such a strategy is indicative of the competition for large audiences and the narrowing of the range of programme making which can be accommodated within such competitive dynamics.

Despite playing this very old game of chasing large audiences, Celador and Liddiment were trying to address the problem concerning an audience profile which advertisers found overly weighted towards the poor and the old; that is, audiences with diminished spending power. In pre-production, the programme was to be called *Cash Mountain*, but it was switched to the title of a song (from the film *High Society*) to give the programme what one ITV controller called a more 'classy, aspirational' quality (Brown, 1999:8). The programme's bid to reach more up-market viewers is also helped by the fact that the prize to be won is money rather than specific consumer goods. The latter inevitably activate questions of taste, which, as we know from Bourdieu, is linked to class. Actually to present consumer goods that would be of interest to the largest section of the audience risks alienating the more up-market viewers whose cultural capital would no doubt frame such goods as 'not for us'. Money, the universal means of exchange, allows consumers to buy into their class or subcultural taste group, but is not itself associated with any particular cultural capital.

The programme is also clearly in the high-budget bracket for a genre which can be produced remarkably cheaply. Not only does it employ an expensive star as Master of Ceremonies (Chris Tarrant), but the production values across the board, in terms of set, camera work and lighting, are above average. Finally, as Adrian Woolf from Celador pointed out, the programme edges itself towards the boundaries of drama and this helps move it away from the downmarket associations of the quiz show genre. The drama is generated in a number of ways. There is the one-to-one intensity between MC and contestant; the way the game moves very quickly into putting many thousands of pounds at risk; and the way the contestant can mobilise, like any narrative character, help to overcome obstacles to his or her goals. The contestant has three lifelines: he or she can phone a friend, ask the audience to vote on the likely answer (a 'novelty' drawn from current affairs programmes such as BBC's *Question Time*) or play 50/50 (and cut the number of possible answers from four to two). So how successful was *Who Wants To Be A Millionaire?* in rehabilitating the genre for the advertisers?

Table 1 shows the socio-economic breakdowns averaged for each of the three series (statistics supplied by Sponsorvision). The As represent the senior professional managerial and executive class; the Bs middle and junior professionals; the C1s skilled workers; the C2s manual workers; and the DEs the low paid, temporarily employed or sporadically or long-term unemployed.

We can see from this that, like the National Lottery, the programme attracts the largest bulk of its audience from the poorest sector of society.

Table 1 The socio-economic characteristics of the audience for *Who Wants To Be A Millionaire?*, 1998–99, averaged for each of the three series

	Class			
	AB (%)	C1 (%)	C2 (%)	DE (%)
Series 1: September 1998	11.6	23	25	40.4
Series 2: January 1999	12.8	23.7	24.9	38.6
Series 3: March 1999	13.5	24	24	38.5

Note: Figures courtesy of Sponsorvision.

While not exactly breaking the mould for ITV's audience profile in this respect, look at the other end of the class spectrum. The programme has marginally increased its AB share over the three series and, taken together, the ABC1s constitute, by the third series, 37.5 per cent of the audience. That's actually very good when *The South Bank Show* achieves 45 per cent across the same socio-economic categories but 'only' racks up between 1 and 5 million viewers.

(cont. p. 214)

'Working through' and US television's second golden age

As John Ellis has pointed out (2000:chapter 6), one of psychoanalyst Sigmund Freud's more informative concepts about the human mind proves to be especially informative about how television works socially and culturally. This is the concept of 'working through'. Indeed Ellis goes so far as to suggest, 'This is television's new role in the era of multiplying consumer choice and escalating social difference and antagonism' (p. 72).

For Freud, working through was the process in which the patient goes over an analytical insight (typically Freud's of course), tossing and turning it in their mind, working it into their experience, relating it to events and feelings and, in the end, benefiting from the balanced state that results. One often senses Freud's own impatience, even boredom, with the everyday detail of this extended process but he recognised its centrality to the therapeutic integrity of the 'talking cure' which he aimed to effect. Setting aside the larger question of psychoanalysis's reliability, there does seem to be a keen insight here into how people make sense of things that might otherwise be only vaguely sensed, experienced as troublesome, contradictory or as fundamentally hard to represent in thought. John Ellis's suggestion is that television has become our collective means of working through such stuff. In place of the analyst's explanatory stories we have the scriptwriters' narratives. Whether insightful and 'true' in any way hardly matters. What matters is that working through then creates a sense of grasping things, of *making sense*.

Among the legacies of twentieth-century television has been the continuing influence of US television's second 'golden age' on TV globally, on our idea of how this working through process should look and feel. American TV has long thought of the early 1950s as its first 'golden age' – when a national audience was being reached, popular content forms had emerged (sitcoms, westerns, 'cop shows', etc.) and new talent was discovering the new medium and giving those forms an early vitality that had worn off by the televisually jaded 1960s (for which film and, especially, popular music compensated). But it is a second period of renewed vitality that has deeply coloured our sense of what good mainstream television is, inaugurated by the work done at MTM Enterprises, described by one employee as a 'Camelot for writers' (Thompson, 1996:47). Starting out as a successful production house for sitcoms (such as *The Mary Tyler Moore Show*, MTM being Moore's initials – she co-founded the company with Grant Tinker), MTM from 1981 to 1988 was responsible for the long-running drama series *Hill Street Blues* and *St. Elsewhere*. More importantly, it developed creative people who went on (outside MTM itself) to make *L. A. Law*, *Twin Peaks*, *thirtysomething* and *Northern Exposure*. Together these MTM-influenced programmes constitute an extraordinarily influential super-genre of 'working through', the long-term impact of which is still clearly detectable in popular series such as *Homicide: Life on the Street*, *E. R.* and *Ally McBeal*. While different genres (the medical drama, the legal drama, etc.) are involved across that range, all of these series shared certain characteristics that become even clearer in retrospect.

This was not to do with increased 'realism' (something that was claimed at the time) so much as with a set of new formal factors – enormous casts (compared with the long-established norm for TV series of two or three main characters) who passed the narrative baton to and fro within and across episodes; an altered balance between self-contained episodic stories and background narrative 'arcs' running through the foregrounded stories; multi-stranded narratives; character change and development (quite new in the hitherto static world of American TV characters); and the frequent use of downbeat moments for closure (instead of always happy resolutions). Simple enough when coldly listed in this way, but these five factors created a new super-genre of popular TV ideally suited to the sustained and expanded role of 'working through' so astutely described by Ellis: 'Its attempt to contain the multiplicity of the world proves the need for television to work through the anxieties and the uncertainties of that world, and to provide the audience with as many means of understanding as possible' (2000:124).

Amid those five formal changes, the characters inevitably seemed slightly decentred – upstaged by others in the ensemble casts, left out of narrative strands, confused by the downbeat epiphanies. So the working through became a function of the ensemble, their multiple storylines, not an individualistic process (a tension that became the very theme of *Ally McBeal*). Although late in the main cycle, a little self-consciously aware of that and less popular as a result (if critically lauded), *Northern Exposure* (1990–95) was perhaps the epitome of the whole super-genre and the example that may best stand the test of time and changing tastes (*Hill Street Blues* already looks badly dated). A young New York doctor (who would have been entirely at home in the *thirtysomething* ensemble) finds himself having to set up practice in the remote town of Cicely, Alaska, a community peopled by the likes of an ex-astronaut, an ex-convict turned new age DJ, a Howard Hawks-style female bush pilot (cf. *Only Angels Have Wings*) and a native American adolescent whose perpetual uncertainties about his identity became an oddly stable centre for the drama on occasion.

Northern Exposure was endearing in many ways – clever, playfully aware of itself as TV, devoted to those five new principles with an ardour that made them into something almost religious – but it all begins to look problematic when we ask in what ways the ensemble cut sufficiently aspirational figures for mainstream TV audiences. *Northern Exposure* and the whole influential super-genre of which it was a part in the 1980s and 1990s managed a process of working through that *worked* for a new, supposedly classless, expanded bourgeois group of thirty-something viewers born in the late 1950s and 1960s, the late 'baby boomer' adults born into post-war affluence and relative stability. The world's larger confusions, a background sense of unease beyond their own comfort zone, could be effectively worked through via the displaced figure of Dr Joel in *Northern Exposure* or any of the others like him in these series. These were aspirational figures in the sense that they aspired – were driven by the aspiration – to *make sense* of life as lived everyday. *Ally McBeal* would later take this to a self-conscious extreme that alienated as many viewers as it attracted, but in *Northern Exposure* it made compelling TV that seemed both to have a lightness of touch, a quirkiness and self-deflating irony and yet to be basically serious. When we come to consider its pleasures and cleverness in relation to those born in the 1970s and 1980s, however, the mis-match starts to look troubling and the working through to look damagingly exclusive. Henry Giroux has put his finger on this in relation to a cinematic spin-off from the TV super-genre described here, Lawrence Kasdan's *Grand Canyon* (1992), which deployed the five formal innovations in modified form for the big screen. Here we have an ensemble cast and multiple storylines dealing with a Los Angeles of dangerous border zones, both geographically and morally. *Grand Canyon* looks, on the surface, to be carefully balanced, liberal, well intentioned. It undoubtedly resonates emotionally with the viewer who was engaged by *thirtysomething* or *Northern Exposure*. Giroux's summary could apply just as readily to those TV programmes:

> Goodwill and choice combine in this film to create a New Age sense of possibility which in the final analysis collapses irreducible differences among blacks, whites, men, and women into the airy recognition that we are all secondary to the larger cosmic forces of good and evil. Thus, the film provides a common ground on which to recognize how goodness can flow out of despair, how agency is limited by nature, and how ethics is powerless against nature's unfolding [. . .] What is missed in Kasdan's New Age ideology, as Michael Dyson points out in a different context, is 'how choice itself is not a property of autonomous moral agents acting in an existential vacuum, but rather something that is created and exercised within the interaction of social, psychic, political, and economic forces of everyday experiences'. (1994:81, quoting Dyson, 1991:75)

American TV's most successful 'second golden age' dramatic form (as adapted by Kasdan) has delivered to popular TV globally a template capable of future development but which works through our anxieties by locating them in an existential vacuum ('out there' beyond the siege mentality of *Hill Street Blues* which started it) and claiming a common ground of experience from where the problems no longer have to be explained in terms of concrete social, psychic, political and economic forces. Instead they impact on that common ground as the bizarre twists of fate and nature, including human nature, as buffeting forces that knock the protagonists off balance and where the downbeat epiphanies represent an acknowledgement of powerlessness combined with an aspirational undercurrent based on stoicism and a continuing, if dented, sense of possibility. It's not surprising that this holds the imaginations of thoughtful, sensitive thirty- and (now) forty-somethings for whom the world's refusal to fall neatly into place is a cause of ongoing unease.

But what happens to young people in their teens and twenties when confronted by these popular and successful TV forms of working through? Surely they – you? – must feel like alienated others, left out completely from the self-absorbed screen fantasies of their – your? – parents? So when we suggest that television has become our collective means of 'working through' we have to stop and ask who 'our' refers to and where those who are not included will need to turn to achieve their own working through of the fractured circumstances we share.

Dan Fleming

We now come to the nub of *Who Wants To Be A Millionaire?*'s reproduction of social inequality. The show's contestants do not mirror the socio-economic spread of its audience. For example, in the last programme of the third series (broadcast 16 March 1999), the three contestants who got into the hot seat were introduced as a computer programmer, a fire protection engineer and a store manager. These are all C1s. Just as with the National Lottery, the poorest pay a greater proportion of their income to play, so *Who Wants To Be A Millionaire?* produces its own medium-specific inequality. The DEs it seems, who constitute the largest audience for the programme, can watch but they cannot play. The C1 contestants function as mediating figures within the class spectrum which makes up the audience. They are not so far removed from either the ABs on the one hand or the C2s and DEs on the other, as to alienate them. If the DEs were on the programme in anything like the proportion of DEs actually watching, this would, I think, provide a problem for the programme. Not only would it lose a proportion of its ABC1s, the programme would also fail to provide the right environment in which to sell commodities to the audience during the advertising break. The DEs, working (if they are working at all) in the poorest paid, most insecure end of the labour market (a 'flexible' labour market, as British Prime Minister Tony Blair would euphemistically call it), would not cut sufficiently 'aspirational' figures for the brave world of ad land.

Another problem which broadcasters have is the difficulty in reconstituting the family audience in an age of multiple channels and where households often have more than one television set. The notion of the 'family audience' is an intriguing category because, while it is central to the organisation of the schedule and while it is the dominant idea which broadcasting institutions have when they imagine who their programmes are being beamed to, it does not necessarily correspond to the empirical audience who are actually watching television (Patterson, 1990:33–4). In the third series here, only 11.6 per cent of the audience were children. Although some of the early questions which contestants have to answer are easy enough for children to have a guess at, this is primarily an adult show and the questions reflect this. The programme does not escape ITV's tendency to attract older viewers, with 36.1 per cent coming from the over 55s, an age when young adults have usually left the family unit. At any rate, 37.3 per cent of the audience are classified as housewives without any children. Despite this, the programme places a fantastic emphasis on the family. The computer programmer's adult daughter is in the audience, while Tarrant refers constantly to the presents which the contestant can buy for his granddaughter whose birthday is imminent. The fire protection engineer's wife and two children are watching at home, Tarrant tells us, and refers at one point to the tension they must be feeling when the contestant has to decide whether he wants to proceed and risk losing money or take what he's won and run. The constestant's brother-in-law, meanwhile, is in the audience, and throughout the game the camera cuts to his expressions and gestures.

Why this emphasis on the family when there is evidence to suggest that it does not correspond to the majority of the audience? There are two reasons I think. The first is indicative of the immediate institutional context. The family is the main frame of reference through which consumer goods are sold. Take the first advertising break in the last programme of the third series. The first advert features a child speaking to his grandmother about pension plans! The child's grandfather and parents occupy the background. (The advert uses a clever bit of digital manipulation that lets the child speak like an adult.) Out of the remaining eight adverts in this break, three focus on women using domestic household cleaning products. This implicitly draws on the traditional division of labour within the family which designates such unpaid labour as women's work. This very traditional gendered division of labour is reinforced by the fact that most of the contestants on *Who Wants To Be A Millionaire?* are men (who do the 'work' of winning the money) even though 10 per cent more women watch the programme than men. Another advert uses a family of cows to sell butter. So five out of nine adverts use the family to make the selling of their commodities seem natural and explicable.

The second explanation for the continual referencing of the family is indicative of the wider socio-cultural context. The huge sums of money which contestants could win risk associating the programme with greed and avarice. The obsessive referencing of the family is an attempt to deflect such negative associations by grounding the contestant within the family unit and via the lifelines ('phone a friend' and 'ask the audience') to ground them within a wider community. It is ironic that the programme uses the title of a song which is about valuing relationships and love over money. The song articulates a wider socio-cultural ambivalence about the corrosive effect money can have on such things. The programme, however, taps into a very late 1990s trend. Like New Labour, *Who Wants To Be A Millionaire?* wants to reconcile the pursuit of money and the embrace of the market economy with family and community values.

Conclusion

I have tried to offer the reader a model for discussing television texts, a model which situates texts in their contexts of production and consumption. Those contexts have to be grasped as dynamic, changing and contradictory. So that contextual analysis moves from being merely descriptive to a critique, I have intertwined the analysis with the key media-related political issue of the moment: how television is being subjected to increasingly commercialised forces and how those forces are eroding public service television. *Who Wants To Be A Millionaire?* is very much a creature of the current trend (and its contradictions) which is well advanced. The endgame has begun.

Stop and think

Broadcasting, narrowcasting and broadcatching

As the long-running contest between public service television and the globalised media economy enters its final phase, we need to stop and think about what the term 'broadcasting' really means. It is deeply implicated in the notion of 'mass' media – of large-scale, one-way flows of communication and big audiences. *Who Wants To Be A Millionaire?* represents one way in which commercial TV is holding on to some of that notion, where public service broadcasting is increasingly having to look to very different models of communication that may soon not be 'broadcasting' at all.

As early as 1969, an American academic, J. C. R. Licklider (in a report for the Carnegie Foundation) came up with the alternative term 'narrowcasting' – aiming for a diversity of good programmes but with smaller audiences for each – and influenced the thinking behind PBS, America's public service television channel. Narrowcasting has been revived as a concept to describe the new world of more fragmented, especially digitally carried, television that began to emerge in the late 1990s. But it is actually quite a misleading – if popularly accessible – term. It suggests that broadcasting stays essentially the same behind the scenes but narrows and multiplies its focus. This may be how established broadcasters would like to think of the way their future is shaping up. Much more accurate, though, is Stewart Brand's concept of *broadcatching*. Here the broadcasters continue to pump out increasing volumes and variety of content but in a sense they are now aimed at everyone and no one. Brand's essential notion instead is that of 'content-specific selectivity and repackaging at the receiving end' (1988:42) – increasingly smart technologies will 'catch' what we want from the passing flows of content and package it according to requirements. (Advertising will not be attached to the content but will be part of the repackaging process.) It is important to think about what this emerging model means for the way television and radio are experienced.

Broadcasting and time–space relations

If we are to understand the conditions of production and consumption in broadcasting, and the distinctive programme formats of radio and television, then it is important for us to consider its temporal and spatial dimensions – to identify the dynamics of location and mediation that are in play. The moments of transmission and reception in broadcasting are virtually simultaneous, yet sounds and images are produced and consumed in places situated at a distance from each other. So while these electronic media offer their audiences an experience of liveness and immediacy, stitching their schedules into the fabric of our everyday routines, the place of the studio or outside broadcast is far removed from the dispersed domestic settings in which listening and viewing are ordinarily done.

This social arrangement of time and space has consequences for the ways in which the listener or viewer is addressed. According to Paddy Scannell (1989), it has given rise historically to a specific communicative ethos of broadcasting. Unlike, say, a theatre performance or public lecture – where speakers and hearers are physically co-present – modes of address in broadcasting have to be designed for absent audiences in the private sphere. The forms of talk produced for household consumption are characteristically relaxed, informal and familiar – and they will often involve an appropriation of those conversational styles that are found in the routine interpersonal encounters of everyday life.

Indeed, back in the early years of television, Donald Horton and Richard Wohl (1956) observed a phenomenon which they referred to as 'para-social interaction' between studio performers and domestic audiences. This was a taken for granted yet quite remarkable cultural encounter in which TV personalities would speak directly to the camera and to the unseen viewer, talking as if in conversation with a close friend rather than an anonymous collection of strangers. Today, we can see such serialised mediated interactions being enacted for us across a range of programmes and genres – including news bulletins and daytime magazine shows (Moores, 1995) – and these relationships of intimacy at a distance may be contributing to a significant shift in experiences of familiarity and estrangement in the modern world.

More generally, broadcasting has had a profound impact on the relationship between private lives and public worlds. Radio and television have made the walls of the home much more permeable (Meyrowitz, 1985) – instantaneously connecting local sites of listening and viewing with image spaces or territories of transmission that are now potentially global in their scale and geographical reach. Inevitably, this tearing of space from place has implications for our senses of social identity and community – for precisely who and where we imagine ourselves to be. As one cultural critic has commented, reflecting on the globalised character of certain media events, we no longer have roots but aerials (Wark, 1994). Of course, the fact of the matter is that most of us have both roots and aerials – so collective identities in late modern society are fashioned at the interface between situated and mediated cultures.

Broadcasting does play a crucial part in the construction of what Benedict Anderson (1991) calls imagined communities. His main concern was with the fictioning of national identity, and he understood the daily newspaper as a symbolic resource which is central to this process. Its individual readers are seen to be engaged in a simultaneous ritual – a kind of mass ceremony that provides them with the confidence of community in anonymity. With radio and television, the simultaneity is greater still – as listeners and viewers tune in to a common schedule of programmes or participate in the life of the nation through their shared reception of various state and sports occasions on the annual broadcasting calendar (Cardiff and Scannell, 1987).

However, following the arrival of new technologies such as cable, satellite television and the internet – and given the increasingly transnational flows of information and entertainment in contemporary culture – private con-sumers now have the opportunity to reschedule their routine participation in public life. They can use a broader range of symbolic resources in the pro-duction of re-imagined communities (Morley and Robins, 1995). An increas-ing fragmentation of audiences for broadcasting – the result of a modern, multi-channel viewing environment – means that future research in media studies must pay close attention to which social groups or market segments are identifying with which image spaces.

Media research must also be prepared to link particular empirical investi-gations to wider debates in social theory concerning the temporal and spatial organisation of daily life and the institutional dynamics of modernity. The work of Anthony Giddens (1990), and especially his concept of time–space dis-tanciation, might help us in thinking about the role of broadcasting both as a means of mass communication and as a cultural institution. Giddens con-tends that social relations in the modern world have been lifted out of situ-ated locales and stretched over sometimes vast distances by a series of disembedding mechanisms – by abstract systems of technical knowledge or symbolic exchange. These social relations are then re-embedded in new types of facework encounter between public institutions and private individuals, in which trust is sought and risk negotiated. Clearly, broadcasting is deeply impli-cated in this process of displacement and re-embedding.

In conclusion, then, we could say that broadcasting both shapes and is shaped by the time–space relations of contemporary social life. On the one hand, radio and television have radically altered our experiences of home and community – connecting everyday routines and domestic geographies with national and international media cultures – but, on the other hand, it is important for us to see these transformations as part of a broader pattern of technological and cultural change. Raymond Williams (1974) sums this up neatly when he calls the current period an era of mobile privatisation – a way of living which is centred on the household unit, yet confers on its inhabi-tants a previously unimaginable sense of mobility. Whether that opportunity for travel is realised literally or electronically, neither self nor society remains the same.

Shaun Moores

Afterthoughts

In 1988, three key articles in the journals *Cultural Studies* and *Critical Studies in Mass Communication* began to put a new spin on reception analysis and audience studies. Larry Grossberg's 'Wandering Audiences, Nomadic Critics', Janice Radway's 'Reception Study: Ethnography and the Problems of Dispersed Audiences and Nomadic Subjects' and Martin Allor's 'Relocating the Site of the Audience', while explicitly or implicitly acknowledging how important the ethnographic turn had been to audience studies, all began to question whether such work allowed too much reality to the very notion of 'audience' itself. There had always been a tendency in some audience ethnography to go out and do observational work in people's daily lives but then to extrapolate from those specific situations to a relatively taken-for-granted concept of audience as something more than the sum of all those particulars but which could nonetheless be grasped through them.

This moment of renewed self examination (it was never a sustained critique from outside) was asking in effect that media research put more effort into connecting its ethnographic case studies of 'audiences' with larger understandings of culture and identity. The content/audience coupling, where a particular package of content (broadcast programme, newspaper, advertisement, etc.) is matched to 'its' audience, is always already structured into how the media work, but ask yourself whether you often actually experience your own media consumption simply as membership of an audience. It happens at live events and their simulation by the media (e.g. when TV shows are taped 'in front of a live audience', whose presence and reactions are orchestrated and integrated into the audio-visual text), but more often you will also be integrating your own media consumption into various niches in the pattern of your daily life – breakfast radio, in-car CD, an evening of TV viewing with friends, Saturday night movie with a partner, magazine at the dentist, and so on. This does not mean that an audience for each of these media forms does not exist, but rather that the concept of 'audience' is criss-crossed by these more personal niches in ways that may undermine many generalisations, especially as media forms have proliferated and found more and more such niches. At the point of intersection between a personal niche of media consumption and the media's construction of a content/audience coupling is your own self consciousness of 'audience' (e.g. when you turn the radio on for 'company').

In a good deal of the excellent ethnographic work in media studies prior to the late 1980s, it was only the researcher who had that self consciousness about 'audience'. The studies largely assumed that the subjects – the media consumers themselves – were just 'doing it', being an audience in an unreflective way. Indeed, media consumption blurred into their everyday activities to such an extent, as viewed by this sort of research, that the media sometimes seemed little different from the manufacturers of the furniture or other appliances that occupy other spaces in people's lives. But if we fix our attention on these points of intersection – where the media's carefully constructed content/audience couplings are criss-crossed by people's own niches of media consumption and use – and at the same time allow for people's self consciousness about being members of various (shifting, changing) audiences, then the media do not dissolve quite so easily into the other furniture of everyday life.

We can take such a point of intersection as an abstract concept (it might be a young woman on her office lunch break reading a men's glossy-style magazine, an elderly woman listening to sport on her kitchen radio or any one of innumerable such moments of intersection, but let's just imagine it as an 'empty' abstraction that then gets filled by such actual circumstances). There is an ideal communicative situation that we can superimpose on our abstract point of intersection. This ideal could be characterised as a point of balance among the four maxims of communicative clarity proposed by Grice (1975): quantity (no more or less information is offered than is required in the situation); quality (the communication aims at maximum truthfulness); relation (only the relevant is included); and manner (ambiguity and disorderliness are kept to a minimum). These maxims define an ideal moment of communicative clarity. The point is, of course, to note that they are a very long way away from being characteristics of the sorts of communication that typically take place within media consumption. Media content and its reception are more often characterised by informational surfeit, the proliferation of competing truth claims in the sheer variety and relativity of perspectives offered, a revelling in irrelevance and the elevation of disorderliness into an aesthetic principle. In short, the media generally flout all four maxims of the ideal communicative situation. (There remains some value, however, in retaining the concept of such an ideal – for example, in Habermas's notion of the ideal speech situation – as a factor in motivating human communication at some deeper level. Grice's faith in these maxims as universal defining features of human communication looks overly optimistic, though.)

In revising the Gricean maxims to account for the inevitability of distortion in communicative exchanges, Brown and Levinson (1987) develop the concept of 'face' (originally proposed by the social psychologist Erving Goffman) around the social and private needs that are maintained in communicative encounters. A social or public 'face' is maintained by fitting in, by going with the crowd. A private face is maintained by exercising one's personal autonomy, by believing oneself to be acting as an individual, making distinctive choices and standing out from the crowd, at least in one's own eyes. The point is that these two dimensions of 'face' are not alternatives but rather aspects which have to be balanced. The effort that goes into achieving such balance in any particular situation can be called 'facework'. This has usually been studied in relation to conversational and interpersonal exchanges but may usefully be developed in relation to the media, especially if located at the points of intersection described above, where public and private, audience and individual, meet. We may, however, need to develop a clearer understanding of the 'quasi-interaction' that occurs via the media.

In interpersonal interactions, participants are always trying to find an acceptable point of balance between compliments, reminders, reprimands, apologies, promises, advice, instructions, and so on. Such exchanged 'messages' have the potential to unbalance public and private face in numerous ways (e.g. by making one person feel inadequate, another appear publicly dominant, etc.). Unsurprisingly, therefore, concepts such as politeness have become a focus of attention for discourse analysts and social psychologists concerned with interpersonal communication (politeness being an achieved, if often rather artificial, balance between public and private face). Among the interesting consequences of adopting this approach is the idea that evidence often has more to do with the maxim of manner than with quality. In other words, I might say to you, 'According to this story in the newspaper, it's unhealthy to eat too much saturated fat' rather than 'You shouldn't eat that cream cake.' The latter threatens face, while the former communicates the same idea but does a more subtle piece of facework. The evidence – the story in the newspaper – is not being used in the interests of truth so much as being deployed to effect a subtle change in the manner of the facework.

Now if we enlarge this situation considerably, to focus on the relationship between the media of public communication and the private individual (rather than on two individuals engaged in interpersonal communication), we can see that some form of facework may also be taking place at our intersection points where the public becomes the audience and the individual is realising particular private niches in his or her daily life for media consumption and use. For example, even though no one may actually be watching, the public act of buying a 'serious' daily newspaper may be barely conscious facework – as if performed in front of public scrutiny – whereas at home the newspaper may become something different, perhaps even something less significant and often just skimmed through inconsequentially. The question is not whether we should see the media or the individual as more 'active' in determining what goes on at such points of intersection but how we can grasp the fact that the facework going on there is already dependent on precisely that question. This is the nature of the individual's self consciousness about 'audience' – people are already bound up in kinds of facework in order to resolve that question for themselves before the media researcher ever arrives on the scene to describe it in theoretical terms. Face is threatened just as much by playing out the herd instincts of the audience as by refusing to join in and consequently feeling out of touch. Most people do not want to feel that they have completely surrendered their individuality to a manipulation of mass response but nor do they feel comfortable with entirely ignoring what appears to be popular taste and the possibilities of shared experience and information. The facework that goes on between media and individuals is, therefore, a complex balancing of these things, on a much larger scale than in interpersonal exchanges but with some of the same processes undoubtedly at work.

For instance, we might consider again the distinction between the public knowledge project and the popular culture project in media studies. It is often assumed that the former is concerned with how the media are used to produce 'knowledge' in the audience while the popular culture project is concerned with how the media are used to produce 'pleasure'. What happens to that sort of distinction when we focus on the facework taking place at the points of media reception? The achievement of a balance in facework (between public and private face) will itself be pleasurable – just as conversation can be pleasurable for the same reason in interpersonal interactions – but this can depend just as much on forms of shared knowledge as on the 'entertainment' value of the conversation or the media content involved in the facework. This becomes clearer if we look again at a media form consistently placed at the centre of the popular culture project in media studies – the TV soap opera.

Robert Allen (1985) has described how TV soap opera typically distils the classic style of film and television visualisation to its barest essentials, avoiding all elaborate camera movements or rapid cutting, opting for an evenness of lighting that does not call attention to itself, and so on. This lack of visual complexity is made up for by the complexity of 'its large community of inter-related characters':

> A great deal might happen to individual characters – multiple marriages, pregnancy, amnesia, temporary blindness, disabling accidents, and so forth, but very little happens to alter the nature of the community. The soap opera community is a self-perpetuating, self-preserving system little affected by the turbulence experienced by its individual members or the fate of any one character. The naive viewer might attend only to the constant state of crisis experienced by individual characters, but the experienced viewer is watchful for the paradigmatic strands that bind the community of characters together and the sometimes glacially slow but far more significant alterations in this network. (pp. 69–70)

'Paradigmatic' may be understood, in this context, as a theoretical term for the sideways movement of a viewer's attention as distinct from the forward push of a narrative towards its resolution – the 'what if?' as distinct from the 'what next?'. Much of the information introduced into any one segment of a soap opera is redundant in terms of forward momentum but significant in activating this sideways movement of speculation and reflection. A character may repeat some piece of information time and again, not to make sure that the audience 'gets it' but to put into play all the nuances of response from other characters in different contexts and in the light of their past histories together.

Again Robert Allen captures this characteristic of the form. Reduced to its forward narrative momentum, 'the soap opera becomes an endless string of excruciatingly retarded subplots, related in episodes whose redundancy gives them an almost Sisyphean tiresomeness. To the experienced reader, however, soap opera's distinctive networks of character relationships open up major sources of signifying potential that are simply unreadable to the naive reader' (1985:71).

Close-up shots of characters often function, in the soap opera, as repositories of this 'depth': on to the face the viewer reads an accumulation of knowledge based on a familiarity with a particular community of characters and their history. A newcomer to the soap opera form in general can find these close-ups perplexing blanks, moments of awkward non-communication that seem to need the performance skills of a cinema actor to endow them with meaning. Maintaining the depth, the complex and slowly shifting network of character relationships, draws the soap opera towards particular kinds of setting – hospitals, bars, offices, housing estates, farming communities, and so on allow for frequent contact among characters and therefore opportunities for talk.

The wandering of the viewer's attention into the depth of the soap opera community is 'that of the uncertain tourist provided with a rather sketchy map, who frequently stops to look back where he or she has been, occasionally takes a side road, and constantly tries to glimpse what lies around the next bend' (Allen, 1985:78). As characters' lives cross in soap opera, all kinds of possibilities occur to the viewer. Some will be realised by the narrative, some won't, while others will be stored away and revived weeks or months later. Thinking about these possibilities entails having access to three kinds of knowledge:

1 Generic knowledge – familiarity with the conventions of soap opera as a genre. For example, expecting discontinuous and cliff-hanging narrative structures
2 Serial-specific knowledge – knowledge of past narratives and of characters
3 Cultural knowledge of the socially acceptable codes and conventions for the conduct of personal life. (Brunsdon, 1981:36)

It is the obvious significance of this latter that prompts Allen to observe: 'To a greater extent perhaps than any other fiction, the soap opera text constantly walks the line between one that can be read as fiction and one that spills over into the experiential world of the viewer' (1985:91). Just what this spillage means has been the object of considerable attention from a number of cultural critics, among them Tania Modleski. Modleski picks up on Allen's point about identification with one character being a 'naive' way of reading soap opera, experienced viewers rejecting the impulse to find one powerful ego in the text from whose point of view everything else can be made sensible: 'soap operas present us with numerous limited egos, each in conflict with the others, and continually thwarted in its attempts to control events because of inadequate knowledge of other people's plans, motivations, and schemes' (1984:91).

It is in accumulating and thinking about characters' plans, motivations and schemes that viewers find the most compulsive pleasures of soap opera. This knowledge is partly generic (certain forms of behaviour tend to turn up in soap operas generally), partly serial specific (the plotting and characterisation of the particular soap opera) and partly cultural (certain issues, problems and dilemmas have a currency at any particular time and characters' attitudes will be tested against prevailing or emerging social attitudes). It is with this latter – cultural knowledge – that we see the distinction between knowledge media (e.g. news, current affairs, documentaries) and popular culture (e.g. soap operas, game shows, situation comedies) breaking down. Where people's social relations in modernity have been plucked out of once more stable and known communities and relocated into a world of looser social bonds, rootlessness among comparative strangers, increased movement (geographically and socially) and lifestyle imagery, the public knowledge proffered by the media is accompanied by the imaginative work of exploring fictional people's plans, motivations and schemes (where once this was likelier to be lives lived more accessibly to public knowledge in the local community).

This – the standard fare of so much television (even game shows where we watch the contestants closely as life-changing sums of money or prizes accumulate or slip away) – is some of the richest material for facework in the expanded sense hypothesised here, where private aspirations, fears and behaviour are delicately balanced with public representations of culturally acceptable aspirations, fears and behaviour, the very stuff of so much media narrative, from soap opera to popular newspapers and popular music.

John B. Thompson (1995) has adapted Goffman's related concept of 'front' and 'back' regions in his account of the rise of mediated interaction, the 'front' region being where facework is done, or where people manage the boundary between 'front' regions (although in fact Thompson does not directly use Goffman's concept of facework). This account is worth quoting at length, especially as it informs one of the few recent attempts at a social theory of television to employ substantive theory, empirical data *and a formal model*, as advocated by Rosengren in chapter 3. Front regions are where the interaction occurs, while back regions are the behind-the-scenes circumstances, ranging from backroom production processes to people's private lives. Thompson is concerned with face-to-face interaction, technically mediated interaction (such as the telephone) and mediated quasi-interaction (such as television):

> The distinction between front region and back region is typical of many action contexts, irrespective of whether they involve the use of a technical medium of communication. But the use of communication media can have quite a profound impact on the nature of front and back regions and the relation between them. Since mediated interaction generally involves a separation of the contexts within which the participants are situated, it establishes an interactive framework that consists of two or more front regions which are separated in space and perhaps also in time. Each of these front regions has its own back regions, and each participant in the mediated interaction must seek to manage the boundary between them. In the course of a telephone conversation, for example, an individual may seek to suppress noises which arise from the physical locale in which he or she is speaking – the sound of a television, the comments or laughter of a friend or colleague, etc. – as such noises may be regarded as back-region behaviour relative to the mediated interaction.
>
> In the case of technically mediated quasi-interaction, the interactive framework is fragmented in a way that distinguishes it from the kind of mediated interaction which occurs in a telephone conversation. Symbolic forms are produced in one context (what I shall call the 'interactive framework of production') and received in a multiplicity of other contexts (the 'interactive frameworks of reception'). Each of these contexts is characterised by its own regions and regional demarcations. Since the flow of communication is predominantly one-way, the front region of the framework of production is typically available to the recipients and is therefore a front region relative to the frameworks of reception. But the

reverse does not hold: that is, the regions in the reception sphere do not directly impinge on the framework of production, and hence are not, strictly speaking, front regions and back regions relative to this framework.

The interactive framework of reception may serve not only as a setting for the quasi-interaction mediated by the television or other technical forms, but also as a setting for face-to-face interaction which bears some affinity to the activity of reception. Individuals watching television or listening to music, for instance, may interact with one another while they participate in the activity of reception. In such cases, the extent to which the activity of reception provides the principal focus of the face-to-face interaction will vary from one instance to another. The conversational content of the face-to-face interaction may be determined largely by the activity of reception, as when individuals are involved in commenting on the messages or images received. In other cases, the activity of reception may be largely peripheral to the face-to-face interaction, and the reception of mediated symbolic forms may be little more than background music or noise for a conversation that takes place face-to-face.

Of course, individuals who engage in interaction, whether mediated or face-to-face, are always drawing on skills and accumulated resources of various kinds. Their action is always part of a structured field of interaction which both creates and limits the range of opportunities available to them. But in the cases of mediated interaction and quasi-interaction, the fields of interaction acquire an additional complexity, since they are now stretched across extended reaches of space (and perhaps also of time), and since the participants may be situated in contexts which are quite diverse in terms of their institutional and structural characteristics. (pp. 88–90)

Now, while apparently quite straightforward, Thompson's model on closer inspection allows us to identify clearly a number of features of broadcasting and its relationship with audiences that we have struggled to conceptualise as clearly without the model. He offers three versions, as shown in figures 12, 13 and 14. In face-to-face interaction there is a shared front region where face-work takes place (all the subtle ways in which people try to control their own self presentation when their social guard is up, in contrast with the sorts of behaviour that occur in the back regions of private spaces and lives). As technology intervenes, the mediated interaction (e.g. the telephone) creates two separate front regions whose boundary now has to be actively managed. Talking to someone on the telephone and hearing them clicking their computer keys in the background as, perhaps, they check their email, unsettlingly allows back-region behaviour to infiltrate the front region, but reminds us that the two front regions (their's and our's) are not in fact the same space. But it is when we move on to the third figure of the model that some very significant features of broadcasting suddenly become clearer. There are three features in particular: (1) discursive elaboration and secondary reception; (2) concerted responsive action; and (3) the absent front region.

Where we now have a more complex picture of various primary reception regions (where people actually watch TV, for instance) and peripheral regions (the attached social and domestic spaces), people will engage in commenting on, talking about (or avoiding talking about if it's socially embarrassing) what they see on TV. This discursive elaboration passes the broadcast content into areas of secondary reception where it is being represented conversationally, retold, summarised, distorted and generally passed around discursively. Ethnographic research techniques (close observation and description of actual contexts of reception) have been very good at tracing these layers of secondary elaboration, where broadcast material is re-used in all sorts of ways.

But we can also now imagine a dense network of communication flows crisscrossing these primary and peripheral regions, as broadcast material gets retransmitted, in a sense, within other forms of social interaction. If we step back from the ethnographer's close attention to detail and to particular settings, we begin to see a 'macro' picture of these flows. One feature of this larger picture identified by Thompson is that of concerted responsive action:

> The revolutionary upheavals in Eastern Europe in 1989 provide [an] example of the ways in which media messages can stimulate and nourish collective action by individuals located in distant contexts. There were, of course, many factors that contributed to the extraordinary events which occurred during the last three months of 1989 . . . But it seems unlikely that the revolutionary upheavals of 1989 would have occurred as they did – with breathtaking speed and with similar results in different countries – in the absence of extensive and continuous media coverage. Not only did television provide individuals in Eastern Europe with a flow of images of the West, portraying life conditions which contrasted sharply with their own, but it also provided Eastern Europeans with a virtually instantaneous account of what was happening in neighbouring countries, as well as in neighbouring cities or locales in their own countries. East Germans had long been able to receive West German television, and the images of refugees crowding into embassies in Prague and Budapest, and eventually being escorted to the West and greeted as heroes, could hardly fail to have an explosive impact in East Germany. When the Berlin Wall fell on the night of 9 November, the images of young people celebrating beneath the Brandenburg Gates and hacking at the wall with pickaxes were transmitted live around the world. (1995:115–16)

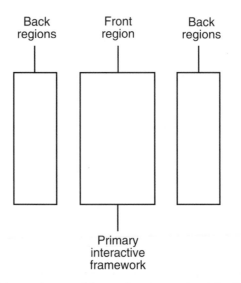

Figure 12 The social organisation of face-to-face interaction (after Thompson, 1995)

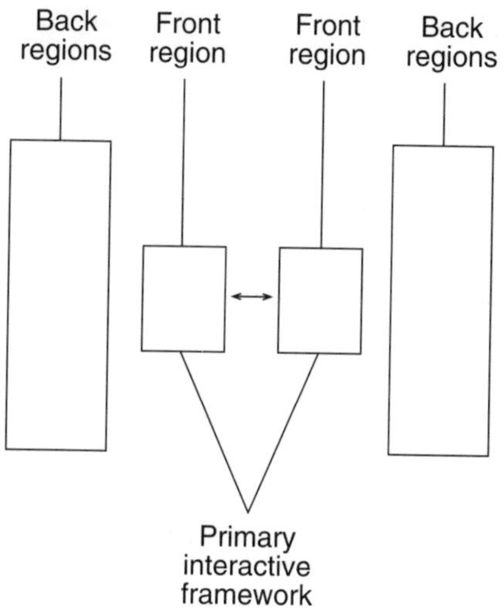

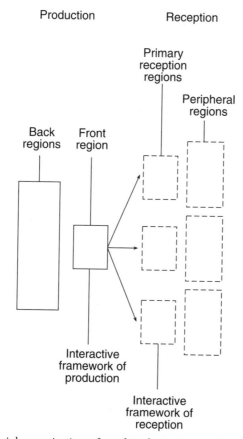

Figure 13 The social organisation of technically mediated interaction (after Thompson, 1995)

Figure 14 The social organisation of mediated quasi-interaction (after Thompson, 1995)

What we have here is a picture of concerted responsive action being fed and amplified by the flow of communication across the various primary reception regions and peripheral regions of Eastern Europe's broadcast landscape. In a sense, then, there was a momentary creation of a shared front region (loosely captured in such phrases as the 'stage of history') where people were aware of their collective 'face', their visibility and effectiveness. This effect – of engaging in responsive activity in relation to the absent front region – is clearer and more sustained, however, on the level of individual behaviour where facework can be thought of as a method for achieving the effect. James Lull (2000) takes the example of a person who wants to gratify their need for self esteem (a typical sort of facework although, again, Lull does not actually use the term):

> The cognitive plan fashioned by the person for this purpose is to become an expert on a topic of cultural interest (world affairs, popular music, fashion, etc.). Developing such expertise could qualify the individual as a possessor of important, useful, or otherwise desirable information. Media activities that could be undertaken to achieve this objective include, for instance, subscribing to specialty magazines, reading the newspaper carefully every day, viewing selected TV programmes, and so on. To the degree that these media acts successfully facilitate the requirements of the method, we can say that the first level of satisfaction has been reached. The person has become an expert. The adequacy of the method is then cognitively tested against the need to achieve self-esteem. (pp. 106–7).

Along with the schemata used by active and resourceful audiences and the contexts that determine how and where TV and its meanings are produced, these further three social phenomena associated with broadcasting – facework (of the sort just described) in the 'absent' front region, the potential for concerted responsive action across a totality of primary reception regions and peripheral regions, and the processes of discursive elaboration and secondary reception – take us a long way towards understanding the widespread impact of broadcasting's mediated quasi-interaction on public and private life.

Part V

Film

12

Film studies

Jim Cook

A historical and conceptual overview

Film studies in Britain effectively began in the 1960s in secondary schools and was part of a new broadly left and 'democratic' interest in revaluing and evaluating works of popular culture. With regard to film, this anti-elitist stance manifested itself critically through including Hollywood entertainment movies among those deemed to be of sufficient artistic quality to be evaluatively 'appreciated', while a more specifically educational concern stressed the curricular relevance of such movies to students' interests and concerns. Hall and Whannel (1964) describe the progressive thrust behind this early work, as well as providing detailed examples of its practice, and Wood (1965) is the first example of a major piece of film criticism arising out of that evaluative and interpretive tradition. Taking an undoubtedly popular film maker, Wood subjected Hitchcock's films to the same rigorous textual and moral analysis as was proposed for great works of literature by his mentor, the teacher and literary critic F. R. Leavis, and in so doing he both offered a particular method of film analysis and secured the director/*auteur* as a key organising principle for film study. He didn't achieve this single-handedly of course: deriving their approach from the French magazine *Cahiers du Cinéma* and sharing a passion for Hollywood cinema, since 1962 writers in the British magazine *Movie* had been proposing new objects of cinematic study and, through their critical practice, providing models of mainly authorial criticism.

In the late 1960s and into the 1970s the provision of advice and models of practice by the then influential Education Department of the British Film Institute (BFI), and its subsequent part-funding of posts in higher education, functioned to train teachers, while the Department's support for a radical publishing programme laid the basis for the intellectual foundations of the subject: see for examples Kitses (1969), Wollen (1969) and McArthur (1972). As part of its support for teachers, the BFI also supported a Teachers' Association, SEFT (The Society for Education in Film and Television), which took a radical change of direction in 1972 and became – through its journal *Screen* – the principal outlet for a range of theoretical writing. Initially offered in translation from French originals and then subsequently homegrown, this material incorporated film into a broader set of concerns about representation and ideology. Drawing its impetus generally from an intellectual tradition very different from the English (if not British) empirical one and fuelled particularly by the political as well as intellectual upheavals of the '*événements*' of 1968 in France, the radical claims made in this French-derived work – both for alternative practices and for the need to destroy older bourgeois-tainted forms – certainly divided, and possibly politicised, film studies.

Beyond accusations about the elitist impenetrability of the language in which it was expressed, the chief consequence of the shift from 1960s film study to 1970s film theory was precisely to displace the object of study, and for a while disputes about the perceived ideological entailment of a particular theoretical 'line' took precedence over any convincing demonstration of the line's potential to illuminate particular film texts. An example of this displacement is the series of debates initiated by MacCabe (1974). Nonetheless, when the dust settled a distinct advance had been made in that the realism/illusionism effect previously considered only in relation to the forms of film texts, was now deemed to be fundamentally linked to how the gendered spectator, sometimes described as the 'viewing subject', makes sense of those texts and constructs coherence out of them. Here the founding and probably most influential text is Mulvey (1975). Inevitably, of course, the advance brought with it also a sense of limitation, in that as soon as you substitute 'audiences' or 'viewers' for 'the viewing subject' then the latter formulation appears a-historical and in need of modification or adjustment through more specific and contexted cases studies (see chapter 15). Consequently, as a reaction to 1970s theory, a lot of subsequent work has concentrated on the importance of age, class, gender and ethnic variables in helping to understand how audiences make sense of films. The most interesting approaches here are those, like that of Stacey (1994), which do not reject the earlier positions but draw on general insights to help construct more specific studies.

Along with the growing diversity of critical approaches to audiences, in recent years film studies has been marked by a return to cinema and a general widening of the areas being researched – from 'third cinema' through children's cinema to 'queer cinema' – and with the concern now being to draw on theory/ies as and when appropriate. This diversity has partly been enabled by the expansion and institutionalisation of the subject, especially within higher education – within secondary education its concerns are now subsumed within those of media studies. Consequently, whereas in the past histories tended to be general overviews written for a general public, since the mid 1980s scholars have profited both from increased access to print and film archives and from a guaranteed higher education readership. These have enabled them to produce more detailed and specific studies ranging from institutional studio histories (Roddick, 1983) through cultural studies periodisation (Hill, 1986) to postmodernist-influenced reconsiderations of previously ignored or dismissed areas (Tasker, 1993). Perhaps the most exciting area to have been substantially recast in a series of revisionist histories is early and silent cinema. In anthologies such as Elsaesser (1990) a much wider range of films than had been available to previous historians is considered but with equal attention being paid also to, for example, exhibition contexts and practices or to the disabling/enabling discourses of censorship. Elsewhere attempts are made to understand cinema across a wide range of social and cultural con-

texts, considering, for example, cinema's hybrid origins and the pervasiveness
of melodrama as a cultural influence (Bratton *et al.*, 1994).

While film studies has followed a logical enough trajectory from textual analysis through debates about critical methods and theory to a diversity of objects of study, it's also true to say that much of this work takes one a long way from the experience of viewing films. This is inevitable and necessary in order to elaborate and clarify the subject area, but it should never be forgotten that film studies is not a branch of history or cultural studies, but a discipline whose central aim is to help us better read and hence understand sights and sounds organised in a variety of ways.

Studying cinema histories: issues and methods

In their introduction, Bordwell and Thompson (1994) identify three key questions that need to be posed in studying the history of cinema: 'How have uses of the film medium changed or become normalised over time? . . . How have the conditions of the film industry – production, distribution, and exhibition – affected the uses of the medium? . . . How have international trends emerged in the uses of the film medium and in the film market?' In formulating their questions in these particular ways, so that the focus is respectively on texts, contexts and spatio-temporal variations, they are not just recommending that prospective histories start from these considerations but attempting also to offer a template for the broad classification of most of the specific film histories which have already been written. Thus the first question leads to considerations of the history of forms (especially narrative), genres and techniques; the second to issues of ownership, the organisation of studio systems and technological developments; and the third to the forms and market conditions which allow films to circulate cross-culturally – broadly either Hollywood hegemony or international art cinema. Examples of histories which address these questions with varying emphases are Bordwell *et al.* (1985), Weis and Belton (1985) and Hayward and Vincendeau (1990).

What Bordwell and Thompson leave implicit in their three central questions are the different types of approach or explanatory framework which can be brought to any history of the cinema, and here Allen and Gomery (1985) is a useful complement. They stress that traditionally film histories have been *aesthetic* – focusing on film form and art; *technological* – focusing on the science and economics of change and development; *economic* – focusing on industrial and business practices; or *social* – focusing on individual biographies, stars, audience studies, cinema and other social institutions. As a case study for each of these approaches they propose respectively: researching the background to a particular production (their example is F. W. Murnau's *Sunrise*, 1927); studying the coming of sound; investigating the formation of the US film industry; and considering the role of the star and the star system. What's interesting about their categories is that more than one approach or framework could be applied to each of Bordwell and Thompson's questions, and indeed the last approach is so broad that arguably its concerns with the links between cinema and society are another – cultural studies – way of thinking about all of the approaches and questions. This is a perspective which has lent itself particularly to studies of national cinemas – Liehm (1984), Barr (1986), Rockett *et al.* (1988) and Elsaesser (1989) are all representative here.

Like many other histories, film histories mainly take the form of a narrative. Across areas ranging from revisionist histories of silent cinema (Tsivian, 1989; Gunning, 1991) to anthologies considering previously neglected genres (Dyer and Vincendeau, 1992) to scholarship revealing previously barely known cinemas (Rajadhyaksha and Willemen, 1995), film historians, like any other historians, marshal their facts around one or more of the questions and approaches outlined above to present arguments and/or offer explanations. Depending on their focus of concern, their evidence will come from the films themselves plus a range of other materials, from production files to memoirs or oral testimony.

What all this amounts to is that, within the structure of questions and frameworks, there are many different types of film history possible – ranging from the overview synoptic one offered by Bordwell and Thompson (1994) to minutely detailed monographs tracing an individual craftperson's career or the history of a particular film print. In the case of these two extremes it's fairly easy to see which would have the wider relevance but, in a situation where cinema is a hundred years old with much of its output irretrievably lost, its form in danger of electronic transformation beyond recognition, and its myriad histories only very partially researched and written, what is currently most positive about cinema history is the very diversity of work being produced and the lack of any strongly proscribed or favoured areas. This is not to suggest of course that issues of historiography (i.e. considerations of how particular histories are structured) are ignored. Indeed the best critical commentaries always build into their accounts a scrutinising of how evidence has been used and attempt to read any history through an awareness of both the original writer's *and* the reviewer's ideological positions, and hence presuppositions.

Cinema: an outline sketch of the twentieth-century medium

Successful projection of moving images happened simultaneously in the mid 1890s in Europe and North America and was the culmination of years of experimentation by scientists with little interest in the commercial 'entertainment' possibilities of their inventions. Even when the first screenings proved so popular that entrepreneurs quickly moved in, it was not the ten one-minute long films, strung together in any order and shown in fairs or at the end of live vaudeville or music hall shows, that were deemed to be of commercial value but the machines for showing them. This situation continued until the turn of the twentieth century, when increasing demand for films as narrative entertainments in themselves led to a realisation of the value of the production content as much as the exhibition hardware.

The years leading up to the First World War were characterised worldwide by massively accelerating growth in the production, distribution and exhibition of films, with British, German, French and Italian cinemas in particular providing tough competition for the highly popular American films, whose makers by 1914 were starting to relocate from New York to the small Californian community of Hollywood. By 1919, however, through vertically integrating its production, distribution and exhibition activities internally and developing horizontally into the rest of the world, American cinema – Hollywood – had achieved the position of international market dominance which it still maintains. In the 1920s what this dominance meant was that, while American stars and stories were being enjoyed across the world in American-owned cinemas (Charlie Chaplin had 'local' names in most of the world's major languages), the only possibility for national indigenous cinemas to survive culturally was through a judicious mixture of state support and conscious aesthetic attempts to be different from Hollywood. As a significant part of their countries' output, both the Soviet silent cinema of montage and German Expressionist films benefited from different types of state support, while French cinema increasingly characterised its difference through the production of 'surreal' artistic non-narrative films guaranteed to appeal to cosmopolitan tastes. Though none of these 'art' cinemas (see above) ever dented the massive popularity of Hollywood imports, they nonetheless created viable alternatives. In Britain, by contrast, despite government regulations in 1927 stipulating that a fixed quota of British films had to be screened annually on British screens and the occasional international successes of someone like Alfred Hitchcock, the industry remained primarily geared to distributing and exhibiting American films.

Many years after its technical feasibility and only when it seemed like a positive commercial gamble, the arrival of sound in 1927 finally consolidated all aspects of the 'software'; that is, sound as well as vision was now exclusively in the hands of the producers (where before music and even effects might have been performed live at a screening). Along with its abrupt ending of the careers of actors whose voices were deemed 'unsuitable' and a marked slowing down of silent cinema's camera mobility in favour of efficient sound registration, sound had more long-term effects. In America the enormous costs of conversion undertaken at the time of the Depression encouraged a greater ideological conservatism on the parts of studio heads and banks, and resulted in the so-called 'Hays Code' of self censorship which producers and directors variously acceded to or subverted, while in non-English-speaking countries there was a marked growth in popular genre cinemas of, especially, comedy and melodrama made in the indigenous language and never intended for subtitled export.

Throughout the 1930s also there was a marked growth in non-fiction 'documentary' film making, often from a broadly reformist or progressive point of view. In Britain, where the documentary has been described as Britain's art cinema, with the coming of the Second World War documentary film making proper became part of the war effort but its influence more generally was also manifest in the production of feature films, some of which for the first time vied in popularity with American pictures. In Italy towards the end of the war and immediately afterwards the documentary impulse was used in a 'neo-realist' fashion to record the struggles against fascism and problems of national recovery, and in so doing to construct the first of the three major cinematic movements which since the war have tried, in their different ways, to negotiate Hollywood's hegemony and construct a cinema with both a specific cultural appeal in its country of origin and broader international appeal. The other two movements are the French New Wave of the early 1960s and the New German Cinema of the 1970s, and the three together constitute a lot of what is known as international art cinema. With the increasing circulation of 'world cinema' since the 1950s, however, the term has been used to include and describe films from a considerably wider range of national sources – Sweden, Poland, Japan, and so on.

Despite the increased accessibility of other cinemas, Hollywood's economic power has never been seriously challenged, nor for the most part has its unique ability to produce at its best considerable numbers of simultaneously complex and popular works. Immediately after the war, although it had to face 'the Paramount decision' (which broke up studios' monopoly control over production, distribution and exhibition), the growth of television and the trauma of investigations regarding 'un-American activities' (i.e. accusations of harbouring communists among its workforce), American cinema was able nevertheless to draw on indigenous popular culture and the talents of many of its émigré personnel to produce the extraordinary Euro-Hollywood hybrid of *film noir* and to enable, in the 1950s, some of the best work of both the older generation of *auteurs* (see above) – Ford, Hawks, Lang, Walsh – and the new – Ray, Fuller, Mann, and so on.

Latterly, what is of interest in the Hollywood/Europe relation is that, while at one level there is a certain fluidity in the traditional geographical locations of the art/entertainment opposition (Scorsese is more art cinema than some of the European attempts at blockbusters), at another the old structures are very much in place; Tarantino is very much American international popular culture, and the most any European film maker can hope to make, no matter how funded, is something viably different. More broadly, what is of immense interest but uncertain outcome is how far 'small' or 'poor' cinemas, for example Irish or Catalan, or larger 'Third' cinemas, for example those of Francophone Africa or South Asia, may be marketable in terms other than those of art cinema and thus find new audiences. Such a reconfiguration is essential for all cinemas and audiences if, at the end of its first century, the thirst for movies is to be met not only retrospectively but in terms of renewal and future developments.

Stop and think

The filmic perspective today

When we look back over a century of cinema, specific films often stand out as especially representative of where cinema was at, in a particular time – say *Birth of a Nation, Battleship Potemkin, Metropolis, Citizen Kane* or *Tokyo Story*. When we try to think of such a film just now, it is tempting to choose something like *Titanic* (a thrilling Hollywood juggernaut) or *Three Colours: Red* (a sublime European art film). But directors Cameron and Kieślowski, while success stories of the 1990s and undoubtedly representative in some important sense, were not making films that seem quite so perfectly turn-of-the-century cinema as – let us say – Pedro Almodóvar. You could usefully stop and look at *The Flower of my Secret* (1995, available on videotape) and think about what it says about cinema today.

In a 1994 interview, leading French post-feminist philosopher Luce Irigaray noted that her work in philosophy had moved through three stages, the first being concerned with 'how a single subject, traditionally the masculine subject, had constructed the world and interpreted the world according to a single perspective' (quoted in Lorraine, 1999:20). This concern was also central to film theory in the 1970s and after. But looking back we can now see that it was in fact cinema that heralded in its own way the ultimate break-up of that single perspective by making it so visible to criticism, by realising it in the cinematic apparatus itself where it became so *obvious*. (This is not to detract from the achievement of film theorists such as Laura Mulvey – seeing the obvious for what it is is not always easy.) Classic Hollywood cinema, of the sort focused on by film theory as film studies began to develop, organised its 'texts', the films themselves, as miniature worlds visually constructed around the male perspective. Always a tendency in visual art, this was now flagrant exhibitionism and, though sustained by film makers for a considerable period and not gone yet, it made visible a large target for a theoretical critique that was actually part of a still larger cultural and social process of becoming self conscious about the 'single perspective' as a way of seeing the world.

Philosophers such as Irigaray were well ahead of the tide and her second phase concerned 'those mediations that could permit the existence of a feminine subjectivity' (Lorraine, 1999:20). Films made by women are conventionally mentioned at this point – say Jane Campion's *The Piano* – but it is rather more interesting to look at a film such as *The Flower of my Secret* where a male writer and director is willingly embroiled in the same 'problem'. The camera, editing and narrative here shift perspective in all sorts of subtle ways, not for any emptily formal effect but because unconstrained by any unitary perspective. The protagonist is a woman who secretly writes successful romantic fiction using an assumed name (as an aside, taking such fiction seriously has been a key move for cultural studies – see Radway's (1987) influential *Reading the Romance* – and as a topic and occupation it undoubtedly has suitably ambiguous connotations, in relation to gender, to suit Almodóvar's purpose). She is increasingly estranged from her husband who is a soldier with the UN and is being posted to Bosnia. Her life and concerns are portrayed in class terms as comfortably bourgeois – her designer apartment comes equipped with cook, she offers a street beggar money only because she needs his help removing her boots (which have got stuck – there's Almodóvar's usual comic streak throughout). Her resentment, about life's injustices towards her, flower into a self-absorbed collapse from which she is rescued by three things: her male editor (at the newspaper where she writes a literary column that viciously attacks her own romance novels) secretly ghost writes further romances for her, saving her career from writer's block; her mother, hitherto a source of endlessly crotchety irritation, takes her home to their rural village of origin where they sit in the sun with the local lace makers; and her cook turns out to be an accomplished dancer whose new show has been financed from jewellery and a story stolen from the writer's apartment by the cook's son during her period of self-absorbed collapse (the story having been sold as a treatment for a film).

What makes *The Flower of my Secret* worth singling out here is that it playfully demonstrates how cinema at the turn of the twenty-first century can transcend the popular/serious distinction (which separates Cameron and Kieslowski); can explore male and female subjectivity without collapsing back into the 'single perspective' visual and narrative structures critiqued by film theory; can weave together the personal melodrama with a sense of time and history (the military husband is a symbolically complex figure in relation to Spain's anti-military movement and Europe's involvement in the former Yugoslavia); and can deal with class in a meaningful way – the segue from the working-class cook's role as part of the furniture to her on-stage transformation into creative energy is visually and thematically unforgettable.

So, surprising as it may seem, *The Flower of my Secret* is not a bad place to stop and think about what film is now, and we have taken Almodóvar's work as a source of further examples in this Part. (Irigaray's 'third phase', to describe 'a philosophy, an ethic, a relationship between two different sub-jects' (Lorraine, 1999:20) is perhaps thinly prefigured by this kind of cinema but is pursuing a fundamental sense of 'difference' beyond 'equality' and remains deeply troubled by questions about the still resolutely patriarchal 'symbolic' (see Sarah Edge, below) and about whether different practices are even imaginable.) Film studies has, to simplify its story somewhat, been espe-cially good at achieving two things. One strand of film studies has focused closely on that whole problem of subjectivity and whether the 'single per-spective' has both structured the filmic text and positioned the spectator in a way that reinforces the latter's social positioning (or ideological interpel-lation in Althusserian terminology). The other, and perhaps in the long term even more important, strand has been more concerned with periodisation, with interpreting films as especially sensitive markers of socio-cultural and historical change (see, for example, Wright (1975), Ryan and Kellner (1988), Orr (1993) and Hill (1986, 1999)). John Orr's chapter, next, is our representa-tive example of that approach.

13

From neo-modern to hypermodern cinema: 1960 to the present

John Orr

Film is an elusive form for any critic and the more critics turn their attention to it the more elusive it becomes. Take a specific instance. The critical orthodoxy of a divide between modernist and 'postmodern', a term derived from architecture, sits uneasily with elements in contemporary film. Cinema has its own history, its own practice, its own perversity. For this reason modernist/postmodern scenarios become misplaced or imprecise and we need a more clinical, exact scenario of recent change in film form. Film, I want to argue, has changed from the 1960s and 1970s, where modernist art was reinvented in film making as *neo-modern* (Orr, 1993:2–10, 15–28), to the 1990s where form has become *hypermodern*, where it has been dominated by technology and spectacle which gloss, often reflexively, the emergence of a new computer-driven global information age in which the distinctiveness of time and place is ever under scrutiny (Augé, 1995:116–20; Castells, 1996). The key changes here are not those usually identified with 'postmodernism', the reinvention of pastiche or nostalgia heralded by Jameson (1991:287–98), or the growing eclecticism of styles noted by others (Andrew, 1987:19). For Hollywood is still largely the epicentre of popular genres based on melodrama and the simplified separation of good and evil, in short of metanarratives now looser in construction than before but still inclusive myths. However, it now creates screen spectacles which are virtual spectacles, which go beyond classic melodrama in order to give a mythic gloss to the speed and movement of the information society. It is this fusion of virtual technologies and spectacle which makes the key difference. Outside of Hollywood, film still inhabits a different world. In it, there are a new breed of maverick *auteurs* with their own agendas. Yet they too must confront the bewildering complexities of the information society and the power of its electronic images. In the 1980s and 1990s this challenge could be seen especially in the films of Atom Egoyan, David Lynch, David Cronenberg, Peter Greenaway, Krzystzof Kieślowski, Wim Wenders and Wong Kar-wai. Thus while Hollywood collectively mythologises the hypermodern, the lone *auteur* of the *fin de siècle* deconstructed it in new and fascinating ways.

Film is a uniquely twentieth-century art with many precursors but little pre-history. It is also the most culturally dynamic medium, technically speaking, of all the major art forms, applying new technology in breathtaking instalments. Sound narrative was not widely used until the 1930s, colour and deep-focus photography were not in widespread use until the 1950s, while the light-weight handheld camera made its mark in features at the end of that decade. This staged transformation of its technologies singles it out in a unique and startling way. It enabled cinema to recycle the modernist impulse of the 1920s in the 1960s while transforming it utterly. Film connected with the 1920s avant-gardes in its silent mode but always at something of a tangent – Sergei Eisenstein with the constructivist movement in Soviet art, Luis Bunuel with the surrealist movement in painting and poetry, Fritz Lang and Friedrich Murnau with the expressionism which embraced nearly every art form in Germany until 1925. In the 1930s, fascist and Soviet censorship broke such connection in many of its European homelands while the populist impulses of the Hollywood studio system constrained it on the American continent. But film had always been a popular art form and modernist forms resurged in the liberal democracies of the Cold War during the 1960s, the new age of mass education and consumer capitalism. Until then experiment had remained at the consumer periphery, prone, because of its sexual and political subversive-ness, to the backlash of censorship – witness the widespread banning of Bunuel's *L'age d'or*, after its abortive debut in 1931, which lasted for all of fifty years.

In the 1960s this peripheral positioning began to change. In the twenty years between 1958 and 1978 (notionally the 1960s and the 1970s), between the release of Welles's *Touch of Evil* and Terrence Malick's *Days of Heaven*, neo-modern film swept to critical acclaim throughout Europe and North America, spurred initially by the French New Wave and appreciated by the educated and critical younger generation of its time. It was to this generation that the filmic vision of veterans Luis Bunuel and Ingmar Bergman appealed so decisively and so became part of durable neo-modern legacy. After the great commercial success of *Bonnie and Clyde* and *Easy Rider*, the focus of attention switched back in the 1970s to the United States, where a handful of Hollywood drop-outs and a new generation of film school graduates, often nicknamed the 'Superbrats', stormed into major film production and changed the nature of American cinema. As we shall see, this challenge to the old authoritarian traditions of the studio system was not fully countered by that system until the revival of science fiction, until the blockbuster successes of *Star Wars* and *Close Encounters of the Third Kind* a decade later. Spearheaded by the sci-fi revival, the Hollywood empire then struck back. Something changed around 1978 and changed utterly. The obsession with spectacle was nothing new but its adroit use of new special effects and computer-controlled cameras was to be decisive. The sudden disappearance of Malick, we might say, marked the rise and rise of Steven Spielberg, for whom even the sky was never the limit. (Malick did not resurface until *The Thin Red Line* in 1998.) Yet this change marks and echoes a further intensification of the processes of Western modernity in the last twenty years of the twentieth century, producing a further transformation in film. If the 1950s saw the transformation from neo-realism to the *neo-modern*, then the start of the 1980s marked the transition from the neo-modern to the *hypermodern*.

Back in the 1960s the neo-modern, modernism's second wave if you like, had been a hothouse of combustible elements – beat poetry, the theatre of the absurd, the French *nouveau roman*, abstract expressionism, pop art, modern jazz and the transformation of rhythm and blues into the rock music of a psychedelic age. All these forms had the eye and ear of the young, the radical and the experimental whose counter-cultures matched a makeshift consumerism to new cults of cultural celebrity. The avant-gardes of modernism's first wave, when revolution and counter-revolution engulfed much of post-war Europe, had gone. The movements which replaced them were cults of the spectacular, such as Andy Warhol's Factory, and the connections between film and other art forms became looser. While the films of Alain Resnais or Michelangelo Antonioni can be linked to the French *nouveau roman*, the connections are at best tenuous. But the power of rock music was more direct. The new rock culture of 'Swinging London' in the late 1960s was captured by Antonioni's *Blow-Up* and then by *Performance*, the startling debut of Donald Cammell and Nic Roeg which starred Mick Jagger as a drugged decadent rock singer in Notting Hill. Thomas, *Blow-Up*'s arrogant young photographer, a working-class Londoner, seemed a composite portrait of David Bailey, Don McCullin and Terence Donovan. His fashion models included Verushka, a major '60s icon, while The Yardbirds – the rock group in the Rhythm and Blues Club sequence – was the forerunner of Led Zeppelin, and the young Jeff Beck who trashes his guitar was to become a major rock guitarist of his generation. In *Performance* Jagger's portrait of the decadent psychedelic Notting Hill recluse and rock singer, Turner, was rumoured to be based on fellow Stones singer Brian Jones, who had just tragically died, while Turner's predatory bisexual lover, a heroin addict who injects in front of the camera, was played by Anita Pallenberg, Jones's ex-girlfriend then linked amorously to Keith Richard and soon to be addicted to the drug herself (MacCabe, 1998:43–6). The incestuous and claustrophobic feeling of both films is derived in part from their closeness to the texture of this rapidly changing culture of the period. Despite the growing use of rock music as soundtrack in counter-culture movies such as *Easy Rider* and *Zabriskie Point* or Vietnam movies such as *Coming Home* and *Apocalypse Now*, the tight intertextuality of the 'Swinging London' dyad has never been repeated elsewhere.

Nonetheless, the dominant structures of feeling in American neo-modernism feature quite starkly the effects and ambience of narcotics, not only in the acid rock of *Easy Rider* and *Zabriskie Point* but through the lyrics of Leonard Cohen which usher in Robert Altman's *McCabe and Mrs Miller* and more especially in the ominous chords of The Doors over which booms the sonorous warning voice of Jim Morrison at the start of *Apocalypse Now*. All four movies evoke, directly or indirectly, the paranoia of the Vietnam period in American life. The war, and the social unrest ever haunting it, now seem like a vital spur to the paranoia and lyrical flight which course daringly through the narratives of Robert Altman, Bob Rafelson, Francis Coppola, Alan Pakula and Martin Scorsese. For sure, these display parallels with their literary contemporaries, the conspiracy narratives of Thomas Pynchon, Don De Lillo and Robert Stone. But they are more. In his powerful reading of the transition from classical to modern film, Gilles Deleuze plays on the proximity of 'balade' (route) and 'ballade' (song) to suggest that the lyrical trip, 'bal(l)ade' is central to the time-image of the new cinema which breaks down the traditional relationship of situation and action in classical narrative (Deleuze, 1989:3–24). The road movie, one could argue, is its prime invention, not only in America in features such as *Bonnie and Clyde*, *Easy Rider*, *Five Easy Pieces* and *Badlands*, but in the films of the New German cinema by Werner Herzog and Wim Wenders. Indeed, Wenders's *Kings of the Road* matches its central German locations to the popular American music which drives its two protagonists ever forward on the road. For sure, film remains a collective artwork but in the neo-modern age it is also more individualistic than ever. In the 1970s Altman, Cassavetes, Coppola, Scorsese, Rafelson and Malick all challenged the sclerotic Hollywood studios, working with independent producers and using *ad hoc* but loyal teams to transform movie making. Needless to say, they often burnt themselves out with the logistical effort of doing so. By the end of the 1970s Altman, Cassavetes and Coppola had suffered burn-out, Malick and Rafelson had disappeared from movie making, and Scorsese was forced in desperation to redeem personal and artistic crisis through the magnificent *Raging Bull*.

Unlike painting or fiction, film's second wave is more defining, more comprehensive and much wider than its original imprint. That is why the term 'neo-modern' defines it as a return of modernism with more breadth of talent, enhanced technologies, larger audiences and more freedom from censorship at its disposal. Although such work was seen as 'arthouse' and 'difficult', all the top European directors had major commercial hits. Fellini was consistently popular from *La Dolce Vita* onwards while Bergman had major hits with *The Silence* and *Cries and Whispers*, Antonioni with *Blow-Up*, Godard with *Pierrot le Fou* and Bertolucci with *Last Tango in Paris*. At a deeper level, the neo-modern turn gave birth to a new poetics best illustrated by the seminal work of the great inventors of its film language – Orson Welles, Antonioni and Jean-Luc Godard. In his two great films of the period, *Touch of Evil* and *The Trial*, Welles created a mobile technology of enhanced speed and image making through wide-angle, deep-focus and a poetic moving camera. His dynamic mise-en-scène was matched by dissonant sound and disruptive montage whose sudden time–space switching is bewildering and exhilarating, claustrophobic and agoraphobic all at the same time. The narrative leap of time and space in Welles is not merely stylistic ellipsis, disassociation of sound and image, or the sharp, unexpected cut which disorients the viewer; it is also a pure visceral displacement of the image from its traditional function of comforting or seducing the spectator. Its force field charged the cinekinetic energies of Truffaut, Bertolucci, Kubrick, Coppola, Scorsese, De Palma, Spielberg and Oliver Stone, all of them profoundly indebted to him. Moreover, Welles's challenge to film language was inseparable from his concern with the burning injustices of the modern world. His work is an aesthetic of shock but also a politics of shock as monumental in sound narrative as that of Eisenstein in silent cinema.

Antonioni and Godard both shared a sense of the screen's limits, its fragility, its failures to show us the events in offscreen space or probe to the full the mysteries of the modern soul. Both directors explored stylistic devices for decentring their subjects, removing them from the centre of the frame or where in any particular montage the audience might expect them to be. This process, referred to by Pascal Bonitzer as 'deframing' (*decadrage*) (Bonitzer, 1985; Aumont, 1997:117–18), thus throws doubt upon the domination by their subjects of their own life-world. Whether these are the dislocations of landscape, modernist architecture or the sheer weight of consumer detritus, deframing throws subjects out of kilter and threatens their ontological status. Both directors also use colour as a form of painting with light which has parallels with developments in modern art. In Antonioni's *Red Desert* there is a level of abstraction in the coloration of the industrial landscape which echoes Mark Rothko's painting of intangible objects, while Godard's use of saturated colour with a hard surface sheen for *Pierrot le Fou*, in the Riviera sequences, shows the clear influence of Roy Lichtenstein's cartoon-strip paintings and pop art (Dalle Vacche, 1996:66–7, 126–7). While Godard was infatuated with its trivia of everyday life and the bewildering speed of its incessant distractions, Antonioni's film language demands a contemplative stance, a viewing mode which became unfashionable in the impatient 1990s where hypermodern speed and motion drown out the aesthetic of contemplation. In its time, however, it did throw into question the whole nature of cinematic meaning. What does the moving image signify? How do we resolve its ambiguities? From *L'avventura* to *The Passenger*, Antonioni's films have engaged in direct ontological puzzles where dialogue is sparse, time lingers, voiceover is non-existent and music is pared to a minimum. Such austerity seems more readable now in Ozu's films, which concern themselves with ritual and tradition, or in Robert Bresson's films, which so often focus on the adversity of the poor and the outcast. What seems unforgivable for contemporary viewers is the melancholia and defeat which pervade a modern, prosperous European bourgeoisie. The early Godard is more appealingly dissonant and disruptive, a visual iconoclast. Antonioni's best work, on the other hand, is an iconographic critique of the limits of Western knowledge. His fractured critique of the bourgeois subject is also what links the diverse and equally powerful styles of Bergman and Wenders, Resnais and Rohmer, Bunuel and Fassbinder, Fellini and Bertolucci. Yet by the 1980s this crisis of the bourgeois subject had been turned round in the Anglo-American world by making him or her no longer the investigated, or even the investigator investigated (as in *Blow-Up* or *The Passenger*), but the hyperactive investigator whose breathtaking speed of movement disallows any such contemplation. This switch from passive to hyperactive mode heralds in effect the beginning of the end for the neo-modern age.

As a result, the liberal melodrama was reborn as a hyperactive ride through the trouble spots of the world. Politics and sexuality had become more explicit while experiments in style were more widely accepted by box-office audiences. Indeed the use of Steadicam, which had been such a novel variation on the mobile camera in *Days of Heaven* and *The Shining*, was to become standard and familiar over the next twenty years. At the same time the liberal hero was resurrected as hyperactive trouble-shooter, flawed but lovable. In genre the crossover is vital. Early 1970s films such as *The Long Goodbye*, *Night Moves*, *The Conversation*, *The Passenger* and *Chinatown* were all classics of the investigator investigated, robbed of heroic status and turned inside out. Starting with *All the President's Men* the process was set in reverse. The investigators are still rough-edged diamonds in risky situations, down on their luck and faced with the forbidding complexities of the modern world, but you can identify with them. They are now heroic. John Travolta in *Blow-Out*, Nick Nolte in *Under Fire* and James Woods in *Salvador* are all flawed and unlikely heroes stumbling on to events of great political importance, a trope which reaches its most complete expression in the squeaky-clean Jim Garrison played by Kevin Costner in Stone's *JFK*. Other films of clear skill and talent fit all too easily into the frame – *The China Syndrome*, *Missing*, *The Year of Living Dangerously*, *The Killing Fields*, *Mississippi Burning* and *Cry Freedom*. The audience gets behind heroes pursuing worthy causes in their uneven quest for justice. For, after the crises of racial unrest, Vietnam and counter-culture revolt, they reinvigorate liberal causes by melodramatic means. Thus the heroic bourgeois subject is recuperated by building on the neo-modern legacy and then crucially altering course. The hyperactive investigator explores the double standards of liberalism at home or abroad, risking the opprobrium of the Establishment in doing so. The stylistic devices of the neo-moderns and the technical changes in shooting are taken up eagerly, the fracturing of narrative, the alternation in the speed of film. Film language becomes sparser, dialogue more elliptical but the bottom line is a new form of heroism which matches physical danger and mental agility in the quest for truth. It is this vein that Spielberg, for example, can reinvent in *Schindler's List*, a hyper-history of the Holocaust, by mythologising the one businessman ever to aid effectively the Jewish prisoners of the Nazi camps. But beyond liberal melodrama always lurked the bankable politics of spectacle which moved away from the actual worlds of modern politics in the virtual worlds of science fiction. *Close Encounters of the Third Kind*, *Apocalypse Now* and *Blade Runner* were experimental forms of spectacle which ushered in the new age of hypermodern film. For they paved the way to a new mythology, a mythic reinvention of virtual computer worlds of the information society destined to work at every level of existence, military, scientific, commercial, artistic, intimate. Such worlds involved, as Paul Virilio has suggested, a derealisation of sense-experience which a revitalised Hollywood makes mythic through science fiction and hi-tech action movies as an exciting and dangerous virtual-reality ride (Virilio, 1997:38–45).

Here the physical increases in speed, movement and density of the information society are fused with the new forms of electronic telepresence and instant communication to create a virtual world onscreen and then reinvent it as a *natural* world. The new professional heroes are mavericks who work within the auspices of the techno-scientific machine. Here there are echoes of earlier genres, the westerner, the private eye, the undercover cop, but now the professionalism is techno-scientific. Sigourney Weaver is the new female executive mythologised as astronaut captain in *Alien*; Harrison Ford is the private-eye-become-blade-runner who has the scientific know-how in 2019 to use the Esper and the Voight–Kampff test in his hunting down of replicants; Jodie Foster is the FBI agent in *The Silence of the Lambs*, who is locked in not only to her profession but by its electronic and computerised surveillance, where serial programming is seen as the effective antidote to serial killing. Elsewhere the action-hero is already biotechnical, the maverick enforcer with a steroid-chemical body locked into new technologies of speed and violence and framed by the new technologies of special effects. If the cyborg is the new heroic – or demonic – figure of the contemporary gloss on a future world, of which James Cameron's *Terminator 2* is the supreme example, this is because the Hollywood star has become a cipher of special effects, an image in the machine, a well-paid victim of techno-entrapment. Just as Deckard can never shake off the fear of being a replicant himself, so the techno-investigator can never shake off the fear of being just another element in a machine. Peter Weller's Robocop and Arnold Schwarzenegger's Terminator are the new cyber-icons of virtual spectacle, their power generated by technology and not by any sense of good and evil. In hypermodern Hollywood the narrative passage of the cyber-icon cues in the perpetual risks and malfunctions of the information society, which are mythologised as the force field of fate in the age of digital interaction and the personal computer. This is the key to the hypermodern which overrides the critique of the futuristic mise-en-scène as postmodern in an architectural sense, for even in *Blade Runner*, cult movie for many post-modern critics, the stylised sets are more clearly evocative of the modernist city (Bukatmen, 1997:59–63).

Where Hollywood glorifies technology-in-general because its success depends upon the addiction to technology-in-particular, upon the empire of special effects and the strategies of simultaneous global transmission, film aesthetics moves in a different direction outside the borders of the empire. Off-world, to use the idiom of *Blade Runner*, is now a different place from what it was. The simultaneous glossing and experimenting with electronic technology in Cronenberg, Egoyan, Wenders, Greenaway and many others, yields to us as viewers a critical fix on its domination in our life-worlds. But it does more. As opposed to the spectacular horrors of Hollywood hypermodern, it chronicles the unspoken terrors of a technical life-world in which speed and motion have generated fragmentation and solitude. The neo-modern 'subject investigated' becomes the hypermodern subject deconstructed, deconstructed, that is, through the ubiquity of technologies which reflexively form the conditions for daily living. Here I propose to examine five keynote films of the 1990s which search in very different ways the core of the hypermodern predicament. These are Kieslowski's *Three Colours: Red*, Egoyan's *Exotica*, Lynch's *Lost Highway*, Cronenberg's *Naked Lunch* and Wong Kar-wai's *Chung-King Express*.

Let us take them in outline one by one. *Red* is the story of a fashion model who meets, literally by accident, a retired judge perfecting telephone voyeurism, monitoring all the calls in his neighbourhood, including her own, and now passing judgement on others by proxy where once he had done so in court (Andrew, 1998:55–62). Through the motif of phone tapping Kieślowski deconstructs the wider voyeurism inherent in daily technologies of communing. In *Exotica*, Egoyan explores the way in which new technologies lure us into re-creating the banalities of everyday life as 'exotic' performance, and his lap-dancing emporium is a transparent hyperreal locale where sexuality is reinvented as a set of disconnected relationships. In *Lost Highway* Lynch takes video surveillance as means and metaphor for the violation of domestic space. The anonymous videotape delivered through the letterbox by unseen hand, with its video images of intrusion through the skylight, visually 'rapes' the intimacy of Bill Pullman and Patricia Arquette, the distraught couple festering in their desolate suburban home. In Cronenberg's film of Burroughs's notorious novel, Peter Weller's narcotic hallucinations of Mugwumps and typewriters turning into beetles suggest, for a bio-technical age, the nightmare vision of transverse crossover between the organic and the mechanical world. Technical objects become living forms and humans are frozen into the posture of machines. In Wong Kar-wai's pyrotechnic version of compressed living in Kowloon, *Chung-King Express*, urban space becomes phantasmagoric, as couples traverse the same locations without meeting and then meet knowing nothing of their adjacency and then finding out even less. Or else they traverse the same spaces at different times in relations of amorous disconnection where neither body or soul will meet. The speed of time passing and camera moving dizzily in handheld motion only exacerbate and never expiate the predicament of distended solitude (Lalanne, 1997:19–27).

Let us now focus in on *Red*. Kieślowski starts with two stunning shot-sequences. In the first a male hand dials a phone number and the camera tracks with a series of disguised cuts the speed of the call through the cable via the exchange and undersea to its receiver in another country, where the engaged tone repeats and the engaged buzzer flashes. An intermediate shot shows a man (later known as law student Auguste) walking his dog out of his Geneva apartment to a nearby café. As he enters the café in high-angle long shot the camera pans and tilts upwards before tracking forward into the apartment window of Valentine (Irene Jacob) to catch the moment at which her phone rings in an empty room. She appears out of nowhere to answer and moves around the flat with the cordless instrument, still in the same shot, answering her boyfriend who has called her from London. As Valentine sits motionless by her bed, Kieślowski finally cuts to facial close-up. We return to the man coming out of the café and making a phone call from his own flat to a weather report call voice. He kisses the female voice down the phone and replaces the receiver, later getting into his jeep before driving off just as Jacob enters the shot and then enters the same café from which he has just departed. While Kieslowski uses offscreen space in a way akin to Antonioni or Godard, the whole sequence intensifies the film experience through its perpetual adjacency. Auguste and Valentine live in adjacent apartments, phone their respective lovers at almost identical times, and use the same local café consecutively. Yet their paths never truly cross, even though it seems from the imprint of the montage on the viewing eye that they are in fact phoning *each other*. This experiential feature of contemporary life becomes a profound form of *simultaneous dislocation*.

We might want to call this the alternate route of the hypermodern. While Hollywood cinema mythologises the hypermodern as virtual spectacle, *auteur* cinema presents it as simultaneous dislocation. Though the hypermodern may be a synonym for 'postmodern' in the eyes of some critics, one important proviso must be made. None of these films vindicates the common criteria of the postmodern. There is little pastiche and no nostalgia. The concern with the reflexive nature of the image, the filmic use of other forms of imaging remains as *visual* as ever, making nonsense of Jameson's claim that in the postmodern the optical gives way to the purely sonic (Jameson, 1992:194). Rather, the fusion of sonic and optical is made more intense by a technical life-world of

simultaneous presence, where different technologies, the car, fax, telephone, computer, camera run in parallel but never in tandem. This is both speed and implosion, the acceleration of which Giddens (1990) speaks when he sees late modernity as a juggernaut in danger of careering out of control, the implosions of telepresence which define for Virilio the invisibility of instantaneous information and for Negroponte (1995) increasing domination by the global network of bits over the tangible world of atoms. In Kieslowski's trilogy, both *Blue* and *Red* are triggered by the fate of the car accident, the technical rendering of a daily fusion of a daily fate, the equation of motorised speed and random encounter. In Egoyan's films, the bourgeois subject lacks definition unless it centres itself amid screens and cameras (*Family Viewing*), or translates daily fate into stylised performance (*Exotica*), or perversely does both (*The Adjuster*). In *Lost Highway* the electronic instrument as video camera or mobile phone is turned into a Gothic monstrosity which violates human privacy and presence, a harbinger of hypermodern rape, a metaphor which the brutal hard-core movie screened towards the end of the film makes distressingly literal. In all these films, simultaneous dislocation creates an implosive density where the co-ordination of the senses is stretched to an almost impossible pitch.

The hypermodern transformation of time is triggered by the electronic revolution which accentuates in late modernity the phantasmagoric and implosive intensity of simultaneous presence, of a world of infinite fragments where everything appears to be happening at once. Here a significant feature of hypermodern film is the rebirth of the cinematic city, a way of filming which colours the reinvention of reality on the plane of city asphalt, the city rendered as a site of instantaneous presence. Here the dilemma is less bourgeois and more subterranean, more the new forms of destitution and crime which inhabit the lower depths, the fragile intersection of working class and underclass which is so difficult to nail down and, after watching this kind of cinema, even more so. If this filmic experience is sometimes amorphous, it is intoxicating for that reason. It is this adriftness or being set adrift which provides the visual phenomenology of post-Godardian Paris, Binoche trying to escape her past in *Blue* by going incognito in Rue Mouffetard, the vengeful unemployed boys from the banlieu in Matthieu Kassowitz's *La Haine*, the risk-taking whores and hustlers of Andre Techine's *J'embrasse pas*. On the streets of London it is David Thewlis, the northern drifter of Mike Leigh's *Naked*, hyperactively violent yet prophesying Blakean apocalypse. It is the phantasmagoric drifting of ex-IRA man Stephen Rea in *The Crying Game* hiding his own persona but discovering that in others too appearances are never what they seem. It is the drifting of casual brickie, Glaswegian Robert Carlyle in Ken Loach's *Riff-Raff*, seeking work to build houses while squatting in a dilapidated flat which is literally falling apart. Here we may also cite the makeshift but even more intense vision of the underclass underworld deployed by Fred Kelemen in Berlin's Kreuzberg in *Fate* or the less than wonderful Copenhagen in the recent film of city drug dealing, *Pusher*. Both films push the low-budget city picture to extremes not seen since the early days of John Cassavetes, the use of handheld following camera, minimal cutting, natural lighting. The camera as mobile witness, itself made hyperactive. Finally we can take in one of the most elegant city films of the 1990s, Gilles Mimouni's debut feature and homage to Hitchcock, *L'ap-*

partement. In the opening sequence, it becomes clear that Vincent Cassel is stranded between two women, one of whom has a perfect double, but equally stranded between the separate time zones they constitute in his life and the separate spaces of their separate apartments. His fate is to live simultaneously in his fruitless odyssey back and forth through city streets between time, place and face, a simultaneous dislocation of season, space and persona. If he endures all this in a state of hyperactive bafflement, that is distantly echoed in our viewing experience as we coast along the edge of the time–space image in watching him. As opposed to the virtual labyrinth of Hollywood science fiction, the actual labyrinth of the European city.

The Blair Witch Project: film and hypertexts

In his prescient book, *Interface Culture* (1997), Steven Johnson draws attention to the remarkable growth of what he terms media 'metaforms' – television programmes, print coverage and so on devoted to other media, rather than to anything outside the circuits of media self referentiality. So we have TV 'review' programmes that consist largely of extracts from cinema films, from other TV programmes, even from computer games. Media celebrities appear in increasing numbers as guests in chat shows. Popular newspapers and magazines find media 'news' as worthy of column inches as many hard news stories, often apparently more so. Johnson's insight is to see these as 'ghosts of technologies to come' (p. 34). In other words, these are not the signs of mere parasitism or self absorption, of a loss of contact with the 'real'. Rather, Johnson argues, they are signs of our increasing need for data that make sense of other data, for information filters and gateways. The fact that this need goes largely unrecognised as the genuine motivation leads many of these metaforms of media output to fail miserably at that task. But they remain evidence of a trend that may – should – lead to useful meta-data and gateways, genuine prototypes of which are actually being developed on the web and will transfer from there with increasing convergence of media technologies.

But there seems to be something else at work here – the elaboration of metaforms just for the sake of elaboration, which apparently offers its own satisfactions. Children's popular culture got to this first, with toy lines since at least the 1970s being developed into TV series or vice versa, spinning off comics, books, sometimes movies, even clothes and wallpaper. Often a 'backstory' develops across these various forms, as notably with the once hugely popular *Transformers* toys which became characters in an increasingly elaborate galaxy-spanning myth, filled out with more and more detail as animated TV series, comics and books proliferated. Adult popular culture trails along behind as usual, but the 'total marketing' of a concept through the whole range of media is now increasingly common. While much of this is just hardheaded money making at work, there are signs that the metaforms are gradually creating a new sort of relationship between audiences and 'text', not least around films.

The Blair Witch Project (1999) was a unique film in many ways. Most obviously, its innovation resided in the use throughout of camcorder footage to create a mock documentary deftly combined with the formula of a horror movie. But, though this is less often noted, *The Blair Witch Project* was much more than the film itself. In fact, looked at in its entirety, *The Blair Witch Project* locates the film as just one artefact in a whole set of elements in print and on the web that sustained an elaborate backstory and an unusually large-scale game of participatory make-believe for its audience. Rather than considering this a one-off phenomenon, stimulated by the odd nature of this particular film, Steven Johnson's perspective might lead us to suppose that metaforms can take on an aesthetic life of their own, no longer secondary in relation to an original, but all caught up in a circuit of self referentiality in which there is no true original any more. For those who have responded enthusiastically to it, *The Blair Witch Project* has become all metaform. Unlike the *Star Wars* films, with their wildly proliferating secondary merchandise (which they are largely responsible for having invented on such a scale), *The Blair Witch Project* is all 'secondary'. The movie itself purports to be found footage shot by the three protagonists themselves before their violent deaths in the Maryland woods at the hands of an unseen maniac possessed by the witch. The 'authorised' book is a dossier of supporting documents, from stained diary extracts to a private investigator's reports. On the web, 'official' and 'unofficial' sites proliferated, the best of them developing the whole scenario and its background mythology in depth and opening it to online discussion by the audience.

For months after the film's success, the web site of the Frederick County Sheriff's Office in Maryland, where the events supposedly took place, carried this message from Sheriff James W. Hagy, prominently displayed: 'Although potentially entertaining, the Blair Witch Project movie is a work of fiction. The events portrayed did not occur in any manner in the town of Burkittsville, Maryland or Frederick County, Maryland.' The town's own web site, promoting the local community and its interests, carried a detailed factsheet provided by Sergeant Thomas Winebrenner, including statements such as, 'There is no APB issued for Josh's car, as it was never reported missing to the Maryland State Police or the Frederick County Sherriff's Office. Besides, we don't call them APBs [All Points Broadcasts], we call them "Lookouts"', or, 'I was working for the Frederick County Sheriff's Office in 1994, and I can confirm that there was no large scale search launched for three missing college students.' Sergeant Winebrenner then goes on to insist – and here one starts to worry about him just a little – 'The non-existent search did not yield a trace of any missing people because there were no missing people.'

This was just the tip of an iceberg of claim and counter-claim about the movie and its 'mockumentary' status, on the web and in print. Many participants clearly felt they were getting into the spirit (*sic*.) of the thing by blurring the distinction between fact and fiction, while others clung tenaciously to that distinction and took pains to protest Burkittsville's innocence of any involvement (while still others, like Winebrenner, evidently started to lose their grip). What becomes strangely disorienting after a while is that game and reality do become increasingly hard to disentangle. The *Project*'s producers generated so much of their own 'police' material and other 'evidence' that even Sheriff Hagy, Sergeant Winebrenner and the 'real' Burkittsville residents came under suspicion as potentially mere artefacts of somebody's imagination. As their statements of their own 'reality' became more strident so, paradoxically, they started to come across as more hollow. On the producers' 'official' web site, entirely convincing scene-of-the-crime photographs and audio interviews with experts vie with the real (?) Sheriff Hagy's amateurish site in terms of projecting convincing truth claims to an audience that evidently revelled in these very ambiguities.

The *Mr. Showbiz* web site (typical of the metaforms that Johnson describes) sustained a popular discussion forum around *The Blair Witch Project* (366 messages in just one topic by the end of 1999), with its own home page based on a suitably grubby map showing the forest area where the three students taped their own haunting and deaths, and where different locations link to further background information. *Mr. Showbiz*'s message is: 'Don't go wandering the Blair Witch woods all alone though – let Mr. Showbiz be your guide. Find out why our critic thinks *The Blair Witch Project* just might be the scariest movie ever made, read our interview with the producer and directors who brought it all together, share your own true tales of terror among the trees, and more.' Among the messages posted to the 'Witch Board': 'What exactly was the slimey crap on Josh's back-pack and practically all of his stuff? I didn't figure that one out'; 'An interview with the directors revealed that they used ky jelly but didn't state what it signified'; 'At the end of the film, when the girl runs into the basement, she sees Mike standing in the corner, and she is knocked down . . . As she falls down the camera turns and gets a shot of something that "looks" like it might be a human head. I re-wound the film a million times and hit "pause" but still can't figure out exactly what it was. Anyone else have any ideas on that?'

There is 'filtering' going on here but much more besides. The metaforms simultaneously filter and elaborate the information. D. A. Stern's book of the film, which plays it entirely straight-faced and insists that the film's producers (i.e. those who had edited and researched the 'found' footage) had been 'looking for someone to help them organize all the vast material related to the disappearance of Heather Donahue, Joshua Leonard, and Michael Williams, and a bizarre and mysterious backstory they weren't able to fit into their documentary' (1999:viii). The resulting book cannot be read on its own in any straightforward sense at all. It is a scrapbook that only makes sense if one knows the main characters and cares enough about their experience to peer into smudgy photocopies of Burkittsville Historical Society documents or hum the tune of 'The Dreary Black Hills' from the reproduced song sheet ('A folk song from the late 1800s, "Tom Kane" in the third verse could be a corruption of "Tom Lang", who was one of the search party victims found bound and disemboweled.') From the whole jigsaw of elements across different media, within which the movie is actually only minimally informative, one can piece together a story arc that runs from the supposed eighteenth-century burning of a witch held responsible for abusing children, the nineteenth-century ritual slaying of a search party looking for another missing child, the mid twentieth-century arrest of a hermit who had lured children to their deaths at the behest of the witch, to the missing college students and the discovery of their unnerving camcorder footage. Plenty of raw material here for further elaborations, perhaps further books and films, but also for the spoofs and parodies that indicate how deeply something has penetrated a popular culture.

What we saw happening around *The Blair Witch Project* in 1999 was the beginning of a hypermedia form that will become more prevalent as it becomes clearer that hypertext – the new aesthetic of the digital – is not just a matter of restructuring existing media forms in some non-linear fashion. Somewhat silly predictions of new forms of 'interactive' or non-linear film (e.g. where the viewer takes decisions about what direction the narrative is going to go in) miss the point entirely. The productive non-linearity is not necessarily going to be happening inside each existing linear medium; rather it is going to be based on hyperlinking across media to create the sorts of metaform of which *The Blair Witch Project* was just a modest but marvellously playful and successful early prototype. That even this early experiment managed to raise such profoundly interesting questions about how public knowledge is constructed, and about how we tell the difference between fact and fiction, suggests that we can look forward to seeing film play a central role within new, dispersed hypermedia 'texts' of a sort that Sergeant Winebrenner can only imagine in his wildest dreams of things that haven't happened. Policing the boundary between fact and fiction can only become more interesting in a post-*Witch* world.

Dan Fleming

14

Woman and the gaze

Efrat Tseëlon

'Is the gaze of cultural representation male?' one may ask, rephrasing the title of Ann Kaplan's 1983 article. She posits the question against a backdrop of feminist literature based on the comfortable binary assumption of a male voyeur and a female object of vision. Binary notions, even in the academy, have an irresistible appeal. And they certainly prove a popular currency in the culture at large. Time and again they survive critical attempts to deconstruct, problematise or destabilise them. The present chapter is one such attempt at rethinking woman and the gaze.

In many studies and interviews I conducted with women on clothes and personal appearance, I came across a prevailing sense of the crucial importance attached to the visible self. It goes beyond the importance of clothes, or making the right impression in certain contexts, or conforming to expectations. Feeling visible, exposed, observed or on show appears to be almost constitutive of their self conception. Yet it is less heightened in an environment where the woman feels approved, accepted, loved, inconspicuous – in short, confident and psychologically less visible. And it is more pronounced where she feels on display, on show, being examined and measured, invaded by scrutinising looks, attention or comments, overshadowed by other people's 'better' presentation or judgement. She then feels threatened and psychologically visible (Tseëlon, 1989).

The visibility factor was further reinforced when I subjected individual accounts by different women, about their clothing concerns, to a statistical analysis that transforms their criteria on to a dimensional space. Using multi-dimensional scaling, the solution shown in figure 15 was obtained. How does one interpret the interconnections between items that are close together or further apart? The structure did not suggest a straightforward interpretation, but the respondents' own reasons suggested that the underlying grouping principle was the visibility/anonymity dimension (Tseëlon, 1995).

But how can we explain the constitutive role of the gaze in the woman's self conception? Part of the reason lies with the long-standing Western tradition of female representation. John Berger (1972) and feminist art historians (e.g. Pollock, 1988) have noted that centuries of Western art have made the female body an object of aesthetic pleasure for the male spectator. More recently, the cinema has been shown to operate similar mechanisms, resulting in a repro-

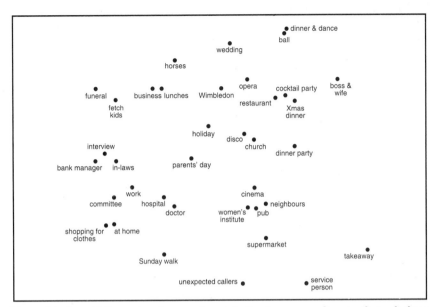

Figure 15 A multidimensional map of social situations according to their clothing concerns (after Tseëlon, 1989)
Note: The top left corner indicates spaces of high visibility. The bottom right corner indicates spaces of low visibility

duction of the woman's specular role. 'Gaze theory' dominated film theory in the 1970s (see also chapter 12). 'Gaze' has been used both literally and metaphorically. Literally it refers to positionality of the camera and the audience. Metaphorically, it refers to subjectivity and identity: a subject position from which a specific individual can speak, look, write, identify or experience pleasure. Using a psychoanalytic position as an analytical tool for deconstructing the patriarchal gaze, gaze theory developed an orthodoxy of a gendered gaze which is eroticising and controlling. It was sparked off by Laura Mulvey's (1975) article which advanced the notion that the cinematic gaze is male, on account of the feminine image it constructs, and the mode of pleasure it offers the female viewer (see figure 16).

According to Mulvey, the options of spectatorial pleasure are limited by the nature of the cinematic medium. The viewing of a film, like peeping through a keyhole, is an act associated with a voyeuristic pleasure, while the positioning of the image of the woman as an object of male desire in the classic Hollywood cinema – to be idolised and either conquered or destroyed – is a form of fetishism. Voyeurism is a conversion of exhibitionistic tendencies from passive pleasure (displaying one's body) to active pleasure in looking. The voyeuristic sadistic look is characterised by a distance between spectator and image allowing the spectator power over the image. It is curious, inquiring, demanding to know. Fetishism is classically understood by psychoanalysis as one solution to castration anxiety. Triggered by the sight of the penis-less woman, the threat of female lack is compensated for by a symbolic 'penis substitute': a part of the body or an item of clothing that belongs to the desired

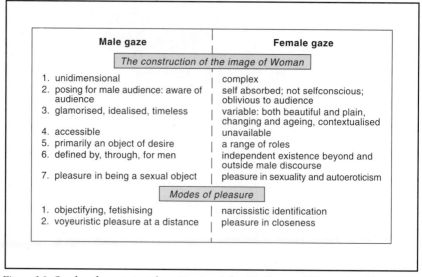

Male gaze	Female gaze
The construction of the image of Woman	
1. unidimensional	complex
2. posing for male audience: aware of audience	self absorbed; not selfconscious; oblivious to audience
3. glamorised, idealised, timeless	variable: both beautiful and plain, changing and ageing, contextualised
4. accessible	unavailable
5. primarily an object of desire	a range of roles
6. defined by, through, for men	independent existence beyond and outside male discourse
7. pleasure in being a sexual object	pleasure in sexuality and autoeroticism
Modes of pleasure	
1. objectifying, fetishising	narcissistic identification
2. voyeuristic pleasure at a distance	pleasure in closeness

Figure 16 Gendered spectatorial positioning (after Tseëlon and Kaiser, 1992)

person. The fetishist look does not wish to inquire further, it is captivated by the display and the spectacular, and transforms the object into a satisfying physical beauty. Both fetishism and voyeurism are sexual male perversions representing solutions to unconscious conflicts (Freud, 1927). As spectatorial positions they exclude the female viewer. Mulvey (1981) later revisited her original analysis and concluded that the woman has another spectatorial position available to her: that of a man in woman's clothes, as it were. This notion of masquerading to denote the position of the feminine is a long-standing one in psychoanalysis. It is based on the idea that femininity is a disguise assumed by the woman in order to disarm the male fear of her power (Riviere, 1929; Doane, 1982).

Correspondingly, analysing the Hollywood genre of the western, Neale (1983) observed that no cultural or cinematic convention allows the male body to be displayed solely as an object of visual pleasure. The specular male body is never coded as an object of erotic display. The male body is a spectacle of fear, hatred or aggression (with obvious consequences for many of the plotlines). As soon as it is made into a spectacle of desire, it is marked in the slot reserved for the effeminate and the gay.

Initially based on analyses of classical Hollywood cinema, the assumptions of gaze theory have been essentialised paradigmatically to all cinema. Assuming a totalising voice that speaks for the category of 'woman' and 'man', and a unitary 'subject', gaze theory theorised all desire as heterosexual male, and woman as just an object devoid of a spectatorial position, except in drag. In recent years, this monolithic, homogenising and heterosexual model of spectatorship – which says that women can adopt either a male or a transvestite position – came under attack (e.g. Williams, 1994). Most of the critique was articulated from within the psychoanalytic framework. Critics wondered whether the characterisation of a Hollywood genre can be extended to all cinematic representations, ignoring more specialised production niches, or, indeed, if a perversion can be used metaphorically as a model for psychic functioning in general. Some were concerned about a practice which, seeking to speak in the name of an assumed 'idealised' spectator, is leaving out marginalised audiences who are neither male nor white, nor heterosexual, and not middle class (hooks, 1992; Mayne, 1994).

Others suggested that the change in modes of address from cinematic viewing to domestic (TV, video) has altered the terms of the cinematic experience so as to render its effects obsolete. With the spell of illusionist absorption of the viewer having been broken by a fragmented and contextualised viewing experience, an aesthetic of the glance is replacing the aesthetic of the gaze (Hansen, 1994). The nature of fantasy, it was argued, cannot be reduced to the literalist assumptions of Mulvey's model (that women can only straightforwardly identify with female screen figures, black men with black male screen figures, etc.). Drawing on 'Fantasy and the Origins of Sexuality' by Laplanche and Pontalis (1968), it had been pointed out that fantasy is not confined to a fixed character or position – and it is not the enactment of a single character's desire. Its pleasure comes from the fluidity of *moving between a range of desiring positions simultaneously*. One of the pleasures of fantasy (Mayne, 1994), as well as pretend play (Bettelheim, 1972) and transgressive fashion (Tseëlon, 1998), which is absent from gaze theory, is the secure space from which to act out the unacceptable without being socially penalised for it, without suffering the consequences. Queer theory has shown that even the genre of horror movies allows the spectator to shift identification between the passive masochistic spectatorial position (through identification with the female victims) and the voyeuristic sadist position (through identification with the monster whose gender identity is ambiguous) (see Clover, 1992; Berenstein, 1996).

Also missing from gaze theory are complex forms of identification: multiple identifications; the plurality, contradiction or resistance that exist among feminine spectators; an active female gaze and feminist erotica (female pleasure in looking outside of male structures); see, for example, Kuhn (1982:65), Betterton (1987:5) and Myers (1988). Finally questioned was the assumption that other forms of spectator identity (race, class, age) are always built upon the model of sexual difference (Mayne, 1994). Consequently, it has been argued that the analysis of desire needs to be extended beyond heterosexual erotic desire. This would apply to films where the look is constructed between two female characters (Stacey, 1988), or in the maternal gaze of mutuality and intimacy (Kaplan, 1983, 1987), which offer different pleasures to the spectator from those criticised by Mulvey. It would also apply to films where desire is understood outside the strictly erotic scene: for example, a desire to see and to know. Indeed, even Mulvey herself has recently allowed the female spectator the active investigative look as a way forward out of the binary impasse (1996). Most of the critique is still framed within the terms of the psychoanalytic equation. So compelling has its paradigmatic gendered assumption of pleasure and control been that it has generated few attempts to move outside the psychoanalytic. Transcending Mulvey's formulation requires replacing the binary with the dialectical, the essential with the constructed, and the single with the multiple. As a result, we might search for shifting, unstable positions of identity and looking, as well as a wider range of looks than the binary sadistic/masochistic, active/passive or controlling/controlled.

Elsewhere (Tseëlon, 1991), I have noted that, in the proposed distinction between the man who is looking and the woman who is being looked at, there is a structural assumption that one position, that of the onlooker, is inherently more powerful than the other. However, a careful examination of the use of 'invisible' and 'visible' shows them to encompass a dialectical rather than a unilateral meaning:

> invisible as ignored, trivialised = powerless
> invisible as the source of gaze (i.e. the one who is looking without being looked at) = powerful

Similarly:

> visible as objectified = powerless
> visible as prominent, dominant = powerful

This formula may seem very similar to that produced by gaze theory (where observer = subject, desiring, masculinised, controlling; and observed = object, eroticised, feminised, controlled), but the concept of (in)visibility is interpreted differently when applied to women and to men. Invisible when applied to women is always used to connote powerlessness. At the same time, invisible when applied to men is always interpreted as signifying power. Consider, for example, how Foddy and Finighan discuss the private sphere: 'the powerful have greater access to the various devices and resources that facilitate the achievement of privacy.' Thus 'access to privacy achieving devices . . . can . . . symbolically define the powerful', while 'the very achievement of privacy can provide the psychological basis for greater power' (1980:10–11). Yet a woman inhabiting the private sphere would rarely be referred to in terms of power. That the power gaze does not inherently belong to the man is well illustrated in the historical convention of courtly love, where the lady is subject to the gaze of her husband and the troubadour. Both males, the meaning of their gaze is nonetheless very different. The gaze of the socially superior husband is that of powerful surveillance. The gaze of the admirer, the troubadour who is her social inferior, is that of the powerless unconsummated desire (Duby, 1992).

The challenge to the objectifying gaze can be mounted from other sources. We might ask: is self conception in the light of the look of the other a uniquely female condition, as feminist theory argues? For Mead (1934) and Sartre (1966), we become selves, or subjects, by virtue of our reflexive capacity to become objects to ourselves, to view ourselves from the standpoint of the other. For Lacan (1981) the gaze represents an object-cause of desire (of the other). It is an illusion of wholeness founded on the repression of the reality of a split subject. Moreover, it is not a specific other but a generalised other whose gaze we internalise (Lacan's 'gaze from the blind spot'; see Žižek, 1996). The generalised other reflects back to us the imaginary gaze of our reference group. Once we have internalised the gaze of the other, all of human behaviour can be seen as acting for an audience, and all subjectivity as performance, as

Goffman (Tseëlon, 1992) and performance theory (Butler, 1990; Case, 1990; Hart and Phelan, 1993) would have it. It is only by being an object to the other's gaze that I become a subject. This is a different notion of objectification from that advanced by feminist theory, where objectification of the woman is viewed as a technology of oppression in patriarchy: 'female subjectivity is most fully achieved . . . when it is most visible' (Silverman, 1988:164; see also Kuhn, 1982; Doane *et al.*, 1984; Betterton, 1987). Clearly, there is a need for a distinction between two conceptions of objectification that get muddled in feminist theories of spectatorship. One is a conception of objectification which is not just a demeaning state exclusive to women, but a precondition of subjectivity, and which applies to men and women. The other is objectification as a technology of commodity fetishism. 'To see objectification in essentialist terms is to deny the possibility of any alternative practice within the representation of women' (Myers, 1988:205).

The feminist discourse on the objectifying gaze is premised on Foucault's analysis of the disciplinary gaze articulated in *Discipline and Punish* (1975). It examines the technology of surveillance developed since the eighteenth century. This technology was modelled on Bentham's Panopticon. The Panopticon is an architectural structure made up of a tower at the centre, surrounded by a ring of cells. The tower is equipped with windows facing the courtyard. The cells have two windows: one on the outside allows light in; the other, facing the courtyard, lays the occupants open to the scrutinising gaze of the supervisor in the tower. The Panopticon principle introduced a new element into power relations. It reversed the principle of the dungeon. Traditionally, power was seen, shown and displayed. This was symbolised by the political ceremony where manifestation of power was spectacular and excessive. It was the objects of power which were in the shade. But disciplinary power is based on invisibility of the subject of power, complemented by the compulsive visibility of its object. Visibility becomes a trap; 'It is the fact of being constantly seen, of being able always to be seen, that maintains the disciplined individual in his subjection' (Foucault, 1975:187).

This permanent visibility becomes an internal feature of the observed in a way which recalls the female self consciousness of her body and appearance. However, the analogy between the principle of the Panopticon and the operation of the male gaze over the female has to be qualified, since there is nothing to imply that the inspector who occupies the observing function in the tower is permanently lodged there. On the contrary. As a metaphor, the Panopticon is a dynamic structure because while 'subtly arranged so that any observer may observe, at a glance, so many different individuals [it] also enables everyone to come and observe any of the observers' (Foucault, 1975:207). And it is Foucault's other conception of power – as being inherent not in hegemonic or sovereign power but in relations between groups – that is more appropriate for this dynamic conception of power and looking. Power, says Foucault, operates from multiple positions in the 'interplay of non egalitarian and mobile relations'(1980:94). It is dynamic, 'the moving substrate of force relations' and *ad hoc*; 'it is produced from one moment to the next'(p. 93).

Appropriating this conception of power, Denzin (1995) goes as far as to broaden the category of the voyeur to include multiple desires (erotic, political, scientific, medical, investigative, criminal, personal) and forms: the clinical gaze of the medical practitioner, the psychoanalyst and the scientist (including archaeologists, anthropologists, sociologists, psychologists, physicists, etc.); the accidental, unexpected gaze of the innocent bystander (including the child); the curious, peering gaze of the tourist; the inquisitive gaze of the apparatus of the law (including the crime detective, the private investigator and the spy); the informational gaze of the journalist (including the reporter and the photographer); the erotic gaze, the violating and violent gaze of the sexual pervert, the psychopath, the murderer and the rapist. Applying his analysis to the category of films he designates as reflexive, Denzin notes that, 'The trajectory of a gaze, male or female, varies by the context in which it is framed. The emotions produced by the gaze (for the onlooker) range across indifference, shame, pride, fear, hysteria, humility, adoration, pleasure, sexual desire. Looks can be open or secretive, commodify or personalise, exalt or dismiss' (1995:5).

One word about method. Much of gaze theory film analysis is based on a selective and rather limited variety of (mostly old) films. No criterion is usually offered for their choice except that they seem to best illustrate the author's thesis. The analysis is conducted as illustrative, metaphorical, paradigmatic, rather than as exhaustive. Rhetorically speaking, it is much more effective to use few examples to challenge a thesis (to show that it does not always apply) than to put forward a thesis (in which case a substantial number of examples is needed). In a previous study, I analysed, together with Kaiser, two films in order to challenge the monolithic notion of power/gaze implied in gaze theory and to illustrate the gaze as a dynamic concept which implies a two-way mechanism. To that end, we drew on two films which take the theme of the male gaze literally through a depiction of a male voyeur (for details, see Tseëlon and Kaiser, 1992; Tseëlon, 1995). These films, *Stakeout* (1987) and *Monsieur Hire* (1989) were not produced as feminist films. Even so, we read them as examples of the dynamic essence of the voyeuristic gaze. In *Stakeout*, police detectives carry out a twenty-four hour surveillance of a woman's house because her boyfriend is an escaped prisoner. One of the detectives falls in love with the woman. When he meets her accidentally and helps her out, she invites him for dinner. 'I was watching the house – from the inside', he apologises to his partner, who had been watching it all from the stakeout point. On another occasion, when he rescues her from an undesirable caller, he yields to passion and spends the night with her. He wakes up the next morning just too late to 'watch from the inside', because in the morning another team has occupied the shift and he becomes entrapped in their gaze, as it were. Unwilling to betray his transgression, the detective tries to leave the house without arousing suspicion, dressed in the woman's pink hat and shawl. This scene is symbolically indicative of the easy transformation from the empowerment of the observer to the disempowerment of the observed (typically dressed as a parody of a woman).

Monsieur Hire tells the story of a lonely man who regularly watches a woman who lives across the courtyard from his upstairs apartment. One stormy night, by the sudden illumination of lightning, the woman realises that the man is watching her. She is initially startled, but later enjoys and exploits it. She watches him watching her and even self-consciously poses for him, at which point the power/gaze structure is reversed. Being exposed in his gaze, the spectator, too, becomes a spectacle. The end of the unidirectionality of the gaze and the shift in the power structure become evident when she comes to visit him. In the beginning he refuses to let her in. Later he does, but when she asks to see the window from where he observed her, and starts inquiring ('What's your favourite moment – when I undress? When I wash?') he drives her away with a scream.

The reading of these films, which I regard as paradigmatic because they actually depict the male voyeur literally (through the male character), can still be criticised. It can be subject to the charge that to read a text against the grain (oppositional or resistive reading) is merely a meaningless intellectual exercise of the privileged few, if performed outside a social context (see hooks, 1990; Bordo, 1993). While I agree that the study of real audiences (as opposed to the imaginary viewer of much of film theory) is important, I do not think that audience research is a necessary precondition of recovering subversive meanings from the text. Nor do I suggest that if a real audience fails to read those subversive meanings when interrogated it renders those meanings invalid. This is particularly so if we adopt the view of Ann Kaplan (1983), Christian Metz, Stephen Heath and other film theorists, that the processes of cinema mimic in many ways those of the unconscious of patriarchy (see *Screen* 16, no. 2, summer 1975 issue on 'Psychoanalysis and Cinema'). If the cinema mimics unconscious processes, film narrative, like dreams, symbolises a latent repressed content. Ordinary methods of social scientific investigation (and audience research), whether qualitative or quantitative, rely heavily on a logical rational discourse. But if one adopts a psychoanalytic epistemology, straightforward questioning is no more enlightening than asking people to reflect on their neurotic symptoms and diagnoses. Psychoanalytically speaking, the subject position of the other (the voyeur in the figure of the therapist or the expert) offers the critical distance that is required to interpret, to guide or to offer an insight. Self reflexivity is hindered by the twin defences of repression and resistance which require a mediator to reach across the various splits that constitute the subject.

In an attempt to bridge the contrary practices of 'let's ask the audience' of ethnographic research and 'we know best' of film criticism, I have chosen a sort of compromise in the form of a film by the Spanish film director Pedro Almodóvar, whose reflexivity and self referentiality are not just projected by the critics, but are actually suggested by the director and by his style. Contemporary reflexive film making, says Anne Doane (1991:166) often addresses itself to the activity of uncoding, decoding, deconstructing the habitual coding of filmic images (see also chapter 13). This project can be about exposing the habitual meanings attached to femininity as a cultural construction. Film makers concerned to achieve something of this are using strategies of demystification as attempts to strip the body of its readings. The Spanish 'cult' movie director Almodóvar is an example *par excellence* of this kind of reflexive cinema, by his own evidence, that of his critics, the audience who vote by buying cinema tickets and, of course, the films themselves. I will refer to the 1991 film *Tacones lejanos* (*High Heels*), although I could have chosen any of his movies, because as a viewer it elicited in me contradictory emotions towards the characters and created a space from where I can simultaneously experience identification and distance, absorption and irony. Indeed, as Paul Smith (1994) points out, no film by Almodóvar has received such contradictory responses as *High Heels*. The subversive goal of this film is to marshal melodrama's full emotional excess, to eroticise and empower it for those traditionally marginalised under patriarchy and to liberate the maternal from the dreaded image of the repressive patriarchal mother.

(cont. p. 263)

The constructedness of gender in the cinema of Almodóvar: a case study

The constructedness of gender in the cinema of Pedro Almodóvar recurs so often as a theme, as varied representations, and even as an aspect of mise-en-scène, that it has become a distinctive marker of the director's authorial signature. Agrado's monologue in *Todo sobre mi madre* (*All About My Mother*) (1999), Almodóvar's latest film at the time of writing, is a suggestive example. Agrado is a transvestite who has left prostitution in order to become an assistant to a famous actress in a production of Tennesse Williams's *A Streetcar Named Desire*. One day the star cannot make it to the performance and Agrado takes over the stage to announce the cancellation of the play and offer a monologue on the story of her life, how she made herself into what she now is. In other words, she presents herself as an alternative production: 'They call me La Agrado because I have always tried to make everyone's life more pleasant', she says; 'Aside from being pleasant I am also very authentic.' She then runs through the full list of surgical operations she has undergone in order to be so authentic, and the corresponding financial cost, before ending with the key sentence. 'It cost me a lot to be authentic. But we must not be cheap in regards to the way we look. Because a woman is more authentic the more she resembles what she dreams herself to be.'

Agrado and her monologue are a useful starting point to discuss some of the complex ways in which Almodóvar depicts the constructedness of gender in his films. First of all, it is significant that Agrado is a transvestite, a figure that recurs throughout Almodóvar's work. The figure of the transvestite inherently raises the issue of gender as a construct because it represents the refusal of a gender role culturally proscribed in relation to sex and a conscious social re-gendering in relation to individual desire. Transvestites and transsexuals in Almodóvar's cinema, so far always male to female, denaturalise femininity by underlining the sartorial, behavioural and emotional codes that constitute its presentation. They show gender as a conscious becoming rather than a natural way of being.

Almodóvar further complicates this by his casting. Agrado is played by Antonia San Juan, a biological woman. Almodóvar has taken this device of casting biological sex against performative gender even further in the past. For example, in *La ley del deseo* (*The Law of Desire*) (1987) young Ada is mothered by transsexual Tina, who is played by Carmen Maura, while her biological mother in the film is played by the transsexual Bibî Andersen. But, as we shall see later, the uses of transvestism and transsexuality are not the only way that Almodóvar shows gender to be a kind of drag. His films attach a moral value to choice and performance. Imaginative re-enactments of socially transgressive gender performance or exaggerated camp performativity of approved social codings are shown to be a source of pleasure to characters and audiences; the unconscious performativity of traditional gender roles is in Almodóvar's work shown to be, at best, a drag and often a crime. The latter represents oppression, isolation and the *ancien régime*; the former represents the modern, the free and the hoped for integration and equality within democratic Western Europe.

It is significant as well that Agrado, whether selling herself on the streets or recounting her life on stage, is a performer. Prostitutes, who earn a (generally meagre) living performing other people's fantasies of who and what they are, recur in Almodóvar's films. For example, in *Que he hecho yo para merecer esto? (What Have I Done to Deserve This?)* (1984), Cristal (Veronica Forqué), the prostitute, fakes sexual desire, sexual preferences and sexual fulfilment to make a living with great success and gusto. The film favourably contrasts her role and her performance of it against a usually more socially revered type, the self-sacrificing housewife, Gloria (Carmen Maura). Cristal is the type of woman society vilifies and yet she is happy; Gloria performs her role as wife and mother unquestioningly and impeccably but is poor, sexually unfulfilled, seemingly unloved and so oppressed that she is driven to murder.

Performers of all stripes appear throughout Almodóvar's work: singers, models, actors. Their performances highlight their characters' emotional states while depicting utopian ways of being and feeling that contrast with that socially prescribed for the characters themselves. In *Mujeres al borde de un ataque de nervios (Women on the Verge of a Nervous Breakdown)*, we are shown Pepa (Carmen Maura) doing a voiceover of Joan Crawford's dialogue in a scene from *Johnny Guitar* (1954). Pepa puts great emotion into her speaking of the dialogue because what Joan is saying is what she feels, what she wants to tell the partner who has left her but cannot because he's playing hard to get. Yet the Joan Crawford Pepa is miming dialogue to, the confident, controlled 'mannish' woman wearing trousers and with a gun, is what the bereft and pregnant Pepa is not. The film thus demonstrates the way one voice can be differently inflected and recontextualised to represent two very different types of 'being women', and in doing so highlights the codes that convey the particularity of each, a strategy typical of Almodóvar.

The representation of the constructedness of gender in Almodóvar is not restricted to femininity. In *Matador* (1986), for example, we are shown three stereotypes of Spanish masculinity – the bullfighter, the cop and the lad; we are told how they should look and behave, and then we are shown how each fails to perform the masculinity indicated by the type: the bullfighter has been gored, rendered unable to exercise his *métier* and is impotent to boot; the policeman is sensitive, gay and his powers of detection are mostly focused on young men's crotches; the lad is sexually confused, faints at the sight of blood and is dominated by his mother. Over and over again Almodóvar's work demonstrates the grotesqueness of *machista* culture. The patriarchal and authoritarian father in *What Have I Done to Deserve This?* is so certain of his social role and of his righteous performance of it that he can flaunt his ignorance, brutishness and lack of hygiene with impunity. But the mise-en-scène will visually condemn him as at least unattractive and the narrative will make him pay for his machismo with his life. His wife will only be able to become a different, freer and more fulfilled type of woman and mother after she kills him. This way of highlighting the codes of macho masculinity, condemning them and narratively punishing the characters for performing them, also extends to gay men in Almodóvar's work.

In *La ley del deseo (The Law of Desire)* (1987), Antonio (Antonio Banderas) cannot reconcile the way of being a man his right-wing family has inculcated into him with his own sexual desires. His appealing initial sexual confusion (and equally appealing subsequent sexual delight) is accompanied by an appalling exhibition of narrow certainty as to how society should be and of his entitlement to patriarchal power within it. His sense of the established order and his place within it lead him to eliminate that which stands in the way of his desire for Pablo (Eusebio Poncela), that is, the character Pablo is in love with, Juan (Miguel Molina). The mise-en-scène where Antonio kills Juan is dominated by phallic imagery, primarily a huge lighthouse complete with a round head that shoots off beams of light. When Antonio has killed Juan, the mournful music is pitched higher while the camera cuts to rest on a long shot of the lighthouse, thus underlining its phallic symbolism. The film makes clear that it is Antonio's attempt at performing the type of oppressive patriarchal masculinity idealised by traditional Spanish culture that has caused Juan's death and will eventually result in Antonio's suicide.

Almodóvar's films highlight the constructedness of gender by positing that inherited ways of being men and women – that is, traditional Francoist norms – are not only not natural but are indeed psychically and socially damaging. In Almodóvar's work a character is indeed most authentic when he or she invents the ways of being men and women that best suit their desire for who and what they want to be. This is demonstrated not only thematically, narratively and in terms of character psychology but, arguably most importantly for someone who is said to 'write on film', at the level of mise-en-scène and tone. An extended discussion of these is not possible here but some aspects from *Tacones lejanos (High Heels)* (1991) may act as illustrative hints (see also Tseëlon below). From the film's first scene, where Rebeca (Victoria Abril) is waiting for her mother Becky (Marisa Paredes) at the airport, we are shown to be in a created world: the chairs in the airport are too red; the images are too consciously composed. Rebeca is also presented as overly composed: the mise-en-scène guides our gaze to the high heels, her Chanel dress and her dangling earrings; the story tells us of her mother and an act that took place in her childhood. Society, pyschological trauma in childhood and ideology are shown to reproduce in Rebeca the same mode of femininity she saw her mother suffer from.

The bright colours, conspicuous set design and theatrical costuming in *High Heels* all highlight that the world we are invited to be emotionally immersed

262

in is a constructed one. The uses of camp in the film also recurringly announce this. *High Heels*, like all of Almodóvar's work, deploys different modalities of camp across different levels of storytelling. Visually, the cut, style and colours of Marisa Paredes's outfits, to take only one example, can – in an exaggerated referencing to the diva couture of classic Hollywood cinema – be seen as camp. Narratively, Rebeca's fulfilling a need to see her mother by watching one of her female impersonators is another example. The many identities of Letal (Judge, drag queen, drug dealer, and the fact that we comprehend them all through the famously ambiguous star persona of actor Mighel Bosé) and that that is who Rebeca falls in love with (her mother's female impersonator) is yet another. On the level of spectacle, the musical number led by Bibî Andersen in the yard of the all-women's prison is camp. And of course, there are the many visual gags – such as when Becky leaves a flamboyant lipstick mark on the Madrid stage she kisses – which arrestingly announce the director's presence but which do not impede emotional involvement. Indeed, it is as if Almodóvar takes Baudrillard's notion of the hyper-real and through his unique play with surface – through highlighting the constructedness of things, people, worlds, ways of being – gets to an emotional engagement and social commentary, a certain kind of 'real', of authenticity, which Baudrillard's own articulation of his concept excludes.

Agrado's monologue applies in a general sense to the representation of the constructedness of gender in Almodóvar's work in that the obviously constructed characters that people his uniquely represented Madrid become most authentic through changing their way of being men and women from a 'natural', socially acceptable model into their own aesthetic ideal. It is through camp pastiche – visual and aural – at the level of narrative and spectacle that Almodóvar's films highlight the constructedness of gender and critique gender subordination. The result is an original commentary on gender and Spanish society that is often intellectually stimulating and usually aesthetically sublime.

José Arroyo

The socio-historical context of Almodóvar's films is the fault line between Francoist and post-Franco Spain. In that period (since 1975) the country has undergone profound political and social transitions. From social and sexual repression that constructed Franco's seamless iconography of monolithic values, to a postmodern deconstruction of those values, Almodóvar's films are a product of the history of the youth culture movement *Movida* which emerged in Madrid after the death of Franco.

Almodóvar challenges the conventional family unit, and the morality of the police and the Church – the trinity that constituted the bedrock of Francoist mythology (D'Lugo, 1995; Vernon and Morris, 1995). He uses comic self reflexivity, tongue-in-cheek humour and irony as a distancing strategy that parodies the spectator's desire for pleasure (and closure), and does not allow any illusion to take hold. Juxtaposition of styles and genres and shots that suspend the narrative flow are used as techniques for deconstructing fundamental values (Morris, 1995). Structurally, *High Heels* contains elements of melodrama, crime detective novel, comedy, soft porn, horror (where the monster signifying the dissolution of sexual difference and stable gender traits is neither man nor woman), musical (a dance routine in prison) and women's films. Thematically, it contains too many disguises, imitations and masquerades to allow anyone a stable and consistent viewing position.

The film's subtle reflexivity was lost on some of Almodóvar's critics, who accused him of appealing to the misogynistic reproduction of patriarchal stereotypes (neurotic career woman and sacrificial mother), harking back to the melodramatic maternal woman's films of the 1940s (Kaplan, 1987). But it has been picked up by others who have applauded it for its 'feminist' deconstruction of gender categories (Smith, 1994). However, the sophistication of Almodóvar's themes and techniques was not lost on his audience, certainly not the Spanish audience. His spectacular success, internationally but especially in Spain, is particularly meaningful. Despite reluctant official backing, unenthusiastic critical reception, a film industry in crisis, and the habitual consumption of and preference for American films, in Spain Almodóvar has gradually managed to occupy a mainstream mass entertainment position with work which initially appealed to a more selective 'artsy' audience (Rolph, 1995).

Almodóvar not only engages in deconstruction and problematisation; he also reformulates cultural and sexual identities and values as well as rewriting the social and moral logic of the past (D'Lugo, 1995). This he achieves by appropriating the language of the old order and turning it against itself to constitute a new Spanishness: the family, Church, the police – the embodiments of traditional patriarchal order – are now the agents of ushering in new cultural desires. 'We have lost the fear of the earthly power (the police), and of the celestial power (the church)', says Almodóvar (Kinder, 1987). Thus his new 'sensitive' policeman is the androgynous hero, just as in his other films the cops are untypically tender-hearted souls who identify with those marginalised under patriarchy. In this way, Almodóvar subverts the dominant ideology by realigning the centre with the marginal. We will look, finally, at *High Heels* in more detail.

High Heels

The film is about a reunion in Madrid of Rebeca, a TV news anchor in a station owned by her husband Manuel, and her absentee actress and singer mother Becky, who abandoned her fifteen years previously to pursue her career in Mexico. A further significant character is Letal, a friend of Rebeca and a female impersonator whose act is based on Becky's pop period. Manuel is found shot in his bed, and Judge Dominguez who investigates the case interrogates three women who visited him on the night before the murder: Becky, Rebeca and Isabel (who 'signs' the news for the deaf with Rebeca on TV). All three women deny the murder. Later, when reading the news, Rebeca confesses to the murder on air and is arrested. In prison she discovers that Letal is a drug dealer, Hugo, who befriends women and then deserts them. She also learns that he is actually a police informer. In the end Judge Dominguez turns out to be Eduardo, who disguises himself as Letal and Hugo as part of his investigative police work. He proposes marriage to Rebeca, who is already pregnant with his child. Such a summary must already suggest how difficult it is to identify a secure 'viewpoint' in this film.

The film is replete with examples of gaze episodes which mock filmic conventions. The object of the gaze is constantly shifting, sometimes looks back, is in disguise, and viewing positions keep changing. In many places the staple voyeuristic poses are twisted, moved around and recast in a different mould. I'll summarise two examples of straightforward gaze scenarios, and one metaphorical one of the voyeur as inquisitive. The first two are Letal's drag show and Rebeca's TV newsreading. The other is the inquisitive look of the representative of state control (investigating judge), something that Almodóvar critiques habitually.

When Letal performs on stage as Becky, three sets of eyes are gazing upon him rather differently. Manuel's look is one of derision for the mock Becky and desire for the real Becky; Becky is absorbed in the music in narcissistic fascination; and Rebeca's look is a combination of pride (in her friend), approval seeking (from her mother) and apprehension as she casts her glance from mama to Manuel, having detected an illicit liaison between them. After the show, when Letal joins them, Manuel is clearly ill at ease. When Rebeca introduces him to Letal he inquires, 'Letal is masculine or feminine?' The camera follows his gaze to Letal's crotch. Letal notices, slowly and emphatically closes his legs together and straightens his skirt in an overstated 'feminine' gesture. The camera then follows his look, which is cast on Manuel's belt at the point where he hid his revolver. Manuel moves his hand uncomfortably to conceal the weapon behind the lapel of his jacket. Only after this mutual exchange of gazes – which reveals Manuel to be just as vulnerable (if not more so) as Letal to the penetrating gaze – Letal delivers his ambiguous reply: 'It depends. For you I am a man.' He straightens his hair in a feminine manner and tilts his head slightly while gazing steadily, evidencing a maintenance of control.

The next type of gaze scenario features Rebeca's newsreading. Women reading the news is a problematic area in a patriarchal society because so often a woman's right to speak in public is diverted by attention to her looks: framed within her 'femininity' she is poised for the pleasure of the onlooker. There are two episodes when Rebeca reads the news and in both of them she uses the medium 'inappropriately', apparently confirming a stereotype of the woman who trivialises a serious situation by introducing emotionality and domesticity. Rebeca does just that, but with a difference. In the first episode her nervousness that her mother may be watching causes her to giggle in the most inappropriate places. Here, unexpectedly, the power of the gaze that matters is that of a judgmental mother. In the second episode she is again misusing the medium, turning it into an instrument of personal confession. The sequence starts off on a serious note and ends with the grotesque. Rebecca first reads the news in an objectively detached 'professional' manner, but soon she begins to depart from the script and abolishes the conventional distance between herself and the viewers by talking about her husband. She confesses on air to his killing and proceeds to show photos she took of the house as memories. By disrupting the newsreading in such a manner, and by being arrested on the scene in front of the viewers, she becomes part of the news herself and in some sense assumes control of the entire situation, and command of the look. She forces the medium to acknowledge her not as a passive newsreader but as an active newsmaker.

Two types of voyeur represent the institutions of the old regime that Almodóvar's comic portrayal targets. Almodóvar positions the once traditionally central powers in marginalised spaces. Thus the Church and the police are mobilised to valorise those sexual activities and marginalised social behaviours they once were instrumental in repressing. Their gaze is intercepted by being forever inverted, destabilised, ridiculed. The official gaze of the judge, for example, is parodied in a scene where, together with two police reporters, he attempts to agree a description of Manuel's body.

The scene starts with a twist on the murder mystery narrative where a dead female body is a ubiquitous trope. Many films hinge on an investigative process triggered by the discovery of a dead female body, a metaphorical investigation of the enigma of the woman. In Almodóvar's *High Heels*, however, this trope is parodically inverted. The image of the corpse is not available for the fetishistic gaze so typical of murder mysteries. Instead, we hear the policemen argue about the description of the corpse without our actually seeing it – what height is it, are the pyjamas of red silk or cherry-coloured satin? What creates the comic effect is not just the contrast between the lax method of verifying facts and the argument about minute details of measurement, but also that it is the policemen who are placed in a discourse usually reserved for the feminine: attention to details of appearance and fine observation of colour tones and hues.

In *High Heels*'s problematising of gender categories, traditional institutions and practices are embodied by the figure of the judge, ambiguously positioned in the overlaid spaces of the maternal, the sexual and the legal, all in disguise. His close alignment with the masquerade goes beyond his drag act. 'For me there is ambiguity in justice', says Almodóvar, 'and that's why I have given it to the character of the judge. I don't know what the face of justice is – sometimes it's masculine, sometimes it's feminine – that is where ambiguity resides: in questions of morality' (Morgan, 1992:29). The judge does not allow the viewer the comfort of a stable viewing position. He assumes many incompatible identities: the representative of law and order, a deviant (drug dealer) and a marginalised performer (drag artist). In the official capacity (the investigative judge) he is a state voyeur, in the deviant capacity he is an undercover voyeur (police informer) who gazes at people when they are unaware, and in a female capacity he is an object of a gaze with a twist.

He reveals his multi-persona to Rebeca and asks her to marry him. She responds, confused, 'Can you explain all this to me?' He replies, 'I've come to explain to you, to ask you to marry me.' Rebeca: 'Who? Hugo? Letal? The judge?' He replies: 'All three.' Not only is it given that he actually enjoys his string of impersonations, but we are even denied the illusion that the judge is the stable identity that anchors the slippage of all the others. In the disclosure scene it turns out that for his 'real' identity he still wears a false beard, a mask that he assumes even in front of his mother. The filmic gaze has changed and there is no going back from this point for any of us.

Images and the self: semiotic 'chora' in recent post-feminist theory

There is a complex relationship between gender construction and patriarchal relations of power. Prior to the development of an adequate set of theories, feminists could only rationalise these inequalities by drawing upon explanations of biological difference. In the late 1970s post-structuralist and post-modern theories of culture offered feminism more complex understandings of women's oppression and the representation of 'natural' femininity (Cowie, 1977, 1978; Pollock, 1977). Central to these developments was Sigmund Freud's proposition of the unconscious. This developing relationship between feminism and postmodernism around psychoanalytic theory is problematic. Nonetheless, there is no doubt that some feminist theory began to draw productively upon post-structuralist (especially Lacanian) theories of the unconscious in order to gain an understanding of patriarchal culture's workings.

The psychoanalytic work of Freud placed gender and gender formation at the very centre of the formation of the patriarchal subject. While few feminists had sympathy for Freud's theories, his contribution to a developing theory of gendered subjectivity was immense (see Mitchell, 1974). In France a new current of psychoanalytic theory emerged which has influenced both feminist cultural theory and creative production practices, in film and photography for instance.

It is to the work of Jacques Lacan (who radically challenged the biological determinism of traditional Freudianism by developing post-structuralist theories of language) that many feminists have been drawn. Briefly, Lacan's reworking of the castration/Oedipal complex proposed a distinction between the penis as an organ (Freudian) and the phallus as a sign (Lacan, 1968). He also theorised a more fluid path to the formation of a gendered subject. This reworking offered a 'logical' rather than biological explanation of patriarchy whereby it is not the having or not having of the physical penis which organises gendered subjectivity under patriarchy, but rather the way in which its presence or absence (lack) functions as a *signifier*; that is, the way in which subjects can make sense of sexual difference is by their possession of the 'sign' (phallus) of patriarchal power, which allows them to place themselves within the symbolic order of patriarchal culture – the so-called Law of the 'Father'. Thus male fear of castration and of the 'lacking' woman is a fear of the loss of that power which the phallus as signifier and 'maker' of language promises to men.

Lacan also proposed that this moment (the acquisition of language and entry into patriarchy) is only the final stage of a series of moments in which the subject is formed. It is to these 'early' stages that feminists looked, for they suggest that, if the child starts to become aware before entry into patriarchy, then a different type of awareness of self and other must exist – one prior to the symbolic structure sketched above. In the theorisation of visual culture, it was Lacan's proposition of 'the mirror stage' (1977a) which was of specific interest (see Metz, 1975; Mulvey, 1975), because this moment was based on specular rather than 'spoken' relationships. This is the moment when the child misrecognises an image of itself as its self, structuring all further

267

misrecognitions of images as reality (the 'Imaginary' in Lacanian terminology). Also of significance is that this is the moment when the child begins to recognise itself as *separate* from the mother and realises it must split from her. However, as Kaplan notes, 'the child/adult never forgets the world of the Imaginary, and he/she continues to desire, unconsciously, the illusionary oneness with the mother he/she experienced' (1991:30). It is this proposition, that the child clings to those heady pleasures of the 'bliss' of pre-Oedipal fusion with the mother, that has been central to the development of a theory of visual culture. Lacan believed that the child never forgets its illusionary oneness with the mother or the '*jouissance*' that this moment entailed – a moment before the intervention of paternal law which requires both the control of 'self' and the denigration/abjection of the feminine (mother) and the pleasures associated with her emotions, feelings, love.

In visual terms, feminists applied these theories to identify the ways in which patriarchal culture naturalises its relationships of power through its symbolic representations of women, as well as exposing how the unconscious of patriarchal culture structures the very forms these representations take. So, for example, Mulvey (1975) demonstrated how the visual style of classic Hollywood film is closed and fixed, rather than open, and is marked by the conventions of realism which 'hide' the processes of signification and are structured around male scopophilic pleasures (or fears). Since the 1980s such feminist theoretical developments (e.g. Kuhn, 1985; Pollock, 1988; Nochlin, 1989) have 'demonstrated the comprehensively patriarchal nature of culture – its institutions and ideologies of production and reception, its regimes of representation, and its formal and textual characteristics' (Wolff, 1990:68).

In French literary theory, *écriture féminine* was evoked as a possible way of recalling the suppressed 'maternal' and as a strategy for disrupting the rules and conventions of the patriarchal symbolic (in the work of Julia Kristeva, Hélène Cixous and Luce Irigaray, for instance). In literary terms *écriture féminine* is based on the idea that 'literary forms can be radically altered in order to accommodate and express women's experience' (Wolff, 1990:67). As a form of experimental writing, its impetus is to inscribe femininity at the moment of reading through its 'difference' from patriarchal/masculine forms. It does this through 'play, disruption, excess, gaps, grammatical and syntactic subversion, ambiguities; by endless shifting register, generic transgressions; by fluid figurative language and myths. They are anti-authoritarian, questioning, unsettling' (Wright, 1992:75). Hélène Cixous and Luce Irigaray promote a more essentialist perception of *écriture féminine* by 'writing from the body', drawing upon female sexuality and libido. Julia Kristeva (1984) proposes a subtly but significantly different relationship between *écriture féminine* and the pre-Oedipal which she terms '*semiotic chora*'. For her, the gender of the producer is not the issue. She discusses the potential of poetically disruptive uses of language in relation to some modernist male writers and to the visual abstractions of some male artists, who have been 'able to evade the apparently monolithic control of the symbolic' through 'texts which are produced from rhythms and pulsions of the semiotic chora – the prelinguistic, pre-Oedipal experience' (Wolff, 1990:74).

Kristeva perceives the semiotic chora as structural – that is, its 'role' is first to make a space in which language (as the underpinning organisation of social–symbolic interaction) can then work. The recalling and momentary revitalisation of this semiotic chora in itself is potentially disruptive to the patriarchal symbolic because it ruptures the latter's normality by recalling a different, pre-linguistic, pre-symbolic sense of self in which the mother of the Imaginary (feminine), and feelings associated with her, are central and compelling rather than peripheral and debased. These 'feelings' (bodily drives, rhythms, pulsions, pleasures, bliss) are never lost and their memory is held precariously in check by the patriarchal symbolic. They can be seen to rise to the surface through cultural forms in different ways. For instance, they have been retrieved in readings of artistic work where their resisting quality may be 'accidental' – for example, in readings of the nineteenth-century photographs of Julia Margaret Cameron (see Mavor, 1996) or the abstract works of Helen Frankenthaler (Pollock, 1992). Feminist cultural theorists have exposed the way in which these memories remain to 'trouble' patriarchy, revealing how cultural practices and stories (films, rituals, fairy tales, myths) replay the moment of patriarchal culture's formation in which the possibilities of 'difference' are continually abjected and repressed (Kristeva, 1992; Creed, 1993; Warner, 1994). Kristeva believes that the subject can gain access more readily to the semiotic chora through creative, musical and poetic practices or even just through vibrant use of colour. She sees these possibilities as already having their origins in the semiotic chora, recalling a more fluid, plural and less fixed perception of meaning and self which reactivates feelings lost in the patriarchal 'rational'. However, Kristeva also makes it clear that the 'feminine' semiotic chora is not something outside or beyond language. She states: 'if the feminine exists, it only exists in the order of significance or signifying process, and it is only in relation to meaning and signification, positioned as their excess or transgressive other that it exists, speaks, thinks (itself) and writes (itself) for both sexes'. Thus it is 'different or other in relation to language and meaning, but nevertheless only thinkable within the symbolic' (cited in Moi, 1986:11). Thus post-feminist interventions that wish to rupture the patriarchal symbolic by recalling this lost 'feminine' cannot assume some form of privileged access to it which will unconsciously show itself in the text or image. Instead a more conscious attempt at manipulating the symbolic, which has been made possible by an informed knowledge of its workings, has begun to emerge; I am thinking of the later photographic works of Cindy Sherman, Helen Chadwick's art pieces and, in cinema, Jane Campion's 1993 film *The Piano*. This may allow post-feminist creative practices to rupture the patriarchal symbolic for their own ends, by calling up resisting and troubling memories of something 'different', something troubling and contesting from the margins.

Sarah Edge

Stop and think

An example of semiotic chora?

It would be rather unfair here if we did not stop and think about finding a specific example from film of semiotic chora at work; or, since it is a highly speculative notion, an example of something that *might* be chora. You should think about what is at stake here: is there something 'different or other in relation to language and meaning, but nevertheless only thinkable within the symbolic', something capable of 'recalling a different, pre-linguistic, pre-symbolic sense of self' (see Sarah Edge above)? What could something like this possibly look like? It is only fair that we should risk an example.

In Pedro Almodóvar's film *The Flower of My Secret* (1995), a pivotal moment in the melodrama of the main character's life comes when she returns to her home village in rural Spain. The film cuts from her bedroom, where her elderly mother has been comforting her (is that scene a clue anticipating the 'feminine' space to which we are about to cut?), to a close-up of lace accompanied by the clackety-clack sounds of the lacemakers' wooden bobbins. As the camera moves over the intricate lace pattern, the brightly coloured pins that hold it in place on the pricking (or pattern template) underneath and the rapidly interweaving threads held taught by their wooden bobbins, have we momentarily entered the space of the semiotic chora? There is no narrative information here, no point of view that turns out to be that of a principal in the action, and the image is located at the film's pivotal emotional turning point. (Interestingly, in the art world many post-feminist theorists have taken to the work of Louise Bourgeois, whose installations of old clothes and materials associated with the textile trade often have something of the same feeling as this cinematic moment.)

However, this image's claim to enter the chora may be more substantial than if based only on visual ambiguity or on narrative and perspectival interruption. If chora is only thinkable within a symbolic order that it attempts to undercut, then the symbolic construction of 'lace' is itself important. The image shows Torchon lace, which has also been called 'beggar's lace' because it is simpler and faster to make than the finery of seventeenth- and eighteenth-century laces made for the garments of the aristocracy. As machine-made lace became economically more viable with the growth of capitalist manufacturing, Torchon was something that the women of village communities could make quickly and cheaply enough to compete with the new factories. Without our necessarily knowing this, does the image nonetheless carry connotations of women's work, creativity and difference that amplify the image's interruptive force in relation to the film's forward movement? The camera moves out to linger on the group of lace makers who burst into song.

15

Reading the American popular: suburban resentment and the representation of the inner city in contemporary film and TV

Cameron McCarthy

This chapter runs contrary to contemporary mainstream and some radical theorising on race and popular culture that tends to place television, film and advertising outside the circuits of social meanings at some self-constituting point from which these technologies then exert effects on a differentiated mass public (Postman, 1986; Parenti, 1992). In what follows, I take a decidedly 'cultural studies' approach to the discussion of the role of television and film in the production and reproduction of contemporary race relations. I situate these social technologies within the turmoil of social life as cultivators and provokers of racial meanings and common sense. I see television and film as fulfilling a certain bardic function, singing back to society lullabies about what a large cross-section and hegemonic part of it 'already knows'.

Like Richard Campbell (1987), I reject the vertical model of communication that insists on encoding/decoding. I am more inclined to theorise the operation of communicative power in horizontal or rhizomatic terms. Television and film, then, address and position viewers at the 'centre' of a cultural map in which suburban, middle-class values 'triumph' over practices that drift away from mainstream social norms. In this arrangement, the American suburb, in the language of Christopher Lasch (1991), becomes 'The True and Only Heaven': the great incubator and harbinger of neo-evolutionary development, progress and modernity in an erstwhile unstable and unreliable world. Our suburban dweller is the great philosophical and semiotic meta-subject of day time and night time radio talk shows, television evening news and tabloid hysteria. He is our contemporary Sweeney Erectus, our last rational man, standing on the pyres of resentment. 'Suburban dweller' here refers to all those agents travelling in the covered wagons of post-1960s white flight from America's increasingly black, increasingly immigrant urban centres. White flight created settlements and catchment areas that fanned out further and further away from the city's inner radius, thereby establishing the racial character of the suburban–urban divide. As taxed-based revenues, resources and services followed America's fleeing middle classes out of the city, a great gulf opened up between that the suburban dweller and America's inner-city residents. Into this void contemporary television, film and popular culture entered, creating the most poignantly sordid fantasies of inner-city degeneracy and moral decrepitude. These representations of urban life would serve as markers of the distance that the suburban dweller had travelled away from perdition. Outside the United States they had the potential to take on a broader status, as representations of a contemporary reality – of modern life – even where local circumstances may actually have been different. Televisual and filmic fantasies would underscore the extent to which the inner-city dweller was irredeemably lost in the dystopic urban core. Within the broad vocabulary of reproductive technologies at its disposal, the preference for the medium shot in television tells the suburban viewer 'We are one with you', as the body of the television subject seems to correspond one for one with the viewer.

As Raymond Williams (1974) argues in *Television: Technology and Cultural Form*, television, film, advertising, textbooks and so forth are powerful forces situated in cultural circuits themselves – not outside as some pure technological or elemental force or some Fourth Estate, as the professional ideology of mainstream journalism tends to suggest. These are circuits that consist of a proliferation of capacities, interests, needs, desires, priorities and commitments – fields of affiliation and fields of association.

One such circuit is the discourse of resentment, or the practice of defining one's identity through the negation of the other. This chapter will call attention to this discourse in contemporary race relations and point to the critical co-ordinating role of news magazines, television, the Hollywood film industry and the common sense of black film makers themselves in the reproduction and maintenance of the discourse of resentment – particularly its supporting themes of crime, violence and suburban security. I also look at the discursive impact of resentment on the sense of capacity and agency among black school youth at a comprehensive high school, Liberty High, in Los Angeles. For this segment of the chapter, I will draw on ethnographic data I collected at this Los Angeles high school some sixth months before the videotaped images of LAPD police beating Rodney King reverberated around the world.

Drawing on the theories of identity formation in the writings of C. L. R. James (1978, 1993) and Friedrich Nietzsche (1967), I argue that the electronic media play a critical role in the production and channelling of suburban anxieties and retributive morality on to its central target: the depressed inner city. These developments deeply informed race relations in late twentieth-century society. These race relations are conducted in the field of simulation as before a putative public court of appeal (Baudrillard, 1983).

Standing on the pyres of resentment

> I feel deadly faint, bowed and humped, as though I were Adam, staggering beneath the piled centuries since Paradise. (Ahab in Herman Melville's *Moby Dick* (1851: 535)

These words, uttered in a moment of crisis in the nineteenth-century canonical text of Melville's *Moby Dick*, might well have been uttered by Michael Douglas as D-fens in the contemporary late twentieth-century popular cultural text of *Falling Down* (1993) or Michael Douglas as Tom Sanders in the anti-feminist, proto-resentment film, *Disclosure* (1994). Douglas is the great twentieth-century suburban middle-class male victim, flattened and spread out against the surface of a narcotic screen 'like a patient etherized upon a table' (Eliot, 1964:11).

In two extraordinary texts written in the late 1940s, *Mariners, Renegades and Castaways: The Story of Herman Melville and the World We Live In* (1978) and *American Civilization* (1993), C. L. R. James made the provocative observation that American popular cultural texts – comic strips, popular film, popular music, soap opera and the detective novel – offered sharper intellectual lines of insight on the contradictions and tensions of modern life in post-industrial society than the entire corpus of academic work in the social sciences. For James, comic strips such as *Dick Tracy* and popular films such as Charlie Chaplin's *Modern Times* (1936) and John Huston's *The Maltese Falcon* (1941) were direct aesthetic descendants of Melville's *Moby Dick*. These popular texts removed the veil which covered social relations in the twentieth century that were 'too terrible to relate', except in the realm of fantasy and imagination (Morrison, 1990:302).

In a remarkable way, popular culture was for James the great storehouse of twentieth-century integrative energies, desires and frustrations – freely mingling the quotidian with the extreme, the mundane with the horrific, didactic moral values with their prurient undersides, the aesthetic with the grotesque. And so, with one brush stroke, James drew a direct line of connection between the canonical work of writers such as Melville and the operation of meaning and values in contemporary popular cultural forms. For James, these popular texts foregrounded the rise of a new historical subject on the national and world stage. This subject was a projection of the over-rationalisation and sedimented over-determinations of the modern industrial age. This new subject was a resentment-type personality who articulated an authoritarian populism: the mutant, acerbic and emotionally charged common sense of the professional middle class (Douglas with a satchel of hand grenades in *Falling Down*). This authoritarian personality was, in James's view, willing to wreck all in the hell-bent prosecution of his own moral agenda and personal ambition. According to James, what was unusual and egregious about the resentment personality type in *Moby Dick* and the nineteenth-century world of Melville had become pseudo-normative by the time of *The Maltese Falcon* in the 1940s – a period marked by the rise of what James called 'nonchalant cynicism' (James, 1993:125).

Thus in *The Maltese Falcon*, detective Sam Spade (Humphrey Bogart) gets to put the woman he loves in jail for the murder of his corrupt partner, Miles Archer. Their love is overridden by the ideology of professionalism and the socio-normative priority of making wrongdoers pay. As the paranoid Spade says plaintively to his lover: 'I don't like the idea that you'd played me for a sucker.' In this version of game theory there are no free riders. Loafers are *persona non grata*. In Sam Spade's case, lovers do not have any special privileges beyond the domestic sphere. Spade is playing by his own ethics and chucking human relations and feelings as encumbering eruptions of irrationality. This is a tart dish of public common sense. He is the eternal stand-in or proxy for middle-American values. Spade holds the line against the threat of invasion by the morally corrupt other, the socially different and the culturally deviant and deprived. The bad guys kill and the good guys kill too. But the good guys kill more efficiently. Morality is on the side of the technologically and materially endowed. The fun and games of law and order are, therefore, part of a deeply ethnocentric and gendered and class-based system of difference – a hierarchy of priorities in the world in which we live. It is a game of exclusions intended to preserve the safety of the suburban domestic space. In popular culture, the public sphere becomes the site of distorted communication and social anxieties and prejudices. By combining detective and gangster rolled into one transcendent subject, Spade enters into the semiotic field, simultaneously, as suburban plaintiff and libidinal cruiser.

Contemporary popular discussion of crime and violence also follows this logic of closed narrative, where the greatest fear is that the enemy will be let into our neighbourhoods. And the greatest stress on public policy may be how to keep the unwanted off the taxpayer-dependent welfare rolls and out of our town, safely in prisons, and so forth. Sam Spade's worries have had a melt down in our time, late in the twentieth century. And they have become a potent paranoid resentment brew that spills over from the fantasy land of television and film into the social world in which we live.

What James's astute comments point us towards is the fact that the filmic and televisual discourse of crime and violence is not simply about crime or violence. Art is not here simply imitating life in some unthinking process of mimesis. Art is productive and generative. Televisual and filmic discourses about crime and violence, as Gerbner (1970) and others argue, are fundamentally urban fables about the operation of power and the production of meaning and values in society. They are about moral re-evaluation, about our collective tensions, crises and fears. They are about how America as a society deals with the social troubles that afflict its soul: sexism, racism and the like. In this sense, popular culture – the world of film noir and the grade B movie, of the tabloids and of the mainstream press – constitutes a relentless pulp mill of social fictions of transmuted and transposed power. At late twentieth century, Sam Spade has been replaced by the towering popular and preternatural intelligence of Sweeney Erectus, our guide into the moral inferno. James wrote almost prophetically about resentment mutations and the time lag in the modern in the late 1940s. The aim of this chapter is to describe the operation of resentment a half-century later in our time – a time in which racial antagonism has been the host of a parasitic resentment stoked in the (cont. p. 282) media and circulating in popular culture.

The ghost citizen and class

Class for the most part is no longer experienced as class, but as constraints (and opportunities) emanating from a variety of sources. Class becomes individualized and expressed through the individual's 'biography'; it is experienced less and less as collective fate . . . The individual relates to the class system not just as a producer but as a consumer. Lifestyle and taste, mobilized in an active way by individuals and groups, become as evident markers of social differentiation as position in the productive order . . . Problems that may originate in, or be strongly influenced by, class factors . . . are not experienced as coming from the past, but as a result of circumstances imping-ing on an individual or group at a particular time. The 'generational trans-mission belt' of class comes to be broken. . . . Class is hence less of a 'lifetime experience' than it was before. (Giddens, 1994:143–4)

Against this background of individualised and circumstantial experiences of social class, one of the great symbolic antagonisms in advanced capitalist soci-eties at the turn of the century is that between an increasingly resentful 'middle class' and an 'underclass' whom the former view as threatening social order, as a burden on welfare systems, as sustained by immigration, as central to drug and crime problems, and increasingly as a 'Third World' on their doorsteps. This antagonism has proved a useful thematic and narrative resource for popular media, thanks to whom we have a generalised picture of siege-mentality suburbs and gang-ridden urban wastelands that can be mapped on to many real cities, from Los Angeles to Glasgow, São Paulo to Berlin.

This middle class/underclass antagonism is, however, in large part a social and cultural construction, a way of imagining contemporary social relations and real social tensions that leaves out many other actors on the social scene – not least the working class. Additionally, the notion of 'middle class' iden-tifies a massively expanded social category in advanced capitalist societies – one that might, therefore, be more usefully considered as *bourgeois* and based largely on consumerist lifestyle – and the key questions then become (1) that of the relation between the bourgeois world and the working class (where 'middle class' evokes an older picture of a more narrowly defined posi-tion in the productive order – the 'white collar' class); and (2) how the 'under-class' is to be understood in relation to this redrawn class map. 'Bourgeois' has always been an ambiguous term that never quite caught on in the English-speaking world, referring to owners, the professional classes who serviced their interests and vaguely defined well-to-do citizens of a public sphere; an ambiguity that can now be useful as the concept of class itself becomes ambiguous. In fact, one of the major areas of uncertainty in contemporary media and cultural studies concerns precisely how to deal with the question of social class. Broadly speaking, there are three ways of thinking about class (see below). While there is agreement, however, that the concept of class has become a complicated one, there is not yet widespread agreement about which, if any, of these three approaches is best. While the social theorists con-tinue to argue this through, you – as a learner – will have to come at least to some pragmatically acceptable understanding in your own mind of whether social class is still a useful concept with which to grasp social relations and their cultural contexts. Certainly, in much of what you will be reading, other concepts – gender, race, ethnicity, and so on, and the 'identity politics' of such categories – will have taken over from class as defining categories of social identity.

The first view is generally thought of as the postmodernist one – social classes as once understood no longer exist. The rather notorious but deeply thought-provoking early statement that fuelled this position was by Ernesto Laclau and Chantal Mouffe (1985) in *Hegemony and Socialist Strategy: Towards a Radical Democratic Politics*. Laclau and Mouffe develop their argument around four terms – articulation, discourse, moments and elements – to which they give quite specific meanings in relation to each other:

> we will call *articulation* any practice establishing a relation among elements such that their identity is modified as a result of the articulatory practice. The structured totality resulting from the articulatory practice, we will call *discourse*. The differential positions, insofar as they appear articulated within any discourse, we will call *moments*. By contrast, we will call *element* any difference that is not discursively articulated. (p. 105)

So the field of social relations can be thought of as containing diverse elements – people, places, economic arrangements, cultural practices, and so on. Relations among these elements are established by articulatory practices – this person in that place within those economic arrangements and receptive to, or engaged in, such and such a cultural practice (you at home watching a rented video paid for by your part-time job in a fast-food restaurant . . .). What results are moments in which particular elements are articulated together (other elements being 'left out', as it were, from the particular arrangements). The totality of articulations and moments makes up a discourse – or perhaps levels of discourse as we move out from the particular moment ('I'm staying in to watch a video tonight') to more generalised levels ('leisure', etc.).

This has been an extraordinarily helpful and influential way of thinking about the social – it replaces a notion of social agents as fixed identities engaged in deliberate pursuit of their transparently understood interests. Instead – and this often proves more useful and explanatory when we actually look more deeply at human activities – we have 'positionalities', people moving from one moment to another, as defined above, and identities and interests depending more on that process than on any absolutely 'fixed' and predetermined factors. Now the difficulty for any notion of social *class* comes when we realise that at this level of generality there is no reason to allow any more 'fixity' to a class of people than we have to individuals. The old notion of a social class, with a fixed identity engaged in deliberate pursuit of its transparently understood interests, dissolves away too into articulations and discourse. A postmodernist tendency to celebrate willy-nilly such dissolutions, of what were previously thought of as fixed, has played into the hands of those who are keen to say that social class – especially the notion of a working class – is simply an outdated idea. Laclau and Mouffe did not quite say that; they pointed to 'the difficulties of the working class in constituting itself as a historical subject, the dispersion and fragmentation of its positionalities, the emergence of forms of social and political reaggregation – "historical bloc", "collective will", "masses", "popular sectors" – which define new objects and new logics of their conformation' (1985:105). But, once you let go of the term 'working class' and find alternative vocabularies for describing various collectivities in various moments, there seems to be an inevitable slippage towards abandoning the idea of social class entirely. This slippage leads us, then, to the first contemporary view – that social classes no longer exist. Whether explicitly argued (and consciously believed) or not, much media and cultural theory is written as if this were the position adopted on class.

The second view is equally thought provoking (for none of these three views, however incompatible they look, can be readily dismissed). It is that the working class has expanded and is everywhere, but not in the sense of 'de-classed' dispersed discursive positionalities with no clear commonality of interest and no way of acting as a coherent 'historical subject'; it is still a collectivity with clear interests that need to be robustly pursued. Tom Lewis has eloquently made this case:

> the working class today is comprised of both 'blue collar' and 'white collar' workers. Displacement of workers from industrial to 'service sector' jobs does not entail a 'de-classing' of workers. Marx's conception of class, for example, stresses two criteria in defining the working class. Individuals form part of the working class if: (1) they must work for a living, as opposed to living off investments or inherited wealth; and (2) they have little or no control over the conditions in which they work and what happens to the products (or outcomes) of their work. On this definition, approximately 70 per cent of the population of an advanced capitalist society structurally belong to the working class (Callinicos and Harman 1987). Not only auto, steel, textile and trucking workers, therefore, but also nurses, schoolteachers, bank tellers, janitors, many engineers, clerical workers, most retail sales floor workers, fast-food workers, a variety of information producers and handlers, and many others – this is the contemporary working class . . . The contemporary working class is also a multiracial and multigendered collectivity. This fact is obscured by those postmodernists who habitually refer to workers as one group among many – women, African-Americans, Latinos, Native Americans, Asian-Americans, gays, lesbians, bisexuals, transgender people, workers, the homeless, the elderly, Quebecois, Palestinians, Tutsi in Rwanda, Hutu in Burundi, etc. – to form a list of oppressions. Such a serial approach to oppression projects a false image of the working class – 'straight white men' – at the same time as it denies the common interests that provide a structural basis for unity in the working class. Indeed, the overwhelming number of lesbians, bisexuals and gays, Native Americans, Latinos, Asians and Blacks, as well as women with jobs, belong to the working class. At a time, therefore, when the limitations of identity politics have become painfully obvious (Smith 1994), the failure to recognize class as offering the most effective subject position through which to organize against racism and sexism is particularly regrettable. (1999:151)

Not only does this make a lot of sense when so clearly stated but it is empirically defensible in relation to the labour market. So the contributors to this book, for instance, whatever their childhood backgrounds, are not now working class – as academics they may have to work for a living but they have a great deal of control over their working conditions, what they produce and what happens to it (this book would be a good example). But look around and we readily start to see Lewis's 70 per cent – working behind the counter at McDonald's, in a hospital ward, at a clerical desk, in a data-processing department, a telephone call centre, and so on. The reality that we seem to be seeing here directly challenges the postmodernist position which tells us that the lesbian girl working in McDonald's has little in common with the black male nurse. On the other hand, recognising that they do have something in common may not be the same thing as claiming an 'effective subject position' that they share and might act upon.

The problem with assuming the existence of this 'subject position' for today's expanded working class becomes clearer when we contrast its situations with those of the old industrial working-class – predominantly the factory workers. Here, from a BBC radio documentary about working-class life in northern England in the 1930s, is a voice that sounds much more like that of a 'subject position' shared by working-class people in general:

> I work in the cotton mill in the card room. I've had to work hard ever since I left school, and me mother and father before me. That's all there is for me – work, eat and sleep. What else is there? If you don't work you don't eat. [. . .] I'm thankful enough to be working now. [. . .] I don't want money and plenty of luxuries. All I want is a comfortable living. But what's the good of looking into the future? I've enough to do to worry about tomorrow.

There is, of course, a discursive convention here – it's not just experience but experience retold with what Michael Pickering (who quotes it) calls the 'poor-but-happy-with-it' message that recodes experience in terms of a self image being deliberately projected to the world, a piece of intentional facework (see Pickering, 1997:214–15). But the commonness of the reported experience and of this way of reporting it clearly suggests the sort of 'effective subject position' available to the working class in that period. It depended in large part on a clear demarcation between what we might term the 'disenchanted' and the 'enchanted' experiences of the social world. This is a disenchanted position ('What else is there? . . . What's the good of looking into the future?'), whereas the world was undoubtedly enchanted by inherited money, investments and freedom from toil for those who had clear answers to both those questions, and in whose houses and property we still find residual enchantment as visitors and tourists mobilised by the heritage industry or viewers of BBC costume dramas. But the world *has become* enchanted for the expanded working class described by Lewis, not least through consumerism and the media. Today's equivalent of that young woman from the mill would have the glossy and aspirational magazine at her lunch break, the video to look forward to in the evening, the shopping trip for fashionable clothes at the weekend or the holiday in Spain to anticipate. As much as anything, it is this re-enchantment of the world that seems to have fractured a unified working-class subject position which once depended to such a great extent on the commonality of disenchantment in drudgery, routine and the vacant sense of future. Indeed the diversity of 're-enchanting' cultural practices available to the nurse, the schoolteacher, the bank teller, the janitor, the retail sales floor worker, will separate as often as they bring together, as tastes and lifestyle choices proliferate. Does this, then, return us to the postmodernist view that shopping has entirely replaced class consciousness (in what Teresa Ebert (1991:115) terms 'ludic' or playful postmodernism and which Peter McLaren (1995:207) distinguishes from 'resistance' postmodernism)? Not

necessarily.

Fredric Jameson offers a third way of thinking about social class, starting by agreeing with Lewis that class is real:

Class is both an ongoing social reality and an active component of the social imaginary, where, with post-Cold War globalization, it can currently be seen to inform our various (mostly unconscious or implicit) maps of the world system. As a dichotomous phenomenon (there are only two fundamental classes in every mode of production), it is able to absorb and refract gender connotations and oppositions (along with racial ones); at the same time it is itself concealed and complexified by the survival of older residual class images and attitudes, aristocratic or (more rarely) peasant components emerging to distort and enrich the picture, so that Europe and Japan can be coded as aristocratic in the face of a plebeian US, while the Third World is joined by Eastern Europe as a generally subaltern area (in which the distinction between working class and peasant is blurred by notions like 'underdeveloped', which do not articulate the surplus-value transformed from Third to First Worlds over the course of history). As soon as the focus changes from a world system to a regional one – Europe or the Middle East, for example – suddenly the class map is rearticulated in new ways, just as it would be even further if the frame were that of a single nation state with its internal class oppositions. The point to be made, however, is not that all such class mappings are arbitrary and somehow subjective, but that they are inevitable allegorical grids through which we necessarily read the world, and also that they are structural systems in which all the elements or essential components determine each other and must be read off and defined against one another. This was of course most notably the case with the original dichotomous opposition itself, whose historical emergence in capitalism has since been shown to involve a constant process whereby a working class becomes aware of itself. (1999:48–9)

In this notion of *class mappings* and in the processes of individual awareness and social imagining we find a third approach to understanding social class today, and one that may seem to absorb the previous two, rendering them less contradictory. We all carry around a sort of empty template of 'class' in our heads – a dichotomous mapping – and apply it 'unconsciously'; that is, as an unreflective way of grasping opposing forces that we sense as loose in our world. This may be in terms of a male/female, affluent/urban poor, white/black, middle class/underclass, developed/underdeveloped, Europe/Third World mapping, some variation of these or some alternative, where what we are doing is imagining dominant and subordinate occupants of the two positions in empirically loose but influential ways. These imaginings are underpinned by the original opposition, so 'working class' becomes a sort of prototype category of social thinking that maps out a space of social subordination that can be differently occupied depending on the frame of reference (world system, nation, city, local community, etc.). The problem with this 'solution', however, is that in turning the category of social class into a kind of 'original' oppositional structure that supports future mappings of subordination through other social categories, we run the risk of reducing the notion of the 'working class' to a historical category which, while remaining important today, does so only as something that allows us to continue thinking the subordinate/dominant opposition which then gets refilled as appropriate. On the other hand, Jameson's notion of class and its 'other' as something 'carried around in the head' (1999:49) is suggestive of a further perspective on the question, one which does still recognise the contemporary reality of the working class.

Towards a working solution to the problem of conceptualising class
Where the great original dichotomous opposition here is that of bourgeois and working class (the old refrain of 'lower', 'middle' and 'upper' classes being simplistic today), each carrying an image of self and other around in its head – 'conflicted by a foreign body it cannot exorcize', in Jameson's startling phrase (1999:49) – we can think of there being two massive and simultaneous class expansions in contemporary societies. The re-enchantment of life through consumerism and the media can be thought of as expanding the bourgeois world, its values and aspirations. At the same time, the expanded working class includes such a great variety of workers and circumstances that it has difficulty recognising itself, as it were. Are these not then different views of the same thing – the same people, caught facing different directions? At one moment the new bourgeois, living the enchanted lifestyles sustained, not by inherited money and investments, but by consumer culture and aspirational media representations; at the next moment caught in the drudgery of work without self realisation or control? What inserts itself between these two takes on contemporary class identity is the set of values, ideas, beliefs and practices of the 'genuinely' bourgeois world – that is, the world where control really resides, where political power operates, where cultural capital accumulates to the greatest degree, where media ownership is located, where white male privilege has its clubs, and also – let's not forget – where reside the rich *in relation to whom* the working class is getting poorer (despite being wealthier in absolute terms). All this, though, is no longer experienced as directly 'other', in relation to which one is materially antagonistic, when the largely politically disengaged populace of the expanded bourgeois world is enchanted by the many satisfactions, luxuries and practices – not least the cultural – it has to offer; but it remains a cognitive 'foreign body' for the fast-food restaurant worker, the clerical worker, the truck driver, the nurse. It entails, we might say, a 'buzzing' in the head when one's own experiences, education, concepts for grasping things are suddenly mismatched with discourses that call for a different sort of experience, different education, different concepts (noting that different does not mean better in any absolute sense) – the ones that underpin and encode real political, intellectual, cultural, technical, racial and economic power. (We used to think also of the 'petty' or aspiring bourgeoisie, the lower middle classes, but this distinction no longer seems adequate given the spread of consumerism and media culture which makes the same symbolic resources accessible to everyone.)

If there is any truth in this perspective – and it may at least be a usable notion that facilitates learning – then each of these class 'identities', sandwiched together in the contemporary inhabitant of the consumerist, media-saturated world, may be experienced as a sort of spectral other in the moments when one or other is more fully experienced. So in the kitchen of the fast-food restaurant there is a spectral other – the leisure-time identity of the media consumer – who was not available to the cotton mill worker of earlier times. But similarly, in front of the TV or on the package holiday to a Spanish beach, is there a spectral other who wonders if there isn't more to life than these everyday and vacation distractions and escapades? Even more importantly, though, in those moments of discursive mismatch – when the articulation suddenly seems awkward or broken jointed – are there opportunities for critical intervention, perhaps especially in the classroom, that might expand into something profoundly transformative for individuals and for the social relations and cultural practices in which they participate? There are ghosts to be laid to rest in the old Marxist notion of class struggle, but also spectral remnants that haunt contemporary class identities with the sense that all is not what it seems or should be. We are using all three perspectives on class here – Laclau and Mouffe's notion of discursively articulated positions helps us to see 'in theory' how someone might occupy a split position as suggested here; Tom Lewis's insistence that 70 per cent of people in capitalist societies should properly (i.e. pre-discursively) be considered working class gives us one of those 'positionalities'; Fredric Jameson helps us to see that class mappings are subtle acts of social imagining these days – and when we put them together we find that the media are deeply implicated in, indeed are the main vehicles of, the re-enchantment of the world that creates the second 'positionality', the one in which the working class no longer recognises itself as such but surrenders to a variety of other, apparently more satisfying, affiliations.

It is to Jameson's notion of class mappings too that we can turn for the next consequence of the view hypothesised here – that by imaginatively mapping all sorts of subordinate others (gay, black, Third World, urban underclass, etc.) on to one's 'working class' identity, the latter itself, if somewhat paradoxically, swims more clearly into view. And interestingly, the media here shift from 'enchanter' to powerful source of public knowledge on which such mappings depend. Indeed, it may be in these extended class mappings, these acts of imaginative empathy, all the way out to recognising the subordination of much Third World labour in the world system, that today's working class in advanced capitalist societies ultimately recognises itself, in some way that is far removed from the disenchanted recognition of exploitation available to the factory workers of an earlier period. Social movements of various kinds are being built on such empathy, as the protestors on the streets of Seattle in December 1999 demonstrated. Their disruption of the World Trade Organisation conference, involving battles with the Seattle police and state national guard, represented a fundamentally unselfish empathy with the world's subordinated (in the interest of limiting unregulated globalised business) on the part of those whose 'enchanted' lives provided the credit cards that paid for the air tickets that enabled them to take to the streets of Seattle, and for the internet connections that allowed them to organise in such large numbers. For those whose educational, social and economic background is 'genuinely', as distinct from 'spectrally', bourgeois – and there will be many among this book's readers – the task is in some ways a more difficult one. The children of the owners of capital (both economic and cultural), and of the professional classes who manage things, feel more instinctively comfortable amid the controlling discourses, which less readily turn into a defensive buzzing in their heads, and may have a liberal sympathy for the world's subaltern peoples (rather than the empathy of a class mapping as described above). But they now rub shoulders with the working class – on the streets of Seattle, in the university classroom (where the working class may no longer be a minority), in the workplace, on the internet – which means that multiple opportunities exist for dialogue around precisely those controlling discourses, dialogue in which intellectual sympathy and felt empathy can cross-pollinate each other and from which everybody can come away a little wiser; not least in terms of an ability to resist the controlling discourses' resentful demonisation of the 'underclass'.

So, as Peter McLaren puts it, '[t]he rhythm of the struggle for educational and social transformation can no longer be contained in the undaunted, steady steps of the workers' army marching towards the iron gates of freedom' (1994:219). But class categories, lived not as pure and self sufficient encapsulations of experience but as 'positionalities' – even split ones as proposed here – become the templates on which are built both politically disengaged self satisfaction (as the new omnipresent consumerist bourgeoisie) *and* politically engaged transformative empathies (as the expanded working class). The key to securing the dominance of the latter over the former, in one's own internal struggle for hegemony, is found in the very process of critical learning in which we are engaged here. The ghost citizen will either be exorcised and permanently laid to rest by consumerist pressures or raised from the dead by a critical pedagogy that knows a good ghost when it sees one.

In the meantime, that struggle for educational and social transformation has to deal with powerful media narratives (from news to films) in which a resentful 'middle class' position is constructed – the wagons are circled, the laager is fortified – against the underclass 'other', because this makes such a good story. Three final points need to be made. First, what we have characterised as a postmodernist caricaturing of 'workers', as only one category in relation to a politics of identity where other social categories are given more weight, is unfair to the best postmodern theorising, which usefully suggests that class is *lived* through those other categories – race, gender, sexuality. Second, while life is re-enchanted by the media and by consumerism there will still be different degrees of re-enchantment – the working-class experience of access to information and consumerist pleasures will still differ in quality and degree from that of the conspicuously wealthy and powerful. Finally, class is not just a matter of structural givens – it is also an individual and collective form of self definition forged through practice on a number of fronts and in a number of pedagogical and cultural sites. It can be learned and unlearned.

Dan Fleming

Dangerous zones

The crisis of the middle class is of commanding gravity . . . The crisis is hardening the attitude of the middle class toward the dependent poor, and to the extent that the poor are urban and black and Latino and the middle class suburban and white, race relations are under a new exogenous strain. (Beatty, 1994:70)

In the early 1990s, *Time* magazine published two articles that together document the contemporary rise of suburban middle-class resentment. In these articles, crime and violence are fetishised, transmuted in the language of the coming invasion of the abstract racial other. Together the articles offer a dystopic chronology in two instalments: in the first phase, indigenous criminal elements take over the small town rural suburbs; and in the second phase, nameless Third World infidels housed in the UN make a final conquering manoeuvre to rush the whole nation, making their first point of attack a leafy Michigan suburb. In this War of the Worlds, 'we' (Sweeney's suburban militias) have to be prepared to liberate the nation. The first article goes by the title 'Danger in the Safety Zone' in which the author notes parenthetically: 'As violence spreads into small towns, many Americans barricade themselves' (Smolowe, 1993:30). In this article, murder and mayhem are everywhere outside the suburban home: in the McDonald's restaurant, in the shopping mall, in the health club, in the courtroom. The article also displays statistics indicating that crime in the major cities has been declining somewhat while crime in the suburbs – the place where the middle classes thought they were safest – is now increasingly engulfing residents in random acts of violence. All of this is happening even in a place like 'small town, U.S.A., Tomball, Texas' – the most unlikely place for post-modernism's final confrontation with the other. The second article is entitled 'Patriot Games'. It is about the mushrooming of heavily armed white militias in training, preparing for the war of wars against the federal government and nameless invading immigrants and political forces that the Clinton administration has somehow, unwittingly, encouraged to think that America is weak and lacking in resolve to police its borders:

The members of the larger patriot movement are usually family men and women who feel strangled by the economy, abandoned by the government and have a distrust for those in power that goes well beyond that of the typical angry voter. Patriots join the militias out of fear and frustration . . . [They] were particularly enraged when Congress passed a crime bill last August that banned assault weapons. . . . Patriots also fear that foreign powers, working through organizations like the United Nations and treaties like the General Agreement on Tariffs and Trade, are eroding the power of America as a sovereign nation. On a home video promoting patriot ideas, a man who gives his name only as Mark from Michigan says he fears that America will be subsumed into 'one big, fuzzy, warm planet where nobody has any borders.' Samuel Sherwood, head of the United States Militia Association in Blackfoot, Idaho, tells followers, absurdly, that the Clinton Administration is planning to import 100,000 Chinese policemen to take guns away from Americans . . . When it comes to organization, however, the [militias] go high-tech. The militia movement, says Berlet [Chip Berlet of the Political Research Association in the United States (ed.)], 'is probably the first national movement organized and directed on the information highway.' Patriot talk shows, such as *The Informed Citizen*, a half-hour program broadcast on public-access TV in Northern California, spread the word that American values are under attack from within and without. Militias also communicate via the Patriot Network, a system of linked computer bulletin boards, and through postings in news groups on the Internet. One recent posting by a group calling itself the Pennsylvania Militia, more specifically the F Company of the 9th Regiment, asked for a 'few good men' to join up and 'stand up to the forces of federal and world tyranny.' (Farley, 1994:48–9)

What does all of this mean? These articles, in some ways, announce a new sensibility and mood in the political and social life in the USA – a mood articulated in suburban fear of encirclement by difference – a mood increasingly being formulated in a language and politics of what James and Nietzsche called 'resentment'. The dangerous inner city and the world 'outside' are brought into suburban homes through television and film, releasing new energies of desire mixed with the fear of the images projected on the home entertainment screen. As we enter the twenty-first century, conflicts in education and popular culture are increasingly taking the form of grand pan-ethnic battles over language, signs and the occupation and territorialisation of urban and suburban space. These conflicts intensify as the dual model of the city, of the rich and poor, dissolves into splintered and fragmentary communities signified by the roaming homeless on network television. For our late twentieth-century Sweeney Erectus, standing on the pyres of resentment in the culturally beleaguered suburbs, the signs and wonders are everywhere in the television evening news. Sweeney's cultural decline is registered in radically changing technologies and new sensibilities; in spatial and territorial destabilisation and re-coordination; in the fear of falling; and in new, ever more incorrigible patterns of segregation and resegregation (Grossberg, 1992). Before his jaundiced eyes immigrant labour, immigrant petty bourgeoisie, now course through suburban and urban streets – the black and Latino underclasses after the Los Angeles riots, announces one irrepressibly gleeful news anchor, are restless. Elements among the white middle classes are experiencing declining fortunes. And the homeless are everywhere.

This new world order of mobile marginal communities is deeply registered in popular culture and in social institutions such as schools. The terrain to be mapped here is what Hal Foster in the *Anti-Aesthetic* (1983) calls postmodernism's 'other side' – the new centres of the simulation of difference that loop back and forth through the news media to the classroom, from the film culture and popular music to the organisation and deployment of affect in urban and suburban communities – Sweeney's homeground.

You will recall that Fredric Jameson, in his now famous essay 'Postmodernism or the Cultural Logic of Late Capitalism', maintained that a whole new emotional ground tone separated life in contemporary post-industrial society from previous epochs. He described this emotional ground tone as 'the waning of affect', the loss of feeling. While I agree with Jameson that emotions, like music, art, film, literature and architecture, are historically determined and culturally bound, I disagree with his diagnosis that contemporary life is overwhelmingly marked by a certain exhaustion or waning of affect. I want to maintain that a very different logic is at work in contemporary life, particularly in the area of race relations. Postmodernism's other side of race relations – of the manipulation of difference – is marked by a powerful concentration of affect or the strategic use of emotion and moral re-evaluation.

Central to these developments is the rise of the cultural politics of 'resentment'. Nietzsche (1967), in *Genealogy of Morals*, defined resentment as the specific practice of defining one's identity through the negation of the other. Some commentators on Nietzsche associate resentment only with 'slave morality'. We are here taken genealogically back to 'literal slaves' in Greek society, who being the most downtrodden had only one sure implement of defence: the acerbic use of emotion and moral manipulation. But I want to argue, along with Robert Solomon (see his 'Nietzsche, Postmodernism and Resentment'), that contemporary cultural politics are 'virtually defined by bourgeois resentment' (1990:278). As Solomon maintains: 'resentment elaborates an ideology of combative complacency [or what Larry Grossberg calls "impassioned apathy"] – a "leveling" effect that declares society to be "classless" even while maintaining powerful class structures and differences' (1990:278). The middle class declares there are no classes except itself, no ideology except its ideology, no party, no politics, except the politics of the centre, the politics of the middle with a vengeance.

A critical feature of discourses of resentment is their dependence on processes of simulation. For instance, the suburban middle-class subject knows its inner-city other through an imposed system of infinitely repeatable substitutions and proxies: census tracts, crime statistics, tabloid newspapers and television programmes, and, lastly, through the very ground of the displaced aggressions projected from suburban moral panic itself (Reed, 1992; Beatty, 1994). Indeed, a central project of suburban agents of resentment is their aggressive attempt to hold down the moral centre, to occupy the centre of public discourse, to stack the public court of appeal. The needs of the suburbs therefore become 'the national interests' or what the Speaker of the House might call the 'legitimate demands of the hard working American tax payers'. By contrast, the needs of the inner city are dismissed as a wasteful 'social agenda' of the out of centre liberal left. Resentment is therefore an emotion 'distinguished, first of all, by its concern and involvement with *power*' (Solomon, 1990:278). And it is a power with its own material and discursive logic. In this sense it is to be distinguished from self pity. If resentment has any desire at all, it is the 'total annihilation . . . of its target' (Solomon, 1990:279). Sweeney in America offers his own homemade version of the final solution: take the homeless and the welfare moms off general assistance; above all, build more prisons! (How the propagation of this popular vision affects social democratic political trends, where they exist elsewhere in the world, would be an important question to explore more thoroughly.)

A new moral universe now rides the underbelly of the beast – late capital's global permutations, displacements, relocations and reaccumulations. The effect has meant a material displacement of minority and other dispossessed groups from the landscape of contemporary political and cultural life. That is to say, increasingly the underclass or working-class subject is contemporaneously being placed on the outside of the arena of the public sphere as the middle-class subject–object of history moves in to occupy and to appropriate the identity of the oppressed, the radical space of difference. The centre becomes the margin. It is as if Primus Rex had decided to wear Touchstone's foolscap; Caliban exiled from the cave as Prospero digs in. Resentment operates through the processes of simulation that usurp contemporary experiences of the real, where the real is proven by its negation or its inverse. Resentment has infected the very structure of abstract value. This battle over signs is being fought in cultural institutions across the length and breadth of American society. The politics of resentment is on the way as the suburbs continue to draw resources and moral empathy away from the urban centres.

Of course, a fundamental issue posed by Nietzsche and James, certainly a fundamental issue posed by their theories of identity formation, is the challenge of defining identity in ways other than through the strategy of negation of the other. This, I wish to suggest, is the fundamental challenge of multiculturalism, the challenge of 'living in a world of difference' (Mercer, 1992). Education is indeed a critical site where struggles over the organisation and concentration of emotional and political investment and moral affiliation are taking place. This battle over signs (resentment) involves strategies of articulation and rearticulation of symbols in the popular culture and in the media. These signs and symbols are used in the making of identity and the definition of social and political projects. Within this framework the traditional poles of left versus right and liberal versus conservative (in the USA, Democrat versus Republican), are increasingly being displaced by a more dynamic and destabilising model of mutation of affiliation and association. A further dimension of this dynamic is that the central issues that made these binary oppositions of race and class conflict intelligible and coherent in the past have now collapsed or have been recoded. The central issues of social and economic inequality that defined the line of social conflict between the left and the right during the civil rights period are now, in the post-civil rights era, inhabited by the new adversarial discourses of resentment. Oppositional discourses of identity, history and popular memory, nation, family and crime have displaced issues concerning equality and social justice. New Right publisher, William Rusher, articulates this displacement by pointing to a new model of material and ideological distinctions coming into being since the 1980s:

> A new economic division, pits the producers – businessmen, manufacturers, hard-hats, blue-collar workers, and farmers [middle America] – against a new and powerful class of non-producers comprised of the liberal verbalist elite (the dominant media, the major foundations and research institutions, the educational establishment, the federal and state bureaucracies) and a semi permanent welfare constituency, all coexisting happily in a state of mutually sustaining symbiosis. (Quoted in Omi and Winant, 1986:124)

Let us examine some manifestations of one of the principal articulations of resentment: the discourse of crime, violence and suburban security. In the next section of this chapter, I will discuss examples from television evening news, film and popular magazine and newspaper features that show the variability, ambiguity and contradiction in this discourse of conflict. We will see that signifiers of the inner city as the harbinger of violence, danger and chaos loop into the mass media and the suburbs and Hollywood, and back again in the constructions by black male directors of the reality of the 'hood' . . . then to the black male youth audience constructed as other to itself.

'Reflecting reality' and feeding resentment

Too often, Black artists focus on death and destruction arguing that it is what's out there so we got to show it! Please!! What needs to be shown is the diversity and complexity of African-American life. (*Syracuse Constitution*, 2 August 1993, p. 5)

The logic of resentment discourse does not proceed along a straight line in a communication system of encoding/decoding. It does not work one-way from text to audience. Its tentacles are more diffused, more rhizomatic, deeply inter-textual. Resentment processes work from white to black and black to white, and white to Asian and Asian to white, and so on, looping in and out and back again as second nature across the striated bodies of the inhabitants of the inner city – the black world available to the black director who delivers the black audience to Hollywood. The inner city is thereby reduced to an endless chain of recyclable signifiers that both allure and repel the suburban classes. The inner city is constantly prodded for signifiers of libidinal pleasure and danger.

But there is also the shared ground of discourses of the 'authentic' inner city in which the languages of resentment and the reality of 'the hood' com-mingle in films of black realism from black directors such as John Singleton and the Hughes brothers. It is a point that Joe Wood (1993) makes somewhat obliquely in his discussion of the film *Boyz 'N the Hood* (1992), which is set, incidentally, in South Central Los Angeles. In an article published in *Esquire* magazine entitled 'John Singleton and the Impossible Greenback Bind of the Assimilated Black Artist', Wood notes the following:

> *Boyz*'s simplified quality is okay with much of America. It is certain that many whites, including Sony executives and those white critics who lauded the film deliriously, imagine black life in narrow ways. They don't want to wrestle with the true witness; it might be scarier than 'hell.' Sony Pictures' initial reaction to *Boyz* is instructive: John confides that the studio wanted him to cut out the scene in which the cops harass the protagonist and his father. '*Why do we have to be so hard on the police?*' they asked. An answer came when Rodney King was beaten; the scene stayed in – it was suddenly 'real.' (1993:64)

Here we see the elements of repeatability, the simulation of the familiar and the prioritisation of public common sense that evening television helps both to activate and stabilise. Hollywood drew intertextually on the reality code of television. Television commodified and beautified the images of violence cap-tured on a streetwise camera. Singleton's claim to authenticity, ironically, relied not on endogenous inner-city perceptions but, exogenously, on the overdetermined mirror of dominant televisual news. *Boyz 'N the Hood* could safely skim off the images of the inner city corroborated in television common sense. For these Hollywood executives, police brutality became real when the Rodney King beating became evening news. As Wood argues:

> What Sony desired in *Boyz* was a film more akin to pornography . . . a safely voyeuristic film that delivered nothing that they did not already believe . . . But how strenuously will they resist his showing how Beverley Hills residents profit

from South Central gangbanging, how big a role TV plays in the South Central culture. (1993:65)

Of course, what even Joe Wood's critical article ignores about a film like *Boyz 'N the Hood* is its own errant nostalgia for a world in which blacks are centred and stand together against the forces of oppression – a world in which black men hold and practise a fully elaborated and undisputed paternity with respect to their children – a world that radically erases the fact that the location of the new realist black drama, Los Angeles, South Central, the memories of Watts, and so on, is now supplanted by an immigrant and a migrant presence in which, in many instances, black people are outnumbered by Latinos and Asian Americans (Davis, 1992; Lieberman, 1992).

Like the Hollywood film industry, the mainstream news media's address to black and brown America directs its gaze towards the suburban white middle class. It is the gaze of resentment in which aspect is separated from matter and substance undermined by the harsh surfaces and neon lights of inner-city life. In the sensation-dripping evening news programmes of the networks – CBS, NBC, ABC and CNN – as they pant and struggle to keep up with the inflamed journalism of the tabloids – black and Latino youth appear metonymically in the discourse of problems: 'kids of violence', 'kids of welfare moms', 'car jackers', the 'kids without fathers', 'kids of illegal aliens', 'kids who don't speak "American"'. The skins of black youth are hunted down like so many furs in the grand old days of the fur trade. The inner city is sold as a commodity and as a fetish – a signifier of danger and the unknown that at the same time narrows the complexity of urban working-class life. You watch network evening news and you can predict when black and brown bodies will enter and when they will exit. The overwhelming metaphor of crime and violence saturates the dominant gaze on the inner city. For example, news coverage of the cocaine trade between the USA and Columbia routinely suggests that only poor and black inner-city residents use cocaine, not rich suburban whites who are actually the largest consumers of the illegal drug.

In the USA, on any given day that Jesse Jackson might have given a speech on the need for worker solidarity, or Henry Cisneros (America's 1993-appointed Hispanic secretary of urban development) on housing, or Congresswoman Maxine Walters on the budget, the news media have been likely to pass over these events for the more sordid images of black crime and mayhem. This selection of images has become the reality of urban America. The inner-city's essence – empty but latent – combines paradigmatically with other images in the newspaper and film culture. It's an essence that has become a powerful crudescence: black bodies as semiotic cargo caught in the endless loop of the electronic media apparatus. The process is one of transubstantiation; so many black bodies ransacked for the luminous images of the subnormal, the bestial, 'the crack kids', 'the welfare brigade'. The mass media's story of inner-city black and Latino people has little to do with an account about the denial of social services, poor public schools, chronic unemployment, the isolation, the hacking to death of the public transportation system, the radical disinvestment in the cities, and the flight of jobs and resources to the suburbs – all of which can ultimately be linked to government neglect and deprioritisation as middle-class issues of law and order, more jail space and capital punishment usurped the Clinton administration's gaze on the inner city. Instead, the inner city exists as a problem in itself, and a problem to the world. This is why it extends well beyond the geographical boundaries of the USA in a construction of contemporary social relations that is increasingly influential elsewhere. The reality of the inner city is therefore not an endogenous discourse. It is an exogenous one. It is a discourse of resentment refracted back on to the inner city itself.

It is deeply ironic, then, that the images of the inner city presented by the 1990s' new wave black cinema corroborate rather than critique mainstream mass media. Insisting on a kind of documentary accuracy and privileged access to the inner city, these directors construct a reality code of 'being there' after the manner of the gangster rappers. But black film directors have no *a priori* purchase on the inner city. These vendors of chic realism recycle a reality code *already in* the mass media. This reality code operates as a system of repeatability, the elimination of traces, the elaboration of a hierarchy of discourses – the fabrication and consolidation of specular common sense. *Menace II Society* (1993), created by Allen and Albert Hughes, places the capstone on a genre that mythologises and beautifies the violent elements of urban life while jettisoning complexities of gender, ethnicity, sexuality, age and economy. Instead of being didactic, like *Boyz 'N the Hood*, the film is nihilistic. The reality of the hood is built on a trestle of obviousnesses. Its central character, Caine Lawson (Tyrin Turner), is doomed to the drug running, car stealing, meaningless violence that claims young men like himself (and before him, his father) from the time they can walk and talk. It is a world in which a trip to the neighbourhood grocery can end in death and destruction. It is a world in which gangbangers demand and enforce respect at the point of a gun. This point is made at the very beginning of the movie when Caine and his trigger-happy buddy, O-Dog (Larenz Tate) feel disrespected by a Korean store owner. The young men had gone to the grocery to get a beer but are provoked into a stand-off when the store owner hovers too close to them. The young men feel insulted because the Korean grocer makes it too obvious that he views them with suspicion. In the blink of an eye, O-Dog settles the score with a bout of unforgettable violence. When Caine and O-Dog leave, the store owner and his wife are dead. And one act of violence simply precipitates another. By the end of the film, Caine, too, dies in a hail of bullets – a payback by the gang of supporters of a young man that Caine had beaten up mercilessly earlier in the film.

This film sizzles with a special kind of surface realism. There is a lot of blood and gore in the hood in *Menace II Society*. And the camera sequences consist, for the most part, of long takes of beatings or shootings. These camera shots are almost always extreme close-ups. Caine's life is supposed to be a character sketch of the inevitability of early death for inner-city male youth reared in a culture of violence. We have already seen it on television evening news before it hits the big screen. Black film makers therefore become pseudo-normative bards to a mass audience, who, like the Greek chorus, already know the refrain. These are not problem-solving films. They are films of confirmation. The reality code, the code of the hood, the code of blackness, the code of Africanness, of hardness, has a normative social basis. It combines and recombines with sub-urban middle-class discourses in the USA such as the deficit, taxes, 'squandering' government programmes, welfare and quota 'queens' and the need for more prisons. It's a code drenched in public common sense. The gangster film has become paradigmatic for black filmic production out of Hollywood. And it is fascinating to see films such as Singleton's *Higher Learning* (1995) glibly redraw the spatial lines of the inner city and the suburbs in a campus town. *Higher Learning* is *Boyz 'N the Hood* on campus. On the other hand, films such as the Hughes brothers' more recent *Dead Presidents* (1995) and Mario Van Peebles *Panther* (1995) set the clock back, nostalgically, to the 1960s and the politics of the Vietnam War and black power – but the inner city remains, translucently, a place of historical ruin and degradation.

It is to be remembered that early in his career, before *Jungle Fever* (1991), Spike Lee was berated by mainstream white critics for not presenting the inner city realistically enough – for not showing the drug use and violence. Lee obliged with a vengeance in *Jungle Fever*, in the harrowing scenes of the drug addict Vivian (Haile Berry) shooting it up at the 'Taj Mahal' crack joint and the Good Doctor Reverend Purify (Ossie Davis) pumping a bullet into his son (Samuel Jackson) at pointblank range (Kroll, 1991).

By the time we get around to white-produced films such as *Grand Canyon* (1992) and *Falling Down* (1993), the discourse of crime, violence and suburban security has come full circle to justify suburban revenge and resentment. In *Falling Down*, directed by Joel Schumaker, we now have a white suburban male victim who enters the hood to settle moral scores with anything and anyone that moves. Mike Douglas as the angst protagonist, D-fens, is completely agnostic to the differences with and among indigenous and immigrant inner-city groups. They should all be exterminated as far as he is concerned – along, of course, with his ex-wife who won't let him see his infant daughter. D-fens is the prosecuting agent of resentment. His reality code embraces Latinos who are gangbangers and Asian store owners who are portrayed as compulsively unscrupulous. In a scorching parody of gang culture, he becomes a one-man gang – a menace to society. In a calculated cinematic twist, the world of D-fens is characterised by a wider range of difference than the worlds of the films of black realism. However, ironically in this world, blacks are for the most part mysteriously absent from Los Angeles (Douglas's character feels more confident beating up on other racial groups). On this matter of the representation of the 'real' inner city the question is, according to Aretha Franklin, 'Who's zoomin' who?'

What is fascinating about a film such as *Falling Down* is that it too is centred around a protagonist, a kind of proto-normative, anomic individual who, as James might put it, is 'out there'. He is the purveyor of what Jacques Lacan in his 'mirror stage' essay calls 'paranoiac alienation' (Lacan, 1977b:5). Single-handedly armed with more socio-normative fire power than any gangbanger could ever muster, D-fens is ready to explode at the seams as everyday provocations make him seethe to boiling point. We learn, for instance, that he is a disgruntled laid-off white-collar employee – a former technician who worked for many years at a military plant. Displaced as a result of the changing economy of the new world order – displaced by the proliferation of different peoples who are now flooding Los Angeles in pursuit of the increasingly illusive American dream – D-fens is a semiotic prototype of a paranoid single white male who is frustrated by failure in the job and in personal relations with women. He is part of a growing anxiety class that blames government, immigrants and welfare moms for their problems. A guy with a couple of chips on his shoulder and a few hand-grenades to throw around. He is the kind of individual we are encouraged to believe a displaced middle-class person might become. As Joel Schumaker, the film's director, explains:

> It's the kind of story you see on the six o'clock news, about the nice guy who has worked at the post office for twenty years and then one day guns down his co-workers and kills his family. It's terrifying because there's the sense that someone in the human tribe went over the wall. It could happen to us. (Morgan, 1993:46)

Newsweek magazine, that preternatural barometer of suburban intelligence, tells us that D-fens's actions, while not always defensible, are 'understandable':

> [The film] packs a pop-sociological punch. The fashionable revisionist reading of American history and culture that makes the white male the bad guy has triumphed, the film seems to argue, and it's made him not just defensive, but paranoid . . . But *Falling Down*, whether it's really a message movie or just a cop film with trendy trimmings, pushes white men's buttons. The annoyances and menaces that drive D-fens bonkers – whining panhandlers, immigrant shopkeepers who don't trouble themselves to speak good English, gun-toting gangbangers – are a cross-section of white-guy grievances. From the get-go, the film pits Douglas – the picture of obsolescent rectitude with his white shirt, tie, specs and astronaut haircut – against a rainbow coalition of Angelenos. It's a cartoon vision of the beleaguered white male in multicultural America. This is a weird moment to be a white man. (Gates, 1993:48)

D-fens's reactions are based on his own misfortunes and anger over disempowerment of the white middle class. Despite his similarities with the neo-Nazi, homophobic, army-surplus store owner in the movie, they are not the same type of social subject. Unlike the neo-Nazi, D-fens reacts to the injustices he perceives have been perpetrated against him. He is the post-civil rights scourge of affirmative action and reverse discrimination.

With *Falling Down*, Hollywood positions the final punctuation marks on a discursive system that is refracted from the mainstream electronic media and the press on to everyday life in the urban centres. Unlike D-fens in *Falling Down*, in *Menace II Society* the central protagonist, Caine, has nothing to live for, no redeeming values to vindicate. He is pre-existentialist – a man cut adrift in and by nature. What the film does share with *Falling Down* is a general subordination of the interests and desires of women and a pervasive sense that life in the urban centres is self-made hell. Resentment has now travelled the whole way along a fully reversible signifying chain as black film makers make their long march along the royal road to a dubious Aristotelian mimesis in the declaration of a final truth. The reality of being black and inner city in America is sutured up in the popular culture. The inner city has no interior. It is a holy shrine to dead black and brown bodies – hyper-real carcasses on arbitrary display.

The Official Cop Catalog

The language and look of the Los Angeles cops are minted and embossed on the tupa-ware and bric-a-brac that you can find in *The Official Cop Catalog* (1992) of the Line Up Police Products Incorporated Company, headquartered in San Luis Obispo, California – a sort of police-exclusive minimart in an emergent culture industry that circulates seductive and fascistic cop images back to the cops themselves. Like the producers of the gangster movies, the police are interested in authentic masculinity. Hence a Christmas *Official Cop Catalog* features 'The Teddy Bear Line Up' of 'Police Bear', 'Mounty Bear' and 'Fire Fighter Bear' for $54.95, $69.95 and $54.95, respectively. The ad tells its prospective audience that Police Bear 'wears a shiny badge, an expert shooter's medal and even has embroidered patches. The bear's .357 [Magnum] is worn in a holster, complete with thumb-break snap' (1992:1). On another page the catalogue features a variety of mugs which portray various parodies of police daily work. On the back of a mug accompanying a picture of a police interrogation scene is the following disturbing message: 'You walk in with a pretty face and information. You can't leave with both' (p. 24). Yet another mug depicts a 'Hooker Lineup' of women before whom a chortling male cop asks his buddy, 'How much for the one on the right?' (p. 25). Like Sam Spade, the police are both in the law and outside it. The displays on these mugs celebrate violence in which the police assert that, as enforcers of the law, they are above it. These mugs celebrate various acts that appear to cross the line of lawful law enforcement and enter the zone of lawless perversity.

Cameron McCarthy

Resentment effects

> But the body is also directly involved in a political field; power relations have an immediate hold upon it; they invest it, mark it, train it, torture it, force it to carry out tasks, perform ceremonies, to emit signs. (Foucault, 1975:25)

As the portrayals of the inner city in these films illustrate, the discourse of resentment not only has powerful rhetorical effects, it also has devastating material effects. Inner-city black school youth are surrounded by this powerful discourse of crime and violence in which they are the constructed other – social objects who grapple with the reality code projected from the popular media culture. Their experience of the reality code is grounded in material practices such as police harassment. Black and brown youth experience the reality code as a problem of representation. The reality code is translated in the discourse of resentment. Democracy asserts its tragic limits in the urban centre. Unlike the cause-and-effect theories of film culture, police harassment reported by high school students in the Los Angeles school system seems random and vicious.

A good example of the material consequences and challenges of representation for minority youth is provided in the stories told by inner-city adolescents at Liberty High School in Los Angeles. Liberty High is itself an extension of the long arm of the state. The LA Unified Public School system has its own police force. The following excerpt, taken from an ethnographic study that I conducted in this inner-city high school about sixth months before the Rodney King beating, gives a sense of the students' experiences with the unyieldingly negative representations of black and Latino male youth generated in the popular media. A switch point of this field of representation is their encounter with the police. This research was conducted in the summer of 1990.

I report on a class that was taught by a Teach for America intern, Christopher Morrison. (Teach for America is a national scheme in the USA, through which recent college graduates commit two years to teach in under-resourced public schools.) Christopher is a white male. He was in his early twenties at the time of the study. His assignment to do a four week teaching stint at Liberty High School was his first 'exposure' to an inner-city school. Christopher's co-operating teacher was a black female, Ms Ruby Marshall. She was in her sixties, anticipating retirement. Of the seventeen students that were in Christopher's classroom, fifteen were African-American and two were Latino. The class under discussion here was taken over by accounts of police violence. Christopher had introduced the topic of police harassment based on some queries made by one of his students, Rinaldo, the previous day. But in the torrent of accounts offered by students, Christopher lost control of his class. So, too, did the co-operating teacher, Ruby Marshall. In effect the classroom had become a site for a therapeutic release – a show and tell on harassment and the 'image problem' that black and brown male youth had with the Los Angeles police. Students detailed acts of police harassment that left them disoriented about their own sense of self and identity. One student reported that he had been stopped by the cops and searched for a gun. But, in his words, 'the cops had no probable reason'. Another reported that he was arbitrarily beaten up, in his view, for walking on the wrong street at the wrong time of night. One girl in the class told of how she knew of friends whose houses, she said, 'was bust into'. Many of them talked of intimidating stares and glares and threatening behaviour on the part of the police.

In this Los Angeles high school classroom, the diffusion of images of the police and the problematic relationship of some kids to the law opened up deep wounds of adolescent insecurity and identity crisis. Students were looking for solutions to problems about self representation from their teachers, who did not seem to have any easy answers. The students were concerned about how to represent themselves in ways that might help them to maintain their sense of adolescent freedom and individual rights and yet avoid the full-court press of the cops. The responses of the adults, Christopher Morrison and Ruby Marshall, were steeped in the common sense of the reality code – the code of mimesis, the code of resentment. Here are some of Ruby Marshall's comments on the students' reports of police harassment:

> I say if you walk like a duck and you hang out with ducks, then you are a duck. I believe that some of the things they [the police] do are not right. But you guys sometimes walk around without any books like the rest of the guys on the street. If you do that, they [the cops] will pull you over . . . One day I saw them [some police officers]. They had this guy spread-eagled against the car. And they were really harassing him. You should not hang out with these guys . . . Don't hang out with the Bloods, or the Crips, or the Tigers! . . . When a group of you guys are

hanging out together that gives them cause for concern. You don't even carry books. You need to be as non-threatening as possible.

To the latter, one student replied: 'You mean to say that if I am going around with my friends at night I need to haul along a big old bunch of books over my shoulder?'

Some of the responses of the white student teacher, Christopher Morrison, conveyed a sense of ambivalence – great sympathy for the adolescent students as they reported examples of police harassment, but also a sense that the police had to go on 'images', that they had to enforce the law, and that school youth had to exercise restraint and respect if they wished to be treated respectfully themselves. In response to the students' questions about free speech and freedom of movement, Christopher pointed them in the direction of the reality code where actions had real consequences; wrong was repaid by retributive sanctions, and personal errors of judgement – associating with the wrong crowd and being in the wrong place at the wrong time – were actions that one had to accept responsibility for. Just as ordinary adult citizens had to accept the consequences of their actions, adolescents who challenge the law ought to be aware of the wrath of the law. There follows an excerpt from a testy but revealing exchange between Christopher and his black students on the topic of the aggressive actions of the police: 'Let me tell you a story about myself. Maybe this will help. Once I had some friends. They were hanging out on the college campus. But they did not look like college students. They were white, but they had long hair.' A number of students interjected, 'You mean like a hippie?' 'Like a hippie', Christopher said. Then he continued with his story:

> They arrested these guys. You have to understand that the police go on images. They rely on images. They need categories to put people into so that they can do their work. And sometimes these categories are right. And if you, Morgan, had a gun [addressing the student who said the cops stopped and searched him for weapons] then you gave them probable cause. You fitted into one of their categories.

Morgan seemed utterly dismayed: 'It wasn't the gun. They were just riding through the hood. If I had given them any trouble they would have sweated me.' Christopher disagreed with this assessment of danger: 'I don't think they would do that to you. You can complain if you feel that your rights have been abused. Look, people are being blown away at a faster rate than ever in this country. Just don't give them cause. If you got something [a gun] on you, then that is giving them cause.'

On the matter of police harassment, the teachers, as representatives of the middle class, moved swiftly towards points of ideological closure. Their students, young and black and Latino and in trouble with the law, passed their adult mentors like ships in the night. They wanted the discourse opened up in ways that would allow their voices to be heard. But the Los Angeles classroom seemed more like a court of appeal in which the students appeared to lose the battle for control over their public identities and self representation. The process of resentment had insinuated itself into the lives of the students. Black and Latino students had to contend with the burden of an always already existent complex of representations that constructs them as outsiders to the law. The inner-city classroom, like the inner-city streets, in the language of Thomas Dunn (1993), has become an 'enclosure' for the containment of the mobility of black and brown youth. The borderline between the suburbs and the trau-matised inner city is drawn in public schools such as Liberty High. And teach-ers such as Ruby Marshall and Christopher Morrison stand guard on the frontlines – agents of resentment guarding the border zone erected around suburban interests.

Conclusion

With the politics of resentment now widely diffused, we have entered a whole new phase in race relations in education and society in the USA, with signifi-cant effects rippling beyond the country's borders thanks to the hegemony of American media. These relations are propelled by the processes of simulation built into historically specific discourses such as crime, violence and suburban security. Of course, it should be noted that both majority and minority groups use resentment discourses. Eurocentrism and Afrocentrism are two such dis-courses that thrive on the negation of the other. Proponents of these two world views attempt to reify moral centres, in opposition to supposed peripheries, not realising that these moral centres are simulations of reality. In popular film and television culture both these discourses have been refracted on to the inner city with a vengeance. In this period of 'the post' there are no innocent or originary identities (Bhabha, 1994).

With the politics of resentment, we are descending down the slippery slopes of the war over signs. Traditional divisions and traditional alliances no longer hold. As Baudrillard (1983) argues, opposition becomes only a hypersimula-tion of opposition. Collusion of supposed extremes is the more common result. The battle lines over signs are now being drawn down in and around pre-dictable constituencies, and whole new categories of association and affiliation enter the fray. The war over signs and symbols pits respectable suburban society against the amoral inner city – the nuclear family residents of the sterilised suburban environments against the urban children without the fathers. It pits supporters of academic freedom against the politically correct; a field of affect in which we see Marxists such as Eugene Genovese form a blood pact with slick proto-capitalist Third World immigrant intellectuals such as Dinesh D'Souza. Together they harangue embattled indigenous First World minorities. So much for the conservative wing of the travelling theorists.

Resentment is, therefore, negative and positive, decentring and recentring. While the inner city flounders under the weight of government disinvestment and the scarcity of jobs and services, old and new patriotic and fundamental-ist groups led by Rambo, the National Rifle Association (the USA's pro-guns lobby) and Teach for America sing conservative icon and broadcaster Rush Limbaugh's refrain: 'We must take back America.'

In a time of the fear of falling, the suburban middle-class subject stabilises itself by dressing in the garb of 'the oppressed' – people whose fortunes have been slipping despite their moral steadfastness. It is the middle class that feels increasingly surrounded by the other, its public space overrun by the homeless, its Toyotas and BMWs hijacked by the amoral underclass. And always there is the question of what to do with urban youth out of control.

Those of us who are privileged but, in some ways, condemned to look at the world as perpetual voyeurs – Sweeneys of the sightless eyes warming in the glow of our ethereal hearths – cannot forever retreat from this tumultuous world of difference. We are part of a world of difference in which our needs and interests must be problematised and our sense of identity and community challenged. We must try to think within but also think beyond our immediate particularities. Those of us who articulate the anxieties repressed in and by our own privileged access to society's cornucopia of rewards – dwellers of the suburban city and the masters of the new fictive hyper-realisms of the hood – are responsible to the urban city which our practices of cultural production and over-consumption both create and displace.

Afterthoughts

Antonio looks down despairingly at the examination paper that sits on the desk before him. He looks up at the back of the candidate in front of him, hunched impenetrably, then around at the ranks of fellow sufferers, among them the half dozen other 'Erasmus' exchange scheme students from elsewhere in Europe, now taking media studies courses at this northern British university. Nobody returns his glance and he looks back at his desk. The examination paper is still there. Film studies. Answer any three questions. He still feels the dampness on his sleeve from the persistent drizzle outside. He thinks of the Spanish sun back home. It seems to have been drizzling continuously, day and night, for the four months that he has been in Britain. He glances across to a window. Still drizzling. He looks back down at his examination paper. Still there.

Question 1 *'While Hollywood cinema mythologises the hypermodern as virtual spectacle, auteur cinema presents it as simultaneous dislocation.' Discuss.*

People around him are beginning to write. Antonio thinks of his new Glaswegian friend, studying environmental sciences at the same university. What would he say? 'Ah'm really fuckin sufferin here, awright?' Not the kind of English his university tutor back in Madrid expects him to be bringing home, but Antonio grins despite his situation as Johnny's habitual refrain comes to mind, 'Away tae fuck, it's goat nowt tae dae wi me mate!' He imagines Johnny's intense expression, Johnny's hand reaching for the pen, Johnny writing, 'Hyper-fuckin-modern shite. Whit you oan aboot?'

Question 2 *It has been argued, by Mulvey and others, that the viewing of a film is an act associated with a voyeuristic pleasure and that the male gaze, as that of the voyeur, structures the visual organisation of the film. With reference to classic Hollywood cinema, explain this argument in detail.*

Even Johnny's voice in his head seems to have been dumbstruck by that one.

Antonio had come close to getting involved in the film industry. Back in Madrid his mother worked as a cook for a writer who went off the rails. His mother, **297**

Blanca, remained stoically loyal but Antonio had little time for the self-absorbed and self-induced anxieties of those who didn't appreciate how well off they were. While his mother cooked meals that were left to go cold, scraping together sufficient money to secure a little independence, Antonio had had enough. He stole some jewellery from his mother's employer and a manuscript of a story that he found in a wastepaper bin in her apartment. He had a friend who knew a movie producer and they managed to sell the story. That and the jewellery paid for Antonio to do what he had been dreaming about – staging a dance drama, with his mother as star. Reluctantly at first – it was a long time since she had danced and she couldn't get much time off from her domestic duties to rehearse – but Blanca had been transformed into a spinning red vision of creative energies. Antonio thought about that story, 'Cold Storage' it had been called, and about the movie that was being made from it even as he sat here confronted by film studies exam questions in this dull British university. Cold storage – it seemed like a statement about his own creative energy. He was a dancer too – lean with long black hair now tied up but on stage swirling wildly and catching the light. He thought about the gaze of the audience as the lights came up on his own leather-clad body. As his boots pounded the stage he always knew that he was a focal point of their desire, even if he didn't have a vocabulary to talk about it with the other dancers. But they all knew what power they had.

Now he felt utterly powerless, his energy sapped by these questions and by everything they represented. Not that he wasn't into film. In fact the next stage of his dream was to transfer the dance production to the screen, if he could find a backer and avoid military service back home. Even here he had had long and surprisingly pleasurable late-night discussions with Johnny and Andrew, a postgraduate student who was taking seminars on the course. The best one had been about *Chung-King Express*, a revelation of a film. Johnny just couldn't get over it ('Awright! Awright!' he had chanted as he watched, rocking back and forward on the edge of his seat) when Andrew brought a tape round to the flat. For Antonio, it was like dance energy transferred into the life of the camera. It had an 'open gaze', as Andrew put it, and Antonio knew what he meant, even though he couldn't find the words to make any connection with Mulvey and the rest. As the night wore on and they'd watched it for the second time, Andrew said something else that was the most important idea Antonio had heard in his whole time at university: 'If, say, you're off to catch a bus and you briefly lose your way in an arcade of shops, Wong Kar-wai's montage style is a bit like the reality of that arcade as you pass the bus driver the fare.' Why couldn't the lecturers talk about film that way? That idea had really stuck in Antonio's mind and a few days later he had bought a copy of the *Times Literary Supplement* because it had a review of a book called *The Arcades Project* by some long-dead German writer. It was the word 'arcades' and the heading that had caught his attention – 'Shops, sewers, boredom, barricades: Walter Benjamin's mappings.' It just seemed to have something to do with what Andrew had said (and had he mentioned Benjamin in a seminar, something about art and mechanical reproduction?) but the review was long and virtually impenetrable. He was disappointed but not surprised. Antonio had long ago accepted that the way these people talk and write, even though his English was excellent, was still like a foreign language to him. It was the same at the university back home. Sometimes he felt like his mother was right – give up the dreams and just make do with a job as a cook or a painter and decorator (his weekend and vacation job). It wasn't so bad after all.

But there was one thing about that review. It quoted Benjamin saying, 'To write history is to cite it'. In Spanish '*citar*' means 'to meet with' and Antonio suddenly understood something as a result of that coincidental insight. He had met with something through *Chung-King Express*, with a bit of help from Andrew, and that something was 'history' happening now.

Question 3 *In 'Brecht and Method', Fredric Jameson argues that we need a method for 'inserting ourselves into history' in an imaginative way. Relate this to Jameson's theory of 'cognitive mapping' in the postmodern world and discuss the film 'Blade Runner' in light of these ideas.*

Antonio looks at his watch. The examination is nearly over. He has written his name on the front of the exam booklet. He smiles as he puts his pen away. He imagines his friend Johnny's catchphrase again, 'It's goat nowt tae dae wi me mate!' Wrong Johnny. Dead wrong.

(With apologies to David Thomson's *Suspects* (1986). Andrew Tomlinson's unpublished doctoral thesis, October 1997, lodged in the library, University of Ulster, Coleraine, Northern Ireland, is called *Windows and Souls: Contrary Imaginations in Film*. Johnny was tear-gassed by police on the streets of Seattle, December 1999, while protesting against the World Trade Organisation.)

Part VI
Method

16

Your own work: research, interviews, writing in media studies

Michael Green

> I remember childhood as time in anguish, as a dark time – not darkness in any sense that is stark, bleak, or empty but as a rich space of knowledge, struggle, and awakening. We seemed bound to the earth then, as though like other living things our roots were so deep in the soil of our surroundings there was no way to trace beginnings. We lived in the country, in a space between country and city, a barely occupied space. Houses stood at a distance from one another, few of them beautiful (hooks, 1999:3)

What makes a first sentence interesting? This requires a writer to think about her or his writing – and think also about who will be reading it.

One of my own favourite writers is bell hooks. I cite her opening sentences in *Remembered Rapture: The Writer at Work* (1999) because they draw you wonderfully into reading the whole of the essay which follows. She describes her upbringing, and her writing as a strategy to cope with it and shape it. Remembering her childhood as 'a dark time' she believed that 'there was light in darkness waiting to be found'. Through much pain and uncertainty she decided 'to be a writer, to seek for that light in words'. Later, in the essay 'remembered rapture: dancing with words' (pp. 35–45) she writes an unusual and passionate tribute to the form of the critical essay. But she observes also, with regret, that 'all academics write but not all see themselves as writers' (p. 37).

My own essay is about working on, and writing – and also enjoying working on, and writing – essays which study aspects of media. To use a far from subtle metaphor, I intend to work through the various 'bread and butter' stages of research and writing – writing research – in media studies.

Your degree course will involve the development of many skills, some taught and some acquired along the way. These will include: effective participation in discussion groups; close attention to a variety of media; critical reading skills; the discovery and investigation of information and sources; interview skills; perhaps media production work; sitting examinations; oral presentations; group work in various forms. Alongside these you will be asked to study towards the writing of essays and projects – perhaps often between 1,500 and 4,000 words long, or dissertations which may be up to a length of 10,000 or 12,000 words.

I shall be thinking here particularly of occasions when you are invited to formulate your own topic or project, rather than those when you work to a tightly specified brief. Even then you may – and should – receive explicit guidelines about what is being looked for and valued. You should know by what criteria the essay is to be assessed. Particular courses will have their own aims, objectives and demands, while what's said here is, unavoidably, general.

This is not, of course, the only piece you might consult on this topic. For example, although my own emphases are partly different, there is a readable and valuable chapter 7, 'Media Research and Investigation', in O'Sullivan et al., *Studying the Media: An Introduction* (1998) which it would be useful to look at.

Work on media should involve you in many kinds of discovery and of pleasure. There are particular interests in finding out how something (whether it be a newspaper front page, a narrative, a photograph, a phone-in, a web page) is constructed, and how it works in detail. There are much broader intellectual interests in seeing how social and cultural issues are focused, shaped, refracted, represented (or distorted, 'mis'represented, ignored) through what media do. Because media are constantly expanding and proliferating and always changing, there is a great diversity of media forms and issues to investigate. Since research can rarely keep up with new developments, there are good opportunities for you to analyse material for the first time or in new ways. It is possible to look at very wide social changes, such as media and globalisation. Equally you could think about very personal stakes and investments, likes and dislikes in media as a way of exploring our own and others' identity (though we know that sociologists such as Bourdieu and Thornton have tried to analyse what determines these apparently private and distinctive tastes).

The other pleasure lies, or should lie, in ways of writing about all this. Essays are not researched and then simply and subsequently 'written up'. Essays are constructed, shaped and even discovered through the act of writing with words. This is an activity which has been transformed – almost entirely for the better – through the possibilities of the word processor. The craft and shape of writing itself, a pleasure and interest and pride in words, sentences, spelling, punctuation, verbal choices and possibilities are at the very centre of what this activity is all about.

I am looking, then, at planning an essay (see 'Planning and preparation' below); and at researching and writing an essay (see 'Areas of the writing and research' below). Planning, research and writing are all important, though the first two culminate in, or are realised only through, a writing process – which will take time, which in turn involves . . .

Planning and preparation

I will discuss some general aspects of planning an essay; then areas which the essay might be working through; issue a couple of cautions; suggest a possible shape for what you're writing; then comment on how best to end it. The skills here should take you on a continuum from undergraduate essays to projects to dissertation and into Master's work, which will interest some of you (and where these experiences of research will stand you in good stead).

It is worth saying (because it seems to be true) that realising best potential in many kinds of activity involves good organisation much much more (for better and for worse) than the interest, ability and motivation which most people have for most of the time (other problems aside). This section is based not only on reading many essays but also on working with students involved in planning and drafting essays, and working with them in discussing a range of study skills. Some people are taught such skills, some pick them up along the way, and some struggle with them. But everyone is able to improve their capacity to do work they're pleased with, and also to time! I hope these comments will be helpful and not obvious. If some of the suggestions are things you already take for granted, I'm glad.

Basics

A writer needs to hand a good dictionary, a thesaurus such as the most up-to-date edition of *Roget*, and a spell checker on screen. It's hard to see, given these facilities, why wrong spellings which can irritate a reader (or employer) should persist. However, even a checker will not pick up one of the most common and irritating mistakes, which involves it's (short for it is), its (belonging to something) and its' (which doesn't – or shouldn't! – exist). Of course it's (N.B.) the case that everything about a language is a matter of its (N.B.) conventions which you may think no more than (boringly) conventional. In practice though, just as sentences 'conventionally' start with a capital, as do proper names (though in fact bell hooks chooses not to do this with her own name), so an essay looks better for using good spelling and layout throughout. This includes paragraphs that aren't a page long: Manchester University Press advises its writers to 're-read each paragraph after writing it and try to clarify and tighten it up'.

A media studies writer could also do with having to hand at least a couple of the many volumes offering clarification of terms, concepts and key writers. There are several good choices to be made, including: for media, O'Sullivan *et al.* (1994 revised); for broader cultural and social terms, Brooker's excellent glossary (1999) or Payne (1996). For your own interest, enjoyment and self respect though, don't just pick up terms at second or third hand when the original writers can be looked at. 'Hegemony' is infinitely richer in the writings of Gramsci (1971); the 'codes' of 'encoding' and 'decoding' deserve tracing to Barthes (1977); writing about the cinematic 'gaze' stems from the complexity of Freud's work on sexuality and on scopophilia. See remarks further on about the introduction of 'theory' into media essays . . .

Timing

The work and time which a piece of writing will involve can be deduced backwards. It has to end by a deadline, but preferably – to avoid self-imposed stress, errors and lack of sleep – an essay can be planned (yes, it can) to be finished, even handed in, before that last minute of that last hour.

The essay is going to involve: planning a strategy for the work and an outline structure of the essay itself; finding materials; analysing them; time for rethinks, pauses, problems and for the unconscious to suggest improvements (it's often good to 'sleep on it', literally); time for rethinking, reworking and rewriting (with a dissertation, comments from other people if possible), which is invariably hugely beneficial. Given that you will be studying an industry with a complex production process, every stage of which has to be rigorously on time, why not treat your own writing as just such a process whose sequence deserves care and attention?

Topic

If the topic is broadly to be self defined, it needs to be both appropriate and productive. To be appropriate, always with regard to the purposes of the course or the assignment, it needs to be of a manageable scale, perhaps involving sharp decisions. Subjects such as 'the media and Kosovo', 'children in film', 'gender and media employment' are all rich areas for book-length or PhD studies. For an essay they are probably quite impossible. It has to be recognised that many excellent books are based on the study of hugely greater amounts of media output than you can deal with, or upon ethnographic observation or interview work over a much longer period of time than you can here possibly envisage. The chosen topic will need to provide the possibility for leading into a sharply focused close-up discussion of some kind, which goes beyond the very important discussion and critique of other writers and avoids writing only at a level of sustained generality. You should expect to be given real credit for finding a topic which is in that way manageable . . . and also productive. You might hope to look carefully into whether and in what ways a critical or theoretical term is helpful to your material. You could show how a particular media text is constructed and works, in detail. You might explain what a particular set of representations constructs or renders invisible. You could seek to understand the resonance of a genre, in detail, with as few as one or two people. In every case you might raise questions which are puzzling, or which might be returned to in other work (for instance, in a dissertation building upon an earlier essay). Both finding a focus for your essay and illuminating an issue through that focus involve serious decisions. The smaller the word length allowed, the sharper these decisions will become.

What kind of essay?

For your own satisfaction you will want to write different kinds of essay during a degree course. One kind of essay may concentrate on looking at a specific author's body of writing about media or at the usefulness and complexities of a specific concept. Another might be concerned with the close study of media texts. A third might try to clarify a complex body of media policy, regulation or law. Another kind again might concentrate on what media users do with or say about the media they use. Elsewhere you might look at the media's role within a particular political debate; or at the place of media within globalisation, or a couple of households; or at ways in which the media are involved in social difference, or in the construction of sexualities, or in the development of ideas of citizenship, or of 'Europe' . . .

These various essays are typically going to involve looking for rather, or very, different kinds of source and material: various ranges of reading in both books and journals; different degrees of study of media texts; at other times autobiographical reflection, or a study of a family, or an effort to seek a particular person for a conversation or interview.

Each essay will also involve a consideration of the balance between two poles. In most cases there will be some comment on some part of the media's output as a particular cultural form. A close analysis will involve looking at: *what* it is (descriptive in an important and valuable sense); *why* it is (at levels from the technical or economic to the ideological); and perhaps *what else* it might have been and why it wasn't (speculative, but often useful and stimulating for ideas). There will in most cases also be some comment on larger cultural and social issues such as identity, or nationalism, or ideas of norms, boundaries and exceptions as they are constructed through news (or sit com or soaps). Essays may be concerned more with one pole than with the other, or seek to balance both; for example, as Ang (1985) – though at book length – connects a particular US drama series with the form of melodrama and then with both feminism and the workings of fantasy.

In real life these two issues and the choices they involve – of topic, of scale, of materials, of emphasis – present themselves simultaneously, untidily, pragmatically, creatively. You'll develop quite quickly (because you'll have to!) some sense of the kind of essay you want to write. You'll think about what you'll need to do it. You'll consider what time and what initiatives the parts of the process will involve. You'll formulate what you're broadly trying to find out or explore that you don't already know. Finding that out involves a learning which, if at times difficult, should be interesting and enjoyable. So too should be the partly subsequent but partly also simultaneous writing itself.

Areas of the writing and research

Setting a context and a framework
This section of your essay or dissertation is in effect a necessity, whereas those which follow involve choices you might make. It is important in showing that you have done relevant reading and research on your topic, and in suggesting issues which may be taken up in the body of what you write.

Unfortunately this section is commonly misunderstood. It is sometimes seen as setting up a 'hypothesis' to be examined or tested, a model from a version of natural science which is rarely helpful or appropriate. More often it is seen as 'the theory section' (or even 'the theory bit'!). This version of 'theory' is one to get rid of. It sets up a dichotomy between theory and analysis (or, on courses with production components, theory and practice) which puts 'theory' on a perch or pedestal. It then separates off analysis or practice as though they don't themselves also involve, as of course they do, at every point, ideas! Nor is it the case that you will somehow necessarily acquire credit or prestige by the citation of major 'names'.

It's a different matter, of course, should a particular assignment actually require you to reflect upon, or consider with respect to an example, a particular model of how media work (e.g. the 'three paradigms' discussed by Stevenson (1995)). It is not, however normally the main point of this section of an essay to 'have a theory', not least because – for many things you might work on – such theories might be extremely general or, in a worthwhile way which generates thoughts about your subject, not yet exist. There are indeed theories of various sorts, but it might be better to think about, and to use instead, the word 'ideas'.

I suggest that this section should not be 'the theory section' but instead do three other things. First, the topic should, if possible, be set in its historical context. Some of this history, which you may be able to refer to only briefly, is a larger social history. Examples might be: the patterns of migration and diaspora which led to settlements in Britain or the USA and the subsequent focus upon something signified as 'race'; the boundaries between the able and 'disabled' which exist in employment and through everyday life as well as in representation; and the New Right ideology which produced deregulation and many of the current tangles in organisational practice and media policy. Some of the history is more closely linked to media themselves, if always in connection with other determinations and with cultural, social and political change. Examples would include the evolution, for financial and a host of other reasons, of phone-ins and talk shows; shifting conventions in the practices of news; and new forms of situation comedy or of sports coverage. Media are very much 'of their time' and times change (I earlier cited Ang on *Dallas* – might that series in fact now need for you an explanatory footnote?). The social world and media change together, at bewildering speed. Indeed, only a few of the media histories we could do with as yet exist. Even so, whatever your subject, it doesn't come from nowhere and setting an appropriate (media specific) and larger (social) context will be useful.

Second, you should read some of what other people have thought and said about your topic and review this. For some topics the literature may be overwhelming and you will have to select drastically; for others you may be hard put to find a couple of articles. Either way, credit will be given for your selection, or for the difficulty of working in a new area. Such work by other people may give you different things: insights (e.g. Williams); suggestive models (e.g. Dyer); various kinds of research strategy (e.g. Radway); exhaustive analysis of a neglected topic (e.g. Cottle); perhaps detailed information. You should show that you know and can summarise some of this work but you should also, especially at dissertation length, look at it critically. Published work is not authoritative or true just because it is published. Rather, like your own essay, it's the result of somebody with a distinctive personal and political agenda using particular resources and a particular research strategy, and so is open to discussion and critique. By all means in your own essay cite, examine and deconstruct a sentence or paragraph really closely and work out its implications – and perhaps its contradictions . . .

Third, you will want to introduce what you are distinctively doing and how you are going to do it. Use other writers, 'theoretical' or otherwise, in dialogue with your particular research. Say which of their concerns you will develop or – especially in a dissertation – what they have not looked at at all which you have yourself chosen to do. In other words, suggest what issues and ways of going about things have interested other writers and locate your own work in dialogue with theirs. Present your purposes and strategy; explain why you chose them; suggest why they will be appropriate and productive for the topic. *(cont. p. 314)*

Models

Models and theories
The human brain is a living machine for creating representations of reality. Good representations of reality have a survival value for their creators. If your representations are bad, you and your progeny won't survive for very long. If they are really good, you may live long and replenish the Earth. It is generally agreed, however, that no representations of this kind are really 'true'. Indeed, as the eighteenth-century German philosopher, Immanuel Kant, showed, we shall never grasp *'das Ding an sich'* – the thing itself. But it seems we can get close enough to survive. And if from two different perspectives you get much the same representation of the phenomenon under study, this is generally held to be a sign that there is something to the two representations. The more different the perspectives, the more valuable the agreement. Thus, to the extent that representations created by deadly enemies agree, there may be something to them. Presumably, the lion and the gazelle do not agree about very much, but the two must have fairly similar representations of the savannah and the wind, of smells and sounds and many other phenomena vital to both of them. Otherwise they wouldn't survive. Similarly, if less dramatically, when two scholars representing two otherwise different research traditions agree about something, chances are that that is the way it is.

When scholars and scientists argue about the world, they discuss three things: (1) observations (often called data); (2) the way observations are to be made (often called methods); and (3) the way the observations or data are to be understood (often called theory and/or model). In such discussions, it is absolutely vital that they be as explicit as possible. A precondition for maximum explicitness is that the discussants heed the distinction between substantive theory and formal model (see also Part I).

Both theories and models are abstract in the sense that characteristics of reality considered to be irrelevant to the ongoing discussion are neglected. The difference between the two is that theories are, by definition, substantive, in the sense that they deal with something which is taken to exist in the real world. Models are much more abstract than theories. They are so abstract, indeed, that they are substantively empty. In principle, that is, they are *absolutely formal*. There are three interrelated languages in terms of which absolutely formal ideas may be expressed and discussed: logics, mathematics and statistics. In order better to understand the sometimes complex argumentation carried out in these three languages, it is often visualised in terms of graphical models. Sometimes these, too, are very complex. But, in principle at least, the simpler the better. 'As simple as possible, as complex as necessary' – that is the catchphrase for both models and theories.

The simplest possible graphical model consists of two boxes, one called *x*, the other *y*, with a one-directional arrow going from the x box to the y box. A corresponding logical, mathematical or statistical model may be written thus: $y = f(x)$. Each in their own way, the two types of model tell us that there is a relationship between x and y. The box model says that variable *x* influences variable *y;* the equation model, that *y* is a function of *x* (i.e. as *x* varies, so varies *y*).

Since models are so general, they fit in with a lot of substantive theories. For instance, the two examples given above – the box and arrow model, and the equation – could be used to discuss the influence of television viewing on small children, expressing, say, a hypothesis that television viewing affects children's behaviour, so that they tend to become more boisterous or aggressive. Their boisterousness is thus a function of their TV viewing. Or they could refer to communication in groups or organisations, expressing, for instance, a hypothesis that the larger the group, the more formalised the communication (type of communication as a function of size of group). And so on.

Since the formal models are substantively empty, their operation is not affected by the substantive content of the various theories. This is a great advantage: the models offer a way of dealing with tricky, sometimes highly controversial, problems in a very detached way, as unaffected as possible by the often controversial substantive contents of the theories. The substantive theories, in contrast, are often couched in verbal language which is notorious for its ambiguity – even among specialists using a language replete with highly standardised terminology. Verbally expressed substantive theories, that is, are more ambiguous than the formal models. On the other hand, they are as a rule more directly related to our observations of reality as we experience it and can measure it in terms of various types of data. The best way to carry out scholarly and scientific studies, then, is to relate to each other these three elements: (1) data about reality, (2) substantive theories, and (3) formal models. As a matter of fact, if we use only two of these three elements in our scholarly endeavour as a whole, we will be severely hampered (although we won't be using all three all of the time). The combination of formal models and data is almost impossible. For how could you relate substantive data to substantively completely empty formal models? You will always need some substantive theory to do that. A better combination is data and substantive theories, but in the long run you may be seriously handicapped by the fact that you will not be able to analyse the data in the precise way which, in their clarity and unambiguousness, only formal models admit.

The combination of substantive theories and formal models is good for theoretical work. By means of the formal models you will be able better to analyse the logical and/or statistical structure of your problems for internal consistency. You may also be able to get some new substantive ideas from the interplay between theory and model. But unless you incorporate also empirical data in order to test the specified hypotheses derived from your substantive theories by means of the formal models, you can never definitively tell whether your hypotheses are false or not. Sometimes elements from the formal model and some empirical data are inserted into the graphical model that visualises it, thus blending elements of theory, model and data in the same representation.

Similarly, tables are built from the different elements. The principles here are easily grasped but many students do not stop and think about what is going on in even a simple table. Look at table 2, for instance. The table tells us how many female and male Swedes there are in three age categories

Table 2 Gender and age in a national population (Sweden), (numbers in thousands)

Age	Gender			
	Male		Female	
	Number	%	Number	%
0–24	1402	32	1335	30
25–64	2268	53	2204	50
65–	651	15	885	20
Total	4321	100	4424	100

(roughly, childhood and youth, middle age and old age). The absolute numbers represent a purely descriptive way of organising data. Not much theory there, is there? Well, already the very variables used in the simplest of tables are always imbedded, implicitly or explicitly, in a theory of sorts. In this case the basic elements in that embryonic theory are the two variables constituting the table: age and gender. How are these variables related to each other?

Obviously, age can hardly affect gender, while gender may affect age or, let us say, length of life. Age, then, is the *dependent variable*, while gender is the *independent variable*. Men and women may have differently long lives to live. Some information about whether that is so may be gained from the percentages also included in the table. We see that although there are relatively more male than female Swedes in the early age groups, it is the opposite in older age, where there are more women than men. Age seems to be a function of gender, then, in the sense that women tend to live longer than men. In the table, this is made manifest by the fact that the percentages are calculated in the direction of the independent variable, not the other way round. If we want to be more precise, the strength of this influence may be expressed in a single coefficient. (There are quite a number of such coefficients that can be derived from statistical techniques; see, for example, Deacon et al., 1999:88–92.) Also note that from a purely formal point of view (where we are not thinking about the 'contents' of these categories but just taking them as formal variables), gender may also be a function of age. From a purely formal point of view, that is, we could have calculated the percentages in the other direction, too. But that does not make much sense in a substantive theory, does it (men are hardly more likely to become women as they grow older are they, notwithstanding the medical possibility of sex changes)? So we discard this formal possibility. We thus realise again that it takes both substantive theory and formal model really to understand empirical data. The relationship between gender and length of life may seem to be a rather simple one. But actually it is a very tricky problem indeed. It takes biological, psychological and sociological theory really to understand it. When we move on to consider problems of media use, influence, and so on, we are dealing with even trickier areas, but understanding how to 'model' problems of this sort is an important first step.

Karl Erik Rosengren

Communication models

In the sciences a good model for a complex system or process identifies the main *elements*, and *relationships* among the elements, that make up the system or process.

In particular, the good model identifies *functional* relationships – what these elements actually do, in which sequence or in some other regulated combination – thereby allowing the observer at least to describe, if not explain, even control, the behaviour of the system as a whole. A model of the communication process, therefore, might identify elements such as source, channel, code, message and destination (note that some of these imply relationships), and functions such as encoding, transmission, reception and decoding.

A good model simplifies, by focusing on what is general if not universal across many different examples of the system or process being studied and many different situations in which specific examples function or behave in specific ways. It therefore tends to ignore exceptions, deviations and special cases. These will be of limited type and number if the model is a good one. To the extent that there are omissions and approximations, any model will be an incomplete representation. The more the modeller tries to capture and include, the more unwieldy and unperspicuous the model becomes.

Models typically represent graphically the elements concerned, in two or three dimensions, and relationships among them are often represented mathematically. Computer models, used, for example, in laboratory testing a new design, are not only three dimensional and mathematically modelled, they may also be dynamic, if the programming allows for simulations of diverse and changing circumstances. They are not models of some existing state of affairs, but construct an *imagined* (in modern terms, virtual) reality which helps us, in various senses, to realise the possibilities.

Lastly, models are essentially metaphorical, or iconic in semiotic terms. They work by creating representations that *resemble* in essentials the immanent elements and structural–functional relationships within some system or process.

By manipulating models, therefore, we can find out about the real world, rather than squander resources in blind trial and error. We can imagine and invent new realities, for example in the genetic engineering of plants or in the creation and use of new construction materials.

We can also, using models, invent new and wholly imaginary dimensions of experience more or less divorced from material reality. The organisational model for a system such as a manufacturing business will typically only approximate to what really happens, not only because it leaves out a lot of detail but because it is a distortion, perhaps deliberately so, in the interests of those publishing the misrepresentation (probably not the workforce). Further into fiction, albeit useful fiction, might be Freud's model for the

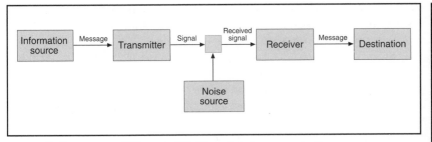

Figure 17 Shannon and Weaver's (1949) model of communication

systems and processes of mental life, or the models we use for political systems and processes (e.g. the body politic and related sub-metaphors, such as 'arm' of the law, 'head' of state).

Stressing the representational, hence imaginative and inventive, dimensions of models and modelling should not obscure the suspicion felt towards all models by scholars in the human and social disciplines. This has various sources. Models are the natural first step towards problem solving in many of the mathematicised, 'scientific' disciplines, which are frequently stigmatised by scholars elsewhere as (among other defects) antithetical to the imagination and irrelevant to its products. These products, so the argument goes, are characterised by idiosyncrasy and originality, generated by essentially mysterious systems and processes (talent, creativity) forever beyond the modeller, or any other form of explanation. Postmodern theorists, hostile not only to science but to the entire programme of rational progress embodied in the Enlightenment and in modernism, cleaving to the particular, the anomalous and the unreconcilable, are especially repelled by the generalising and positive features of modelling: revealing the essential, 'scientific' truth about how a dimension of reality works, mostly or even universally, is anathema to them. Equally, the idea that a model may specify how things *ought* to be or work (a model is something we are expected or required to follow) does not commend itself to those in permanent opposition to established ways and wisdoms.

All of the concerns above are raised by the most famous model of communication in the literature, the Shannon Model of 1948 (see Shannon and Weaver, 1949, and figure 17; also MacKay, 1972). Shannon's early work was carried out in the laboratories of the Bell Corporation, a US telecommunications conglomerate. He was concerned with maximising the efficiency with which electronic signals could be transmitted from one point to another in a system, such as a telephone exchange. His work was scientific in the sense that he developed a particular form of applied statistics, known as 'information theory'. This caused great excitement among social and behavioural scientists at a time when the fashion was to 'scientise' these disciplines (see McQuail and Windahl, 1981; Heath and Bryant, 1992).

This model has been widely used and much criticised, as has Lasswell's not dissimilar, contemporaneous, summary: Who says what to whom through what channel with what purpose and effect (Lasswell, 1948). Linear, static, mechanistic and one-way models privileging action by the source, such as

Shannon's and Lasswell's, were quickly supplemented by two-way, dynamic 'process' models stressing interaction (not necessarily collaborative), interpretation and the negotiation of meaning (Berlo, 1977).

To produce a perspicuous and tidy diagrammatic representation of these more and more inclusive accounts of 'communication' is very difficult and few serious attempts have been made in recent times. This should serve to remind us that a model is, above all, an abstract simplification, a set of starting points for investigation. That investigation should be reflexive in the sense that good models display their own shortcomings as clearly as they depict the key elements and relationships of the system or process to which they refer. It should also be reflexive in the sense that innocent-seeming labels for elements, functions and relationships may conceal highly contentious assumptions.

Bill Scott

Working on media texts

The word 'text' is not straightforward and in some ways we know it to be deceptive. You or I can listen or see or read in certain ways, but others may do so quite differently. Dahlgren commented that the text is 'polysemic; offering an array of possible readings . . . [T]o analyse meaning is to take aim at a moving target' (1992:207). Similarly, Radway came to ask how her own account and analyses of romance fictions looked alongside those obtained – through a variety of research strategies – from a number of women reading them. Still, for the moment let's assume that the 'text' as produced through a process by a media organisation is in some sense available to be analysed; and is of potential interest. Should you think of looking at texts, the obvious questions are: how much to look at, and in what way?

The answers to these questions are connected. You might, for instance, want to consider a content analysis of the kind which is excellently presented in O'Sullivan *et al.* (1998) or by Konczal in chapter 17 of this volume. This analysis will require a sample of some scale in order to be significant. If you do not use content analysis (the problems of which you will realise) then you will, in the length you have (a dissertation is more than an essay), want to get at some detail through a close analysis. You will also want to feel that your examples are not idiosyncratic or unique (though that might make them interesting in other ways). There are no definable rules or procedures here. You will want probably several examples but not to be overwhelmed by too many of them. These could be episodes, or contrasted instances from different films, newspapers or radio channels, which give you some feeling for the flow and range of how what you're looking at is handled. At the same time, close attention to spoken language in radio, or to written language in newspapers, or to the ways in which photographs signify, will certainly require significant time, space and detail. The balance of range, contrasts and very thorough analysis is to be considered with care.

You will find ideas on various ways of carrying out such an analysis in the reading which you do. Try, though, to set up headings which encourage you to think in depth about your material. By way of example, think of how news is reported. Here five areas of questions will take you a long way into what is going on:

1 *Selection*: what news items have been selected, how have they been relatively weighted, how juxtaposed?

2 *Visualisation*: how (in print or on television) are events represented visually, what has been visually selected for attention and how has the visual been given a verbal framing which offers a preferred meaning?

3 *Voices*: who gets to speak, and what voices are used with what relative weight?

4 *Language*: what kinds of language are used, what kinds of sentence, what metaphors, with what kind of address to the listener or reader or viewer?

5 *Explanations*: what explanations for events are given, and whose accounts of what causes, meanings and significance are offered?

There is also, for any example and not just news, a sixth set of questions – *what is not represented*: what other forms of representation or ways of constructing this text might there have been – and why, here, was it so and not otherwise? Whatever you do in this way, give your reasons positively – and reflect in a last section of the essay about your choices.

Finding out about media production

In practice this is not easy to do. Much of what goes on, whether in the public service or commercial sectors (despite our 'democratic society'!) is not very accountable and not simple to get at. You are unlikely, while a student, to have the good fortune to work for any length of time inside a media organisation. If you do you are richly placed to see and think about what goes on. More likely you may possibly be able to talk to somebody who works in media, preferably in a recorded interview of up to about an hour. Try to ignore the fact that your interviewee may be a greatly experienced interviewer – it might provoke in them a wish to help!

You should set up any interview (another example would be with media users) in much the same way. Make sure that your audio recorder is working and if need be test it with the interviewee – it is part of the process, not an embarrassment. Take with you – and again, why conceal this which only the most experienced of interviewers would try to do – a card or sheet with some main headings you hope to address. Don't phrase these as set questions to be woodenly read out: do improvise on the spot, in a way which feels appropriate, the wording of main questions and follow-up questions. Don't start with a difficult or general question which may have the interviewee on the defensive ('how can you possibly justify spending time working on ——'): do begin by asking about the person's background and how it led to the present job. This, after all, is a conversation in which you are interested, with another person you should be directly looking at (rather than anxiously at the recording level or at your notes).

If the direction of the discussion (in which you can be equal, not just a 'neutral' questioner) isn't one you expected, don't over-control it since the 'tangents' may prove unexpectedly rich. At the same time, don't encourage a monologue, and make it politely clear that there are other issues you want to address or get back to. Don't be too thrown or bothered if the answers seem to be to a different question, or if an issue is evaded or refused, since you will later be able to reflect upon this in the light of Willis (1980:92) 'Why are these things happening? Why has the subject behaved in this way? Why do certain areas remain obscure to the researcher? . . . It is time to ask and explore, to discover the differences between subjective positions . . . a time of maximum disturbance to researchers, whose own meanings are being thoroughly contested'. The whole of Willis's essay, though difficult, is worth reading.

Some of those working in the media will be able to talk with insight and in detail about their work: but by no means all. What may be hardest to get beyond is the 'common sense' or 'intuitive feel' about why things are done as they are. 'It's a good picture'; 'that was the right story to lead on'; 'this was the strong theme we needed'; 'the audience wouldn't take to it'. . . In these cases, rather than show your frustration (there are areas of what we all do which we take for granted and can't imagine otherwise) try other tacks. Suggest another way it could have been done and ask for reactions, or ask how differently things might have gone in a different context. Persevere. Getting to the ideas which those in media organisations themselves have about their work is rarely done, challenging and highly valuable.

Working on uses made of media

This is an area with a rich potential for satisfying, and at times original, research, and for the exploration of research strategies. This is partly because of the centrality of media to everyday life and to the discussion of most social issues, and partly from the usually willing readiness of those who use media to talk about them.

Research could investigate investments in, and attachments to, particular media forms; the media's role in lives and in households; responses to, and uses of, the media as technologies (see Gray, 1992); memories and recall of media in general or media-specific oral histories and autobiographies; talk about media; and people's critiques of media and suggestions for change.

Again, the question is not only who to talk to but to how many. Again, this is related to time and to length but good material will take time to produce, report on and analyse: six good interview discussions might be enough or more than enough. Once again, the point, purpose and selection and their rationale should be positively set out. Opinions could be sought through casually prompted discussions, even overheard conversations; through interviews including group interviews; or on occasion be prompted by an invitation from a local newspaper or through a particular group you might contact and seek views from. Internet discussion forums can also be useful, particularly if investigating fans. There is great interest in seeking out a group you have little connection with, but you could also draw upon a group you have (or had) contact with and where you have a good sense of what's involved and at stake.

Don't ask questions which are too general, or which sound like an examination paper, or which you might struggle to answer yourself ('so just why do you like this soap opera?'). Instead, prompt and listen to a flow of discussion, as Buckingham (1987) did. Try to locate media use, and opinions refracted through media or directly about the media, within people's lives and experiences (see the study by Pursehouse, 1997). Treat your respondents primarily as people living particular lives in distinctive ways, and only within that as members of an 'audience'. You may also want to test – or invent – particular methods such as what recall people have of media coverage: for this and other ideas see, for instance, Philo (1990).

In analysing this material and reflecting upon it, remember to 'put yourself in the picture', as Walkerdine (1986) did so memorably (and as others have also done fruitfully); interviewing is a relationship and a social process of a distinctive kind. Remember the remarks by Willis about what is at stake in 'mis'understanding. Look at the essays by Frazer (1992) and by Dahlgren (1992) which show in what different ways, in what different linguistic 'registers', the same person might be able to discuss the same issue. Think all the time about what kind of occasion, process and relationship produced these particular views. Cite interviews and draw issues from them – but don't, don't, normally attempt the gigantic labour of transcribing them.

A couple of cautions!
There are two things to be more wary of. You may quickly think you need information or ideas or leads which you can't get from a library or on your own. You may want to try *making contact* with an individual or group or organisation. You may think of writing them a letter asking them to contact you, or to give you materials or opinions. If so, be aware that there are long odds against this being productive. Larger organisations and individuals in senior positions may receive many such letters and have neither the time nor the inclination or motivation to reply. It is very easy to put a request for help from an unknown person (particularly if it involves some thought) to the bottom of a things-to-do pile. A friendlier and more colloquial email, if you can get the right address, may ease the situation, though not necessarily.

You should normally expect to gain help of this kind by making personal contact – possibly a phone call, more usually a face-to-face request, if necessary with the 'front desk' person – to engage interest, sympathy and support. You might perhaps also make it clear that you can be politely persistent! Cases vary, but while it is often extremely easy to disregard an anonymous written request it is less common to want to refuse help to an individual caller.

More problematic still is a common resource for essay writers: *the questionnaire*. There are many clear guides to the construction of questionnaires in media research, including that in O'Sullivan *et al.* (1998:335–9). An essay writer may feel that the questionnaire provides some relatively 'hard' evidence and that it constitutes without doubt a known research method. Perhaps, but there are good reasons to be wary and sparing about their use in an essay of limited length.

Questionnaires are normally held to have two main strengths. Carefully constructed, they can provide a 'representative' sample of the attitudes or actions of a wide range of people. This, though, means using questionnaires on a scale quite beyond the time capacity of an essay. Questionnaires are also at their best in providing more factual evidence, allowing for correlations between, say, choice of newspaper and age or social class. Yet many of the issues likely to interest us, about values and meanings and investments in media use, are inherently almost impossible to put into questionnaire form or to be usefully answered in that mode.

In addition, you would have to motivate potential respondents to go through what is, after all, rather like an examination and not necessarily a very interesting one. You presumably cannot offer prizes; you cannot, or probably should not, 'doorstep' people's houses; you would be hard put to take respondents through a questionnaire in the street. These problems, and the typically low rate of return for questionnaires, risk your ending up with a small number of frankly not very interesting answer sheets from a quite definitely, even absurdly, limited group of people.

If a questionnaire is to be useful to you at all, you should be reasonably sure that, for whatever reason, you will get a high rate of return – and that the answers will give you one or both of two things. The first would probably be some mainly factual material (e.g. you persuade a youth group leader to get the group to tell you what access to the internet they have and, if you can achieve frankness, what use they make of it). The second, probably more fruitful, use would be to identify a small number of people who might be worth talking to in a much more detailed way on specific issues for particular reasons. I once asked a large group of people to write down the titles or subjects of the three documentaries they remembered most clearly from the past few years, with intrinsically interesting results which also suggested which of them I might want to talk to further.

Otherwise, the main interest of the questionnaire in media studies is to try and get at how questionnaires are used in society for various purposes, including market research on media, and to note how media reporting may make highly selective use of questionnaire evidence. The questionnaire matters as a cultural form and as a strategic organisational tool – but in researching for an essay, its value has to be limited and its effective use very carefully considered.

An outline and a shape

Writers vary and their habits vary. Still, having considered a topic and what kind of essay you are writing, you will know what kinds of area you want to cover and where to start looking for, or constructing, relevant resources. You will need a rough working outline or chart of the issues you're following up. There are some people who acquire the ability (even taking lecture notes in this way) to construct 'spider charts' (also called 'pattern notes' or even 'mind maps'), where boxes or circles link across to others and the topic's range is shown as a set of connections in a mosaic (something I just cannot do!). Others will construct a more linear set of headings with subheadings beneath, fitting their reading and research to these headings as they go.

Use whichever of these works, but try to use one of them (or your own ingenious third way). It shows, to bad effect, if a writer 'just starts', plunges in and on and, with material whirling throughout, abruptly just stops. It's painful, too, when people with good ideas and material end up rather helplessly juggling with it, uncertain which points are main and which secondary, 'not seeing the wood for the trees'.

Good and helpful working practice will almost certainly involve making, and as need be revising, a short (at the very most two page) outline of topics, issues and details of each, in some kind of order. This will get revised in the light of reading and research – in the case of dissertations, probably revised many times. Alongside this there could be a small notebook (perhaps a research diary or learning log, which some courses now use as a form of assessment) or ideas sheet – perhaps kept in the bathroom, perhaps by the bed – where other issues, ideas, thoughts, that don't yet obviously 'fit in' and may or may not become relevant, are recorded.

From this beginning stage you will be envisaging the likely shape of the essay itself. Here I rather take the word processor for granted, as an investment and because it should significantly enable your writing (except those cut-and-pasted bits you should remember not to repeat – it happens!). You are able to construct sentences and chunks of the essay in draft in the course of research, not all at once when the research is finished. This helps take pressure off, especially with the amount of material you will have gathered for a dissertation. It also brings home – to repeat a remark made at the beginning of this piece – that much is discovered and made sense of during writing which happens through and in (not before or outside) the writing process. If we all write 'but not all see themselves as writers' it might help to do what writers often do – that is, write on a regular basis: research is in part, but importantly, constituted in and through the writing process.

Essays and their shapes vary too. Still, there is often a typical shape (this is, after all, a genre!) once you've looked also at the stated assessment criteria:

- Whether or not you prefer an 'Introduction' so labelled, the opening of the essay should say what its topic is; probably why it was chosen (including, if you wish, your personal reasons – the essay has an author who is 'coming from somewhere' after all); and why the topic matters. You will want to explain briefly your purpose and what you're trying to do – and outline the essay's structure (perhaps with subheads later) to guide the reader (and yourself).
- The topic doesn't come from nowhere: as I suggested earlier, it needs to be framed within several contexts, historical and intellectual, so that your own approach is located next to other work. This will involve saying what you chose to do (perhaps among various strategies you considered and lay out briefly).
- You will want to bring forward the substantive material on which you're basing the essay. This will be as full and detailed an exploration as possible, if possible always using at times a close focus on something quite particular.
- Out of such analysis and interpretation there should be developed the issues which arise, inferences and evaluations you want to make, if possible something of a distinctive and clear argument. There is a place for good and careful description (particularly of what may have been little written about before); for interpretation and evaluation and analysis; and then for taking a point of view which is your own.

- The essay can productively close with a very useful end section, which I discuss as my own way of ending this essay in a moment.
- There should of course be a bibliography or, since more than the written word is involved, a list of references. Those to video materials, to radio programmes, to web site sources, newsgroups or emails, to interviews you've carried out and recorded, can be cited in any way that's clear and consistent (subject to consulting course or departmental style sheets): this is a new area where the 'Harvard' and other style sheets haven't caught up with new media. If a press article, video extract, internet discussion room exchange or section of an interview are really central to your essay and analysed in detail, it's helpful to include them (if you can do this without being too cumbersome) with the essay.
- There is occasionally a place for an informative footnote on an issue you think worth referring to though not central to the essay; occasionally too for an appendix containing information (an internal memorandum, a packed email) which is worth keeping – particularly if not readily found elsewhere. This might be true especially given the length of an investigative dissertation which has come across new or inaccessible source materials, which others might treat as a resource.
- Otherwise a dissertation is not likely to differ in kind from an essay or project, though at every point more so developed: a fuller account of other writers; a more nuanced account of the research strategy and process; a more developed substantial section; and a fuller concluding section.

Reflections and conclusions

Not mine on this occasion – but what you should want to do towards the end of your own essay (allowing proper space for this in your planning of word lengths). This section is strangely often ignored or, because of time, reduced to a minimal (and often slightly pointless) recapitulation of what the essay has already said. You should allow some space here, not for a cursory afterthought, but to look back on and think about what you've done.

Consider further issues and questions which arose but you did not have time and space to pursue (as you certainly didn't) but which might be followed in other work. Reflect upon the problems which arose, which all research has, and present them not defensively but in a positive way, showing what was learned from them. A dissertation writer who took three months failing, despite hard work, to obtain a single interview she wanted, later wrote about this with great insight. In this section even the most fraught of experiences can be put to fruitful use!

Above all, *treat your research itself as a social process of interest* which can be thought about. Think back on what happened (and what else was necessarily omitted and couldn't happen) through the particular mode of research which you chose. If you did or tried something distinctive, assert and argue this with verve. Then (because you've made time for this) re-read, get other comments and rewrite.

320   Good luck with your research. Enjoy writing it!

Stop and think

How do we make knowledge?

OK, more manageably, how do we make knowledge about the media? Part II was concerned with how the media themselves are deeply implicated in the construction of public knowledge. This book as a whole is concerned to support the construction of knowledge within media studies as pedagogical practice and as a form of learning. But you, as a reader, are concerned independently with making your own knowledge about the media. Stop and think about how this is done, about the process of knowledge construction and some of its key features.

Where does knowledge come from? What resources do you need to make it? What principles are involved? Let's take a few specifics in order to highlight what's at stake in this.

Content analysis has been much maligned among many on the 'textualist' side of media studies – those mostly concerned with interpreting texts. They have argued that it produces crude knowledge, raw quantifications of things that really need subtle interpretation. But, in fact, content analysis is more usefully thought of in terms of levels of knowledge construction in media studies, where a base level of fairly raw, but potentially informative, data is often needed to ground the interpreter's more subtle attempts to read media texts for their multiplicities of meaning. It isn't always the case, of course, that specific studies have to start with content analysis, but media studies as a field would do well to remember that the content analysts are producing often highly reliable evidence of a particular sort, especially where we wish to fill in our models and theories with empirical detail (as we should more often than we do, perhaps). Indeed, a 'textualist' can tie him- or herself up in all kinds of knot trying to explain something that suddenly becomes clear, if on a simpler level, from a good piece of content analysis. Content analysis here means categorising and then quantifying the occurrences of particular media content. So a content analyst might count the number of occurrences in a large number of western movies of a 'professional group' of protagonists (think of *El Dorado* or *The Wild Bunch*). It is, of course, much more interesting in many ways to interpret a filmic text in detail, but it helps to know how common such a feature is in the genre as a whole. Indeed, such information can be used to locate the genre against its social background and to periodise its development. (Wright (1975) did exactly that to good effect.)

So content analysis illustrates something important about the construction of knowledge in media studies. It is frequently useful to have large-scale, reliable data about significant categories of media content. That we so often do without such data leaves media studies open to the charge of over-reliance on interpretive analyses that on occasion can be little more than guesswork. Even intelligent, or theoretically informed, guesswork can gain from being grounded, where appropriate, in some raw data; especially when those data actually confound taken-for-granted assumptions or add their own complexity to a situation where interpretive presuppositions turn out to be oversimplifications (as perhaps with the representation of minorities in the USA, see chapter 17).

In addition to some raw but reliably gathered data, media studies often finds itself deploying some existing explanatory framework, model or theory. It is an important principle (not always followed) of knowledge construction that such things should be explicitly presented, not just wheeled on as a *deus ex machina*, and preferably presented in relation to any significant alternatives that may also be available in the circumstances.

Further, media studies almost always finds itself having to consider *institutions*. If it fails to do so, the results are frequently so much the poorer. Consideration of institutions does not always have to occupy the foreground, of course, but there are few occasions when it will not supply at least some informative background details. So it's helpful to know that Kieślowski's film *La double vie de Véronique*, an 'art cinema' favourite and splendidly receptive to the textualist's closest attentions, was part financed by the French TV channel CANAL+, whose 1991 annual report describes its film financing initiatives as securing 'an optimum match between programming supply and consumer demand': so we would want to think about how Kieślowski's film was, in a sense, designed to match a demand for 'art cinema' of this kind among a particular socio-economic group of CANAL+ viewers.

Finally, constructing knowledge in media studies will involve a scrupulous avoidance of unsupported generalisations (the student's most frequent failing, it has to be said). The right to make generalisations has to be earned, by precisely the sorts of careful work we are proposing here. But, once properly supported, generalisations become themselves a key feature of knowledge production. Victor Sampedro's chapter on the Spanish anti-military movement and its treatment by the media is offered here as exemplary in this regard (see chapter 18): it moves from theoretical models to content analysis to consideration of institutional factors to generalisations. The serious student of the media needs to stop and think about how this can be achieved – it's the difference between scholarship and guesswork. In particular, Victor Sampedro demonstrates how to combine a content analysis and a historical account with substantive theory capable of explaining the media's role in a significant example of political and social change.

17

Content analysis

Lisa Konczal

Content analysis collects various forms of communication, including newspapers, journals, television, radio and the internet, and quantifies it into units that can be recorded and counted (Krippendorff, 1980; Harless, 1985; Priest, 1996). As an analytical tool, it can itself take on many forms depending on the research question involved and the form of communication being analysed (Barken and Gurevitch, 1991). In general, content analysis is a research method for making inferences by systematically analysing frequencies of media or other content. Like any proper component of a study, it should retain a strong sense of the importance of relating a particular analytical component, such as frequency counts, to all other areas of the research question. In that respect, good content analysis should be both statistical and ethnographical. At its best, it is both quantitative and qualitative (although often dismissed by qualitative researchers as mere 'counting').

If recorded matter on a research question exists, content analysis could well be the best method of collecting data to investigate it. Like any research method, content analysis should be systematic or should follow certain procedures that can feasibly be repeated for other samples or populations. Although content analysis has taken various forms, the general technique can be summarised using five steps, after selecting a research question. These steps are: choosing a sample, defining categories, reading and coding, analysing data, and making inferences and drawing conclusions based on patterns. To illustrate the steps of content analysis, this summary will use a research question posed by a group of researchers in Miami: What are the recent images being portrayed by the local print media in South Florida about Hispanic immigrants?

Choosing a sample

As noted above, there are various forms of media that can be sampled. Obviously, it would have to be an accessible form – ideal is a collection of material that the researcher might obtain through an electronic database in a library, for example. Since the research question here specifies 'printed news' as the communication source, the 'population' is all available newspapers in South Florida. The *Miami Herald* was chosen not only because of accessibility, but also because it is a widely read publication (Soruco, 1996).

Following the selection of the media source, it is necessary to choose para-meters to limit the sample of articles, such as with time lines and units of analysis. Again, referring to the research question is key. In this example the researchers inquired about *recent* articles (from the previous two years) and selected articles only about Cubans and Nicaraguans (the two largest Hispanic immigrant groups in South Florida). 'Cubans' and 'Nicaraguans' are the 'units of analysis'.

In order to select only those articles that mention the units of analysis, 'key words' were used to pull articles from a CD-ROM database (even word proces-sors can do this, with their 'find' commands applied to a set of texts). In the *Miami Herald* example, all articles were obtained using the key words 'Cuban' and/or 'Nicaraguan' along with their plurals and home countries ('Cuba', 'Nicaragua'). In some cases, researchers included related terms such as 'Contra' and 'Sandinista' – terms that would include the association of 'Nicaraguan'.

The sample can be narrowed down further if too large. For example, the total number of articles about Cubans between August 1992 and August 1994 was about 5,500. From this population, a random sample could be selected using a table of random numbers. A general rule for a feasible quantitative study is using a sample size of at least 100.

Defining categories

Given the magnitude of such a study, consisting of numerous articles to be selected, read and dissected, subject categories should start off being broad and branch out into subcategories. For the *Miami Herald* study, sixteen broad categories were chosen, such as crime, immigration, politics, and so on. They were then broken down into subcategories (e.g. 'crime' included subcategories 'violent crime', 'drug trafficking', 'police brutality', etc.). Basic utilitarian cat-egories that would apply to most content analyses of newsprint material are page number, section, title and date. These categories will be useful later when asking questions such as 'Was the article on the front page or less conspicu-ously located somewhere in the back?', 'Was the article in the main section?' or 'Are there patterns in article titles?'.

Reading and coding articles

Following the selection of categories, the next step is to read each article and assign it category codes. This may be the most tedious and time-consuming step of content analysis. Articles should be read thoroughly and coded accord-ingly. It will be helpful later if extensive notes about the articles' content are jotted down as they are read.

As with any type of quantitative coding, various measures of *intercoder reli-ability* are used in content analysis to ensure that everyone involved in the research (given there is more than one researcher) understands the categories in the same way. In its simplest form, this means taking the percentage of the instances that two or more researchers agree on the appropriate classifications to be used.

Other questions to be considered for accuracy are: Are the content categories reliable, or is assignment too arbitrary? Are they valid encapsulations of the abstract concepts that the researcher is really interested in (whether 'violence' or 'educational' or 'political' themes)? Regardless of how the data have been collected, the results will be easily (albeit time consumingly) coded (or converted into simple numerical form) for analysis. Coding can be as simple as assigning a number to each article category. For example, an article could be assigned '1' for 'main' section or '2' for 'local' section; and '5' for 'violent crime' or '6' for 'homeland politics'. To keep track of what all the numbers mean, researchers create a code book that describes the meaning assigned to each numerical value for the content analysis.

Analysing data

Computers today tabulate most numerical data quickly and easily. SPSS® (Statistical Package for the Social Sciences) is probably the best-known computer software for this purpose in mass communication studies. It can run frequencies, cross-tabulations and multiple regressions to draw patterns. This step will involve at least some knowledge of statistics and statistical software.

Making inferences and drawing conclusions based on patterns

Conclusions from the data findings are usually presented in terms of percentages and proportions. For example, in the *Miami Herald* study it was found that 25.8 per cent of the total Cuban article sample appeared in the 'Local' section, while only 15.6 per cent of the total Nicaraguan article sample appeared in the 'local' section. The researchers hypothesised that this result had emerged because Cubans have stronger political and economic influence in the local scene than do Nicaraguans (Masud-Piloto, 1988; Portes and Stepick, 1993).

Content analysis in its final stages involves taking an overview look at all the material and data collected. Again, this is a step involved in many forms of study. It involves not only presenting the data, but also making strong interpretations of it to answer the original research question. Conclusions should be supported, not only by the numbers, but by a relationship between the numbers and an understanding of the readerships, audiences and communities the investigated medium is serving. The following case study will make this clear.

Case study: minority images and the US media

Media analysis in the USA has developed a dominant framework for understanding how minorities are portrayed (Gans, 1992). Usually the media are criticised for representing minorities unfairly by portraying them as criminals and deviants, or ignoring them altogether. For example, an analysis of the major US television news networks examining news stories from the full year of 1995 found that Hispanic minorities were 'symbolically annihilated' in terms of their presentation in the news (Carveth and Averio, 1996:5). They were only seen occasionally, for example when receiving 'undeserved' benefits of affirmative action. Another study of two daily newspapers in New York showed Puerto Ricans to be presented mostly in 'problem oriented' stories and at least two other studies have found similar results when analysing news content about Mexican Americans (Fishmen and Casiano, 1969; Greenberg and Burgoon, 1983). These bodies of research examining popular news media have found a preponderance of stories about immigrants focused on conflict and crime. These and other studies of US news media that profess minority misrepresentation pose two important theoretical questions: Who are the *minorities* in today's multiethnic US cities? And do media images of US minorities vary depending on the distinct local setting? These questions have become ever more significant for media analysts looking at the USA – a nation where cultures are diverse and unevenly distributed, and the 'majority' in a particular city may be the 'minority' in the rest of the USA.

When used in its statistical sense, the term 'minorities' refers to groups small in number and less than majority – a term often applied to people of colour in the USA, such as blacks, Hispanics, Asians and Native Americans. Over time, this term became a convenient category under which to place any population that the US census would not call 'white'. It is, however, a misleading label in many of today's metropolitan US cities such as Miami. The so-called 'minorities' among readers of the *Miami Herald*, in terms of population size make up the majority (Soruco, 1996:35). A content analysis of the *Miami Herald*, one of the twenty largest US newspapers in terms of circulation, illustrates how Cuban immigrants succeeded in moving out of 'minority' status – in both the literal and discursive sense.

Cubans in Miami are an ideal example of a large ethnic group in the USA gaining influence over the media. Having started as a large group of political refugees over fifteen years ago, Cubans in Miami have developed into an immigrant enclave with immense political and economic influence in the Miami community (Portes and Rumbaut, 1990; Portes and Stepick, 1993). It was no surprise that during the 1990s the city and county elected Cuban mayors, and a majority of the commissioners are Cuban. Their influence became great enough to make dramatic changes in the *Miami Herald*. In recent years, the newspaper saw the hiring of more Hispanic-American journalists, covering more issues concerning Cubans in Miami and thus presenting a new image of minorities in the USA – an image usually reserved for the 'white' or Anglo majority (Soruco, 1996:90).

Although Cubans were successful in changing one of the most popular printed news sources in the USA, other 'minority' groups continued to be victims of media bias. To illustrate this anomaly in minority representation, a content analysis was conducted involving images of Cubans and Nicaraguans in the *Miami Herald*.

Like Cubans, Nicaraguans are considered 'Hispanic' by the US census – 'people of colour' and an immigrant group who sought political asylum in the USA. In Miami, Nicaraguans are smaller in population size than the Cubans, but are the second largest Hispanic group, right behind the Cubans. Furthermore, Nicaraguans have a difficult time obtaining legal US residency, whereas Cubans are issued legal residency relatively easily. For political reasons, the US government does not welcome Nicaraguans into the country as it does Cubans (Masad-Piloto, 1985; Loescher, 1983; Portes and Stepick, 1993).

A content analysis of both groups in the *Miami Herald* found that articles about Cubans far outnumbered articles about Nicaraguans (population proportions taken into consideration). It also found that 25.8 per cent of the total Cuban article sample appeared in the 'local' section while only 15.6 per cent of the total Nicaraguan article sample appeared there. On average, Cubans appear in 10 per cent more front-page stories than do Nicaraguans. Nicaraguans were usually labelled in news stories as part of a general minority group such as 'Hispanics' or 'immigrants', in contrast with Cubans who usually appeared in articles either as individuals or simply as 'Cubans'.

One common term found in articles during the political elections in Miami is 'non-Cuban Hispanic', a label used to describe Nicaraguans and other minorities not of Cuban origin. An article entitled 'Non-Cuban Hispanics Uniting for Power', about the Miami mayoral election, reads: 'Tired of feeling powerless, Miami non-Cuban Hispanics are acting on an old adage: there is power in numbers'. That the 'non-Cuban Hispanic' label is frequent during election time illustrates the political potency the Cubans have in this community and that the media have designated to them an identity apart from the other Hispanics.

Analysis of story topics in the *Miami Herald* concludes that there is a significantly greater percentage of stories dealing with crime in articles about Nicaraguans than in articles about Cubans (3 per cent of Cuban articles versus almost 7 per cent of Nicaraguan articles). Also, there are almost three times more articles covering conflict and violence in Nicaragua than in Cuba. These Nicaraguan 'homeland' articles usually have a negative tone, blaming its people for the strife; such as an article entitled 'Nicaraguans Make Discontent a Way of Life' which describes endemic political unrest in Nicaragua.

Cuban articles focused on the topic of immigration almost three times more frequently on average than did Nicaraguan articles. Immigration articles about Cubans were most often presented in a manner that sought to elicit sympathy for Cuban refugees, such as 'Cuban Orphan becomes Symbol of Tragic Exodus' and 'Neither Waves, nor Sharks, nor Disability Deterred Him [a Cuban Refugee]'. The result of this angle being promoted was reported as intensified support for Cuban immigrants: 'Pastors Unite in Campaign to Free Rafters' and 'Lawyers Suing Government on Behalf of Rafters Visit to Guantanamo'.

In comparison, the few Nicaraguan articles about immigration argue over the issue of granting immigrants legal residency, as in the following editorial discussing deportation and border control:

> The answer to the [immigration] problem is twofold: a strenuous effort to control our borders, and deportation of the tens of thousands here on extended residency carried over from now-ended strife in El Salvador, Nicaragua, and Haiti. These refugees were granted temporary asylum, promising to go home when their wars were over. Well, they're over. The federal government must send them back. Otherwise, the law is a mockery.

The view propounded in this article parallels the US government's attitude towards legal residency policies for Nicaraguans. The *Miami Herald* reflects US media generally by presenting a negative image of disadvantaged 'minorities', such as Nicaraguans, compared with those who are more affluent, such as Cubans.

It would be inaccurate to say that there has not been progress in the portrayal of immigrants and minorities in the US media. Although the *Miami Herald* is typical of US media generally in propagating an image of one group taking precedence over another, it is a Hispanic ethnic group rather than the 'white' mainstream in the case of the *Miami Herald*. While the potentially positive consequence of Cubans controlling a major US media source is nonetheless a change in the unspoken rules for other media in other US cities, still this example indicates that subordinate minorities such as Nicaraguans are no longer pressured by media coverage to assimilate into the ethnically white majority, but rather into another immigrant group – one with power and status.

Positive media coverage of Hispanics may not apply for Mexicans (the ethnic 'majority' of the south-western USA) or for Puerto Ricans (the ethnic 'majority' of New York), as studies of their local media have demonstrated. On the other hand, Miami may not be utterly unique in this respect. In parts of California, Asians have come to dominate the media agenda in a way that parallels Cubans in Miami. In Monterey Park, California, in particular, Asians are a powerful influence in politics, economics and in their effect on the local media. With the presence of these large 'minority' groups, media have made unavoidable alterations in their representations of ethnic groups. Metropolitan newspapers now recognise that, at least in some instances, ethnic groups can establish sufficient power in the local media to affect the course of dominant media representations. Furthermore, the content analysis of media on a local level has illustrated their new role in generating representations of 'minorities' as the new mainstream – a significant finding for today's multiethnic US cities.

Qualitative research methods

Critical researchers in media studies usually employ qualitative methods of inquiry when they are investigating cultural constructions of meaning and power. In contrast to the quantitative techniques which are typically employed in mainstream mass communications research, the emphasis of qualitative approaches is on matters of interpretation and experience rather than on issues of measurement or quantification. So critical media studies have been concerned with the forms and meanings of texts – or the interpretations and experiences of audiences – rather than with measuring the content of media output or counting the heads of viewers, listeners and readers. It is important for us to remember that qualitative and quantitative research methods can be used together, and one set of techniques is in no way inherently more critical than another, but we must also recognise that academics working in these two paradigms tend to operate with quite different purposes as well as different practices.

There is a large body of qualitative media research which could be placed under the broad heading of 'textual analysis'. For example, this includes those academic readings of print and audio-visual texts which have been made within the tradition of semiotic and structuralist thought. Using analytical principles borrowed from modern structural linguistics, the key purpose here is to approach media texts as sign-systems – identifying the processes through which meanings are produced and the narrative forms or structures that characterise various genres of output. In addition, there may be an attempt by the analyst to identify the cultural myths or ideologies that are at work in a text – and which offer media audiences particular ways of knowing the social world.

A major figure in the development of this tradition was Roland Barthes (1977, 1993). He pioneered a semiological perspective on popular culture and a structural analysis of narrative fictions, and his work has inspired many others in the field of media studies. Those who follow most closely in his footsteps pursue an interest in the production and circulation of contemporary mythologies (Coward, 1984; Masterman, 1984; Easthope, 1986), looking at the connotations of media texts and cultural artefacts – asking how these representations serve to construct our social identities or to mask relations of power between various groups in modern society. However, while this semiotic approach has certainly been valuable in raising questions to do with meaning and signification, it has also been criticised by some qualitative researchers who see it either as limited or flawed.

One of these critiques actually comes from within the broad area of media text and discourse analysis – from a group of researchers who are primarily interested in the use of spoken language in radio and television. Paddy Scannell (1991), a leading member of this faction, argues that a semiotic model of communication – though it is derived from the discipline of linguistics – has made it difficult to discover talk as an object of study in relation to broadcasting. He and his colleagues have chosen to draw instead on different strands of linguistic theory, favouring those perspectives such as pragmatics and conversation analysis which focus on the contexts of utterances or on the turn-taking practices of language users (Scannell, 1991; Hutchby, 1996).

A further critique of semiotic textual analysis, launched from another site altogether, is to be found in an approach which is often called 'audience ethnography'. In critical media studies, this type of research originally arose out of a dissatisfaction with any narrow focus on the text itself as the source of meanings – and began by investigating differential interpretations of television content made by viewers from a range of socio-economic and cultural backgrounds (Morley, 1980). The purpose was to understand dialogical interactions that are played out between texts and audiences, where meaning is made in a process of encoding and decoding (Hall, 1980). So texts may prefer certain readings of the social world over others, but they can never finally close down interpretation – because of the polysemic or multi-accentual character of televised sounds and images, and the interrogative nature of media consumption.

Audience ethnographers have gone on to explore the dynamics of media consumption in the home (Bausinger, 1984; Morley, 1986; Lull, 1990); the tastes and preferences of viewing or reading formations for particular genres (Ang, 1985; Radway, 1987); and the social uses and meanings of technologies such as the video recorder (Gray, 1992) and satellite television (Moores, 1996). **329**

Here, the previous emphasis on power relations and social inequalities is retained – yet translated into new concerns with the politics of domestic life, and with an uneven distribution of competences in what sociologist Pierre Bourdieu (1996) would term the 'cultural economy'.

Ethnography is a research method with its origins in anthropology and over recent years there has been a marked self-reflexive turn in certain parts of that discipline – with practitioners looking critically at their own relations to, and representations of, other cultures (Clifford and Marcus, 1986). This politics of the act of research has also been introduced into media reception studies by Valerie Walkerdine (1986) and Ien Ang (1989) – who have each posed some difficult yet necessary questions to do with the voyeurism of ethnographic observation, the styles of academic writing and the dynamics of knowledge production. A possible danger with their line of argument is that too much reflexivity might actually hinder rather than help qualitative inquiries into everyday media use – but they are quite right to connect epistemological matters with issues of social power and control.

Finally, it is worth mentioning another qualitative method which has been employed in investigations of media and everyday life – the technique of oral history. Initially developed by radical social historians as a means of recovering subordinated memories and experiences – thereby challenging the dominant narratives of the past – oral history interviews have since enabled audience researchers to challenge, or at least to supplement, existing institutional histories of the modern mass media. So in an attempt to reconstruct the entry and incorporation of television (O'Sullivan, 1991) or early radio (Moores, 1988) into the domestic sphere, viewers or listeners are asked to recall the place of those technologies in their daily routines and situated activities.

Shaun Moores

18

Media, social movements and history: an agenda-building case study

Victor Sampedro

Many social movements aim to influence policy agendas by defining new social problems through media coverage of their protest activities. Instead of lobbying or negotiating, social movements tend to 'display' protest activities. By resorting to demonstrations or civil disobedience, movement activists challenge the control that institutional actors (e.g. governmental, administrative, political and lobbying agencies) exert upon politics and mainstream media. Indeed, the effectiveness of social movements might be assessed by measuring: (1) how political elites set policy agendas that either reflect or ignore social movements' demands; and (2) how media agendas are either shaped by or unresponsive to social movement tactics (Klandermans, 1989:387–9).

I will present here the interdependence of policy agenda building, media agenda building and social movement mobilisation as they apply to a major, yet under-reported, European social movement: the Spanish anti-military movement. The analysis focuses on how social movements, institutional actors and the media all bring to bear distinctive resources, strategies and alliances in an evolving and interrelated way. The outcome of media/movements relations can be located in terms of models of power that help media scholars to organise other case studies.

Building agendas for new politics

The agenda-building approach addresses the core questions of the two major schools for studying social movements. *New social movements* theorists (Touraine, 1981; Offe, 1985; Melucci, 1989, 1996) consider that protest mobilisation denounces structural problems in a society and challenges dominant ideologies. Changing social consensus moves the activists to search for a 'space of public representation' in the media (Melucci, 1996:218–28). The news may shape public opinion and how social issues are discussed (Gamson and Modigliani, 1989). Then, social movements use the media to project certain events and features in a particular 'public image' of their ideology and goals (Van Zoonen, 1996:213–14).

From a different perspective, the school of *resource mobilisation* examines social movements as policy entrepreneurs that demand access to official agendas (McCarthy and Zald, 1977, 1987). In order to attract support, protesters must consider the external conditions that hinder or facilitate their success. A favourable 'political opportunity structure' consists of stable political alignments, formal channels of access and intra-elite conflict (Tarrow, 1988), where dominant groups do not have their own seamless consensus. In the same vein, the factors that affect the media agenda might be labelled the 'media opportunity structure' (Sampedro, 1997a) that helps social movements to challenge public policies, to demand access to institutional agendas and to attract potential supporters (Snow and Benford, 1988).

Recent research connects the ideological and the political dimensions of social movements. The use of rhetorical argument is assumed to increase the opportunity to act in a given political context (Diani, 1996; Tarrow, 1998), especially through 'master frames' – dominant arguments and associated images – which characterise cycles of protest (Snow and Benford, 1992). The basic idea here is that social movements energise their peculiar tension between claims for broad ideological change (vital to any 'master frame' of protest) and concrete policy demands when questioning official agendas and frames, both in politics and in the media. This perspective has always characterised the policy agenda literature.

Seminal authors, Cobb and Elder (1971; Elder and Cobb, 1984; Kingdon, 1984), pointed to three processes for insinuating new issues into governmental plans. First comes the ideological process of framing: attributing causes for collective privation, personifying responsibility and offering solutions. Second, movements' grievances cannot be attributable 'to fate, or nature' if they are to call for governmental action (Stone, 1989:299). For example, feminism and pacifism present their causes as issues of real politics linked to discrimination and militarism, respectively. Finally, social movements must advance policy solutions and find political authorities potentially receptive to the new policies.

As suggested, most political science and social movement theorists adopt a constructionist perspective when addressing the dynamics of social movements. Media scholars join the constructionist perspective when they study *agenda building* instead of agenda setting. Agenda-setting research (McCombs and Shaw, 1972; Protess and McCombs, 1991) intends to demonstrate that news organisations offer audiences the issues *to think about* and the frames for *how to think about* them (Iyengar, 1991; McCombs, 1993:62). Media coverage could, in that sense, help activists to persuade the public (and even the political elites) of their demands and arguments. But most movement/media studies question that hypothesis (Kielbowicz and Scherer, 1986) against the background of work that demonstrates how striking differences exist among the frames presented by the media and those held by the audience (Graber, 1988; Neuman *et al.*, 1992). Especially important are the news frames that might influence the audience's perception of its own capacity to affect institutional politics (Gamson, 1992). Media frames (Altheide, 1976; Entman, 1993) function, as social movement studies suggest: 'as forms of political rhetoric rather than as belief systems' (Diani, 1996:1057–8). As part of this rhetoric, news sources tend to impose their agendas and frames to position the audience as passive and detached from events and from the creation of public discourse – to demobilise the public (Gitlin, 1980; Entman and Rojecki, 1993).

On the other hand, the agenda-*building* approach (Gandy, 1982) also reveals the privileges that the media grant to certain groups as active agents that monopolise public discourse. Media coverage may offer social movements a discursive platform for interacting with other such policy actors. The mass media have become 'the arena for the contended definition of what is political, of what belongs to the *polis* . . . transforming . . . the society's inner dilemmas . . . into politics (literally into something concerning the *polis*)' (Melucci, 1996:221). In fact, mass media are critical levers to foster and reallocate both public and institutional attention upon new issues. For example, social movements may go from police repression of protest activities to court litigations and then – or simultaneously – to political debates over their demands. This chain would hardly occur without media coverage of protest activities. Crucially, the social movement has here broken on to the discursive platform where the 'audience' as such is never represented.

In looking at this more closely, we need to know to what extent social movements can access, and frame their demands in, mainstream media. This implies studying the 'agenda game' (Protess *et al.*, 1991) as it is played out among different policy actors and the media themselves through a symbolic struggle that filters new political issues and ways of thinking about them. More than stressing a coincidental history of different disciplines, the discussion here sustains a *parallel* analysis of political and communicative, or discursive, power.

Models of political and communicative power

Depending on the political context, newsworthy issues and events may be fixed by the controlling elite, through open debates or through institutional patterns for news and policy making. Following Michael Mann (1993:44–91), we can think of movements/media relations in terms of three models of power: pure elitism, pluralism and institutional elitism. These models are ideal-typical in that they locate real-world relations in terms of pure models based on the nature and degree of elite control (see table 3). They provide an analytically convenient way of organising and systematising complex relationships which are far from static. Regarding the Spanish anti-military movement, these models represent distillations of complex state–media relationships that exist over time.

Pure elitism depicts an exclusionary control of the political and media agendas by relatively cohesive ruling groups (Mills, 1956). Political access and freedom of expression are both curtailed. Officials respond to social protest by vetoing or delaying decision making that may threaten their interests. If protest cannot be ignored, authorities may simply *repress* it. Favourable publicity in support of a movement is greatly reduced, given the repression of coverage.

Media outcomes for protest are either *silence* or *marginalisation*. Silence typically results from authoritarian legal proscriptions or internal censorship. Journalists are forced to ignore those social demands dubbed 'irrelevant' or 'too risky' for official action. Frequently, common interests and/or background ties among political, business and media elites account for a material and ideological convergence (Herman and Chomsky, 1988; Parenti, 1993). Marginalisation means that, if official repression occurs, mainstream media

Table 3 Policy and media outcomes of social protest by models of media–state relations

Model of power	Policy agenda	Media agenda
Pure elitism	(a) Inactivity (b) Repression	(a) Silence (b) Marginalisation
Pluralism	Political innovation	Coverage of protest and/or of official controversy
Institutional elitism	(a) Co-option (b) Institutional marginalisation of conflict	(a) Institutionalisation of social movement sources. Sensationalism (b) Indifference

will frame protesters as anti-systemic, extreme, anarchic, inconsistent and uncohesive, or lacking public support (Entman and Rojecki, 1993).

Classic elitism was refined by theories of neo-Marxist hegemony and social control. Hegemony – the ideological dominion of ruling classes – implies that news organisations veil class struggle (Goldman and Rajagopal, 1991) or marginalise protesters (Gitlin, 1980). Social control research also shows the media imposing 'deviant' frames on unconventional collective action (Cohen, 1972; Young, 1990; Van Zoonen, 1992). Thus elitism explains why activists see the media as a target as much as a means of communication (Gamson and Wolsfeld, 1993). Ironically though, '[m]ost movement activists are media junkies' (Gamson, 1995:85); they seek news coverage constantly. Pluralism could explain why.

Pluralism is based on Robert Dahl's well-known description of democratic political competition between interest groups in which resources play a large role in determining success (Dahl, 1961). Exclusive control over the agendas becomes a minor problem because policy and news making respond to diverse competing interests without any pre-established bias. This bottom-up model contradicts the top-down model of elitism. Media coverage of social protest may reflect and/or foster popular support. If representative of meaningful social demands, a movement would gain the attention of the journalists who grant activists access (e.g. interviews, letters to the editor, opinion columns) and give ample coverage (sometimes favourable) to their demands. This happens before a policy innovation takes place and during mobilisations to challenge old policies. Pluralist media also report on conflict and controversy within established policy communities because these debates are accessible and are thought to be newsworthy. In this way, the movement's demands are legitimised to some degree.

In pluralist competition, movement organisations mobilise the media like a resource at their disposal. It has been suggested that a rational exchange of information for publicity – one that mirrors rational market transactions – occurs beween journalists and news sources (Blumler and Gurevitch, 1981). Movements want exposure and the media want sensationalism, often exchanged in a 'transaction model' (Wolsfeld, 1984, 1991). Protest activities provide the media with personalised, emotionally laden and conflictive dramas. These are highly valued media commodities which deserve high-visibility coverage, sometimes enabling a handful of activists to achieve broad public attention. However, a fair exchange between movements' sources and conventional journalists seems far from common. As Gamson and Wolsfeld (1993:117) argue, 'those who are most needy have least access to the media services they desire and pay a higher price for them – an example of the principle of cumulative inequality'. The pluralist exchange model, on the other hand, tends to consider the media as themselves neutral resources for reaching the audience, while acknowledging that institutional and political constraints can distort the exchange of news information.

In order to manage news coverage effectively, a social movement needs (1) stable networks for media relations (e.g. established connections to responsive journalists); (2) internal division of labour between those members devoted to activism and those designated to press relations; (3) control over supporters to schedule and sustain protests easily covered by the journalists; and (4) a clear-cut collective 'identity' and demands to project to the media. Instead social movements typically produce 'cultural modes not governed by cost–benefit calculations but by symbolic waste' (Melucci, 1996:359). Often social movements pose ambiguous agendas in different and sometimes contradictory ways (Van Zoonen, 1996). Gamson (1995:104) observes that: '[media discourse] . . . often obstructs and only rarely and unevenly contributes to the development of collective action frames'. Negative media effects upon social movements are rooted in journalistic working routines and professional news values. In particular, the explanation rests on the media's institutional 'logics'.

Institutional elitism is the model most characteristic of Western democracies. This recognises that news production is an institutionally embedded process, conditioned by political context, which has its own routines and norms. The media privilege certain interests while, at the same time, creating specific kinds of space for the expression of social demands. In a sense, the institutional model combines elitist and pluralist elements because it emphasises asymmetries of power and the unintended consequences of institutional patterns (Hall and Taylor, 1996). Power is distributed unevenly across social groups, and it tends to be monopolised by networks of the best-positioned actors. States, parties, courts, and so on – and media organisations themselves – structure power relations, since they maintain distinctive forms of interaction with pressure groups. Official agenda building often lurches from one extended phase of stability to another, as short periods of change are followed by new equilibria that re-establish the position of dominant groups. Agenda building reflects continually reorganised systems of 'limited participation' (Baumgartner and Jones, 1992). Officials and journalists establish new routines or alter existing ones to support their interests. Then the role of social movements is to demand new policies that have yet to become routinised and institutionalised. In limited cases, major mobilisations can break policy monopolies.

The institutional model also recognises how state structures shape social movements. David Meyer (1991) observes that social movements can be *co-opted* by being incorporated into existing institutions, for example putting leaders of movements on advisory committees. One might also speak of *institutional marginalisation* in which conflict is managed by commissions of experts, detoured to the courts or confined to bureaucratic proceedings (at a bureaucratic pace). Enmeshing movements in the legal system is a common practice. The net effect of these official strategies is to shuttle movement demands out of the public eye.

The power of institutional structures also biases media agendas. Media coverage of protest is shaped by news organisations' organisational and epistemological features (Van Zoonen, 1996). Institutional conventions ingrained in daily journalistic practices structure the contest for representing policies in favour of those groups that already possess institutional resources. Mainstream media are 'path dependent' on 'legitimate politics' (Hallin, 1986) because official sources provide constant and reliable routes for obtaining new information and for making 'different' news stories on a regular basis. Institutional actors usually set the parameters of political conflict through the media because of their accessibility and predictability. More subtly, journalistic routines find legitimation in institutional sources because their social authority implies objectivity (Tuchman, 1978; Gans, 1980; Fishman, 1988). In contrast, social protest must always carry the weight of proving its legitimacy. All this means that media agendas are more accessible to elites than to social activists. So, the political opportunity structures shape media opportunity structures (Sampedro, 1997a,b) and vice versa in a self-reinforcing spiral.

However, journalistic routines may also *facilitate* coverage of movements. Social movements may influence news agendas by moderating their demands and adopting a more consensual frame or working closely with official agencies that are regularly followed by journalists. In this case, the co-optation of a social movement often occurs in the form of institutionalising movement 'sources' ((a) in the bottom-right box of table 3). Such 'sources' can even attain brief celebrity status (as with anti-road-building protestors in rural England in the mid 1990s). When a movement refuses to moderate, another variety of co-optation derives from media structures. I have in mind activists' strategies to generate shocking and novel events that fit the news values of dramatisation and shock, and capitalise on journalists' attention. In these cases, it is a real possibility that journalists frame protestors as sensationalists, not because of state directives or elitist ties, but simply because of the commercial imperative to win market share. Shocking news stories are easier and faster to 'manufacture' than background reports, and they sell better. The result is that the movement is sensationalised, trivialised and then also co-opted. If movement leaders become media 'stars', increasingly preoccupied with gaining attention, they can further contribute to sensationalisation (Gitlin, 1980:146–78) and their own co-option. In sum, through media institutionalisation social movements may be co-opted by becoming either conventional or eccentric news sources.

Finally, institutionalised media agendas may react to social movements with indifference. This corresponds to the shift of contention to bureaucratic processes sketched above. Contention that is shifted to judicial or administrative arenas where conflict simmers without resolution, claims are asserted without drama and debates rage without clear villains or victims, is not often newsworthy. Lengthy and intricate institutional proceedings obscure the broader storyline and make a news plot that is hard for audiences to follow (Cook, 1996). If any storyline is forthcoming at all, it will coincide with the 'trail of power' (Bennett, 1996), drawing upon institutional and bureaucratised politics. If activists are unable to generate elite disagreement or innovative reframings of their demands, protest will fade from the media.

In the remainder of this chapter, I will apply these three models in a longitudinal study of incremental – although not continuous – institutionalisation of relations between the anti-military movement and the Spanish media. Some of the processes observed will be generalisable to other issues and other political contexts, but the chapter is also intended as a working example of how knowledge can be reliably produced about the media and their role in a society. So it is important that we are not generalising here; we are focusing on a particular historical moment and a particular social context. Prior to 1976, the Spanish anti-military movement was effectively marginalised by Francoist dictatorship and media control. At the other end of the study's temporal frame (1996), we encounter news agenda building integrated into institutionalised relations with political elites but opening public discourse to anti-draft protests. *(cont. p. 339)*

Method

Media history

Everyday, familiar contact and interaction with the various media is very much a part of modern cultural life. This contact plays an important part in the process of 'anchoring' the social present, synchronising the here and now of the moment, the day, week, year or season, marking the passage of social time, of self and generation. Contact with mediated information and imagery plays an important role in the construction of a sense of the past, of history and of speculation about the future. The role of the media in the construction of social time and identity and media representations, especially of national history, are significant topics for study. We all have biographies and belong to generational cultures which are in part defined by a familiarity with a particular range of media at a particular phase of their technical, economic and social development. In other words, our taken-for-granted daily media contacts are historically contingent, dependent upon the institutional, political and technological forms which the media assume in any given era. Compare, for example, the forms and patterns of media consumption and production characteristic of the 1990s with the 'mediascapes' – the media environments – of the 1950s, the 1920s, the 1890s and the 1820s. You will find that the range and types of media available to audiences have changed considerably in the last two hundred years.

As a result, the analysis of the historical development of the media is an essential component of media studies. But so, too, is the analysis of media histories themselves, which cannot always be taken for granted as the only possible accounts of this development. The underlying rationale here suggests that the study of the historical formation and evolution of the various media – how they have emerged and under what conditions – makes possible a more informed understanding of their present forms of organisation, regulation and use, and of their likely patterns of development and change in the future.

If this broad rationale is accepted, there are a number of issues which warrant further consideration.

The first of these concerns the nature of historical study and analysis. The study of history is often associated with identifying and uncovering lists of dates: successions of undeniable, often isolated, historical events. 'Great Media Inventions' and the lives and work of 'Great People' (often men): press proprietors and editors, film directors and stars, for instance, have frequently been presented in this way. Many modern historians have argued, however, that historical study involves much more than the uncritical listing of self-evidently important dates, people and events. From this point of view, historical analysis always entails a sense of how certain events and processes, and their dates, are *selected* as significant and how their significance should be interpreted and understood. In other words, historical analysis is not solely concerned with the 'cult of facts'; it should be motivated by theories, ideas and debates which go beyond the purely descriptive and attempt to offer explanations of large-scale institutional process and change.

In approaching the study of media history it is useful, as Golding (1974:14) has suggested, to remember that: 'The growth of mass communications is a dual process. On the one hand it describes the development of an industry, on the other the evolution of an audience. The relationship between the two is one of supply and demand for two basic social commodities; leisure facilities and information'. Although this model of supply and demand is a deceptively simple one, it directs attention to the most general factors which have shaped and historically determined this fundamental relationship. It also enables specific historical concerns – for instance, understanding shifts in radio programming during the Second World War or press coverage in Spain after Franco – to be related and situated with regard to the broader picture or historical context.

Factors and forces which have historically conditioned the activities of media producers, their products and processes of media production – *supply*, in the model above – can be reduced to three principal areas of concern. These include: the economic organisation and consequences of *commercial* market forces; and the structure and operations of legal, statutory and *political* powers and their interaction with the *technological* conditions and developments prevalent at any one point in time. If these factors combine to constitute the historical conditions of media production, there are others that need to be considered in assessing the historical formation of media consumption – *demand*, in the model above. The conditions of media consumption have been related to what at first sight might seem mundane considerations: the *time* available to social groups in their use of the media; the amounts of *money* that they have been able and willing to spend on media consumption; and a number of related and important *cultural factors* – ranging from literacy to lifestyle – which have structured the access, use and reception of media products by readers and audiences.

The real challenge to historical analysis of the media is to relate the specific to the general, to do justice to the local and the particular, and at the same time to the global and the all-embracing. This is best accomplished by consideration of some particular historical case studies and instances. In approaching these, it is important to bear in mind that the particular focus of historical analysis and the questions posed may entail attention to very different kinds of *source material* as well as to the use of different kinds of *research method*. Sources may include large-scale quantitative or statistical data and records (wherever and however they have been compiled) concerning industrial production, circulation, attendance, ratings or news promoters, for example. They may also include work on archives of the films, newspapers, radio or TV programmes, or the media texts themselves (wherever and however these have been archived). In addition, historical studies will often draw on biographical and other literary sources and records, and may well utilise the resources and the methods of oral history.

In a period when the 'end of history' has been proclaimed, it should be noted in conclusion that history as a discipline faced, in the 1990s, a series of totalising critiques and challenges associated with the rise of postmodernism. These have foregrounded and amplified the idea of history as a narrow, ideologically constructed and privileged set of discourses, rather than as an objective discipline. The positions, motives and possibilities for historical study and analysis have, as a result, been called into question in the context of postmodern times. From the point of view of media studies, there are at least two related issues which deserve consideration. The first concerns the tendency for media history to have focused on media production at the expense of forms of media reception or social use. Finally, media histories have also tended to mean histories of media in the West, to the exclusion of other cultures and national media systems.

Tim O'Sullivan

Anti-militarism, politics and information as a social commodity

Military service for adult males is still compulsory in Spain. Serious consideration of conscientious objection (hereafter CO) as an alternative was denied for fifty years: during the Francoist dictatorship (1939–75), during Spain's democratic transition (1976–82) and during the democratic consolidation (1982–96). Policies ranged from repression and imprisonment under Franco to bureaucratic stonewalling, symbolic pronouncements and temporary deferments after Franco's death (1975). The first cases of CO were mostly religiously inspired. After 1975, politically oriented CO appeared, with numbers of objectors growing each year.

The military was the major antagonist against the democratic transition and considered CO as a direct attack. Even though the 1978 constitution provided a right to CO, and a CO law had been passed in 1984, it took until 1989 to put into effect a civilian service in the place of military conscription. The main social movement, the Movimiento de Objeción de Conciencia (MOC), and other anti-military organisations, responded by launching a campaign of civil disobedience (*insumisión*) against all compulsory military and civilian service, thereby risking imprisonment. They argued that accepting the alternative service continued to legitimate not only the draft but the military itself. As a result, the Spanish anti-draft movement grew at an unprecedented rate (see table 4).

Table 4 Recognitions of conscientious objectors by the Spanish state, 1986–97

1986	1987	1988	1989	1990	1991	1992	1993	1994	1995	1996	1997
6,407	8,897	11,049	13,140	27,389	28,051	42,454	68,209	77,121	72,832	93,272	127,304

Source: *El País*, 17 February, 1998, p. 18.

Spanish CO rates are the highest in the world. By 1993, those choosing total rejection of the conscripted system, including compulsory civilian service (called *insumisos*), reached 9,000 and enjoyed broad popular support (Ibarra, 1992; Sampedro, 1997b; Ibarra *et al.*, 1998). Forced by this pressure, in 1996 the government announced the end of military conscription by 2000. Spain may be considered the first case where a social movement forced the transition to a fully professional armed forces in peacetime.

Agendas of protest and information

Figure 18 shows the media coverage of the CO issue and the changing ability of the different actors to promote their position as measured by main 'news promoters' (a concept defined by Molotch and Lester, 1974), in terms of what activities, statements, and so on, had prompted journalists to write the news stories. We coded all CO coverage of the three main national newspapers from 1976 to 1996. The influential *El País* (aligned with the socialists), *ABC* (conservative) and *El Mundo* (a more popular and adversarial daily that began printing in 1989) were here taken to set the agendas for other media to some degree through a 'cascade effect' (Noelle-Neumann and Mathes, 1987).

Figure 18 also shows the relationship between news coverage and CO numbers increasing rapidly after 1989, when the *insumisión* campaign began. Also, it represents a further influence on news coverage: the level of elite disagreement, measured by the parliamentary initiatives from opposition parties. The dates are grouped below according to five periods that distinguish different media agenda/policy agenda models. I will discuss how the main players' strategies to influence both CO politics and public debate evolved across these five periods.

Period I: transition from Francoism (1976–77)
Francoist repression was replaced by benign governmental inactivity. In 1976 an executive decree recognised CO on religious grounds only, and condemned secularly motivated conscientious objectors to prosecution. Coverage of protest demanding new legislation peaked in 1977, suggesting a pluralist model. Because of movement resistance and media attention to innovative non-violent protests, the 1976 decree was never implemented. In November 1977, the Ministry of Defence privately provided for the 'unofficial exemption' of all the objectors who dared to apply, while maintaining a hard-line position against protesters. This measure was never printed in official bulletins and its publication was punishable as an offence against the armed forces, effectively

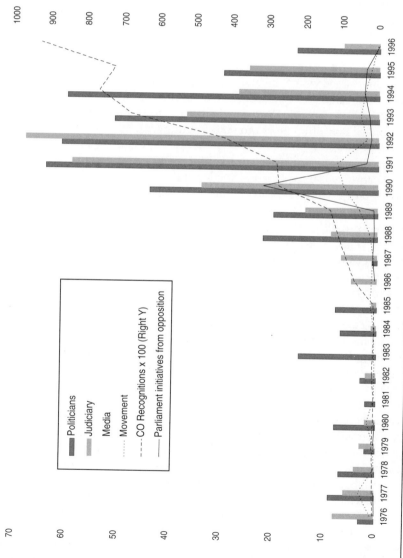

Figure 18 News promoters in *El País* and *ABC* (May 1976–June 1993) and *El Mundo* (Oct. 1989–June 1996)

silencing the media for the next six years and ending pluralistic coverage (with two exceptions that I discuss below).

Period II: conflict management by 'hidden agenda' (1978–84)
Most senior officers were holdovers from Francoism, and gave rise to continuous rumours of *coups d'état*. On 23 February 1981, the Spanish Parliament was seized by a colonel in the Civil Guard. The government avoided a permanent political solution to CO while simultaneously implementing a 'hidden agenda': between 1977 and 1984, many objectors were amnestied and subsequent objectors were exempted from military duty until 1989 – a policy of 'concealment by postponement'. This way, politicians placated the military by sidestepping the pressure of a social movement that had already defined itself as 'anti-militaristic'.

The policy of 'unofficial exemption' noted above was kept secret by pressure, self censorship and threat of military tribunal. As figure 18 demonstrates, media reaction was to avoid or deny coverage except for two peaks in 1980 and 1983. The first represented coverage by *El Pais* of twenty CO activists who had been imprisoned for making public the 'unofficial draft exemption'. The second peak occurred in 1983 during heated parliamentary debates over the first secular CO law presented by the socialists. Figure 18 shows that politicians predominated over other news promoters at this time.

Period III: enlargement of conflict and debate (1985–88)
Media coverage suggests pluralist competition during this period. The movement's presence in the news resulted from mobilisations against yearly draft calls that preceded the *insumisión* campaign. The Spanish socialist party swept into office in 1982 but, contrary to the hopes of many activists, its policy was intransigence and stonewalling rather than accommodation of the movement's demands. The Ministry of Defence imposed severe limitations on the right to claim CO in 1985. Facing the movement's mobilisation, the socialists shifted the movement's challenges to bureaucratic agencies. Moreover, changes to the CO laws had to be sanctioned by the highest courts, further delaying a resolution and removing the issue from public scrutiny until 1988, when lengthy CO legislation was concluded. In the end, this legislation was challenged by the *insumisión* campaign (1989). Mobilisation of increasing numbers of CO and total objectors made it impossible to keep the conscription issue on the back burner of the official agenda any longer.

Period IV: outburst of conflict and debate (1989–92)
News coverage increased significantly each year during the *insumisión* campaign and peaked in 1991. Figure 18 shows that movement organisations reached their peak as news promoters. The substantial news share on the part of the politicians and the judiciary reflected heated parliamentary debates over the model for the armed forces, and ongoing judicial proceedings against the *insumisos*. A second peak of information occurred in March 1992 when a 'not guilty' sentence was passed, generating an impressive news share for the judiciary.

Period V: institutionalisation (July 1992–March 1996)
Media coverage now declined, ignoring the increase of activism, judicial proceedings and court sentences – some favourable to *insumisos* and others upholding their prosecution. Several news-making patterns account for the news decline. Journalistic routines and professional norms led to some indifference towards the movement because of the shift of conflict to the less easily reported judicial arena. Influential political elites agreed in late 1991 that the movement's goal of draft abolition was simply unattainable. Many journalists evidently accepted the official definition of the movement as 'unrealistic' and no longer relevant. Reports about new CO policies in 1994 and electoral promises in 1996 generated the high news shares of politicians and of media (see figure 18). But the overall decline of coverage suggests a characteristic pattern of 'either feast or famine' (Baumgartner and Jones, 1992) in which the media remain attentive to intense conflict but soon become saturated. How this process played out warrants closer attention.

Feast, famine and indifference

No newspaper could avoid reporting the impact of the *insumisión* campaign when it coincided with Spain's participation in the Gulf War during 1991. News shares of the movement peaked. Coverage in 1992 changed dramatically, with judicial and political elites becoming the primary news promoters. Social protest was replaced by institutional conflicts within the political class and between the government and the judiciary. In March 1992 a judge absolved a young Catholic *insumiso* – the first to be set free – but socialist President Felipe González asked the Attorney General to imprison all *insumisos*. A year later, a second activist was found not guilty. A breakdown of news coverage for these two trials demonstrates the media saturation by 1993. The sentence of March 1992 attracted sixty news stories in the three newspapers, compared with just five stories for the next acquittal. *El Pais* and *ABC* offered just one story each (four and three paragraphs long, respectively). However, this last case deserved much more media attention because of its social implications. The 1993 sentence applied to 200,000 draftees because the *insumiso* had refused to perform military service. Previously, the 1992 sentence had been more limited in its impact, affecting only 40,000 men, because this *insumiso* was tried for refusing to perform the alternative civilian duty, but the story was more extensively covered.

A plausible explanation must take all the actors into account as shown in table 3. First, the government decreased the media appeal of the *insumisión* by shifting the debate to judiciary processes. Contradictory court sentences (which did not carry the message of either imprisonment or freedom for all *insumisos*) blurred the differences between civil disobedience, CO and draft dodging. Officials took advantage by simply ignoring the sentences that threatened their own position, thereby marginalising or confusing the successes of the movement. Second, in 1991 a parliamentary consensus was reached on attaining a semi-professional army by 2000. This was an apparent success for the movement, but it was accompanied by an increase in penalties for *insum-*

Table 5 Promoters of news stories for the first two *insumiso* acquittals

Insumiso trial	CO movement	Politicians	Judiciary	Media
March 1992	9	19	22	10
February 1993	0	1	4	0

isión and new legislation to decrease the number of CO recognitions. After these laws were passed, the number of parliamentary initiatives from the opposition decreased dramatically (see figure 18), leading effectively to media silence.

Third, 'judicial marginalisation' was reflected in news-gathering routines. Journalists increasingly turned to institutional sources, such as those associated with the judiciary, as shown in table 5. Figure 18 also shows how political news promoters and the judiciary elites enjoyed the highest shares from 1993 onwards. In 1995 and 1996 the movement achieved the smallest news share, while the trials of *insumisos* and recognitions of CO outnumbered those of previous years. Compared with the drama of the Gulf War mobilisations and the first trials, subsequent judiciary episodes evidently seemed uninteresting.

In sum, the institutional patterns that had previously impelled the movement's media presence lost strength. The CO movement was thwarted by a mix of political strategy, media saturation and journalistic routine. The all-volunteer armed forces, announced in 1996, demanded an enormous military budget and full integration into NATO, both contrary to majority public opinion. The fortunes of the anti-military movement in questioning this policy agenda were shaped by a constricting media agenda which clearly gave advantage to the political class as the main news promoter during the last five years of the study (see figure 18).

It is important to emphasise, however, that the media are not just a simple tool of politicians. Had it not been for the CO stories of *El País* between 1978 and 1988, the movement would probably have been heading for extinction. The climax of the *insumisión* campaign (1989–91) set in motion a wave of media interest (open to different proposals for draft abolition), of court trials and journalistic efforts to report, comment on and measure the turmoil. Thus the media were *both* the vehicles by which the movement was brought into the public arena and the means that officials used to stake out their own positions.

An intensive content analysis of the 1988 coverage in *El País* and *ABC* traced how the media may have helped the movement in framing the *insumisión* campaign (Sampedro, 1997b:263–94). We found that the media played a partially positive role for activists. Half of the relevant paragraphs, both in *El País* and *ABC*, framed *insumisión* as legitimate social protest. Most policy proposals that were printed demanded alternative CO policies. Moreover, only 2 per cent of policy proposals presented by *El País* and 6 per cent in *ABC* defended legal punishment. The compulsory military conscription was labelled as too conservative and militaristic. Clearly, this coverage opened the policy debate when it had seemed to be closed.

While the mainstream press performed as a 'space of opposition', during 1988 it nonetheless privileged institutional sources. Routine news such as press conferences, leaks and press releases amounted to almost half of the information provided by both dailies. They also preferred sources closest to their editorial lines. The Ministry of Defence relied on conservative *ABC* to criticise the initiatives of the Ministry of Justice, which were all advanced by *El Pais*. Journalistic routines and editorial bias imposed additional constraints. The newspapers printed stories about peaceful demonstrations on pages dominated by stories of terrorism or on the crime pages. Evidently the media considered only the activities of professional politicians worthy of the political pages. Movement-related stories grouped with coverage of military issues occurred only 20 per cent of the time in *El Pais* and a scant 2 per cent in *ABC*. Thus the movement was *framed by juxtaposition*, suggesting a conscious editorial decision by *ABC*. Established options on draft policy were clearly favoured in both newspapers, which never portrayed the *insumisión* master frame as globally anti-militaristic (i.e. not 'No to the armed forces' but only 'No to the draft'). The general conclusion is that while news coverage of a social movement might play a key role, it must nevertheless pass through several filters: routine practices of journalism, constraints of layout, sequencing and composition, and congruence with institutional elites aligned with the media.

Until 1991, the media *opened* the policy agenda by introducing new issues, participants and solutions that officials were forced to take into consideration. Media coverage also *reset* the official agenda by discussing flaws and fissures in official policy, thereby rekindling debate that had been artificially dampened down. And, ultimately, the media's critical coverage *blocked* the official plans for implementation of CO laws. Media coverage clearly influenced the political agenda. But powerful structural constraints, such as elite alliances, economic considerations, news-making routines and political inertia, cushioned media effects.

What we might call 'a media politics of social protest' (Sampedro, 1997a) consists of spreading and accelerating policy controversies in front of the public; that is, strategically positioning certain demands in order to encourage political debates and competition among policy actors. This strategy may eventually result in policy innovation but, as the case of the CO movement in Spain demonstrates, change is incrementally slow and may not necessarily coincide with the movement's core demands.

Conclusion

In contemporary societies, the best that a social movement might expect is that protest mobilisation demonstrates (and in some cases deepens) contradictions or insufficiencies in existing policy alternatives. Through media coverage of protest, the activists might open the institutionalised controversy, reset its contents or block unpopular initiatives. Rarely are the activists able to determine the policy agenda. For short pluralistic periods, movements may react to and counteract the elitist control of the agenda, but in the long run they are faced with institutional pressures to close the policy agendas they have opened to **345** challenge. These institutional pressures are reinforced by parallel processes in the media. Political elites have resources that enable them to co-opt movements by bureaucratising protest and diffusing original demands. Under these circumstances, media attention reaches saturation point quite soon. Another response is to trivialise and sensationalise a movement, although we did not see much of this in the present case.

News organisations can be active contributors to the policy agenda. While institutional constraints are always at work, the media may offer a *space of representation* for new ideologies or even a *space of opposition* by injecting alternative issues into decision-making circles. Because journalistic attention focuses mainly on official activities, media opportunities of which a social movement might take advantage are typically dependent on existing political opportunities, especially the level of institutional controversy. When the state exercises greater influence over the media, as in the elitist model, 'symbolic politics' based on artificial consensus and mere rethoric (Edelman, 1987) – or 'placebo politics' which mask social injustices (Stringer and Richardson, 1980) – can easily close the media agenda.

The general conclusion is that political control and news management usually go hand in hand, guaranteeing the stability of official agendas. A 'soft' version of the elite hegemony model consequently seems most appropriate here. In advanced democracies, elites do not baldly 'manufacture consent' through the media nor are the major media simply propaganda organs of the state or parties. But mass communication mostly inhibits the expansion of ideological alternatives and collective action through its own rules and practices. The media's institutional rules undeniably tend, in the long run, to dilute social protest. Nonetheless, change occurs, and it remains important for media studies to document, detail and analyse – to produce knowledge about – how social movements, institutional actors and the media all bring to bear their resources, strategies and alliances in the interrelated ways demonstrated by this case study.

19

Interpretation, semiology and the 'Warriors of Democracy'

Tereza Batista

The late Roland Barthes, famed French cultural critic and semiologist, had this to say about our understanding of the *text*: 'We now know that the text is not a line of words releasing a single "theological" meaning (the "message" of an Author-God) but a multi-dimensional space in which a variety of writings, none of them original, blend and clash' (1977:146). It is quite difficult for us to recover in 2000 and beyond just how exciting that was for cultural and media studies in the second half of the twentieth century. Barthes did not originate the idea of course – his text is not itself exempt from the insight – but he articulated it in especially influential ways. Others extended the insight to audio-visual texts as well as written ones, and much adventurous thinking then went into developing ways of understanding the 'multidimensional' spaces of broadcast texts, filmic texts, photographic texts, and so on. In fact, even thinking of some of these things as 'texts' (rather than, say, 'pictures') is itself dependent on recognising them as multidimensional spaces criss-crossed by the ebb and flow of multiple meanings.

For some, the resultant 'blending and clashing' was entirely circumstantial and unpredictable; for others it derived from the power struggles among different discourses for dominance; for still others it represented something that true Author-Gods attempted to contain and master. So it was still possible to pursue authorship studies (the works of this film director, that TV dramatist, etc.) but such scholarship has had to work much harder to demonstrate authorial intentions and achievements, as texts are now widely held to spill beyond any individual control. Indeed, some of the most rigorous textual studies (sometimes styling themselves 'deconstructionist') have focused closely on the ways in which seemingly coherent texts lay traps for themselves and unravel like intertwined strings when pulled apart in the right places. ('Deconstruction' is not just a fancy word for analysis and should only be used to refer to such work of textual unravelling around texts' own internal contradictions and their secret dependence on things that have seemingly been excluded in the interests of coherence.) So not only is authorial coherence challenged but, even where the idea of authorial control is largely abandoned, textual coherence is itself now questioned as reliant on carefully papered over cracks.

All of this is exciting and different from the older approach of reading a novel and, by extension, a film or TV drama for example, as straightforwardly the intended meanings of a creative author (in which regard the film director's claim had to be argued for in the early days of film studies over that of, say, the screenwriter or even the cinematographer). Of course, part of the fun was for professional 'readers' such as academics, who suddenly found that everything had not already been said about well-commented upon texts and they were still in business. More seriously, though, the general insight captured by Barthes has genuinely revitalised the activity of interpretation in ways that have been not only productive (producing more interpretations) but informative: they have often, if not always, told us things about the relations between text and world that do seem to be helpful in trying to understand what it means to be a human being in these times of textual proliferation.

But therein lies a problem for media studies as a field. The revitalisation of interpretive approaches has left them so buoyant and superficially confident, and so well staffed by a flow of suitably apprenticed graduates, that what is often termed 'critical' media studies has been in danger of thinking that it needs no other approach. Critical media studies, for instance, tends to distinguish itself from schools of mass communication, staffed largely by sociologists and political economists, precisely on the (by no means universally accepted) grounds that 'critical' means interpretive and interpretive means focused largely on texts. The 'multidimensional space' of the text is now understood to be carrying the traces of institutional, economic, historical and other factors traditionally the concern of the mass communication scholar. So – the claim often seems to be – the critical, interpretive, text-based approach can comprehend all these other things without having to spend much time looking at them independently or directly. There is some justice in this claim on occasion; the best interpretive work has been stunningly informative about all sorts of things not traditionally thought of as being 'in' texts at all. One thinks of the writings of Fredric Jameson, for example, or Edward Said. But those are hard acts to follow and it would be preferable to have a good measure of other approaches within media studies rather than a plethora of overcooked interpretive readings of texts that unconvincingly squeeze any vestige of significance from every passing detail.

Worse, student writing in the tradition of critical, text-based media studies is too often not an apprenticeship for subsequent interpretive craftsmanship but a plateau of mediocrity where interpretations are offered on the thinnest of evidence. I would go so far as to suggest – based on a decade of teaching in this context and reading at least a couple of thousand student essays – that most student writing within this sort of media studies is seldom much more than unsupported generalisations informed by a few 'theoretical' concepts that are trundled on stage as *deus ex machina*, devices to intervene and 'explain' everything. These devices are often just caricatures of ideas, and frequently incompatible at that – the media are run by powerful elites who use them as ideological apparatuses to dupe and dope the masses, or media output is 'polysemic' and can mean everything to everybody, or women are turned into passive objects by patriarchal image-making machines, or Rupert Murdoch is the Devil – but are typically latched on to early in a student's short career in media studies and are then routinely deployed in essays and examination answers without much thought of further development. This tendency stems in part from the sometime arrogance of the interpretive, 'textualist' school of media studies, once largely defectors from or graduates of English literature or fine art departments but now largely self perpetuating from within media studies departments themselves, increasingly staffed by their own graduates. What is arrogant is the assumption that media students only need to be exposed to the interpretive approach and left to get on with it. Where well done, the interpretive approach requires a depth of theoretical knowledge and a skill at fashioning a 'reading' in written form (the latter sometimes taking on its own status as a primary text that overshadows the original object of the reading – many of Edward Said's readings are more interesting than the texts he is interpreting). Where students are not learning about the available theories in sufficient depth (which may be more properly an aim for the research student instead) or being trained in the rhetorical skills required to fashion a good piece of interpretive writing, the result will almost inevitably be a laboured and unconvincing emulation of such writing. Where some of the writing being emulated is not itself very good, the problem escalates rapidly.

With a massively expanded intake into universities in most advanced countries (in recognition of the turn towards an information economy requiring higher levels of education in the workforce), there is no longer recourse to the argument that an apprenticeship in critical reading and writing is a skill for life. Those few who genuinely take to the proffered apprenticeship will indeed probably end up having lives as research students and then academics themselves, but this will now be a tiny percentage and the remainder will pass through largely unacquainted with the peculiar pleasures of getting the interpretive approach right, turning out instead superficial 'readings' of a few films, TV programmes, magazine advertisements, star images, news stories, and so on, on their way to a second-class degree.

What is quite disheartening about this is that it dilutes the potential of the interpretive approach by spreading it too thinly. Where it is the only approach adopted (a few occasional curricular gestures towards sociology or political economy notwithstanding), it cannot carry the weight of learners' expectations. For I am convinced that the student writers I have characterised above arrive in our universities wanting to do much better. Offered an insufficient range of intellectual tools to achieve this, they soon tire of their own pale critical readings of texts, of the ineffectiveness of much of the theory *in their own heads*, and they make do. In fact, I wish to argue, interpretation is the lifeblood of good media studies but is properly one activity among several, especially for students. This book has evidently been designed from the outset to have a broader range, but we encountered a reading of a British TV text – *Edge of Darkness* – early on by way of signposting the power of interpretation to reveal things that are barely accessible to other approaches and to pull things together. Equally, though, those moments of interpretive insight and comprehension need to be scaffolded with other work, without which they can easily become mere guesswork. We need to know the media in a whole range of ways. At the right moments, with the right preparation and the right objectives, we will turn to the interpretation of texts, not as a bludgeoning routine, but as an exciting way to discover really meaningful things.

Now there is another side to this. There are departments of mass communication or 'communication studies' where textual interpretation is marginalised in favour of these other approaches (content analysis, institutional economics, studies of media policy and regulation, media and social history, audience research, etc.). While students on such courses – and here again I am relying largely on my own experience – often routinely produce more competent work than is the norm on many determinedly 'critical', textually oriented courses, they do so because the techniques are clearer, are more objectively taught as skills that can be mastered, and the learner is apprenticed to things that seem more transferable to the outside world of jobs and careers. The negative side is that a gaping hole is often experienced where the learner is looking for some purchase on the pleasures and 'multidimensional spaces' of meaning making that are actually so central to how media culture really works. Texts are indeed central; they are how most media content is organised. We all know this when engaged by the media and our learning has to reflect it.

So what is to be done? The obvious answer might seem to lie in some sort of institutional 'peace process' to unite the two communities, the (qualitatively oriented) textualists and the (more often quantitatively oriented) mass communications scholars. In fact, of course, through accident or design, there are university departments where forms of media studies are pursued and taught that do not fall foul of the extreme positions evoked here, positions which I have in any case caricatured a little to make the point. But we are not concerned so much here with the institutional arrangements and the locations available for academic careers as with the learner's perspective – your perspective. The caricatured positions above are caricatures in part because that is how the learner is likely to experience them. Even fairly slight institutionalised biases towards the textualist or the mass communications perspectives can be amplified into dominant routines of thinking, reading and writing on the part of students. No, the best way forward is not to present some utopian argument for a better sort of media studies department in universities, but to re-situate interpretation within the learning process in such a way that its particular utility there becomes clearer; rather than either ignoring it or – worse, as I have argued – simply assuming that it is self evidently *the* way to go about media studies. In the latter instance it too quickly becomes little better than the stale air in a seminar room. So back to Barthes.

What does 'What does it mean?' mean?

Roland Barthes helpfully marks a point in the development of cultural and media 'criticism' when interpretation was both still possible and yet simultaneously being challenged from within because now so ambitiously expanded from its old focus, on authorial intentions, to the newly recognised 'multidimensional spaces' of often unruly texts. (The post-patriarchal hints here are not inappropriate – in a sense the text grew up, become problematic and moved out of the author's house to make a life of its own.) While continuing to write interpretive essays, Barthes could simultaneously push well beyond the outer limits of interpretation in studies such as his unpacking of a Balzac novella in *S/Z*. This sort of French post-structuralism became increasingly hostile to the very idea of interpretation, which was seen as still too tainted by 'totalising' thinking, the ambition still to master textual unruliness and to reduce the multiplicities of the textual space to a single interpretive narrative – in short, to explain or reveal its true meanings. (Post-structuralism took its bearings particularly from the 'structuralist' version of totalising thought that attempted to identify common structures underpinning various cultural forms, such as the basic structures of myth that are shared by many traditional stories across numerous cultures.) The Freudian model of interpretation was taken as a particular target. Where the text in question is what the analysand says on the couch, Freud sought to construct in interpretation a reductive explanatory narrative. This is presented as the unconscious meaning of the text. Similarly, the post-structuralist critics argued, interpretation in general is devoted to uncovering some sort of 'unconscious' in other texts – whether literary or media – and presenting it as a distillation with a claim to truth. One thinks of Gilles Deleuze and Felix Guattari in the vanguard of the objectors to this, arguing instead that the old question 'What does it mean?' has to be dismantled entirely in recognition of the newly discovered fact – as they would have it – that *meaning is nothing other than use.*

When he evoked God in summarising the new understanding of what a text is, Barthes was not using merely a loose metaphor (the 'God like' status of the author as creator of the text). He was signposting the inevitable deployment in interpretive work of a philosophy of history, a particular understanding of where meaning comes from if it pre-exists 'use'. Augustine's *City of God*, in the first century AD, articulated a powerful philosophy of history (it comes from God) and Fredric Jameson acknowledges this in noting: '[G]enuine philosophies of history have never been numerous. And few survive in workable, usable form in the contemporary world of consumer capitalism and the multinational system' (1981:18). Once we do away with God as source of meaning, as ultimate author, then His texts, in the absence of any other philosophy of history, might indeed be surrendered to 'use' – they mean different things to different peoples who use them (e.g. in the form of the Christian Bible) in different ways (and they then slyly evoke God to justify their particular use of the texts). This rings true. So no meaning pre-exists use, then, only the texts from which meaning is made in particular contexts.

Unless, that is, one can think of another viable philosophy of history that somehow puts meaning into things such as texts even before they get to specific contexts of use. It may be tempting at this point, however, just to throw up one's hands and say 'OK, so God is dead but long live the author' and to set about re-establishing authorial intention and creative expression now freed from the shadow of God the Author of Everything. Why does the notion of authorship in that sense necessarily collapse along with God's demise? In fact, it does not *necessarily* collapse (authors continue to exist) but it has a hard job surviving the realisation that texts have their own independent lives, unlegitimised in a totalising sense by the intentions of a controlling creator. There are really two visions of the author here and it's only one of them that's dead. There is the Author-God who is the authority for all the meanings that a text contains and there is the actual, historically grounded author or authors who made the text, laboriously and with little sense of how it might ultimately be used, what it might mean in use. So the many authors of the Christian Bible might be rediscovered in this way (and some have been) but the odd fact that almost nobody, however familiar with the texts, can readily think about those real authors indicates the force of the other vision. The problem arises when we apply that other vision to the way we read texts in general, elevating the author to an impossibly clever, prescient and controlling status. Once we localise the author and realistically limit his or her responsibility for the meanings that circulate in the multidimensional spaces of texts, we are returned to the question of whether *any* meaning can properly be thought to pre-exist use. Is the author a constructor of texts, rather than a giver of meaning, a circus ring-master who brings all the elements together for us but stands back while we then make sense and take pleasure out of it? This is, we should note, an immediately persuasive picture in relation to 'authorship' in the media, where production teams are usually involved in making texts.

The Marxists did, of course, replace God with History as the source of meaning that pre-exists use. Marxism is precisely a philosophy of History as an underpinning socio-economic process that forms and shapes all cultural epiphenomena. So the 'unconscious' that can be revealed underpinning texts is then a political one, and narrative structures, characters, styles, and so on, can all reveal at particular historical moments the underlying workings of the great productive forces, of the markets and of the class structures on which it all depends. (In 1937 Christopher Caudwell produced, in *Illusion and Reality*, perhaps the epitomising piece of interpretation of this sort when he linked in poetry the 'elegant corset of the eighteenth-century heroic couplet' to trade restrictions (p. 86).) But even less than God can this survive the realisation marked by Barthes that there is too much going on in texts for it all to be reduced to a single 'meaning', and this Marxist version of the critical project never managed to prove the worth of its substitute player, History on in place of God, while it stuck to the rules of the established game. On the other hand, as Fredric Jameson has demonstrated, it may be possible to change the rules, or rather to reveal the old interpretive rules as themselves superseded by the new move towards meaning-in-use. This has the advantage that it also side-steps Deleuze and Guatarri's attempt to render the very idea of interpretation redundant. What is redundant is interpretation as an uncovering of hidden meanings (appropriately epitomised by the classic Freudian model just before it became redundant). This approach may have lingered on embarrassingly in the new workplace of bright young scholars pursuing new sorts of critical activity but there are signs that it is finally accepting retirement. The idea of interpretation need not go with it; it can be reinvented.

Before we do some interpretation of the newer sort, we might stop and think about where this leaves today's student when confronted by texts for which she or he is expected to produce 'readings'. At first sight, it leaves her or him a lot worse off. Apparently gone is the Freud-like approach of laying the text down on a couch, sitting beside it with a notebook and analysing it to reveal some hidden meaning, in relation to which much of the text can then be discarded as mere incidentals. So today's student critic tends, instead, to take some pre-existing theory (it might be to do with narrative structures or the gaze or even the castration complex, for psychoanalysis is still around) and then to apply it, often cudgel fashion, to the particular text, which soon surrenders to the role of being mere illustration for the theory. Not surprisingly, then, the same bit of 'theory' is found time and again in the texts being read; the irony being of course that this tends now to send on the Theorist to play extra time when History went off injured, having replaced God in the second half (or third quarter as American readers might prefer).

We need something better, in the particular sense of an approach to interpretation and texts that gives today's learner a clear sense of purpose, a robust opportunity to deal non-reductively with texts and a genuine experience of performing productive critical work from which they see some pay-off in addition to the grades they are given. That pay-off has everything to do with the production of knowledge and with experiencing one's activity – one's critical work – in those satisfying terms. It seems to me that I have seen, persistently, one major problem in student critical writing in media studies. It concerns the lack of method, especially regarding the *signifying processes* at work in texts – the ways in which meaning is supported and organised around features of the text. With this problem dominant, it is not too difficult to understand why so much student writing in the critical, text-based tradition of media studies is inconsequential, reliant on unsupported generalisations and guesswork, thinly 'illustrative' of some caricatured theoretical idea and unexpressive of any personal engagement.

Semiological method

So I want to suggest here an example of the sort of thing we need in our media pedagogy, if we are to address this widespread failing. It is a deliberate focus on identifiable signifying processes and practices, for which I propose Roland Barthes's semiological reading method as a model or prototype. This focus is being urged here, not as a theoretically comprehensive category into which all work of interpretation should fall – it is most definitely not that – but as a pragmatically important and useful stage through which a learner should pass in this field of ours. There may well be just as useful alternatives, but my point here – and I can't urge this too strongly – is that learning in media studies, especially within the critical study of mass cultural texts, must pass through some helpful method for the organised 'reading' of signifying practices and, with that, some explanatory moment that points beyond the negative, the textual dismemberments, the takings apart, to grasp a positive, creative promise in all of this effort (and in the texts that are subjected to it). What I have in mind, especially, are students who have undertaken some serious introductory work in media studies, of the kind sustained by O'Sullivan *et al.*, *Studying the Media* (1998). They then move on say, given the text-based interests of critical media studies, to look at national cinemas, genres, TV soap opera and issues of gender, advertising, news, and so on – a whole range of objects of study that are organised into this or that specific curricular framework (courses, 'modules', etc.). Assuming that a further move will take them to more specialised topics, such as those pursued in dissertation work, I am thinking of my particular pedagogical area of concern here as falling in the middle, where, as I understand it, this whole book is particularly intended to be effective (a 'middle' that has been ill served, it has to be said, making this such a welcome initiative).

One further issue in contemporary media studies that requires note before we try our hand at interpreting something, is the perception sometimes encountered outside the field that it is a 'Mickey Mouse' subject (usually in reference specifically to the critical, text-based sort of media studies rather than the 'harder' mass communications approach, a distinction, of course, which we wish to break down here). In idiomatic English this accusation seems to imply triviality and a lack of method or intellectual seriousness. Unfortunately, this characterisation, as I have suggested, often seems apt when applied to the work actually produced by many students, so perhaps we have to live or die by the achievements of those we teach. On the other hand, those of us who have worked in Latin America do not find Mickey Mouse so trivial after all: ever since Dorfman and Mattelart (1976) famously subjected Donald Duck to an ideological critique, it has been impossible not to see Disney's role in relation to the global expansion of American influence in far from innocent terms. So being a 'Mickey Mouse' subject is not all bad, if the everyday and its 'common sense' are genuinely subjected to serious critique.

Indeed it is in that very spirit that I want to take for interpretation a very particular mass cultural artefact – the soldier doll called GI Joe/Action Man. More specifically, I want to look at a picture, a contrived photographic tableau from Dan Fleming's *Powerplay: Toys as Popular Culture* (1996), which shows GI Joe in Gulf War uniform (American not Iraqi of course) posed before a British newspaper story with the headline 'The Hour Has Come' (figure 19). In fact the soldier doll seems to have stepped directly out of the newspaper photograph of US soldiers. On the other side of the newspaper layout we see Saddam Hussein (looking at his watch) and here, in the foreground, Fleming has positioned a children's party mask of Saddam, grossly caricatured. Assorted toy tanks and aircraft, all with Persian Gulf War associations, litter the lower

(*cont. p. 358*) foreground.

Semiotics

Semiotics is the body of theory that studies signs and sign systems. The core concept is that of the 'standing for' relationship: a sign is an arrangement where something (a signifier) stands for something else (a signified). A sign system, or code, comprises at least two distinguishably different signs, groups of which may be formed by using rules, such as the grammar of a language, the rules of arithmetic or the conventions of a particular style of music. The 'standing for' relationships to be found in nature and culture are extremely diverse and complex. Attempts to identify basic principles of signification, and to categorise classes of signs and sign systems, notably in the lifelong efforts of the American philosopher Charles Sanders Peirce (1839–1914), have produced work much criticised for its intricacy and abstraction. However, it is in Peirce's work that one of the most widely used accounts of the 'standing for' relationship is to be found. If we ask how something may stand for (or stand in for) something else, three types of signifier–signified relationship proposed

Figure 19 'The Warriors of Democracy' by Dan Fleming, in *Powerplay: Toys as Popular Culture*, Manchester University Press (1996)

by Peirce are generally agreed to be present, at least in human experience and practice.

First, there are signs, called iconic in Peirce's terminology, where the signifier relates to the signified by some form of resemblance: photographs look more or less like selected key features of what the photograph is 'of'. Statues, busts and portraits offer further examples of attempts, by means of visual simulation, to represent some original, perhaps very literally, as in forensic photography, or idealised, as in the efforts of taxidermists, morticians and beauticians. Maps, plans, diagrams, scale models, replicas, copies, imitations, signatures, fingerprint matching, mime, games such as charades, impersonation, many aspects of decor and decoration, 'renderings' of scripts and scores, all share this common principle of resemblance, between something – noises, visual images, and so on – which is present to our senses, and something else, which is not directly present, and which it, the signifier, is not. 'Live' television pictures are not the real thing, though real enough in themselves.

Even the signified is not necessarily the real object that the photograph or other form of simulation is 'of'. A selective abstraction is conveyed by the visual stimulus, which the interested viewer recognises, that is, compares with some existing notion. For example, the general 'aircraft' shape we see on roadsigns near an airport looks fairly like our mental image of the objects we particularly associate (to anticipate the next type of signification) with such places. We need never have seen a real aircraft to make sense of the sign, just as we may recognise a person from a photograph (and vice versa in the case of passports). Signification is thus a two-step operation: from sensory stimulus (e.g. a visual image) to generalised concept, perhaps another image; from concept to the specific object or end point of the signifying/interpreting process.

While signifiers are real enough in themselves, for they must be perceptible, it is in their nature to be not-the-real-thing, but to be stand-ins, substitutes. Inauthenticity is thus at the root of semiosis – the process of signifying. More developed forms of inauthenticity are evident in the use of cosmetics and prosthetics by humans to create a semblance of what was (perhaps) once there naturally and for real (e.g. skin texture and colour, hair, teeth). Such examples forbid the assumption that iconic signification is more faithful to the reality represented than the others discussed below, just because the signifier directly maps the signified, and the object if any. The animal and plant worlds, for example, are replete with deceit, with misrepresentation or dissemblance that nonetheless still operates iconically. Many species use camouflage, mimicry, decoys and lures, in all 'sense modalities' not only the visual. Among humans, the deceitful use of iconicity also extends across all the channels and transmitters/receptors. It is frequently benign and desirable: imitation leopard-skin or mahogany is preferable to destruction of the real thing, as is artificially minty breath to halitosis, fragrance to body odour. Many of us enjoy performers who impersonate in living reality expensive or remote originals otherwise known to us only by their representations on film or disk. Indeed, our appetite, in the industrialised world, for substitutes, for the artificial – particularly with regard to the texture, taste and smell of foodstuffs, but in all sense modalities and most domains of experience – is noteworthy and has been much discussed (Eco, 1986; Baudrillard, 1988:ch. 7).

Less benign, however, are other forms of deceit in which the basic semiotic principle of iconicity is at work. Counterfeits of all kinds – for example, fake spare parts or fake medicines, as well as the various sorts of counterfeit currencies – endanger all of us. Lies of all sorts typically embody the basic principle we are discussing, in that their plausibility often stems from a close approximation to what is considered normal and reasonable in the community in which the lie functions. Tact involves constructing a selective approximation – a likeness of sorts – to the whole and only truth. (Eco (1976) goes so far as to define semiotics as the study of whatever can be used to tell lies.) This raises another important aspect of the iconic sign, and indeed of all signs. To expand the definition given in the first paragraph, a sign is an arrangement in which something stands somehow for certain aspects of something else, for someone, or for some community of users. We need signs to make sense together, within and among interpretive communities, thus creating, sustaining and re-creating those communities in the content of our myriad signifying practices.

The second way in which signifiers relate to signifieds is by association, either natural and relatively fixed (e.g. weather signs, some medical symptoms) or cultural and more flexible/revisable (e.g. indicators of social class or stylishness). Peirce called such signs 'indices', or 'indexical signs'. The key concept is that, given X, we can infer Y, and vice versa: as with icons, either partner in the conjunction can function as signifier or signified, depending on where the observer starts from. In both the natural and cultural worlds, this attentiveness to regular co-occurrences is crucial in enabling sign-using species (i.e. all sentient beings) to cope with their environments and to solve their problems. 'Clues' and 'evidence' of all sorts, for instance those of the classic detective novel (Eco and Sebeok, 1983), are good examples of the indexical sign. Typically, a seemingly innocent object, with no significance beyond its own existence, is seen by the forensic genius (above all, Sherlock Holmes) to be significant, that is, to signify: it points to other links in a deductive chain leading to the unique solution. Here again, we can be misled – by false trails or by mistaken beliefs enshrined in custom and practice, including medical practice – about what goes with what for what cause or reason, and hence about how to interpret and deal effectively with the worlds we inhabit.

The third way in which signs relate signifier to signified is by allocation: the users agree among themselves that certain units of the code will have certain meaning(s) and, if the code is to be productive, that certain combinations will be created by the use of constructive rules. All languages, for example, combine and re-combine a small number of semantically empty sounds to create much larger numbers of larger units (e.g. word parts, words, compound words, etc.) which are then re-combined non-randomly, and so on to the infinity of verbal texts with which the speaker-listener must contend. The key concepts here are arbitrariness (anything can stand for anything, in principle) and conventionality (the signifier–signified associations we in fact use are overwhelmingly ready-made, certainly at word and often phrase level, and learned in the process of socialisation). Peirce called this third class of signs 'symbolic'. (This was an unfortunate choice, as everyday use of the term is closer to the notion of the iconic. We commonly refer to the familiar blindfold figure holding up scales as 'symbolic' of the disinterested weighing of evidence that the judicial process is said to offer. In fact this visual metaphor, like most metaphors, operates on the basis of a similarity between two processes, and is iconic in Peircian terms.)

The value of these three basic semiotic concepts may briefly be illustrated by considering how they interact in the use of signs. Words, for example, are essentially symbolic, but many words depend for their operational meaningfulness upon associations with other words, whether bi-valent (husband–wife; high–low) or polyvalent (number or colour words, for example, and many other semantic fields and sets). Other sorts of association (connotations) gather around specific words, phrases, styles and other semiotic materials in cultural life: the phrase 'the final solution' and the iconic image of the swastika remain powerful signifiers of Nazism, and all that is associated with it, at least for older people in Western cultures. Similarly, relatively recent usage has given associations to the word 'queer' that impact upon colloquial expressions such as 'being on queer street' or 'queering someone's pitch'. The ancient rhetorical concepts of metonymy and synecdoche are, of course, captured in this broad perspective, where we are emphasising signification by the use of association in some form or degree. Resemblances of many sorts also operate in language use: for example, onomatopoeia, alliteration, rhyme, rhythm, certain euphemisms ('gosh' for 'God') and, above all, metaphor.

Allusion, allegory, plagiarism, pastiche, faking and forgery are to be found in texts of every sort, not merely or mainly linguistic. There is a mimetic element in many texts, even those that renounce realism but which contain enough recurring samenesses or internal patterning to allow some measure of understanding. Moreover, signs which are originally or fundamentally iconic, indexical or symbolic, may be used in either or each of the other modes, as may entire texts: books are in themselves symbolic, but signify differently when burned, brandished or used as a fashion detail. Also, many everyday signs (e.g. traffic signs) are composites, mixing all three sorts of signification. Airport signs often carry the word 'airport', and perhaps a directional arrow, as well as the image already discussed.

The above account considers just one of three interlocking classification systems for, or perspectives upon, signs, each similarly three way, offered by Peirce. It does so by focusing on whatever 'objects' these may refer to. The two other trichotomies emphasise the nature of the signifier and the signi-fied (called the 'interpretant' by Peirce), respectively. As any particular sign will embody aspects of each trichotomy, a minimum of twenty-seven poten-tial combinations is generated, and so on into the unmanageable complexity that has caused many sympathetic to Peirce's project to give up in despair (see Hervey, 1982:section 1.3). One other complaint about the Peircian legacy must be noted. For Peirce, the ultimate form of signification was to be found in those philosophical discourses (including the sciences) wherein the mind engaged with the most potent and telling generalisations about experience and reality; for example, the laws of geometry or of rational thought itself. His semiotic enterprise embraced these superordinate considerations con-cerning the making of sense, as well as, potentially, all subordinate domains, particularly those where some sort of codedness is evident. In its scope would therefore be the object domains (and scholarly discourses) of all the arts and all the sciences, especially the life sciences where the most fundamental coding of all – genetic coding – operates. Consequently, semiotics has been accused of rampant immodesty and of banality, on the argument that we make scholarly sense somewhere between saying absolutely everything about hardly anything (the specialist perspective of normal scholarship) and hardly anything about absolutely everything (the alleged semiotic perspective).

Lastly, this account of semiotics ignores the body of work often gathered under the title of 'semiology'. The key figure here is Peirce's near contempo-rary, Ferdinand de Saussure, whose relatively sparse and speculative com-ments on the possibility of a science of signs have since been appropriated into the tradition that moved from structuralism, through post-structuralism, to postmodernism, with its very different account of how meaning might be stabilised and widely shared. The main difference is that this alternative per-spective seeks to deny the universalising, positive pursuit of enduring essen-tials of the broadly Enlightenment tradition adopted by Peirce (and in the account here), emphasising instead relativity, oppositionality, deviance, con-tingency, and so on.

Bill Scott

To begin thinking about the mass cultural object GI Joe and about the striking picture from *Powerplay*, we can go back to Barthes's collection of exemplary essays in cultural criticism, *Mythologies* (1993: a recent edition of collected essays first published in French periodicals in the 1950s). One of these short essays is simply called 'Toys'. Barthes says: 'Toys here reveal the list of all the things the adult does not find unusual: war, bureaucracy, ugliness, Martians, etc.' (p. 53). He goes on to note that the child can only understand herself or himself as recipient and user of these things, not as a creator (for which she or he has to go back to wooden blocks). Toys '*always mean something*' insists Barthes (his italics) and this something includes centrally the 'myths . . . of modern adult life' (1993:53). Now the whole point of Fleming's book on the contemporary toy, as I understand it, is to argue that in fact today's toys are precisely constructional like the old building blocks, except that now the components are cultural meanings that can be built up, rearranged, knocked over by the child. But this interesting difference of opinion notwithstanding (and Barthes was writing before the emergence of the 'new toy' described by Fleming), Fleming shares with Barthes a conviction that the myths of adult life need to be grasped in relation to the toys that carry them so successfully into the hands of children. The value of the book *Powerplay* is that it documents the way in which today's toy has become so thoroughly a mass cultural object, inextricably bound up with television, comics, and so on, which gives us all the justification we need to look at GI Joe here.

So here we have a GI Joe soldier doll, relaunched in Gulf War uniform after several years out of production. First appearing in 1964, GI Joe did not survive the trend towards collections of small 'action figures' stimulated by the spin-off toy range from the *Star Wars* films. So in the late 1970s and 1980s, GI Joe contracted in stature and proliferated in identity into dozens of little figures. Quite clearly, as an image of American military confidence, he had also been badly shaken by defeat in Vietnam. By the mid 1970s it was simply not possible to 'buy' the myth of the soldier-hero, essentially a Second World War myth relayed via the comic books of the 1950s and 1960s, without being deeply troubled by some sense of his fundamental failure as an icon. But while the United States rediscovered a role as global policeman and learnt where and how to play it out without actual and symbolic risk (no more Vietnams, but high-tech interventions with limited entanglement on the ground), GI Joe could make his reappearance without embarrassment. His 1993 relaunch as the large soldier doll once more reasserted the power of the old, briefly interrupted, myth, with the military success of the Persian Gulf War as apparent historical evidence of his renewed capability, and replacing Vietnam in cultural memory as it were.

So far so good. This angle allows us to situate our mass cultural object – GI Joe – in some sort of historical context, where his role does not seem to be an innocent one at all; his disappearance and reappearance not mere marketing decisions but synchronised with the peaks and troughs of both American military realities and associated cultural myths. But what to do next? The student writer will typically give up at this point, having offered a few generalisations, an appropriate quotation or two, the 'discovery' of a meaning not superficially available at first glance. What is missing is any proper explanation of the signifying processes at work, whether in the original object, GI Joe, or in Fleming's picture, itself worthy of closer examination for the 'argument' it embodies.   **359**

Barthes's *Mythologies* again proves instructive. Our brief interpretive sketch above might easily become a short essay of the sort Barthes offers on toys, wrestling, Einstein's brain in a jar, and so on. But, as his translator points out in her introduction, Barthes's essays look at first to be idiosyncratic and underdeveloped while gradually revealing the presence of an underpinning *method*, one which he presents more clearly in the longer essay 'Myth Today' which finishes the collection. Barthes had just read Saussure's founding suggestions about semiology and took them to offer a method with which to 'go further than the pious show of unmasking' the objects of mass culture (1993:9) in order to explain more precisely the signifying processes at work through such objects. So Barthes's readings become trial exercises in interpreting in this more ambitious way. What I am suggesting is that the learner can usefully repeat this stage in Barthes's own development (he would go on to fuller, more worked over, post-structuralist dissertations of his own such as *S/Z*, but these 1950s essays are an exemplary middle phase of interpretive insight and *reproducible* method). At the heart of this early, useful method was Barthes's adaptation of a broadly Sausurrean terminology to describe the 'imbricated system' or nested levels of signifying process through which cultural objects carry 'myths'. By 'myth' Barthes means the third level of this system of signifying strata, so we cannot really understand this particular notion of myth until we grasp the whole system, which is actually quite simple though very powerful in its explanatory potential.

Following Saussure, Barthes understands meaning to be organised through signs, or signifying units. Now the first nice insight embodied by Barthes's method here is that our recognitions of what constitutes a sign change with our angle of interpretive attack. This is where he draws up a three-levelled signifying system and uses a cover picture from the magazine *Paris-Match* (no. 326, June 1955) to clarify it. The picture shows a young black boy in uniform (one takes it to be a French youth organisation uniform). He is looking up, out of the frame, and saluting. He looks keen and proud (the cover photograph is reproduced in Deacon *et al.*, 1999:145). In Saussure's terms every sign is made up of the relation between a signifier and a signified, or both the material carrying the meaning and the meaning carried. So here we have a first-level signifier: the materiality of the photographic image, the colours and outlines on paper, the tones, the highlights and shadows, the grain, all of which have been photographically reproduced and printed. But human beings are so adept at reading signs that what we 'see' immediately is the image of the boy – that is, the signified at this first level. And the key next move in this method of reading signifying processes is to see that the sign on this first level then becomes in its turn a new signifier at a second level. So meaning continues to accumulate as we look at the magazine cover. Now we have a signifier that consists of the first-level sign (which we can still decompose back into its own signifier and signified as we did above). Here the total effect, as it were, of the image at a second level of signification is to 'suggest' pride, patriotism (we surmise that the boy is saluting a flag) and an imagined scene in which a uniformed youth group is gathered ceremonially together.

A characteristic feature of the signifying process at work in cultural objects is that we find it difficult to 'stick' at that first level of signification; to say, as it were, it's just a uniformed black boy saluting. Instead we move almost without effort to the second level, where we are actually reading a new signifier for *its* signified and creating a new sign, all built on top of the first. So the cover picture becomes a sign of that surmised ceremonial occasion, of the boy's participation in a collective event, of the pride that it occasioned. But – and here we get to the really exciting and useful part of Barthes's simple interpretive method – there is yet a further level! The signifying process is the same. We take the second-level sign as just described and it becomes in its turn another signifier on this third level. Barthes describes the signified now (he's glancing at the magazine while waiting to get a haircut):

> whether naively or not, I see very well what it signifies to me: that France is a great Empire, that all her sons, without any colour discrimination, faithfully serve under her flag, and that there is no better answer to the detractors of an alleged colonialism than the zeal shown by this Negro in serving his so-called oppressors. (1993:116)

And in this process of nesting, or imbricating, one level of sign relation within another, we see the signifying process through which, in Barthes's terminology, 'myth' is created, the third-level significations where the material stuff of a picture's composition now carries ideas of national greatness, and so on (We might want also to say, therefore, that ideological factors come particularly into play on this third level.)

Once we set out deliberately to recognise these third-level significations for what they are, we find that we have a helpful method in place to disentangle them from all the other things that are going on in the 'multidimensional' spaces of the texts we are considering. So let us look at GI Joe again with this in mind and see if we are still satisfied with having simply uncovered the connotation of the contemporary American soldier-hero, revitalised (at least to eleven inch stature) by success in the Persian Gulf. The problem with stopping at this 'discovery' is that the soldier doll might then just as well be thought of as a mere symbol, like the French tricolour or the Stars and Stripes, symbolising patriotism. Undoubtedly there is a sense in which GI Joe can be a symbol of that kind, as a mass produced object, but he (it?) is much more as well. The black boy saluting might be taken for a symbol, for example if reproduced enough, put on a stamp, instantly recognised, but, Barthes notes, in the actual photograph where he appears for the first time,

> [t]he form of myth is not a symbol: the Negro who salutes is not the symbol of the French Empire: he has too much presence, he appears as a rich, fully experienced, spontaneous, innocent, *indisputable* image . . . If I read the Negro-saluting as symbol pure and simple of imperiality, I must renounce the reality of the picture. (1993:118, 129)

What Barthes is insisting upon here is that the third-level significations we identify must not be reductions to the status of crude symbols – the boy means imperial assimilation, GI Joe means US military power – but have to be allowed their own particularity and expressive complexity, their own reality, the very basis of their apparent indisputability (whereas a symbol is obvious as such and can be fairly swiftly rejected if one feels so inclined). These third-level significations are much more persuasive.

This is where so many student readings of mass cultural texts and objects fall down. The discovered meanings are typically presented in just the way Barthes denies, as if they were 'symbolism' slyly carried by the text or object, rather than as third-level significations that cannot simply be read off without paying attention, not just to the reality of the text or object itself, but to the underpinning levels of signification on which the whole process of meaning making actually depends. So if we 'read down' from GI Joe's third-level signification what we find is a second level where the signifier is 'GI Joe' and the signified is 'Second World War' (an associative or indexical relationship). Until his temporary departure from the scene in the late 1970s, the GI Joe soldier doll was steeped in the imagery and associations of the Second World War. Most of his costume sets (sold separately) were from that conflict (including Nazi uniforms) and his place in popular culture generally was very much among Second World War comic book characters (Fleming recalls *Sgt Rock* from DC Comics, for instance) and John Wayne movies such as *The Sands of Iwo Jima* (an award-winning TV commercial for the toy's launch in 1964 had, in fact, intercut shots of the doll with scenes from Hollywood war movies). GI Joe never shook off these associations with that older conflict, which is why he had difficulty surviving Vietnam, along with many Americans' illusions that war would always be like the 'remembered' simplicity and heroism of the Second World War as re-imagined in popular culture. So his reappearance in 1993, wearing the name 'Duke' (John Wayne's nickname) on his desert uniform, was not his reinvention for a modern war but the rediscovery of that Second World War myth and its reassertion in relation to contemporary conflict.

This reassertion of a Second World War myth depends on that second-level signification – 'after' the first (iconic) level where we recognise the materiality of the object as a soldier doll and toy but 'before' the third-level signification of America's 'heroic' answer to the challenge, when 'The Hour Has Come', to step back on to the world stage armed and ready. On this second level the toy is recognised as 'GI Joe/Action Man' (the signifier at this level) and the connotations of the Second World War come flooding back (the signified). So what? Well, the reactivation of a Second World War storyline was not confined to Joe's revival. It characterised CNN reporting of the Gulf War, which may have reached one billion viewers worldwide, as something rather like a re-run of the battles in North Africa between the heroic 'desert rats' and the Nazis. It crept insidiously into the way news media reported the conflict, with Saddam Hussein as a Hitler figure (sometimes quite explicitly, as in the case of the London *Evening Standard* which labelled him as such). It even surfaced in the widespread characterisation of Saddam as 'The Thief of Baghdad', an almost subliminal recalling of a spectacularly popular film of that name made during the Second World War, in which a German-American actor played the evil Arab to a schoolboyish Anglo prince. So our simple interpretive method is starting to reveal a good deal more about the signifying process at work in this apparently straightforward example of a mass cultural object. But there is a further twist to the interpretation, not one conjured cleverly out of thin air but clearly there in Barthes's own description of the process. The fully experienced, innocent, indisputable object here is still a toy, the signified on the first level.

Unlike the *Paris-Match* photograph of the saluting boy or the newspaper picture of Gulf War soldiers arranged by Fleming behind the toy in his photograph, the reality here is not that of a boy who actually saluted, a soldier who actually disembarked into the desert, but of a popular toy. This makes the signifying process different from that operating through the newspaper photograph, no matter what the striking similarities. And, consequently, when we turn to interpret Fleming's photograph, something else floats into our interpretive view. The whole edifice of media reporting of the Gulf War depended on a second level signifying process in which the media of photography and video claimed as a signified the *immediacy* of access to signifiers that were actually there – battlefront footage and first-person images as substitute experiences for the viewers at home. CNN reporters pushed themselves into the thick of the action, their participation there being more important than any information they were reporting. At its most insistent, this came from cameras mounted on the very bombs that homed in on Iraqi targets, relaying their pictures until the moment of impact. So in the newspaper photograph in the background of Fleming's image it is not so much the first-level signification that matters (the particular materiality of a newsprint image and its reading as a picture of soldiers) as the second level, which is, in effect, a claim to have been there, the key claim that the media want to make in these times of *immediacy* with satellite technology to back it up. But before the third level locks neatly into place (where the signified is American greatness, etc.), Fleming interferes with that second level by juxtaposing the toy version. This simple alignment introduces the question of any image's constructedness. What actually is the difference between the toy and the photojournalist's picture that so resembles it? In the end we can't resist the movement through the second level where the claim to presence, to having recorded something real, is being made, but even the brief interruption is informative. Not least it serves to remind us that there *is* a signifying process here and not just, in that hackneyed phrase, a 'window on the world'.

Beyond the text

We could shift attention also at this point to a different cultural object or objects, less familiar this time – the photographs of David Levinthal. Levinthal has courted controversy by using toys to 're-create' imagined scenes from American history, most controversially of the Nazi persecution of the Jews. His images of blurred colours and shallow focus from which emerge little fragments, shards of meaning, such as bleached white plastic toy skeletons heaped up by little Nazi toy soldiers, offend some people's sense of decency, of appropriateness; but they also interfere with the signifying process in much the same way as Fleming's more clearly didactic staging here. They insert an interruptive second level of signification into the smooth transitions that normally characterise the movement from image to history and force us to see that process as always one of construction, no matter how terribly real the events being retold, represented. A principal task of interpretation is to ask how that construction works in particular instances, particular moments, particular circumstances. It's with the other half of Fleming's visual argument that we must, then, conclude – the party mask of Saddam Hussein. Surely the point here is that the gross caricature is the 'reality' of the West's understanding of this man, a new Hitler to set against GI Joe? The newspaper photograph is, then, a mere cipher of this constructed reality and the man himself is nowhere to be found. More importantly, in the person of that absent but actual man, in his history, his family, his motivations, his policies, reside largely inaccessible truths about the Middle East. W. J. T. Mitchell expresses this clearly (writing about the CNN version of the Gulf War). Think about the caricature here as the third-level signification, the 'myth' in Barthes's sense, and it suddenly becomes clear that that mask *is* our 'reality', here revealed in all its plastic unreality:

> I don't mean to deny, of course, that Saddam Hussein was (and still is) an evil, vicious, and dangerous tyrant. I only want to note that his characterization as Hitler, as the Butcher of Baghdad, as a man whose very name on American lips elicits echoes of sodomy and sadism, has more to do with the strategies of a public relations war than it does with any political or historical analysis of the real aims and consequences of our war in the Middle East. The main function of this caricature was reductive and emotional – to simplify the issues to a straightforward moral choice, to whip up war fever and mass hatred against the enemy, and to make rational debate and opposition to the war seem like an act of treason. (Mitchell, 1994:404)

A final three points, then, about method. I want to emphasise again that I am not urging a rediscovery of Barthes's semiology as the best method of interpretation for mass cultural texts. What I am proposing is that it is an especially helpful method for the learner to adopt at a particular stage in her or his development as a student of the media, in what I have characterised broadly as a middle phase between introductory concepts and later work of more subtlety, theoretical and methodological variety, and analytical sophistication. Setting about pursuing a series of essays in the 'mythologies' of media culture, looking for and unpacking the third-level significations at work in them, is a good and disciplined way of shifting interpretation off mere guesswork. A note on terminology: semiology and semiotics are often taken to be different terms for the same thing, but I am thinking of semiology here as an interpretive method rather than as a 'science of signs' and would suggest that it is very unhelpful to confuse the two. The grand ambitions of semiotics as totalising thought, as a science of communication, have not in the end been especially helpful in media studies, but Barthesian-style semiological method still has much to recommend it in pedagogical practices concerned with meaning in use. The third point is that, having recognised the reductive and emotional functions of the signifying practices that caricatured Saddam Hussein, the learner could usefully set about examining the construction of public knowledge about the Middle East through content analyses of news reports, studies of the professional and organisational routines of CNN or other news media, the mechanisms of public relations or audience research, to discover what sorts of understanding people actually have. These methods take us outwards to embed representational 'myths' in cultural, social and historical realities (the informing dimensions that make texts multidimensional) which can be approached from many angles; rather than having us forget that interpretive findings are not secret messages hidden away inside texts for us to find. In short, the interpretive focus on texts and on related mass cultural objects, even such unexpected ones as GI Joe, is necessary and revealing but only one dimension of media studies.

So I will end with an example from outside the mass cultural object we have interpreted here, GI Joe; an example that makes the point with particular clarity. At the end of 1999 Time Warner, one of the big seven global media empires, presented and profiled the 'Time 100' people of the century on its popular Pathfinder web site. Among the chosen one hundred, rubbing shoulders with Einstein, Mother Teresa and Martin Luther King, was 'The American GI'. The online profile in this instance was written by Colin Powell, US Gulf War general turned politician:

> As Chairman of the Joint Chiefs of Staff, I referred to the men and women of the armed forces as GIs . . . Several years earlier, the Army had officially excised the term as an unfavorable characterization derived from the designation 'government issue' . . . I persisted in using GIs and found I was in good company. Newspapers and television shows used it all the time . . . When you added one of the most common boy's names to it, you got GI Joe, and the name of the most popular boy's toy ever, the GI Joe . . . GI is a World War II term that two generations later continues to conjure up the warmest and proudest memories of a noble war that pitted pure good against pure evil – and good triumphed . . . The GI was the wisecracking kid Marine from Brooklyn who clawed his way up a deadly hill on a Pacific island. He was the black fighter pilot escorting white bomber pilots over Italy and Germany, proving that skin color had nothing to do with skill or courage . . . They were truly a 'people's army', going forth on a crusade to save democracy and freedom, to defeat tyrants, to save oppressed peoples and to make their families proud of them. They were the Private Ryans, and they stood on the thin red line . . . For most of those GIs, World War II was the adventure of their lifetime. Nothing they would ever do in the future would match their experiences as the warriors of democracy, saving the world from its own insanity. [The American GIs] soldiered on through the twilight struggles of the cold war and showed what they were capable of in Desert Storm. The American people took them into their hearts again.

This is an astonishing pronouncement of the myth, weaving together references to late twentieth-century Hollywood revisitations of the Second World War (*Saving Private Ryan* and *The Thin Red Line*) with that war's evocation as a dehistoricised and almost Biblical struggle between 'pure' good and evil (perhaps two generations of distance were needed in order for this to work, as detail fades from collective memory). It is among the clearest examples we are likely to get of what is at stake in linking interpretation to broader forms of analysis. The general's alliance here – newspapers and TV, the toy industry, Hollywood, Time Warner – is marshalled in defence of a myth that takes the world into the twenty-first century with its most powerful military presence thus motivated and legitimised. In all questions of representation we must be determined to ask whose interests and needs are being represented.

Strategies of communications policy research

Communications policy is a key ingredient of the total policy mix within advanced post-industrial societies, in which policy is constructed as the governance of the public interest. In general, policy may manifest itself at specific sites of contestation, or as consensually agreed economic and social formations. Communications policy is extraordinary in this general domain, due to powerful vested interests which are challenging the consensual conceptualisation of social life. Nevertheless, contemporary societies incorporate an assortment of policy objectives which are marked by the rapid transformation of social and economic and community needs, which can be met by rationally generated knowledge. Communications of all types serve to meet, advance and challenge these needs. It is for reasons such as this that communications policies are primary features of general policy formulation in contemporary advanced societies.

Contemporary societies have progressively moved beyond their reliance on traditional 'bricks and mortar' industries, such as heavy industry, and factory-based labour for economic growth and development. Service industries, including media activities, operate at every level of these societies which promote the confluence of industrial activities within a nexus of media, communications and new technology concerns. This is generally referred to as the 'information economy', with suggestions that a new entertainment economy is also emerging. Increasingly significant in the convergence of information, media and entertainment is the mediating logic of communications policy.

Working across these converged sectors, communications policy is the site for concerted debate about the democratic flow of information and the ways in which it operates in appropriate spaces in which to meet public needs. Communications policy research functions as an important adjunct to the management and control of changes in the communications industry. A variety of issues cluster around communications policy research, which deserve both localised and generalised (global) theorisation, together with a diverse range of methods and strategies. Rudimentary, yet always necessary, questions can be asked about the fundamentals of research and its outcomes. A methodology drawn from the tradition of normative social science has been an effective tool in establishing and setting goals in the overall process of communications policy formulation. Normative social science recognises that suitable methods of measurement can be tested against established and new theories, which are informed by public policy objectives.

Despite the influence of the normative approach, numerous alternative approaches to communications have been proposed (McQuail, 1987). Foremost among the discussions is the binary model of critical and administrative research. Controversial issues in communications policy arise from the interventionary logic of the normative approach which sets a research agenda by undertaking focused inquiry which, in turn, seeks to directly inform and influence communications activity. This approach seeks to maintain a distance from the vested interests – capital, labour and government – in an effort to provide an independent perspective on the issues, coupled with policy objectives which serve the public.

Alternatively, opponents of this approach maintain that research should be responsive to the needs of existing communications and government interests. Such administrative approaches *follow* industrial and government (regulatory) activity at a distance, seeking to inform policy with ameliorative measures, rather than creatively to construct it.

Massification of media and communications industries combined in the telecommunications, computing and entertainment sectors has challenged the binary reading of the policy options condensed around the critical and administrative approaches. An influential response – in the critical tradition – was made by James Carey, who suggested that new communications technology and government interests had produced a 'high communications policy' (1981). Capitalist models of competition theory created government, policy, institutional and corporate programmes aimed at removing spatial and cultural obstacles to communication (Innis, 1950). National outcomes overwhelmed local and community interests, as the previous constraints of distance evaporated with the ubiquitous appearance of satellite, cable and digital information compression technologies. A key feature of Carey's proposal was the concept of the disempowering of localised and national communication. This global–national model has been used in a number of recent studies to explain how media industries are incorporated as weapons in a new form of information imperialism, while indicating how differentiated local issues need not be constrained by the US experience (Berland, 1991; Cunningham 1992; O'Regan, 1993).

Optimistic normative readings of communications policy could describe Carey's formulation as defeatist, offering localised and national perspectives that suggest socially beneficial possibilities (Sinclair *et al.*, 1996). Many of these approaches are premised on the belief that contemporary communications technology offers an increasingly broad range of options for communications policy. Price and availability of communications technologies have produced fragmentation, which offers its own possibilities for operating in new social spaces, and which appropriate policies can support. This is especially the case with indigenous, self-managed models (Molnar, 1993). Furthermore, readings of post-modernity suggest that a 'low theory' of contemporary popular media production and consumption produces configurations where empowered audiences engage with cultural commodities using sophisticated strategies learned over time in the market economy (Frow, 1995).

Compelling theories must, however, remain conscious of the social, cultural, economic and industrial forces that converge in communications policy. One way of conceptualising this relationship in the social democratic context has been proposed with the 'cultural policy formulation' model (Breen, 1999). The nature of policy itself may be that it is a mechanism for moderating the extreme interests of any participants in society in general, as information becomes more closely aligned with market interests. The formulation of specific policies will vary with the prevailing political economy of the national and local circumstances and technological capacities.

Qualitative public communications policy formulation will seek to operationalise research that reflects the interests and concerns of producers, users and governments in a variety of localities and sites that are frequently contradictory. Establishing informed questions is a key ingredient. The questions may be ranked according to the interests represented: user/audience demand, infrastructure, market supply, equipment, network, content, applications. A single priority issue may serve as a useful indicator of policy objectives: Does the communication policy under consideration involve a Universal Service Obligation and why? What challenges are involved in new digital (or converged) communications that Universal Service or Universal Access may struggle to include? Related issues concern the emergent online digital economy and the availability of transactions within the global economy. Normative research will suggest appropriate policy measures to provide answers to these questions and developments (Brock, 1998; Tsagarousianou *et al.*, 1998).

Communications policy is a key component of the general formation of social, cultural and economic structures in society. Research strategies can challenge conventional readings of government and corporate behaviour in the emerging information economy, by identifying whose interests are represented, and draw attention to new possibilities for human interaction and betterment. The precise characteristics of the research will inform policy in different ways depending on the country, region and circumstances in which the investigation is undertaken and put to use.

Marcus Breen

Afterthoughts

In the face of powerful, barely comprehensible forces loose in our world we turn to books. If this is not to seem like the ultimate evasion, we need considerable faith in the power of reading. *How to Read a Book?* That was the title of Mortimer J. Adler's surprise success on the American bestsellers' list in 1940 but, despite the appearance of a revised edition of Adler's guidebook in 1972, the whole idea of taking advice on reading has fallen rather out of favour. As a consequence, many students who present themselves in our classes do not know how to read. Worse still, they do not know that they do not know.

We can still take Adler as a reliable guide but, with a view to addressing the particular requirements of media studies as a field, the following notes are both highly selective and skewed towards reading media studies books. It helps if one has a good book to read. So the serious student here should go out immediately and obtain for themselves a copy of James Lull (2000) *Media, Communication, Culture: A Global Approach* (Cambridge: Polity, and New York: Columbia University Press). Learning how to read a book such as Lull's may be the single most important thing that a student can do in the middle phase of his or her studies in order to consolidate introductory work and to anticipate more specialist later engagements. How, then, does such a book fit into your understanding of things media related?

As Adler notes early in his own guidebook to reading, many people undoubtedly have the growing feeling that the book is only one, decreasingly important, source of information these days. You may feel that you have plenty of information about things without spending much time on serious reading. As a result, reading tends to become a hunting and gathering exercise for tidbits that you use in an essay or examination answer, except when you are reading for pleasure, which may seldom involve media studies books. That is partly our fault – we do not write enough books that can be read for pleasure as well as for information. But, mostly, it is probably a matter of your own different expectations of academic and 'light' reading and your feeling that the modern media themselves are sufficient sources of information most of the time. A good thought experiment here, though, is to imagine that cinema, broadcasting and the web had somehow managed to come into existence before we invented the book. If somebody now presented us with a book as a brand new innovation, we would be mightily impressed. Here would be an adaptable, portable object **369** capable of carrying large amounts of information, all accessible randomly and non-linearly when required (open at any page and browse), easily stored and exchanged, relatively cheap to own. Further, when writers mastered the required techniques of inputting information into this new medium, we might even sense that we had minds alive in our hands every time we opened a good book. Although millions of writers *have* mastered those techniques, it is the book's misfortune (1) to have been around for so long that newer media seem better, and (2) to be so taken for granted that readers now fail to see that there are techniques to good reading also.

Moreover, as Adler says, 'Too many facts are often as much of an obstacle to understanding as too few' (1972:4). The modern media saturate our lives with information but the book remains a principal tool for sorting, sifting, developing perspectives upon and ultimately understanding things. As the online bookseller Amazon has found, the book is becoming more not less important, perhaps because people sense this mismatch between information and understanding. But acquiring the right books is only the first step. Next comes knowing how to read them.

So let's take just a few of Mortimer J. Adler's sensible principles. First, a book can be read for information. For many students this can create as many problems as it solves. Confronted by an essay question or revision for an examination, it is possible to scour the library shelves, not for books to be properly read but for snippets of information. These are, as it were, heaped up along with lecture notes and perhaps videotapes of primary source material such as TV programmes or films, and then confronted by the panicked learner as a mass of information from which some sort of extraction process has magically to occur. The commonest approach is, then, a sort of random hunting and gathering – just wade in and grab anything that comes to hand that seems to link together, however loosely, and stop when it feels like you have enough. To set against this unsatisfactorily shallow approach, let us offer this thought: if seriously read, with time devoted to doing it well, a book such as James Lull's *Media, Communication, Culture* will prove to be genuinely helpful for – no matter how surprising this may seem – literally dozens of different essay topics and examination questions. This is not because the author has somehow cleverly anticipated all the questions you might be asked, but because most of those questions will be probing issues which, at a different level of generality, characterise the whole field of media studies and so inevitably are addressed by a serious author such as Lull who has things to say about that field. You will still have to make the connections through to more specific topics (perhaps using some of that heaped-up information) but your work will be informed by genuine understanding; because that is the other way in which a book can and should be read – not just for information but for understanding. The good news is that there are methods for achieving this.

First, savour the book. Take time to handle it, leaf through it, catch glimpses of what's to come, feel its promise, begin to sense the author's presence in your own mind. Contemporary theories of interpretation reinforce the idea that this is *your work*. The author is not actually there any longer and much of the text, in your hands, may escape his or her specific intentions. But you can still establish a dialogic relationship in your mind, with the book in your hands. So when

James Lull begins by quoting his plumber or writing about his own thoughts drifting off while listening to the 'drone' at an academic conference, there is an offer of engagement with another, an imagined mind here. You will miss it if your aim is only to find, as quickly as possible, something that you can paraphrase in throwing together an assigned essay. So the proper sort of reading cannot be done under pressure. That is why most university courses leave you with so much non-timetabled time. *You need time to read well if you are then to write essays well.* This is not some pious advice from representatives of an older generation who just don't 'get it', whose own lives are so stuffed with books that they can't see there's more to life! It is simply an incontrovertible fact that has been known at least since Michel Eyquem de Montaigne wrote the first essays in the sixteenth century, and there is no reason to suppose it will ever change.

Of course, if you think of the essay as nothing more than an external requirement, a given exercise that simply has to be mechanically got through, rather than as an opportunity to demonstrate, develop and communicate your understanding, then reading for understanding will seem pointless too. That's up to you.

There is an inequality of understanding here. The book's author understands some things better than you do. Reading carefully involves raising yourself to that level, so far as this is attainable. Often, therefore, you need some outside assistance. First, you need to have been assisted towards reading the right book at the right time, in terms of your own intellectual development. (If recommendations from your teachers do not find this match, tell them so and ask for alternatives until you find books that work for you. James Lull's book should work if we are imagining you correctly as we write this.) But, even more importantly, your reading needs to be embedded in an organised process of learning, involving the course you are on, what you make of the lectures and other classes, the discussions you are participating in or attending. At the heart of this are *interconnections* which, to a very great extent, you have to make for yourself as you go along, sometimes looping back to connect something that didn't fit when you first came across it. (We will look further into the question of interconnections, hyperlinkage and related ways of working in Part VII.)

But now down to reading James Lull's book. Having given yourself time to get into the book and having adopted the right frame of mind, the next step is *inspectional reading* (here we are following Adler's stages). 'Skim' or pre-read the book. Look at the Table of Contents – ten chapters with clear titles. Some key words emerge even at this stage – hegemony, audiences, globalisation, etc. What do you know of such topics already, what else have you read, how is this book going to fit in? You will not have many definite answers at this stage but you are starting to think about the book seriously. Flick through the chapters, not carelessly but spotting words and phrases that catch your eye, stopping to read a few sentences here and there. There's a brief discussion, unexpectedly perhaps, of Finland in relation to globalisation, with mention of a Finnish basketball star; the words 'structure' and 'agency' in frequent juxtaposition (you may already know the sort of debate this signposts); there are interesting photographs; brand names stand out in the pages about ideology (Coke, Kodak

. . .); the word 'I' jumps out at you from time to time ('I can tell you from per-sonal experience that growing up in the farmlands of Minnesota . . .'); there are short boxed sections of text throughout (one on Microsoft for example, another on the sex scandal that threatened US President Clinton) which clearly offer case studies related to the main text; there are a lot of references to Brazil and China; there are neat Conclusions sections at the end of some chapters (stop and read one or two); subheadings every few pages begin to give you a clear sense of the topics being covered as you skim; you pause over a section on 'ebonics' (a word you've never seen before) with its examples and discus-sion of black American speech. You begin to sense the way in which James Lull may be handling 'culture' – perhaps as a vast pool of resources for meaning making, criss-crossed by powerful limiting currents but energised by people's capacity to make meanings in their own ways, to swim in their own direction even if against a tide. Only reading the book carefully will allow you to find out if this is indeed the sort of thing he is thinking and saying.

After skimming the book, the second stage of inspectional reading is *super-ficial reading*. Go back and read that section on the Finnish basketball star, read the Clinton sex scandal bit, pick out and read one of the passages on China, and so on. Let your superficial reading spill over into the adjacent pages. Take about thirty minutes on a book of this length and read some sections, drawn by your earlier skimming, quickly and for a general impression rather than to learn anything specific. Many avid readers will do this with every book they obtain but then shelve it and only return to a full reading later, when they need to read something on that particular subject (either because their own think-ing has reached a point of receptiveness to it or because they have some purpose in mind, such as writing on the subject). A crucial point here is that works of non-fiction do not have to be read like novels, beginning at page one and not skipping ahead for fear of spoiling the plot. There is rarely any plot to spoil in this way with non-fiction, and academic books are usually more recep-tive to a method that works its way down from inspectional and superficial to deep readings, rather than adopting a page-by-page approach from the very beginning. This is not to say that such books have no progressively elaborated structure of argument. Hopefully they will have, but it does not have to be encountered in a state of readerly virginity.

Next, either right away or later when you have determined that you really want to read this particular book, you will move on to the serious work, that of *analytical reading*. You will already by now have a good feel for the book, as analytical reading is hard to do from 'cold', as it were. When you begin reading an academic book slowly and carefully the coming pages can seem weighty and threatening if you have never looked at them; inspectional reading will have broken through this psychological barrier for you and you may even be looking forward to seeing how precisely that Clinton scandal fits into the devel-oping argument. Vital here is fine tuning your own ability to find the book's main *propositions*. A book will offer a lot of detail and typically plenty of tan-gential detours into interesting but supporting material. If it has been well written, however, you will be able to pick out the main propositions as you go along. Of what is James Lull trying to persuade you? What are the various

kinds of example and evidence actually examples and evidence of? You may want to make pencil marks in the margin when you locate these propositions or begin keeping separate notes. Lull is quite helpful in signposting his own key propositions, sometimes even with italics for emphasis (although not every author will do this work for you). So when he says in chapter 5 that 'media audience fragmentation leads to fewer common experiences for any society', you will be fairly sure that this proposition emerges from the examples and evidence in that chapter. But you can do more with propositions than merely locating them in this way. While they need their supporting material to function as a book, they can also be abstracted in your own thinking and recombined to form a more general argument or set of analytical insights into the book's 'big' topics – media, culture, agency, and so on. In your own long-term memory it is likely to be this more formal structure of logically interconnected propositions that you retain and continue to use as a learner (along with a few colourful examples perhaps, which can form useful hooks on which to hang the memories). If you are not reading analytically you may find that almost nothing of the book enters long-term memory (which might be OK for tomorrow's examination but a waste of your own effort beyond that).

Adler has two especially good points to make about analytical reading: (1) you are, in a way, X-raying the book for its skeleton of propositions and the main argument or explanation that is constructed from them; and (2) you should in the end be able to 'state the unity of the whole book in a single sentence, or at most a few sentences' (1972:75–6). You may well have had a stab at that after your inspectional reading (as we did above) but now you should be in a position to have a seriously informed attempt at getting such a summary right. It's only for your own satisfaction that you should do so. It is often fun to compare this with the publisher's blurb on the back of the book. This is written to sell it, thus the overused phrase 'This will be essential reading for . . .' (which should be banned forthwith), and seldom captures the book's import in the way that you should be able to achieve after a proper analytical reading (although students have been known to quote the blurb in essays, suggesting an overly superficial approach to superficial reading!). More importantly, in fact, the synoptic sentence or two that you come up with may actually capture *what the book now means to you*, which does not have to be a universally acceptable summary. So we will not offer a summary of Lull's book here (except to say that our first stab at it, after an inspectional reading, was not too far off the mark).

That's you finished now, right? Not quite. The final point to emphasise is that reading one book in media studies is not (or hopefully not!) an isolated event. Reading to learn is a larger process than the reading of one book at a time; it is more than the sum of its parts. So the final stage of reading is the *synoptic*, or what (deviating slightly from Adler now) we will call the *connectively synoptic*. Adler pinpoints the key difference at this level. Where before you were coming to terms with an author, now '*it is you who must establish the terms, and bring your authors to them rather than the other way round*' (1972:318, emphasis in original). But you must know what you want in order even to come close to achieving this. What 'terms' can you establish? These are the terms of your own pursuit of understanding within the field of media studies and, more generally, the terms on which you are forming knowledge for yourself. You may not always formalise these into questions or into descriptions of things that you currently do not understand, but they should be there nonetheless. *Formations* is, in the end, about creating a context in which a learner – a reader – may 'establish the terms' for themselves. Know what you want to understand, what you want to learn about, and you can proceed confidently towards taking your analytical readings of book after book (and journal articles, too, of course) and interconnecting your synoptic understandings of each to form your own personal network of ideas, propositions, evidence, analyses, arguments and hypotheses, the very raw material of knowledge making. Here, reading intersects clearly with method, with the other forms and techniques of knowledge making with which you are coming to terms as a student of the media. Knowing how to read (itself a method) underpins it all. As that personal network grows it will largely determine what you read next (usually several things simultaneously and across subject boundaries) – you will sense where the network needs or will support further extension and where any gaps are. After a while it becomes a part of your life, independent of any institutional requirements, and you have become a learner rather than merely a student.

Part VII
Pop tech

The electronic back tier

Turbo-capitalist media seem to rush ahead, unstoppably, with AOL Time Warner in the lead. It is easy to sit back and just experience the ride, giving up all notion of being anything other than a passenger, a spectator, or maybe even just a bystander getting left behind (as some are). But the insistence in Part VI was on the importance of *method* as an alternative to such passivity. People use media in methodical ways – to make sense, to negotiate meaning, to construct knowledge (where method shades into methodology in media studies), to sustain or counter social movements, to affect policy. Indeed the latter, in the form of communications policy, can seem like the only significant way of applying brakes, of getting the careering juggernaut under some sort of control. You may even have encountered Marcus Breen's short account of issues in communications policy research (the last boxed section above) as a blockage in your own reading here, just as you were starting to think it was all falling neatly into place. Marcus introduces a whole new set of terms and ideas to those already deployed in previous sections, because communications policy is a highly problematic area of contemporary media studies and cannot be neatly dropped into place here with a few accessible generalisations.

Recently revived interest in the 1920s Chicago School of communications research has been based on our recognising the pertinence of its main concerns: how communication technologies might transform societies into communities (starting with the moment when the printing press created 'the public'), because the media of public communication might be *cohesive* in their effects; its interest in studying communications in relation to history and in interdisciplinary ways (rather than with a 'formalism' that reduced it to techniqiues); its version of the 'frontier hypothesis' (America's myth of its own making) in which strangers come together in new spaces to build democratic forms of public life; and its insistence that communication is more than the transmission of information – it is a set of cultural processes. This was an auspicious start for communication studies, but it was burdened by considerable romantic idealism and ultimately crippled by a key contradiction – that the very media which promised so much in terms of new cohesiveness and culture making also had the potential to pull communal life apart, to re-fragment the 'public' they had created. So American communication studies took a different course, into social and interpersonal psychology and linguistics, into emulations of the physical sciences, often subsequently demonstrating a fear of the big cultural questions that so excited Robert Park and his students in Chicago. (This short account draws on James Carey's important 1981 essay.) That intervening history has placed a chasm between much communications research and media studies as described in the present volume, but the Chicago School remains a significant sign of potential for rapprochement, not least since its main concerns now look rather contemporary in the era of the internet. The idea which we can no longer entertain, of course, is that a society might become one big community, its cohesiveness sustained perpetually by its media.

As Carey explains, it was one of the Chicago School's students, Harold Innis, who pointed out that every frontier has a back tier. The American frontier's was first Europe and then its own cities – dense complexes of interests and politics, power and policies – that actually underpinned the frontier communities, which only *seemed* to be inventing themselves anew out there in open spaces. So the larger vision of communication spaces has to recognise its 'back tier' as well. If we can strip out and discard the American 'frontier hypothesis' from the Chicago School's agenda, some vital questions remain, especially about communication 'as a container of human interaction that allows for the persistence and growth of culture' (Carey, 1981:84). Interest in the latter was discarded along with the frontier-inspired romanticism when American communication studies took its turn into social psychology. But media studies later in the century began to revisit it as an increasingly central concern.

Carey notes: 'The United States, then, at all levels of social structure pursued what I call high communications policy, one aimed solely at spreading messages further in space and reducing the cost of transmission' (1981:83). This is the communications policy – focused on the techniques of better, faster, more far-reaching media – that has produced satellite systems, the internet and AOL Time Warner, dominant features of the global media environment today. But what would 'low' communications policy look like? It would have to revisit issues of community and cultural identity but now with a comprehensive recognition of the 'back tiers' that inform all culture-making and identity-making activity.

James Carey offers a striking example that should help to make this clear. It's the 'sabbath', in which he is interested in a secular way. Set aside, for a moment, any religious views you may have and think of Sunday as a social phenomenon. It is a temporal phenomenon. Sundays are not in any particular place or space, they are defined in time. Communications, later sustained by that 'high policy' of constant improvement and extension, first had space to occupy, but as this looked like it was well on the way to being achieved (e.g. with the telegraph system, the nineteenth-century's internet) time became the next target:

> For purposes of communication, the effective penetration of the sabbath came in the 1880s with the invention of the Sunday newspaper. It was Hearst with his New York Sunday *World* that popularized the idea of Sunday newspaper reading and created, in fact, a market where none had existed before

– a sabbath market. Since then the penetration of the sabbath has been one of the 'frontiers' of commercial activity. (Carey, 1981:88–9)

So time, then, became increasingly the target for penetrative communications progress (twenty-four hour supermarkets, night-time radio and TV, global financial markets, video-on-demand, personalised time-shifting digital TV). But what gets penetrated and filled are also the potential spatio-temporal, social 'containers' for human interaction based on other notions, such as community. (The sabbath was one such container, only given a privileged status by believers, but unbelievers need to stop and think too about what is lost if all such potential 'containers' disappear.)

So a 'low' approach to communications policy might focus on whether, where and how secular 'sabbaths' in both time and space may need to be created and protected (if this is still possible at all) from the penetrative progress of AOL Time Warner's turbo-charged media capitalism. As Marcus Breen points out, above, we once thought that policy could either be administrative (following along behind the AOL Time Warners and making adjustments to their impact while not impeding their overall interests) or critical (independent of vested interests). But it is no longer clear where the vantage point for the latter might be. From where is an 'independent' overview going to be exercised? And, in any case, Carey's description of communication technology's total spatio-temporal penetration leaves no room for anything else, does it? On the other hand, if we abandon the administrative/critical distinction, it no longer becomes a question of finding a critical position somehow outside or above administrative interests, but of contributing in a whole range of ways to local, national and global media 'ecologies' constituted in a complex interplay of interests. As Marcus Breen puts it, 'The formulation of specific policies will vary with the prevailing political economy of the national and local circumstances and technological capacities' (p. 367).

For this reason, communications policy is not a matter of some grandly independent policy-making organ (whether governmental or other) to which we can point to see policy making in action. Rather, there is a vast diversity of policy agents at work in the sphere of contemporary media, from government-appointed regulators to non-governmental organisations, lobbying and special interest groups, professional associations (e.g. of journalists), public relations firms, community organisations, social movements and legal institutions. If there is not some outside position of critical independence from all of this which academic knowledge producers can adopt, and from where they might seek to advise on matters of communications policy, you might wonder what role, if any, is left to them. It's just that perhaps – to *be* knowledge producers, through research and teaching, rather than to presume to advise from some imagined position outside vested interests. Communications policy will be the better (and perhaps pitched usefully 'lower' too) for having to work itself out, across multiplicities of interest, in a context in which robust knowledge about the media is being produced and circulated.

This is back tier work and necessarily so. It also renders that old Chicago School dream of community through communications technology as a new, more limited but just as important, sort of interest. In AOL Time Warner's world do we want to – can we? – create times and spaces for something called 'community'? To answer that question we have to think about what the word means, what the alternatives are, where and when such 'containers' could be created, what sorts of intervention would be needed to achieve them. These too are back tier sorts of question, not those concerned with some imaginary electronic frontier of boundless opportunity. Strangers can still come together in new mediated times and spaces and, although they are a lot less free to do what they want there than we once thought, the question of whether they can overcome their estrangement from each other remains vitally interesting.

Dan Fleming

20

Pop tech and pedagogy
(or, 'I link, therefore I am')

Tereza Batista

> Lights and screens blinked on spasmodically in houses all along the empty streets, his own included; the world was plugging in. Urquhart didn't see the need. He stood in the scrub, down in this pocket of quiet darkness banked on all sides by the spreading radiance. He felt as if he'd just turned on some sharp vector, bearing into a kind of adjacency, another world . . . Back in that other world of time and violence the frayed voices were spilling from the media, filling the rooms . . . He could try to be Outside but it wasn't happening. The voices would find him here. Things didn't sound promising back in the other world. Though Urquhart could not make out a single word, the tones of voice told him everything. The news hounds had their blood up. Something nasty was in the offing.

This is near the beginning of Stuart Moulthrop's hypertext fiction *Victory Garden* (1991). Published for the 'Storyspace reader', perhaps the most highly regarded environment for hypertext writings, *Victory Garden* may be read fairly traditionally by paging through the text on-screen. But each 'page' holds multiple links from which that particular progression in the reading gives way to others.

So, in the extract above, the words 'plugging in' yield to:

> We stumbled from room to room flicking on TVs, radios, tape decks, VCRs . . . While it was happening all we wanted was to be multiply channeled and networked . . . We yearned to hear all those voices around the dial, not out of distrust or skepticism so much as a hunger for input . . . It was a reflex burned in somewhere between Dallas and the Sea of Tranquility. The event must be grasped in all its multiplicity, it must be broken down and remembered. We must match the frequencies, we must get in tune.

Whereas the words 'his own included' yield to: 'Urquhart stepped back into the light again and it was like walking back through the doors of an asylum . . . In the living room, deep in the heart of it all, sat . . .' And this time the conventional narrative route, of accompanying the actions of a protagonist while introducing further characters, continues, at least for a while. Not that the branching optional routes are mere tangents; rather, they loop around the 'story' in ways that each elaborate its significance. The 'something nasty . . . in the offing' turns out to be the Gulf War. It is the winter of 1991. Boris Urquhart is a deeply unsettled, middle-aged academic who is loved by Emily, **381** now serving with US forces in the Gulf. Emily had been involved with Victor Gardner, one of Urquhart's graduate students, to whom she has sent a letter breaking off their relationship. As the tangle of personal relationships unravels, the reader can move to and fro across both that story's particular textual manifestations and other material, including reflections on the war and on the media. Roland Barthes's 'multidimensional space' of the text here becomes concretely realised. One has to relearn the reading process to a degree – it is easy to feel the fragments slipping away into randomness and to let them go, clicking arbitrarily through links – but if carefully done by the reader the cumulative effect is quite startling and informative. 'The voices would find him here', says Moulthrop. The voices find the reader too, voices from elsewhere(s) that coexist within this remarkable textual space.

Stuart Moulthrop is one of a group of Eastgate authors ('Storyspace' is a product of publishers Eastgate, which maintains a thriving community of hypertext scholars and readers around its catalogue), including Michael Joyce, Shelley Jackson and Stephanie Strickland. These authors have been pushing forward our still underdeveloped understanding of hyperfiction and gradually finding readers who are willing to retrain themselves to read in this new way. What *Victory Garden* demonstrates is that a particular strength of these new narrative forms may be their capacity to interconnect different levels of experience, from the personal to the historical, without recourse to the compressive, foreground/background trick of the great nineteenth-century novelists. In *Victory Garden* the Gulf War is not 'background' – it breaks into the reading of the story in multiple and (genuinely) unpredictable if determinate ways, precisely because that reading is itself a deliberative, constructional process.

Now this is, perhaps, the great challenge facing both the media and media studies today. How do we stop clinging to the illusion of the comprehensively all-embracing univocal work (whether the great film or TV drama series, the great work of theory, the great textbook or the great instance of pedagogical comprehensiveness) without surrendering to random fragmentation, collage, cut-and-mix assemblages that lead us nowhere? What is deeply helpful about *Victory Garden* and similar experiments is that they demonstrate how such a surrender is the outer limit, an always present risk inherent in moving away from the old univocal ambitions. It is possible to read *Victory Garden* as a series of gradually disintegrating fragments, a chatter of multiple voices. But with effort this need not happen. It becomes in large part *the reader's responsibility*.

So, if we extend this insight, what responsibility now confronts us when we find ourselves faced by Walter Salles's Brazilian cinematic work *Central Station*, one of the closest things we have to a traditionally 'great' film of the late twentieth century, and *The Sopranos*, an indisputably 'great' TV drama series, when these are juxtaposed with the new forms – say, British film maker John Akomfrah's 'black sci-fi documentary' *The Last Angel of History* (1996); or DJ Spooky's 'illbient' albums *Songs of a Dead Dreamer* (1996) and *Riddim Warfare* (1998). Or, and let us take this as a primary emblem of pop tech, Mariko Mori's 'photograph' *Birth of a Star* (1996)? To put it bluntly, is media studies any good to us now?

Media studies as an urgently needed field of scholarship and pedagogy can easily run scared from all of this. It is populated by many academics and teachers who were revolutionising the humanities in our universities when they first began thinking and teaching about the films of John Ford, or even the music of Bob Dylan, in the 1960s. Studying Ford's film *The Searchers* today is to take seriously a Hollywood film in a popular genre, the western, that might have been dismissed as mere escapist entertainment. It is a film that continues to raise some profound questions about American culture, about cinema itself and about narrative in history. But it is also now safely contained by the passing of time, by the accumulation of largely agreed scholarship concerning it and by its cultural irrelevance when set alongside the contemporary examples quoted above. But can today's Boris Urquharts be expected to reinvent themselves in middle age as listeners to DJ Spooky, never mind teaching in some way that seriously addresses the contemporary? Probably not, although of course there will always be bright young graduate students coming off their PhD programmes to replace them, bringing the flipside of that problem – can *they* be expected to take *The Searchers* seriously?

The solution – for I wish to say that there is one – is already prefigured in the implications of *Victory Garden*. Pedagogy has to transform itself into something like hypertext writing and shift responsibility on to the learner to 'read' – to learn – in ways that cut close at times to the arbitrariness, the senseless fragmentation, but pull back to something else, something that does ultimately hang together. There simply does not appear to be any alternative, except the conservative and nostalgic retreat to having students do no more than sit in lectures where the professor expounds on the interpretation and cultural context for media stuff that fossilised long ago (which with media history's pace may be a mere decade ago or less). What this means is that media studies has to recognise it is teaching media history much of the time (and preferably call it that). To take on Spooky, Mori or Akomfrah, and to situate the 'great' contemporary media content (say, *Central Station* and *The Sopranos*) in relation to them, is something else entirely. But get it right and media history then falls into place as the indispensable adjunct, or hypertextual other level, of living media studies.

The narrator in *The Last Angel of History* says this at one point: 'If you find a crossroads, any crossroads, this crossroads, if you can make an archaeological dig into this crossroads, you'll find fragments – technofossils – and if you can put those elements, those fragments together, you'll find the code. Crack that code and you have the key to your future.' This forty-five minute 'art' film concerns a futuristic character, the Data Thief, who is sent back to our time to 'dig' for cultural fossils and unlock the secret of black culture. Armed with metal sunglasses and a black box, the Data Thief goes in search of people, including DJ Spooky, who can help him assemble his fragments. The film's computer-assisted collage style reflects this quest. There is, of course, no magic code, no single future in that sense (not least because there are so many crossroads). The film is about constructing one. Technofossils in the making are the stuff of contemporary media cultures. Quickly sedimented into our individual and collective experience, they are the stuff too of a recombinant pedagogy that finds itself having to discover and employ the best method of the new media; not so much cut and mix (which implies too little responsibility on the reader's, viewer's, listener's, recipient's, learner's part) as 'ergodic' construction (which we will define in due course).

But first to Mariko Mori, the Japanese photographer and artist working in New York, whose *Birth of a Star* (1996) we are taking as a pop tech emblem. This is a large transparency set into a light box, with an accompanying pop tune that burbles along jauntily. The image shows Mori, full length, colourfully costumed, half like a cellophaned *Barbarella* space chick, half a mini-skirted Japanese comic-book teen, while colourful spheres (bubbles? balloons?) float around her. It is a striking image, evoking in some ways the 'Film Stills' of Cindy Sherman but without Sherman's edge of menace and irony. Bright, airy and cheerful, *Birth of a Star* has a lingering afterglow that proves unsettling in its own peculiar way. Mori has said in interview:

> I can be a Japanese, or a New Yorker or even a 'transcended' person – regardless of race, gender, sexuality, etc. Using images of myself originates from when I was a fashion model, at around age sixteen. Often I designed my own clothes and made them myself – I studied at a fashion college – and I asked a photographer to take a photograph of myself wearing the clothes that I made. Some way my work is the extension of those experiences. Further back into my childhood, my father loved to take photographs of me. (online interview, *Journal of Contemporary Art* on the web, 1998).

It is this combination of 'transcended' identity and DIY teen fashion-model exhibitionism that proves usettling – the cut and mix here is largely empty, except for the inhabiting of the images by Mori's own 'Japaneseness' as a self-consciously exhibited otherness. This is close to being a sort of self-imposed techno-orientalism, where 'Japanese' is offered as already quintessentially techno pop in orientation, in its superficial otherness, its exoticism, its surrender to technologised popular culture, its glossy geekishness. But Mori's work is intelligent and knowing – like the knee-socked Japanese schoolgirls who flounce past the grey-suited salarymen, all too conscious of their widespread Lolita complex – and the point about her techno-orientalism is that it presents itself this way, it is not the invention of a coloniser's fascination. Still, she forces the central techno pop question clearly into view. Is there nothing more, is it all a recombinant game, a playful acting out of 'transcended' identities in the realm of cut and mixed images?

That question is at the centre of DJ Spooky's equally self-conscious work with sound. Spooky (real name Paul Miller) began his DJ-ing career while at college (sedate Bowdoin College in Maine, on whose web site he is not currently listed among the notable alumni), moving on to clubs in Washington, DC and New York. New York's 'illbient' music scene in the 1990s took ambient music (immersive soundscapes) and added a twist of more hard-edged hip hop influence (ambient soured by urban malaise?). Miller's particular interest was in including in the mix elements from a highly diverse range of sampled popular cultural sources, including TV and movies. While he returned to hip hop's early focus on the turntable and DJ (rather than emphasising studio production), his diverse range of materials, and his retention of an overall commitment to realising the socially imprecise ambient notion of aural 'space', distanced him from the street where hard-core rap was increasingly caught up in violence and turf wars. Miller's middle-class college background and wide reading in cultural theory (he took French literature and philosophy at Bowdoin) further distanced him from the social realities of the hip hop scene outside his door, on which he nevertheless drew for his method. Among the other influences Miller acknowledges on his thinking and practice is the Afro-Brazilian syncretic religious tradition where music, especially in north-eastern Brazil, is central to a cut-and-mix fusion of Roman Catholic and West African mythologies. DJ-ing becomes a syncretic method: 'it's a way of creating a weave or a fabric of sounds' (demonstration and talk given at Harvard University, 30 November 1998).

Spooky makes it clear that his work is not intended to create 'really clean, smooth mixes that respectfully reference established styles', but rather to make abrasive assemblages (*ibid.*). Do these go beyond the formal practice of construction and reconstruction? Do they 'mean' anything more? There is not, of course, any extractable message from a Spooky track, any idea merely carried or transmitted by the musical and aural assemblages. Nor, to his credit, do the tracks 'illustrate' any of the theoretical concerns about which Miller can be highly articulate on other occasions (e.g. in the albums' sometimes awkwardly pretentious liner notes). Rather, the work challenges listeners to put non-trivial effort into, not intellectualising meaning, but grasping the mix and *feeling* how it works as a pop tech soundtrack in which they are involved, and the elements of which they can recognise in principle. This is what differentiates his pop tech practice from the careful studio constructions of, say, Dogon (Miguel Noya and Paul Godwin), whose *The Sirius Expeditions* and *redunjusta* (both 1998) are masterpieces of sound collage and 'smooth mixes'. With Dogon one can intellectualise the use of a poem read in an Arkansas schoolhouse by a thirteen-year-old girl. With Spooky this sort of stuff is just grabbed because it is there and then mixed so that it barely carries any of its original meanings at all, except hints and traces, evocations and half-grasped recognitions, things overheard in passing, thoughts more felt than articulated, invitations.

Among the material cut and mixed in *Riddim Warfare* (1998) are a Buddhist chant performed by Mariko Mori and a tape made in Brazil where Spooky jammed with the Bahian percussionists Nação Zumbi (drums are at the heart of the Bahian *candomblé* cult in whose temples women engage in slow, circular, swaying dances awaiting 'visitation' by one of the gods). When talking about the work, Spooky has a habit of identifying such elements' claims in the overall mix with the phrase 'Check it out!', as if each momentarily asserts itself, not so much in the sense of a quotation as of an invitation. His tracks are invitational machines and the always implicit 'Check it out!' implicates the listener in an acknowledgement of the fact that they already know, in principle, how all this hangs together. Otherwise it would be impossible to listen to, as undoubtedly would be the case with a listener from a century ago. It is the fact that the listener already knows how to listen to Spooky's materials that is their final signified, after all the specific recognitions dissolve back into the mix. So Mori and Nação Zumbi do not need to be explicitly recognised, their cultural contexts acknowledged; rather, they present recognisable invitations to 'Check **385** it out!' and we know that they are *potentially recognisable* themselves. They are of our world as we know it, not 'out there' somewhere but inside our heads and bodies.

At this point we need to turn things around and suggest that DJ Spooky, Mariko Mori and John Akomfrah are models, not for the media in general to follow into some hypermedia future, but for pedagogy. They mark at long last the emergence of a zone of overlap between media and media studies, production and pedagogy, practice and theory, where a method is clarifying itself that will break down those binary oppositions that have so debilitated media studies' evolution from its promising beginnings in our universities. That media practitioners should have opened up this pedagogic space is perhaps, in the end, only just; partly because academic media studies has had long enough to do so and has failed fairly miserably, but mostly because it is time to see the tools and techniques of media production as themselves available to a pedagogy that intends to be more than mere 'production training' (which is only questionably a part of media studies anyway if pursued as a separate activity).

The essential point to emphasise here is that I am not advocating some sort of 'experimental media' zone of student work in media studies, where practical work indulges itself in open-ended formal and conceptual experimentation of a sort that might claim to be 'theoretically informed' but which usually ends up merely as evidence that our students cannot competently write a script, edit a video, mix a track, use a photographic darkroom or authoring software. Technical and formal incompetence cannot be helpfully disguised by claims to experimental adventurousness. Spooky, Mori and Akomfrah are all very much in charge of their different media. In order to make clear where the alternative lies we need to find a new model, one that captures something of what these practitioners are doing, and a model other than the implicit one which locates a zone of experimental liberation somewhere on the outer edges of mainstream production and allows students to head straight there, which usually takes them off the pedagogic map entirely. We have one candidate for such a model in Espen Aarseth's work.

Aarseth's book *Cybertext: Perspectives on Ergodic Literature* (1997) is especially concerned with new forms of writing such as that produced by the Eastgate authors. He has developed the first really comprehensive agenda for thinking about hypertext (and his work should be closely read by any serious student of the media on those grounds alone), but, along the way, Aarseth also finds himself in the position of having to rethink accepted models of media communication. He offers a simple alternative (see figure 20) which just happens to be precisely what we need in rethinking pop tech pedagogy. He also develops the idea of an ergodic relationship between text and reader/recipient. The current dictionary definition of this term runs something like, 'pertaining to the probability that in a system any state will occur again' (derived from the Greek *ergon*, work, and *hodos*, way). Aarseth pushes this notion in a particular direction: he argues that ergodic texts involve the reader/recipient in actively discovering the different available 'states' of a text by the ways they read them. Such texts have multiple states – like the different routes through *Victory Garden* – and it is the reader's responsibility to realise them. These are not

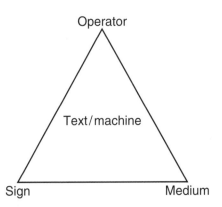

Operator

Text/machine

Sign   Medium

Figure 20 Espen J. Aarseth's 'textual machine' (after Aarseth, 1997)

unlimited or randomly discovered states; any such text will have a determinate set of possible states that will recur in different readers' encounters with them – hence ergodic rather than simply multiple. Now while Aarseth's discussion of these ideas in relation to hypertext literature repays close attention, our purpose here is to bend the same ideas in a slightly different direction by suggesting that Moulthrop's *Victory Garden* and its like can in fact join DJ Spooky's cut-and-mix creations, Mariko Mori's blissful pop tech imagery and John Akomfrah's video excavations as examples to media pedagogy of how things can and should be done these days.

The point is that Aarseth's deceptively simple model of the textual machine opens up these new possibilities in ways that Spooky, Mori and Akomfrah could not have been consciously aware of but were already *doing*. Once creator/ author and reader/recipient are combined in the new term 'operator', our understanding of media communication is transformed. The term seems clumsy and forced at first, but this is the effect of unfamiliarity. In hypertext fiction such as *Victory Garden* it is clear that the reader has to operate the 'storyspace' in order to read the text, but the latter is itself a definite sort of operation. And when we apply the same term to Spooky, Mori and Akomfrah it becomes a question of recognising them as operators of textual machines made up of found elements, pop tech excavations, technofossils dug out of the media environment and recomposed, not as authors sending us messages. Akomfrah thematises this in his narrative, Spooky does it self consciously and Mori just does it. This maps out a spectrum from the intellectualised to the blissfully immediate and superficial, but they are all at it, one way or another. So, too, their viewers and listeners are operating the text/machine to make sense of what they are confronted with, to feel its resonances, to activate their own pop tech memory and understanding.

Now I have no intention here of getting into the question of how extensible this model might be to media at large as they go digital and perhaps develop increased 'interactivity' (a highly problematic concept anyway). What I want to do instead is to raid Aarseth's text (sample it even?) and take the model off in a different direction, as the basis for some propositions about pop tech pedagogy. First, to be clear about this, I am suggesting that twenty-first-century media studies = media history + pop tech pedagogy. A great deal of what currently goes on in media studies is actually what I would call media history. What is missing is a leading edge that takes the field (1) into contemporary media experience, and (2) into practice. Interpretive and analytical work will be appropriate to both media history and pop tech pedagogy (employing, for example, the semiological method suggested by Roland Barthes – focusing on the 'sign' in Aarseth's model – in addition to forms of content analysis, reception studies, etc.). But, just as the particular focus of media history is ultimately on historical understanding, the particular focus of pop tech pedagogy is on practice, understood as an intensified form of *operation* (in Aarseth's terminology). The organic link between the two parts of media studies comes from the fact that media history delivers to pop tech pedagogy its historical sediments, its layers of material, its stuff for archaeology, for cutting and mixing.

So what is pop tech pedagogy as 'operation'? For the purpose of discussion, I want to propose that it has a practical method and a related point of focus where we always have to ask how practice fits into our broader concepts and theories: the question of the public sphere (which in turn raises questions of media power and institutional economics, etc.). Learners engaged in the practical method should always be required to undertake related 'contextual' work concerned with understanding the role of cultural practices in the public sphere if their learning is to be effective and their practical work is not to degenerate into mere technicism (i.e. learning to use the technologies but in ways entirely limited to their inherent functionality – using a camera to take any photograph because that illustrates mastery of the camera's functionality). The point to be made about a pop tech practice without any deliberate consideration of the public sphere is that it is no longer fully a pedagogical practice: Mori's photographs are not engagements with a pop tech pedagogy (although are useful models for it). Pedagogy *assumes* a public sphere, an assumption which then has to be acknowledged in, or in relation to, the work itself. Pedagogy operates between the private realm of family and personal life on the one hand, and the public realm of the state (or other public authorities, depending on one's model of society) on the other. Therefore, whatever our precise understandings of the public sphere, its organisation and potential, pedagogy already operates in that space and must take its larger concerns into account. The university seminar room is already operating, in principle, in the same space as the town squares or coffee houses of previous times, where we understand those spaces to bear the potential for public discourse. But even more importantly, media practice in the university, practice of the kind proposed here, assumes viewers and listeners in that space (actually co-operators in this model), it assumes the possibility of communication (as distinct from self-absorbed experimentation for its own sake). Some forms of communication will contribute to the characterisation of those spaces as pedagogical, while others will not. Clearly the former should be developed.

Communicating from the practical position of 'operator' in relation to the text/machine is one of those forms. It requires an understanding of the other poles of the triangle – the operation of signs and the operation of media (specifically the technologies being used). And it also requires a consciousness of one's co-operators in the pedagogical space and, beyond them, of a public sphere of other, more numerous potential co-operators, of which these are just a sample. The field of practice is the text/machine marked out by these poles and here it is possible to be much more specific about the sorts of work that can be done there, having already set up three practitioners as exemplary:

- The central procedure is one of sampling, of recombinant cutting and mixing from the whole media environment. This can be as primary material (the use of actual fragments) or secondary (the referencing, quotation or connotation of such material) – see DJ Spooky, culturally acquisitive and inquisitive.
- Technical proficiency is necessary in order to give one's material expressive power – see Mariko Mori, blissfully competent.
- There must be principles of organisation for the 'found' or excavated material from the media environment and for its combination with personally generated material – see the method of John Akomfrah's Data Thief, which is really the same method as Stuart Moulthrop: the deliberate and careful layering of personal, cultural and historical material in new and more accessible arrangements, new configurations (rather than the less readily penetrable sediments in which they were laid down historically).

This sort of work is possible in audio and video form. But it is especially possible now using the emerging digital media that combine elements of the previous technologies and facilitate real communication with them, for example on the web. It is this development that lends particular urgency to questions of the public sphere. Where audio and video have raised similar issues (e.g. in the debates around access and community media), the internet now provides an unparalleled opportunity to reach audiences. In reality, audio and video practices outside the main institutional frameworks could seldom hope to discover such opportunities, notwithstanding much effort that has gone into community-based activity and outlets over the years since access to the technologies themselves became easier. Audio and video work in a pedagogic context has tended to be limited to the audience of peers afforded by particular courses and educational institutions. The web changes all this, not just as a transmission and distribution medium but because its formal organisation and emerging aesthetic principles are well attuned to the practice of pop tech pedagogy as broadly defined here; and therefore to engaging co-operators, even unanticipated ones via the web, in a collaboratively pedagogical practice. It is there for the taking, if only we can make the leap from teaching and learning media history to a genuine and ongoing engagement with contemporary pop tech realities. And as DJ Spooky has said somewhere, if we're going to approach life as a mix, we'd better make sure it's a good one.

(cont. p. 393)

Mystory: inventing a genre for practical media studies

It has become clear as the field of media studies develops within the university that it needs urgently to transcend the sterile tension between, on the one hand, its critical, interpretive and analytical intentions and, on the other, media practice as mere technical or production training. The latter, when attempted, is seldom, if ever, well done in media studies degree programmes (it requires too much time, too costly resources and teaching staff with up-to-date production skills – a combination almost impossible to achieve or sustain within a university department that is also striving to maintain critical-analytical range and excellence in its work with students). What has been missing, perhaps, is the concept of a heuretic practice to set alongside interpretive and analytical work – in other words, a use of media technologies and forms of production in a critically *inventive* mode.

Tereza Batista, here, outlines three broad objectives for such work: (1) that it should be centrally a recombinant practice, reconstructing the material of media culture as a way of investigating that material; (2) that some technical skills are necessary, not as ends in themselves (a training emphasis) but as means of expressive effectiveness; and (3) that a 'method' needs to be devised for heuretic practice capable of drawing together personal, cultural and historical material. One candidate method that fits the bill is that of the 'Mystory', first devised and practised by Gregory Ulmer (1990, 1994) and his students at the University of Florida, but subsequently taken up and developed by others. The informing idea here is, in fact, derived from theological practices. Scriptures, taking a very broad view, could either be interpreted or developed. In the former – the hermeneutic tradition – a fixed object of study was closely examined for its meanings and explanation. In the latter – the heuretic tradition – the object never became fixed in quite that way but continued to be developed. The hermeneutic tradition has long been dominant in Western theology and in the practices of cultural interpretation that, in part, developed from it. But the heuretic tradition has been maintained within certain approaches to both 'art' and 'theory'. Psychoanalysis is a good example. Freud's interpretations of Greek myths, for instance, are not offered as mere readings of stories by Freud the hermeneutic critic but are the raw material for his own 'inventive' practice – the construction of psychoanalysis itself. In turn, psychoanalysis has been redeployed in inventive ways, both within popular culture (e.g. playfully by Hitchcock) and by avant-garde, theoretically aware art practices (beginning with surrealism). This is, perhaps, why psychoanalysis refuses to go away in contemporary cultural and media theory, despite our now being deeply unsure whether it is objectively useful as a science of the mind (probably not) or is a colourful, imaginatively elaborated and insightfully fictional account that approximates to, and renders accessible, certain human truths. Within the heuretic tradition this sort of problem matters less; it is the continuing process of invention and elaboration that matters, for so long as the material in question offers expressive and explanatory potential. The matter of strictly scientific explanation can be left to other disciplines. Much of the writing by philosopher and theorist Jacques Derrida has this heuretic quality; hence his critical texts never seem secondary to some interpreted original or primary text but have their own expressive life and inventive capacity.

But the hermeneutic or interpretive tradition is so absolutely central to how the humanities and social sciences are pursued in universities that it would be foolish to imagine doing without it. Heuretics would not be an alternative to critical study and analysis but its complement, or perhaps better a component in a new articulation where interpretive and inventive intentions more deliberately inform each other. The model here would most definitely not be that of 'theoretically informed practice', a dubious formulation at best where it is claimed that learners somehow use their practical work to explore what they have learned theoretically. This is sometimes reduced, for example, to applying *film noir* lighting in a video after studying Hollywood film of the 1940s (i.e. reducing 'theory' to stylistic analysis). Where theory retains its more robust content and concerns, its supposed 'application' can then produce portentously intellectualised practice that only makes sense (if at all) as a rather pointless demonstration of some theoretical concept (let's say Lacan's mirror-phase in a photographic exercise using multiple reflections). This is twisting hermeneutics into a debased, circular, emptily self-referential caricature of a heuretic practice. Hermeneutics' findings are not secret messages implanted in texts that, once identified, can then be extracted and deliberately re-implanted in new texts to demonstrate our understanding. What breaks us out of any such largely useless tail chasing in the theory–practice relationship will be a genuine heuretic inventiveness. This will have the added advantage of freeing learners from having to 'express' any leaden theoretical content in their practice, allowing instead a lighter approach and more space for creativity and pleasure (not innocent terms, of course, but they should still be permitted their existence). On the other hand, what prevents this from slipping in turn towards the vacuous demonstration of technical skill in, say, a pop video or a short horror film, with all their clichés intact, will be the deliberate maintenance of a proper relationship of heuretics to critical, analytical work.

That relationship turns on our devising *genres* of practice that carry, or dramatise, the heuretic intention. In other words, we need new genres with which to replace the popular ones to which students will naturally turn if freed from any deliberately theoretical 'content' for expression or illustration through their practical work – the music video, and so on. Media pedagogy, then, has a clear responsibility to invent new genres for student practical work. The 'Mystory' is one such invention. A key distinction here is between (1) dealing with the already known, and (2) wishing to find out. It is wishing to find out that leads the 'Mystory' and similar practices towards the recombinant method. Something can be found out about the stuff of media culture by sampling it and constructing new combinations, especially if the learner can somehow be 'inserted' into the construction. This insertion or positioning of oneself is, in part, why the genre is called the 'Mystory'. While there are now several variations on the generic conventions, a common approach is as follows:

1 In the spirit of Barthes's *Mythologies*, choose a popular figure that has become 'mythical' through media representations, say Nelson Mandela, Eva Peron (Evita) or Michael Jackson.
2 In the form of an anecdotal account, scenes for a performance or some other appropriate device, write his or her story in summary form.
3 Research the mythical figure in more depth, examining available media

representations from as many angles as time allows, and gathering resource material.

4 Sort the accumulated material and select an image or a fragment that is especially striking (in Barthesian terms, perhaps, something that 'pricks' your attention, that has the power of the *punctum*). Let the image or other fragment (sound, piece of text) turn over in your mind; sleep on it; see what develops.

5 Compose a new baseline narrative which explains how you, the 'Mystorian' here, first encountered and became interested in your chosen figure. The account should elaborate on how this figure 'hailed' you or caught your attention (in something like the process Althusser termed *interpellation*, or calling into place).

6 Select a professional discourse (say, politics in the case of Nelson Mandela) and/or a sequence of historical events (the founding of the new South Africa?) and gather or pick out further material on your chosen subject from this 'objective' or analytical perspective.

7 Using the image or fragment chosen in step 4 as a centrepiece or guide, rearrange the material – the outline story of the chosen figure, your baseline explanation of your own involvement, the professional or historical explanations, the raw material of images and texts drawn from the media – by cutting and mixing it together. Your assemblage should move back and forwards across the three levels: the personal (your involvement or engagement), popular culture (media representations) and the historical or disciplinary account, letting both links and unexpected juxtapositions emerge.

8 Depending on the choice of presentation medium, shape the 'Mystory' into something like a finished form – say, a video or a set of web pages.

That simple eight-step recipe somewhat disguises the more general potential of an approach to constructing exploratory media artefacts that draws its strength from the deliberate interconnection of personal, cultural and historical material. Within the broad parameters of the approach, the 'Mystory' genre has proved itself adaptable and powerfully enabling. The web has, to some extent, become its ideal medium, given the ease with which varied material can be interlinked there. But other approaches are possible. For several years at the University of Ulster I ran a 'Mystorical' project based on a William Trevor short story 'Events at Drimaghleen', filmed by the BBC in 1991 (produced and directed by Robert Cooper). With the BBC's help we produced a resource pack of materials about the supposed 'events' of the title, the violent deaths of three people at an isolated Irish farm. An incident room was set up for students with scene-of-the-crime photographs, pathologist and police reports, newspaper cuttings and background files on the various people involved, including audiotaped interviews with friends and family members – all contrived to create the raw material for the 'original' occurrences as if they had actually happened. The short story deals with a magazine journalist's reconstruction of the events. The BBC version adapts this to tell the story from the point of view of a TV documentary crew. The students were given the resource material and asked to apply a version of the 'Mystorical' procedure to it, using audio or video as their medium for re-presenting and extending the material. Reading the Trevor story and viewing the BBC adaptation were held back until students had produced their own versions. (Some of the resource material appeared in the BBC version, adding to a strange sense of overlapping realities that the project generated.) The exercise was planned to encourage students to engage with one of the key figures – the visiting reporter (played by Sophie Ward in the TV version, but into whose role they could insert any celebrity journalist with whose work they were familiar) – and also to deal with professional discourses (journalistic, legal, police and medical) and with issues around the different versions of the 'truth' that the police, the community, the Church and the media sought to articulate. The 'interpellation' was readily there for these students because of the Irish location and Trevor's deep-rooted sense of how such communities formulated their own acceptable truths.

The point here, though, is not necessarily to advocate adoption of the 'Mystory' genre, or a variation on it such as the Drimaghleen project, but to propose that inventing a heuretic genre in this way is a key step in shifting media practice in the university beyond the debilitating tension between critical-analytical work and technical training.

Indeed it is possible to see something of the 'Mystory' in other cultural forms that had no contact with it as a concept, suggesting a deeper fit with the times we find ourselves in and with the available resources. Black gay artist Isaac Julien's film *Looking for Langston* (1988) has something of this quality – it is a sort of archaeological investigation into an identity – and so too do young photojournalist Dan Eldon's journals.

Dan Fleming

Finally, what do we do with those media products that seem so much more continuous with, more in keeping with, the ideas, debates, methods and objects of study discussed in previous Parts of this book, say, *Central Station* in the cinema and *The Sopranos* on TV? This is precisely where it becomes important not to mistake DJ Spooky, Mariko Mori, John Akomfrah or Stuart Moulthrop for the future of the media. They are instructive occupants, to be highly valued, of a liminal zone between mainstream media and media pedagogy. The cut-and-mix practices I have advocated for the latter will continue to influence mainstream media too, and will spill over into other areas (subcultures, amateur erotica), but they are not *the* future of the contemporary media. So we have to stop and think about how a pop tech pedagogy centred around recombinant, hypertextual practices will relate to the continuing necessity of studying *Central Station* or *The Sopranos*, deeply representative as these are of the best cinema and TV traditions. Are we to permit today's learners to see these only as throwbacks to an older genetic code, as it were? Or – and this might seem to be the logic of what I have been proposing – as raw material to be sampled and recombined in some other mix?

We already sense an answer to this question in the emerging relationship between hypertext fiction and 'regular' fiction. *Victory Garden* is not displacing the novel as currently understood, but nor is the latter likely to remain entirely unaffected by developments in hypertext. So in Geoff Ryman's stunning 253 *the print remix* (1998) we have a novel that could not have been written before hypertext drifted into public consciousness as a possibility, no matter how vaguely sensed (Ryman traces the connections across life fragments from 253 imagined people carried by a London subway train). But even writing in less obviously experimental guise will not remain unaffected by these possibilities. Sebastian Faulks's *The Fatal Englishman* (1997) tells three short lives with an economy of style and a straight reportage of personal experiences and historical contexts that leave the reader vividly sensing the 'hypertextual' links which are not literally there but which were clearly intended to be available in the reading. Irene Vilar's *A Message from God in the Atomic Age* (1996) weaves Puerto Rican history into personal tragedy with an alternating focus that is similarly hypertextual in conception if not in literal form. And Tomás Eloy Martínez's *Santa Evita* (1997) constructs around the corpse of Eva Peron a collaged story that is affected, or infected, from the start by Evita's own pronouncement, 'I want to take a look at the world the way a person takes a look at a postcard collection.' The work that serious writers now have to do to continue *containing* their subjects is exactly the point. The pull of other connections, other ways of connecting, becomes greater and greater and has to be acknowledged. So too, I would suggest, with *Central Station* and *The Sopranos*. What makes these so good is that the work of containment is so much a part of their very substance; because, as it were, DJ Spooky is out there somewhere wanting to pull them apart.

What is at stake here is what Ronald Dworkin, albeit in a very different field (legal philosophy) has called *articulate consistency* (1977:88). We now realise that the sort of containment referred to above is not a totalising comprehensiveness – somehow packing everything in – but a matter of maintaining an articulate consistency against the forces of fragmentation and cognitive disintegration that we have let loose by that very realisation. To make things somehow hold together is a matter of achieving some consistency in how we articulate those things. In Salles's film *Central Station* articulate consistency is achieved by telling the simplest of stories (an important gesture for cinema at the end of its first century). Dora is a cynical middle-aged woman who cheats illiterate people at her stall in Rio's railway station by writing letters for money and never posting them. When one of her customers is killed by a bus outside the station, Dora finds herself taking increasing responsibility for the woman's young son, Josué. The two, compelled by various circumstances, set out to find the boy's lost father in the *sertao*, the arid scrubland of north-eastern Brazil. They never find the man but do find his two abandoned other sons, now making a life for themselves from a patch of land and a makeshift carpentry workshop. Dora leaves the boy with his brothers. Along the way they have both discovered things about themselves. This film is an important achievement. One option, indeed a still necessary and helpful one, for achieving articulate consistency is to find the seemingly simple stories that can still hold together. The story of Dora and Josué is not sentimentalised Disney-fashion (the largely phony consistency of sentimentality being a perpetual risk in mainstream popular culture) but nor is it subjected to a cynically detached irony that would undermine its consistency. Other elements criss-cross the pair's journey (primarily the letters but also encounters with other people whose own stories are glimpsed, with violence and child abuse, with the dizzying religious ritual and fervour of the north-east, with housing policy, etc.), and while these are not followed off in other directions they are sufficient to give the film much larger resonances than the storyline would suggest.

Being able to find or imagine – or make – stories that still have articulate consistency in today's world would be a significant learning outcome for our students. *The Sopranos* demonstrates a different solution. This astonishing achievement from the very heart of commercialised TV production (Home Box Office) optimistically reminds us that TV drama can still find its own appropriate forms of articulate consistency from time to time. Produced by writer-director David Chase (family name Cesare, changed by his grandmother in the 1920s), the series focuses on an Italian American family of petty mobsters in New Jersey. In a space opened up by the MTM legacy in American TV (*Northern Exposure*, etc.), *The Sopranos* achieves its articulate consistency by moving back and forwards across its ensemble cast's involvement in mob activities and their personal lives (running gangster genre and a darkly disjointed soap opera side by side), but 'hinges' the two around moments that transcend the conventions and limitations of both genres, beginning with family *capo* Tony Soprano's nervous collapse (and ongoing psychotherapy) when a family of wild ducks that has been living in his swimming pool flies away. This trope – hanging an implied significance on 'surreal' moments – is now well established in American TV drama (*Ally McBeal* depends upon it) but *The Sopranos* deploys it especially effectively to bore connecting tunnels between its two genres.

But the final point I want to make here is that achieving articulate consistency is an ongoing problem in media culture. We have to be able to grasp how film and TV makers are responding to this problem, while at the same time seeing the 'problem' as itself deeply productive for us if it can be liberated within a pop tech pedagogy of the sort proposed. Even a story such as that of Dora and Josué could be placed within a project of hypertextual elaboration, where the materials of mass culture and the historical situation could be productively linked together, where the text's own crossroads were deliberately followed in multiple directions, were thought laterally, and where articulate consistency then explored its outer limits through the *rhizomatic* cut-and-mix method of pop tech, without crossing over into senseless fragmentation or vacuously ironic detachment.

21

The internet as public sphere

Liza Tsaliki

Introduction

> The revolution will not be televised, but the proceedings will be available on line.
> (From the signature file of a netizen, cited in Ogden, 1994:713)

The issue of the public sphere lies at the heart of any reconceptualisation of democracy. As 'traditional' loci of interactive practice, such as the agora, the New England town hall, the village church, the coffee house, the tavern and the public square, continue to shrink in modern times, attention has shifted to other, this time electronic, places of political discussion and action. The search for the new public sphere took a different turn with consideration of computer-mediated communication (CMC): 'In a democracy, people believe that every-one should be included on equal terms in communication; no one should be excluded from free exchange of information. New communication technology is suprisingly consistent with Western images of democracy' (Sproull and Kiesler, 1991:13). More specifically, it is the internet, with its anti-authoritarian, anarchistic nature – without any central authority – that has emerged as the new springboard for democracy. This is the view of the cyber-libertarians who see cyberspace as the promise of a new, global and anti-sov-ereign social space where anybody can express their beliefs without fear (Barlow, 1996). According to this approach, the information superhighway will be able to support a wide range of new services which will allow the cir-culation of information, empower citizens and provide for their full participa-tion in an emerging 'digital democracy'. This is the view of the internet as a new public sphere.

Towards a theory of the democratising potential of the internet: reasons to be cheerful . . .

Equality of participation

One of the main tenets of this perspective is that the internet can lead to par-ticipatory parity through the accommodation of 'subaltern counterpublics' (see the accompanying case study, p. 405). The argument is that, as a result of increasing urban fragmentation, the traditional notion of a universal public realm has become problematic, and digital computer networks have emerged as carriers of new types of public, social and cultural exchange – a 'new public realm' (Aurigi and Graham, 1998). Cyberspace has, therefore, become an arena for participation in public life wherein the notion of traditional *Gemeinschaft* can be restored and retrieved through CMC. It is perceived and experienced as a place where people share a sense of belonging and community, ways of expression, meanings and emotions, which are as genuine as their real-life counterparts (Harasim, 1993; Rheingold, 1993; MacKinnon, 1995). Cyberspace has thus been seen as a new public sphere, wherein Internet Relay Chat, usenet groups, listservers and other subscriber bulletin boards serve as institutionalised forums for public debate and exchange on a variety of issues (Fernback, 1997). It becomes a realm, therefore, in which public debate helps to shape participatory democracy, especially if we accept that it is a medium which allows coexisting public spheres of 'subaltern counterpublics' (Fraser, 1994:84) to form, where the central claim is one of . . .

Extending access and democratic practice: the circulation of information
If we want to understand the democratic potential of new communications technologies and examine their ability to extend the public sphere, we need to look at the actual uses of networks of communication, at the dynamics of real social movements engaged in local problem solving, and at the democratic traditions that underpin them, rather than at technology itself. The reason for doing so is that, although new digital technologies are embedded in an oligopolistic capitalist market-place, they may actually be used in ways that extend democratic practices. As networks become decentralised, ever wider publics gain access to them, thus increasing public exchange and undermining any centralised control of information (Friedland, 1996).

In that respect, a variety of citizen- and community-based networks, facilitated by CMC, act as brokers of democratic information and have formed a civic networking movement. Initiatives may range from the use of city hall web pages in order to make political information available to citizens, to experiments in electronic voting, or to the organisation of interest groups and neighbourhood alliances. Although state apparatuses have experimented with the new media (see, for example, the supposedly direct e-mailing facility to President Clinton at the White House (Hacker and Todino, 1996)), it is initiatives at the local level (e.g. civic networks) that offer genuinely new patterns in political communication. These projects offer a substantial diversity in their organisation and management, but share the same democratic belief in active political citizenship.

In order to avoid the emergence of an 'information aristocracy', the development of new services and applications must reach and benefit more people than it does already. There are increasing calls for public support at the local level to ensure a 'development from below' approach in the new infrastructure, whereby the distinction between producers and consumers of information blurs and every individual can potentially be a 'politician' themselves. The proliferation of such politically 'grassroots' services can compensate for the dominant pattern of 'development from above', whereby new services and applications are controlled by the multinational corporate sector (Carter, 1997). Experimentation at the local level, for example, can lead to the establishment of learning networks for people in relation to consumer needs, citizenship and wider democratic interests. However, if there are any benefits to be gained from the development of the information economy, then the key principle here is *universal access* to telematics services: these new media facilities must be accessed as a public service, just like public transport, if any of these radical aspirations is to be realised.

At the end of the twentieth century, we saw these aspirations take form in a number of experiments, for example digital cities. Among numerous attempts to create 'virtual metaphors' for modern cities and their citizens, good examples come from Amsterdam (Brants *et al.*, 1996; Aurigi and Graham, 1998; Francissen and Brants, 1998), Bologna (Aurigi and Graham, 1998; Tambini, 1998), 'Telecities UK' (including Birmingham, Bradford, Edinburgh, Glasgow, Manchester and Newcastle, among others) (Carter, 1997), Berlin (Schmidtke, 1998) and Athens (Tsagarousianou, 1998). Other initiatives in the sphere of participation in local politics include the Public Electronic Network of the city of Santa Monica (Dutton and Guthrie, 1991; Docter and Dutton, 1998), Neighborhoods Online in Philadelphia (Schwartz, 1998), the Seniorweb in the Netherlands (Jankowski and Van Selm, 2000), UK Communities Online, the European EPITELIO network and the Democr@acy Forum.

. . . and reasons to be worried

A matter of vocabulary: the problem of the 'highway' metaphor
The euphoria enveloping the literature on the democratising potential of the internet is moderated once the darker side of cyberspace is admitted. A concerned perspective will point out the uneasy relationship between the information 'superhighway' and that earlier modern invention, the interstate highway system or motorway. It may be feared that the information superhighway will have the same detrimental effects on social formation as the interstate highway:

> [Highways] have had monstrous side effects. They have often rolled . . . through cities, splitting communities off into ghettos, displacing people, and crushing the intimacies of old cities . . . While promising to bring us closer, highways in fact cater to our sense of separateness. (Patton, 1986; cited in Jones, 1995:11).

If, however, it is the highway metaphor that is inadequate, it should perhaps be replaced. There is the railroad metaphor (interesting where the railroads are privately owned while the highways are publicly owned) (Sawhney, 1996). Alternatively, the digital infrastructure can be visualised in terms of a pipeline metaphor. For sceptics such as Herbert Schiller, the pipeline metaphor stresses the potential for one-way flow of, and control over, information by the state and corporations (in Sawhney, 1996:304). Or again, the metaphor of cyberspace as an electronic frontier reflects an image of the Wild West where cowboys, law and lawlessness (in the form of hackers and their pursuers), as well as railroad companies (large US corporations), reign over both actuality and the imagination (Jordan, 1999). The frontier metaphor is also related to a highly gendered moment in American history, resonating with the classic western narrative. The image of cyberspace as such a frontier invokes a need for its defence, while also allowing the construction of 'imperilled women and children' (Miller, 1995:52).

Stop and think

Pornography revisited

The moral panic currently raging over internet porn (see O'Toole, 1998) is, in many ways, a re-run of previous panics about photography, film and video. While none of those media became primarily distribution channels for pornographic material, they did of course enlarge the scope of porn and increase its accessibility. So, while one would not wish to think of the internet as the major vehicle for porn, it is difficult to deny that it is having its own significant impact on the scope and accessibility of pornographic material. On the other hand, the internet is potentially too valuable to the producers and distributors of porn for them to allow its unregulated movement over the networks. To make money from the new medium they have to introduce their own controlled gateways where they can establish a business model that works for them. Already most porn sites on the web require a credit card number to be entered for access, even to free material: after all, the producers and distributors are only interested in attracting paying customers in the long run. Indeed, if the millions of children suspected by the morally panicked of accessing internet porn were actually using the pornographers' servers they would be hogging connections that the latter would much rather see being used by paying adults.

Even a cursory exploration of supposed porn sites on the web reveals two categories – a number of genuine porn sites, a few with free 'preview' areas but most only accessible with a credit card; and an extraordinarily large number of adolescent 'soft porn' sites that are little different in content from lingerie catalogues or tabloid newspaper 'glamour' photographs. Whatever one's views on the value of the latter, these can hardly be construed to be a disturbingly new vehicle for pornography in any strict sense of the term. There are a lot of teenage boys out there with internet connections in their bedrooms, posting material that they have under their beds already.

In fact, many of the scare stories about children stumbling across – or actively seeking? – pornography confuse bulletin boards and newsgroups, on the one hand, with the much more accessible web on the other. It is the web that children often have ready access to but it is the less easily accessed computer network world of the former (where images are circulated as downloadable files) that sustains the organised pornography 'rings', very much as an inevitable extension of the existing porn industry, aimed at much the same customers and serviced by the same providers. (This is also where paedophilic pornography is exchanged, of the sort that forced the 1987 closure of the Lille-based *Ballet Rousse* bulletin board on France's Minitel system.) That organised industry merits separate attention, but the web does not yet furnish much convincing evidence that it is being widely turned over to the porn industry's use, except occasionally as a 'shop window' advertising hard-core material elsewhere or behind credit card-requiring firewalls that children are no more likely to cross than the threshold of a porn shop.

This may change, of course, and the issue of children's access to inappropriate sexual material needs to be monitored sensibly, but what *is* worth stopping and thinking about in more depth now is the question of the web's impact on adult erotic lives. From webcams in bedrooms to chat rooms for flirting or erotic conversation, the web is offering increasing opportunities for such experience, not least because identities can be disguised, genders swapped, preferences explored. There is a thriving subculture of *Star Trek* eroticism, where characters from the popular TV series are reinvented in gay and lesbian relationships by their fans. In fact, 'slash' or 'queer fan-fiction', based on the various *Star Trek* series and movies, was a strikingly popular growth area of web eroticism in the late 1990s, centred around home-produced web sites displaying the authors' stories, poems, scripts and (much less frequently) visual material. (To find this material you have to know what you're looking for – for example, by searching on specific homoerotic vocabulary – which tends to preclude most children browsing randomly looking for thrills.) This on one well-known slash site gives some sense of the intentions:

> We are aware that 'slash' as a cultural phenomenon is beginning to see the light of day in the mainstream. And though we at Slashcity appreciate that more people are trying to understand what we do, we are also painfully aware that this very thing endangers the hobby we love so much. As slash writers we are not seeking the limelight. We do not want our favourite leisure activity to be shoved into the faces of people who are not ready to accept it.

What the internet has brought is not a world of new and, sometimes, unsettling content 'broadcast' to a mass public that may throw up its hands in horror at what it's being offered, but rather an environment of rapidly multiplying spaces for semi-private experimentation. In the realm of the erotic this raises new questions about where the responsibility lies for any offence that might be caused.

A further weakness of the cyber-libertarian perspective is that it often treats cyberspace as somehow parallel to, but separate from, the 'real' world. However, such a tendency ignores the fact that the very same technologies which have enabled 'virtuality' have been developed for specific purposes within military, educational and increasingly commercial contexts. The origins, development and ethos of the internet are therefore directly associated with all too real government policy making and public expenditure (Loader, 1997). In addition, because of the postmodern tendencies that circulate around the notion of cyberspace, the fragmentation of its multiple 'narratives' may in effect inhibit the consolidation of electronic democracy, dependent as the latter is on sustaining its own narrative of effective citizenship. CMC may make individual participation in collective dialogues possible, and may facilitate interactive communication around the globe, but is this what public space is all about? In the end, most of what is discussed 'in' cyberspace has more to do with sound-bite politics – epitomising the commodification of political discourse – rather than with informed political dialogue.

The fragmentation of internet narratives inhibits electronic democracy in another way. Internet users engage in scattered, small-scale personal exchanges which may be larger in scale when compared with the exchanges taking place in eighteenth century salons and coffee houses, but only give the 'illusion of participatory democracy' since, with these internet exchanges, a larger scale does not translate into increased participatory effectiveness (Jones, 1997:26). Moreover, some 'conversations' are being carried out by 'bots', programs acting as human surrogates, and it is becoming difficult to know whether or not one is talking to a person (e.g. in a chat forum)! More fundamentally, the internet's claim to freedom does not guarantee its effectiveness beyond its users' circle of activities. It may be that the internet allows us to shout more loudly, but whether our fellow citizens or the politicians will listen remains a different issue and is not guaranteed by the technology's exponential growth.

What kind of access?

If the internet is to become an alternative public sphere, then it will need to be accessible to the many. However, there are serious structural inequalities in access to the communication and computing infrastructure which has become an integral part of contemporary cities and their hinterlands. These inequalities testify that the internet remains the incontestable domain of the economically well-off and the socially privileged. In fact, the profile of the 'average' internet user is still white, middle class, male and well educated (Aurigi and Graham, 1998).

Gender further complicates the matter of access. Research on the position of women in the labour market of information and communication technologies (ICTs) has shown that gendered divisions of labour are actually reinforced with the introduction of ICTs (Adam and Green, 1998). In light of this, it should not come as a surprise that – despite the cyberfeminist contention that women can bend gender boundaries through 'cyborg' identities and make cyberspace a space where women take control (Haraway, 1991) – the reality is that traditional gender interactions remain persistently present in cyberspace (Herring, 1996; Squires, 1996).

There are also reasons to believe that the technology of cyberspace will widen existing social cleavages between the information rich and the information poor rather than leading to a greater equalisation of power structures, especially as information has so clearly become a market-driven commodity. In that respect, disparities of access between the developed world and developing countries will continue to grow. Internet use in the developing countries is more likely to be restricted to the privileged metropolitan elites. These elites will develop an increasingly specialised knowledge of information technology and its social rules (tailored to them), while the majority of the rural populations in the developing world will be marginalised and excluded from the networking revolution (Haywood, 1998). As increasing amounts of trade shift into cyberspace, we face yet another risk: that these divides between information haves and have-nots become self reinforcing. Here, we are not only dealing with 'information poverty', but with 'material poverty' as a result of the lack of access to communication technologies (Holderness, 1998). In this sense, we should not underestimate what may be the pending material impoverishment of large segments of the world population by those who are not only better equipped to take advantage of ICTs but also able to maintain this privileged position. In effect, what we may be witnessing is 'a social and economic process which has much in continuity with previous epochs' (Loader, 1998:8).

A realm for active political citizenship?
The notion that digital cities form a new, discourse-driven urban public realm has been over-hyped, not least because the majority of the civic web sites are in fact merely set up as urban databases where residents (and non-residents) can browse for information about entertainment, leisure and travel. Most digital cities are characterised by uni-directionality and a lack of opportunity for authentic interactivity. In some of these digi-domains we may experience the virtual simulation of the postmodern city: exciting, inticing, fragmented, self parodying. Yet this is a sanitised city where crime never happens and pollution and social and racial cleavages are also blatantly absent (Aurigi and Graham, 1998).

A closer look at the Dutch De Digitale Stad (Digital City) project reveals that, although democratic in principle, the reality of access is different: the majority of users are young, well educated, employed and male. Discussions on computer technology, on art, on the theoretical relationship between information technology and democracy, are better visited than those concerning specific political issues in Amsterdam. This seems to imply that the Digital City is more of a place for a new cultural elite and some 'techno freaks' rather than for everyday Amsterdammers. Further, it would be worth investigating the extent to which the demographics and debates represent the local citizens rather than (as one suspects) the wider internet population (Brants *et al.*, 1996; Aurigi and Graham, 1998; Francissen and Brants, 1998). In other words, these digital cities may be drifting free of their geographical locations, where politics has real effects.

There are similar problems in the Iperbole initiative (the online community in Bologna), as the number of subscribers is very small when compared with the total population. In addition, discussion groups have focused more on leisure than on political issues. Despite a great number of electronic inquiries between citizens and local officials, the majority of them have been ignored, undermining the interactive claims and the supposedly democratising potential of the initiative (Aurigi and Graham, 1998).

In general though, the most serious threats to the notion of the internet as a public sphere come from its heavy and ongoing commodification and privatisation, which are threatening to replace public interaction and deliberation with individual consumption (Dahlberg, 1998).

Afterword

To this point, we have considered the relationship between new technology and democracy in terms of dominant hopes and fears. Contrary to technological optimism – regarding the democratising potential of the internet and its ability to form an alternative public sphere – a more bleak picture emerges, where cyberspace has a good deal in common with the Habermasian public sphere, showing signs of elitism, exclusion and commodification. All may not be lost, however.

Although there is no 'easy fix' solution, there is a way to make sure that an alternative, digital public sphere takes effect. We need to revisit our understanding of the public sphere itself, and 'we are advised to abandon Habermas' concept of the public sphere in assessing the internet as a political domain', as the question of democracy must now take into account the new electronically mediated forms of interaction themselves, rather than assuming that they are only a new setting or location for an existing conception of the public sphere (Poster, 1995). We need to construct a 'socially useful' cyberspace at the local level, and provide connectivity through community-based initiatives in order to construct a digital civil society. The strengthening of community access and the civic networking movement may still be a way forward, especially for subaltern publics. (*cont. p. 405*)

Media and the public sphere

Although there is a general sense in which the 'public sphere' can be understood as referring simply to the formation of public opinion in modern democracies (Dahlgren, 1991:2), the term is now pretty much inseparable from the sense given to it in Jürgen Habermas's classic discussion (Habermas, 1989).

The more precise concept at stake here is of a social sphere distinct from the 'public authority' of the state on the one hand and the 'private sphere' of economic relations and intimate family relations on the other. Habermas's thesis in *The Structural Transformation of the Public Sphere* was that such a sphere emerged briefly among the bourgeoisie of eighteenth-century Europe – in the coffee houses and salons of London and Paris and informed by the emerging print media, the journals and periodicals of the day. Although it was in practice restricted to those qualified by property, education and leisure to engage in critical discourse, Habermas maintains that the bourgeois public sphere embodied a more general principle of 'publicness': that rational debate in an open, critical and uncoerced context could produce public opinion as a democratic force, out of the personal views and opinions of private individuals.

The bourgeois public sphere rapidly declined following its brief flowering. This decline and ultimate demise Habermas attributed partly to a progressive blurring of the distinction between the state and civil society, as private interest groups became more involved in the political process and as the state became more interventionist in the private lives of individuals. Thus the available 'space' for a public sphere of critical debate became eroded. Accompanying this process, Habermas points to a degradation in the means of communication, most importantly the commercialisation of the mass media and their consequent transformation into an aspect of the 'culture industry'. Here Habermas's critique follows the familiar contours of critical theory of the early Frankfurt School (Adorno, 1991). Public opinion formation, he claims, degenerated from being the outcome of active critical debate into the consumption of media products. The potential for radical participatory democracy opened up in the bourgeois public sphere thus remains unrealised and, indeed, Habermas argues that public life has regressed to a 'quasi-feudal' character in which the role of private individuals is reduced to that of spectators in an increasingly managed ritual of political display to which they are intermittently required to provide acclamatory assent via the ballot box.

Habermas's ideas have been widely influential (Dahlgren and Sparks, 1991; Calhoun, 1992). In the UK, Nicholas Garnham has been a consistent and persuasive advocate of Habermas's general case in relation to the mass media and the democratic process (Garnham, 1992) and also in more policy-oriented debates about public service broadcasting (Garnham, 1986).

However, Habermas has also been widely criticised on both the details of his historical analysis of the bourgeois public sphere and his theoretical stance on its transformation. He has been accused of idealising the bourgeois public sphere; of ignoring the parallel (and oppositional) development of a 'plebeian public sphere' based, for example, in the trade union movement; of being blind to issues of gender and patriarchy (see Fraser, 1987); of propagating an over-abstract and rationalistic model of human communication; and of exaggerating the manipulative potential of the mass media over a passive and malleable audience. (See Dahlgren, 1991; Garnham, 1992; Thompson, 1993, for summaries of these criticisms.)

Though many of these criticisms were justified in relation to *The Structural Transformation of the Public Sphere,* some have lost their force in the years since it was first published in 1962. This is first because Habermas has responded by shifting his position on certain of these issues (see, for example, his reply to his critics in Calhoun, 1992), and second because his general theoretical stance has moved on considerably since then, incorporating the concern with the public sphere into a much broader social-theoretical analysis (Habermas, 1984, 1987).

One line of criticism is, however, worth more detailed attention since it has more general implications for the way we think about the relationship between communications media and 'publicness' in late-modern societies. John Thompson has argued, convincingly, that Habermas's position in *The Structural Transformation of the Public Sphere* is unsustainable since it trades on an inappropriate dialogical conception of communications as face-to-face 'conversational' interaction in shared locales: the Greek market-place, the eighteenth-century salons and coffee houses. This model, Thompson argues, is redundant since it has little in common with the way most of us now relate to public affairs, through the mass media. He goes on to suggest that we need to divorce our view of what the public sphere *can be* in late modernity from this neo-classical model of local dialogue:

> We shall not arrive at a satisfactory understanding of the nature of public life in the modern world if we remain wedded to a conception of publicness which is essentially dialogical in character, and which obliges us to interpret the ever-growing role of mediated communication as an historical fall from grace. We should instead recognize from the outset that the development

of communication media . . . has created a new kind of publicness which . . . has become detached from the sharing of a common locale. It has become *despatialized* and *non-dialogical*, and it is increasingly linked to the distinctive kind of visibility produced by, and achievable through, the media (especially television). (Thompson, 1993:187)

Contemporary public life thus has to be thought through in the essentially *monological* communicational conditions of what Thompson elsewhere calls 'mediated quasi-interaction' (1994:35f.). Thompson's point is that most people's participation in public debates cannot realistically be as dialogue partners in the way Habermas's model suggests. Mostly people participate simply by watching and listening to the debates on television. This may be far from the 'ideal' of direct participatory democracy but it should not necessarily be seen as the loss of political involvement. What we have is a different *kind* of public sphere, one which, as Roger Silverstone (1994) puts it, has become 'suburbanised'. As a result of the mass mediation of public debates, the public sphere now extends to vastly more people, much better informed politically but 'participating' in different, more diffuse ways. Though Thompson is undoubtedly right in his analysis of the significance of this communicational shift for Habermas's argument, it remains an open question whether a form of public life lived through the 'mediated quasi-interaction' of media representations can deliver the democratic and rational politics which remain the goal of Habermas's critical theory.

John Tomlinson

Women and the digital public sphere: background to a case study

The ongoing development of a network computer culture has given rise to enthusiastic claims that the new media, especially in the form of the internet, have the potential to reinvent our understanding of deliberative democracy, by facilitating interaction on public issues and by enabling increased information provision and sharing. The internet has been equated with a virtual agora, a place where the notion of the public sphere can be revitalised and revolutionised. To test these claims, this case study aims to explore the democratising potential of the internet from the point of view of women, and argues that, although 'it may take more than a new medium to provide for [gender] equality' (Ebben and Kramarae, 1993:18), cyberspace can and does provide for an alternative, post-feminist public sphere of a sort.

In order to provide a conceptual backdrop for this case study, I will offer again a brief rehearsal of the theory of the public sphere and an outline of its major theoretical deficiencies as seen from a feminist perspective. I will then discuss cyberspace as a place for the construction of a new, digital public sphere where women can be equal participants. This will be followed by a less optimistic view of cyberspace, where inequalities of access and participation, and increasing commodification, reign.

The work of Jürgen Habermas on the bourgeois public sphere (1989) has become central to the theorising of the relationship between media and democracy. According to this theory, the development of mercantile capitalism in the sixteenth century, along with the changing institutional forms of **405** political power, led to the creation of the 'bourgeois public sphere', a space substantially free of state and corporate interests, where private individuals came together as equals to debate about the regulation of civil society and the conduct of the state. The medium of this deliberative interaction was the public and unconstrained use of reason (Thompson, 1993).

The emergence of the bourgeois public sphere was facilitated by the development of the periodical press as well as the rise of new centres of sociability (salon and coffee houses) in early modern Europe, from around the mid seventeenth century on. The institutions of the public sphere, and the periodical press in particular, practised informed critical discussion, thereby gradually transforming the institutional form of modern European states. The bourgeois public sphere did not last for long though, as the institutions that provided the forum for the public sphere were transformed: salons and coffee houses declined in significance, the periodical press became part of large-scale media institutions with overriding commercial interests, and the separation between the state and civil society (which had created the space for the public sphere in the first place) started to break down. Gradually, instead of being a forum of rational and critical debate, the bourgeois public sphere became a forum of cultural consumption and state management, where public relations and image creation reigned. In effect, according to Habermas, this 'refeudalisation' of the public sphere in modern times has turned politics into spectacle, and excludes citizens from public discussion and decision-making processes (Thompson, 1993, 1995).

Habermas's concern with the possibility of free and rational communication as the basis of a healthy democracy has been sustained within a rich philosophical debate about communicative competence. An interest in the concept of the public sphere has been particularly evident in debates about the changing role of the mass media in public life (Dahlgren, 1991), which coincided with the crisis in public service broadcasting (and the public sector at large) in the UK and in Western Europe. Hence the idea of 'a forum for open and rational critical debate of public processes inevitably chime[d] with the possibility of such a public sphere' (Golding, 1995:26).

The theory of the public sphere has been criticised on a number of counts (Calhoun, 1992; Golding, 1995; Thompson, 1995) which go beyond the scope of this case study. However, one particular aspect of the critique needs to be mentioned at this point. Habermas has been attacked for idealising the institutions of the bourgeois public sphere since, despite the rhetoric of accessibility, the *official* public sphere was constituted by exclusion. Contrary to the founding principle of universal access by peers, the public sphere was in practice restricted to those individuals who had the education and the financial means to participate in it. Not least, the institutions of the public sphere were not merely bourgeois but male.

Feminist criticism addresses the essentially gendered nature of the theory of the public sphere, and stresses that the Habermasian account was blind to any appreciation of difference within the 'public' (Golding, 1995). In that sense, the exclusion of women from the public sphere was not a mere historical contingency. Instead, it was constitutive of the notion of the public sphere, since the latter was understood as a domain of reason where men were uniquely equipped to take part, while women were better suited to domestic life (Landes, 1988). Gender exclusions were also class and race related, as full accessibility to the public sphere was never realised by women of any class, by plebeian men, or by women and men of racialised ethnicities (Eley, 1991; Ryan, 1991). Habermas's original account of the public sphere fails to realise the existence of *other*, non-bourgeois, competing public spheres in the nineteenth century (for instance, bourgeois women forming women-only voluntary associations, working-class women taking part in male-dominated protests, or women's rights advocates). This not only shows that 'declaring a deliberative arena to be a space where extant status distinctions are bracketed and neutralized is not sufficient to make it so' (Fraser, 1994:78), but it also implies that concurrently with the bourgeois public sphere there was 'a host of competing counter-publics . . . from the start, not just from the late nineteenth and twentieth centuries' (Fraser, 1994:79).

From the above it follows that the bourgeois public sphere does not foster participatory parity. It rather amplifies the marginalisation of subordinated groups. The ideal of participatory parity is therefore better served by a plural-ity of competing publics than by a single, comprehensive public. These 'subal-tern counterpublics . . . signal that the[re] are parallel discursive arenas where members of subordinated social groups invent and circulate counterdiscourses . . . thereby reducing, although not eliminating, the[ir] disadvantage in official public spheres' (Fraser, 1994:84).

Democracy in crisis: a call for an alternative public sphere

At the heart of modern democratic politics lies the argument that liberal democracy has failed to engage citizens in the political process. Citizen disillu-sionment has built up as a result of a variety of factors, not least because of the lack of channels for free democratic communication both among citizens and between representatives and voters within a monological broadcast-based culture; centralised government management of public information; and a political agenda determined by party spin doctors and media professionals (Coleman, 1999). Furthermore, the increasing lack of public spaces, the growing size of contemporary political communities, along with the colonisa-tion of the public sphere by the state and political parties, and its dominance by the logic of commercialisation and commodification, have all contributed to an atrophied political culture (Negroponte, 1995; Rheingold, 1995; Bryan *et al.*, 1998).

Technology gradually came to be considered as the 'way out' of this 'demo-cratic deficit', offering unprecedented opportunities for the revitalisation of the political process through various versions of 'electronic democracy'. The concept of 'electronic democracy' has a relatively long history, being part of a technological utopia proposed by New Left activists since the 1960s and exem-plified in the case of pirate radio stations. The debate over the advantages and disadvantages of new information and communication technologies for the political process was later transferred to remote computing, telephone confer-encing and interactive cable television technology (Becker, 1981; Arterton, 1987; Abramson *et al.*, 1988). In the mid 1980s, the debate on teledemocracy focused on interactive television, while developments in technological convergence and the proliferation of computer networks such as the internet in the 1990s shifted attention on to CMC: 'For many, CMC holds the key to the enhancement of the democratic aspects of the political process and to the creation of new opportunities for citizen participation in the local and national political spheres' (Bryan *et al.*, 1998:2).

CMC is expected by some to revitalise citizen-based democracy and bypass the commodified, mass media-dominated public sphere, as the ongoing proliferation of civic networking initiatives indicates. Advances in digital technology aside, the development of civic digital activism occurs at a time when national telecommunications have been privatised (leading to debate as to whether or not they can provide universal service), public service broadcasting has been in turmoil (with discussion about the replacement of citizens' rights by consumers' rights), and levels of political apathy are rising. Amid widespread belief that traditional political communication stuctures and the old media are inadequate for democratic practice, the general premise is that the existing social infrastructure for public debate and political action has been eroded and undermined, and that CMC can undo the harm done to politics by the old media. Thus the emergence of the new media, and the internet in particular, presents the possibility of a qualitative shift in communicative and democratic interaction (Bryan *et al.*, 1998). The internet becomes the place where hopes for the revivification of the public sphere, congenial to the democratic process, can be realised. Taking into account that the ideal of participatory parity is better served by multiple publics than by a single, comprehensive one, then the internet, by means of CMC, accommodates a multiplicity of vigorous public spheres. Cyberspace turns into a public forum where various 'subaltern counterpublics' coexist outside state apparata, and where conflicts and demands can take place, both essential features for any successful democratic project (Melucci, 1989; Keane, 1995).

It is within this context that cyberspace can be seen as an alternative public sphere where subaltern publics can take part in the political process, interact and deliberate. I will now turn to the democratising potential of the internet as a public discursive forum for one of these subaltern publics: women.

The internet as public sphere: a forum for women?

The relationship between women and technology has always been an uneasy one, since the traditional perception of technology is heavily weighted against women. In most cases, the symbolic representation of technology reproduces the stereotype of women as technologically ignorant and inept. It is men who are in control of technology since women are usually excluded from an understanding of technique and the physical principles by which machines operate. This is because technical competence is central to dominant perceptions of masculinity which see a 'natural' polarity between male/female, rationality/emotion, hard/soft. This social construction draws from a wider system of sexual stereotypes within Western culture which identify men with culture and science, and women with nature and intuition. Feminist research has long argued about the traditional process of women's socialisation into relationships with technical objects, thus resulting in the notion of technology as masculine culture (Kramarae, 1988; Wajcman, 1991; Cockburn and Furst-Dilic, 1994).

The introduction of computer technology into everyday life brought with it expectations that the gender stereotyping of technology would decrease. Computers, for example, could have been gender free, with no differentiation between their male and female users. The harsh reality, though, is that Western culture has already contextualised computer culture as masculine culture. Girls are seriously outnumbered by boys when it comes to computer use and expertise, usually because computers are associated with maths and science – traditionally constructed as male subjects (Turkle, 1988; Wajcman, 1991; Cockburn, 1992). Even when girls use computers, their interaction with and experience of them is different from that of boys (Haddon, 1992) and therefore from the dominant form of interaction. As a result of this process of socialisation, women learn as young girls that the domain of computers belongs primarily to the male.

Things are, though, subject to change and women have started to explore the new technologies with their own interests in mind. We are now living in a world marked by 'a movement from an organic, industrial society to a poly-morphous, information system – from all work to all play, a deadly game' (Haraway, 1991:161), where computer technology is everywhere. Within this networked reality, polarities such as nature/culture and animal/human/machine are redefined in boundary-shifting terms. Enter the internet and the world of cyberspace wherein technology is opening up some possibilities for female reassertiveness.

Public participation through cyborg imagery
One way to understand the internet as a place for public discussion and po-litical action for women is through cyborg imagery. The icon of the cyborg offers women a powerful voice and identity in cyberspace. In her now clas-sic 'A Cyborg Manifesto', Donna Haraway, partly inspired by the gender-free utopias of feminist science fiction, identifies a new feminism and invokes the image of the cyborg – 'a cybernetic organism, a hybrid of machine and organ-ism' (1991:149). She concludes by saying that she 'would rather be a cyborg than a goddess' (1991:181). Her vision is that the blurring of boundaries between human and machine will eventually make the categories of male and female obsolete, and open up the way towards a world of freedoms beyond gender.

The cyborg imagery suggests that electronic technology makes possible an escape from the confines of the body, and from the boundaries that have separated organic from inorganic matter. The merging with the computer in-volves a change from the 'physical, biological space of the embodied viewer to the symbolic "consensual hallucination" of cyberspace [where there is a] desire for refigured embodiment' (Stone, 1991:108–9). In other words, when humans interface with computer technology, the self is transformed into some-thing entirely new, combining technological with human identity. As the boundaries between technology and nature are in the midst of a deep restruc-turing, Cartesian principles no longer hold, and the distinctions biological/

technological, natural/artificial and human/mechanical become unreliable. It is at this point that cyborg consciousness can be understood as the technological embodiment of a particular and specific form of oppositional consciousness. An oppositional cyborg politics, then, could very well bring the politics of the alienated, white male subject into alliance with the subaltern politics of the Third World and of feminism (Sandoval, 1995:408–9). The cyborg metaphor, in this line of thought, provides a way to overcome divisions among feminists, alienated white males and the Third World in a movement where oppression is overthrown and egalitarianism becomes feasible. Therefore, it is no coincidence that many social groups have embraced the computer, and cyberspace by extension, as a cultural icon wherein physical distinctions of gender, race or sexual orientation become obsolete.

One feminist response to emerging CMC, influenced by discussions on gender fluidity by feminist and queer theorists, is that of 'liberal cyberfeminism' (Hall, 1996). This approach sees the computer as plugging into a liberating utopia that goes beyond the polarity of male/female, heterosexual/homosexual, and cyberculture as a new frontier of sexual activism and rebellion. Liberal cyberfeminism has extended the notion of cyberspace as a democratic forum wherein users are freed from the constraints of the physical world on sexuality – a notion already identified within the cyberpunk movement. In this sense, cyberspace allows 'gender fluidity' rather than 'gender categorisation', thereby liberating participants from the binarism of maleness/femaleness. Despite, then, a long-standing feminist tradition claiming that technology is inscribed in masculine terms, the cyborg metaphor is not just another toy for the boys, and many feminists have turned to cyberspace at large in search of liberation and agency (Squires, 1996).

Participation in practice

One of the common threads in the discussion over the relationship between democracy and new communications technologies is the debate between plebiscitary and deliberative democracy (Arterton, 1987). In the first instance, members of the public cast their vote directly through the use of interactive technologies. The underlying rationale is that 'the sum of individual votes will allow for the rapid expression of the common will' (Friedland, 1996:187). The plebiscitary model has been used in Britain (in the New Labour 1997 electoral campaign) and even more extensively in the USA, where both the Republican House Speaker, Newt Gingrich, and the Clinton Democrats embraced the new technology. The irony, though, is that despite the view that electronic communication is a democratic end in itself, the first impact of ICTs on the political process 'was for the old political élite to appropriate them as parasitical tools in the more efficient service of the existing media' (Coleman, 1999:68). On the other hand, the deliberative approach examines ways through which representative democracy can be strengthened and become more participatory. This model – sometimes referred to as 'strong democracy' – considers the political involvement of citizens as an ongoing, lifelong enterprise in which communication is the core of the democratic process (as opposed to the periodic election of representatives) (Friedland, 1996; Jankowski and Van Selm, 2000). The embracing of new digital technology and the use of the internet by previously marginalised publics, such as women, can play a central role in this process, allowing women, for example, to participate actively in the public sphere. Women quickly appropriated the web and created electronic networks that function to set up a 'virtual sisterhood', linking together women's groups, feminist activist groups and social forums: 'Networking, activism and support are interwoven as we push ourselves to learn to work with the new electronic tools we are encountering. Together we anticipate a future where growing numbers of women can access and use the global connections to promote women's equality' (*Women's Space* web page, in Wakeford, 1997:60).

Recent research shows that the number of women using the internet has been rising. The latest figures expect women soon to account for half of the online community, which indicates that computer technology is not an exclusively male affair any longer. For the time being, one of the recent surveys on internet demographics presents female usage in the USA at 35.8 per cent and male usage at 64.2 per cent. This balance in Europe is 18.4 per cent for women and 81.6 per cent for men, and in the rest of the world 23.6 per cent for women and 76.4 per cent for men (GVU Seventh User Survey, April 1997; the Graphics, Visualization, and Usability Center is an interdisciplinary research laboratory affiliated with Georgia Tech in the USA). It is expected that the gender split will have diminished by 2001, with women representing 45 per cent of the world's internet users. In North America, where the largest number of internet users is concentrated, the number of women online will surpass that of men. The projected female usage in 2001 is 51 per cent as opposed to 49 per cent male usage. The equivalent participation for women in Europe is 40 per cent and for men 60 per cent (CyberAtlas Archive: Internet Statistics and Market Research for Web Marketers, 11.11.99 – an online information service and newsletter from internet.com). Although the above figures selectively represent findings from two different surveys, the future is generally pictured in optimistic terms for female users of the internet.

A number of cyber-presences created by women have come in direct response to stereotypical understandings of computing culture. Sites such as Cybergrrl, geekgirl and Netchick explore the possibility of a close relationship between women and computer culture wherein a discourse of 'problems' is not reproduced and traditional stereotypes are defied. In fact, grrrls – echoing a post-feminist rhetoric – dissociate themselves from 'an older style feminist rhetoric', and 'don't blame men for anything. [I]nstead [they] focus on ways to improve and strengthen [them]selves. Grrrls enjoy their femininity and kick ass at the same time . . . without acting like women are victims' (Wakeford, 1997:61).

One of the biggest and most popular networks in the USA is iVillage. It was set up in 1995 targeting baby boomers, though it is now aimed at women between twenty-five and fifty-four. The network consists of some seventeen sub-sites, offering a mix of information channels (anything from health, fitness and food to parenthood, relationships, travel, career and teleworking) and commercial channels (as in the case of the ecommerce iBaby.com and iMaternity.com shops). The entire network is about 'busy women sharing solutions and advice', who have fostered loyal, interactive communities through a number of bulletin boards and chat forums. iVillage invites women to 'speak their mind' and become active members of its online communities. There were 4.9 million members by the end of April 2000. iVillage is well on its way to reaching 10 per cent of US internet users on a regular basis.

Another successful site is electra.com, with its content categories covering money, career, mind and body, style and relationships. The Glass Ceiling web site has a slightly different emphasis, its mission being 'to assist all women in their pursuit of excellence in their business as well as personal lives'. Created in 1996, it sprang from *Shatter the Glass Ceiling*, a 'working woman's magazine' and, although conceived as a place for women trying to gain equality in their workplace, the site evidently became an online home for men as well. It has web pages on business and 'how to succeed' tips, health, employment, family, specific 'glass ceiling' issues and more. The site's demographics show a population of 75 per cent women and 25 per cent men, many of whom are business women, college students, college professors, male and female business owners, members of women's organisations and government personnel. This is a highly interactive site, where users (of either sex) can offer and receive advice on a wide variety of problems and needs.

FeMiNa is another women-related directory of 'sites for, by and about women' offering web links in arts, business, computers, education, motherhood, girls, health, media, society, leisure, and regional links (which open up a whole new directory of women's sites across Europe, for instance). The site has a 'Cybrarian' who offers assistance to women with their online searches. Also included is FeminaNet, a list where members can ask other women online for help regarding personal issues, academic research, employment needs, and so on. FeMiNa is linked to other women's networks such as cybergrrl.com and webgrrls.com. Chickclick is a directory with 'intelligent, sassy, progressive content'. It targets the 'anti-*Cosmo* girl crowd' (a reference to the glossy magazine *Cosmopolitan*) and presents links to a number of e-zines such as Riotgrrl, Razzbery, Hissyfit, Wench and Disgruntled Housewife. The site is the home of several bulletin board debates and hosts homepages. The majority of its users are between eighteen and twenty-four, with a quarter aged from twenty-five to thirty-five; its total population coming up to 1.4 million visitors per month.

These examples have been heavily US dominated. UK-based online networks for women are a fairly recent phenomenon, although the market is opening up. One of the leaders is PlanetGrrl, which was set up in 1998 as 'a resource by women and grrls from the UK in or interested in new media and technology for chicks everywhere'. The menu features various sites on life, love, sex ('Tired and sick of stupid books like *Men are From Mars, Women are From Venus*? Sick of magazines of 15-year-olds looking unhappy? What you won't find here . . . how to please your man'), including a polling debate on the pros and cons of forming online relationships. There is also an internet-related page with instructions for 'newbies', along with pages on clubbing and employment. Handbag is another relatively new British site, preparing its launch at the time of writing, and 'containing everything a woman needs, from health and beauty, to arts and relationships'. It positions itself as 'the ultimate destination for women of all ages who want to be informed, empowered and entertained'. These examples and brief descriptions indicate, at the very least, a rapidly developing demand for online 'communities' or 'networks' of this kind.

The strong (or strengthening) presence of women in cyberspace is not merely, however, a result of the proliferation of these women-related sites, since growing by numbers is not necessarily equivalent to the existence of a public sphere inclusive of women. Online networks for women provide their users with a common sense of belonging and a multiplicity of virtual communities (Harasim, 1993; Rheingold, 1993). These become, in turn, social networks where the critical communicative functions of the public sphere might be served (Garnham, 1990): we have seen examples of how information is disseminated to, and exchanged among, members, and how electronic communities provide a forum for public debate and shared decision making outside the state apparatus (through consultation, polls, referenda). Third, women are able to communicate with each other and participate in the various communities as equals. In fact, research on the discursive styles of the internet shows that there are a distinct style and mode of address among women which are characterised by expressions of support and appreciation, and serve to empower and encourage women users (Herring, 1996). Men, on the other hand, tend to feature more adversarial styles in cyberspace interactions, thus conveying a feeling of inhospitability to women. Without implying that all women in cyberspace are inevitably polite and supportive of each other, or that men are necessarily aggressive and adversarial, the trend remains evident in the 'virtual commons' that 'women thank and men flame' (Herring, 1994). As a result, women's networks, by their ethos and the encouraged styles of interaction, seek to bracket and neutralise inequalities in participation.

Does it really work for women?

In this case study I have discussed the internet as a public space for women, following a historical tendency to look for democratic channels within newly emerged communication technologies. Network technology, however, is Janus faced and cyberspace can stand for visions of both communicational Heaven and Hell. Hope for a reinvigorated public sphere is not the same as substance, and democratic optimism regarding participation, deliberation and equality can be tempered by a number of factors.

First, the dominant way the internet is currently envisaged may be problematic for women. The metaphor of cyberspace as an electronic frontier draws on a concept of war, conquest and extermination, and often reflects a specific image of the American West. Hackers and their pursuers then represent cowboys, law and lawlessness, while large corporations, which take an increasing interest in constructing networks in cyberspace (and tried, in some cases, to construct proprietary ones, such as Microsoft's MSN, in the early days of the internet), become the equivalent of the railroad companies in the West who encouraged people to settle in frontier lands near the railroad (being thus responsible for the pioneers' total dependence on the railroad for communication and supplies) (Jordan, 1999). Furthermore, the frontier metaphor is related to a specific moment in American history which was highly gendered. No wonder that women in cyberspace are positioned as lacking in agency: they exist within a classic western narrative of individualistic masculinity.

Then there is the question of access. Despite the rhetoric (and some evidence) of increasing gender equality in internet usage, there is a large number of women in the less developed world whose first priority is not surfing in cyberspace. Apart from the conception of 'surfing' as a sporting activity enjoyed by a specific social, economic and geographical group (Wakeford, 1997) – after all, *who* goes surfing in Africa? – evidence shows that the position of women as internet users in Africa, the Middle East and South America will remain low. The projected female usage by 2001 in these regions (which among themselves will account for only 3 per cent of the total internet use worldwide) is 28 per cent, 15 per cent, and 30 per cent, respectively (Cyber-Atlas: Internet Statistics and Market Research for Web Marketers).

The dystopic image of cyberspace becomes more pronounced once we take into account that the internet has inherited a problematic relationship with gender originating from its roots within the military-industrial complex. Given this inheritance, it comes as no surprise that many women experience the internet as 'male space':

> Many of the engineers currently debating the form and nature of cyberspace are the young turks of computer engineering, men in their late teens and twenties, . . . preoccupied with the things with which postpubescent men have always been preoccupied. This rather steamy group will generate the codes and descriptors by which bodies in cyberspace are represented. (Stone, 1991:103–4)

Given the ever-increasing complexity of digital technology, power in cyberspace is based on expertise and is available to technologically adept users – in itself leading towards the creation of a cyber-elite (Jordan, 1999), which remains primarily male dominated. The archetypical computer user is male, in paid employment in a well-defined organisational setting. On the other hand, women in the ICT labour market are segregated into low-paid, low-status, clerical jobs, while they are seriously under-represented in managerial and scientific posts (Diamond, 1997). Furthermore, the use of subcontracted female labour in the software industry means that women in many Third World countries are employed for the lower-level, standardised tasks of routine programming at rates of pay which are much lower than in the West. This reality strengthens the traditional perception of women's office work as 'deskilled', resulting in limited agency and autonomy for women in relation to men (Adam and Green, 1998).

Despite the fact that the overall position of women as internet users is improving, access to network technology can take place at a number of levels, with unevenness across these levels. Women need to have access to computer technology, either at home or at work, which implies that they must have considerable control of their time in order to use and become proficient in ICTs in either environment (Adam and Green, 1998). At the same time, though, simple access to computer infrastructure does not guarantee any advantages for its users. Heavy users, for example, may merely represent routinised telework (e.g. working from home) on piece rates, in non-unionised conditions, and bearing the responsibility of heating and lighting costs (Massey, 1993 in Aurigi and Graham, 1998). Therefore, actual circumstances of 'use' of digital technology need to be taken into account.

Moreover, there is the problem of discursive inequalities in CMC, imping-ing on the 'public sphere' features of participatory parity and unconstrained deliberation. Contrary to claims that CMC neutralises gender distinctions 're-cent empirical studies of computer-mediated interaction suggest that gen-der differences online reproduce and even exaggerate gender differences found in face-to-face interaction' (Herring, 1996:118). Experience suggests that many computer network forums are dominated by men who claim much more time and space than women, criticise women when they do the same and ignore topics introduced by women. Women are constructed as the other even within academic computer networks, where men monopolise the talk and make female participants feel 'irrelevant', on the statistical evidence that an increase in male participation is usually followed by a drop in the partici-pation of women (Ebben and Kramarae, 1993; Kramarae and Taylor, 1993). This situation is more accentuated with the male propensity towards 'flam-ing' (antagonistic exchanges), sometimes taking the form of extreme sexual harassment, even rape, as in the case of Mr Bungle in LambdaMOO (Dibbell, 1994). (This was an alleged verbal 'rape' of four people by a participant in a text-based online multi-user domain – a precursor of today's internet chat rooms – first reported as a 1993 cover story in New York's *The Village Voice* (Ed.).)

Finally, the creeping commercialisation of the internet and its colonisation by capital casts a shadow on the vision of a virtual public sphere. Increasing privatisation of the internet means cyberspace is now marketed to network consumers, and has become 'the perfect market-place' by offering new ways of reaching niche markets and expanding 'direct points of sale' (Dahlberg, 1998). As a result, there is growing concern that 'another potentially liberat-ing technology has been engulfed by the still rampant forces of the free market' (Golding, 1996:76). This impacts heavily on the concept of the internet as an alternative public sphere since the optimism around increasing numbers of female participants is moderated by the fact that many of them have emerged as powerful consumers on the web. Internet adoption by consumers is being driven, for the first time, by women, who represent 41 per cent of today's 55 million internet shoppers (CyberAtlas: Females Lead Online Growth Spurt). Women, who also tend to control household spending, are the driving force in the growth of e-commerce, a tendency which has not been overlooked by advertisers, sponsors and entrepreneurs. The proliferation of tips on online sales and of links to shopping sites on all the women's networks offers further testimony to this trend. Hence, contrary to hopes that cyberspace would be a differently feminine space, the internet is rapidly being swept up by capitalism's business as usual. In that respect, there is the risk of misreading the inclusion of the culturally marginal (e.g. women) as democracy instead of 'the insatiable hunger of commercial culture for new images and markets' (Diamond, 1997:83).

Conclusion

In this case study, I have explored the democratising potential of the internet by looking at it as a public forum for women. Technological utopia has been contrasted with the stark reality of privatisation and commercialisation. The question then arises: where does this leave women? Given the various constraints around the notion of cyberspace as public sphere, is there a digital future that women can claim as their own?

My answer to this is yes – as long as we allow for a looser definition of the public sphere. We need not only a multiplicity of public spheres (which will in turn accommodate a multitude of publics), but also to reconfigure the concept of the public sphere in a way that moves away from equality – for, let us not forget, even the original version of the public sphere was far from being egalitarian. In congruence with post-feminist politics, where women have shifted from debates around equality to debates around difference (Brooks, 1997), the debate on the digital public sphere should also focus on difference. In a post-feminist era, not all women experience gender inequalities in the same way across the globe. Without underestimating the generally bleak overall picture of internet participation, we need to realise that this will affect women to varying degrees, in different circumstances.

However, instead of concentrating on women 'networking', we should perhaps talk about women 'weaving' the net. Haraway argues that 'weaving' is for oppositional cyborgs, whereas 'networking' can be both a feminist practice and a multinational corporate strategy (Haraway, 1991:171). Around the intriguing icon of the weaving cyborg, women on the internet can, perhaps, construct both oppositional identities and electronic and social networks (Wakeford, 1997:63). It remains to be seen what forms this might take in practice.

As regards fear for the changing political economy of the internet (which will impact on its ability to become a digital public sphere), we should be reminded that, in the Habermasian public sphere, the press, far from embodying a disinterested rationality, was an engine of bourgeois propaganda (see Golding, 1995), in itself a result of the growing commercial viability of the press industry. In this context, arguments bemoaning the growing commodification of the internet not only promote a romanticised version of a public sphere which never existed, but portray women users as passive – and irrational – consumers. This, however, echoes some earlier views in communication studies (aired by male academics) which viewed women as passive readers of media texts such as magazines or romantic fiction, and which later led to the emergence of critical feminist media studies and the re-evaluation of those forms. Furthermore, concerns over commercialisation fail to recognise that the inherent interactivity of digital technology nonetheless remains appropriate for a notion of a public sphere in cyberspace, locating female participants as *active* consumers, in charge of technology, their time, tastes and pleasure.

22

New media convergences: some research issues

Julia Knight

Introduction

The 1990s was undoubtedly the decade of 'new media technologies' (NMTs) – not only in terms of the development and diffusion of the actual technologies, but with regard to the explosion of material written about them. The number of books, magazines and journals addressing some aspect of digital technology grew from a mere trickle into a veritable flood. And as co-editor of one of those publications – *Convergence: The Journal of Research into New Media Technologies* – I was responsible for contributing to that flood. Part of the reason for this wealth of material was that it soon became clear that what was being termed the 'information revolution' was rapidly impacting on all areas of human endeavour. But, as Andrew Murphie has observed:

> Revolutions have always been the best and worst of times for theory, and the information revolution is no exception. In such times it almost seems as if one can say anything one wishes – and receive an audience – yet it is also all too easy for vested interests and . . . 'false prophets' to hijack the debate. (Murphie, 1997:5).

In launching *Convergence* in 1995, our aim was to provide a much-needed forum for the careful and sustained critical analysis of the developing field of NMTs. (*Convergence* is edited from the Department of Media Arts at the University of Luton, England; from its launch until 1999 by Julia Knight and Alexis Weedon, when Jeanette Steemers joined as third co-editor. This chapter intentionally adopts the perspective of the journal editor in judging how, where and why key 'issues' are formulated in media studies.)

The word 'convergence' has since become something of a buzz word, but we chose the name because it seemed to sum up so much of what was happening within the mass media and media industries in the late twentieth century: not only technological convergence, but the changes in industrial structures and networks of ownership, the erosion of boundaries between distinct media forms, and the collapse of the traditional distinction between producer and consumer. And, importantly for us, it was also apparent that if we, as media researchers, were to fully explore the creative, social, political, economic and pedagogical issues raised by digital technology, we needed a convergence of academic disciplines. As we stated in our first editorial, we would have to 'draw on and pursue a range of academic approaches in order to develop the critical frameworks and methodologies that will enable us to analyse the specific implications of the new media' (Knight and Weedon, 1995:5–6). In short, *Convergence* set out to develop NMTs into a new area of study in its own right.

Developing an interdisciplinary approach, however, necessarily gave rise to a heterogeneous range of perspectives and critical frameworks. Both our editorials and those by guest editors were forced to acknowledge this diversity when a single issue of *Convergence* might combine theoretical, empirical and philosophical approaches and have contributors from the fields of mass communications, library studies, French studies, computer science and media arts. Yet without exception, amid the diversity, common issues would emerge and have come to constitute central research issues in the field of NMTs. Although it is impossible to explore here all the issues that have been raised in the pages of *Convergence*, what follows is an attempt to identify some of the major recurring concerns.

The search for clarity and appropriate analytical tools

In view of the excitement and hype surrounding the new technologies and their status as a developing field, the terms used to discuss them have often been used imprecisely. In a discussion of virtual reality and telepresence, for instance, Ken Goldberg has asserted: '[T]here is no universal agreement on the definitions of VR and telepresence. Unfortunately, they are sometimes used interchangeably in studies of electronic immersion' (1998:33). Thus an obvious and crucial concern has been to clarify the terminology.

The term that has probably been subjected to most scrutiny is 'interactivity'. It has been appended to NMTs to suggest that something new has been added, but the term has been an endless source of confusion. As Erkki Huhtamo argued in an early issue of *Convergence*, it has been used to describe such a range of 'things interactive' that '[i]f it ever had any conceptual integrity, it is quickly disappearing' (1995:81). In an effort to unpick some of the issues, Luke Hockley pointed out that, '[t]ypically we think about two types of interactivity' (1996:10). The first, he asserts, is where the user can exert a degree of control over, or help create, what they engage with by physically interacting with the technology. Yet the consumer has always been able to do this to a certain extent by, for instance, selecting which parts of a newspaper to read or by choosing to re-watch certain parts of a film on video. The second form of interactivity is based on the idea of reciprocal communication between producers and consumers. Again, however, this is hardly new: the feedback systems of letters' pages, radio phone-ins, right-of-reply programmes, and so on, have long facilitated two-way communication and have on occasion allowed audiences to influence plot lines and programming decisions.

The popular belief is that NMTs will enhance and expand these traditional forms of interactivity to offer a qualitatively different experience, one that puts the user on an equal footing with the producer so that it is their combined input, their mutual collaboration via the technology, which creates the end product. However, Hockley argues that this is merely an illusion:

[A]t their very best, the current implementations of interactivity merely broaden the paradigmatic set from which the viewer makes choices. Control rests firmly within the institutions or individuals of creation; it is they who determine the limits of the interactivity . . . Interactivity is actually about power. It is about persuading users that they are powerful when in fact they are powerless. (1996:10)

According to Jonathan Roper, part of the problem lay in our obsession with interactivity:

Interactivity became the touchstone of multimedia because it was technically possible. Multimedia has given us an opportunity to combine and interact with materials that has never been possible before in such an easy format. And given that interactivity became a possibility, it then quickly progressed to being the *raison d'être* for multimedia. (1995:24)

Thus, for Roper, multimedia was essentially a form with no content; or rather the technological interactivity – the user's ability to push a button or click a mouse to select options and so on – *was* the content. Consequently, for him, '[t]he very word "interactivity" which used to promise so much now carries the smell of death: death to feeling, intelligence and experience' (1995:25). Roper has not been alone in making this kind of observation, but others have taken issue with such an analysis. Neither Hockley nor Roper addressed new media art and, in different ways, both Huhtamo and Martin Rieser have suggested artists are in fact doing much to develop our understanding of what 'interactivity' could – or indeed should – be (Huhtamo, 1995:81–104; Rieser, 1997:10–19). What becomes clear from their discussions is that 'interactivity' is not a pre-existing given – hence the hype and confusion. *Technological* interactivity is a reality, but any other level of interactivity – how the technological capability can be used to develop meaningful content, to enable *psychological* interactivity – is something which will have to be worked for, or even – according to Huhtamo – struggled for, and artists have been at the forefront of this struggle.

Amid these debates around the terminology, and alongside those working to develop the potentialities of NMTs, some researchers have also taken the next step and tried to develop, or at least to point the way to, the critical frameworks within which to analyse new media products. As part of a research project evaluating the effectiveness of multimedia in museums, for instance, Mary Dyson *et al.* identified the need to create an analytical framework within which to classify the experience of, and degrees of, interactivity in multimedia installations. In 'Multimedia in Museums: The Need for a Descriptive Framework', they discuss the criteria they used to develop such a framework and explain the problems in classifying the extensive range of technical possibilities which are currently employed by multimedia developers (Dyson *et al.*, 1995:105–24). While they acknowledge that the framework may need adapting or expanding for use in other contexts, it offers a useful starting point for comparing the characteristics of a range of multimedia systems and as such constitutes an important research tool.

In 'The Psychology of New Media Technologies', Greg Boiarsky productively shifts the focus from the technologies themselves to their users: 'No matter how powerful a technology is, its use always occurs within the context of the psychology of the user' (1997:121). Hence he argues that a thorough understanding of the impacts, usability and adoption of NMTs 'must involve an understanding of the "mental processes" of the user' (1997:110). Drawing on widely accepted concepts in cognitive psychology, he shows how these concepts have been productively applied in the past to study the impact of word processors on writing ability and how they might be usefully applied to understanding the impact of hypertext, hypermedia and multimedia computer applications on their users.

The internet: an enhancement of democracy?

No discussion of NMTs can avoid addressing the internet, and one of the issues that has recurred in the pages of *Convergence* has been that of its democratic promise. The claims made for the net's potential to promote social and political democracy stem in part from its interactive nature. As Lincoln Dahlberg explains, 'The electronic linking of computers enables the formation of a virtual meeting place, cyberspace, whereby participants can interact' (1998:70). According to net enthusiasts, this facilitates information sharing and can allow individuals to debate issues of common concern in a manner that will revitalise Habermas's notion of the public sphere. Furthermore, online we lack the visual information afforded by face-to-face contact and this identity 'blindness' is thought to undercut social hierarchies and power relations, allowing people to interact as if they were equals. Also, as an increasing number of organisations go online, it means that users and consumers can have direct and reciprocal communication with producers, politicians, managing directors and the like. Overall, there is supposedly greater opportunity for a wider range of voices to be heard and for more communities to influence the decision-making processes that affect them.

It is indisputable that the internet has allowed some of this democratic ideal to be realised. In 'Revolution Goes Global', Michael Hoechsmann recounts how in Mexico, after a brief armed uprising in January 1994, the Zapatista National Liberation Army (EZLN) used the internet to further its fight for indigenous rights and social justice (1996:30–5). Press releases and open letters from Subcomandante Marcos, EZLN's political and spiritual leader, were regularly posted on the internet and circulated on bulletin boards worldwide. This exposure rallied international support for the Zapatistas and gained the attention of the international media. According to researcher David Ronfeldt, cited by Hoechsmann: 'the Internet had provided immediate international pressure on the Mexican government to negotiate with the Zapatistas and not to simply defeat them by force' (1996:33).

From a different perspective, Ananda Mitra analyses how the 'space' offered by the internet has opened up a new set of possibilities for community and nation formation by those groups whose communal and national roots have been disrupted by the processes of migration and immigration. His analysis is based on the specific example of the Usenet group soc.culture.indian, and he found two forces at work in imaging a nation on the net:

On one hand, there are the centralising tendencies through which members of the virtual community are using the electronic space to develop a certain fraternity around the place of origin and their identities in the New World . . . On the other hand, the centrifugal forces generated by the variety of discourses that create a range of alternative images of India always expose the differences between the members of the community and often lead to the disruption of community membership. (1996:66)

Mitra views this as a positive feature since it creates a genuine dialogue which questions and reflects on the segmentation that exists within the Indian networks – a dialogue which is only possible because, according to Mitra, 'the space cannot be co-opted by any particular point of view' (1996:66).

This democratic ideal is not without its flaws, however. Not only has Habermas's public sphere model been exposed as exclusionary, but as Dahlberg argues: 'Net enthusiast rhetoric tends to emphasise the technical aspects of the net. Yet in order to understand the medium's potential to enhance the public sphere, its technological form must not be separated from the context shaping its development, deployment and uses' (1998:70). Dahlberg focuses on just one aspect of that context, but one he considers may be the single most important factor structuring the net's democratic potential: 'the rapid colonisation of cyberspace by capital' (1998:70). Now almost entirely funded by private enterprise, the way the net is developing has three major implications which Dahlberg believes are threatening to undermine any potential it may have to enhance democracy. As privatisation leads to corporate control, he argues, 'People do not necessarily get what they want but what the market deems most profitable to produce and sell' (1998:75). Second, with interaction on the net increasingly determined by commercial imperatives, '[i]nstead of citizens actively seeking some form of "the public good", participants in privatised cyberspace are constructed as consumers encouraged to maximise their individual pleasure' (1998:78). And third, Dahlberg raises the issue of how many may be excluded from cyberspace due to '[t]he fixed and variable charges of networking, along with the skills required to network' (1998:76).

Although some may disagree with Dahlberg's analysis, access is an issue that has been raised repeatedly. In 'E-mail in African Studies' (1996), Handel Kashope Wright is critical of Western media theorists who take the widespread availability of computers in educational institutions for granted. While they focus their attention on critiquing the use to which computers are put, Wright is concerned with an area where digital technology is still not widely available. His description of the problems facing one of the two sister university colleges in Sierra Leone – although written in 1995 – is indicative of impediments to a fully wired 'global village' that have all too often been overlooked by the visionaries:

There is currently no electricity supply to the campus (because of rebel sabotage of the system) . . . Both funding to purchase and materials to upkeep computers are in short supply. It would be difficult to install computers somewhere where they can be kept at an appropriate temperature (the area is hot and dusty), and be made safe from theft and yet accessible to students (much of the infrastructure of the campus has been destroyed in two rebel raids). [C]omputers . . . would be nothing but white elephants. (1996:27)

However, it is not just technical and practical issues that present a problem – which are not necessarily insurmountable. As Nyaki Adeya has asserted, 'it's possible to argue that the need for political will and commitment poses a greater obstacle' (1996:25). Although the situation varies between African countries, in 'Beyond the Borders: The Internet for Africa', she argues that politicians fear an uncontrollable flood of information which could propagate anti-government ideas and hinder government plans. Thus rather than gearing up for connectivity, some African governments have instead introduced discouraging measures, such as putting strict import controls on computers and related equipment.

Adeya also raises the issue of what you have access to online. She argues there is a widespread concern in Africa that the internet is simply another means by which the West is propagating its own culture and subjugating others. In a report from the Baltic 'cyber-corridor', Eric Kluitenberg echoes this concern:

> The so-called culture of the net is not reflected in the quantity of native tongues in the global 'infosphere' as it is still heavily dominated by the hegemony of anglo-saxon culture and the English language. In small nations such as the Baltic states, this inspires fears of a loss of a newly regained national identity and the net can become an easy target of hatred and scepticism, being perceived as an invasive force rather than a cultural life-line. (1998:23; see also Dauncey, 1997)

And just as Anglo-Saxon cultural hegemony has been replicated in cyberspace, so too has a real-life gender imbalance. Although Rhiannon Bury (1999) argues that in North America the situation is improving, in 1998 Stephen Lax observed that '[a]ll demographics available about internet access and computer ownership suggest that the majority of users and owners are wealthy, young and male' (1998:33). Even where women have access, many have frequently been discouraged from using the internet due to the masculine image that has attached itself to NMTs and to the aggressive behaviour that can be encountered in multi-user domains and on newsgroups (see, for instance, Cherny and Weise, 1996).

Nevertheless, the internet does provide access to information, which is vital in a political democracy. As a newspaper editor expressed it: 'You can explore so many things that you didn't have access to otherwise . . . The world is at your fingertips like it's *never* been before' (quoted in Singer, 1997:81). Yet as Jane Singer's research with metro reporters and editors on three US newspapers demonstrated, at one level all the so-called information revolution has done is bring about '[the] realisation of just how much junk is out there' (1997:80).

The internet enables such access because the technology allows anyone effectively to become a 'publisher', able to disseminate information all over the world. On a more productive level, this means that social and campaigning groups which have been under- or misrepresented by the traditional media, have the possibility of representing themselves and their views on a global stage, thus raising awareness of their concerns within the mainstream of society. A good example of this is OneWorld Online, which provides a collective gateway on the web to human rights organisations and groups campaigning around global issues:

> It precisely offers (at least potentially) the kind of access to the means of information dissemination that older technologies such as broadcast and print do not. The Internet has allowed OneWorld Online to create . . . 'citizen spaces', a means of information dissemination which is not channelled through journalists or broadcasters, that allows a diverse range of people to speak on their own terms. (Knight, 1997:130)

However, internet connectivity has also facilitated virtually the opposite. Under- or misrepresented by the traditional mass media, some people have used the internet to seek out like-minded people and group together in their own discussion forums. When Rhiannon Bury conducted ethnographic research online with female fans of *The X-Files*, for instance, she found that they had joined the all-female David Duchovny Estrogen Brigades lists primarily because 'they were interested in building "private" women's communities which offered support, solidarity and friendship' (1998:60; see also chapter 21). While the group members may find much-needed support, the emphasis on 'private' means that the concerns of women and other groups can remain marginalised.

(cont. p. 424)

Playing video games

I am a twenty-one-year-old father of a six-month-old baby girl, engaged to her mother, and a partner in a small, independently owned video shop. I received my first Sony PlayStation as a Christmas present in 1998. One might assume from my circumstances that I should not have had much time to devote to playing video games. This was not the case. A long romance with the PlayStation began with my acquisition of a game called *Oddworld: Abe's Exodus*, the third in an 'Oddworld' series.

The aim here is to guide Abe, a small alien-looking creature, in rescuing others of his kind from a factory where they are enslaved to make a drink produced from their bones. I am rather ashamed to admit that – despite the responsibilities to which I should have been attending (my then two-month-old daughter, a floundering relationship with another family member, a fledgling business, college exams pending) – Abe took precedence. Many entire nights were spent playing Abe. Often I would rise early, with my daughter, to play Abe. My typical examination revision schedule that year consisted of 20–25 minutes' revision interspersed with 35–40 minutes' playing Abe, typically right through the night.

Initial reactions from family members to my immersion in video games included the standard 'toys for the boys' charge. While I had been interested in gadgets as a teenager, my relationship with video games seemed very different to me, even as others moved on from that charge to more serious suggestions about 'addiction'. I retaliated with feeble justifications – I was just trying to reach the next level, then I'd stop; it was good for hand–eye co-ordination; I was studying it for college! Privately, I just accepted that if I was addicted so be it.

I was delighted to find that a friend had bought a PlayStation. Thus began marathon video-gaming sessions with four friends, two taking turns on each console – we would spend at least four hours a night, three or four nights a week, playing one game through as far as we could get. The first major challenge was *Gran Turismo* – a racing game, very technical, with tournaments and hidden levels of complexity – then *Warped*. As we sat playing games one evening I looked at the group and thought about how our lives previously had crossed only in casual, insignificant ways. Now we seemed almost like a family, as I imagined people gathered round the first TV sets sharing vicarious experiences together. The intensity seemed palpable and strange. There was nothing reclusive about video games here.

I started to use the web to support my immersion in video games. I found a chat network for gamers, where information and reviews circulated widely. Communication of tips, secrets and cheats was pursued with intense enthusiasm and breaking through difficult levels of particular games was celebrated. I found myself writing and submitting long explanations of how to progress through certain games, eager to be the first person to reply to a query or solve a problem and display my mastery. Exposed to others' devotion, I was no longer ashamed of my own 'addiction'.

Control – this, I have figured out, is the ultimate reason why I play video games. I came across Freud's description of the child's 'gone/back' game (throwing an object away every time it is brought back) and recognised there something of my own compulsive use of video games. I have played 'fort-da' with the PlayStation not, I think, through any kind of infantile regression, but as an antidote to uncontrollable things in my own life. (The game of 'fort-da' was observed by Sigmund Freud when his grandson, then one-and-a-half years old, played with a piece of string attached to a wooden spool which he threw away with an 'oooh', then pulled back saying 'da'. The child's mother interpreted the first sound as a version of 'fort' ('gone away'), the second as German for 'there it is!'. To Freud this demonstrated a human compulsion towards repetition in order to achieve mastery. (Ed.)) The pleasures of immersive, hard-won control were not so much escapist for me as compensatory. They reminded me that I could think and try hard and win, that I could bond in friendship with like-minded others. Where life had been doing its best to teach me otherwise, to push me into passivity, into hollow and empty reactions, into tired resignation, video games gave me back energy, confidence and strength.

Conor Beattie

Regulation and control

A further problem of the internet as an open-access publishing medium is that groups that are racially intolerant, such as the neo-Nazis, or infringe human rights, such as child pornographers, are equally free to disseminate their material. Whereas in the traditional media, editors, laws, industry regulators and complaints procedures, and so on, act as 'gatekeepers' to monitor and control the flow of information that enters the public domain, no such controls exist for the internet. There have been attempts to instigate some forms of control, but as yet these have proved problematic.

This lack of control has given rise to fears about children in particular accessing inappropriate information. As Amy Bruckman asserts: 'A tremendous volume of obscene, racist, and violent information is available on-line. While such information generally appears only when one actively looks for it, it is possible to stumble across it accidentally' (1999:29–30). She relates how a twelve-year-old pupil of hers accidentally accessed a collection of lawyer jokes that were largely obscene and included ones about anal sex. Although little harm may have been done, most parents don't want their children to see such material. Others, however, have argued that the freedom of speech and the freedom to read are absolute. Amid these debates, a number of software products have been launched which aim to make net access more suitable for children, such as SurfWatch, Cyber Patrol and Net Nanny. These products allow parents to decide what their children can have access to, but in doing so neglect the competing rights of children, parents and educational systems: 'For example, should teenagers be able to access information about gay teen support groups if their parents and school system don't want them to?' (Bruckman, 1999:31).

In the USA digital technology has similarly been used to introduce a new form of regulation into the broadcasting arena. Manufacturers are now required by law to incorporate a microchip circuit device – the V-chip – into all TV sets. Using a remote control programmed according to a ratings system, viewers can blank out any programming that exceeds their desired level of violent, sexual or indecent material. A seemingly ideal solution to controlling *children's* viewing, Matthew Murray (1997:27) argues, however, that the V-chip 'will likely limit choices *for most users* as a result of the ideological commitment to "family values" underlying its practical implementation' (my emphasis). Rather than precipitating a broader range of TV representations and user choice, Murray asserts that it actually 'operates to privilege certain viewers' values over others' (1997:27).

Both SurfWatch *et al.* and the V-chip are blocking devices designed to protect the user from unwanted material invading the home. Journalists, however, have approached the matter from almost the opposite perspective. In view of what has become an information overload, they believe that before long there will be an inevitable shift of emphasis from quantity to quality:

> Playing up the volume of information available on-line is 'a natural initial marketing ploy', said a *Sun* editor. 'But at some point, someone's going to have to realise . . . it's not just quantity that counts, but maybe some quality control, too. I mean, who wants to wade through tons of crap?' (Singer, 1997:80)

According to Singer, journalists' gatekeeping role will become less about selecting what information to make public and more about 'helping people figure out which of the millions of bits of information available on-line are important – or even true' (1997:80). Thus the problem is not so much about barring *unwanted* information from your home as about finding ways of seeking out the information that you *do want*. Although software is being developed along these lines, journalists see themselves as playing a key quality control role in directing people to the credible and important information in an online world.

Although this by no means exhausts the issues around control and regulation, it is nevertheless evident both that some forms of control are inevitable and that technology alone cannot satisfactorily regulate information access. Using the analogy of a city, Bruckman argues that, in the case of children using the internet, it is only by monitoring the users – rather than the information – that we can develop sensible and appropriate forms of regulation:

> You don't let a very young child go into the city alone, but you might let them play alone in the yard . . . As children grow older, you need to educate them on how to be street smart. Eventually, you need to trust them to venture off on their own and use good judgement. The internet brings some of the complexities of the real world onto your desktop. Parents need to stay involved to help children learn to negotiate those complexities. (1999:31)

What do we want?

The idea of educating the *users* of NMTs about what they are using implies we have a clear understanding of both what those technologies can do and what we want them to do. However, this is not always the case. As Roger Silverstone observes, 'technological change is neither determined in its development nor determining in its use' (1995:11), and hence the future is to some extent uncertain. As discussed above, the internet has the potential to enhance democracy, yet Dahlberg's analysis suggests that this is being eroded by its increasing commercialisation. Similarly, online publishing was thought to foreshadow the 'death of the book', yet, in an analysis of experiments in internet publishing by book and journal publishers, Alexis Weedon found that 'the book trade is developing the net as a promotional and marketing tool rather than exploiting it as a distribution system' (1996:76). And clearly the field is developing and changing all the time.

What is apparent is that we have a series of competing hopes and fears around NMTs. We hope they will benefit humankind; hence the enthusiastic claims for the democratic potential of the net. According to Amy Bruckman, there is almost equal enthusiasm for the educative potential of computer networking, but as yet little concrete evidence of its educational value (1999:24). In 'The Day After Net Day', she suggests that this is because the educational use of the internet is often like the 'horseless carriage' – an attempt to understand and utilise a new medium in terms of the old one, without recognising that the internet opens up different possibilities (1999:43). Bruckman cites technological samba schools – a virtual space offering a context in which interaction, meaningful interrelationships and learning can take place for people who would otherwise not meet – as one such possibility. Developing these new possibilities, as Dina Iordanova (1997) outlines in 'On-line Teaching in International Communication', can be fraught with institutional difficulties, enormously time consuming and disappointing. However, both agree that results of preliminary experiments have nevertheless been promising, but stress that 'innovative thinking and careful, self-critical research is (*sic.*) required to understand how to use this new medium to its best advantage' (Bruckman, 1999:44).

The fears we have about new technologies are most evident in the narratives we tell ourselves. Quite contrary to the enthusiastic claims made for NMTs, a number of films suggest that we fear they will de-humanise us, will invade our lives and change them for the worse. As Paul Young (1999) argues in 'The Negative Reinvention of Cinema', there has been a cycle of Hollywood films addressing digital media that can be described as specifically mediaphobic, and he cites Brett Leonard's *The Lawnmower Man* (USA, 1992) as exemplary. In the film the mentally disabled Jobe, guided by Dr Angelo, gains superior intelligence through the use of consciousness-altering drugs with computer learning tools such as CD-ROMs and virtual reality. In a Frankenstein-like scenario, however, Jobe becomes subsumed by the technology and threatens to take over the global telecommunications network. More recently, in Irwin Winkler's *The Net* (USA, 1995), computer software consultant Angela Bennett finds herself up against an unscrupulous corporation and discovers that:

> for all the perks of on-line existence, the traces of identity one leaves behind in all phases of an information society – credit card numbers, identity records, server accounts, consumer profiles – invite disaster by allowing anyone with the right skills and equipment to manipulate those traces. Among other disasters, the terrorist corporation transforms Angela into a fugitive prostitute named 'Ruth Marx' by vandalising her identity records, and arranges the death of her only friend. (Young, 1999:30)

Conclusion

There are, of course, many other aspects of NMTs that have been raised in the pages of *Convergence* which have not been discussed here, such as the impact of digital television, identity in cyberspace, special effects in film and their impact on linear narrative realism, emerging economic models on the internet, and virtual reality. At the risk of overgeneralising, however, in many cases the issues they raise are not new; it is simply that the technological innovation gives them a new immediacy. In some instances, of course, new possibilities do emerge – such as Bruckman's technological samba schools – and professional roles may change – as Singer finds with journalists. In 'The Case for Lateral Thinking', Peter Braunstein also reminds us that, according to some critics, the information age is even changing how we think, that 'growing up in a media saturated environment is producing distinctive effects among the under-30 generation in terms of intellectual inclinations and thought processes' (1999:10). The contention is that lateral thinking – drawing associations between diverse ideas – is starting to replace vertical thinking – the ability to think in linear patterns. What is clear, however, is that we cannot predict developments with any absolute certainty, and that our understanding of NMTs and their development into something productive cannot be taken for granted; rather, it is something for which we have to strive.

Media power and institutional economics

Questions of media power have circulated throughout the previous Parts of this volume, so what follows is a summary and a recapitulation. Which social actors control the media? And what effect does media power have upon audiences? These two questions have stimulated media research from the outset and the answers provided subscribe to three paradigms of power which are virtually canonical in the social sciences. The mass media have been studied as if empowering the elites – *elitism* – the people – *pluralism* – and social institutions, including themselves – *institutionalism*.

The elitist approach conceives of the media as instruments in the hands of the elite groups whose position of power is guaranteed by the effects of the media upon the behaviour and beliefs of the audience. By contrast, the pluralistic paradigm argues that media control is open to competition among different groups that represent the main interests in a society. Thus pluralists tend to speak of minimal media effects and they emphasise the power of the audience to use and make sense of media content. Finally, the institutional paradigm of power sustains the view that the media display their own goals and norms, although linked to other powerful institutions, especially those of the state and the market. Powerful media effects can be detected at the institutional level when media reinforce (and sometimes weaken) the functioning and the legitimacy of other social institutions. These three alternative views of media power inform most research traditions about mass media control and its effects.

Elitism depicts exclusionary control of the media, fortressing the interests of cohesive ruling groups that limit social debate to whatever is most convenient for their advantage (see Mills, 1956). Challengers are either silenced or marginalised by the media as being anti-systemic, extreme and lacking support. In authoritarian states, most media silence or condemn protest. In democratic societies, common interests among the elites' enterprises and the main news organisations often explain why the media sustain the status quo (see Herman and Chomsky, 1988).

Two schools of media effects have assumed the elitist paradigm: much early empirical research into the effects on audiences of media content, and the critics of the ideological hegemony that media build in favour of capitalism. The seminal mass communication research of the 1920s applied the notion of mass society and the principles of behaviourist psychology to the models of the 'hypodermic needle' and 'bullet' theories for immediate media effects. It claimed that the media 'injected' or 'shot' messages into the helpless and atomised audience in order, say, to steer mass consumption and electoral preferences. After being abandoned for a time, the powerful effects thesis was recovered in some quarters during the mid 1970s and 1980s in empirical studies based on cognitive psychology that claimed long-term media effects on the public's belief system. The main thesis was that the media generated a 'pseudo-reality' on which the public was fully dependent to formulate its opinions (see Adoni and Mane, 1984).

The most vigorous theories of the cognitive 'dependency model' at present are the agenda-setting theory, complemented with framing and priming effects, and the 'spiral of silence'. All of these share with elitism a top-down model. Media agendas are built by elites (experts, journalists and officials) securing the conformity of the audience's perception of public issues. (For reviews of agenda setting and related issues see Protess and McCombs, 1991.) In addition, the mass media suppress debate over certain issues and opinions, and spin the spiral of silence upon ever-receding minority factions (Noelle-Neumann, 1980).

In contrast, many critical scholars addressed the ideological hegemony of the mass media, the main effect of which was to guarantee that the dominant ideology coincided with the ideology of those who held power. Drawing upon Marx, the Frankfurt School and later followers studied how the media 'manufactured' consent in favour of a political status quo and capitalist values. Neo-Marxist theories of hegemony, and social control studies, claim that news organisations veil the class struggle in the interests of those with economic power and marginalise challengers to the social order. Mainstream media infuse this bias into the belief systems of most citizens. The Gramscian version of hegemony was more dynamic, admitting some degree of audience resistance to ideological manipulation. But the outcome was again that the media impeded the working class from gaining consciousness of its oppressed position, building instead a 'false consciousness'. (For an excellent reader of Marxist and neo-Marxist texts, see Mattelart and Siegelaub, 1979.)

From an entirely different perspective, *pluralists* maintain that power is the shifting result of resource mobilisation by interest groups in an 'inclusive' and 'relatively open' system (see Dahl, 1961). Thus the media respond to competing interests, diversely and without any necessarily pre-established bias. It is a bottom-up model of media power, contradicting the top-down model of elitism. Pluralistic media content mirrors the values and views of the most influential and representative social groups. Even anti-elite factions could, in this view, mobilise publicity against the status quo by having their activities covered by conventional media.

Two traditions finding weak or minimal media effects support a pluralist view. They are the school of 'uses and gratifications' of the 1970s and the current research into 'active' audiences. While the first maintained that the audience used the media to satisfy certain needs or gratifications, nowadays an increasing number of studies shows the audience interpreting the media in different contexts and building personal and social meanings. The studies of uses and gratifications took a functionalist approach in which the media fulfilled public needs for information, social interaction and entertainment. This thesis was consonant with the dominant idea that reinforcement of the public's preferences was the principal media effect. Current ethnographic work, focused on the so-called 'active' audience, links specific patterns of media consumption to different 'interpretive communities' that are defined by, say, class, gender or race. In this way, media effects may seem to dissolve into multiple 'negotiations of meanings' from the same media content. If the studies of uses and gratifications usually concluded with the sovereignty of media users, much current research tends to picture the 'active' audience as the ultimate interpreter of media communications. Consumers' power to use the media for their gratifications has given way to the power to decode media messages. (For a critical review of the pluralist schools see Curran, 1990.)

Elitism over-emphasises the power of ruling groups to control the media and their effects, while pluralism over-emphasises the capacity of the audience to use the media and extract specific meanings at its convenience. The modern media, as will be clear from many of the contributions to this volume, are neither elite transmission belts nor unbiased platforms for pluralist representation and meaning building. Considering the media as a contemporary institution (or a set of interlocked institutions) drives our attention towards media organisations and their conventional practices. These media norms and routines result from power inequalities and tend, in turn, to reproduce them. So *institutionalism* is the third and last paradigm of media power. The media institutional 'logics' – formal or informal procedures, routines and norms embedded in media production – are tied to powerful institutions and favour the groups that already count on other institutional resources. Although the media privilege certain interests, they may also provoke unintended consequences. For example, most political leaders have been drawn into self-promotional strategies in order to achieve media impact, often with unpredictable results in relation to their parties' interests. A general effect is that modern parties have lost ground as institutions for political socialisation in favour of the mass media, with their focus on individuals (see Patterson, 1993).

Indeed, the 'mediatisation' or imposition of media logics on other institutions is perhaps the most powerful overall effect (Beniger and Herbst, 1990). The media constitute a key institution of modern societies but often display contradictory institutional logics while pretending to perform as entertainers and enlighteners of the public, watch-dogs of government and of powerful enterprises, all at the same time.

Media power over the audience will depend in turn on the economic and socio-cultural resources of the various groupings that make up 'the public', as well as on certain institutional features of the media. Those with more *cultural capital* are in a better position to demand, to choose and to resist media messages (Morley, 1992). In any case, those sectors of audiences with the highest purchasing power and political influence consume and influence the media with greater gusto (Ettema and Whitney, 1994). On the other hand, the less favoured or subaltern publics may display a 'paradoxical creativity' (Silverstone, 1994), robustly reinterpreting the media in their own contexts despite apparently limited resources for doing so.

Victor Sampedro

Institutional economics as a framework

In the search for appropriate theories, methodologies and strategies with which to undertake media studies, institutional economics offers a range of analytical frameworks.

Born out of wide-eyed disbelief in the capability of late nineteenth-century mass-producing global capitalism, its appeal stems from two traditions: the critical and the pragmatic. In establishing a critical path for a 'new' economics of mass market capitalism, institutional economics provides a vehicle for entering into the historical task of critique. Thorstein Veblen (1857–1929), the recognised founder of the 'school', was virtually estranged from the entire US academic establishment as a result of his efforts in generating theories of evolutionary capitalism. This did not hinder his substantial contribution to the literature of engaged economic thought.

The tradition which Veblen established has concerned itself with a non-Marxist approach, where idealist and utopian class and philosophical concerns carry less currency than the everyday problems of equity, access and resource allocation. Nevertheless, institutional economics shares with some contemporary liberal-Marxist thought a heterodox approach to the formation and extension of opportunity within contemporary society. Implicit in this approach is the acknowledgement that participation in, and reform of, capitalism is possible. This approach incorporates a deeply held scepticism of key tenets of the theory of the market economy, together with a conceptual and promotional role for established public and emerging institutions of advanced, post-industrial society. This theme was given prominence in the work of Joseph Schumpeter (who was not, however, a recognised institutional economist), in his classic 'mapping' of the evolving shifts in nineteenth-century society in *Capitalism, Socialism and Democracy* (1942).

The pragmatism inherent in this approach incorporates a moral dilemma for the critique – it emboldens practitioners who recognise that the questions raised by contemporary capitalism are always a site for contestation. Furthermore, the institutional economist's pragmatism recognises that the inherent characteristics of contemporary society – its culture – are in a constant 'feedback' relationship with economy. Where economy may appear to triumph in one instance, the emerging institutions and practices of social life challenge and defeat any determinist reading of economy. The best-known advocates of the pragmatic view applied in the public sphere are John Maynard Keynes and John Kenneth Galbraith.

Significant sub-themes of increasing relevance to media studies which have become prominent in contemporary institutional economics include the battle over the corporate economy and neo-classical economics. Both issues mark the debate over the evolutionary nature of corporations within the national and global economy, together with their alliance with government and the regulatory regimes established to maintain business and public interest. Considerable public attention has been directed to the monopolistic nature of media corporations and their ability to deliver programming content which may prejudicially benefit (e.g. in relation to ownership and control issues) the corporations offering those programmes. Institutional economics takes a pragmatic position in recognising the inevitability of this dimension of the corporations, and a critical position in probing the control and content issues.

In many respects, institutional economics carries within its critique the characteristics of a moral science. That is, the positioning of the critique functions as an expression of a quest for moral behaviour in public and social life. The synergistic relationship between a quest for morality within a democratic programme of culture, economy and industrial progress finds its moment in what

Gruchy (1990) refers to as social (or human) provisioning. In this model, the quest to provide agreed upon resources to all members of society is undertaken by acknowledging the recognised failure of the market economy, and the responsibility of government, together with the ability of society to meet the needs of its citizens. Democratic planning in a mixed economy is one extension of this model (Hodgson, 1984). This approach has been attempted by social democratic governments in countries as diverse as Australia, Austria, Sweden and Spain, and more dramatically in South Africa.

A key interpretive manoeuvre of institutional economics has seen a 'culturalist' perspective put as the preferred direction for its critique. The culturalist view values social/cultural activity as the first-order priority of society and recognises that human welfare can only proceed if democratic planning accepts this pre-eminence. Critics of institutional economics would view this as naive and formalistic. Liberal and neo-conservative critics would see it as a reinvented socialism which sought to deny the prominence of economy. Whatever the case, institutional economics provides numerous opportunities for media studies. By working within the acknowledged terrain of corporate developments from a pragmatic perspective, it is possible to participate in the making and management of civil society. The sites for intervention are numerous, but can be gathered around the following nodes: (1) corporate economy, (2) technology, (3) convergence, and (4) cultural policy studies.

Questions can be raised from within the theoretical resources offered in the literature that shine a progressive light on the nature of capitalism and its evolving institutions. That may include detailed analysis of global corporations and their involvement with government. Indeed, evidence suggesting that corporations are becoming supra-national raises many challenging questions about the future of national governments in relation to international conventions and treaties. Recognising that *social provisioning* is the objective of a civilised society, institutional economics offers opportunities for media studies to construct models for intervening in the needs of citizens within the democratic process. The sites for investigation require precise approaches, which an institutional economic framework can enrich.

Marcus Breen

23

An endnote on popular music's leading light

Marcus Breen

Sectoral studies of media activity have often failed to build on the constructive interdisciplinary work undertaken in closely related areas. Popular music studies is one such domain. While, for example, film and television studies have flourished, there has been a slower progression in popular music studies. This endnote is not the place to enter into a detailed discussion of the issue, for which there may be a number of reasons. Certainly the ubiquity of popular music, coupled with the sheer volume of its production, should, on a quantitative assessment of products manufactured, have prompted more writing on popular music. Alternatively, it may be that other media sectors offer more confined spaces in which to undertake research. One major limitation has been that popular music has had to grapple with interrelated definitions, such as those thrown up by genre questions described by such terms as jazz, folk, pop, rock, and the diffusion of styles and categories following the punk rock explosion of 1976–77.

One consequence of this limitation is that it is only since the early 1990s or so that popular music has been offered as an object for study within the academy. Undoubtedly this reluctance was due in part to the Frankfurt School analysis published by Theodore Adorno (1990), which characterised popular music as an industrialised cultural form, co-opted by the market and thus devoid of its creative 'aura'. The influential work undertaken by Adorno on the cultural industries was both definitive and debilitating. It has more recently been closely researched and analysed through a contemporary perspective (Jameson, 1990).

Adorno's critique of cultural industries was bound up with the historical constraints of the rise of globalisation and new technologies, such as the radio and gramophone. Adorno argued that the liberating experience of live music performance was lost when disseminated through new communication technologies and the emerging social and economic organisation of culture. This produced in him a sense of despair, due to the effectiveness of capitalism in denying popular music its authenticity.

Issues that relate directly to Adorno's analysis of industrialisation and the accompanying commodification of popular music are features of popular music studies (Frith, 1983). They have found a profound analysis in Jacques Attali's theoretical study, *Noise: The Political Economy of Music*. Attali suggests

433

that popular music engages prophetically with contemporary society, announcing and thereby revealing what is happening in society at large:

> Music is prophecy. Its styles and economic organisation are ahead of the rest of society because it explores, much faster than material reality can, the entire range of possibilities in a given code. It makes audible the new world that will gradually become visible, that will impose itself and regulate the order of things. (1985:11)

This interpretation suggests why a highly engaging theory of popular music can be indicative of a sort of avant-gardist approach for other fields of media and cultural studies. Because popular music happens so quickly in response to social and economic events, it contains the seeds of theoretical and practical explanation which can be applied in other sectors of cultural production.

There are, however, several existing categories of investigation in the popular music literature from which students, researchers and writers can draw. Much of this material has originated in the UK and the USA. For example, Frith and Goodwin have suggested a set of macro and micro categories for organising popular music theory: sociology, including subcultural and cultural studies theory, music industry analysis and pop music production; textual analysis, including musicology and semiotics; hermeneutics – sexuality, stardom and meaning; fans (1990:x–xi).

The rich vein of possibility inherent in each of these categories is vast. One issue that has received considerable prominence since the mid 1980s is the changing place of popular music in the political struggles of advanced societies. The use of popular music as a mobilising tool in undeveloped nations and territories is under-researched, with the principal exceptions of Wallis and Malm (1984, 1992) and Feld (1996).

Some studies of popular music in advanced capitalist societies have considered the collapse of categories of pop music and rock into different sets of concerns which are characterised by a new set of possibilities and limitations (Street, 1986). This debate has taken place within a broader discussion of post-modernity, where the previously identifiable articulation of youth with popular music and political behaviour has become less clear as changing demographics have made commercialised popular music the key cultural activity within advanced societies. Issues that have been highlighted by this discussion include the dimensions of multinational music production, together with globalised media coverage (Garofalo, 1992). The changing nature of youth culture, observed in the incorporation of political resistance within conservative domains, thereby denying popular music its power to generate emerging social movements, has been a particularly strong site for discussion (Grossberg, 1992). Such concerns appear in equivalent, yet divergent, discussions of new feminist formations and youth culture (Kearney, 1998). Furthermore, rap music and hip hop culture have marked the contemporary awakening of a new form of popular music innovation, generated from African American realities. Rap continues the extraordinary history of black American contributions to popular music. Expanding the new sonic soundscape even more, new dance and rave scene music has pushed the boundaries of sensory possibility, tapping into independent local–global music production and youth culture formation, articulating digital technology with music and youth. Both rap and rave have established independent organisational structures for music production and distribution, including dance parties and extensive use of internet resources.

Other issues that have been the focus of detailed study include: indigenous and localised music production for national and export markets (Breen, 1987; Feld, 1991); heightened involvement by all levels of government in popular music policy initiatives in support of national activity (Bennett *et al.*, 1993); and the emergence of detailed analysis of copyright laws and the regulation of popular music production and dissemination (Frith, 1993). More generally, discursive overviews of popular music now provide a basis for new perspectives as well as appeals for integrating academic traditions such as textual media studies and musicology (Shepherd and Wicke, 1997; Shuker, 1998). The provocative nature of popular music appears in its energetic and inherent musical characteristics as well as its leading role in social movements (Ross and Rose, 1994; Lipsitz, 1998). For these reasons alone, it should be recognised as a significant indicator for the further development of media studies.

Stop and think

Fidelity to festive things

That phrase, 'fidelity to festive things', comes from Albert Borgmann's book, *Holding on to Reality: The Nature of Information at the Turn of the Millennium*, one of the most serious recent attempts to stop and think about the technologies that underpin pop tech culture. Borgmann develops a persuasive argument – one that many, perhaps especially older people, will find deeply attractive. In the end he says that we will be all right if we can correct the balance between reality and information, something for which he finds ideas of community, collaborative celebration and 'festive resolution' in the face of acknowledged misery and pain indispensable. Borgmann says of the communal, celebratory, festive moment, 'As a thing it has the presence of self-warranting clarity, as a sign it refers us to the darkness of contingency that constitutes its periphery' (1999:228). He gives as one example: Pavarotti bringing together '[h]alf a million often surly New Yorkers' in a concert while the homeless and street muggings remained visible beyond that particular periphery. 'The warm and luminous moments of festivity are forever surrounded and threatened by darkness' (1999:228). In relation to information technologies, to media and contemporary culture, Borgmann is looking for that 'fidelity' in moments when other people and material reality are re-experienced through or beyond the immateriality with which the media cloak them. In short, perhaps, we have to get together more and get out more! Except that Borgmann gives this curt prescription much greater resonance than that.

But we might stop and think about whether this prescription can survive the most glaring paradox it faces. Hip hop, house (Chicago, acid, progressive, hard), Detroit techno, trip hop, trance, speed garage, US garage, Balearic, electro – these, and more, are the contemporary designations of fidelity to

435

festive things among young people today. These musics, inevitably to be replaced by others, mark their moments of getting out and getting together. But one imagines (and perhaps we do him an injustice) that Albert Borgmann would not experience one of their clubs as the sort of celebration he has in mind nor that their – perhaps your – sorts of 'community' could be extended to others and across generations in the ways he envisages.

Is this, then, a central irony of contemporary media: that the media create both a mainstream leisure culture and participatory, deeply involving, communal reactions to it, which are driven by the very same dissatisfactions that motivate Borgmann's critique, but that the reactions are found so strange and inexplicably different by the inhabitants of the former that they can never join in? (On contemporary musics, see Reynolds, 1998, and Ogg, 1999.) Which does the following statement come from, a participant in one of Borgmann's festive events or a raver? 'What I got from those few experiences is a profound sense of connectedness with people, especially people whom I had never met before. I carried that feeling into my daily life . . .' (Alissa, 1994, posted on the web).

Afterthoughts (on alter/natives)

One of the curious features of the way that the internet was talked about at the end of the twentieth century was the vagueness and generality of the vocabulary, as if a natural phenomenon such as the weather were being described. The internet often seemed to have arrived as a globe-enveloping network of wires, cables and computers that just existed, somehow floating free of institutions and of any real anchorage in specific spaces or interests. So one of the next tasks for media studies has to be an institutional economics of the internet and, more specifically, of web applications (the use of internet technology to communicate new media content), in order to reveal the underpinning realities of cyberspace as locatable within essentially the same institutional spaces as the other twentieth-century media. Only then will we be in a position to judge how the new media are reshaping those spaces and reorganising the relationships among the various media, as each new medium has always done.

The first histories of the internet and web (e.g. Hafner and Lyon, 1996; Reid, 1997) concentrated on the technological and commercial narratives that were falling into place around key figures such as Vinton Cerf and Robert Kahn (authors of the blueprint paper 'A Protocol for Packet Network Intercommunication') or Marc Andreeson and Jerry Yang (originators of the first web browser and the web's most influential portal site, respectively). But these tended still to be highly individualised narratives, such as those developed around Baird and the early days of television, rather than institutional analyses, which media studies has found rather more useful in the longer term for understanding how media actually work in the contemporary world, not least where and how power gathers. Indeed, where News Corporation's Rupert Murdoch is seen as the powerful bogeyman of publishing and TV, Microsoft boss Bill Gates is emerging as the internet's equivalent figure, despite being largely absent from any of the accounts of the new medium's early rise and development, where the stories are instead of 'pioneers' and their struggles (Gates came fairly late to the internet). Power, we know all too well from our understanding of the twentieth century's other media, seldom follows such groundbreaking individual effort, but rather emerges and consolidates in 'back tier' places that can only be properly understood by adopting institutional and economic perspectives (otherwise we tend to slip towards an individualist understanding of power as well, as indeed we have seen with the demonisation of Murdoch and Gates). From the Hollywood studios to broadcasting titans such as AOL Time Warner's CNN and the computer operating-systems empire of Microsoft, we know that we are dealing with a complex admixture of evolving institutions, economic interests, audience engagements, communications policy and social provisioning. We are going to have to grasp the internet and web in this way too and, beyond them, new forms of digital media.

In fact the internet may be only the momentarily most striking component of a more general reconfiguration of contemporary media, spearheaded globally by AOL Time Warner; a reorganisation around altered power relationships and aesthetic forms, 're-purposed' content and relations of cultural capital that have seen us move from a period of tension between high and popular culture, through a period of popular culture hegemony (the heyday of mass TV), to the present situation where a consensual mainstream culture (spanning *Titanic* and Pavarotti) is surrounded and reduced by the proliferating cultural alternatives of pop tech, or post-mass media. Digital TV may take over from the web as a primary driver of these changes (or may hybridise with the web in ways that we cannot yet quite foresee) but, in any case, the changes present media studies with some fresh challenges if they are not to go unexamined. And if we care to believe that media studies, understood as both an intellectual project and a domain of pedagogical practices, has some role to play in the making and management of civil society at the beginning of the twenty-first century, then the challenges are so much more urgent. So let us end this textbook with two snapshots of the sorts of thing that are going on in the emerging world of pop tech. These particular afterthoughts are meant, not as rounded analyses, but as signposts towards matters that require our further attention as teachers and learners.

First, popular music and the web. MP3 represents a revealing moment in the development of both the internet and the popular music industry. As a particular technology the moment may pass quickly enough, but what it reveals are some of the reconfigured relationships evoked above. MPEG-1 Audio Layer 3, to give it its full title, is a 'codec' or compression–decompression algorithm for digitally compressing, or packing, and then decompressing, or unpacking, audio content that otherwise is too 'large' for convenient transmission on the internet. Effectively, it allows music to be packaged for transmission via the web. (Originated at the Fraunhofer Institute in Germany in the late 1980s, MPEG-1 was adopted as a standard in 1992 by the Moving Picture Experts Group – MPEG – which operates as an industry standards authority for audio-visual technologies on the internet. Audio Layer 3 was a subsequent refinement of the audio-visual codec and was then developed independently for audio-only use.) What MP3 facilitates is the posting of audio files on web sites for downloading and playing by users, either on their computers (using downloadable player software) or on small dedicated player machines, much like portable stereos (which may well be in widespread use by the time this book is published, with Casio even promising a wristwatch version). By late 1999 it was estimated that 17 million MP3 files were being downloaded every day and the web search engines were reporting that the term 'MP3' was the second most frequently used search term on the web (after 'sex'). Ninety-eight per cent of music available on the web was by then using the MP3 format. Given 1999's average home computer capability and dial-up internet access speed in the industrialised world, it was taking around four minutes to download every minute of music, an attractive trade-off between time and accessibility, especially in the realm of popular music, where vastly more material is actually available than can be carried by any music store. So-called 'CD-ripper' software soon appeared, allowing users to grab and encode music off their own CDs. Napster led the MP3 'revolution' on the web.

It is not too difficult to see how suddenly and profoundly this could change many of the existing relationships in the popular music industry. While the established industry – based around its cycle of band acquisition by labels, promotion, album production, cross-media marketing and distribution via retail outlets – was continuing seemingly unaffected by MP3 in the late 1990s, the new technology opened up a gaping hole in those established procedures, through which we were able to glimpse a startling alternative, whether or not MP3 turns out to be the full realisation of that alternative in the longer term. Not only will the alternative eventually take shape more clearly, perhaps around subsequent technologies rather than MP3, but it will be only part of the broader shift towards a pop tech world of largely altered relationships among producers and consumers generally, as well as between mainstream culture and proliferating alternatives. Musicians and bands could bypass the labels and go straight to listeners via the web, new economic models could be developed around payments per track (or even micro-payments per sample?), the distinction between producer and consumer of popular music could become blurred (as computers become effective recording 'studios'), and at the heart of these changes would be the new concept of the listener's own 'album', compiled in a personalised way from the vast range of available choices and with a coherence based on something very different from a band's intentions. For this to work within the music industry, as it must do to be sustained in the longer term, new sorts of promotion, marketing and advertising would need to be devised, constructed more centrally around the listener's preferences and 'profile' rather than the performer's identity, career and output. (Web bookseller Amazon has pioneered sophisticated profiling of this sort by cross-referencing millions of book buyers' purchases and providing each with an automated recommendations service of often striking accuracy.)

Now what this reveals, in part because the music industry is, as Marcus Breen puts it, a potential 'leading light' for new media studies, is the way that the media in general are moving, if rather more ponderously and hesitantly than the hype about digital TV, web TV, and so on, might suggest. The Me-album of music promised by MP3 is only one vision of a shift that appears to be leading towards Me-TV and, beyond that, a whole reorganisation of the media landscape around personalisation techniques and the pulling out and reassembling by audience members of whatever they want from the passing flows of digital media content of all sorts (a reassembling that may be increasingly performed by smart 'agents' or bits of software that learn about us and collect suitable material). Putting the 'me' into media may be the pressing agenda for media institutions in the next couple of decades. Sony's Memory Stick concept, a multi-functional audio-visual storage device not much bigger than a stick of chewing gum, is conceived as a handy means of plugging in and out of various media flows and grabbing content; but the underpinning vision of the direction things are going in may be more important than whether the Memory Stick itself becomes as successful as the Sony Walkman was.

Still, the institutional questions inevitably remain paramount here. How can we move towards such a future when the content producers depend for their survival (and therefore their ability to continue producing content) on controlling distribution and aggregating consumers to a sufficient degree that they can profit from it? Listeners 'ripping' tracks from their CD collections and posting these on the web for others to download freely (as was happening widely, particularly among the vast US college student population in 1999 and 2000) may seem like a radical subversion of big business interests in the interest of the listener, but could eventually destroy the business model that generates the content without replacing it with any equally effective alternative. (It is not at all clear that artists selling directly to listeners is a model that could survive in a totally deregulated industry. The similar model of 'shareware' computer software, for instance, has long remained an economically unreliable and marginal feature of the software industry.) The music industry in fact quickly anticipated this threat, as they perceived it, in late 1998 when they set up the Secure Digital Music Initiative (SDMI); 'they' being the five largest music companies (Sony, BMG, Warner, Universal, EMI), the International Federation of the Phonographic Industry, the Japanese recording industry federation and Microsoft, with other IT industry representatives. The SDMI aims to introduce mandatory protocols for the technologies and for the distribution of digital music that will constrain users to downloading only from authorised web sites (e.g. by 'watermarking' content so that it will only be recognised there) and will prevent the redistribution of 'ripped' material off commercial CDs. While not finalised at the time of writing, these sorts of standard will eventually provide a working compromise between the popular music industry and its listeners, who have briefly flirted with anarchic alternatives that were bound to be regulated sooner or later in the interests of the institutions that dominate the field. But that those institutions are being forced to find such compromises is an indication of the altered relationships which are emerging.

Let us switch, though, to a second snapshot of these changes, in order to come at them from a different angle. This is the case, reported by Rosemary Coombe (1998:199–207), of the Crazy Horse brand. Crazy Horse Original Malt Liquor, a brand of whisky, was launched in the USA in 1992 by Ferolito, Vultaggio & Sons, an Italian American firm that specialises in developing distinctive brands for beverages that may otherwise be barely distinguishable from each other: 'Like many postmodern entrepreneurs, they trade in imagery and symbolism to create new distinctions for goods that have become more or less functionally indistinguishable' (Coombe, 1998:200). Out of the bottle, Crazy Horse whisky tasted like many others (indeed it may have been the same product re-branded in many instances). From our point of view here, we can see that Crazy Horse whisky was being promoted as a lifestyle choice for 'lifestyles' that are themselves largely media creations: whole agglomerations of advertised products, TV programmes, movies, types of popular music, newspapers and magazines loosely co-operating to define a particular lifestyle that is in reality little more than the sum of those parts (co-operation based less on deliberate planning than on the economic logic that sends a range of producers in pursuit of the same consumers). So Crazy Horse whisky was sold on the basis of its imagery, as evoked on the bottle labelling: 'The Black Hills of Dakota steeped in the History of the American West, home of proud Indian Nations, a land where imagination conjures up images of . . .'. The reader can probably guess the sorts of thing that are listed next (because they are already themselves products of media culture) – Indian warriors, Sitting Bull, Custer, intrepid pioneers, wagon trains, blue-coated cavalry, frontier bravery, tradition, and so on. And also, of course, Crazy Horse, who has had a place in the popular imagination at least since his name appeared on the cover of the bestseller *Bury My Heart at Wounded Knee* in 1971, if not before thanks to numerous appearances in Hollywood westerns.

The real Crazy Horse, Tasunke Witko, a leader of the Lakota peoples, was bayoneted to death by a US soldier during a scuffle at an army post in September 1877, when he had been arrested. His body was displayed on a scaffold to announce the forced removal of his people to a barren reservation. His father and mother escaped with his bones, hoping to find freedom in Canada (Brown, 1972:245–6). 'Descendants of the Lakota statesman Crazy Horse, angered to learn of the appropriation of their revered ancestor's name and image as a trademark by a manufacturer of malt liquor, have invoked the legal process to oppose this use of their heritage and to politically assert the legal significance of their own understandings of property and propriety' (Coombe, 1998:199–200). Particularly poignant about this case were the facts that Crazy Horse in his own day had condemned the introduction of whisky into Native American communities as a 'pacifying' agent, that the modern brand still deliberately targeted Native Americans in its advertising campaigns, and that Crazy Horse himself had carefully guarded against the reproduction of his own image in drawing and photography.

Coombe describes the case as '*one of the more fascinating instances of historical others interrogating the claims of postmodern authors*' (1998:204). The latter, Ferolito Vultaggio, adopted a variety of not uncontradictory strategies. They dismissed the objection to their branding as trivial. They then claimed to have chosen the name without knowing of the historical figure's significance. Then a press release claimed that their choice was a deliberate tribute to the Indian leader. Then they suggested that Crazy Horse was a 'true American', implying that he should not be claimed by partisan interests. Penultimately they suggested that Native Americans were not in agreement about Crazy Horse's significance, and finally they claimed that they were referring to another Crazy Horse entirely, a man named Curly who had adopted the Indian leader's name as a colourful nickname! Notwithstanding this attempted postmodern rejection of origins, the US Patent and Trademark Office refused to register the Crazy Horse brand, implicitly acknowledging the descendants' case based on propriety when they found that the brand brought significant persons, beliefs **441** and symbols into 'contempt or disrepute' (Coombe, 1998:202). The claimants pursued the case in court seeking damages – symbolically, a braid of tobacco, a horse and a blanket for each month and US state in which the whisky had been sold prior to the refusal of its brand. Rather than on contempt in the portrayal, however, the case for damages was based on Crazy Horse's descendants' ownership of his name, essentially an assertion of theft. The action is unresolved at the time of writing. Given the legal strategy adopted by the claimants, Rosemary Coombe speculates on a logical, if unlikely, outcome, based on the fact that rock musician Neil Young's backing band is called Crazy Horse: 'Sioux peoples might even publicly designate Neil Young to be their first "authorized licensee" and seek his assistance in denouncing disrespectful usages of the Crazy Horse name' (1998:205).

Now the point about that interesting case is this: as Rosemary Coombe expresses it, the case testifies 'to new dimensions of what we might deem the politics of mass publicity in a consumer society – strategies of property and impropriety and tactics of publicity and counter-publicity – in which authors and alters engage in dances of mimicry that simultaneously mask and reveal real financial and political stakes' (1998:206). What is really interesting in the Crazy Horse case is not so much that a blow of some sort has been struck for Native American honour as that the 'alter' or subaltern here, the Native American, has joined the semiological dance so effectively. It is not that there is some larger principle outside particular circumstances – say, the inviolability of Crazy Horse's honour as a minority statesman – but that the scales are more evenly matched within those particular circumstances and that the outcome rests on the force of argument deployed there. Of course, things might look very different were the defendant AOL Time Warner rather than a Brooklyn marketing firm. But one could argue that AOL Time Warner, or other large corporations these days, would not get themselves in this position anyway because, based on their organisational experience of surviving and prospering in this new world, they would have anticipated the problem. The Native American (who can represent here many subaltern publics) has so successfully joined the politics of publicity and counter-publicity in the new media culture that the big corporations are always already second guessing them to avoid trouble (which is in no way to deny the very real social and economic injustices to which they are still subject).

Coombe again: 'The postmodern celebration of pastiche and montage – mimetic juxtapositions of alterity in recodings and reworkings of regimes of signification – must remain cognizant of the imperialist histories in which many commodified forms of available cultural difference were originally forged' (1998:206–7). In other words, the recombinant possibilities of pop tech are not, or should not be, freely available with no anchorage in history. Alongside the new regulatory regimes of institutional economics in the media sphere (such as SDMI) there will have to emerge *regulatory regimes based on historically informed propriety*, not because every point of tension will come to court (at least we might hope not) but because the politics of the public sphere is altering in ways that both Gramsci and Volosinov would have recognised, given their sensitivity to the ongoing struggle over the connotative reach of cultural signs and symbols. Media studies is without doubt one potential contributor to the regime of historically informed propriety; this is one way in which it can contribute to the making and management of civil society. Put more simply, media studies needs to pay close attention both to the recombinant games of pop tech (where Curly can be invented to short circuit the historical realities of Crazy Horse) and to devising its own inventive practices, its own heuretic forms of practical work, in pedagogical contexts where learners are guided to a full and careful appreciation that a historically informed propriety must accompany every snippet they sample from the cultural flows that surround them, every new juxtaposition they attempt to cut and mix together in order to deepen their understanding of media culture by intervening in it. This sort of effort is only possible where understanding has been cultivated of how the media are deeply implicated in matters of public knowledge and cultural identity, how film and broadcasting continue to feed imagination and aspiration (sometimes but not always with junk food), of how method resists madness and how pop tech presents profound challenges as it reconfigures the media world. With such effort and understanding might the ghost citizen who haunts the modern media of public communication approach material form.

Now, while one does not wish in any sense to reduce particular struggles by generalising about them, it remains nonetheless possible to see a common narrative thread that connects Crazy Horse's descendants with other subaltern groups, such as gays, of whom Crimp (in Wallis *et al.*, 1999:151) says: 'Having learned to support and grieve for our lovers and friends; having joined the fight against fear, hatred, repression, and inaction; having adjusted our sex lives so as to protect ourselves and one another – we are now reclaiming our subjectivities, our communities, our culture . . . .' There is a more widely applicable periodisation of struggles here – from grief for past injustices, through fighting for rights and making adjustments, to reclaiming and remaking cultural identities – that allows us to see where today's pop tech resources intersect with projects of *becoming*.

The so-called 'culture wars' in the United States have clarified what is at stake in this (when, starting in the late 1980s, works such as Andres Serrano's *Piss Christ*, Robert Mapplethorp's photographs of gay black and white men, and Martin Scorsese's film *The Last Temptation of Christ*, and the interests these represented, were attacked by a loose but potent confederation of traditionalists, right-wing politicians and religious leaders). '[T]hose of us who think of ourselves as progressive are stuck in a process of becoming, because, unlike the right, we don't see where we would like to end up as a fixed point' (Wallace, in Wallis *et al.*, 1999:180). While, more generally, the anti-becoming, stasist world view, and the dynamist world view that it opposes, are transcending the old right/left distinction that characterised the US's culture wars (there are stasists and dynamists on both sides of the political spectrum; see Postrel, 1998), the distinction marks something profoundly important for media studies in the pop tech world. The ghost citizen introduced in Part I may never fully materialise – the utopian wish for a better 'fixed point' in the future – but remains an important way of understanding the sort of becoming to which we are attached.

Bibliography

Aarseth, E. J. (1997), *Cybertext: Perspectives on Ergodic Literature*, Baltimore, Johns Hopkins University Press.

Abercrombie, N., S. Hill and B. S. Turner (1980), *The Dominant Ideology Thesis*, London, Allen and Unwin.

Abercrombie, N., S. Hill and B. S. Turner (eds) (1990), *Dominant Ideologies*, London, Unwin Hyman.

Abramson, J. B., F. C. Arterton and G. R. Orren (1988), *The Electronic Commonwealth: The Impact of New Media Technologies on Democratic Politics*, New York, Basic Books.

Adam, A. and E. Green (1998), 'Gender, agency, location and the new information society', in B. Loader (ed.), *Cyberspace Divide: Equality, Agency and Policy in the Information Society*, London, Routledge.

Adeya, N. (1996), 'Beyond the borders: the internet for Africa', *Convergence*, (Autumn) 2:2, 23–37.

Adler, M. J. and C. van Doren (1972), *How to Read a Book* (revised and updated), New York, Touchstone.

Adoni, H. and S. Mane (1984), 'Media and the social construction of reality: toward an integration of theory and research', *Communication Research*, 11:3, 323–40.

Adorno, T. W. (1990), 'On popular music (1941)', in S. Frith and A. Goodwin (eds), *On Record: Rock, Pop and the Written Word*, New York, Pantheon Books.

Adorno, T. W. and M. Horkheimer (1979), *Dialectic of Enlightenment*, London, Verso.

Adorno, T. W. (1991), *The Culture Industry: Selected Essays on Mass Culture* (ed. J. M. Bernstein), London, Routledge.

Ahmad, A. (1992), *In Theory: Classes, Nations, Literatures*, London, Verso.

Allen, R. and D. Gomery (1985), *Film History: Theory and Practice*, New York, Random House.

Allen, R. C. (1985), *Speaking of Soap Operas*, Chapel Hill, University of North Carolina Press.

Allor, M. (1988), 'Relocating the site of the audience', *Critical Studies in Mass Communication*, 5, 217–233.

Altheide, D. (1976), *Creating Reality: How TV News Distorts Events*, Newbury Park, Sage.

Amin, A. (1997), 'Placing globalization', *Theory, Culture and Society*, 14:2, 123–37.

Althusser, L. (1971), *Lenin and Philosophy and Other Essays* (trans. B. Brewster), London, NLB.

Althusser, L. (1976), *Essays in Self Criticism* (trans. G. Lock), London, NLB.

Althusser, L. (1993), *The Future Lasts a Long Time* (ed. O. Corpet and Y. M. Boutang, trans. R. Veasey), London, Chatto and Windus.

Anderson, B. (1991), *Imagined Communities: Reflections on the Origin and Spread of Nationalism* (revision of 1983 edition), London, Verso.

Anderson, E. (1994), 'The code of the streets', *Atlantic Monthly*, May, 80–94.

Anderson, J. A. (1983), 'Television literacy and the critical viewer', in J. Bryant and D. R. Anderson (eds), *Children's Understanding of Television*, New York, Academic Press.

Andrew, D. (1984), *Concepts in Film Theory*, Oxford, Oxford University Press.

Andrew, D. (ed.) (1987), *Breathless*, New Brunswick, Rutgers University Press.

Andrew, G. (1998), *The 'Three Colours' Trilogy*, London, British Film Institute.

Ang, I. (1985), *Watching 'Dallas': Soap Opera and the Melodramatic Imagination*, London, Methuen.

Ang, I. (1989), 'Wanted: audiences. On the politics of empirical audience studies', in E. Seiter, H. Borchers, G. Kreutzner and E. Warth (eds), *Remote Control: Television, Audiences and Cultural Power*, London, Routledge.

Ang, I. (1991), *Desperately Seeking the Audience*, London, Routledge.

Appadurai, A. (1996), *Modernity at Large: Cultural Dimensions of Globalisation*, Minneapolis, University of Minnesota.

Arato, A. and E. Gebhardt (eds) (1978), *The Essential Frankfurt School Reader*, Oxford, Blackwell.

Arrighi, G., T. K. Hopkins and I. Wallerstein (1989), *Antisystemic Movements*, London, Verso.

Arterton, F. C. (1987), *Teledemocracy: Can Technology Protect Democracy?* (Sage Library of Social Research vol. 165), London, Sage.

Attali, J. (1985), *Noise: The Political Economy of Music*, Manchester, Manchester University Press.

Augé, M. (1995), *Non-Places: An Introduction to an Anthropology of Supermodernity*, London, Verso.

Aumont, J. (1997), *The Image* (trans. C. Pajackowska), London, British Film Institute.

Aurigi, A. and S. Graham (1998), 'The "crisis" in the urban public realm', in B. Loader (ed.), *Cyberspace Divide: Equality, Agency and Policy in the Information Society*, London, Routledge.

Axford, B. (1995), *The Global System: Economics, Politics and Culture*, Cambridge, Polity.

Bachelard, G. (1969), *The Poetics of Space*, Boston, Beacon Press.

Barker, M. (1989), *Comics: Ideology, Power and the Critics*, Manchester, Manchester University Press.

Barkin, S. M. and M. Gurevitch (1991), 'Out of work and on the air: television news of unemployment', in R. K. Avery and D. Eason (eds), *Critical Perspectives on Media and Society*, New York, Guilford Press.

Barlow, J. P. (1996), *A Declaration of the Independence of Cyberspace*, Electronic Frontier Foundation, http://www.eff.org.

Barr, C. (ed.) (1986), *All Our Yesterdays: 40 Years of British Cinema*, London, British Film Institute.

Barrett, M. and A. Phillips (eds) (1992), *Destabilizing Theory: Contemporary Feminist Debates*, Oxford, Polity.

Barthes, R. (1975), *S/Z* (trans. R. Miller), London, Jonathan Cape.

Barthes, R. (1977), *Image–Music–Text*, New York, Hill and Wang.

Barthes, R. (1982), *Camera Lucida: Reflections on Photography*, London, Jonathan Cape.

Barthes, R. (1993), *Mythologies* (selected and trans. A. Lavers), London, Vintage.

Bartlett, F. C. (1932), *Remembering: A Study in Experimental and Social Psychology*, Cambridge, Cambridge University Press.

Bassnett, S. (1997), *Studying British Cultures: An Introduction*, London, Routledge.

Baudrillard, J. (1983), *Simulations*, New York, Semiotext(e).

Baudrillard, J. (1988), *Selected Writings* (edited and introduced by M. Poster), Oxford, Polity.

Bauman, Z. (1991), *Modernity and Ambivalence*, Cambridge, Polity.

Bauman, Z. (1996), 'From pilgrim to tourist: or a short history of identity', in S. Hall and P. du Gay (eds), *Questions of Cultural Identity*, London, Sage.

Baumgartner, F. R. and B. D. Jones (1992), *Agendas and Instability in American Politics*, Chicago, University of Chicago Press.

Bausinger, H. (1984), 'Media, technology and daily life', *Media, Culture and Society*, 6, 343–51.

Beatty, J. (1994), 'Who speaks for the middle class?', *Atlantic Monthly*, May, 65–78.

Becker, K. E. (1992), 'Photojournalism and the tabloid press', in P. Dahlgren and C. Sparks (eds), *Journalism and Popular Culture*, London, Sage.

Becker, T. (1981), 'Teledemocracy: bringing power back to the people', *Futurist*, December, 6–9.

Bell, M. (1998), 'The truth is our currency', *The Harvard International Journal of Press/Politics*, 3:1, 102–9.

Beniger, J. R. and S. Herbst (1990), 'Mass media and public opinion', in M. T. Hallinan, D. M. Kelin and J. Glass (eds), *Change in Societal Institutions*, New York, Plenum Press.

Benjamin, A. and P. Osborne (1991), *Thinking Art: Beyond Traditional Aesthetics*, London, ICA Books.

Benjamin, W. (1973), 'The work of art in the age of mechanical reproduction', in *Illuminations* (edited H. Arendt, trans. H. Zohn), London, Collins.

Bennett, T., S. Frith, L. Grossberg, J. Shepherd and G. Turner (1993), *Rock and Popular Music: Politics, Policies, Institutions*, London, Routledge.

Bennett, W. (1994), *The Book of Virtues*, New York, Simon and Schuster.

Bennett, W. L. (1988), *News: The Politics of Illusion*, New York, Longman.

Bennett, W. L. (1990), 'Toward a theory of press–state relations in the United States', *Journal of Communication*, 40:2, 103–26.

Bennett, W. L. (1996), 'An introduction to journalism norms and representations of politics', *Political Communication*, 13:4, 373–84.

Berenstein, R. J. (1996), 'Spectatorship-as-drag: re-dressing classic horror cinema', in J. Belton and R. J. Berenstein (eds), *Attack of the Leading Ladies: Gender, Sexuality and Spectatorship in Classic Horror Cinema*, New York, Columbia University Press.

Berger, J. (1972), *Ways of Seeing*, London, Penguin/BBC.

Berland, J. (1991), 'Towards a creative anachronism: radio, the state and sound government', *Public*, 4:5, 9–21.

Berlo, D. K. (1977), 'Communication as process: review and commentary', in B. D. Ruben (ed.), *Communication Yearbook 1*, New Brunswick, Transaction Books.

Bettelheim, B. (1972), 'Play and education', *School Review*, 81, 1–13.

Betterton, R. (ed.) (1987), *Looking On: Images of Femininity in the Visual Arts and Media*, London, Pandora.

Bhabha, H. (1987), 'Interrogating identity', in L. Appignanesi (ed.), *Identity, ICA Documents No.6*, London, ICA.

Bhabha, H. (1994), *The Location of Culture*, London, Routledge.

Bhabha, H., S. Feuchtwang and B. Harlow (1987), 'Remembering Fanon', *New Formations*, 1 (Spring), 118–35.

Blonsky, M. (ed.) (1985), *On Signs: A Semiotic Reader*, Oxford, Blackwell.

Blumler, J. G. and E. Katz (eds) (1974), *The Uses of Mass Communications: Current Perspectives on Gratification Research*, Beverly Hills, Sage.

Blumler, J. G. and M. Gurevitch (1981), 'Politicians and the press: an essay on role relationships', in D. D. Nimmo and K. R. Sanders (eds), *Handbook of Political Communication*, Beverly Hills, Sage.

Blumler, J. G., M. Gurevitch and E. Katz (1985), 'Reaching out: a future for gratifications research', in K. E. Rosengren, L. A. Wenner and P. Palmgreen (eds), *Media Gratifications Research: Current Perspectives*, Beverly Hills, Sage.

Boiarsky, G. (1997), 'The psychology of new media technologies: lessons from the past', *Convergence*, 3:3 (Autumn), 107–26.

Bonitzer, P. (1985), *Decadrages*, Paris, Editions de l'Etoile.

Bordo, S. (1993), *Unbearable Weight: Feminism, Western Culture and the Body*, Berkeley, University of California Press.

Bordwell, D. and K. Thompson (1994), *Film History: An Introduction*, New York, McGraw Hill.

Bordwell, D., J. Staiger and K. Thompson (1985), *The Classical Hollywood Cinema: Film Style and Mode of Production to 1960*, London, Routledge and Kegan Paul.

Borgmann, A. (1999), *Holding on to Reality: The Nature of Information at the Turn of the Millennium*, Chicago, University of Chicago Press.

Bottomore, T. (1984), *The Frankfurt School*, London, Tavistock.

Bourdieu, P. (1996), *Distinction: A Social Critique of the Judgement of Taste*, London, Routledge.

Bowden, C. (1998), *Juárez: The Laboratory of Our Future*, New York, Aperture.

Boyd-Barrett, O. (1982), 'Cultural dependency and the mass media', in M. Gurevitch, T. Bennett, J. Curran and J. Woollacott (eds), *Culture, Society and the Media*, London, Methuen.

Brand, S. (1988), *The Media Lab: Inventing the Future at MIT*, Harmondsworth, Penguin.

Brants, K., M. Huizenga and R. van Meerten (1996), 'The new canals of Amsterdam: an exercise in local electronic democracy', *Media, Culture and Society*, 18, 233–47.

Bratton, J., J. Cook and C. Gledhill (eds) (1994), *Melodrama: Stage, Picture, Screen*, London, British Film Institute.

Braunstein, P. (1999), 'The case for lateral thinking: discerning new thought patterns in the contemporary info-sphere', *Convergence*, 5:1 (Spring), 10–17.

Breen, M. (1987), *Missing in Action: Australian Popular Music in Perspective Vol. 1*, Melbourne, Verbal Graphics.

Breen, M. (1989), *Our Place, Our Music, Aboriginal Music: Australian Popular Music in Perspective Vol. 2*, Canberra, Aboriginal Studies Press.

Breen, M. (1995), 'The end of the world as we know it: popular music's cultural mobility', *Cultural Studies*, 9:3, 486–504.

Breen, M. (1999), *Rock Dogs: Politics and the Music Industry in Australia*, Sydney, Pluto (Australia).

Brock, G. W. (1998), *Telecommunication Policy for the Information Age: From Monopoly to Competition*, Cambridge, MA, Harvard University Press.

Bronfen, E. (1992), *Over Her Dead Body: Death, Femininity and the Aesthetic*, Manchester, Manchester University Press.

Brook, P. (1968), *The Empty Space*, Harmondsworth, Penguin.

Brooker, P. (1999), *A Concise Glossary of Cultural Theory*, London, Arnold.

Brooks, A. (1997), *Postfeminisms: Feminism, Cultural Theory and Cultural Forms*, London, Routledge.

Brosius, H. B. and H. M. Kepplinger (1993), 'Linear and nonlinear models of agenda setting in television', *Journal of Broadcasting and Electronic Media*, 36, 5–24.

Brown, A. (1986), *Modern Political Philosophy: Theories of the Just Society*, London, Pelican.

Brown, D. (1972), *Bury My Heart at Wounded Knee*, London, Pan.

Brown, M. (1999), Editorial matter, *The Guardian (Media section)*, 8 March, p. 8.

Brown, M. E. (ed.) (1990), *Television and Women's Culture: The Politics of the Popular*, London, Sage.

Brown, P. and S. C. Levinson (1987), *Politeness: Some Universals in Language Usage*, New York, Cambridge University Press.

Brownlow, K. (1968), *The Parade's Gone By*, London, Secker and Warburg.

Bruckman, A. (1999), 'The day after net day: approaches to educational use of the internet', *Convergence*, (Spring) 5:1, 24–46.

Brunsdon, C. (1981), ' "Crossroads": notes on soap opera', *Screen*, 22:4, 32–7.

Brunsdon, C. and D. Morley (1978), *Everyday Television: 'Nationwide'*, London, British Film Institute.

Brunvand, J. H. (1981), *The Vanishing Hitchhiker: Urban Legends and their Meanings*, London, Pan.

Bryan, C., R. Tsagarousianou and D. Tambini (1998), 'Electronic democracy and the civic networking movement in context', in R. Tsagarousianou, D. Tambini and C. Bryan (eds), *Cyberdemocracy: Technology, Cities and Civic Networks*, London, Routledge.

Bryant, J. and D. Zillman (1991), *Responding to the Screen: Reception and Reaction Processes*, Hillsdale, L. Erlbaum Associates.

Buchanan, P. (1992), 'We stand with President Bush', in C-Span Transcripts *1992 Republican National Convention*, Lincolnshire, IL, Tape Writer.

Buchler, J. (ed.) (1950), *The Philosophy of C.S. Peirce (Selected Writings)*, London, Routledge and Kegan Paul.

Buckingham, D. (1987), *Public Secrets: 'EastEnders' and its Audience*, London, British Film Institute.

Buissac, P. (1998), *Encyclopaedia of Semiotics*, Oxford, Oxford University Press.

Bukatmen, S. (1997), *Blade Runner*, London, British Film Institute.

Burrell, G. and G. Morgan (1979), *Sociological Paradigms and Organisational Analysis*, London, Heineman.

Bury, R. (1998), 'Waiting to X-hale: a study of gender and community on an all-female X-Files electronic mailing list', *Convergence*, 4:3 (Autumn), 59–83.

Bury, R. (1999), 'Women on-line (review)', *Convergence*, (Autumn) 5:3, 121–3.

Butler, J. (1990), *Gender Trouble: Feminism and the Subversion of Identity*, London, Routledge.

Butler, J. G. (1994), *Television, Critical Methods and Applications*, Belmont, Wadsworth.

Calhoun, C. (ed.) (1992), *Habermas and the Public Sphere*, Cambridge, MA, MIT Press.

Campbell, R. (1987), 'Securing the middle ground: reporter formulas in "60 Minutes" ', *Critical Studies in Mass Communication*, 4:4, 325–50.

Cardiff, D. and P. Scannell (1987), 'Broadcasting and national unity', in J. Curran, A. Smith and P. Wingate (eds), *Impacts and Influences: Essays on Media Power in the Twentieth Century*, London, Methuen.

Carey, J. (1981), 'Culture, geography and communications: the work of Harold Innis in an American context', in W. H. Melody, L. Salter and P. Heyer (eds), *Culture, Communication and Dependency: The Tradition of Harold Innis*, Norwood, Ablex.

Carey, J. W. (1989), *Communication as Culture*, London, Routledge.

Carter, D. (1997), ' "Digital democracy" or "information aristocracy"?', in B. Loader (ed.), *The Governance of Cyberspace*, London, Routledge.

Carveth, R. and D. Averio (1996), *Network Brownout: The Portrayal of Latinos in Network Television News*, report for the US National Association of Hispanic Journalists, June.

Case, S.-E. (1990), *Performing Feminisms: Feminist Critical Theory and Theatre*, Baltimore, Johns Hopkins University Press.

Castells, M. (1996), *The Rise of the Network Society*, Oxford, Blackwell.

Caudwell, C. (1937), *Illusion and Reality*, London, Lawrence and Wishart.

Caws, P. (1994), 'Identity: cultural, transcultural and multicultural', in D. T. Goldberg (ed.), *Multiculturalism: A Critical Reader*, Oxford, Blackwell.

Cherny, L. and E. R. Weise (eds) (1996), *Wired-women: Gender and New Realities in Cyberspace*, Seattle, Seal Press.

Chippindale, P. and C. Horrie (1990), *Stick It Up Your Punter!*, London, Heinemann.

Christenson, P. G. (1986), 'Children's perceptions of moral themes in television drama', in M. L. McLaughlin (ed.), *Communication Yearbook*, Beverly Hills, Sage.

Cixous, H. (1981), 'The laugh of the Medusa', in E. Marks and I. de Courtivran (eds), *New French Feminisms*, New York, Schocten Books.

Clarke, J., C. Critcher and R. Johnson (1979), *Working Class Culture: Studies in History and Theory*, London, Hutchinson.

Clifford, J. and G. Marcus (eds) (1986), *Writing Culture: The Poetics and Politics of Ethnography*, Berkeley, University of California Press.

Clover, C. J. (1992), *Men, Women and Chain Saws: Gender in the Modern Horror Film*, Princeton, Princeton University Press.

Cobb, R. and C. D. Elder (1971), 'The politics of agenda building: an alternative perspective for modern democratic theory', *Journal of Politics*, 33, 892–915.

Cobb, R. and C. D. Elder (1981), 'Communication and public policy', in D. D. Nimmo and K. R. Sanders (eds), *Handbook of Political Communication*, Beverly Hills, Sage.

Cockburn, C. (1992), 'The circuit of technology: gender, identity and power', in R. Silverstone and E. Hirsch (eds), *Consuming Technologies: Media and Information in Domestic Spaces*, London, Routledge.

Cockburn, C. and R. Furst-Dilic (1994), *Bringing Technology Home: Gender and Technology in a Changing Europe*, Buckingham, Open University Press.

Cohen, S. (1972), *Folk Devils and Moral Panics*, Oxford, Blackwell.

Coleman, S. (1999), 'The new media and democratic politics', *New Media and Society*, 1:1, 67–74.

Collins, J. (1989), *Uncommon Cultures: Popular Culture and Post-Modernism*, London, Routledge.

Collins, R. (1990), 'Broadband black death cuts queues: the information society and the UK', in *Television: Policy and Culture*, London, Unwin Hyman.

Collins, R. (1993), 'Public Service versus the market ten years on: reflections on Critical Theory and the debate on broadcasting policy in the UK', *Screen*, 34 (Autumn), 243–59.

Collins, W. A. (1983), 'Interpretation and inference in children's television viewing', in J. Bryant and D. A. Anderson (eds), *Children's Understanding of Television: Research on Attention and Comprehension*, New York, Academic Press.

Collins, W. A. and H. M. Wellman (1982), 'Social scripts and developmental patterns in comprehension of televised narratives', *Communication Research*, 9:3, 380–98.

Collins, W. A., H. M. Wellman, A. H. Keniston and S. D. Westby (1978), 'Age-related aspects of comprehension and inference from a televised dramatic narrative', *Child Development*, 49, 389–99.

Cook, T. E. (1996), 'Afterword: political values and journalism values', *Political Communication*, 13:4, 469–81.

Coombe, R. J. (1998), *The Cultural Life of Intellectual Properties: Authorship, Appropriation and the Law*, London, Duke University Press.

Cormack, M. (1992), *Ideology*, London, Batsford.

Cormack, M. (1994), *Ideology and Cinematography in Hollywood, 1930–39*, London, Macmillan.

Corner, J. (1991), 'Meaning, genre and context: the problematics of "public knowledge" in the new audience studies', in J. Curran and M. Gurevitch (eds), *Mass Media and Society*, London, Methuen.

Corner, J. (1995), *Television Form and Public Address*, London, Edward Arnold.

Corner, J. (1996), 'Reappraising reception: aims, concepts and methods', in J. Curran and M. Gurevitch (eds), *Mass Media and Society* (second edition), London, Edward Arnold.

Corner, J. (1999), *Critical Ideas in Television Studies*, Oxford, Oxford University Press.

Corner, J., K. Richardson and N. Fenton (1990), *Nuclear Reactions: Form and Response in Public Issue Television*, London, John Libbey.

Corner, J., S. Harvey and K. Lury (1994), 'Culture, quality and choice: the re-regulation of TV, 1989–1991', in S. Hood (ed.), *Behind the Screens: The Structure of British Television in the Nineties*, London, Lawrence and Wishart.

Cottle, S. (1993), *Television News, Urban Conflict and the Inner City*, Leicester, Leicester University Press.

Coward, R. (1984), *Female Desire: Women's Sexuality Today*, London, Paladin.

Cowie, E. (1977), 'Women, representation and the image', *Screen Education*, 23, 15–23.

Cowie, E. (1978), 'Women as sign', *m/f*, 1, 46–63.

Creed, B. (1987), 'From here to modernity: feminism and postmodernism', *Screen*, 28:2, 47–68.

Creed, B. (1993), *The Monstrous Feminine: Film, Feminism, Psychoanalysis*, London, Routledge.

Culf, A. (1995), editorial matter, *The Guardian*, 3 October, section 2, p. 2.

Culf, A. (1996a), 'Crisis? What crisis?', *The Guardian* (media section), 24 June, p. 12.

Culf, A. (1996b), editorial matter, *The Guardian*, 12 October, p. 10.

Culf, A. (1997), 'Crisis for ITV as BBC wins ratings battle', *The Guardian*, 28 May, section 2, p. 11.

Cunningham, S. (1992), *Framing Culture: Criticism and Policy in Australia*, Sydney, Allen and Unwin.

Curran, J. (1990), 'The new revisionism in mass communication research', *European Journal of Communication*, 5:2–3, 135–64.

Curran, J., A. Douglas and G. Whannel (1980), 'The political economy of the human-interest story', in A. Smith (ed.), *Newspapers and Democracy*, Cambridge, MA and London, MIT Press.

Dahl, R. A. (1961), *Who Governs? Democracy and Government in an American City*, New Haven, Yale University Press.

Dahlberg, L. (1998), 'Cyberspace and the public sphere: exploring the democratic potential of the net', *Convergence*, 4:1, 70–84.

Dahlgren, P. (1988), 'What's the meaning of this?: viewers' plural sense-making of TV news', *Media, Culture and Society*, 10:3, 285–301.

Dahlgren, P. (1991), 'Introduction', in P. Dahlgren and C. Sparks (eds), *Communication and Citizenship: Journalism and the Public Sphere*, London, Routledge.

Dahlgren, P. (1992), 'What's the meaning of this? Viewers' plural sense-making of TV news', in P. Scannell, P. Schlesinger and C. Sparks (eds), *Culture and Power: A Media, Culture and Society Reader*, London, Sage.

Dahlgren, P. and C. Sparks (eds) (1991), *Communication and Citizenship: Journalism and the Public Sphere*, London, Routledge.

Dalle Vacche, A. (1996), *Cinema and Painting: How Art is Used in Film*, London, Athlone Press.

Danesi, M. (1994), *Messages and Meanings: An Introduction to Semiotics*, Toronto, Canadian Scholars' Press.

Dash, J. (1992), *Daughters of the Dust: The Making of an African American Woman's Film*, New York, The New Press.

Dauncey, H. (1997), 'A cultural battle: French Minitel, the internet and the superhighway', *Convergence*, 3:3 (Autumn), 77–89.

Davis, H. and P. Walton (1983), 'Death of a premier: control and closure in international news', in H. Davis and P. Walton (eds), *Language, Image, Media*, Oxford, Blackwell.

Davis, M. (1992), 'Urban America sees its future: in LA, burning all illusions', *Nation*, 254:21 (1 June), 743–6.

Deacon, D., M. Pickering, P. Golding and G. Murdock (1999), *Researching Communications: A Practical Guide to Methods in Media and Cultural Analysis*, London, Arnold.

Debord, G. (1977), *The Society of the Spectacle*, Detroit, Red and Black.

Deely, J. (1990), *Basics of Semiotics*, Bloomington, Indiana University Press.

Deleuze, G. (1989), *Cinema 2: The Time-Image* (trans. H. Tomlinson and R. Galeta), London, Athlone Press.

Denzin, N. K. (1995), *The Cinematic Society: The Voyeur's Gaze*, London, Sage.

Diamond, S. (1997), 'Taylor's way: women, cultures and technology', in J. Terry and M. Calvert (eds), *Processed Lives: Gender and Technology in Everyday Life*, London, Routledge.

Diani, M. (1996), 'Linking mobilization frames and political opportunities: insights from regional populism in Italy', *American Sociological Review*, 61, 1053–69.

Dibbell, J. (1994), 'A Rape in cyberspace: or how an evil clown, a Haitian trickster spirit, two wizards and a cast of dozens turned a database into a society', in M. Derry (ed.), *Flame Wars: The Discourse of Cyberculture*, Durham, Duke University Press.

Dirlik, A. (1994), *After the Revolution: Waking to Global Capitalism*, Middletown, Wesleyan University Press.

D'Lugo, M. (1995), 'Almodóvar's city of desire', in K. M. Vernon and B. Morris (eds), *Post-Franco, Postmodern: The Films of Pedro Almodóvar*, Westport, Greenwood.

Doane, M. A. (1982), 'Film and the masquerade: theorising the female spectator', *Screen*, 23:3/4, 74–87.

Doane, M. A. (1991), *Femmes Fatales: Feminism, Film Theory, Psychoanalysis*, London, Routledge.

Doane, M. A., P. Mellencamp and L. Williams (eds) (1984), *Re-Vision: Essays in Feminist Film Criticism*, Los Angeles, American Film Institute.

Docter, S. and W. H. Dutton (1998), 'The First Amendment online: Santa Monica's Public Electronic Network', in R. Tsagarousianou, D. Tambini and C. Bryan (eds), *Cyberdemocracy: Technology, Cities and Civic Networks*, London, Routledge.

Dolar, M. (1996), 'At first sight', in R. Salecl and S. Žižek (eds), *Gaze and Voice as Love Objects*, Durham, Duke University Press.

Dorfman, A. and A. Mattelart (1975), *How to Read Donald Duck: Imperialist Ideology in the Disney Comic*, New York, International General.

Dorr, A. (1986), *Television and Children: A Special Medium for a Special Audience*, Beverly Hills, Sage.

Drabman, R. S., S. J. Robertson, J. N. Patterson, G. J. Jarvie, D. Hammer and G. Cordua (1981), 'Children's perception of media-portrayed sex roles', *Sex Roles*, 7, 379–89.

Du Gay, P. (1997), *Production of Culture/Cultures of Production*, London, Sage.

DuBois, M. (1991), 'The governance of the Third World: a Foucauldian perspective on power relations in development', *Alternatives*, 16, 1–30.

Duby, G. (1992), 'The courtly model', in C. Klapisch-Zuber (ed.), *A History of Women in the West, Vol. 2: Silences of the Middle Ages*, London, Harvard University Press.

Dunn, T. (1993), 'The new enclosures: racism in the normalized community', in R. Gooding-Williams (ed.), *Reading Rodney King*, New York, Routledge.

Dutton, W. H. and K. K. Guthrie (1991), 'An ecology of games: the political construction of Santa Monica's Public Electronic Network', *Informatization and the Public Sector*, 1, 279–301.

Dworkin, R. M. (1977), *The Philosophy of Law*, Oxford, Oxford University Press.

Dyer, R. (1981), 'Entertainment and utopia', in R. Altman (ed.), *Genre: The Musical*, London, Routledge and Kegan Paul/BFI.

Dyer, R. (1987), *Heavenly Bodies: Film Stars and Society*, London, Macmillan Education.

Dyer, R. (1992), *Only Entertainment*, London, Routledge.

Dyer, R. and G. Vincendeau (eds) (1992), *Popular European Cinema*, London, Routledge.

Dyson, M. (1991), 'Growing up under fire: "Boyz N the Hood" and the agony of the Black man in America', *Tikkun: The Bimonthly Jewish Critique of Politics, Culture and Society* 6:5, September/October, 74–8.

Dyson, M., M. Andrews and S. Leontopoulou (1995), 'Multimedia in museums: the need for a descriptive framework', *Convergence*, 1:2 (Autumn), 105–24.

Eagleton, T. (1990), *The Ideology of the Aesthetic*, Oxford, Blackwell.

Eagleton, T. (1991), *Ideology: An Introduction*, London, Verso.

Eagleton, T. (2000), *The Idea of Culture*, Oxford, Blackwell.

Easthope, A. (1986), *What a Man's Gotta Do: The Masculine Myth in Popular Culture*, London, Paladin.

Ebben, M. and C. Kramarae (1993), 'Women and information technologies: creating a cyberspace of our own', in H. J. Taylor, C. Kramarae and M. Ebben (eds), *Women, Information Technology and Scholarship*, Urbana, Centre for Advanced Study.

Ebert, T. (1991), 'Political semiosis in/of American cultural studies', *American Journal of Semiotics*, 8:1/2, 113–35.

Eco, U. (1976), *A Theory of Semiotics*, Bloomington, Indiana University Press.

Eco, U. (1979), 'Introduction: the role of the reader', in *The Role of the Reader: Explorations in the Semiotics of Texts*, Bloomington, Indiana University Press.

Eco, U. (1986), *Faith in Fakes*, London, Secker and Warburg (re-issued as *Travels in Hyper-Reality*, London, Pan Books, 1987).

Eco, U. and T. A. Sebeok (eds) (1983), *The Sign of Three: Dupin, Holmes, Peirce*, Bloomington, Indiana University Press.

Edelman, M. (1987), *Constructing the Political Spectacle*, Chicago, University of Chicago Press.

Elder, C. D. and R. W. Cobb (1984), 'Agenda building and the politics of aging', *Policy Studies Journal*, 13, 115–29.

Eldon, K. (ed.) (1997), *The Journey is the Destination: The Journals of Dan Eldon*, San Francisco, Chronicle Books.

Eley, G. (1991), 'Nations, publics and political cultures: placing Habermas in the nineteenth century', in C. Calhoun (ed.), *Habermas and the Public Sphere*, Cambridge, MA, MIT Press.

Eliot, T. S. (1964), 'The love song of J. Alfred Prufrock', in *Selected Poems*, New York, Harcourt Brace.

Elliott, P. (1974), 'Uses and gratifications: a critique and a sociolgical alternative' in E. Katz, J. G. Blumler and M. Gurevitch (eds), *The Uses of Mass Communication*, Beverly Hills, Sage.

Ellis, J. (2000), *Seeing Things: Television in the Age of Uncertainty*, London, I. B. Tauris.

Elsaesser, T. (1989), *New German Cinema: A History*, London, Macmillan/BFI.

Elsaesser, T. (ed.) (1990), *Early Cinema: Space, Frame, Narrative*, London, British Film Institute.

Entman, R. M. (1989), *Democracy without Citizens*, New York, Oxford University Press.

Entman, R. M. (1993), 'Framing: toward a clarification of a fractured paradigm', *Journal of Communication*, 4, 51–8.

Entman, R. M. and A. Rojecki (1993), 'Freezing out the public: élite and media framing of the U.S. anti-nuclear movement', *Political Communication*, 10, 155–73.

Ericson, R., P. Baranek and J. Chan (1987), *Visualizing Deviance*, London, Sage.

Ettema, J. S. and D. C. Whitney (1994), *Audiencemaking: How the Media Create the Audience*, Thousand Oaks, Sage.

Ettema, J. S., J. W. Brown and R. V. Luepker (1983), 'Knowledge gap effects in a health information campaign', *Public Opinion Quarterly*, 47, 516–27.

Faris, R. E. L. (1970), *Chicago Sociology 1920–1932*, Chicago, University of Chicago Press.

Farley, C. J. (1994), 'Patriot games', *Time*, 19 December, 50–1.

Featherstone, M. (1990), 'Global culture: an introduction', *Theory, Culture and Society*, 7, 1–14.

Fedarko, K. (1993), 'Holidays in hell', *Time*, 23 August, pp. 50–1.

Fejes, F. (1981), 'Media imperialism: an assessment', *Media, Culture and Society*, 3:3, 281–9.

Fejes, F. (1984), 'Critical mass communications research and media effects: the problem of the disappearing audience', *Media, Culture and Society*, 6:3, 219–32.

Feld, S. (1991), 'Voices of the rainforest', *Public Culture*, 4:1, 131.

Feld, S. (1996), 'Pygmy POP: a genealogy of schizophonic mimesis', in D. Christensen (ed.), *1996 Yearbook of Traditional Music*, New York, Columbia University Press.

Ferguson, M. (ed.) (1990), *Public Communication: The New Imperatives, Future Directions for Media Research*, London, Sage.

Fernback, J. (1997), 'The individual within the collective: virtual ideology and the realization of collective principles', in S. Jones (ed.), *Virtual Culture: Identity and Communication in Cybersociety*, London, Sage.

Findahl, O. and B. Hoijer (1976), *Fragments of Reality: An Experiment with News and TV Visuals*, Stockholm, Swedish Broadcasting Corporation.

Fishman, M. (1988), *Manufacturing the News*, Austin, University of Texas Press.

Fishmen, J. and H. Casiano (1969), 'Puerto Ricans in the press', *Modern Language Journal*, 33:3, 157–62.

Fiske, J. (1986), 'Television: polysemy and popularity', *Critical Studies in Mass Communication*, 3:4, 391–408.

Fiske, J. (1989a), *Understanding Popular Culture*, London, Unwin Hyman.

Fiske, J. (1989b), *Reading the Popular*, London, Unwin Hyman.

Fiske, J. (1989c), 'Moments of television: neither the text nor the audience', in E. Seiter, H. Borchers, G. Kreutzner and E.-M. Warth (eds), *Remote Control: Television Audiences and Cultural Power*, London, Routledge.

Fiske, J. (1990), *Introduction to Communication Studies*, New York, Routledge.

Fiske, S. T. and S. E. Taylor (1984), *Social Cognition*, New York, Random House.

Fleming, D. (1996), *Powerplay: Toys as Popular Culture*, Manchester, Manchester University Press.

Flynn, T. R. (1984), *Sartre and Marxist Existentialism*, Chicago, University of Chicago Press.

Foddy, W. H. and W. R. Finighan (1980), 'The concept of privacy from a symbolic interactionist perspective', *Journal for the Theory of Social Behaviour*, 10, 1–17.

Foster, H. (1983), *The Anti-Aesthetic*, Seattle, Bay Press.

Foster, H. (1985), *Recodings: Art, Spectacle and Cultural Politics*, Port Townsend, Bay Press.

Foucault, M. (1974), *The Archaeology of Knowledge*, London, Tavistock.

Foucault, M. (1975), *Discipline and Punish: The Birth of the Prison* (trans. A. Sheridan), New York, Pantheon Books.

Foucault, M. (1977), *Language, Counter-memory, Practice* (trans. D. F. Bouchard and S. Simon), Ithaca, Cornell University Press.

Foucault, M. (1980), *The History of Sexuality, Vol. 1: An Introduction* (trans. R. Hurley), New York, Vintage.

Francissen, L. and K. Brants (1998), 'Virtually going places: square-hopping in Amsterdam's Digital City', in R. Tsagarousianou, D. Tambini and C. Bryan (eds), *Cyberdemocracy: Technology, Cities and Civic Networks*, London, Routledge.

Fraser, N. (1987), *Unruly Practices: Power, Discourse and Gender in Contemporary Social Theory*, Cambridge, Polity.

Fraser, N. (1994), 'Rethinking the public sphere: a contribution to the critique of actually existing democracy', in H. A. Giroux and P. McLaren (eds), *Between Borders: Pedagogy and the Politics of Cultural Studies*, London, Routledge.

Fraser, N. and L. Nicholson (1988), 'Social criticism without philosophy: an encounter between feminism and postmodernism', *Theory, Culture and Society*, 5:2/3, 373–94.

Frazer, E. (1992), 'Teenage girls reading "Jackie"', in P. Scannell, P. Schlesinger and C. Sparks (eds), *Culture and Power: A Media, Culture and Society Reader*, London, Methuen.

Freud, S. (1926), 'The "uncanny"', in *Standard Edition, Vol. 17*, London, The Hogarth Press.

Freud, S. (1927), 'Fetishism', in *Standard Edition, Vol. 21*, London, the Hogarth Press.

Friedland, L. (1996), 'Electronic democracy and the new citizenship', *Media, Culture and Society*, 18, 185–212.

Frith, S. (1983), *Sound Effects: Youth, Leisure and the Politics of Rock 'n' Roll*, London, Constable.

Frith, S. (ed.) (1993), *Music and Copyright*, Edinburgh, Edinburgh University Press.

Frith, S. and A. Goodwin (1990), *On Record: Rock, Pop and the Written Word*, New York, Pantheon Books.

Frow, J. (1995), *Cultural Studies and Cultural Values*, Oxford, Oxford University Press.

Fukuyama, F. (1993), *The End of History and the Last Man*, New York, Viking.

Gadamer, H.-G. (1979), *Truth and Method* (2nd edition, trans. G. Barden and W. G. Doerpal), London, Sheed and Ward.

Gamson, W. A. (1992), *Talking Politics*, Cambridge, Cambridge University Press.

Gamson, W. A. (1995), 'Constructing social protest', in H. Johnstone and B. Klandermans (eds), *Social Movements and Culture*, Minneapolis, University of Minnesota Press.

Gamson, W. A. and A. Modigliani (1989), 'Media discourse and public opinion on nuclear power: a constructionist approach', *American Journal of Sociology*, 95:1, 1–37.

Gamson, W. A. and G. Wolsfeld (1993), 'Movements and media as interacting systems', *Annals of the American Association of Political Science*, 528, 114–25.

Gandy, O. H. (1982), *Beyond Agenda-Setting: Information Subsidies and Public Policy*, Norwood, Ablex.

Gans, H. J. (1980), *Deciding What's News: A Study of CBS Evening News, NBC Nightly News, Newsweek and Time*, New York, Pantheon.

Gans, H. J. (1992), 'Multiperspectival news', in E. D. Cohen (ed.), *Philosophical Issues in Journalism*, Oxford, Oxford University Press.

Garnham, N. (1983), 'Public service versus the market', *Screen*, 24:1, 6–27.

Garnham, N. (1986), 'Media and the public sphere', in P. Golding, G. Murdock and P. Schlesinger (eds), *Communicating Politics*, Leicester, Leicester University Press.

Garnham, N. (1990), 'The media and the public sphere', in N. Garnham (ed.), *Capitalism and Communication: Global Culture and the Economics of Information*, London, Sage.

Garnham, N. (1992), 'The media and the public sphere', in C. Calhoun (ed.), *Habermas and the Public Sphere*, Cambridge, MA, MIT Press.

Garnham, N. (1993), 'The future of the BBC', *Sight and Sound*, February, pp. 26–8.

Garofalo, R. (ed.) (1992), *Rockin' the Boat: Mass Music and Mass Movements*, Boston, South End Press.

Gates, D. (1993), 'White-male paranoia', *Newsweek*, 29 March, pp. 48–53.

Gavin, N. (ed.) (1998), *The Economy, Media and Public Knowledge*, London, Leicester University Press and Cassell.

Geertz, C. (1975), *The Interpretation of Cultures*, New York, Basic Books.

George, S. (1988), *A Fate Worse Than Debt*, Harmondsworth, Penguin.

Gerbner, G. (1970), 'Cultural indicators: the case of violence in television drama', *Annals of the American Association of Political and Social Science*, 338, 69–81.

Giddens, A. (1973), *The Class Structure of the Advanced Societies*, London, Hutchinson.

Giddens, A. (1989), *Sociology*, Cambridge, Polity.

Giddens, A. (1990), *The Consequences of Modernity*, Cambridge, Polity.

Giddens, A. (1991), *Modernity and Self Identity: Self and Society in the Late Modern Age*, Cambridge, Polity.

Giddens, A. (1994), *Beyond Left and Right: The Future of Radical Politics*, Cambridge, Polity.

Giddens, A. (1996), 'Affluence, poverty and the idea of a post-scarcity society', *Development and Change*, 27:2, 365–77.

Gifford, B. and D. Perry (1998), *Bordertown*, San Francisco, Chronicle Books.

Gillespie, M. (1995), *Television, Ethnicity and Cultural Change*, London, Routledge.

Giroux, H. A. (1994), *Disturbing Pleasures: Learning Popular Culture*, New York, Routledge.

Giroux, H. A. (1997), *Pedagogy and the Politics of Hope: Theory, Culture and Schooling*, Oxford, Westview Press.

Gitlin, T. (1980), *The Whole World is Watching. Mass Media in the Making and Unmaking of the New Left*, Berkeley, University of California Press.

Goffman, E. (1974), *Frame Analysis*, Boston, Northeastern Press.

Goldberg, K. (1998), 'Virtual reality in the age of telepresence', *Convergence*, 4:1 (Spring), 33–7.

Golding, P. (1974), *The Mass Media*, London, Longman.

Golding, P. (1995), 'The mass media and the public sphere: the crisis of information in the "information society"', in S. Edgell, S. Walkgate and G. Williams (eds), *Debating the Future of the Public Sphere*, Aldershot, Avebury.

Golding, P. (1996), 'World Wide Wedge: division and contradiction in the global information infrastructure', *Monthly Review*, 48:3, 70–85.

Goldman, R. and A. Rajagopal (1991), *Mapping Hegemony: Television News Coverage of Industrial Conflict*, Norwood, Ablex.

Gowing, N. (1994), 'Real-time TV coverage from war: does it make or break government policy?', European Film and Television Society Conference, NFT, London, July.

Graber, D. A. (1988), *Processing the News: How People Tame the Information Tide* (2nd edition), New York, Longman.

Graddol, D. (1994), 'The visual accomplishment of factuality', in D. Graddol and O. Boyd-Barrett (eds), *Media Texts: Authors and Readers*, Clevedon, Multilingual Matters/Open University.

Gramsci, A. (1971), *Selections from Prison Notebooks* (ed. and trans. Q. Hoare and G. Nowell-Smith), London, Lawrence and Wishart.

Gray, A. (1992), *Video Playtime: The Gendering of a Leisure Technology*, London, Routledge.

Greenberg, B. S. and M. Burgoon (1983), *Mexican Americans and the Mass Media*, Norwood, Ablex Publishing.

Greenfield, P. M. (1984), *Mind and Media*, Harvard, Harvard University Press.

Grice, H. P. (1975), 'Logic and conversation', in P. Cole and J. L. Morgan (eds), *Studies in Syntax: Speech Acts*, New York, Seminar Press.

Grossberg, L. (1988), 'Wandering audiences, nomadic critics', *Cultural Studies*, 2:3, 377–92.

Grossberg, L. (1992), *We Gotta Get Out of This Place: Popular Conservatism and Postmodern Culture*, New York, Routledge.

Gruchy, M. (1990), 'Three different approaches to institutional economics: an evaluation', *Journal of Economic Issues*, XXIV:2, 361–9.

Gunning, T. (1991), *D. W. Griffith and the Origins of American Narrative Film*, Urbana, University of Illinois Press.

Haavelsrud, M. (ed.) (1995), *Kunnskap og Utvikling*, Tromsø, University of Tromsø.

Habermas, J. (1984), *The Theory of Communicative Action V. 1: Reason and the Rationalization of Society*, Cambridge, Polity.

Habermas, J. (1987), *The Theory of Communicative Action V. 2: Lifeworld and System*, Cambridge, Polity.

Habermas, J. (1989), *The Structural Transformation of the Public Sphere: An Enquiry into a Category of Bourgeois Society*, Cambridge, Polity.

Hacker, K. and M. Todino (1996), 'Virtual democracy at the Clinton White House: an experiment in electronic democratization', *Javnost/The Public*, 3:1, 71–86.

Haddon, L. (1992), 'Explaining ICT consumption', in R. Silverstone and E. Hirsch (eds), *Consuming Technologies: Media and Information in Domestic Spaces*, London, Routledge.

Hafner, K. and M. Lyon (1996), *Where Wizards Stay Up Late: The Origins of the Internet*, New York, Touchstone.

Hall, K. (1996), 'Cyberfeminism', in S. Herring (ed.), *Computer-Mediated-Communication: Linguistic, Social and Cross-Cultural Perspectives*, Amsterdam, John Benjamins.

Hall, P. and R. Taylor (1996), 'Political science and the four new institutionalisms', *Political Studies*, 44:5, 936–57.

Hall, S. (1980), 'Encoding/decoding', in S. Hall, D. Hobson, A. Lowe and P. Willis (eds), *Culture, Media, Language: Working Papers in Cultural Studies, 1972–79*, London, Hutchinson.

Hall, S. (1982), 'The rediscovery of "ideology": the return of the repressed in media studies', in M. Gurevitch, T. Bennett, J. Curran and J. Woollacott (eds), *Culture, Society and the Media*, London, Methuen.

Hall, S. (1989), 'New ethnicities', in K. Mercer (ed.), *Black Film, British Cinema*, ICA Documents No.7, ICA, London.

Hall, S. (1990), 'Cultural identity and diaspora', in J. Rutherford (ed.), *Identity*, London, Lawrence and Wishart.

Hall, S. (1991), 'The local and the global: globalization and ethnicities', in A. D. King (ed.), *Culture, Globalization and the World System*, London, Macmillan.

Hall, S. (1992), 'The question of cultural identity', in S. Hall, D. Held and T. McGrew (eds), *Modernity and its Futures*, Cambridge, Polity, in association with The Open University.

Hall, S. (1995), 'Negotiating Caribbean identities', *New Left Review*, 209, January/February, 3–14.

Hall, S. (1996a), 'Gramsci's relevance for the study of race and ethnicity', in D. Morley and K.-H. Chen (eds), *Stuart Hall: Critical Dialogues in Cultural Studies*, London, Routledge.

Hall, S. (1996b), 'Introduction: who needs identity?', in S. Hall and P. du Gay (eds), *Questions of Cultural Identity*, London, Sage.

Hall, S. and P. Whannel (1964), *The Popular Arts*, London, Hutchinson.

Hall, S., C. Critcher, T. Jefferson, J. Clarke and B. Roberts (1978), *Policing the Crisis: Mugging, the State, and Law and Order*, London, Macmillan.

Hall, T. (1999), 'Best of British', *The Guardian*, 10 April, p. 22.

Hallin, D. C. (1986), *The Uncensored War*, New York, Oxford University Press.

Hamelink, C. (1994), *The Politics of World Communication*, London, Sage.

Hammersley, M. (1989), *The Dilemma of Qualitative Method: Herbert Blumer and the Chicago Tradition*, London, Routledge.

Hansen, M. (1994), 'Early cinema, late cinema: transformations of the public sphere', in L. Williams (ed.), *Viewing Positions: Ways of Seeing Film*, New Brunswick, Rutgers University Press.

Harasim, L. M. (ed.) (1993), 'Networlds: networks as social space', *Global Networks: Computers and International Communication*, Cambridge, MA, MIT Press.

Haraway, D. (1991), 'A cyborg manifesto: science, technology and socialist-feminism in the late twentieth century', in *Simians, Cyborgs and Women: The Reinvention of Nature*, London, Free Association Books.

Harindranath, R. (1998), 'Documentary meanings and interpretive contexts: observations on Indian "repertoires" ', in R. Dickinson, O. Linne and R. Harindranath (eds), *Approaches to Audiences*, London, Edward Arnold.

Harless, J. D. (1985), *Mass Communication: An Introductory Survey*, Dubuque, W. C. Brown.

Harrison, P. (1993), *The Sociology of Modernization and Development*, London, Routledge.

Hart, L. and P. Phelan (eds) (1993), *Acting Out: Feminist Performances*, Ann Arbor, University of Michigan Press.

Hartley, J. (1982), *Understanding News*, London, Methuen.

Harvey, D. (1989), *The Condition of Postmodernity*, Oxford, Blackwell.

Hayward, S. and G. Vincendeau (eds) (1990), *French Film: Texts and Contexts*, London, Routledge.

Haywood, T. (1998), 'Global networks and the myth of equality: trickle down or trickle away?', in B. Loader (ed.), *Cyberspace Divide: Equality, Agency and Policy in the Information Society*, London, Routledge.

Heath, R. L. and J. Bryant (1992), *Human Communication Theory and Research: Concepts, Contexts and Challenges*, Hilldale, Erlbaum.

Herman, E. A. and N. Chomsky (1988), *Manufacturing Consent: The Political Economy of the Mass Media*, New York, Pantheon.

Herring, S. (1994), 'Politeness in computer culture: why women thank and men flame', in M. Bucholtz, A. Liang and L. Sutton (eds), *Communicating In, Through and Across Cultures: Proceedings of the Third Berkeley Women and Language Conference*, Berkeley, Berkeley Women and Language Group.

Herring, S. (1996), 'Posting in a different voice: gender and ethics in CMC', in C. Ess (ed.), *Philosophical Perspectives on Computer-Mediated-Communication*, Albany, State University of New York Press.

Hervey, S. (1982), *Semiotic Perspectives*, London, Allen and Unwin.

Hill, J. (1986), *Sex, Class and Realism: British Cinema 1956–1963*, London, British Film Institute.

Hill, J. (1999), *British Cinema in the 1980s: Issues and Themes*, Oxford, Oxford University Press.

Himmelweit, H. T., A. N. Oppenheim and P. Vince (1958), *Television and the Child: An Empirical Study of the Effect of Television on the Young*, London, Oxford University Press.

Hirsch, J. (1981), *Family Photography: Context, Meaning and Effect*, New York, Oxford University Press.

Hockley, L. (1996), 'Inter-between: actus-done', *Convergence*, 2:2 (Autumn), 10–12.

Hodge, R. and G. Kress (1988), *Social Semiotics*, Oxford, Polity.

Hodge, R. and D. Tripp (1986), *Children and Television: A Semiotic Approach*, Cambridge, Polity.

Hodgson, G. M. (1984), *The Democratic Economy: A New Look at Planning, Markets and Power*, Harmondsworth, Penguin.

Hodgson, G. M. (1991), *After Marx and Sraffa: Essays in Political Economy*, London, Macmillan.

Hoechsmann, M. (1996), 'Revolution goes global: Zapatistas on the net', *Convergence*, 2:1 (Spring), 30–5.

Hoggart, R. (1957), *The Uses of Literacy*, London, Chatto and Windus.

Hoijer, B. (1990), 'Studying viewers' reception of television programmes: theoretical and methodological considerations', *European Journal of Communication*, 5:1, 29–56.

Hoijer, B. (1993), 'Reception of television narration as a socio-cognitive process: a schema-theoretical outline', *Poetics, special issue: Audience Research*, 21, 283–304.

Holderness, M. (1998), 'Who are the world's information-poor?', in B. Loader (ed.), *Cyberspace Divide: Equality, Agency and Policy in the Information Society*, London, Routledge.

Holland, P. (1996), 'When a woman reads the news', in P. Morris and S. Thornham (eds), *Media Studies: A Reader*, Edinburgh, Edinburgh University Press.

Holub, R. C. (1984), *Reception Theory: A Critical Introduction*, London, Methuen.

hooks, b. (1990), *Yearning*, Boston, South End Press.

hooks, b. (1992), *Black Looks: Race and Representation*, London, Turnaround.

hooks, b. (1999), *Remembered Rapture: The Writer at Work*, London, Women's Press.

Horne, H. and S. Frith (1987), *Art into Pop*, London, Methuen.

Hornig Priest, S. (1980), *Doing Media Research: An Introduction*, Beverly Hills, Sage.

Horton, D. and R. Wohl (1956), 'Mass comunication and para-social interaction: observations on intimacy at a distance', *Psychiatry*, 19, 215–29.

Huhtamo, E. (1995), 'Seeking deeper contact: interactive art as metacommentary', *Convergence*, 1:2 (Autumn), 81–104.

Hume, M. (1997), *Whose War Is It Anyway?: The Dangers of the Journalism of Attachment* (a *Living Marxism* special), London, Informinc (LM) Ltd.

Hutchby, I. (1996), *Confrontation Talk: Arguments, Asymmetries and Power on Talk Radio*, Hillsdale, Erlbaum.

Hutton, W. (1995), *The State We're In*, London, Jonathan Cape.

Hutton, W. (1999), editorial matter, *The Observer*, 21 March, p. 30.

Ibarra, P. (ed.) (1992), *Objeción de Conciencia e Insumisión. Claves Ideológicas y Sociales*, Madrid, Fundamentos.

Ibarra, P. *et al.* (1998), *La Insumisión: Un Singular Ciclo Histórico de Desobediencia Civil*, Madrid, Tecnos.

Inglis, F. (1990), *Media Theory: An Introduction*, Oxford, Blackwell.

Innis, H. (1950), *Empire and Communications*, Oxford, Oxford University Press.

Innis, R. E. (ed.) (1985), *Semiotics: An Introductory Reader*, Bloomington, Indiana University Press.

Instrell, R. (1992), 'Blade Runner: the economic shaping of a film', in J. Orr and C. Nicholson (eds), *Cinema and Fiction*, Edinburgh, Edinburgh University Press.

Iordanova, D. (1997), 'On-line teaching in international communication', *Convergence*, 3:3 (Autumn), 10–16.

Irigaray, L. (1985a), *Speculum of the Other Woman* (trans. G. C. Gill), Ithaca, Cornell University Press.

Irigaray, L. (1985b), *This Sex Which is Not One* (trans. C. Porter and C. Burke), Ithaca, Cornell University Press.

Irigaray, L. (1996), *I Love To You: Sketch of a Possible Felicity in History* (trans. A. Martin), New York, Routledge.

Iser, W. (1980), 'Interaction between text and reader', in S. R. Suleiman and I. Crosman (eds), *The Reader in the Text: Essays on Audience and Interpretation*, Princeton, Princeton University Press.

Iyengar, S. (1991), *Is Anyone Responsible? How Television Frames Political Issues*, Chicago, University of Chicago Press.

James, C. L. R. (1978), *Mariners, Renegades and Castaways: The Story of Herman Melville and the World We Live In*, Detroit, Bewick.

James, C. L. R. (1993), *American Civilization*, Oxford, Blackwell.

Jameson, F. (1979), 'Class and allegory in contemporary mass culture: "Dog Day Afternoon" as a political film', *Screen Education*, 30 (Spring), 75–92.

Jameson, F. (1981), *The Political Unconscious: Narrative as a Socially Symbolic Act*, London, Methuen.

Jameson, F. (1984), 'Postmodernism, or, the cultural logic of late capitalism', *New Left Review*, 146, July–August, 59–82.

Jameson, F. (1990), *Late Marxism: Adorno, or, the Persistence of the Dialectic*, New York, Verso.

Jameson, F. (1991), *Postmodernism, or, The Cultural Logic of Late Capitalism*, Durham, Duke University Press.

Jameson, F. (1992), *Signatures of the Visible*, London, Routledge.

Jameson, F. (1998), *Brecht and Method*, London, Verso.

Jameson, F. (1999), 'Marx's purloined letter', in M. Sprinker (ed.), *Ghostly Demarcations: A Symposium on Jacques Derrida's 'Specters of Marx'*, London, Verso.

Jankowski, N. and M. Van Selm (2000), 'The promise and practice of public debate in cyberspace', in K. Hacker and J. van Dijk (eds), *Digital Democracy: Issues of Theory and Practice*, London, Sage.

Jauss, H. R. (1982), *Towards an Aesthetic of Reception*, Minneapolis, University of Minnesota Press.

Jenkins, R. (1994), 'Rethinking ethnicity: identity, categorization and power', *Ethnic and Racial Studies*, 17:2, 197–223.

Jensen, K. B. (1991), 'When is meaning? Communication theory, pragmatism and mass media reception', *Communication Yearbook*, 14, Newbury Park, Sage.

Jensen, K. B. (1986), *Making Sense of the News: Towards a Theory and an Empirical Model of Reception for the Study of Mass Communication*, Aarhus, Aarhus University Press.

Jensen, K. B. (1987), 'Qualitative audience research: toward an integrative approach to reception', *Critical Studies in Mass Communication*, 4, 21–36.

Jensen, K. B. and N. W. Jankowski (eds) (1991), *A Handbook of Qualitative Methodologies for Mass Communication Research*, London, Routledge.

Jensen, K. B. and K. E. Rosengren (1990), 'Five traditions in search of the audience', *European Journal of Communication*, 5, 207–39.

Jhally, S. (1990), *The Codes of Advertising: Fetishism and the Political Economy of Meaning in the Consumer Society*, London, Routledge.

Johansson, T. and F. Miegel (1992), *Do the Right Thing: Lifestyle and Identity in Contemporary Youth Culture*, Stockholm, Almqvist and Wiskell.

Johnson, S. (1997), *Interface Culture: How New Technology Transforms the Way We Create and Communicate*, New York, Basic Books.

Johnsson-Smaragdi, U. (1994), 'Models of change and stability in adolescents' media use', in K. E. Rosengren (ed.), *Media Effects and Beyond: Culture, Socialization and Lifestyles*, London, Routledge.

Johnsson-Smaragdi, U. and A. Jönsson (1994), 'Self-evaluation in an ecological perspective: neighbourhood, family and peers, schooling and media use', in K. E. Rosengren (ed.), *Media Effects and Beyond: Culture, Socialization and Lifestyles*, London, Routledge.

Jones, J. (1992), 'The accusatory space', in G. Dent (ed.), *Black Popular Culture*, Seattle, Bay Press.

Jones, S. (ed.) (1995), 'Understanding community in the information age', in *CyberSociety: Computer-Mediated Communication and Community*, Thousand Oaks, Sage.

Jones, S. (ed.) (1997), 'The internet and its social landscape', in *Virtual Culture: Identity and Communication in Cybersociety*, London, Sage.

Jordan T. (1999), *Cyberpower: The Culture and Politics of Cyberspace and the Internet*, London, Routledge.

Jöreskog, K. G. and D. Sörbom (1988), *LISREL 7: A Guide to the Program and Applications*, Chicago, SPSS Publications.

Kahin, B. and E. Wilson (1997), *National Information Infrastructure Initiatives: Vision and Policy Design*, Cambridge, MA, MIT Press.

Kahneman, D., P. Slovic and A. Tversky (eds) (1982), *Judgment under Uncertainty: Heuristics and Biases*, New York, Cambridge University Press.

Kaplan, A. E. (1983), 'Is the gaze male?', in A. Snitow, C. Stansell and S. Thompson (eds), *Desire: The Politics of Sexuality*, London, Virago.

Kaplan, A. E. (1987), 'Mothering, feminism and representation: the maternal in melodrama and the woman's film 1910–40', in C. Gledhill (ed.), *Home is Where the Heart Is*, London, BFI.

Kaplan, E. A. (1991), *Motherhood and Representation: The Mother in Popular Culture and Melodrama*, London, Routledge.

Katz, E. (1968), 'On reopening the question of selectivity in exposure to mass communications', in R. P. Abelson *et al.* (eds), *Theories of Cognitive Consistency: A Sourcebook*, Chicago, Rand McNally.

Katz, E. (1979), 'The uses of Becker, Blumler and Swanson', *Communication Research*, 6:1, 74–83.

Katz, E. (1996), 'Viewers' work', in J. Hay, L. Grossberg and E. Wartella (eds), *The Audience and its Landscape*, Boulder, Westview.

Katz, E., M. Gurevitch and E. Haas (1973), 'On the uses of mass media for important things', *American Sociological Review*, 38, 164–81.

Keane, J. (1995), 'Structural transformations of the public sphere', *Communication Review*, 1, 1–22.

Kearney, M. C. (1998), ' "Don't need you": rethinking identity politics and separatism from a grrrl perspective', in J. Epstein (ed.), *Youth Culture: Identity in a Postmodern World*, Oxford, Blackwell.

Kelley, H. H. (1972), 'Attribution: perceiving the causes of behaviour', in E. E. Jones, D. E. Kanouse, H. H. Kelley, R. E. Nisbett, S. Valins and B. Weiner (eds), *Attribution in Social Interaction*, Morristown, General Learning Press.

Kellner, D. (ed.) (1989), *Postmodernism/Jameson/Critique*, Washington, DC, Maisonneuve.

Kellner, D. (1992), *The Persian Gulf TV War*, Boulder, Westview.

Kennedy, L. (1992), 'The body in question', in G. Dent (ed.), *Black Popular Culture*, Seattle, Bay Press.

Kerr, P. (1991), 'Opportunity knocks?', *Screen*, 32:4 (Winter), 357–63.

Kielbowicz, R. and C. Scherer (1986), 'The role of the press in the dynamics of social movements', in *Research in Social Movements, Conflicts and Change: An Annual Compilation, Vol. 9*, Greenwich, JAI Press.

Kinder, M. (1987), 'A conversation with Pedro Almodóvar', *Film Quarterly*, 41, 33–43.

Kinder, M. (1995), 'From matricide to mother love in Almodóvar's "High Heels" ', in K. M. Vernon and B. Morris (eds), *Post-Franco, Postmodern: The Films of Pedro Almodóvar*, Westport, Greenwood.

Kingdon, J. W. (1984), *Agendas, Alternatives and Public Policies*, Glenview, Scott, Foresman and Co.

Kitses, J. (1969), *Horizons West*, London, Thames and Hudson/BFI.

Kitzinger, J. (1993), 'Understanding AIDS: researching audience perceptions of Aquired Immune Deficiency Syndrome', in J. Eldridge (ed.), *Getting the Message: News, Truth and Power*, London, Routledge.

Klandermans, B. (1989), 'Introduction: organizational effectiveness', *International Social Movement Research*, 2, 383–94.

Kluitenberg, E. (1998), 'Connectivity, new freedom, new marginality: a report from the Baltic cyber-corridor', *Convergence*, 4:2 (Summer), 20–6.

Knight, J. (1997), 'Art and activism: engaging with body and space', *Convergence*, 3:3 (Autumn), 129–35.

Knight, J. and A. Weedon (1995), 'Editorial', *Convergence*, 1:1 (Spring), 4–8.

Knightley, P. (1982), *The First Casualty*, London, Quartet.

Kramarae, C. (ed.) (1988), *Technology and Women's Voices: Keeping in Touch*, London, Routledge.

Kramarae, C. and H. J. Taylor (1993), 'Women and men on electronic networks: a conversation or a monologue?', in H. J. Taylor, C. Kramarae and M. Ebben (eds), *Women, Information Technology and Scholarship*, Urbana, Center for Advanced Study.

Krampen, M. (1987), *Classics of Semiotics*, New York, Plenum.

Krippendorff, K. (1980), *Content Analysis: An Introduction to its Methodology*, Beverly Hills, Sage.

Kristeva, J. (1980), 'Motherhood according to Bellini', in *Desire in Language: A Semiotic Approach to Literature and Art* (trans. L. S. Roudiez), Oxford, Blackwell.

Kristeva, J. (1984), *Revolution in Poetic Language*, New York, Columbia University Press.

Kristeva, J. (1986), 'Women's time', in T. Moi (ed.), *The Kristeva Reader*, Oxford, Blackwell.

Kristeva, J. (1992), *Powers of Horror: An Essay on Abjection* (trans. L. S. Roudiez), New York, Columbia University Press.

Kroll, J. (1991), 'Spiking a fever', *Newsweek*, 10 June, pp. 44–7.

Kubey, R. and M. Csikszentmihalyi (1990), *Television and the Quality of Life: How Viewing Shapes Everyday Experience*, Hillsdale, Lawrence Erlbaum.

Kuhn, A. (1982), *Women's Pictures: Feminism and the Cinema*, London, Routledge and Kegan Paul.

Kuhn, A. (1985), *The Power of the Image: Essays on Representation and Sexuality*, London, Routledge and Kegan Paul.

Kumar, K. (1996), 'Home', in K. Kumar and G. Weintraub *Public and Private in Thought and Practice*, Chicago, University of Chicago Press.

Lacan, J. (1968), 'The mirror phase as formative of the function of the "I" ', *New Left Review*, 51, 71–7.

Lacan, J. (1977a), 'The signification of the phallus', in *Écrits: A Selection* (trans. A. Sheridan), New York, Norton.

Lacan, J. (1977b), 'The mirror stage as formative of the function of the I', in *Écrits: A Selection* (trans. A. Sheridan), New York, Norton.

Lacan, J. (1981), ' "The line and light" and "What is a picture" ', in *The Four Fundamental Concepts of Psycho-analysis* (trans. A. Sheridan), New York, Norton.

Laclau, E. and C. Mouffe (1985), *Hegemony and Socialist Strategy: Towards a Radical Democratic Politics*, London, Verso.

Lal, V. (1996), *South Asian Cultural Studies*, Delhi, Manohar.

Lalanne, J.-M. (1997), 'Images from the inside', in *Wong Kar-wai*, Paris, Dis Voir.

Lambert, A. (1994), *The Crimean War: The War Correspondents*, London, Sutton.

Landes, J. (1988), *Women and the Public Sphere in the Age of the French Revolution*, Ithaca, Cornell University Press.

Laplanche, J. and J. B. Pontalis (1968), 'Fantasy and the origins of sexuality', *International Journal of Psychoanalysis*, 49, 1–18 (reprinted in V. Burgin *et al.* (eds) (1986), *Formations of Fantasy*, London, Routledge).

Larrain, J. (1979), *The Concept of Ideology*, London, Hutchinson.

Larrain, J. (1983), *Marxism and Ideology*, London, Macmillan.

Lasch, C. (1991), *The True and Only Heaven: Progress and Its Critics*, New York, Norton.

Lasswell, H. D. (1948), 'The structure and function of communication in society', in L. Bryson (ed.), *The Communication of Ideas*, New York, Harper.

Latour, B. (1996), *Aramis or The Love of Technology* (trans. C. Porter), Cambridge, MA, Harvard University Press.

Laurie, P. (1974), *Meet Your Friendly Social System*, London, Arrow Books.

Lax, S. (1998), 'Democracy and communications technologies: superhighway or blind alley?', *Convergence*, 4:3 (Autumn), 30–7.

Lazarsfeld, P. F. (1941), 'Remarks on administrative and critical communications research', *Studies in Philosophy and Science*, 9, 316.

Lee, A. J. (1976), *The Origins of the Popular Press 1855–1914*, London, Croom Helm.

Lele, J. (1993), 'Orientalism and the social sciences', in C. A. Breckenridge and P. van de Veer (eds), *Orientalism and the Postcolonial Predicament*, Philadelphia, University of Pennsylvania Press.

Levy, M. R. and S. Windahl (1985), 'The concept of audience activity', in K. E. Rosengren, L. A. Wenner and P. Palmgreen (eds), *Media Gratifications Research*, Beverly Hills, Sage.

Lewis, J. (1985), 'Decoding television news', in P. Drummond and R. Paterson (eds), *Television in Transition*, London, British Film Institute.

Lewis, J. (1987), 'The framework of political television', in J. Hawthorn (ed.), *Propaganda, Persuasion and Polemic*, London, Edward Arnold.

Lewis, T. (1999), 'The politics of "hauntology" in Derrida's "Specters of Marx"', in M. Sprinker (ed.), *Ghostly Demarcations: A Symposium on Jacques Derrida's 'Specters of Marx'*, London, Verso.

Lieberman, P. (1992), '52 per cent of riot arrests were Latino, study says', *LA Times*, 18 June, p. B3.

Liebes, T. (1992), 'Decoding TV news: the political discourse of Israeli hawks and doves', *Theory and Society*, 21, 357–81.

Liebes, T. and E. Katz (1986), 'Patterns of involvement in television fiction: a comparative analysis', *European Journal of Communication*, 2:1, 151–71.

Liebes, T. and E. Katz (1993), *The Export of Meaning*, Cambridge, Polity.

Liehm, M. (1984), *Passion and Defiance: Film in Italy from 1942 to the Present*, Berkeley, University of California Press.

Lineup Police Products (1992), *The Official Cop Catalogue*, San Luis Obispo, Lineup Police Products Inc.

Lipsitz, G. (1998), 'The hip hop hearings: censorship, social memory, and intergenerational tensions among African Americans', in J. Austin and M. N. Willard (eds), *Generations of Youth: Youth Cultures and History in Twentieth Century America*, New York, New York University Press.

Livingstone, S. (1996), 'On the continuing problems of media effects research', in J. Curran and M. Gurevitch (eds), *Mass Media and Society* (second edition), London, Arnold.

Livingstone, S. (1998), *Making Sense of Television: The Psychology of Audience Interpretation* (2nd edition), London, Routledge.

Livingstone, S. and M. Bovill (1999), *Young People, New Media*, London, London School of Economics, final report of the project, 'Children, young people and the changing media environment'.

Livingstone, S. and P. Lunt (1994), *Talk on Television: Audience Participation and Public Debate*, London, Routledge.

Loader, B. (ed.) (1997), 'The governance of cyberspace', in *The Governance of Cyberspace: Politics, Technology and Global Restructuring*, London, Routledge.

Loader, B. (1998), 'Cyberspace divide', in B. Loader (ed.), *Cyberspace Divide: Equality, Agency and Policy in the Information Society*, London, Routledge.

Loescher, G. D. (ed.) (1983), *Global Refugee Problem: U.S. and World Response: American Academy of Political and Social Science Annals, Vol. 467*, Beverly Hills, Sage.

Loescher, G. and J. A. Scanlan (1989), *Calculated Kindness: Refugees and America's Half-Open Door, 1945 to Present*, New York, The Free Press.

Lorraine, T. (1999), *Irigaray and Deleuze: Experiments in Visceral Philosophy*, Ithaca, Cornell University Press.

Lowenthal, L. (1961), *Literature, Popular Culture and Society*, New York, Doubleday Anchor.

Luckmann, T. (ed.) (1978), *Phenomenology and Sociology*, Harmondsworth, Penguin.

Lukes, S. (1974), *Power: A Radical View*, London, Macmillan.

Lull, J. (1988), *World Families Watch Television*, Newbury Park, Sage.

Lull, J. (1990), *Inside Family Viewing: Ethnographic Research on Television's Audiences*, London, Routledge.

Lull, J. (2000), *Media, Communication, Culture: A Global Approach* (revision of 1995 edition), Cambridge, Polity.

Luttwak, E. (1995a), 'Économie Americaine: les risques du "turbo-capitalisme"', *Politique internationale*, no. 69, 257–68.

Luttwak, E. (1995b), 'Turbo-charged capitalism and its consequences', *London Review of Books*, 2 November, pp. 6–7.

MacCabe, C. (1974), 'Realism and the cinema: notes on some Brechtian theses', *Screen*, 15:2, 7–27.

MacCabe, C. (1998), *Performance*, London, British Film Institute.

MacDonell, D. (1986), *Theories of Discourse: An Introduction*, Oxford, Blackwell.

MacKay, D. M. (1972), 'Formal analysis of communicative processes', in R. A. Hinde (ed.), *Nonverbal Communication*, Cambridge, Cambridge University Press.

MacKinnon, R. C. (1995), 'Searching for the Leviathan in Usenet', in S. Jones (ed.), *CyberSociety: Computer-Mediated Communication and Community*, Thousand Oaks, Sage.

Madison, G. B. (1990), *The Hermeneutics of Postmodernity: Figures and Themes*, Bloomington, Indiana University Press.

Mandelson, P. and R. Liddle (1996), *The Blair Revolution: Can New Labour Deliver?*, London, Faber and Faber.

Mandler, J. M. (1984), *Stories, Scripts, and Scenes: Aspects of Schema Theory*, Hillsdale, Erlbaum.

Mann, M. (1993), *The Sources of Social Power*, Cambridge, Cambridge University Press.

Mansell, R. (1993), *The New Telecommunications*, London, Sage.

Marshall, T. H. (1956), *Citizenship and Social Class*, Cambridge, Cambridge University Press.

Marshall, T. H. (1965), *Social Policy in the Twentieth Century*, London, Hutchinson.

Marshall, T. H. (1981), *The Right to Welfare and Other Essays*, London, Heinemann Educational.

Marwick, A. (1980), *Class: Image and Reality in Britain, France and the USA Since 1930*, Glasgow, Collins.

Marx, K. and F. Engels (1974), *The German Ideology, Part 1* (second edition), London, Lawrence and Wishart.

Masud-Piloto, F. R. (1988), *With Open Arms: The Evolution of Cuban Migration to the US*, Lanham, Rowman and Littlefield.

Massey, D. (1993), 'Power-geometry and a progressive sense of place', in J. Bird, B. Curtis, T. Putnam, C. Robertson and L. Tickner (eds), *Mapping the Futures: Local Cultures, Global Change*, London, Routledge.

Masterman, L. (ed.) (1984), *Television Mythologies: Stars, Shows and Signs*, London, Comedia.

Masterman, L. (1985), *Teaching the Media*, London, Comedia.

Mattelart, A. (1979), *Multinational Corporations and the Control of Culture*, Brighton, Harvester.

Mattelart, A. and S. Siegelaub (eds) (1979), *Communication and Class Struggle*, New York, International General.

Mavor, C. (ed.) (1996), *Pleasures Taken*, London, Tauris.

Mayne, J. (1994), 'Paradoxes of spectatorship', in L. Williams (ed.), *Viewing Positions: Ways of Seeing Film*, New Brunswick, Rutgers University Press.

McAllester, M. (1991), *Gaston Bachelard, Subversive Humanist*, Madison, University of Wisconsin Press.

McArthur, C. (1972), *Underworld USA*, London, Secker and Warburg/BFI.

McCarthy, J. D. and M. N. Zald (1977), 'Resource mobilization and social movements: a partial theory', *American Journal of Sociology*, 82, 1212–41.

McCarthy, J. D. and M. N. Zald (1987), 'Appendix. The trend of social movements in America: professionalization and resource mobilization', in M. N. Zald and J. D. McCarthy (eds), *Social Movements in an Organizational Society*, New Brunswick, Transaction Books.

McClintock, A. (1994), 'The angel of progress: pitfalls of the term "postcolonialism"', in F. Barker, P. Hulme and M. Iversen (eds), *Colonial Discourse/Postcolonial Theory*, Manchester, Manchester University Press.

McCombs, M. E. (1993), 'The evolution of agenda-setting research: twenty-five years in the marketplace of ideas', *Journal of Communication*, 43, 58–67.

McCombs, M. E. and D. L. Shaw (1972), 'The agenda-setting function of the mass media', *Public Opinion*, 36, 176–87.

McGuigan, J. (1992), *Cultural Populism*, London, Routledge.

McLaren, P. (1994), 'Multiculturalism and the postmodern critique: toward a pedagogy of resistance and transformation', in H. A. Giroux and P. McLaren (eds), *Between Borders: Pedagogy and the Politics of Cultural Studies*, New York, Routledge.

McLaren, P. (1995), *Critical Pedagogy and Predatory Culture: Oppositional Politics in a Postmodern Era*, London, Routledge.

McLellan, D. (1995), *Ideology* (second edition), Buckingham, Open University Press.

McLuhan, M. (1987), *Understanding Media: The Extensions of Man*, London, Ark (original 1964).

McPhail, T. L. (1987), *Electronic Colonialism: The Future of International Broadcasting and Communication*, Beverly Hills, Sage.

McQuail, D. (1987), *Mass Communication Theory* (second edition), London, Sage.

McQuail, D. and S. Windahl (1981), *Communication Models for the Study of Mass Communications*, New York, Longman.

McQuail, D. and S. Windahl (1993), *Models of Communication* (second edition), London, Longman.

Mead, G. H. (1934), *Mind, Self and Society*, Chicago, Chicago University Press.

Meehan, E. R. (1993), 'Conceptualizing culture as commodity: the problem of television', in H. Newcombe (ed.), *Television: The Critical View*, Oxford, Oxford University Press.

Meese Commission (1986), *US Attorney General's Commission on Pornography, Final Report*, July.

Meinhof, D. (1994), 'Double talk in news broadcasts', in D. Graddol and O. Boyd-Barrett (eds), *Media Texts: Authors and Readers*, Clevedon, Multilingual Matters/Open University.

Melody, W. H. and R. Mansell (1983), 'The debate over critical versus administrative research: circularity or challenge', *Ferment in the Field: A Special Issue of the Journal of Communication*, 33:3, 103–16.

Melucci, A. (1989), *Nomads of the Present: Social Movements and Individual Needs in Contemporary Society*, London, Century Hutchinson.

Melucci, A. (1996), *Challenging Codes: Collective Action in the Information Age*, Cambridge, Cambridge University Press.

Melville, H. (1851), *Moby Dick, or The White Whale*, New York, Harper.

Mercer, K. (1992), '"1968": periodizing postmodern politics and identity', in L. Grossberg, C. Nelson and P. Treichler (eds), *Cultural Studies*, New York, Routledge.

Metz, C. (1975), 'The imaginary signifier', *Screen*, 16:2, 14–72.

Metz, C. (1990), 'Photography and fetish', in C. Squires (ed.), *The Critical Image*, Seattle, Bay Press.

Meyer, D. S. (1991), 'Peace movements and national security policy: a research agenda', *Peace and Change*, 16:2, 131–61.

Meyrowitz, J. (1985), *No Sense of Place: The Impact of Electronic Media on Social Behavior*, New York, Oxford University Press.

Miller, L. (1995), 'Women and children first: gender and the settling of the electronic frontier', in J. Brook and I. A. Boal (eds), *Resisting the Virtual Life: The Culture and Politics of Information*, San Francisco, City Lights.

Miller, W. L. (1991), *Media and Voters: The Audience, Content and Influence of the Press and Television at the 1987 General Election*, Oxford, Clarendon.

Mills, C. W. (1956), *The Power Elite*, New York, The Free Press.

Mitchell, J. (1974), *Psychoanalysis and Feminism*, London, Allen Lane.

Mitchell, W. J. T. (1994), *Picture Theory*, Chicago, University of Chicago Press.

Mitra, A. (1996), 'Nations and the internet: the case of a national newsgroup, "soc.cult.indian"', *Convergence*, 2:1 (Spring), 44–75.

Mitra, A. (1997), 'Diasporic web sites: ingroup and outgroup discourse', *Critical Studies in Mass Communication*, 14:2, 158–81.

Modleski, T. (1984), *Loving with a Vengeance: Mass-Produced Fantasies for Women*, New York, Methuen.

Moi, T. (ed.) (1986), *A Kristeva Reader*, New York, Columbia University Press.

Molnar, H. (1993), 'Remote Aboriginal Community Broadcasting (Australia)', in P. Lewis (ed.), *Alternative Media: Linking Global and Local*, Paris, UNESCO.

Molotch, H. and M. Lester (1974), 'News as purposive behaviour: on the strategic use of routine events, accidents and scandals', *American Sociological Review*, 39, 101–12.

Moores, S. (1988), '"The box on the dresser": memories of early radio and everyday life', *Media, Culture and Society*, 10, 23–40.

Moores, S. (1993), *Interpreting Audiences: The Ethnography of Media Consumption*, London, Sage.

Moores, S. (1995), 'TV discourse and "time–space distanciation": on mediated interaction in modern society', *Time and Society*, 4, 329–44.

Moores, S. (1996), *Satellite Television and Everyday Life: Articulating Technology*, Luton, John Libbey Media.

Morgan, R. (1992), 'Dressed to kill', *Sight and Sound*, 1, 28–9.

Morgan, S. (1993), 'Coastal disturbances', *Mirabella*, March, 46.

Morley, D. (1980), *The 'Nationwide' Audience: Structure and Decoding*, London, British Film Institute.

Morley, D. (1981), 'The "Nationwide" audience: a critical postscript', *Screen Education*, 39, 3–14.

Morley, D. (1986), *Family Television: Cultural Power and Domestic Leisure*, London, Comedia.

Morley, D. (1992), *Television, Audiences and Cultural Studies*, London, Routledge.

Morley, D. and K. Robins (1995), *Spaces of Identity: Global Media, Electronic Landscapes and Cultural Boundaries*, London, Routledge.

Morris, B. (1995), 'Almodóvar's laws of subjectivity and desire', in K. M. Vernon and B. Morris (eds), *Post-Franco, Postmodern: The Films of Pedro Almodóvar*, Westport, Greenwood.

Morris, C. W. (1971), *Writings on the General Theory of Signs*, The Hague, Mouton.

Morrison, T. (1990), 'The site of memory', in R. Fergusson, M. Gever, T. T. Minh-ha and C. West (eds), *Out There: Marginalization and Contemporary Cultures*, New York, The Museum of Contemporary Art.

Mulvey, L. (1975), 'Visual pleasure and narrative cinema', *Screen*, 16:3, 6–18.

Mulvey, L. (1981), 'Afterthoughts on "Visual pleasure and narrative cinema" inspired by "Duel in the Sun"', *Framework*, 6, 15/17 (reprinted in C. Penley (ed.) (1988), *Feminism and Film Theory*, London, Routledge/BFI).

Mulvey, L. (1996), *Fetishism and Curiosity*, London, British Film Institute and Indiana University Press.

Murdock, G. (1990), 'Television and citizenship', in A. Tomlinson (ed.), *Consumption, Identity and Style*, London, Routledge.

Murdock, G. (1992), 'Embedded persuasions: the fall and rise of integrated advertising', in D. Strinati and S. Wagg (eds), *Come on Down? Popular Media Culture in Postwar Britain*, London, Routledge.

Murdock, G. (1994), 'Money talks: broadcasting finance and public culture', in S. Hood (ed.), *Behind the Screens: The Structure of British Television in the Nineties*, London, Lawrence and Wishart.

Murphie, A. (1997), 'Editorial', *Convergence*, 3:2 (Summer), 5–8.

Murray, M. (1997), 'Technological thresholds: the V-chip, the family and media regulation', *Convergence*, 3:1 (Spring), 26–50.

Myers, K. (1988), 'Towards a feminist erotica', in H. Robinson (ed.), *Visibly Female: Feminism and Art Today: An Anthology*, New York, Universe Books.

Nandy, A. (1994), 'Culture, voice and development: a primer for the unsuspecting', *Thesis Eleven*, 19, 1–18.

Nandy, A. (1997), *A Secret History of Our Desires*, London, Zed Books.

Neale, S. (1983), 'Masculinity as spectacle: reflections on men and mainstream cinema', *Screen*, 24, 2–16.

Neale, S. (1990), 'A question of genre', *Screen*, 31:1, 45–66.

Neale, W. C. (1987), 'Institutions', *Journal of Economic Issues*, XXI:3, 1177–206.

Negroponte, N. (1995), *Being Digital*, London, Hodder and Stoughton.

Neuman, W. R., M. R. Just and A. N. Crigler (1992), *Common Knowledge: News and the Construction of Political Meaning*, Chicago, University of Chicago Press.

Neumann, J. (1996), *Lights, Camera, War!*, New York, St. Martin's Press.

Nietzsche, F. (1967), *On the Genealogy of Morals* (trans. W. Kaufman), New York, Vintage.

Nochlin, L. (1989), *The Politics of Vision*, New York, Harper and Row.

Noelle-Neumann, E. (1980), *The Spiral of Silence: Our Social Skin*, Chicago, Chicago University Press.

Noelle-Neumann, E. (1991), 'The theory of public opinion: the concept of the spiral of silence', *Communication Yearbook*, 14, 256–87.

Noelle-Neumann, E. and R. Mathes (1987), 'The "event as event" and the "event as news": the significance of "consonance" for media effects research', *European Journal of Communication*, 2, 391–414.

Noth, W. (1990), *Handbook of Semiotics*, Bloomington, Indiana University Press.

O'Carroll, L. (1994), 'Fortune favours ITV–Sun tie-in', *Evening Standard* (London), 13 July, p. 49.

Offe, C. (1985), 'New social movements: challenging the boundaries of institutional politics', *Social Research*, 52:4, 817–68.

Ogden, M. R. (1994), 'Politics in a parallel universe: is there a future for cyberdemocracy?', *Futures*, 26:7, 713–29.

Ogg, A. with D. Upshal (1999), *The Hip Hop Years: A History of Rap*, London, Channel 4 Books/Macmillan.

O'Malley, T. (1994), *Closedown? The BBC and Government Broadcasting Policy, 1979–1992*, London, Pluto Press.

Omi, M. and H. Winant (1986), *Racial Formation in the United States*, New York, Routledge.

O'Regan, T. (1993), *Australian Television Culture*, Sydney, Allen and Unwin.

Orr, J. (1993), *Cinema and Modernity*, Cambridge, Polity.

Orr, J. (1998), *Contemporary Cinema*, Edinburgh, Edinburgh University Press.

O'Sullivan, T. (1991), 'Television memories and cultures of viewing, 1950–65', in J. Corner (ed.), *Popular Television in Britain: Studies in Cultural History*, London, British Film Institute.

O'Sullivan, T., B. Dutton and P. Rayner (1998), *Studying the Media* (second edition), London, Arnold.

O'Sullivan, T., J. Hartley, D. Saunders, M. Montgomery and J. Fiske (1994), *Key Concepts in Communication and Cultural Studies*, London, Routledge.

O'Toole, L. (1998), *Pornocopia: Porn, Sex, Technology and Desire*, London, Serpent's Tail.

Owens, C. (1985), 'The discourse of others: feminism and postmodernism', in H. Foster (ed.), *Postmodern Culture*, London, Pluto.

Palmer, P. (1986), *The Lively Audience: A Study of Children Around the TV Set*, London, Allen and Unwin.

Parenti, M. (1992), *Make Believe Media: The Politics of Entertainment*, New York, St. Martin's Press.

Parenti, M. (1993), *Inventing Reality*, New York, St. Martin's Press.

Parry, B. (1987), 'Problems in current theories of colonial discourse', *Oxford Literary Review*, 9, 27–58 (selection reprinted in B. Ashcroft, G. Griffiths and H. Tiffin (eds) (1995) *The Post-Colonial Studies Reader*, London, Routledge).

Patterson, R. (1990), 'A suitable schedule for the family', in A. Goodwin and G. Whannel (eds), *Understanding Television*, London, Routledge.

Patterson, T. (1993), *Out of Order*, New York, Knopf.

Payne, M. (ed.) (1996), *A Dictionary of Cultural and Critical Theory*, Oxford, Blackwell.

Phillips, W. (1995), 'There may be trouble ahead', *The Guardian*, 3 July, section 2, p. 16.

Philo, G. (1990), *Seeing and Believing: The Influence of Television*, London, Routledge.

Philo, G. (1993), 'Getting the message: audience research in the Glasgow University

Media Group', in J. Eldridge (ed.), *Getting the Message: News, Truth and Power*, London, Routledge.

Piaget, J. (1968), *Structuralism*, London, Routledge and Kegan Paul.

Pickering, M. (1997), *History, Experience and Cultural Studies*, London, Macmillan.

Pingree, S. (1978), 'The effects of nonsexist television commercials and perceptions of reality on children's attitudes about women', *Psychology of Women Quarterly*, 2:3, 262–77.

Pollock, G. (1977), 'What's wrong with "Images of Women"?', *Screen Education*, 24, 25–33.

Pollock, G. (1988), *Vision and Difference*, London, Routledge.

Pollock, G. (1992), 'Painting, feminism, history', in M. Barrett and A. Phillips (eds), *Destabilizing Theory: Contemporary Feminist Debates*, Oxford, Polity.

Portes, A. and R. G. Rumbaut (1990), *Immigrant America: A Portrait*, Berkeley, University of California Press.

Portes, A. and A. Stepick (1993), *City on the Edge: The Transformation of Miami*, Berkeley, University of California Press.

Posner, R. *et al.* (eds) (1997), *Semiotik/Semiotics* (3 vols), Berlin and New York, Mouton de Gruyter.

Poster, M. (1995), *CyberDemocracy: Internet and the Public Sphere*, http://www.hnet.uci.edu/mposter/writings/democ.html

Postman, N. (1986), *Amusing Ourselves to Death*, New York, Penguin.

Postrel, V. (1998), *The Future and Its Enemies*, New York, The Free Press.

Press, A. L. (1991), *Women Watching Television*, Philadelphia, University of Pennsylvania Press.

Priest, S. H. (1996), *Doing Media Research: An Introduction*, Beverly Hills, Sage.

Protess, D. and M. E. McCombs (eds) (1991), *Agenda-Setting: Readings on Media, Public Opinion and Policy Making*, Hillsdale, Lawrence Erlbaum.

Protess, D., F. L. Cook, J. Doppelt, J. S. Ettema, M. T. Gordon, D. R. Leff and P. Miller (1991), *The Journalism of Outrage*, New York, The Guildford Press.

Pursehouse, M. (1997), 'Looking at the "Sun": into the nineties with a tabloid and its readers', in T. O'Sullivan and Y. Jewkes (eds), *The Media Studies Reader*, London, Arnold.

Raboy, M. (ed.) (1996), *Public Broadcasting for the 21st Century*, Luton, John Libbey Media/University of Luton Press.

Radway, J. (1985), 'Interpretive communities and variable literacies: the functions of romance reading', in M. Gurevitch and M. R. Levy (eds), *Mass Communication Review Yearbook*, Beverly Hills, Sage.

Radway, J. (1987), *Reading the Romance: Women, Patriarchy and Popular Literature*, London, Verso.

Radway, J. (1988), 'Reception study: ethnography and the problems of dispersed audiences and nomadic subjects', *Cultural Studies*, 2:3, 359–76.

Ragin, C. C. (1987), *The Comparative Method: Moving Beyond Qualitative and Quantitative Strategies*, Berkeley, University of California Press.

Rajadhyaksha, A. and P. Willemen (1995), *Encyclopaedia of Indian Cinema*, London, British Film Institute.

Rajan, R. S. (1997), 'The third world academic in other places, or, the postcolonial intellectual revisited', *Critical Inquiry*, 23, 596–616.

Reed, A. (1992), 'The urban underclass as myth and symbol: the poverty of the discourse about the discourse on poverty', *Radical America*, 24:1, 21–40.

Reeves, B. and G. Garramone (1982), 'Children's person perception: the generalization from television people to real people', *Human Communication Research*, 8:4, 317–26.

Reeves, B., S. H. Chaffee and A. Tims (1982), 'Social cognition and mass communication research', in M. E. Roloff and C. R. Berger (eds), *Social Cognition and Communication*, London, Sage.

Reid, R. H. (1997), *Architects of the Web*, New York, John Wiley and Sons.

Reynolds, S. (1998), *Energy Flash: A Journey Through Rave Music and Dance Cultures*, London, Picador.

Rheingold, H. (1993), 'A slice of life in my virtual community', in L. M. Harasim (ed.), *Global Networks: Computers and International Communication*, Cambridge, MA, MIT Press.

Rheingold, H. (1995), *The Virtual Community: Homesteading on the Electronic Frontier*, London, Minerva.

Rieser, M. (1997), 'Interactive narratives: a form of fiction?', *Convergence*, 3:1 (Spring), 10–19.

Ritzer, G. (1999), *Enchanting a Disenchanted World: Revolutionizing the Means of Consumption*, Thousand Oaks, Pine Forge.

Riviere, J. (1929), 'Womanliness as masquerade', *International Journal of Psychoanalysis*, 10, 303–13.

Robertson, R. (1992), *Globalization: Social Theory and Global Culture*, London, Sage.

Robinson, J. P. and M. R. Levy (1986), 'Interpersonal communication and news comprehension', *Public Opinion Quarterly*, 50:2, 160–75.

Rockett, K., L. Gibbons and J. Hill (1988), *Cinema and Ireland*, London, Routledge.

Roddick, N. (1983), *A New Deal in Entertainment: Warner Brothers in the 1930s*, London, British Film Institute.

Rogers, E. M. (1997), *A History of Communication Study: A Biographical Approach*, New York, The Free Press.

Roget, P. M. (1998), *Roget's Thesaurus* (revised B. Kirkpatrick), London, Penguin.

Rojecki, A. (2000), *Silencing the Opposition: Antinuclear Movements and the Media in the Cold War*, Urbana, University of Illinois Press.

Rolph, W. (1995), 'Afterword: from rough trade to free trade: toward a contextual analysis of audience response to the films of Pedro Almodóvar', in K. M. Vernon and B. Morris (eds), *Post-Franco, Postmodern: The Films of Pedro Almodóvar*, Westport, Greenwood.

Roper, J. (1995), 'The heart of multimedia: interactivity or experience?', *Convergence*, 1:2 (Autumn), 23–5.

Rosaldo, R. (1993), *Culture and Truth: The Remaking of Social Analysis*, London, Routledge.

Rosengren, K. E. (1987), 'The comparative study of news diffusion', *European Journal of Communication*, 2, 227–55.

Rosengren, K. E. (1993), 'Audience research: back to square one – at a higher level of insight?', *Poetics, Special Issue: Audience Research*, 21, 239–41.

Rosengren, K. E. (ed.) (1994a), *Media Effects and Beyond: Culture, Socialization and Lifestyles*, London, Routledge.

Rosengren, K. E. (1994b), 'From field to frog ponds', in M. R. Levy and M. Gurevitch (eds), *Defining Media Studies: Reflections on the Future of the Field*, Oxford, Oxford University Press.

Rosengren, K. E. (1995), 'Substantive theories and formal models: Bourdieu confronted', *European Journal of Communication*, 10, 7–39.

Rosengren, K. E., L. A. Wenner and P. Palmgreen (eds) (1985), *Media Gratifications Research: Current Perspectives*, Beverly Hills, Sage.

Ross, A. and T. Rose (1994), *Microphone Fiends: Youth Music and Youth Culture*, New York, Routledge.

Rowe, W. and V. Schelling (1991), *Memory and Modernity: Popular Culture in Latin America*, London, Verso.

Ryan, M. (1991), 'Gender and public access: women's politics in nineteenth century America', in C. Calhoun (ed.), *Habermas and the Public Sphere*, Cambridge, MA, MIT Press.

Ryan, M. and D. Kellner (1988), *Camera Politica: The Politics and Ideology of Contemporary Hollywood Film*, Bloomington, Indiana University Press.

Said, E. (1979), *Orientalism*, New York, Routledge.

Said, E. (1993), *Culture and Imperialism*, London, Chatto and Windus.

Sakwa, R. (1999), *Postcommunism*, Buckingham, Open University Press.

Salecl, R. (1994), *The Spoils of Freedom: Psychoanalysis and Feminism After the Fall of Socialism*, London, Routledge.

Sampedro, V. (1994), 'Periodismo, conflicto simbólico y fetichismo. Tipología y tensiones de las relaciones entre periodistas y políticos', *Revista de Ciencias de la Información*, 10, 99–121.

Sampedro, V. (1997a), 'The media politics of social protest', *Mobilization*, 2:2, 185–205.

Sampedro, V. (1997b), 'Movimientos sociales: debates sin mordaza', in *Desobediencia Civil y Servicio Militar 1970–1995*, Madrid, Centro de Estudios Constitucionales.

Samuel, W. J. (1987), 'Institutional economics', in J. Eatwell, M. Millgate and P. Newman (eds), *The New Palgrave: A Dictionary of Economics*, London, Macmillan.

Sandel, M. (ed.) (1984), *Liberalism and Its Critics*, Oxford, Blackwell.

Sandoval, C. (1995), 'New sciences: cyborg feminism and the methodology of the oppressed', in C. H. Gray (ed.), *The Cyborg Handbook*, London, Routledge.

Sartre, J. P. (1966), *Being and Nothingness* (trans. H. E. Barnes), New York, Washington Square Press.

Sartre, J. P. (1976), *Critique of Dialectical Reason, Part I: Theory of Practical Ensembles* (trans. A. Sheridan-Smith), London, NLB.

Sawhney, H. (1996), 'Information superhighway: metaphors as midwives', *Media, Culture and Society*, 18, 291–314.

Scannell, P. (1989), 'Public service broadcasting and modern public life', *Media, Culture and Society*, 11, 135–66.

Scannell, P. (1991), *Broadcast Talk*, London, Sage.

Schiller, H. (1979), 'Transnational media and national development', in K. Nordenstreng and H. Schiller (eds), *National Sovereignty and International Communication*, Norwood, Ablex.

Schiller, H. I. (1976), *Communication and Cultural Domination*, New York, Sharp.

Schiller, H. (1991), 'Not yet the post-imperialist era', *Critical Studies in Mass Communication*, 8, 13–28.

Schlesinger, P. (1978), *Putting Reality Together*, London, Constable.

Schlesinger, P. (1991), *Media, State and Nation: Political Violence and Collective Identities*, London, Sage.

Schmidtke, O. (1998), 'Berlin in the Net: prospects for cyberdemocracy from above and below', in R. Tsagarousianou, D. Tambini and C. Bryan (eds), *Cyberdemocracy: Technology, Cities and Civic Networks*, London, Routledge.

Schorr, D. (1995), 'Ten days that shook the White House', in R. E. Hiebert (ed.), *Impact of Mass Media: Current Issues*, White Plains, Longman.

Schrøder, K. C. (1994), 'Audience semiotics, interpretive communities and the "ethnographic turn" in media studies', *Media, Culture and Society*, 16, 337–48.

Schumpeter, J. (1942), *Capitalism, Socialism and Democracy*, New York, Harper and Row.

Schumpeter, J. (1976), *Capitalism, Socialism and Democracy* (fifth edition), London, Allen and Unwin.

Schutz, A. (1967), *The Phenomenology of the Social World* (trans. G. Walsh and F. Lehnert), Evanston, Northwestern University Press.

Schwartz, E. (1998), 'An internet resource for neighbourhoods', in R. Tsagarousianou, D. Tambini and C. Bryan (eds), *Cyberdemocracy: Technology, Cities and Civic Networks*, London, Routledge.

Seaman, W. R. (1992), 'Active audience theory: pointless populism', *Media, Culture and Society*, 14, 301–11.

Sebeok, T. A. (1976), *Contributions to the Doctrine of Signs*, Bloomington, Indiana University Press.

Sebeok, T. A. (1991), *Semiotics in the United States*, Bloomington, Indiana University Press.

Sebeok, T. A. (1994), *Signs: An Introduction to Semiotics*, Toronto, University of Toronto Press.

Seiter, E., H. Borchers, G. Kreutzner and E. M. Warth (1989), *Remote Control: Television Audiences and Cultural Power*, London, Routledge.

Selby, K. and R. Cowdrey (1995), *How To Study Television*, Basingstoke, Macmillan.

Seymour, G. (1998), *The Waiting Time*, London, Bantam.

Shannon, C. E. (1948), 'A mathematical theory of communication', *Bell Systems Technical Journal*, 27, 379–423, 623–56.

Shannon, C. E. and W. Weaver (1949), *The Mathematical Theory of Communication*, Urbana, University of Illinois Press.

Shaw, M. (1996), *Civil Society and Media in Global Crises*, London, Pinter.

Shepherd, J. and P. Wicke (1997), *Music and Cultural Theory*, Cambridge, Polity.

Shiva, V. (1989), *Staying Alive: Women, Ecology and Development*, London, Zed Books.

Shuker, R. (1998), *Key Concepts in Popular Music*, London, Routledge.

Silj, A. (1988), *East of Dallas: The European Challenge to American Television*, London, British Film Institute.

Silverman, K. (1988), *The Acoustic Mirror: The Female Voice in Psychoanalysis and Cinema*, Bloomington, Indiana University Press.

Silverstone, R. (1994), *Television and Everyday Life*, London, Routledge.

Silverstone, R. (1995), 'Convergence is a dangerous word', *Convergence*, 1:1 (Spring), 11–13.

Silverstone, R. (1999), *Why Study the Media?*, London, Sage.

Sinclair, J. (1992), 'The decentering of globalization', in E. Jacka (ed.), *Continental Shift: Globalisation and Culture*, Double Bay, NSW, Local Consumption Publications.

Sinclair, J., E. Jacka and S. Cunningham (1996), *New Patterns in Global Television: Peripheral Vision*, Oxford, Oxford University Press.

Singer, J. (1997), 'Still guarding the gate? The newspaper journalist's role in an on-line world', *Convergence*, 3:1 (Spring), 72–89.

Skinner, Q. (1984), 'The idea of negative liberty', in R. Rorty and J. B. Schneewind (eds), *Philosophy in History*, Cambridge, Cambridge University Press.

Skinner, Q. (1986), 'The paradoxes of political liberty', in *Tanner Lectures on Human Values, Vol. VII*, Cambridge, Cambridge University Press.

Sless, D. (1986), *In Search of Semiotics*, New York, Barnes and Noble.

Smith, A. (1979), *The Newspaper: An International History*, London, Thames and Hudson.

Smith, P. J. (1994), *Desire Unlimited: The Cinema of Pedro Almodóvar*, London, Verso.

Smolowe, J. (1993), 'Danger in the safety zone', *Time*, 23 August, pp. 29–32.

Snow, D. A. and R. D. Benford (1988), 'Ideology, frame resonance, and participant mobilization', in B. Klandermans, H. Kriese and S. Tarrow (eds), *From Structure to Action: Comparing Social Movements Research Across Cultures*, Greenwich, JAI Press.

Snow, D. A. and R. D. Benford (1992), 'Master frames and cycles of protest', in A. D. Morris and G. McClurg (eds), *Frontiers in Social Movement Theory*, New Haven, Yale University Press.

Solomon, R. (1990), 'Nietzsche, postmodernism and resentment: a genealogical hypothesis', in C. Koelb (ed.), *Nietzsche as Postmodernist: Essays Pro and Con*, New York, SUNY.

Somby, Á. (1995), 'Joik and the theory of knowledge', in M. Haavelsrud (ed.), *Kunnskap og Utvikling*, Tromsø, University of Tromsø.

Soruco, G. R. (1996), *Cubans and the Mass Media in South Florida*, Miami, University Press of Florida.

Sparks, C. (1988), 'The popular press and political democracy', *Media, Culture and Society*, 10:2, 209–23.

Sparks, C. (1992), 'Popular journalism: theories and practice', in P. Dahlgren and C. Sparks (eds), *Journalism and Popular Culture*, London, Sage.

Spence, J. (1987), *Putting Myself in the Picture*, London, Camden Press.

Spence, J. and P. Holland (eds) (1991), *Family Snaps: The Meanings of Domestic Photography*, London, Virago.

Spivak, G. (1988), 'Can the subaltern speak?', in C. Nelson and L. Grossberg (eds), *Marxism and the Interpretation of Culture*, London, Macmillan.

Sproull, L. and S. Kiesler (1991), *Connections: New Ways of Working in the Networked Organization*, Cambridge, MA, MIT Press.

Squires, J. (1996), 'Fabulous feminist futures and the lure of cyberculture', in J. Dovey (ed.), *Fractal Dreams: New Media in Social Context*, London, Lawrence and Wishart.

Sreberny-Mohammadi, A. (1991), 'The global and the local in international communications', in J. Curran and M. Gurevitch (eds), *Mass Media and Society*, London, Arnold.

Stacey, J. (1988), 'Desperately seeking difference', in L. Gamman and M. Marshment (eds), *The Female Gaze: Women as Viewers of Popular Culture*, London, The Woman's Press.

Stacey, J. (1994), *Star Gazing: Hollywood Cinema and Female Spectatorship*, London, Routledge.

Steinfield, C., J. Bauer and L. Caby (eds) (1994), *Telecommunications in Transition: Policies, Services and Technologies in the European Community*, London, Sage.

Stern, D. A. (1999), *The Blair Witch Project*, London, Boxtree.

Stevenson, N. (1995), *Understanding Media Cultures*, London, Sage.

Stone, A. R. (1991), 'Will the real body please stand up? Boundary stories about virtual cultures', in M. Benedikt (ed.), *Cyberspace: First Steps*, Cambridge, MA, MIT Press.

Stone, D. A. (1989), 'Causal stories and the formation of policy agendas', *Political Science Quarterly*, 2, 281–300.

Storey, J. (1993), *An Introductory Guide to Cultural Theory and Popular Culture*, London, Harvester Wheatsheaf.

Storey, J. (1999), *Cultural Consumption and Everyday Life*, London, Arnold.

Strauss, A. and J. Corbin (1990), *Basics of Qualitative Research: Grounded Theory Procedures and Techniques*, London, Sage.

Straw, W. and J. Shepherd (eds) (1991), *Cultural Studies Special Issue: The Music Industry in a Changing World*, 5:3.

Street, J. (1986), *Rebel Rock: The Politics of Popular Music*, London, Blackwell.

Strinati, D. (1995), *An Introduction to Theories of Popular Culture*, London, Routledge.

Stringer, J. K. and J. J. Richardson (1980), 'Managing the political agenda: problem definition and policy making in Britain', *Parliamentary Affairs*, 33, 23–39.

Stubbs, M. (1983), *Discourse Analysis*, Oxford, Blackwell.

Suleiman, S. and I. Crosman (eds) (1980), *The Reader in the Text*, Princeton, Princeton University Press.

Swanson, D. L. (1993), 'Understanding audiences: continuing contributions of gratifications research', *Poetics, Special Issue: Audience Research*, 21, 305–28.

Swanson, D. L. (1996), 'Audience research: antinomies, intersections, and the prospect of comprehensive theory', in J. Hay, L. Grossberg and E. Wartella (eds), *The Audience and Its Landscape*, Boulder, Westview.

Syracuse Constitution, editorial matter (1993), 'A menace to society', *The Syracuse Constitution*, 2 August, p. 5.

Tambini, D. (1998), 'Civic networking and universal rights to connectivity: Bologna', in R. Tsagarousianou, D. Tambini and C. Bryan (eds), *Cyberdemocracy: Technology, Cities and Civic Networks*, London, Routledge.

Tarrow, S. (1988), 'National politics and collective action: recent theory and research in Western Europe and the U.S.', *Annual Review of Sociology*, 14, 421–40.

Tarrow, S. (1998), *Power in Movement: Social Movements, Collective Action and Politics* (revised edition), Cambridge, Cambridge University Press.

Tasker, Y. (1993), *Spectacular Bodies: Gender, Genre and the Action Cinema*, London, Routledge.

Taylor, C. (1985), 'Interpretation and the sciences of man', in *Philosophical Papers Vol. 1*, Cambridge, Cambridge University Press.

Taylor, S. J. (1991), *Shock! Horror! The Tabloids in Action*, London, Bantam.

Thompson, J. B. (1990), *Ideology and Modern Culture*, Cambridge, Polity.

Thompson, J. B. (1993), 'The theory of the public sphere', *Theory, Culture and Society*, 10:3, 173–89.

Thompson, J. B. (1994), 'Social theory and the media', in D. Crowley and D. Mitchell (eds), *Communication Theory Today*, Cambridge, Polity.

Thompson, J. B. (1995), *The Media and Modernity: A Social Theory of the Media*, Cambridge, Polity.

Thompson, R. J. (1996), *Television's Second Golden Age*, New York, Continuum.

Thomson, D. (1986), *Suspects*, London, Picador.

Thomson, D. (1999), Review of *South Park: Bigger, Larger and Uncut*, *The Independent*, 7 July, review section p. 1.

Thornton, S. (1995), *Club Culture*, Cambridge, Polity.

Tomlinson, J. (1991), *Cultural Imperialism: A Critical Introduction*, London, Pinter.

Tomlinson, J. (1994), 'A phenomenology of globalization? Giddens on global modernity', *European Journal of Communication*, 9, 149–72.

Touraine, A. (1981), *The Voice and the Eye: An Analysis of Social Movements*, Cambridge, Cambridge University Press.

Tsagarousianou, R. (1998), 'Back to the future of democracy? New technologies, civic networks and direct democracy in Greece', in R. Tsagarousianou, D. Tambini and C. Bryan (eds), *Cyberdemocracy: Technology, Cities and Civic Networks*, London, Routledge.

Tsagarousianou, R., D. Tambini and C. Bryan (eds) (1998), *Cyberdemocracy: Technology, Cities and Civic Networks*, New York, Routledge.

Tseëlon, E. (1989), *Communication via Clothes*, PhD Thesis (unpublished), University of Oxford, Department of Experimental Psychology.

Tseëlon, E. (1991), 'Women and the private domain: a symbolic interactionist perspective', *Journal for the Theory of Social Behaviour*, 21:1, 111–24.

Tseëlon, E. (1992), 'Is the presented self sincere? Goffman, impression management, and the postmodern self', *Theory, Culture and Society*, 9:2, 115–28.

Tseëlon, E. (1995), *The Masque of Femininity: The Presentation of Woman in Everyday Life*, London, Sage.

Tseëlon, E. (1998), 'Fashion, fantasy and horror: a cultural studies approach', *Arena Journal*, 12, 107–28.

Tseëlon, E. and S. B. Kaiser (1992), 'A dialogue with feminist film theory: multiple readings of the gaze', *Studies in Symbolic Interaction*, 13, 119–37.

Tsivian, Y. (co-ordinating ed.) (1989), *Silent Witnesses: Russian Films 1908–1919*, London, British Film Institute.

Tuchman, G. (1978), *Making News: A Study in the Construction of Reality*, New York, The Free Press.

Tudor, A. (1976), 'Genre and methodology', in B. Nichols (ed.), *Movies and Methods Vol. 1*, Berkeley, University of California Press.

Tunstall, J. (1993), *Television Producers*, London, Routledge.

Turkle, S. (1988), 'Computational reticence: why women fear the intimate machine', in C. Kramarae (ed.), *Technology and Women's Voices*, London, Routledge.

Turner, G. (1990), *British Cultural Studies: An Introduction*, London, Unwin Hyman.

Turner, G. (1993), *Film as Social Practice* (second edition), London, Routledge.

Ulmer, G. L. (1990), *Teletheory: Grammatology in the Age of Video*, New York, Routledge.

Ulmer, G. L. (1994), *Heuretics: The Logic of Invention*, Baltimore, Johns Hopkins University Press.

Van Dijk, T. A. (1987), *News as Discourse*, Hillsdale, Lawrence Erlbaum Associates.

Van Zoonen, L. (1992), 'The women's movement and the media: constructing a public identity', *European Journal of Communication*, 7, 453–76.

Van Zoonen, L. (1994), *Feminist Media Studies*, London, Sage.

Van Zoonen, L. (1996), 'A dance of death: new social movements and mass media', in D. Paletz (ed.), *Political Communication in Action: States, Institutions, Movements, Audiences*, Cress Hill, Hampton Press.

Vernon, K. M. and B. Morris (1995), 'Introduction: Pedro Almodóvar, postmodern auteur', in K. M. Vernon and B. Morris (eds), *Post-Franco, Postmodern: The Films of Pedro Almodóvar*, Westport Greenwood.

Virilio, P. (1997), *Open Sky* (trans. J. Rose), London, Verso.

Volosinov, V. (1976), *Marxism and the Philosophy of Language* (trans. I. R. Titunik), New York, Seminar Press.

Vorderer, P. and N. Groeben (1993), 'Audience research: what the humanistic and the social science approaches could learn from each other', *Poetics, Special Issue: Audience Research* (edited by K. E. Rosengren), 21, 361–76.

Wajcman, J. (1991), *Feminism Confronts Technology*, Cambridge, Polity.

Wakeford, N. (1997), 'Networking women and grrrls with information/communication technology: surfing tales of the world wide web', in J. Terry and M. Calvert (eds), *Processed Lives: Gender and Technology in Everyday Life*, London, Routledge.

Walker, S. (1998), editorial matter, *Television Business International*, March, p. 47.

Walkerdine, V. (1986), 'Video replay: families, films and fantasy', in V. Burgin, J. Donald and C. Kaplan (eds), *Formations of Fantasy*, London, Methuen.

Wallace, M. (1992), ' "Boyz N the Hood" and "Jungle Fever" ', in G. Dent (ed.), *Black Popular Culture*, Seattle, Bay Press.

Wallis, B., M. Weems and P. Yenawine (eds) (1999), *Art Matters: How the Culture Wars Changed America*, New York, New York University Press.

Wallis, R. and K. Malm (1984), *Big Sounds from Small Countries*, London, Constable.

Wallis, R. and K. Malm (1992), *Media Policy and Music Activity*, London, Routledge.

Wark, M. (1994), *Virtual Geography: Living with Global Media Events*, Bloomington, Indiana University Press.

Warner, M. (1994), *From the Beast to the Blonde: On Fairy Tales and their Tellers*, London, Chatto and Windus.

Wasserman, S. and K. Faust (1994), *Social Network Analysis: Methods and Applications*, Cambridge, Cambridge University Press.

Waterhouse, K. (1989), *Waterhouse on Newspaper Style*, London, Viking.

Waters, M. (1995), *Globalization*, London, Routledge.

Wayne, M. (1998), 'Counter-hegemonic strategies in "Between the Lines"', in M. Wayne (ed.), *Dissident Voices: The Politics of Television and Cultural Change*, London, Pluto Press.

Weedon, A. (1996), 'The book trade and internet publishing: a British perspective', *Convergence*, 2:1 (Spring), 76–102.

Weedon, C. (1987), *Feminist Practice and Poststructuralist Theory*, Oxford, Blackwell.

Weis, E. and J. Belton (eds) (1985), *Film Sound: Theory and Practice*, New York, Columbia University Press.

White, I. (1999), editorial matter, *Broadcast*, 12 February, p. 21.

White, M. (1994), 'Playing on television', *Journal of Communication*, 44:1 (Winter), 117–21.

White, R. (1998), *How Computers Work* (fourth edition), Indianapolis, QUE.

Whitford, M. (ed.) (1991), *The Irigaray Reader*, Oxford, Blackwell.

Williams, L. (1994), 'Introduction', in L. Williams (ed.), *Viewing Positions: Ways of Seeing Film*, New Brunswick, Rutgers University Press.

Williams, R. (1974), *Television: Technology and Cultural Form*, New York, Schocken Books.

Williams, R. (1975), *Drama in the Dramatised Society*, Cambridge, Cambridge University Press.

Williams, R. (1977), *Marxism and Literature*, Oxford, Oxford University Press.

Williams, R. (1983), *Towards 2000*, London, Chatto and Windus.

Williams, R. (1988), *Key Words*, London, Fontana.

Williams, R. (1989), *What I Came to Say* (ed. N. Belton, F. Mulhern and J. Taylor), London, Hutchinson.

Willis, P. (1980), 'Notes on method', in S. Hall, D. Hobson, A. Lowe and P. Willis (eds), *Culture, Media, Language*, London, Hutchinson.

Willis, P. (1990), *Common Culture*, Milton Keynes, Open University Press.

Wolff, J. (1990), *Feminine Sentences: Essays on Women and Culture*, Oxford, Polity.

Wollen, P. (1969), *Signs and Meanings in the Cinema*, London, Secker and Warburg/BFI.

Wollen, T. (1991), 'Institution', in D. Lusted (ed.), *The Media Studies Book*, London, Routledge.

Wolsfeld, G. (1984), 'Symbiosis of press and protest: an exchange analysis', *Journalism Quarterly*, 61, 550–5.

Wolsfeld, G. (1991), 'Media, protest and political violence: a transactional analysis', *Journalism Monographs*, no. 127.

Wolsfeld, G. (1997), 'Fair weather friends: the varying role of the news media in the Arab–Israeli peace process', *Political Communication*, 14:1, 29–48.

Wood, J. (1993), 'John Singleton and the impossible greenback of the assimilated black artist', *Esquire*, August, 59–108.

Wood, R. (1965), *Hitchcock's Films*, London, Tantivy Press.

Wren Lewis, J. (1983), 'The encoding/decoding model: criticisms and developments', *Media, Culture and Society*, 5, 179–97.

Wright, E. (ed.) (1992), *Feminism and Psychoanalysis: A Critical Dictionary*, Oxford, Blackwell.

Wright, E. and E. Wright (eds) (1999), *The Žižek Reader*, Oxford, Blackwell.

Wright, H. K. (1996), 'E-mail in African studies', *Convergence*, 2:1 (Spring), 19–29.

Wright, W. (1975), *Sixguns and Society: A Structural Study of the Western*, Berkeley, University of California Press.

Young, A. (1990), *Femininity in Dissent*, London, Routledge.

Young, P. (1999), 'The negative reinvention of cinema: late Hollywood in the early digital age', *Convergence*, 5:2 (Summer), 24–50

Žižek, S. (1996), ' "I hear you with my eyes": or, the invisible master', in R. Salecl and S. Žižek (eds), *Gaze and Voice as Love Objects*, Durham, Duke University Press.

Index